British-American Committee's
unanimous decision. Pg. 306

U.N. Assembly on Nov. 29) 94-
voted in favor of Partition in
Palestine 33 for, 13 against, with
9 abstentions. 4/ Salvador abstained.
pg. 363.

Israel's Declaration of
   Independence - pg. 404

Admission by U.N. 33-11 with
13 abstentions - pg. 447

IF I FORGET THEE O JERUSALEM:

American Jews and The State of Israel

by ROBERT SILVERBERG

WILLIAM MORROW AND COMPANY, INC.

New York 1970

Contents

Illustrations appear following page 80

List of Maps

Introduction

IT TAKES a measure of boldness to present a work of history to the public today. One must be willing to be looked upon in certain quarters as somewhat square. History is not fashionable for either the partisans of revolutionary destructiveness or for the followers of the expedient and their intellectual apologists, who rationalize the "ethic of the possible."

For the former, the existent situation contains all the ingredients needed for decision-making; history is invoked to justify or to polemicize. For the latter, the test of the validity of a decision or of a position is the measure of its capacity to serve one's own interests or those of one's group effectively. Both prior commitments and theoretical justice must bow to the requirements of the moment.

This situational approach, as contrasted with the historical or evaluative approach, is the one most commonly taken—and possibly always has been. It is the approach of problem-solving. It entails a minimum of evaluation, for the actual values applied are self-serving and the general human values become useful for argumentation and rationalization rather than for judgment.

Men and nations normally turn away from historical or depth factors in their dealings with international problems. Power and strategic position are the effective determinants of decision. Long before the label "pragmatic" was given to it, this was the stance of the Machiavellis of all ages. Thucydides baldly recorded it twenty-five centuries ago in the address of the Athenians to the people of Melos: "You know as well as we do that right, as the world goes, is only in question between equals in power, while the strong do what they can and the weak suffer what they must." And when he has the Athenians describe the Lacedaemonians as being "most conspicuous in considering what is agreeable honorable, and what is expedient just," he speaks in terms easily understood by any intelligent newspaper reader of 1969.

These considerations make all the more welcome the appearance of a volume which, while emphasizing the role of the United States and of American Jewry in the creation of the State of Israel, sets the fact of Israel's contemporary re-emergence in the frame of the millennial history of the land cherished and claimed by the Jewish people and regarded as "holy" by both Islam and Christianity.

One cannot make an adequate judgment in the matter of the existing issues arising out of the Arab-Israeli confrontation without placing them in this historic frame. "Historic," here, does not necessarily mean two thousand years. Even the context of the last twenty years is decisive. Let me cite one specific example: the general press today customarily refers to Nablus and Hebron and other "West Bank" locations as "Israeli-occupied Jordan" and to East Jerusalem as "occupied" territory. In fact, these locations were occupied by force of Jordanian arms twenty years ago. Through the entire twenty years since the armistice-without-peace, Jordan has persisted in regarding itself as being in a "state of war" with Israel. Yet these territories were not referred to as "occupied areas" during the two decades that preceded the six days of June, 1967. It may be added that fifty-some years ago, on the eve of World War I, the Jews constituted the majority of the population of Jerusalem. These are but two historic facts that must inevitably bear some relationship to decisions that are made today.

Only yesterday my little girl came home from school to proclaim, "My teacher says the Arabs were there first!" Evidently history does have something to do with claims and the determination of their justice. And the concern generated by the teacher had to be answered with historic fact.

The truth is that the Jewish people, contrary to the impression that is widespread, never abandoned what they have through the ages lovingly called *Eretz Yisrael,* the land of Israel. Their continuing and courageous physical presence in the land is another historic fact. There has never been a time in the last two thousand years when the land of Israel has been without a *yishuv,* a settlement of Jews. One finds the remains of beautiful third- and fourth-century synagogues in the upper Galilee. In the tenth and eleventh centuries Jerusalem was the seat of the Palestinian Gaonate. During the Crusades there was a Jewish population in Jerusalem large enough for a synagogue to have been built—the synagogue in which the Crusaders burned the Jews of Jerusalem to death to the last man, woman, and child. Safed became the home of Jewish mystics and sages in the sixteenth century and was for an extended period the center of a large Jewish population and the focus of a continuing settlement until the establishment of the State. Despite fire, sword, and proscription, there were always *Neturei Karta*, pious "guardians of the city," dwelling as close to the sacred Temple precincts as the foreign overlords would permit.

The miraculous revival after eighteen hundred years was not a new planting but the miraculous sprouting of the seed that had lain almost dormant in the soil. The land was restored to life by those who most deeply loved it after it had been abused, pillaged, and neglected by those who had successively conquered it.

I have recently refreshed my memory of what Palestine had been reduced to by the mid-nineteenth century, rereading the description of the land in Mark Twain's *Innocents Abroad*. Writing in a serious vein that underscores his disillusion, Mark Twain speaks of the tininess and desolation of Palestine; he tells of traveling for miles and encountering only three persons; of villages which were "ugly, cramped, squalid and filthy," of "sore-eyed children"; of Jerusalem with a population of only 14,000; "hardly a tree or shrub anywhere"; and as for the "Holy Places"—"clap-trap side-shows and unseemly impostures." His final evaluation is that "Palestine sits in sackcloth and ashes"; "Palestine is desolate and unlovely."*

This was the truth behind the Zionist aphorism of the late nineteenth century: "The land without a people was waiting for the people without a land." And as that people returned they lavished on that land toil and fervor born of memory and love.

To whom does the land belong? At least a portion of the answer to this question goes beyond United Nations resolutions and military victories. The land belongs to those who loved it through the centuries and nourished and revived it into its contemporary flowering and promise.

The vital core of the story of Israel's re-emergence in our time is not the eighteen hundred years of sentimental attachment and

* *The Complete Travel Books of Mark Twain*. New York: Doubleday and Company, 1966. Pp. 316–380.

yearning but what that attachment was able to accomplish in the practical movement of redemption. In the seventy years that separated the first modern settlers, the "Biluim," from the declaration of independence of the new State, the land was made healthy and whole. The land that nobody had loved, if love is expressed only in care and responsibility, now flowered in response to Jewish concern. This is the greatest miracle: the new forests, the newly fertile valleys, the new cities, the trees, the industry, the beauty. And as Britain was violating its Mandate by keeping Jews out, Arabs came in a steady flow from the desert kingdoms and the poverty-stricken nation-states of the vast Arab territories, seeking to share in the revival, increasing the Arab population, and intensifying the Arab-Jewish problem.

More than love, however, lies behind the fact that only a Jewish Palestine was acceptable to the Jewish people. The long years of Jewish exile had convinced our people that no haven in which Jews constituted a minority would ever provide the assurance of a genuinely creative Jewish life. The Jews were tired of running from *golah* to *golah*—from one place of exile to another like it. Only Palestine offered the possibility of enduring statehood.

The British White Paper of 1939 was a mockery of Jewish hopes because it sought to consign the Jews to minority status even in the land of Israel. It spat upon those Jews who were condemned to die in Europe. Worse, it was issued in a world setting in which every door was closed to those Jews. No wonder then that when the British attacked on the high seas ships bearing their tragic cargoes of doomed refugees, the protest of the Jewish world reached anguished heights and the hatred of Britain was an immeasurable fury.

If the Zionist thesis was that Jews would know no security until in courage and dignity Jews themselves had wrested it from fate, British bloodshed and cruelty demonstrated once again the truth of that thesis. But no Zionist, even in the crucial years after the end of World War II, ever welcomed the death of young heroes on the Exodus or the broken heads of those who resisted the British at Hamburg. All the more puzzling is the speed with which Israel has been able to forget the ignominious role which Britain played in seeking to frustrate its own Balfour Declaration.

The story is far from ended. The war that began on November 30, 1947, is still raging. But the determination which marked the long struggle of the Jewish people to rebuild the land is matched only by their determination to defend it and to preserve the promise which their own achievement brought them.

Any venture into history must be evaluative to be meaningful, but it must also seek to marshal the facts without favor to any thesis or preconception. The book to which these words are an introduction is written with integrity and tells the story as the author has come to understand it. It is not a book that will make any partisan wholly happy, but it sheds the clear light of earnest scholarship on the material which has been gathered with painstaking care. Jews and non-Jews will find it bright and lively reading on a subject of compelling importance.

Perhaps Isaac Deutscher* is correct in viewing the rebirth of a Jewish nation-state in our time as a "paradoxical consummation" of Jewish history. The nation-state, he says, may be "fast becoming an anachronism and an archaism." But it is also possible that the establishment of Israel can be the harbinger and example of that maturation of human dignity that demands world order, world law, and world peace, founded on a new conception of the relationship of plural cultures to a sovereignty invested in a world body. This was, after all, the vision of Isaiah: not that nations and peoples would disappear but that they would together look up to a higher authority and, then, would learn war no more.

ARTHUR J. LELYVELD

---

* *The Non-Jewish Jew and Other Essays.* New York: Oxford University Press, 1968. P. 40.

. . . for David's sake did the Lord his God give him
a lamp in Jerusalem, to set up his son after him,
and to establish Jerusalem: because David did that
which was right in the eyes of the Lord . . .

I KINGS 15:4–5

Six Days in June

ON MONDAY morning, June 5, 1967, I was awakened as usual by the sound of my radio-clock, automatically turning itself on to deliver the 8 A.M. news. The news that morning was grim. "War has broken out in the Near East," the announcer said. "Aircraft of Egypt, Jordan, Syria, and Iraq have bombed Israel. Radio Cairo reports that Tel Aviv is in flames and an oil refinery near Haifa has been destroyed. Algeria, Morocco, Tunisia, the Sudan, Kuwait, Yemen, Lebanon, and Saudi Arabia have announced declarations of war against Israel. There has been no word as yet from the Israeli government on conditions there."

Scarcely awake yet, I felt a sudden chill of terror. It's happened at last, I thought. Pearl Harbor Day once more, this time for Israel. I pictured waves of Arab planes streaking in from the Mediterranean or from the desert and smashing, in a few hours, what had taken so long to build. I saw the Russian-built tanks of Egypt rolling through the shattered streets of Tel Aviv. I saw the troops of Jordan bursting across no man's land into sleek Jewish Jerusalem. I saw Syrian infantrymen descending like locusts on the little farming settlements of the Galilee. And I felt a sense of personal anguish and loss, as though the enemy were marching up my own street toward the comfortable house where I lay still abed.

Even in that moment of fear and despair, I paused to wonder at my own presumptuousness. By what right did I allow myself the luxury of these emotions? What, after all, did Israel mean to me, that I should be so deeply concerned? Some friends of mine lived there, but no close relatives. Up to that time I had never visited the place, never contributed a penny toward its development, never recognized in myself any special involvement with its fortunes. As a secularized New York Jew, more familiar with the tenets of Buddhism or Hinduism or even Roman Catholicism than with those of Judaism, I certainly could claim no mystic religious bond with the land of the Bible. It was reasonable for me to react to the Arab attack as I would to any act of violence, to any suppression of freedom, to any destruction of a cherished homeland. Yet I trembled for Israel, and mourned for her devastated cities, in a way that was entirely different in depth from my response to the crushing of Hungary in 1956, to the invasion of South Korea from the north in 1950, to the overthrow of the Benes government in Czechoslovakia in 1948. I had not earned my feelings, but in that first instant it seemed to me that by attacking Israel, the Arabs had attacked some extension of myself. And I was baffled by the source of that powerful emotion.

Other American Jews felt a similarly intense response to the news from the Near East that Monday morning. A novelist whose home is in Ohio was driving eastward through Connecticut, shortly after dawn, heading toward a summer of work at a writers' colony in New England. As the news of war came over his automobile radio, he experienced an immediate impulse to turn back, drive to Kennedy Airport, board the first plane to Israel, and offer his services to the army. His family did not expect to hear from him for the next three months anyway; no one would be the wiser until he returned. A moment later, he realized the foolishness of the idea. Only two days earlier Israel's new Minister of Defense, Major General Moshe Dayan, had declared that his country could win the impending war without the aid of foreign volunteers. "I would not like American or British boys to get killed here in order to secure Israel and I don't think we need it," Dayan had said. The novelist knew that Israel certainly would have no need of a sedentary, unmilitary American in his middle forties. But his impulse had been sincere; he had genuinely wanted to offer himself to Israel.

As Monday spread westward across the United States, Israeli consulates and U.S. passport offices were besieged by Americans of all ages—many, but by no means all, Jewish—who wished to volunteer to fight for Israel, or else to take the places of the Israeli farmers and workers who had been called into action. The flow of such volunteers had been increasing all during late May and early

June, as prewar tensions built up, but on the first day of the war itself at least 10,000 Americans presented themselves, more than half of them at the New York offices of the Jewish Agency, an important Zionist body. Repeated Israeli insistence that a deluge of foreign volunteers would only complicate a difficult situation did not keep people away, nor did the American government's announcement that, for the time being, American citizens were forbidden to travel to the war area.

At the Jewish Agency, the would-be volunteers were asked to fill out registration forms. At the suggestion of Dr. Arnulf M. Pins, executive director of the Council on Social Work Education, these forms included questions on the Jewish educational and organizational background of the volunteers and their involvement in such causes as Zionism, the civil rights movement, and opposition to the war in Vietnam. Dr. Pins found that the earliest volunteers—those of May—had mainly been educated in Jewish parochial schools and had strong religious or Zionist backgrounds. However, the later ones, though most were Jewish and had conventionally liberal attitudes toward race problems and the Vietnam issue, had never felt any particular attachment to Judaism or to Israel. "What seemed to be happening to them," Dr. Pins suggested, "was that a dormant loyalty had suddenly been stirred and had become at that moment an overriding passion."

It was, for some American Jews, a day of curious conflicts. Vehement opponents of the American interventions in Vietnam and the Dominican Republic found themselves demanding an American intervention to protect Israel, and then looked with confusion on their sudden hawkishness. (Some, like Arthur Schlesinger, Jr., refused to sign an advertisement in *The New York Times* calling on President Johnson to "act now with courage and conviction" to defend Israel. "I think it inconsistent to favor unilateral intervention in one part of the world when I'm already opposed to unilateral intervention in another part of the world," he said. Others, despite similar misgivings, signed.) The passionate young leaders of the New Left movement, many of them Jewish, were awkwardly torn between their pacifist tendencies and their admiration for Egyptian President Nasser as a "progressive" neutralist leader. And that minority of influential American Jews that had long expressed strong opposition to American Jewish involvement in Israeli affairs discovered itself in the most difficult position

of all. These anti-Zionist Jews, severe critics of many Israeli policies and of the entire concept of a Jewish national homeland, could
nevertheless not deny, that day, that they feared for the lives of
Israel's two and a half million Jews; and in the first moments of
the crisis, most members of this usually vocal group found it desirable to refrain from making public statements about the war.

Other American Jews had no such complexities with which to
cope, and their reaction was instant and visceral. As one official of
the Jewish Agency arrived for work early Monday morning in
New York, a cab pulled up and a middle-aged man stepped out,
followed by two younger men. Stopping the Israeli official, the
man said, "I have no money to give, but here are my sons. Please
send them over immediately."

Making cash contributions—"dollar Zionism," Israelis sometimes call it, in a faintly mocking way—has long been the customary method by which American Jews gratify their desire to share
in building the Jewish homeland. *Tzedakah*—charity, philanthropy—is regarded as a sacred duty by the Orthodox Jews, and
is an ingrained cultural trait among the prosperous secularized
ones. Even during the Depression one found, in the poorest
American Jewish home, the little blue-and-white metal collection
can, the *pushky,* in which pennies for Palestine were deposited. In
more recent, happier times, wealthy Jewish industrialists have
vied openly to outdo one another in making large cash donations
that are frankly intended as declarations of status. Through private
contributions, America's Jews had raised more than $1,500,000,-
000 for Israel between the founding of the Jewish state in 1948 and
the outbreak of the 1967 war, so that it could fairly be said (and
too often was) that Israel had been built with the dollars of America's Jews. On the first day of the June War, however, the impulse
toward *tzedakah* became a kind of hysteria of charity. Unable to
order American troops into the field to rescue Israel, American
Jews plunged into an extraordinary frenzy of philanthropy.

It began with such spontaneous acts as that of the New York
youngster who went into the streets with a Manischewitz borscht
bottle and collected $72.79 from passers-by. Jewish children with
plastic buckets, cardboard boxes, and tin cans improvised fund-
raising campaigns of this sort in many American cities. By midday
on Monday the fifth the formidable machinery of Jewish professional fund-raising was in action. The United Jewish Appeal, a

major philanthropic organization, set up an Israel Emergency Fund with a luncheon of 200 community leaders in New York; within fifteen minutes they had pledged $15,000,000 to the cause. One businessman promised $1,550,000; there were four million-dollar gifts. In Boston, 50 families opened the drive by contributing $2,500,000. In Beverly Hills, a luncheon of Hadassah, an important women's Zionist group, drew pledges of $250,000 from its 500 attendees. The 20 Jewish families of Okmulgee, Oklahoma, sold their synagogue for $4,000 and sent the money to Israel. Seven men in Dayton, Ohio, contributed $500,000. The Jews of St. Louis raised $1,200,000 overnight; those of Cleveland, $3,100,000; those of Toledo, $530,000. Jewish power in its most basic form—the power of the dollar—was coming instantly to Israel's rescue.

Nor were the dollars exclusively Jewish; the emotions unleashed that day in June crossed religious boundaries. Local 299 of the Paper Box Makers Union in New York, of mixed ethnic origin, raised $4,000. A Christian businessman in Rapid City, South Dakota, where Jews are scarce, gave $1,000. The president of New York's Fordham University, a Catholic organization, sent a check for $5,000 to the emergency fund. Robert T. Stevens, head of a textile-manufacturing concern and Secretary of the Army under President Eisenhower, donated $250,000. A girl in Minnesota called a rabbi and asked, "How can I become Jewish?" A Gentile shipping magnate was in so much of a hurry to contribute $100,000 that he sent it direct to Tel Aviv, though he was advised that he might forfeit his tax deduction if he did not make his gift through regular philanthropic channels.

Overseas, of course, other Jewish communities were doing their share. Baron Edmond de Rothschild and his friends in Paris raised $1,500,000 at a private party, and other French Jews added $8,500,000 more. In London, the baron's cousin, Lord Rothschild, gave a party of his own at which he contributed $2,800,000 to Israel; his 30 guests pledged another $17,000,000. But it was in the United States, where the world's largest and wealthiest Jewish community is found, that the fund-raising efforts were most astonishing. Even the professional fund-raisers of the United Jewish Appeal, skilled in the techniques of wringing ever greater gifts from American Jews, were amazed at the ease with which the money flowed. In a few days an amount came in that was substantially greater than the usual annual intake—itself substantial—of the UJA. During the first three weeks of this whirlwind campaign, American donations to Israel exceeded $100,000,000.

Pro-Israeli Jewish power manifests itself in the United States in another characteristic form: direct political agitation. There was plenty of agitation that morning, on all levels, from spontaneous street demonstrations to statements by recognized Jewish organizations calling for American support of Israel. The existence of an American commitment to defend Israel was taken for granted by many Americans, and by nearly all American Jews; and when, in the initial confusion of the war, a State Department spokesman released a clumsy statement to the effect that the United States was going to remain "neutral in thought, word, and deed," the political effects were explosive. Thousands of telegrams descended on the White House and the Congress, and President Johnson, himself incensed at the State Department's blunder, clarified his position by saying he was "concerned" over Israel's fate. Nevertheless the campaign continued.

There is nothing new or unusual about ethnic lobbying in the United States. Irish-Americans, resentful of Great Britain's control of their homeland, succeeded many times in influencing American relations toward Britain in the nineteenth and early twentieth centuries. German-Americans attempted in 1888 to have the United States settle a dispute involving Germany, England, and the United States over the island of Samoa in a way favorable to Germany. At the beginning of the twentieth century Dutch-Americans tried to bring about American intervention in the Boer War. American Catholics, to some extent, urged the United States not to intervene in the Spanish Civil War. American Protestants successfully prevented President Truman from appointing an ambassador to the Vatican. Americans of Polish, Ukrainian, Hungarian, Czechoslovakian, and Cuban extraction have, since the Communist takeovers of their ancestral countries, worked toward sustaining anti-Communist philosophies in the United States. And there are numerous other examples.

American Jews, though most of them can look upon the Holy Land as their "ancestral country" only in an abstract and theoretical sense, have practiced this kind of politics in a particularly dedicated and intense way. Five Presidents have experienced the cajolery, threats, pleas and lofty appeals—often inextricably mixed in a single statement—of Zionist organizations. United States policy toward the nations of the Near East, contradictory and confusing though it has often been, has taken careful heed of American Jewish thinking. Perhaps Israel would have come into being without the aid of these American pressure groups. But her road would have been even thornier than it has been.

American Jews came late to the movement to found a Jewish homeland—there was little Zionist activity in the United States before World War I, and not much of real significance until World War II—but, through unremitting pressure, they played important roles first in trying to open Palestine to immigration by Jewish war refugees, then in helping to bring forth the State of Israel out of the mandated territory of Palestine, and then in the not always successful effort to ensure a consistently pro-Israeli foreign policy on the part of the United States.

Certainly there was a vigorous display of Jewish pressure at the outbreak of the June War. Certainly a troubled President, already burdened with one overseas military adventure and looking uneasily toward an unpromising election day seventeen months away, wondered how he could avoid a second commitment of troops and yet manage to placate the fiercely partisan, politically influential American Jewish community. But the demonstrations, the desperate rush to volunteer, the pledges of support—everything, in fact, except the cash contributions—proved to be unnecessary. Before the people and government of the United States had been able to gain a clear perspective on the events in the Near East, Israel had won the war by herself.

In the early hours of the war the only communiqués had come from Radio Cairo and other Arab outlets, which delivered news of a series of Moslem triumphs: Israeli cities in flames, dozens of Israeli jets shot from the skies, the Arab brethren united in a joyous holy war. Israel remained silent behind a tight barrier of censorship. By noon in New York, while the United Nations Security Council met in urgent session and Jewish magnates pledged millions to defend the cause of Zion, night had settled over the battlefield, and the first fragmentary reports from the Israeli side began to filter through. They said little except that damage to Israeli territory had been slight.

We were not yet able to realize that the Arab communiqués were self-inflating fantasies, wholly false, which served only to instill misleading and misplaced confidence in the Islamic allies. We did not yet know that Israel had launched an astonishing series of pre-emptive air strikes early Monday morning, Mirage-3 and Super-Mystère jets swooping low to avoid radar and smashing dozens of military airports in Egypt, Jordan, Syria, and Iraq. We were unaware that the entire Arab air force, hundreds of jets, had been destroyed on the ground; that Israeli aircraft had undisputed command of the skies over the whole Near East; that the Arabs had managed to drop only a scattering of bombs on Israeli suburbs before they lost their few remaining planes; that Israel was unscathed and the struggle was over.

Late Monday night in London the BBC carried a report by its American-born correspondent in Jerusalem, Michael Elkins, who said, "Less than fifteen hours after fighting began Israel has already won the war. Egypt is no more a fighting factor. . . . It's the most instant victory the modern world has seen." The Elkins report was relayed around the globe, but it was too fantastic to believe.

On Tuesday and Wednesday all doubt disappeared. Israeli tanks were grinding through the Sinai wasteland, on their way toward the Suez Canal, in a replay of the 1956 war. A second front had been opened in Jordan, with Arab troops falling back as the Israelis battled for the most cherished prize of all, Jerusalem. The Syrians were being driven from their long-held positions on Israel's northeast frontier. Algeria, Kuwait, Yemen, the Sudan, and the rest of that long list of declarers of war had neglected to send soldiers into the fray. There was indeed no Arab air force left, and gleeful Jewish aviators buzzed the Arab capitals with impunity. It seemed as though Israel would be dictating cease-fire terms in Cairo, Amman, and Damascus by the weekend—as in fact she was.

As the details of this miraculous transformation of terrible defeat into glorious victory emerged, I felt anguish give way to wonder, and then to a pride in Israel's victory that was as totally unearned as my earlier sorrow had been. How splendidly "we" had fought, I told myself; how fine it was that "we" had once again foiled the villainous Arabs. *We!* I, no Zionist, hardly even a Jew except by birth, was amused by an audacity in identifying myself with the Israeli warriors. Yet the identification was there, for me, for virtually all other American Jews, for hundreds of millions of Gentiles throughout the world. It was easy to see why. Once again David had slain Goliath; and the valor of Israel held an emotional appeal that few could resist trying to share.

For Jews there was a special pleasure in so thorough a victory, for Jews bear a twenty-century-long heritage of defeat. Driven out of their homeland by the Romans, hounded by persecutors across the face of Europe, set apart by special laws, special taxes, special badges and clothes, they came finally to the depths of existence in Hitler's death camps, and—many of them—waited meekly, resignedly, for their turn to enter the gas chambers. That meekness in the face of unspeakable evil, that sad shrug and easy acceptance of one more round of atrocities, seemed all too characteristically Jewish. So, too, was the urge to be inconspicuous, to keep out of harm's way, that typified many American Jews, transforming Epsteins into Epworths, Feldsteins into Fieldstones.

Now, abruptly, there was no need to conceal one's background, and that long career as victim had been obliterated by Jewish guns, Jewish tanks, Jewish planes. "I really do feel prouder today," said a 26-year-old Jewish graduate student at Brooklyn College. "There is new meaning in being Jewish." But he was quick to add, "I'm reluctant to express pride. It has to do with humility, with not being boastful, with the Jewish feeling of walking humbly with God, with the Jew's reluctance to assert himself in America."

Others spoke the same way. "Moshe Dayan is another Moses," declared a 34-year-old New Yorker, a survivor of the Auschwitz death camp. He had always been proud to be a Jew, he said, but he admitted that he was a good deal prouder this day than while he had been in Auschwitz. And a 30-year-old woman, neither a religious Jew nor a Zionist, said, "I felt a pride in being Jewish that I've never felt. . . . It was a real change from seeing the Jews as the long-suffering victims."

That week of fear giving way to vicarious pride was a strange week for many Americans—a week for inward voyages of discovery. It brought a number of difficult questions to the surface. What was there about Israel's movement of peril that aroused such passions in Jews who are citizens of another nation, Jews who speak no Hebrew, Jews who in many cases are strangers not only to the synagogue but to God? What is this mysterious dual loyalty that emerged so unexpectedly that week? What hold is it that Israel has on Jews of this country?

My own response, so surprising to me, led me into a quest lasting more than a year. It took me to Israel itself, where I found my reservoir of undeserved pride even deeper than I had suspected during the June War; it took me into the archives of Zionism; it brought me into conversation with many people, Jews and Gentiles, Americans and Israelis, whose attitudes toward this small Near Eastern land formed a broad and complex spectrum. I wanted to learn what role Americans had played, as fund-raisers, as political lobbyists, as smugglers of weapons, and as soldiers, in the creation and sustenance of Israel. I wanted to trace the intricate web of circumstances out of which the concept and then the reality of a Jewish national home had come. Until those six days in June, Israel's origin, growth, and future prospects had seemed to mean no more to me than the origin, growth, and future prospects of, say, Ghana, Burma, Paraguay, or Portugal. During the course of a single news broadcast on a Monday morning I discovered that the case was otherwise; and it was my desire to comprehend how I had become so involved in the destinies of a nation that was not my nation, a people that I did not consider my people, that I undertook my quest.

Millions of Americans share some of these feelings and some of this bewilderment. Since the June War, we have virtually all become Zionists; a movement that a majority of American Jews once opposed is now supported by a majority of Americans both Jewish and Gentile. There is something impudent about the American Jew's self-proclaimed unofficial citizenship in Israel, and the Israelis themselves are both amused and angered by it; but nonetheless it exists. Let Goliath growl at David once again, and we will once again rush to stand at David's side, and probably will try to take some of the credit for his next amazing victory. No other nation holds quite the same relationship to the United States. I have tried to uncover the nature of that relationship, and some of the reasons for its existence.

ONE

The Dream of Herzl

ISRAEL AS a modern state goes back only to 1948; but the wedge of land at the eastern end of the Mediterranean occupied by that modern state is encrusted by thousands of years of history. According to the present possessors of the land, the weight of that history gives the Jews of the world valid title to it. According to the Arab enemies of Israel, the Jews have neither a legal nor a moral claim to that land, and hold it only by virtue of conquest and through the chicanery of Western politicians. No easy middle path is available for compromise of these irreconcilable beliefs, for there is justice on both sides. The Israelis, like all previous rulers of the Holy Land, are there by force of arms, having staked a claim and successfully defended it against the Arabs after the withdrawal of British occupation troops in 1948. As Robert Graves wrote that year, "There are no modern title-deeds to Palestine except the Mandate which the British are now surrendering. They seized the country from the Turks, who had seized it from the Arabs, who had seized it from the Crusaders, who had seized it from the Jews, who had seized it from the Canaanites, Perizzites, Philistines and others."

The Israelis do not see themselves merely as one of a dozen transient holders of this dusty scrap of territory. They produce the argument from theology: that Palestine was bestowed upon them by the Lord Almighty, who is also the God of the Moslems, as a homeland for all time. They offer the cultural argument: that during their first occupation of Palestine they created a society and a culture whose beliefs and scriptures influenced the future course of Western civilization, and so they are entitled to return to the

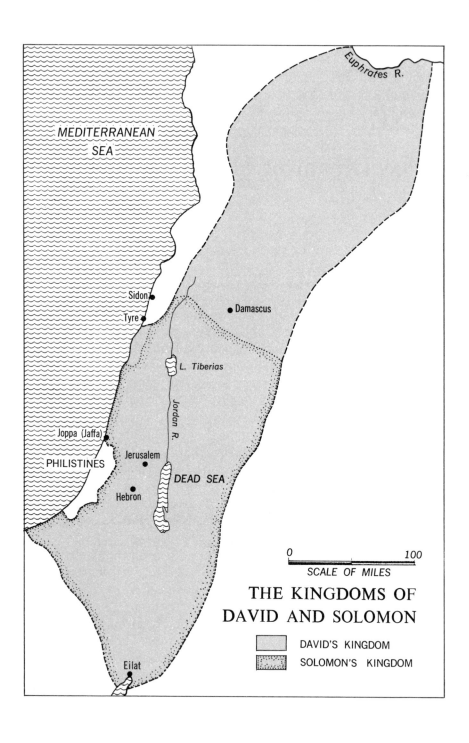

MEDITERRANEAN
SEA

Euphrates R.

Sidon

Tyre

Damascus

L. Tiberias

Jordan R.

Joppa (Jaffa)

PHILISTINES

Jerusalem

DEAD SEA

Hebron

0   100
SCALE OF MILES

THE KINGDOMS OF
DAVID AND SOLOMON

DAVID'S KINGDOM
SOLOMON'S KINGDOM

Eilat

land where such powerful ideas were generated. They cite the economic facts: that the Turks and Arabs had managed to turn this land of milk and honey into a desert, and that the Jews, during their brief present occupation of it, have made it fertile again. They present the argument of moral compensation: that the Jews, homeless wanderers for twenty centuries, deserve some small place where they may live in their own special way, and that the Arabs, masters of so many thousands of square miles, can easily spare this unimportant patch. When all else fails, they resort to the blunt argument from possession: the Holy Land is once again theirs, and they mean to keep it, or die to the last man in its defense.

The origin of this passionate commitment is shrouded in myth, or, as the Orthodox would prefer to say, in religious tradition. But archaeological findings of the past century have shown that the chronicles of the Old Testament correspond in outline, if not necessarily in close detail, to historical events. The Hebrews, most scholars believe, were one of the many nomadic desert tribes who inhabited the Near East about 2000 B.C. These wandering shepherds spoke a language of the linguistic family we call Semitic, so that the Hebrews were related linguistically, though not necessarily otherwise, to such contemporary peoples as the Canaanites, the Assyrians, the Babylonians, the Edomites, and many others.

About 2000 B.C. the Hebrews—who appear in the written chronicles of their neighbors as Habiru, Khabiri, or 'Apiru—lived in southern Mesopotamia, what is now Iraq. Led by one Abraham, perhaps an actual sheikh of the tribe, they migrated westward into northern Syria, and then drifted downward into Canaan, or Palestine. The Bible says that divine promises were made to Abraham: "I will make thee exceeding fruitful, and I will make nations of thee, and kings shall come out of thee. . . . And I will give unto thee, and to thy seed after thee, the land wherein thou art a stranger, all the land of Canaan, for an everlasting possession; and I will be their God."

This Canaan, this promised land, was no paradise, except in contrast to the desert. In the north, in cool, green Galilee, the land was good, and so it was also in the fertile strip of lowland along the Mediterranean coast, dominated by the powerful Canaanite mercantile ports, Byblos, Tyre, Sidon. (The Greeks would later call these Canaanites of the coast "Phoenicians.") But the Hebrews of Abraham's tribe settled along the gray, sandy spine of the land, the hilly country inland, where dry streambeds wound through a harsh terrain blighted by salty swamps. Evidently they met little resistance from the sparse population of herdsmen there. Exalted by his covenant with Jehovah, the patriarch Abraham dwelled there with Sarah his wife and Isaac the miraculous child of his old age. (Abraham had had an older son, Ishmael, by his wife's Egyptian handmaid Hagar; but when Isaac was born, Sarah forced Abraham to drive Hagar and Ishmael into the wilderness. The Arabs claim Ishmael as their ancestor, saying that he sired twelve Bedouin tribes in the desert, and so they revere Abraham as progenitor of their progenitor. The hatred of Arab for Jew, then, can be seen as sibling rivalry, the sullen hatred of the outcast brother.)

Migrations of Semitic tribes continued for several centuries, reaching a climax about 1700 B.C. when the desert princes known as the Hyksos conquered mighty Egypt. Not long afterward, the Biblical tale goes, famine came over the land of Canaan. Existence was particularly difficult for the family of Abraham's grandson Jacob, the younger son of Isaac. Jacob—whom the Lord had re-named Israel, "he who prevails with God"—sent ten of his sons into Egypt to purchase grain. He kept Benjamin, the eleventh son, home "lest peradventure mischief befall him." Mischief had al-ready befallen the twelfth son, Joseph, Israel's favorite. Joseph's brethren had sold him into slavery to ease their envy of him, reporting to their father that he had been devoured by a wild beast. But when they reached Egypt, Israel's ten sons were seized as spies, and taken before a high official of Pharaoh, who turned out to be Joseph himself, now a favorite at the Egyptian court. Joseph forgave them, and, as the famine deepened, found land in Egypt for all of his brothers and for old Israel himself. Thus the family of Israel left Canaan for Egypt.

The Hyksos rulers of Egypt eventually were overthrown, and the Hebrews in Egypt suffered grievously as native Egyptian dynasties assumed power. Now began the years of bondage for the children of Israel, fulfilling another of God's promises to Abraham, that the land of Canaan would not belong to the Hebrews until they first had spent four hundred years of affliction in another land. In time a leader arose—Moses—to bring the Israelites out of Egypt and back to Canaan. They made a tortuous exodus through the Sinai Desert, entering Canaan and finding it occupied by Semitic cousins who had not chosen to sojourn in Egypt. Under their brilliant general Joshua, the Israelites seized southern Canaan about 1200 B.C., driving out a people called the Philistines, who left their name behind, at least, in the word *Palestine.* The Hebrew invaders did not attempt to make war against the strong and wealthy Phoenician-Canaanite cities of the coast; it is one of history's ironies that modern Israel's most valuable territory, the coastal zone from Haifa to Tel Aviv, was not originally a part of the ancient Hebrew realm. Instead the Israelites took care to maintain friendly relations with the Phoenician kings.

They founded in Canaan a sovereign Jewish state that evolved painfully from a quarrelsome confederation of tribes, and was ruled at first by judges, then by kings. We know these kings well from the Old Testament: Saul the misguided, David the valiant and crafty, Solomon the wise and opulent. It was David, ruling from 1010 to 970 B.C., who finished the task of trouncing the Philistines, and it was Solomon his son, reigning in oriental splendor from 970 to 930 B.C., who brought the kingdom of Israel to the height of its power.

David chose as the capital of the kingdom the hilltop city of Jerusalem, far inland, which he took by force from its inhabitants, the Jebusites. Jerusalem bore a secondary name, Zion, whose origin is uncertain. Perhaps it was the name of the fortress built by the Jebusites to defend Jerusalem. By metaphorical extension the name became attached to a hill within the city and then to the city itself, so that "Zion" came to mean Jerusalem, and "the dwellers of Zion" the Israelites. There were various other metaphorical uses of the word; Jerusalem was poetically personified as a woman, "the daughter of Zion," but "the sons and daughters of Zion" was a way of referring to the Hebrew population as a whole. In time Zion acquired powerful mystical and emotional overtones, carrying a symbolic charge of meaning to which every Jew responded.

Within Jerusalem David selected a site for a great temple, and Solomon brought it into being, with the aid of his Phoenician ally, Hiram of Tyre. Solomon purchased from Hiram timber of cedar and timber of fir, and hired Phoenician craftsmen, and erected a lavishly decorated edifice on Mount Moriah in Jerusalem, with a brazen altar and doors of gold, and inlays of precious stones, and veils of blue, and purple, and crimson, and fine linen, with cherubim wrought thereon. The Great Temple of Solomon was nothing that the simple desert patriarch Abraham would have understood. It was a trumpet blast of magnificence, announcing the arrival on the world scene of a new and important nation. Its site became, and remains, the holiest place in the Hebrew world.

Upon the death of Solomon the kingdom, little more than a century old in its unified form, split into a pair of mutually hostile states. The ten tribes of the northern half of the country proclaimed their own kingdom under the name of Israel; the two remaining tribes formed the kingdom of Judah in the south, centered on Jerusalem and the temple. These small, weak realms managed to maintain a precarious independence for several centuries, until their invasion late in the eighth century B.C. by the Assyrians. Judah, aided by a timely plague in the enemy camp, managed to stand off the militaristic giant in 726 B.C., and survived thereafter by submitting to Assyrian dictation. But the northern kingdom, invaded in 721, was utterly defeated and its whole population carried off captive to Assyria. Nothing further ever was heard from the ten tribes of Israel—the Ten Lost Tribes of much pseudoanthropological mythology—and from then on the Hebrews were known as *yehudim*, "men of Judah," from which our word *Jew* is derived.

The catastrophe that befell the kingdom of Israel was the first of a melancholy repetitive series. In 586 B.C. the kingdom of Judah fell to Nebuchadnezzar's Babylonians, successors to the Assyrian empire. Nebuchadnezzar's men sacked the Temple of Solomon and hauled the citizens of Judah to Babylon. No Jews now remained in Palestine, and one product of this Babylonian captivity was an eloquent literature of lament for the lost land. In captivities to come, Jews would turn for consolation to such poems as Psalm 137—

By the rivers of Babylon, there we sat down, yea, we wept, when we remembered Zion.
We hanged our harps upon the willows in the midst thereof.
For there they that carried us away captive required of us mirth, saying, Sing us one of the songs of Zion.
How shall we sing the Lord's song in a strange land?
If I forget thee, O Jerusalem, let my right hand forget her cunning.

If I do not remember thee, let my tongue cleave to the roof of my mouth; if I prefer not Jerusalem above my chief joy. . . .

In 539 B.C. Babylonia fell to Cyrus of Persia, and the following year the tolerant Cyrus permitted the exiled Jews to return to their homes. Only 40,000 accepted the offer, a small fraction of the number carried off to Babylon half a century earlier. This loyal remnant, these few who had not forgotten Jerusalem, rebuilt the looted temple and founded a new Jewish kingdom, which enjoyed self-government for centuries under the auspices first of the Persians, then of the Greeks after Alexander the Great's conquest of Persia. Gone now were the pretensions to splendor of Solomon's day. Yet this chastened latter-day Jewish kingdom was responsible for the greatest cultural achievements of Judaism: the codification of various sacred texts into the Torah, the Five Books of Moses; the construction of the historical sections of the Old Testament; and the composition of the poetic and philosophical masterpieces of the Bible—Job, Ecclesiastes, the books of the prophets, the Song of Songs. This period is known as the time of the Second Temple.

The empire of Alexander split apart when the conqueror died in 323 B.C., and the Near East, including Palestine, passed into the power of Seleucus, one of Alexander's generals. It was a king of this Seleucid dynasty, Antiochus IV Epiphanes, who in 168 B.C. desecrated the Second Temple by using it to sacrifice to Zeus, and this outrage touched off the first of the four Jewish revolts to which modern Israelis look with warm respect. An aged priest named Mattathias, of the priestly family of Hasmoneans, defied Antiochus' order to establish altars to the Greek gods in Palestine, and himself slew an apostate Jew who was about to offer a pagan sacrifice. It was the signal for a general uprising against the Seleucids, led by the five sons of Mattathias, and in particular by Judas surnamed the Maccabee, "the appointed one." By 165 B.C. the Seleucids were routed, and Judas the Maccabee himself lit the candles of rededication at the cleansed Second Temple. This is the event the Jews commemorate in their annual festival of Hanukkah. Political freedom took somewhat longer to gain than religious freedom, and two decades of warfare followed before Simon, last survivor of the sons of Mattathias, was able to inaugurate the Hasmonean dynasty of a sovereign Jewish state in 143 B.C.

The Hasmoneans ruled successfully at first, expanding their

power until for a while they controlled much the same territory that had comprised the kingdom of David and Solomon. But quarreling factions within the Jewish community and within the Hasmonean family itself sapped the vitality of the kingdom, and it fell to the Roman general Pompey in 63 B.C. Shortly the Romans extinguished the Hasmonean line and founded their own puppet dynasty by naming Herod, a Palestinian Jew of Roman citizenship, as King of Judaea in 37 B.C. Herod, who is no hero to Israel, was a weak man of strong ambitions, and gratified his hunger for immortality in grandiose construction projects. The Temple in Jerusalem, which had fallen into dilapidation, he rebuilt to something like Solomonic splendor; he created a whole new city on the coast, Caesarea; and he sprinkled the realm with palaces for himself, of which one of the most impressive was atop a desert peak called Masada, near the Dead Sea.

The Romans preferred to remain aloof from the people they had conquered, and they interfered as little as possible in the daily life of the Jews of Palestine. So long as taxes were remitted regularly to Rome, the Jews might do as they pleased. It was in the spirit of this hands-off policy that a Roman official allowed a faction of conservative Jews to obtain the execution of a young Jewish prophet, Jesus of Nazareth, whose unorthodox teachings and blasphemous claims disturbed them.

But in time the Jews came to chafe under Roman rule; taxation increased, religious fanaticism took command, and an eruption of nationalistic spirit led to a revolt against Rome in A.D. 64. This uprising, too, has potent meaning for today's Israelis, though unlike that of the Maccabees it ended in complete disaster. The Romans, caught off guard at first by unexpectedly fierce Jewish resistance, ultimately demonstrated their usual military skill and, after years of bitter fighting, captured Jerusalem in A.D. 70. Emperor Vespasian had placed his son Titus, a future emperor, in command of the war against the Jews. Aware of the symbolic value of the Temple, Titus sealed his victory by destroying it beyond hope of rebuilding. He left nothing but some fragments of its outer wall chiefly along the western side. The mighty stone blocks of the western wall, some of them probably part of Solomon's original edifice, became the Wailing Wall at which Jews for nearly 1,900 years would bemoan the obliteration of the Holy of Holies.

Some fight was left in the Jews, though, and another symbol emerged. A last outpost of resistance remained atop the rock of Masada, where about a thousand Jewish defenders held out in Herod's fortress. In A.D. 72 a Roman legion undertook the siege of Masada, and after great effort managed to find a way to the summit; but the Jews took their own lives before the Romans could capture them. To a modern young Israeli, Masada is more holy even than the Wailing Wall, for it represents the grandeur, rather than the sorrow, that can come with defeat. The spirit of this resurrected nation is contained in the slogan engraved on a coin commemorating the recent archaeological restoration of the mountain stronghold: "Masada Shall Not Fall Again."

Jewish nationalism revived in the century after the destruction of the Temple and the fall of Masada. There were rebellions against the Romans in 113 and in 132; this last revolt was led by a latter-day Maccabee, the charismatic Shimon Bar-Kochba, whose desperate and briefly successful war against the Romans was the final flicker of Jewish might until our own time. Bar-Kochba was slain in 135, and the coins struck by his regime became bitter souvenirs of lost sovereignty. Jerusalem was hammered to rubble and a plow drawn across its site. The Romans forbade the practice of Judaism in the new Roman city of Aelia Capitolina that rose where Jerusalem had been, and decreed that no Jew might set foot in the city more often than once a year. Zion was lost. Dreams of one more revolt were foolish fantasies. Palestine now cast forth its Jews once again, but not to any brief Babylonian exile of fifty years. The long migration was beginning, the scattering, the Diaspora, the dispersal of the Jews, who would spill out now into Asia and Europe, into every land, a strange and despised people keeping apart from others and carrying with them everywhere their Book, their creed, and their sad memories of the unforgotten Jerusalem, of the forfeited Zion.

2.

Palestine remained Roman until Rome's metamorphosis into Byzantium in the fourth century A.D., and then it was a Byzantine province until 636. Byzantium found it a profitable possession, for now it was a magnet for Christian pilgrims. The followers of that Palestinian prophet Jesus, having inherited Rome and the rest of Europe, came in hordes to see the places where their Saviour had lived and the place of his death. The pilgrims paid tolls to the Byzantines and crowded toward such wonders as the cup of the Last Supper, the Crown of Thorns, the bones of the apostles, and other holy relics. The dispersed Jews, to whom the Holy Land had been sacred a thousand years before Jesus, were excluded from the privilege of making pilgrimages to their own revered places in Palestine. Those places were tended only by the small Jewish population that had managed to remain in the country despite catastrophe and adversities.

Early in the seventh century a prophet arose among the sons of Ishmael. He was Mohammed, a merchant of the Arabian city of Mecca, who as a young man drew away from the idolatry of his people and embraced the Judaeo-Christian idea of One True God. "There is no God but God, and Mohammed is his Prophet," his followers declare to this day. He made himself the voice of Allah, and men listened. The religion that he preached owed much to Judaism and Christianity, which Mohammed did not deny; he recognized Moses and Jesus as great prophets. His creed, simple and direct, went to the hearts of the Arabs. It had no rituals, no elaborate doctrines, no priesthood. Mohammed called on all men to bow to God, to accept Allah's will, and to recognize all other men as brothers. The name of the religion, *Islam*, means "surrender," and Mohammed's followers are *Moslems*, "those who surrender themselves."

Driven from his own city in A.D. 622 by enemies of the new faith, Mohammed established himself in another Arabian city, Medina, and formed an army of men willing to shed blood in Allah's name. The Moslem conquests began. Islam was a strange combination of the austerely religious and the bloodthirsty; the wars of the Moslems were pious wars that used the sword to bring the message of Allah's justice to unbelievers.

Mohammed sent a message to Heraclius, the Byzantine Emperor, asking him to embrace Islam. Heraclius paid no attention to the desert prophet; he was busy with a war against the Persians, who had occupied Palestine. The Emperor drove the Persians out and returned to his mighty city of Constantinople. But then the Moslems advanced out of Arabia, under Mohammed and his successors. The trumpet sounded; the curved swords gleamed in the sun; Moslems swept onward through North Africa, Egypt, Syria, Palestine. A clash with Byzantium was inevitable. In 636,

Moslem troops met Christian troops near the Sea of Galilee, and in a blinding sandstorm the men of the desert massacred the Byzantines. So the Holy Land passed into Arab rule.

The tide of Moslem expansion surged on until they were in Europe itself, conquering Spain in the early eighth century and nearly taking France as well. After their defeat by Charles Martel at the battle of Tours in 732, they halted their outward drive, and turned their energies toward building a rich and complex civilization; the Arabs of the ninth and tenth centuries experienced an astonishing cultural upsurge that made them the intellectual leaders of the world.

Except in occasional moments of fanaticism, they tolerated Christians and Jews in the lands they had conquered. The inhabitants of the Holy Land found them easy masters. Taxes were lower than they had been under the rule of Byzantium, and the Moslem sense of justice created an atmosphere of tranquility. The meager Jewish community in Palestine was able to sustain itself, although there was no migration of Jews back into the old homeland, and certainly no suggestion of a Jewish military campaign to recapture Palestine. As a military force, as a nation, the Jews had ceased to exist.

The Holy Land changed hands once more in 1071, when the Arabs lost it to a newer and more vigorous band of Islamic warriors, the Seljuk Turks. The Near East now was fragmented, with Egypt remaining in Arab control and various Turkish chieftains establishing principalities in Syria and Palestine. This political chaos resulted in the effective closing of the Holy Land to Christian pilgrims from Europe, and led to the commencement of the Crusades, a fitful series of wars in which European princes sought to place Palestine under Christian rule.

This strange episode of history was of little significance to the Jews, who had no reason to regard the Crusaders as their friends. When the troops of the First Crusade marched eastward across Europe in 1096, they amused themselves along the way by massacring the Jews of Germany; and when they seized Jerusalem from the Turks in 1099, it was of no benefit to the sons and daughters of Zion. The Crusaders held Jerusalem until 1187, and continued to rule other parts of Palestine for a century after that. In 1291 they were driven out by the Egyptians, and in 1517 the Egyptians gave way to the Ottoman Turks. Down to the early twentieth century

Palestine remained a sleepy, decaying, half-forgotten corner of the vast, mismanaged Ottoman Empire. Through all of those years the Jews of the world faithfully mentioned Palestine in their prayers, and at the annual feast of the Passover inevitably spoke of celebrating the festival "next year in Jerusalem," but next year never came.

In fact there was little realistic expectation among Jews that Palestine would ever be theirs again. The longing for Zion was a conditioned reflex, not a political program. The Jews had settled far from the land of David, establishing communities in the Diaspora that had taken on an air of permanence, whether they were miserable ghettos or substantial, comfortable islands of Judaism.

The oldest of these communities was the Babylonian one, which could trace its origin back to the fall of Judah in 586 B.C. The Babylonian Jews were the descendants of those who had been carried off by Nebuchadnezzar and who had not chosen to return to Palestine after the fall of Babylonia in 539 B.C. They had outlasted not only Babylonia but the city of Babylon itself, which over the centuries crumbled and was replaced by the new Arab capital of Baghdad a few miles away. The expulsion of Jews from Palestine after the Bar-Kochba revolt of A.D. 132–135 had greatly swollen the Babylonian community, and it was the center of Jewish life and scholarship for centuries thereafter, flourishing particularly during the golden age of Arab life in the seventh to tenth centuries.

The other great early Jewish center was in Alexandria, Egypt, which dated from Second Temple times. It, too, prospered after the Arab conquest, and many Egyptian Jews attained positions of power and responsibility in Moslem society, while retaining their ancient faith. There was no reason why the Alexandrian Jews or those of Mesopotamia could not have gone back to Palestine at any time during the Arab era. But there was also no reason, except that of sentiment, why they should. Life was good where they were.

Other Jews of the Diaspora were less fortunate. They had spread into Europe in the first three centuries after Christ, settling in the major cities of what was then the Roman Empire. Jewish communities were founded in Italy and Greece, in France, in Spain. Rome was tolerant of alien religions and these Jews met no hardships at first. But eventually an alien religion—Christianity— conquered Rome, and Judaism suffered. The Christianized Roman

emperors of the fourth century denounced the "nefarious sect"
and its "sacrilegious gatherings," and persecutions followed that
were interrupted only by the barbarian invasions of the empire.
Later, when the barbarians also became Christians, the Jews suffered again; the seventh century saw a particularly fierce campaign
of forced conversions of Jews to Christianity all across the continent.

Soon, though, they found sanctuaries of Arab tolerance in Spain
and North Africa. In the ninth century, too, Europe began discovering uses for these curious people, and Jews were invited into
France, Germany, and Italy to organize commerce. In Palestine
they had been farmers and shepherds, but those callings were
forgotten, and the medieval Jews became Europe's middle class,
engaging in banking activities that were forbidden to pious Christians. There was no room for Jews in Europe's peasantry, but a
definite need for them as merchants, peddlers, moneylenders.
When William the Conqueror took England in 1066, he brought
Jews along to aid in the transformation of that predominantly
agricultural country into a commercial power.

But in the centuries that followed, European Christians took
over most of the Jews' mercantile functions, leaving them only the
trade of moneylending, since Christians were forbidden to make
loans at interest. Increasingly Jews became targets of abuse. Their
distinctive clothing, the odd language that they spoke among
themselves, and their refusal to accept Christianity drew upon
them the fear and hatred that those who are different always
inspire; and the belief that Jews of all eras bore continued burdens
of guilt for the death of Christ made it almost an act of piety to
cheat, injure, or even kill a Jew. The ignorant hated them because
Jews were strange; the upper classes hated them because Jews
were everyone's creditors. It is easy to despise Shylock.

Jews were forced to live in specific quarters, the ghettos; they
were subjected to special heavy taxation; periodically their wealth
was confiscated altogether to meet the expenses of some spend-
thrift feudal prince. Rumors frequently spread that the Jews,
mumbling in their synagogues, drank the blood of Christian infants, or practiced even more ghastly rites. Waves of Jew-slaughter
were the customary consequences of such whisperings. When the
Black Death decimated Europe in 1348, Jews were accused of
having poisoned the wells. Ordinarily, though, no such intricate

excuse was needed to touch off a new round of Jew-baiting.

To many rulers it seemed simplest to get rid of these troublesome people, especially after Italian bankers started to risk their immortal souls by making loans. In the thirteenth century the Jews were banished from England, in the fourteenth from France, in the fifteenth from Spain and most of Italy. Except for parts of Germany and Italy, Western Europe now was closed to them.

Always resilient, they found havens elsewhere. Most of them went to Turkey or Russia, although many Spanish Jews settled in North Africa. No political barriers prevented them from undoing the whole Diaspora and returning to Palestine, but they did not go there; the Holy Land had become a wilderness of marshes and deserts during the Moslem centuries, and it had small need of merchants and moneylenders, while the Jews were now a wholly urban people. In theory, they longed for Zion; in practice, a return to the homeland was unimaginable.

The Jews who flooded into Eastern Europe in the fifteenth and sixteenth centuries were not usually permitted to live in the cities. They went out into the countryside and created an extraordinary new culture, neither urban nor rural, based on the *shtetl*, the tiny village. In these hermetically sealed communities the Jews lived in a completely self-contained way. They produced enough food to keep themselves going; they managed to support a vast nonproductive population of rabbis and Biblical scholars; they hedged themselves in with rigid dietary laws and customs of daily life which, though based on scriptural precedent, would have amazed the Palestinian Jews of the past. It was a world of long beards and dark clothes, of scrupulously modest wives who avoided all show of glamor, of a nightmare folklore of golems and dybbuks.

Shtetl life was something rich and strange, an airless environment born of isolation and inbreeding. Hebrew, the traditional language of the Jews, was reserved only for religious purposes. They spoke Yiddish, a mongrel tongue based on German and Hebrew, outside the synagogue. To the *goyim*—the Christians about them—the *shtetl* folk seemed unutterably bizarre, and the Russians and Poles in particular expressed their amazement in the form of frequent violent invasions of the Jewish villages, the infamous pogroms. The Jews, united by the powerful solidarity of their new culture, withstood these onslaughts and simply drew closer together, so that *shtetl* life grew ever more involuted and hermetic.

By the seventeenth century, a more liberal climate of thought made Jews again welcome in Western Europe, and a great many, mostly descended from the exiled Spanish Jews, moved into France, England, and the Netherlands. (The most enterprising ones of all went to the New World.) These returning Jews quickly became assimilated into the mainstream of Western European life. They adopted Western clothing and Western languages; the ghettos were no more; the old laws governing and limiting Jewish freedoms were repealed or simply forgotten, so that the difference between Jew and non-Jew grew slight. Religious dedication among these Westernized Jews slackened with their emancipation. Many left the synagogue, and some even found it convenient to become Christians. They attained positions of power in the arts and sciences and especially in banking and commerce.

The escape of the Jews from the ghetto was best symbolized by the rise of the Rothschild family of bankers to international prominence, great wealth, and titles of aristocracy in several countries in the nineteenth century, or by the ascension of Benjamin Disraeli, a convert to Christianity whose name proclaimed his thousands of years of Jewish ancestry, to the prime ministership of Great Britain. These sophisticated, assimilated Western Jews looked upon their cousins of the *shtetl* as quaint and primitive backwoodsmen with whom they had little in common.

It was not to be expected that the enlightened and emancipated Jew of Paris or London or Berlin of the 1850's would show much interest in moving to Palestine. No one was persecuting them where they were, and opportunities were boundless. Look at the Rothschilds! Look at Disraeli! Besides, Palestine was a distant and uncomfortable land, ruled by the barbaric Turks and occupied mainly by ignorant, filthy Arabs. Should one give up one's café and one's newspaper and go to live among the Bedouin tribesmen, merely to be close to the place where the Temple of Solomon had been? Furthermore, the current Turkish administration clearly did not want Jews settling in Palestine, and interposed all sorts of bureaucratic obstructions to block the entry of those few who wished to return to Zion.

The call to return was much more likely to come from Eastern Europe, out of the stifling world of the *shtetl*. Conditions were growing cruel there. The Jews of Eastern Europe tripled in number between 1800 and 1850, and doubled again in the next 50 years, but there was no corresponding increase in community

income. The Jewish villages of Russia, Poland, and Rumania became backwaters of poverty. A few Jews escaped to the cities to
become laborers in the new industrialized society, but most remained trapped in despair. To some rabbis of the nineteenth century a return to Zion seemed the only hope, although the return
that they preached was based more in mystical thought than on
practical grounds. Their appeals had little impact in the *shtetl*,
where the journey to Palestine seemed as impossible as a journey
to the moon.

Only after the assassination of the liberal Tsar Alexander II in
1881 unleashed a new series of pogroms, the most terrible since
the Middle Ages, did the *shtetl* folk begin to think seriously of once
again seeking some more hospitable place. For many, that place
was the United States, and soon a crowded new *shtetl* was taking
form on New York City's Lower East Side; in the generation prior
to World War I more than two million Eastern European Jews
entered this country.

Others—only a few—looked toward Palestine. In 1881, Leo
Pinsker, a Jewish physician from Odessa, published a pamphlet
that argued that the only solution to the problem of Jewish persecution was migration to some place where Jews could form a
nation of their own. As it was, they comprised a "ghost nation"
within other countries, forever vulnerable. Pinsker did not specifically propose Palestine as the site for this Jewish state, but it was
a logical choice, and by 1882 a group of Russian Jews had founded
the first Zionist organization, Choveve Zion, "the Lovers of Zion."
Under the auspices of Choveve Zion a trickle of Jews made their
way from the Tsarist realm to Palestine: about 25,000 in all between 1882 and 1903.

The Eastern European Jews' yearning for Palestine was a profoundly emotional thing, almost mystical, virtually incomprehensible to the Gentile. Chaim Weizmann, a *shtetl* Jew from Russia
who was eight years old when the Choveve Zion movement began
in 1882, and who would become, 66 years later, the first President
of Israel, declares in his autobiography, *Trial and Error*, that the
Jews of his village "were separated from the peasants by a whole
inner universe of memories and experiences. In my early childhood Zionist ideas and aspirations were already awake in Russian
Jewry. My father was not yet a Zionist, but the house was steeped
in rich Jewish tradition, and Palestine was at the center of the

ritual, a longing for it implicit in our life. Practical nationalism did not assume form till some years later, but the 'Return' was in the air, a vague, deep-rooted Messianism, a hope which would not die."

Choveve Zion, Weizmann indicates, was hardly a well-organized political movement:

"Looking back from the vantage point of present-day Zionism, I can see that we had not the slightest idea of how the practical ends of the movement were to be realized. We knew that the doors of Palestine were closed to us. We knew that every Jew who entered Palestine was given 'the red ticket,' which he had to produce on demand, and by virtue of which he could be expelled at once by the Turkish authorities. We knew that the Turkish law forbade the acquisition of land by Jews. Perhaps if we had considered the matter too closely, or tried to be too systematic, we would have been frightened off. We merely went ahead in a small, blind, persistent way. Jews settled in Palestine, and they were not expelled. They bought land, sometimes through straw men, sometimes by bribes, for Turkish officialdom was even more corrupt than the Russian. Houses were built, in evasion of the law. Between *baksheesh* and an infinite variety of subterfuges, the first little colonies were created. Things got done, somehow; not big things, but enough to whet the appetite and keep us going."

These pioneer Zionists came into a dismal land, malarial, eroded, unproductive. Its population in 1882 was about half a million, mostly Arab. There were 25,000 Jews, nearly all of them descended from the remnants of Palestine's two million Jews of Roman times, although some were pious, elderly European Jews who had made individual migrations so that they might die on the soil of Zion. This existing pre-Zionist community of Palestinian Jews lived mainly in the cities of Jerusalem, Hebron, Tiberias, and Safed. Their only occupation was the study of the sacred books and the commentaries on those books. They were unfit by age and training for agriculture, and Palestine had no industry or commerce. This anachronistic community of aged scholars was supported entirely by contributions from the Jews of Europe, who regarded it as an act of the highest charity to sustain them regardless of their own poverty.

The Jews who now entered Palestine with the help of Choveve Zion were altogether different: young, energetic, idealistic, ro-

mantic colonizers who proposed to break from the *shtetl* traditions
and become farmers and manual laborers. They would return to
the old Palestinian ways and—literally—send fresh air sweeping
through Jewish life. To symbolize their adherence to the vigor of
ancient times, they chose to make Hebrew their everyday language, which horrified the older inhabitants, among whom Hebrew was spoken only in the rites of the synagogue. Those rites
themselves meant little to the newcomers. They were impatient
with the endless droning recapitulations of past oppressions and
with the maze of dietary laws and other restrictions that gave
structure to orthodox Jewish life. These would-be Jewish farmers
felt they could not spare the time for such things when there was
farming to be done.

The Choveve Zion immigrants were not the first to come to
Palestine with such ideas. In 1878, a group of Hungarian Jews had
established an agricultural colony called Petach Tikvah, "The
Gate of Hope," eight miles from the port of Jaffa. A few years
earlier a French group had founded an agricultural school, Mikveh
Yisrael, "The Refuge of Israel," near Jaffa. But Petach Tikvah
failed, and the agricultural school produced few alumni.

The new pioneers failed also. They reopened Petach Tikvah and
set up half a dozen new colonies, but they knew little about tilling
the soil and were hard put to cope with the demands of corrupt
Turkish officials, the enmity of their Arab neighbors, and the
hostility of the orthodox Jewish community. Within a few years
they had to be rescued by the philanthropy of Baron Edmond de
Rothschild of Paris, who paid their debts, bought them new tools,
and sent experts in farm management from France to instruct
them. The Rothschild-reorganized colonies survived, but only by
hiring cheap Arab labor; the Jewish pioneers became dealers in
oranges instead of farmers, and found themselves middle-class
merchants even here in Palestine. This was not what the enthusiastic idealists had anticipated when they left Russia.

3.

In Europe, Jewish intellectuals looked with disapproval on the
experiment in Palestine. They knew it could not succeed. It depended entirely on Rothschild's bounty; the widely scattered little
settlements would perish the moment the baron decided to cut his
losses. To survive in the Holy Land, they insisted, Jews must learn

to be farmers themselves, not mere overseers to the Arabs.

Some went beyond that. Survival, they said, depends on achieving political independence in Palestine. Persuade the Turks to let go of that worthless sliver of land, buy out the Arabs somehow, establish a real Jewish state, and draw the exiles home.

This proposal scandalized many European Jews, notably the assimilated Western ones, but also those of the *shtetl*. The Easterners had spiritual objections to political Zionism. Why dilute Judaism, they asked, with strivings toward sovereignty? Why compel ourselves to worry about a national budget, a postal service, a diplomatic corps, and other such things, irrelevant to man's dialogue with God? So long as free immigration of Jews to Palestine can be assured, let the Turks continue to handle the machinery of government, and let us concern ourselves only with spiritual matters, with the return of wanderers to sacred soil.

Western Jews had more practical fears. They believed that a campaign for a Jewish national state would draw uncomfortable attention to them and might encourage anti-Semitism. If such a state materialized, they could be exposed to charges of divided allegiance, and would be asked if their loyalty to the Jewish state went beyond the loyalty they should feel to the countries of which they were citizens. By all means let there be Jewish settlements in Palestine, but let us not try to create a nation there!

It was a debate destined to continue for decades, and echoes of it are sometimes heard today, even though the ambitions of political Zionism have been fulfilled. In the 1890's, though, it was a topic of passionate concern among European Jews, particularly after the emergence of the prophet of political Zionism, Theodor Herzl.

He was an improbable prophet, an assimilated Jew, a literary dilettante, proud of his emancipation from the ghetto and wholly detached from the traditions of Judaism. Born in Budapest in 1860 to a well-to-do bourgeois family, educated in Vienna, a connoisseur of opera and a brilliant essayist for Austrian newspapers, a successful author of boudoir comedies, Herzl had turned his back completely on his Jewishness and, until the age of 34, managed to avoid a confrontation with any of the special problems the world holds for Jews.

He was well aware of the existence of anti-Semitism, which now was resurgent in the Germanic countries. In Germany itself Jews were openly accused of dominating national life, of holding unhealthy control over finance, and of conducting themselves in an alien, insufficiently German manner. The Anti-Semitic League, a public organization, had in 1881 asked Bismarck to disenfranchise the Jews and halt their further immigration into Germany. An Anti-Semitic Congress had been held in Dresden the next year to discuss implementation of this program. Herzl's private solution for anti-Semitism was assimilation: dress like a Gentile, talk like a Gentile, live like a Gentile, and the Gentiles will not despise you.

But in 1894, while serving as the Paris correspondent of the *Neue Freie Presse* of Vienna, Herzl had a disquieting close-range look at anti-Semitism when he covered the Dreyfus court-martial. The Dreyfus affair, involving an Austrian Jew in the French army who was charged with being a spy for Germany, exposed the raw Jew-hatred of the time as a widespread popular sentiment. "We are a people living perpetually in enemy territory!" Herzl wrote. Nothing could save the Jew from anti-Semitism; he was hated because he was strange.

Herzl's first attempt at solving the problem was grotesque. If all Jewish children were baptized, he said, anti-Semitism would necessarily disappear in a single generation. He imagined "a solemn procession accompanied by the pealing of bells" proceeding to the cathedral of St. Stephen in Vienna. "There shall be no furtiveness and no shamefacedness. . . . Our children will pass over to Christianity before their conversion can bear the character either of cowardice or interested scheming."

Herzl's Viennese editor, a Jew, refused to publish the absurd proposal. As the Dreyfus trial reached its bitter climax, Herzl came to understand the silliness of what he had suggested. Dreyfus, after all, had been an assimilated Jew, proud of his military uniform, and what good had it done him? Though clearly innocent, he was on his way to Devil's Island! Assimilation was no answer. It would bring an end to Judaism, but not to anti-Semitism. The only real solution to the problem was a mass exodus of Jews to a land where they might live apart from Gentiles. Herzl the literary playboy abruptly became Herzl the Zionist.

He was not the first cosmopolitan Jew to undergo this metamorphosis. An important predecessor was the Franco-German Jew Moses Hess, who had drifted into socialist atheism and nearly into Christianity before realizing he was doomed to be scorned as a Jew no matter what disguise he donned. In *Rome and Jerusalem,* published in 1862, Hess observed, "No reform of the Jewish religion, however extreme, is radical enough for the educated German Jew. But the endeavors are in vain. . . . The German hates the Jewish religion not less than the race; he objects less to the Jews' peculiar beliefs than to their peculiar noses." It was self-destructive folly, Hess asserted, to give up Jewish culture and religion and try to camouflage one's self as a *goy*. A Jewish state in Palestine was the only answer.

Herzl apparently knew nothing of Hess, nor of the Choveve Zion movement, nor of any of the other pamphleteers and theoreticians of the back-to-Palestine faction. So remote was he from Jewish thought that he was compelled to invent Zionism independently. In the summer of 1895 he produced his first manifesto, *Der Judenstaat*, or *The Jewish State*, a document in many ways as naïve as his essay in favor of mass baptism, yet at the same time the first significant step that was taken on the road toward Israel.

In *Der Judenstaat* Herzl called for a self-governing Jewish republic outside Europe. Palestine was a preferable location for historical reasons, but Herzl had no strong commitment to the ancient Zion, and said that Argentina might be just as satisfactory. ("We shall take what we are offered," he wrote.) Lower-class Jews would be shipped out first to build roads and houses; the middle class would follow when accommodations were ready. There would be a Jewish army of defense. Thrift and hard work were to be encouraged in every way. Each citizen would continue to speak the language he knew best, in "memory of the native land out of which we have been driven." Herzl rejected the idea of Hebrew as a national language: "We cannot converse together in Hebrew. Who amongst us has a sufficient acquaintance with Hebrew to ask for a railway ticket in that language?" A corporation would be set up in London to handle the raising of capital for the project.

It was a dream of a tidy Jewish Switzerland far from the obsessive bigotry of Europe. It might have remained no more than a dream, except for Herzl's new-found Messianic fervor. He was a man of great presence, formidably bearded, theatrically handsome, magnetic, charged now with a sense of mission, and he was irresistible. The year 1896 saw him publishing his pamphlet, pounding on the doors of the great Jewish bankers, reading his theories to gatherings of Viennese intellectuals, wangling inter-

views with the Grand Duke of Baden, with Bismarck, with the
papal envoy in Vienna, with any high figure who might lend
influence, even hurrying off to Istanbul in his first doomed attempt
to persuade the Sultan of Turkey to give him Palestine. Herzl's
frantic quest was so desperately energetic that he drew the numerous armchair Zionists out of their lethargy. In 1897 he called them
to the First Zionist Congress in Basel, Switzerland, and Jews from
all over the world answered the call.

Many of them detested Herzl. His flamboyance, his curious
mixture of sophistication and naïveté, and his furious energy irritated them. Some resented him as a late-comer, bursting into the
vineyard of Zionism that they had tended peacefully for fifteen or
twenty years. Yet they came, and they listened. And though they
made jokes about Herzl's beard and his style of prose, they were
swayed. Zionism was alive. It had found its prophet. At the end
of August, 1897, two hundred delegates gathered for the First
Zionist Congress. Clad in full evening dress, they heard Herzl say,
"We are here to lay the foundation stone of the house which is to
shelter the Jewish nation." He called for acquisition of an internationally recognized legal right to colonize Palestine, the formation
of a permanent Zionist organization uniting all Jews, and the
promotion of large-scale migration to Palestine. A debate on ends
and means followed. It lasted five and a half hours. Finally the
exasperated novelist and philosopher, Max Nordau, offered a one-
sentence statement of policy that avoided the worst point of con-
tention, whether the Jewish homeland should be a sovereign state
or merely a refuge for coreligionists: "Zionism seeks to secure for
the Jewish people a publicly recognized, legally secured homeland
in Palestine." Then the congress adjourned.

Herzl noted in his diary, "At Basle I founded the Jewish State.
If I were to say this today, I would be met by universal laughter.
In five years perhaps, and certainly in fifty, everyone will say it.
The State is already founded in the will of the people to the State."
He saw the future clearly, and missed the date of his prophecy by
only one year. At another time he wrote, "If you will it, it is no
dream."

4.

But how to implement the Zionist program? There was little
money available, no political leverage, and not even a united fol-

lowing. Many of the assimilated Jews, who were also the wealthiest Jews, wanted nothing to do with Zionism in any form. The *shtetl* Jews of the East were suspicious of this project devised by worldly Western sophisticates, whose attitude toward them seemed insufferably patronizing. Zionists themselves quarreled over whether they were building a Jewish "state" or a Jewish "home," and a majority opposed the idea of nationhood. Herzl himself, though never relinquishing the dream of sovereignty, tactfully allowed the euphemism "homestead" to be used to avoid arousing the sensitive.

One step was to form a World Zionist Organization, with Herzl as its first president. Out of this, he hoped, would evolve the governmental structure of the eventual state. Within two years, the World Zionist Organization had 114,000 members, but growth thereafter was slow. By 1914 there were only 130,000 members, and that slender increase had come only after a steep decline from the original number.

The next step was to raise money. Herzl told the Second Zionist Congress, held at Basel in 1898, that he had founded a bank, the Jewish Colonial Trust, in London; it would serve as the agent for eliciting contributions from the rich Jews. He was sure that the Jewish philanthropists, the Rothschilds, Montefiores, Hirsches, and the rest, would give generously so that their impoverished brethren might go to Palestine. In this expectation he was wrong. The big philanthropists gave, somewhat reluctantly, but Zionism could not attain solvency until it had reached into the less capacious but more numerous pockets of the Jewish middle class.

Then, a way had to be found to persuade Turkey to give up Palestine—for the consensus of the First Congress had been that Palestine was the only acceptable homeland. But Turkey was a crumbling monarchy, decadent and bankrupt, whose fuddled old Sultan and sinister viziers had no sympathy toward any kind of change. Already stained with the blood of thousands of Armenian nationalists, were the Turks likely to be any more inclined toward Jewish nationalism?

Herzl did his best. Kaiser Wilhelm II of Germany was vaguely favorable to Zionism, and was about to visit Sultan Abdul-Hamid in Istanbul as one stop in a tour of the Near East; Herzl spoke to the Kaiser's ministers, asking if the Kaiser would intercede with the Sultan on behalf of the Jews. An audience with Wilhelm was arranged for Herzl in Istanbul. The Zionist prophet met the German Emperor three times in October and November, 1898: once in the Turkish capital, once at the Jewish agricultural school of Mikveh Israel near Jaffa, and once in Jerusalem itself. For a while the Kaiser seemed interested in putting pressure on the Sultan and even in offering German protection to the new Jewish state. But then he reflected on possible international consequences of interfering in internal Turkish affairs and politely withdrew from the project.

Herzl struggled on, making the rounds of diplomats, dukes, and financiers. He felt time running out for him, for his heart was weak and he had already had several serious attacks. Drained by fatigue, troubled now by growing skepticism among his followers, he found strength somewhere to continue, and in May, 1901, succeeded in obtaining an audience with the Sultan. The old potentate hinted slyly that if the Jews could help him find the $150,000,000 he needed to settle the national debt, he might let them found small colonies in various parts of the Turkish Empire. After weeks of tragicomic negotiations it became clear that the Jews were not being offered unrestricted immigration into Palestine at all, but merely a chance to settle in the wastes of Mesopotamia. Herzl abandoned the Istanbul talks.

In October, 1902, he shifted his attention toward Great Britain, beginning an involvement between Britain and Zionism that was to last 46 years, commencing in hope and ending in bitterness. The British were powerful, tolerant, and progressive, Herzl felt; they seemed to abhor that dark, mystic anti-Semitism that kept creeping out of hiding on the continent of Europe; and they controlled such a vast empire that surely they could spare a little of it for the Jews. They could not give him Palestine, but they did have a protectorate over Egypt as a result of their interest in the Suez Canal, and perhaps they could be persuaded to lop off the Sinai Peninsula, the tract of land separating Egypt from Palestine, and give it to the Jews. This too was Biblical territory; Moses had set foot here. Most of the Sinai was a terrible desert, to be sure, but the Mediterranean coastal strip held promise, especially in the area around the town of El Arish. And the Sinai was just a few days' journey by camel from Jerusalem. It would do as a substitute for Palestine. Another possibility was the British-held island of Cyprus, in the eastern Mediterranean not far from the Holy Land.

The British government was willing to listen to Herzl because it sensed a potential Jewish problem developing in London: thousands of refugee Jews from Russia were piling up in the tenements of the East End, creating such fear of aliens that some Englishmen were talking of restrictions on immigration. It would avoid an ugly and un-British show of prejudice if these Jews had some other place to go. So Herzl was able to present his thesis to Joseph Chamberlain, the Colonial Secretary. Chamberlain at once rejected the Cyprus plan. Cyprus was already full of contentious Turks and Greeks, and introducing Jews would be an impossible complication. El Arish, though, had possibilities, and Chamberlain referred Herzl to the Foreign Office, under whose jurisdiction Egyptian affairs lay.

The Foreign Office investigated the possibility of giving El Arish to Herzl, and Herzl sent a Zionist committee to El Arish to see if the place was really suitable. The committee found El Arish lacking a reliable water supply. The Foreign Office found that it could not transfer Sinai territory to anyone without the permission of Turkey, which nominally had sovereignty over Egypt, and that in any case the Egyptians looked coldly on the notion of planting a Jewish state next door to them.

All options were closed to Herzl now. Though hardly past 40, he was mortally ill, and exhausted by the sniping coming at him from Eastern European Zionists who wanted Palestine or nothing. Where to turn? In 1903, a pogrom in the Russian town of Kishinev took 45 Jewish lives, injured hundreds, and left millions of Eastern Jews in terror. The pressures on Herzl to find a land of refuge increased. Where? Where? Joseph Chamberlain had an idea: The Jews could have Uganda.

It was a valid offer, and the Colonial Secretary's word was binding. In August, 1903, Herzl came before the Sixth Zionist Congress with a written commitment from the British government. He admitted that Uganda was not the true Zion; but times were harsh, the Russian Jews were in distress, and this tract in Africa offered an immediate answer, a resting place on the road back to Palestine. As Max Nordau put it, it was a *Nachtasyl*, a shelter for the night. Herzl asked the congress to authorize a committee to explore the Uganda offer.

The Eastern Europeans, the "Zion Zionists," were aghast. The idea of building a new Zion in an African wilderness seemed preposterous, and they feared that if they did take Uganda, they would lose all hope of someday getting Palestine. Herzl was accused from the floor of being a traitor to Zionism. Thirty-year-old Chaim Weizmann, who had left his Russian *shtetl* to take up a career in chemistry in Switzerland, made an impassioned anti-Ugandist speech. The congress was savagely divided; 295 voted in favor of investigating the British offer, 175 were opposed, about 100 abstained, and after the votes were recorded, the anti-Ugandists, mainly Russians, ostentatiously stalked out.

Herzl was amazed by their stubbornness. "These people have a rope around their necks, and still they refuse!" Haggard, drained, he tried in vain to end the secession.

And Uganda was a mirage after all. The British settlers there were alarmed at the prospect of being engulfed by a torrent of Jewish paupers. They set up an outcry, and, when Chamberlain left the Colonial Office, the offer was quietly withdrawn. Herzl, a broken man, went to Italy in search of a Zion in North Africa, collapsed in May, 1904, and died in July, at the age of 44.

Time has made his mistakes, his miscalculations, his opportunism, look less important; the intensity of his vision and the power of his dream are all we need to remember. Like Moses, he was denied the privilege of leading his people into the promised land, but he took them a long distance on the way.

5.

The World Zionist Organization survived the loss of its leader. Some of the Ugandists seceded permanently, but most returned to the group, and it continued to function, although at first in a lame, paralyzed way. Max Nordau and other eloquent Jewish intellectuals shied away from the responsibilities of running the organization, and finally its presidency went by default to one of Herzl's closest friends, David Wolffsohn of Cologne. He undertook the tasks of raising funds, of pressing for freer entry of Jews into Palestine, and of organizing world-wide support for the Zionist movement among political leaders. But in the decade following Herzl's death the center of Zionism gradually moved away from Wolffsohn and the official organization, now headquartered in Berlin, and toward the house in Manchester, England, where Chaim Weizmann had settled.

Weizmann was Herzl's antithesis in most respects: a *shtetl* Jew, fluent in Hebrew, deeply rooted in the traditions of Judaism, modest, reserved, with little liking for showmanship or pretentiousness, and wholly dedicated to the idea of a Jewish homeland in Palestine, nowhere else. Because he had been educated in the West and to some degree had taken on Western ways, Weizmann was ideally suited to span the gulf between the Eastern and Western Jewish communities, as well as to deal with the Gentile political leaders of Europe. Suave and diplomatic, at home in French, German, and English as well as in Hebrew, Yiddish, and Russian, a brilliant scientist and a shrewd negotiator, he seemed, in the eyes of the West, someone apart from the often uncouth Easterners. Yet, he never forgot the sufferings, the poverty, the despair of the villagers from whom he had sprung. As David Ben-Gurion expressed it, "Weizmann was the greatest Jewish emissary to the Gentile world, the most gifted and fascinating envoy the Jewish people ever produced. There was no one quite like him. With his Jewish grandeur, his Jewish profundity, his sense of history, his genius for expressing the centuries-old longings of Jewry, he represented to the non-Jewish world the very embodiment of the Jewish people."

After beginning his career as a chemist in Geneva, he moved to England in 1904—on the day of Herzl's funeral, as it happened. He had already distinguished himself as a scientist, though only 40, and had an intuitive feeling that his career would flourish more happily in England than in small, crowded Switzerland. He obtained a research scholarship at Manchester University, established contact with the English Zionists (whose continued fascination with Uganda he deplored), and gradually, without seeking it, found himself becoming a leader of the Zionist movement.

While still without any official position in the World Zionist Organization, Weizmann unexpectedly was thrust into an interview with Arthur James Balfour, the former Prime Minister of England, early in 1906. Balfour, a Conservative, was one of England's most vigorous leaders. He had become Prime Minister in 1902, had fallen from power at the end of 1905 after a split in his party, and now was struggling to regain his place in the general election of January, 1906. His own Parliamentary seat was in Manchester, and one of Weizmann's new English friends, the Zionist chemical manufacturer Charles Dreyfus, was chairman of the Manchester Conservative Party. In the midst of the campaign Dreyfus arranged for Weizmann to meet Balfour, hoping that the young Russian's sincerity and passion might sway Balfour toward some public commitment to the Zionist cause.

Weizmann, whose English was still uncertain, came before Balfour in a London hotel room. Balfour at once asked him why so many Jews were opposed to the Uganda offer. The British government, he said, really wished to do something to relieve Jewish misery, but was puzzled by the angry debate over the innocent proposal.

"In reply," Weizmann wrote, "I plunged into what I recall as a long harangue on the meaning of the Zionist movement. I dwelt on the spiritual side of Zionism, I pointed out that nothing but a deep religious conviction expressed in modern political terms could keep the movement alive, and that this conviction had to be based on Palestine and on Palestine alone. Any deflection from Palestine was—well, a form of idolatry. I added that if Moses had come into the Sixth Zionist Congress when it was adopting the resolution in favor of the Commission for Uganda, he would surely have broken the tablets once again."

Dismissing the Uganda idea as a misplaced and overhasty snatching of opportunity, he explained "the magic and romantic appeal" Palestine has for the Jews, and suddenly said, "Mr. Balfour, supposing I were to offer you Paris instead of London, would you take it?"

"But, Dr. Weizmann, we have London," Balfour replied.

"That is true," said Weizmann. "But we had Jerusalem when London was a marsh."

Balfour began to glimpse the meaning of the Zionist cause for the first time, and became Weizmann's first convert among the British ruling class. But the Conservatives lost the election, Balfour lost his own seat in Parliament, and nearly a decade would pass before he would be in a position to speak out on behalf of Zionism. During those years Weizmann continued his propaganda activities in England, and became involved in the activities of the World Zionist Organization, helping to ease the well-meaning but ineffectual Wolffsohn out of the presidency and replace him with another Herzl associate, Otto Warburg. But there was little sense of forward movement toward the attainment of a Jewish national state in Palestine.

However, Jewish migration into Palestine had begun again.

What Israelis call the second *aliyah* was under way. In Hebrew *aliyah* means "ascent"; in a literal sense one "goes up" to Jerusalem, that hilltop city above the Holy Land, and in a spiritual sense a Jew "ascends" when he settles in Palestine. The first *aliyah* had been the migration of 25,000 Eastern European Jews to Palestine, beginning in 1882, to found agricultural colonies. That movement had been virtually completed by the end of the nineteenth century. In 1904, impelled by the Kishinev pogrom and its bloody successors, a new wave of emigrants left Russia for the Holy Land. Between 1904 and 1914, when the coming of war shut off the flow, 40,000 more Russian Jews found their way into Palestine.

These newcomers were even more radical, more firmly pledged to a socialist-agrarian society, than the men and women of the first *aliyah* had been. Those were the old settlers now, comfortably established as managers of orange plantations employing Arabs; they had lost the impulse toward farming life with which they had left Russia. Now came *chalutzim*—pioneers—of great vigor, high ideals, strongly nationalist, Jews more in name than in practice, who went out into the fields and had the staying power to remain. They developed cooperative enterprises and mutual aid societies according to socialist theory; they triumphed over calluses and malaria to make dead soil fertile again; they built a Jewish homeland in Palestine with sweat and stubbornness. Out of the nucleus of the second *aliyah* came the men who would create the State of Israel and who would live on to guide it through its first decades: David Ben-Gurion, Itzhak Ben-Zvi, Zalman Shazar, Levi Eshkol. All of Israel's early premiers and presidents and political leaders, with the conspicuous exception of Weizmann himself, were members of this group.

One tangible accomplishment of the second wave of immigrants was the founding of a town called Tel Aviv, "Hill of Spring," on a 32-acre tract of sand dunes just north of Jaffa in 1906. Meir Dizengoff, the leader of the founding party, predicted that someday 25,000 Jews might live in the new community. Today it has half a million, and the ancient city of Jaffa is merely a squalid appendage to the giant Jewish city, but no one would have dared to make such a prediction the day the first cornerstone was laid.

The work of building the fledgling state continued. Turkish officials were bribed to turn their backs as Jews bought land from the Arabs, and the Arabs were persuaded that the newcomers meant no harm and might even bring prosperity for everyone.

The land was purchased through the Jewish National Fund, established by the World Zionist Organization for the specific purpose of buying Palestine piecemeal, tract by tract. The fund kept title to all the land bought; the Jewish pioneers did not permit private ownership, and the fund gave out its land on 49-year leases, which would revert if the lessee did not work his land himself. The use of hired labor was cause for reversion. (The policy is still in effect; 94.5 percent of the land of Israel is owned by the state's National Land Company, successor to the titles of the Jewish National Fund.)

Overseas, the World Zionist Organization kept to its double tasks of raising money for the Palestine colonists and of seeking political leverage to pry loose the Turkish grip on the Holy Land. There were many obstacles: the indifference of many Western Jews to the Zionist cause, the outright hostility of some, the governmental persecution of Zionist officials in Russia, and the hairsplitting factionalism within the movement itself.

Yet there was hope. By 1914 the Jewish populaton of Palestine had grown to 100,000, the agricultural colonies were taking root, and Weizmann's patient toil in England had won several more government leaders to a sympathy for Zionism.

On June 28, 1914, an event occurred that seemed little related to the problems of a Jewish homeland: a Slav nationalist assassinated Archduke Franz Ferdinand, heir to the Austro-Hungarian throne, who had been visiting the city of Sarajevo, Serbia, in what now is Yugoslavia. But the assassination served to catapult Europe into war. At the urging of Germany, the Austro-Hungarian Empire served an ultimatum on Serbia on July 24, demanding heavy reparations for the assassination. Serbia ignored the ultimatum and called on her protector, Russia, for help. On July 29, Austria-Hungary declared war on Serbia, and when Russia moved to Serbia's aid, both Austria-Hungary and Germany declared war on Russia. On August 2, German troops invaded France without formal declaration, violating the neutrality of Belgium in the process, and two days later Great Britain, outraged by the entry of the Germans into Belgium, announced a state of war with Germany and Austria-Hungary.

"Yes, but what does it mean for the *Jews?*" is the traditional Jewish response to any earth-shaking event. In the case of the events of the summer of 1914, what it meant for the Jews was that

Turkey, which owned the Holy Land, was sympathetic to Germany in the war. Though she attempted to maintain a strongly pro-German neutrality for a few months, Turkey was maneuvered into the war by early November, when Russia, Great Britain, and France declared war against her.

From the point of view of the Jews, the most progressive nation in the world—Great Britain—had taken up arms against one of the most backward—Turkey. A plausible outcome would be the defeat of Turkey and the dismemberment of her sprawling empire. Quite possibly Palestine, as a prize of war, would soon be in British hands, and available to the Zionists. In England, Weizmann began to make plans for that eventuality, remote though it might be. And across the Atlantic in America there suddenly emerged a powerful new Zionist spokesman, who might well be in a position to help at the critical moment. For the first time, the United States mattered to Zionism.

TWO

Zion in the New World

THERE ARE nearly 6,000,000 Jews in the United States today, if we apply the most liberal definition of "Jew." (Defining "Jew" can be a difficult matter, and in Israel is a problem of the most complex kind, involving a person's legal rights and degree of citizenship. In the United States it is simplest to count as a Jew anyone who regards himself as a Jew, or whose parents did.) The American Jewish community is the largest, wealthiest, most secure, and most powerful group of Jews in the world. It includes not much less than half of the total world Jewish population of about 14,000,000. The next largest group, some 2,600,000, lives in the Soviet Union under conditions of uncertain freedom. The Jewish population of Israel was about 2,436,000 in 1969. A million Jews live in Western Europe, 700,000 in South America, 500,000 in the Moslem world, chiefly North Africa.

The heavy concentration of Jews in the United States is something relatively new, dating only from the beginning of the twentieth century, and their statistical importance to world Jewish distribution is even newer, resulting mainly from the German campaign of genocide against the Jewish population of Europe under Hitler. (Before World War II, 58 percent of the world's Jews lived in Europe; today only 30 percent do, the majority in Russia. The total world population of Jews is still 2,000,000 less than that of 1939.)

The American Jews are found in all 50 states, but they live predominantly in the large cities and their suburbs. Some 2,000,000 of them dwell in and around New York City, which has a greater Jewish population than any other city in history; there are nearly as many Jews in New York as in all of Israel. In cities with 100,000 people or more, Jews make up about 11 percent of the population; in smaller cities they amount to 1 percent to 3 percent of the population, and in rural areas they represent less than ½ of 1 percent. (The American population as a whole is slightly less than 3 percent Jewish.)

The concentration of Jews in the urban areas is often extraordinary. Nearly 80 percent of the entire Jewish population of the United States lives in the 14 largest metropolitan regions, and in those cities solidly Jewish neighborhoods are still found, though they are breaking up in the migration to the suburbs. Brooklyn has 10,000 Jews per square mile. (Israel: 575 Jews per square mile.) Nassau County, Long Island, a major suburban gathering place for Jews, has 374,000 of them, more than there are in Poland, Austria, Hungary, Germany, Rumania, Greece, Algeria, and Iraq combined. (Before World War II those nations had more than 7,-000,000 Jews.) Hartford, Connecticut, with 26,000 Jews out of 160,000 residents, itself outnumbers in Jews half a dozen major European countries.

A survey taken in 1936 showed that 68 percent of the total Jewish population of the United States was to be found in just six states: New York, Pennsylvania, Illinois, Massachusetts, New Jersey, and Ohio. More than 90 percent of American Jewry lived in those states and seven others: California, Connecticut, Michigan, Maryland, Minnesota, Missouri, and Texas. Making such religious surveys is more difficult today, now that it is no longer customary to require data on religious preference in all kinds of questionnaires. But it is a safe assumption that those 13 states still contain the bulk of American Jewry, despite a heavy migration of elderly Jews to Florida. This has been a factor in domestic politics, as we will see repeatedly in examining the political influence of American Jews. The 13 states of high Jewish concentrations controlled, in the 1968 election, 281 electoral votes, or more than enough to elect a President.

Though Jews do not constitute a majority of the voters in any of those states, they are regarded as an active, articulate group who through energetic campaigning and their own monolithic vote can sway a national election. Much of America's official policy toward the development of a Jewish homeland has taken the "Jewish vote" into consideration. (Whether there really is a monolithic

Jewish vote is another matter. In 1968 eight of the states supposedly dominated by Jewish voters gave their electoral votes to Mr. Humphrey, and five to Mr. Nixon. But politicians *believe* there is a powerful Jewish vote, and shape their public statements accordingly.)

Because of their generally high interest in the functions of the government, their predominant commitment toward progressive causes, and their willingness to participate enthusiastically in public debate, America's Jews certainly do hold political influence out of proportion to their numerical strength in the national population. The same disproportionate influence can be found in the business world, the arts, and the professions.

The compulsion of the American Jew to make something of himself stems, most surely, from the conditions of life in the impoverished Eastern European society from which his parents or grandparents most likely came. The vast majority of America's Jews are only two or three generations away from the *shtetl* or the ghetto. Most are unable to trace their ancestry back before 1900, when everything disappears into the recordless obscurity of Poland or Russia. The immigrants who came here at the turn of the century worked as butchers or laborers or tailors, but were determined that their children should be doctors and lawyers and professors, and so it came to pass. The success-oriented American Jew (and his success-oriented parents) have become stock figures of fiction and comedy; but the determined rise of a mass of penniless Jews into the professional upper middle class has its awesome and impressive as well as its comic side, and unquestionably has given those Jews immense intangible power. In medicine, the law, and the academic world, Jews far exceed the statistical just-under-3-percent distribution of their presence in the population as a whole, and Jewish "establishments" exist in all three environments, protecting Jewish professionals against what is seen as the hostility of an envious Gentile world. In the communications industry—television, radio, the movies, advertising, and book, magazine, and newspaper publishing—Jewish leadership goes beyond any statistical spread. The three major television networks, most of the movie studios, many of the national magazines, and close to half the major publishing houses are run by Jews. In the world of business, the highest executive levels of many large corporations show few if any Jews, but this residual anti-Semitism has not hampered the development of a Jewish industrialist class in the past few generations. Jews have formed their own corporations, banks, and brokerage houses. They have penetrated the lingering barriers of the older enterprises, and have helped in a number of ways to reshape the traditions and practices of the business community.

The examples could be multiplied: the prevalence of Jewish novelists and orchestra conductors, the extraordinarily high proportion of Jews in the faculties and student bodies of American colleges and universities, the great number of Jewish judges, public administrators, scientists, engineers, entertainers, scholars. American Jews themselves, naturally, are proud of these achievements, and happily produce a list of famous American Jews—from Nobel laureates to baseball stars—at the slightest encouragement.

It is clear that Jews form an elite group in the United States, above average in education, professional attainments, income, and family stability. Some unique quality in Jewish culture, coupled with bitter memories of past persecutions and the relative freedom from such persecutions in the United States, has served as an inner goad pushing America's Jews to an unusual position in this country. As in any ethnic group, the American Jewish community has a great many ignorant, shiftless, poor, criminal, unstable, drunken, foolish, or unsuccessful members; but little is said about them either by Jew or Gentile. The statistically disproportionate number of outstanding American Jews is what is noticed. It is the Arthur Goldbergs, the Leonard Bernsteins, the Sandy Koufaxes, the Jonas Salks, the Arthur Millers, the Norton Simons, who get the publicity.

It should be added that many American Jews save their recitations of Jewish accomplishment for one another, and refrain from making boastful statements to Gentiles. They fear that they may provoke the old, familiar cry that the Jews are too smart and are getting too wealthy, too powerful. The root of much modern anti-Semitism has been simple envy, rather than distaste for the strange (for modern assimilated Jews look and dress and talk like everybody else). The sting of past pogroms still throbs, even in the friendly Jewish suburbs, even in the luxurious Jewish country club. The old enemy may yet awaken on these shores. And so the Jew does not speak out as a Jew in the United States, except when he feels Jewish interests are threatened. He will defend those interests, but he will not otherwise call attention to his Jewishness.

The numerous Jewish organizations that were formed in the nineteenth and early twentieth centuries devoted themselves largely to charitable work among the poverty-stricken new Jewish immigrants, and to campaigns against anti-Semitism in America. When poverty became a rarity instead of the rule among American Jews, and when anti-Semitism perished or at least went underground in the United States, the Jewish organizations discovered a new zone of activity: as champions of the State of Israel. Secure in their New World Zion, needing an outlet for the political and economic power they have amassed, no longer immediately concerned with self-defense on the conscious level, America's Jews have become vicarious Israelis. They are free to boast of the exploits of Jews *as Jews* in Israel, although it still seems like tempting fate to show the same kind of overt ethnic pride on the home front.

2.

So powerful beyond their numbers today, American Jews were long a statistically insignificant feature of life in the New World. In 1790 there were only 3,000 Jews in the United States, out of a total population of 4,000,000. Though the rate of growth of the Jewish community, swelled by two waves of emigration from Europe, exceeded that of the American population as a whole, the number of Jews in the United States remained small all through the nineteenth century: 50,000 in 1850 (national population: 23,-000,000), 250,000 in 1880 (national population: 50,000,000), and 1,000,000 in 1900 (national population: 76,000,000).

There were Jews in the crew of Columbus; there is even a story of shaky probability to the effect that Columbus himself was a Spanish Jew. However, none of the men who helped to discover the New World were practicing Jews. In 1492, Ferdinand and Isabella of Spain had promulgated a decree banishing all Jews who would not be baptized, and the five or six men of Jewish birth who sailed with Columbus were all converts, voluntary or otherwise, to Christianity.

The decree of 1492 had smashed the most glittering Jewish culture since the fall of Jerusalem. The *Sephardim*, the Spanish Jews, had begun to settle in the Iberian Peninsula in the wake of its conquest by the Arabs in the eighth century A.D. The society of the Spanish Moors, as these Arabs were known to the rest of

Europe, was exceptional in its degree of enlightenment, serving as the funnel through which the science and culture of the flourishing Moslem world entered Europe; and the Jews of Spain were an integral part of this Iberian intellectual aristocracy. During the reconquest of the peninsula by Christians—a task that began in the eleventh century and took four hundred years—both the Moors and Jews were at first able to retain their positions of distinction. The Christian kings of Spain depended on the Moors and Jews to be their doctors, their professors, their geographers, their astronomers. Elsewhere in Western Europe the dark night of medieval Jew-hating had settled in, but in Spain, where Jews were allowed to own land and hold high rank at court, a powerful Sephardic elite, wealthy and highly cultivated, enjoyed a golden age.

All this ended in 1492. In that year the last stronghold of Moorish Spain, Granada, fell to the troops of Ferdinand and Isabella, and in all of Spain a persecution of Moslems and Jews began. In a burst of nationalistic fervor the monarchs told their Moslems and their Jews to convert or get out. Spain was thenceforth to be wholly a Christian realm. The harsh fanatics of the Inquisition had something to do with bringing this about, but so, too, did the financial problems of the Spanish government: the long war had depleted the royal treasury, and confiscating the estates of banished Jews was a quick way of replenishing it.

Of Spain's 300,000 Jews, some 50,000 saved their property by embracing Christianity. Many of these, though, practiced Judaism secretly, and some, detected at it by Inquisition spies, died at the stake for their relapse into the forbidden creed. The rest of the Sephardim abandoned homes and possessions and poured out of Spain in a new Diaspora, settling in Portugal (from which they would soon also be expelled), North Africa, Italy, Turkey, or France.

Wherever the Sephardim went they conducted themselves with lofty bearing quite unlike that of the timid, oppressed ghetto Jews of the northern lands. These Sephardim had a Mediterranean outlook on the world; they were sensual, luxury-loving, a people of the sun and the sea. They had little in common with the *Ashkenazim*, the drab, dismal, defeated people crammed into the ghettos to the north. The Sephardim were the aristocrats of the Jewish world. They spoke Ladino, a Spanish dialect, as their private language, not the guttural Yiddish of the ghetto folk, and even their pronunciation of Hebrew and their religious rituals differed from those of the Ashkenazim. In the sixteenth century, when most of the Ashkenazic Jews of Central Europe were being driven eastward, where they would create the *shtetl* culture of Poland and Russia, Spain's outcast Sephardim were unaffected, and maintained their separate way of life around the rim of the Mediterranean. Some found their way to the Spanish settlements of the New World. Judaism was banned there too, but outposts of secretly practicing Jews sprang up in Peru, Mexico, and Brazil.

In the seventeenth century many Sephardim settled in the Netherlands, formerly a Spanish province, now suddenly free and a bastion of tolerance as a result of a dramatic war of independence. The Protestant Dutch, who had felt the flames of the Inquisition themselves, welcomed the Jews. Amsterdam became an important Jewish city, with many rich merchants and a number of profound thinkers. (Baruch Spinoza was the most famous of those, but his people excommunicated him for heresy.) As the Dutch built a maritime empire, the Sephardic Jews followed them to the New World, especially after the Dutch conquest in 1631 of Recife, then the capital of Brazil.

The first openly acknowledged Jewish community in the Americas developed in Recife. At its peak it numbered about 5,000, with an economy based on sugar manufacture. Then in 1654 the Portuguese recaptured Recife and ordered the Jews out. Some returned to the Netherlands, some settled in the West Indies, and 23 of them chose to go to the Dutch colony of New Amsterdam, far to the north. Peter Stuyvesant, New Amsterdam's governor, had little fondness for Jews and asked the mother country that "the deceitful race be not allowed further to infect and trouble this new colony," but he was overruled, and the Jews stayed. Thus the first Jewish settlement in what would one day be the United States was planted.

Ten years later New Amsterdam became New York, but the English were reasonably tolerant of Jews, and the tiny Sephardic outpost held firm. Slowly it grew; and later in the seventeenth century a second Sephardic group settled in Rhode Island. From these pioneers comes an American Jewish aristocracy so exclusive that many American Jews are unaware of its existence. Jews with names like Pinto, Seixas, Lopez, Cardozo, Touro, and Dandrada —names scarcely recognizable as Jewish by those who think all

Jews are called Cohen, Katz, or Levy—maintain their distinctive traditions to this day, conscious of three centuries of American history behind them.

At the outbreak of the American Revolution the handful of American Jews, most of them important importers and merchants, sided with the colonists against the British. They did not care for Britain's restrictive mercantile policies, and also felt that they had a better chance to attain full equality and freedom under the government of the colonists. (In most of the colonies Jews had been denied the right to vote or hold citizenship, though these laws had been ignored by certain liberal administrations. Even so, the status of Jews in colonial America was far more secure than in Europe.(Some Jews, such as Haym Salomon of Philadelphia, functioned as financiers to the Revolution, and there were about 50 Jewish officers in the Continental army. The leaders of the Revolution were grateful for such support and promised that Jews would have complete civil rights in the new nation. After independence, the old colonial restrictions were in fact carried over into the constitutions of the new states. That of Georgia required all legislators to be Protestant. That of Massachusetts declared it was the "duty of all men in Society publicly and at stated seasons to worship the Supreme Being . . ." and specified, "Every denomination of Christian shall be equally under the protection of the law," leaving Jews excluded.

At the urging of Jefferson and Madison such discriminatory laws were quashed in Virginia in 1786, and gradually the other states fell in line with the guarantees of religious freedom of the federal Constitution, although in some states Jews remained second-class citizens for another 50 years. (A New Hampshire law prohibiting Jews from holding public office stayed on the books until 1877.)

The Sephardic Jews prospered, became important businessmen in the young nation, and became indistinguishable except in religion from other Americans. Though they took up residence in every major Atlantic port, they were spread thinly, a dozen in this town, twenty in that. By 1840 there were about 15,000 of them in the United States, five times as many as at the beginning of the Revolution, but scarcely a substantial number.

Then a new exodus of Jews began in Europe, and the Sephardim found themselves suddenly engulfed by German Jews whom they scorned and detested. A few Ashkenazim had reached America in the eighteenth century and had joined Sephardic congregations, even intermarrying with the Sephardim. But these were unusually enterprising men of the upper bourgeoisie. The kind of German Jew who started coming to the United States about 1837 was proletarian: undernourished, poorly dressed, and, from the viewpoint of the Sephardim, grubby, uncouth, noisily aggressive. The Sephardim, horrified by these "foreigners," closed their synagogues to them and, pulling away haughtily like lofty grandees, pretended that they did not see their shabby coreligionists.

The migration of German Jews was a result of the period of chaos in Europe following the fall of Napoleon. Chaos has always been an enemy of Jews. Napoleon had imposed a single unified government on the dozens of German-speaking states. Upon his defeat in 1815 this unified government was allowed to collapse into a collection of semiautonomous states, in which, by way of preserving their autonomy and thwarting constitutional change, all the old demons of repression were let loose—including official anti-Semitism. Medieval laws against the Jews, long suspended, were revived. Jewish tradesmen and workers, seeing no hope, began to flee toward the New World. (They were not the only victims of this oppression. Many Christian Germans also fled, settling mainly in the American Midwest.)

The movement accelerated in 1848, when Europe was swept by liberal revolutions in which Jewish leaders played a prominent part. The stifling of this movement touched off massive Jewish emigrations to the United States; more than 100,000 arrived here between 1848 and 1860. The Sephardim were transformed into a curiously antiquated oligarchy, thereafter isolated from the mainstream of what was to be American Jewish life.

The new American Jews were universally poor and often poorly educated, but they were ambitious and the opportunities were limitless, particularly inland, where the Sephardim had not gone and where a class of merchants was needed. Thus the German Jews, beginning as peddlers carrying their assets in packs on their backs, became shopkeepers, then merchants on a still larger scale, and ultimately bankers and brokers.

Within a generation a new Jewish aristocracy took form, wholly apart from the old Sephardic enclaves. Names like Lehman, Straus, Seligman, Goldman, and Sachs predominated; later came the Lewisohns, Guggenheims, Loebs, and Schiffs, and then the Kahns and Warburgs. An elaborate social stratification developed within this group, governed by the date of a family's immigration to the United States and its degree of wealth in the old country. But such fine distinctions should not be allowed to conceal the essential fact that the German Jews who came to the United States between 1837 and 1860 forged, by intermarriage and other kinds of alliance, a tight, powerful mercantile class, affluent, cultured, self-perpetuating. Only in America could an aristocracy be created in a single generation.

By no means did most of the German Jews become millionaires, nor was the building of a Jewish *haut monde* in the New World their only achievement. A German-Jewish middle class was also emerging. By founding a network of fraternal lodges and mutual-aid societies to ease the path for one another in this strange new world, these Ashkenazic immigrants gave American Jewry that intensely *organized* nature that is its most typical trait. The Sephardim had not needed to do this, for they had arrived at the dawn of the settlement of the thirteen colonies and never felt like strangers here; the synagogue was a sufficient center for their lives. But the Ashkenazim, organizers by inner nature, gloried in writing constitutions, inventing purposes for extrareligious lodges and societies, and indulging in quasi-political sniping at one another's organizations.

The first to appear was the Independent Order of B'nai B'rith, "Sons of the Covenant," formed in New York in 1843 by twelve poor German Jews. Its purpose was to provide a social life within the lodge hall (complete with secret rituals) and mutual aid (such as insurance and loans) outside. The ritualism dwindled as the order grew. By 1858 there were 3,000 members, and after the Civil War there were 20,000, in several parts of the country. Philanthropy became its major aim as its now prosperous members turned to helping less fortunate Jews. Orphanages and old-age homes were founded, then hospitals; affiliates in schools and universities encouraged the study and development of Jewish culture; an Anti-Defamation League was created to combat anti-Semitism. Other fraternal orders soon arose: the Independent Order of the Free Sons of Israel in 1849, B'rith Abraham in 1859, Kesher Shel Barzel in 1860, and so on. But B'nai B'rith remained the stronghold of the German Jew in the United States.

By 1890 the position of the German Jews in the United States
had become quite remarkably secure, both in the lofty society of
the Seligmans and Schiffs and in the more modest world of B'nai
B'rith. A report of the Census Bureau published in that year,
studying 10,000 Jewish families of German origin that had come
to the United States between 1850 and 1880, showed that 40
percent had at least one servant, 10 percent had three servants or
more. About half the heads of households were in business, chiefly
in retail or wholesale trade; 10 percent were salesmen, 20 percent
were white-collar workers, 5 percent bankers, 2 percent professional men, 2 percent farmers and ranchers. Though one Jew out
of eight was a manual worker, these were employed in highly
skilled occupations: watchmaking, printing, tailoring. One Jew
out of a hundred was still an unskilled laborer or domestic servant.
As a group, they had done well for themselves. But now they were
to be subjected to a trauma not unlike that which their fathers and
grandfathers had inflicted upon the Sephardim earlier in the century. Out of Eastern Europe came thousands upon thousands of
Russian and Polish Jews, bitterly poor, ignorant of everything
except the teachings of the Hebrew sages, unwashed, loud,
ragged, crude.

This colossal migration, ultimately involving millions of Eastern
European Jews, had been stimulated by the severe anti-Semitic
laws decreed by the Russian government after the assassination of
the Tsar in 1881, and the furious, officially countenanced pogroms
that followed. Each year freighters and cattle ships from Europe
disgorged from their steerage holds torrential outpourings of these
Jewish refugees, who swarmed into New York and settled in
self-made ghettos where they could continue to speak Yiddish and
practice the customs of the old country. They worked as common
laborers or as pushcart peddlers, or at best as tailors, for they knew
no other trades and had no capital. There was a tremendous dyna-
mism among these people, unleashed after centuries of oppression. Here in America they saw opportunities opening, if not for
themselves then for their children, and amid the noise and squalor
of their raucous tenements they struggled to learn English, to rise
above the filth in which they lived, to fulfill their vaulting ambitions.

The German Jews were aghast. "Those people" seemed barbaric, grotesque, medieval—"the dregs of Europe" was the usual

phrase. German-Jewish newspapers spoke of the "un-American ways" of the "wild Asiatics" and called the Easterners "a piece of Oriental antiquity in the midst of an ever-Progressive Occidental Civilization." The *Hebrew Standard* declared, "The thoroughly acclimated American Jew . . . has no religious, social or intellectual sympathies with them. He is closer to the Christian sentiment around him than to the Judaism of these miserable darkened Hebrews."

Something more than mere snobbery motivated this Jewish anti-Semitism. The German Jews feared that the influx of uncouth ghettoites would injure their own position in the United States. Gentile America more or less accepted the German Jews, as it had the Sephardim before them, though there were certain resorts and neighborhoods where even the wealthiest and most refined Jews were unwelcome. But these new Jews were so alien, so strange, so grimy, so uncivilized, that their arrival might well lead to a wave of anti-Jewish feeling and restrictive practices that would sweep the Americanized Jews under as well.

Furthermore, these penniless immigrants of the working class were trade-unionists, socialists, even wild Bolsheviks calling for the destruction of the whole capitalistic system. This too was hardly likely to win admirers in conservative America, and the German Jews, themselves successful capitalists, showed little sympathy for the nihilistic ideas the Russians and Poles brought with them.

Since they were unable to prevent the Easterners from entering the United States, the established German Jews resolved to purify and Americanize them as rapidly as possible. The fraternal orders devoted themselves to the uplift of the sweatshop workers, providing them with free medical care, clothing, lectures on American culture, English lessons, and food, doling out philanthropy in a patronizing way that did not go unnoticed by its recipients.

As soon as they were self-sustaining—by 1905 or so—the Eastern Jews spurned this charity and began to set up their own philanthropic organizations. They also kept their characteristic culture alive by founding Yiddish-language newspapers, schools of theology, Yiddish theaters, and Jewish labor unions. And in time they left their New York ghetto and climbed into the middle class. The Lehmans, Warburgs, Kahns, and Schiffs retained their power in the financial world and their private environment of mansions and estates, but the Eastern European Jews, by force of numbers, came to dominate American Jewry.

The traits that the average American thinks of as "Jewish"—a certain manner of phrasing, a certain accent, a way of gesticulating, a comic self-deprecation, a cuisine of borscht, pot roast, and gefilte fish—are those of the Russian and Polish Jews. The stereotyped Jewish families of the Broadway stage, with their domineering, devouring mothers and baffled, shrinking fathers, are exaggerations of Eastern Jewish family structures. The majority of American Jews today did indeed have parents or grandparents who talked and acted something like the stage Jews. But these supposedly Jewish characteristics are as alien to the two submerged minorities of Jews within American Jewry, the German Ashkenazim and the old Sephardim, as they are to Swedish-Americans or Italian-Americans. Equally alien to these engulfed American Jewish aristocrats was another importation of the Yiddish-speaking Eastern Jews: Zionism.

3.

Zionism had been irrelevant to the early Jewish settlers in the New World. They had found their land of milk and honey here, and the gates were open; why think of giving up America for a backward corner of the Ottoman Empire, however sanctified by tradition it might be? If they gave any thought to Palestine at all, it was as a recipient of their charity, not as a possible place of migration. When *meshullachim*—messengers—from the tiny population of pious Jews in Palestine toured the congregations of wealthy American Sephardim in the eighteenth century, contributions flowed freely. But there was no talk of founding a Jewish nation there.

The first American Jewish exponent of Zionism—long before the term was coined—was the curious Mordecai Manuel Noah (1785–1851), Philadelphia-born, a journalist, playwright, politician, orator, and visionary. He was an early member of Tammany Hall and a fierce political battler, an active Mason, a major in the New York State militia. At various times he was sheriff of New York County, a judge of the New York Court of Sessions, surveyor of the Port of New York, and United States consul in Tunis. In his travels through Europe and Africa he had seen the sad state of most of the world's Jews, and decided that their only salvation lay in the creation of a Jewish homeland.

From former President John Adams he elicited in 1818 the first pro-Zionist statement from a high official of the United States: "I really wish the Jews again in Judaea, an independent Nation, for, as I believe, the most enlightened men of it have participated in the amelioration of the philosophy of the age; once restored to an independent government, and no longer persecuted, they would soon wear away some of the asperities and peculiarities of their character. I wish your nation may be admitted to all the privileges of nations in every part of the world."

But it was clear to Noah that the chances of regaining Palestine were poor, and in 1825 he set out to found a Zion in the New World. Proclaiming himself governor and judge over Israel, he persuaded a Christian friend to buy land for a Jewish republic on Grand Island, in the Niagara River near Buffalo, New York. A formal dedication ceremony was held in an Episcopal church in Buffalo, in which Noah named his colony Ararat. Addressing an audience of fellow Masons, militiamen, and politicians, he invited Jews from all lands to settle there—along with the American Indians, whom he believed to be descended from the Ten Lost Tribes of Israel.

"I do revive, renew, and reestablish the government of the Jewish Nation," Noah declared, but neither Jew nor Indian ever settled in Ararat, and in his late years he returned to his original dream of a Jewish state in Palestine.

Something closer to the modern American attitude toward Zionism was expressed in the 1850's by Isaac Leeser, the German-born rabbi of a Sephardic congregation in Philadelphia. Leeser called "for a time when the land of Israel is again to be ours, to be occupied by the sons of freedom and industry, sitting each under his own vine and under his own fig-tree, with none to make him afraid." But he did not suggest that American Jews settle there. Rather, he saw Palestine as a place of refuge for the oppressed Jews of Russia, Germany, and Hungary. The role of America's Jews would be simply to provide financial support for the establishment of agricultural colonies that eventually would become self-sustaining.

The German Jews who were reaching the United States about this time had even less interest than the Sephardim in the destiny of Palestine. A definite component of *anti*-Zionism was their contribution to American Jewish life. They were eager to assimilate, to obliterate all distinctions between themselves and other Americans, and talk of resurgent Jewish nationalism seemed harmful to their ambitions.

They had even gone to the extent of modifying Judaism to make it more compatible with their new American image of themselves. Reform Judaism, an explicitly non-Zionist movement, became their creed. The Reform movement had originated in Europe in the early nineteenth century as part of the great liberalizing wave that swept the Continent; it called upon Jews to shed many of their confining traditions and adopt a freer, more forward-looking, more humanistic kind of religion.

In the United States, where Reform Judaism won a foothold about 1840, English replaced Hebrew as the language of religious service. The dietary laws that make it so difficult for an Orthodox Jew to venture into Christian territory were discarded. Also banned was the whole uniform of worship—skullcaps, prayer shawls, phylacteries—that seemed so bizarre to Gentiles. Traditional Judaism's main thrust was toward the ritualistic repetition of the sacred texts within the synagogue, and the painstaking study of those texts and the commentaries on them outside it; the Reform movement was more concerned with the ethical precepts to be found in the Bible than with recitations of the ancient persecutions and tribulations. The books of the prophets, those stern exhortations to virtue, now were deemed more significant than the chronicles of the vanished Jewish kingdom.

The new kind of Judaism seemed, to the adherents of the old, very much like a species of Protestant Christianity without Christ. There was a Presbyterian starkness, a rejection of ritual and pomp, about a Reform service; and there was a familiar Protestant ring to the sermons of Reform rabbis, who were fond of preaching the virtues of hard work and thrift. But the new Judaism was simpler and more responsive to an altered environment than the old, and the German Jews in America adopted it in large numbers.

Inherent in the Reform idea was the concept of Judaism as a spiritual, nonsecular force. We are not citizens of a Jewish nation, temporarily waiting out in America our exile from the Holy Land; we are American citizens of the Jewish faith. The Diaspora ceased to matter. The Jewish nation was something out of the past, one with Nineveh and Tyre, and could hold no claim to the loyalties of a proud American. As Gustav Poznanski, the rabbi of a congregation in South Carolina, declared at the dedication of America's first Reform temple in 1841, "This country is our Palestine, this city our Jerusalem, this house of God our Temple." To the Reformers, Zionism was a subversive movement. An American citizen had no business advocating the establishment of a foreign state that might lay claim to his allegiance. Above all else the Reform Jews wanted to be accepted as good Americans by the Gentile world, and at every opportunity they openly denounced the follies of "Ziomania." It was an offense to their Americanism, an obstacle to their assimilation.

They even opposed, to some extent, giving aid to the few existing Palestinian Jews. This was not a matter of political strategy but of quasi-Protestant distaste for "indolence"—as is shown by this statement published in the *Jewish Times* in 1871:

"We have no doubt they are starving there, and the hungry is entitled by right of nature to receive his bread from those who can give it. But have the majority of these people any business to be there and starve? . . . Had they employed the same amount of energy to reach a place where they could find work and employment and a proper sphere for their physical and mental energies, they would, without a doubt, be dispensers instead of receivers of alms.

"As long as these pious fanatics are encouraged by other pious people, who merely lack the intensity of purpose and the courage to follow their example, they will continue to flock there. Starvation in their eyes is one of the steps to heaven. . . . That will not deter them as long as contributions pour in to alleviate their misery."

This stern approach was not typical of all the Ashkenazim. Most of them were willing to give generously for the Palestinian Jews, however they regarded their lack of productivity. B'nai B'rith was providing financial aid to Palestine as early as 1865. Only when the suggestion of support for a political movement in Palestine arose did the Reform Jews grow defensive. As Zionist stirrings began among Europe's Jews late in the nineteenth century, anti-Zionists in the United States responded with manifestoes of their own, such as the Pittsburgh Platform of 1885, issued by a council of Reform rabbis:

"We recognize, in the era of universal culture of heart and

intellect, the approaching of the realization of Israel's great Messianic hope for the establishment of the kingdom of truth, justice, and peace among all men. We consider ourselves no longer a nation, but a religious community, and therefore expect neither a return to Palestine, nor a sacrificial worship under the sons of Aaron, nor the restoration of any of the laws concerning the Jewish state."

However, not every Reform leader shared this dread of "Ziomania." Gustav Gottheil of New York's Temple Emanu-El, Bernhard Felsenthal of Chicago, and the rabbinical professor Max Schloessinger all spoke out in favor of a return of Jews to Zion. They refused to see Zionism as a menace to American Jewish security, nor did they believe that to advocate a Jewish homeland in Palestine was to give ammunition to the anti-Semites who maintained that every American Jew was a secret traitor to America. But they were a minority within Reform, and anti-Zionist resolutions and proclamations continued to emanate from the Central Conference of American Rabbis, through which the Reform establishment spoke.

By the early 1900's, though, the prosperous, acceptance-seeking German Jews who were the pillars of the Reform movement were surrounded in the United States by hordes of Russian and Polish Jews who were orthodox in their religious practices, socialist in their economic theories, and Zionist in political belief. Neither they nor the Tsarist administration had ever thought of them as Russian citizens in the old country; they were classed as members of "the Jewish nation" who resided in the Russian realm. Centuries in Russia had taught them to regard themselves as the wandering remnant of an exiled and landless people, held together in the Diaspora only by their traditions and their religion. Thus, while still in Russia, they formed their Choveve Zion ("Lovers of Zion") groups, dreamed of emigration to Palestine, and managed to send a few of their number actually to settle there.

But the Turks made it difficult for Jews to enter Palestine; the United States offered an open door to the "huddled masses yearning to breathe free"; and each year brought new pogroms. An accident of politics in a time of emergency, then, carried the Eastern Jews to America instead of to Zion. Nevertheless they did not forget Jerusalem. They brought Choveve Zion to the United States; and when Herzl sounded his call for a Jewish state, they responded enthusiastically. A Chicago group called the Knights of Zion sent a Jewish journalist named Leon Zolotkoff as a delegate to Herzl's First Zionist Congress at Basel in 1897. A year later, a Zionist convention was held in New York at which the Federation of American Zionists was founded. Its leaders, oddly, were two young Reform Jews of German origin: Professor Richard Gottheil of Columbia University and Rabbi Stephen S. Wise. But the core of its membership came from the Russian immigrant group.

As the new century opened, Zionist activities proliferated in the United States. Zionist organs in Yiddish and English appeared; recruitment programs reached into the ghettos of the big American cities; a host of subsidiary organizations emerged. Herzl was invited to visit the United States and aid the propaganda efforts. He was too busy to come, though he sent an inspiring message in June, 1901: "A crucial moment has arrived in the history of the Jews. Shall they miss this unprecedented opportunity of laying the ghost of the Jewish question, of ending the tragedy of the wandering Jew? Will the Jews of America, in particular, forget in their own happiness in the glorious land of freedom, how heavy is the bondage of their brethren?" In 1902, Herzl sent a close associate, Jacob de Haas, to assist the American Zionists. He became secretary of the Federation of American Zionists and editor of *The Maccabean*, its official organ, and served as liaison with the international Zionist movement.

An inner contradiction is evident in all this Zionist fervor on the part of American Jews, a contradiction that remains a source of friction today. As Herzl had noted, these Jews had just recently reached "the glorious land of freedom" and were safe from pogroms. Now they were feverishly learning English, applying for American citizenship, dreaming of sending their sons to Columbia and Harvard. How deep, how sincere, could their commitment to Zionism be? Did the rapidly Americanizing refugees from Russia and Poland really plan to abandon the New World for Palestine as soon as the goals of Zionism were achieved? Did they want their relatives still in the Tsar's land to escape to Palestine, or to New York? Unquestionably the American Zionists of 1900 did want a Jewish homeland in Palestine, and worked with tremendous zeal to bring it into being—but for whom was this homeland intended? For themselves, or for "other" Jews, unspecified and unknown? The question was a harsh one, and it went unanswered. And today it remains unanswered even though the Jews of Israel, eager to see every Jew in the world living in Zion, continue to ask it.

Herzl correctly sensed that the Jews of the United States would find it difficult to give up the new comforts and security they had found there. They would form innumerable Zionist organizations and issue innumerable manifestoes, they would contribute millions of dollars, they would bombard political leaders with pro-Zionist propaganda, but they would not return to Zion themselves. And so a cruel but accurate joke emerged: "A Zionist is a Jew who gives money to a second Jew so that a third Jew can go to live in Palestine."

In truth, the American Zionists at the start of the twentieth century were no more than a handful of zealots. As late as 1914, there were only 12,000 dues-paying Zionists among the 3,000,000 Jews of the United States. The annual budget of the whole American movement was $12,150. The members of the Federation of American Zionists were Zionists out of theory, out of sentiment, or simply out of reflex. They believed that there *ought* to be a Jewish homeland in Palestine, and so they worked to attain it, without trying to explore the question of whether they intended to settle there themselves. The great majority of the Eastern European Jews who had flooded into the United States were vaguely sympathetic to the movement, but the goal of rising out of the squalid tenements was more immediate than the goal of creating a sovereign Jewish state.

Among the new Eastern European immigrants were many who were as hostile to Zionism as the assimilated German-Jewish gentry. Particularly strong opposition came from the Marxist Jews, who rejected Zionism as a movement irrelevant to the only real problem of mankind—the class struggle. The idea that Jews constitute a distinct people with nationalistic aspirations struck the radicals as "reactionary," "bourgeois," and "obscurantist," and they termed Zionism "a mirage, compounded of religious romanticism and chauvinism." They wanted a world-wide brotherhood of workers, not an isolated nation founded on religious lines.

The young intellectuals who dominated the big Jewish labor unions of the garment trades, such as the International Ladies' Garment Workers Union and the Amalgamated Clothing Workers, were belligerently anti-Zionist well into the 1920's, as well as being antireligious and anticapitalistic. The rank-and-file members, however, shared their leaders' economic radicalism without sharing their militant atheism or their distaste for Zionism, and created their own Zionist organizations within the framework of the labor movement but outside the labor unions themselves.

While the godless Bolsheviks among the Eastern European immigrants opposed Zionism, the religious traditionalists were divided on the issue. Most leaders of the Orthodox branch of Jewry favored Zionism, regarding it as a unifying force that would serve to remind Jews of their ancient heritage and to keep them from succumbing to the temptations of Reform. Devout Jews tended not to have a great interest in the political aspects of Zionism, but desired Palestine as a cultural and spiritual center for the world's Jews. Thus in 1902 a movement called *Mizrachi* was founded by the leaders of Lithuania's Jewish community as the voice of Orthodox Zionism; *mizrachi* literally means "eastern," but the name also was a portmanteau combination of the Hebrew words *merkaz ruhani*, "spiritual center." By 1913 there was an American branch of Mizrachi, which found many members among the immigrants who did not care to join the more secularly oriented Federation of American Zionists.

But the most orthodox of the Orthodox would have nothing to do with any Zionist group. Zionism, said the most pious of all, was a blasphemous attempt "to force the hand of God." Some day the long exile would end and the wanderers would go home; but it would happen only in God's own time. When He had chosen to end the sufferings of His people, He would send a Messiah to let that fact be known. Then would the Diaspora be undone and the priesthood restored in Jerusalem. Obviously no Messiah was currently at hand; and so Zionism was a sacrilegious shortcut and a secular heresy.

4.

The American Jewish community in the early years of the twentieth century, therefore, presented anything but a united front on the subject of a Jewish homeland in Palestine. The Sephardic Jews remained outside the controversy. The well-to-do Jews of German descent feared that "Ziomania" would cause most Americans to doubt the patriotism of all American Jews, and used the Reform movement as a vehicle to denounce Herzl and his followers. Among the newcomers from Russia and Poland, the

Marxist extremists reviled Zionism as a bourgeois irrelevancy, and the ultra-Orthodox assailed it as a shameful anticipation of the will of God. Only a small core of activists kept Zionism alive in America.

They received some support from "renegade" Reformers, such as Gustav Gottheil and Max Schloessinger, who declared in 1907, "Reform Judaism will be *Zionistic* or it will *not be at all*"— Schloessinger promptly lost his professorship at the Reform seminary, Hebrew Union College—but such defections were rare. As the veteran Zionist leader Louis Lipsky put it, the conversion of a Reform rabbi to Zionism was an "occasion for great rejoicing: it meant that a breach had been made in the enemy's citadel."

More substantial was the aid that came from the new middle-of-the-road Conservative Judaism movement. The Conservatives, who emerged late in the nineteenth century, offered a brand of Judaism for those who felt that Reform Jews looked a little too much like Presbyterians. They conducted their services partly in Hebrew and partly in English, and while they preferred to use prayer shawls and skullcaps, they left the observance of dietary laws and other Orthodox restrictions up to the individual conscience. Thus the Conservatives developed a streamlined, Americanized kind of worship that partook of traditional Orthodoxy while accepting some of the flexibility of Reform.

Conservative Judaism swiftly attracted hundreds of thousands of followers who found Orthodox Judaism obsolete and Reform Judaism too radical a departure. The Conservatives regarded Zionism as an agreeable way of affirming their link to traditional Judaism. They viewed Palestine, said a leading Conservative rabbi, Israel Goldstein, in 1927, with "an intuitional, unreasoning, and mystic love," and looked upon the return to Zion "as an ultimate, a thing that is good in itself, whose welfare we seek for its own sake."

The chief Zionist advocate in their midst was the scholar Solomon Schechter, who came from Europe to head the Jewish Theological Seminary in New York. The seminary had been founded in 1887 by Reform Jews who felt the dejudaizing aspects of Reform were going too far. These Reform Jews asked Schechter to find a way to bring the Russian Jews of New York into the Reform movement. He did it by adopting the Conservative program and, to the horror of his anti-Zionist sponsors, creating a faculty of Zionists at the seminary.

Even so, Zionism's hold on American Jews was precarious. Louis Lipsky, chairman of the Executive Committee of the Federation of American Zionists, described the problem at the federation's fifteenth annual convention in Cleveland in 1912:

"A large plan of Zionist propaganda is impossible under the conditions that hem us in. A large plan, a movement that would impress and strike the entire Jewish community, is impossible without a large corps of energetic workers, backed by a capital fund of ample proportions to make the expenditure of energy worthwhile.

"This capital fund we have not. The large corps of energetic workers we have not. What we do possess is a small band of enthusiastic men and women. . . . What we have done this year, little as it seems to be, has been possible because of the existence of this small group, each bringing his mite of self-sacrifice. Zionism is as yet no mass movement."

If it were ever to become one, it needed a charismatic leader, an American Herzl, an American Weizmann, someone to draw the splintered factions together, to reassure the uncertain and capture the imaginations of the apathetic. It found that leader in 1914 in the person of Louis Dembitz Brandeis.

Brandeis, born in Louisville, Kentucky, in 1856, came from a well-known family of German Jews. His uncle, Lewis Napthali Dembitz, was an early leader of the Republican Party, and was one of Abraham Lincoln's three nominators at the Republican Convention of 1860. (American Jews in the nineteenth century were nearly all Republicans. They flocked to the party as soon as it was founded in 1856, admiring both its strong antislavery stand and its conservative, business-oriented economic philosophy.) Dembitz was an ardent Zionist who several times was elected to office in the Federation of American Zionists, but the nephew who bore his name was a typical young assimilationist, and showed no interest in Jewish problems throughout the first half of his life.

After studying law at Harvard, Brandeis went into legal practice in Boston, and won national attention by his advocacy of liberal causes, gaining the nickname of "the People's Attorney." He fought before the Supreme Court for legislation limiting the length of the working day, defended workers against the great corporations, helped to organize the Massachusetts system of cheap savings-bank insurance, and served as a judicious arbitrator in labor disputes. In 1910 the Zionist leader Jacob de Haas, then editor of the Boston *Jewish Advocate,* interviewed Brandeis about his insurance program. De Haas then mentioned the Zionist activities of Lewis Dembitz and led the discussion toward the ideas of Herzl. Brandeis, who apparently had never given much thought to the Zionist cause, allowed himself to be quoted in the *Jewish Advocate*'s issue of December 9, 1910, to the extent of saying, "I have a great deal of sympathy for the movement, and am deeply interested in the outcome of the propaganda. The so-called dreamers are entitled to the respect and appreciation of the entire Jewish people."

In 1911 and 1912, Brandeis contributed to Zionist funds and attended a few meetings of a Boston Zionist group. And in March, 1913, he agreed to serve as chairman at a reception honoring Nahum Sokolow, an official of the World Zionist Organization who was touring the United States on a propaganda campaign. Sympathy for the movement, belatedly awakened, was rapidly growing in him, perhaps as a result of his professional contacts with the Jewish garment workers of New York. But Brandeis still hesitated to become more deeply involved in Zionism. Late in April, 1913, the newly organized Zion Association of Greater Boston invited him to join its board of directors, but Brandeis declined, pleading the burden of "my other engagements."

Among those other engagements was one he had contracted only two days earlier: President Woodrow Wilson, who had just taken office, had asked Brandeis to accept the post of Chairman of the Commission on Industrial Relations, which was to investigate the labor unrest that was one of the chief problems of the United States in those years. Wilson had evidently planned an even more important appointment for Brandeis—a seat in the Cabinet as Attorney-General—but had been discouraged by his closest adviser, Colonel Edward M. House.

Wilson owed a considerable political debt to the Jews, for they had deserted their customary Republican allegiance in great numbers to vote for him in the 1912 election. That complex election pitted the Republican incumbent, William Howard Taft, and a former Republican President now heading a third party, Theodore Roosevelt, against Wilson, who had been a Princeton professor and was now governor of New Jersey. Taft was unacceptable to most Jews for his failure to live up to certain campaign promises to deal with Russian anti-Semitism. Roosevelt, who had once been highly popular among Jews (he appointed the Jew Oscar Straus to his Cabinet as Secretary of Commerce and Labor) had lost favor on account of his big-stick jingoism; his blustery belligerence frightened many Jews. Wilson, urbane and professorial, seemed altogether different from the machine Democrats who long had controlled that party, and his idealism and culture won a great deal of Jewish support.

He responded by naming one of his major Jewish backers, Henry Morgenthau, as his ambassador to Turkey, where Morgenthau would be able to intercede on behalf of Palestinian Jews. Another, financier Bernard Baruch, became openly identified as an adviser to Wilson. And a week after the election the President-elect began to consider a post to give Brandeis. Colonel House met with Brandeis and surveyed him as a possible Attorney-General. House reported to Wilson that "his mind and mine are in accord concerning most of the questions that are now to the fore," but a few weeks later the colonel had second thoughts about giving the post to a Jew, particularly such a controversial Jew identified with liberal, not to say radical, causes. In December, House noted in his diary that he and the President-elect "discussed again the Attorney General-ship and he asked about Brandeis. I told him that it was with much regret that I had to advise against him, that I liked him personally but he was not fit for that place." House similarly foreclosed the possibility of making Brandeis Solicitor-General, and finally the chairmanship of the Commission on Industrial Relations was found for him.

The struggling American Zionist movement continued to hope it could attract Brandeis into activity. Not only was he one of the best known and most widely respected Jews in the country, but he had access to President Wilson, and Wilson was considered sympathetic to Jewish aspirations; while still governor of New Jersey, he had spoken out vigorously against the oppression of Jews in Russia and had praised "our Jewish fellow-citizens from whom have sprung men of genius in every walk of life."

In the summer of 1914, with the world at the edge of war and Zionism in disarray, a new attempt was made to draw Brandeis into the movement. An American Provisional Executive Committee for Zionist Affairs was organized within the Federation of American Zionists; its purpose would be to protect Jewish interests in the coming war and, if possible, obtain Palestine as the Jewish homeland at war's end. On August 26, 1914, in the early days of the war, Jacob de Haas wrote to Brandeis, saying, "I should like to have your authority for proposing your name as the Chairman or Directing Head of the Committee which will have to take charge at this time of practically the whole Zionist Movement. . . . I think that the Jews of America will accept your leadership in this crisis, and that an army of zealous workers will be at your disposal to carry out the manifold policy that in my judgment the situation demands. It is not too much to say that everything depends on American Jewry, and that Jewry has to be led right."

Brandeis accepted the nomination and was unanimously elected. On August 30 he offered an official acceptance, declaring, "I have been to a great extent separated from Jews. I am very ignorant in things Jewish. But recent experiences, public and professional, have taught me this: I find Jews possessed of those very qualities which we of the twentieth century seek to develop in our struggle for justice and democracy; a deep moral feeling which makes them capable of noble acts; a deep sense of brotherhood of man; and a high intelligence, the fruit of three thousand years of civilization. These experiences have made me feel that the Jewish people have something which should be saved for the world; that the Jewish people should be preserved, and that it is our duty to pursue that method of saving which most promises success. . . ."

The defensive tone of Brandeis' words, the apparent need to justify the preservation of Jews before an audience of Jews, marked him as an outsider; they could almost have been the words of an enlightened, sympathetic Christian. The Zionists assumed that Brandeis would be merely a prestigious figurehead, lending his lofty name and thereby showing American Jewry that Zionism was no mere conspiracy of ghetto-bound agitators.

But, to their immense surprise, he demonstrated at once that he was going to take his responsibilities seriously. From his office there poured a torrent of memoranda, requests for progress reports, letters, exhortations. He studied the history of Zionism as though he had to prepare a brief on it for the Supreme Court. He held endless conferences with Zionist officials, spoke at synagogues and before Jewish student groups in high schools and colleges, maintained contact with the European Zionist movement, and reshaped the entire American organization to make it more dynamic, more efficient. "Organize, organize, organize," he begged, "until every Jewish American must stand up and be counted, counted with us, or prove himself wittingly or unwittingly one of the few who are against their own people."

One problem to which Brandeis gave particular attention was that of a divided national allegiance, which so deeply distressed his fellow Jews of German descent. In the summer of 1915 Henry Hurwitz, the editor of a newspaper for Zionist student groups, wrote Brandeis to tell of a discussion he had had with Judge Irving Lehman of the New York State Court of Appeals, a member of one of New York's most important Jewish families:

"The Judge declared that the instant a Jewish state should be established (he didn't believe it could ever be, but if it were) he would without hesitation turn Unitarian! He is not opposed to what he termed spiritual Zionism; on the contrary, he would warmly welcome a Jewish University in Jerusalem and still more he wants to see the ancient Temple literally rebuilt upon Mount Zion. But he declared that no American citizen could work for the Zionist political program without violating his legal as well as moral duty to the United States. Certainly, he believed, the naturalized citizen who has expressly abjured other sovereigns and taken an oath of allegiance to the United States is guilty of violating this oath if he endeavors to set up or help in setting up another sovereignty. I have been thinking that we ought to have ready for use when deemed proper a formal and authoritative answer, from a legal point of view, to such and similar contentions."

This was formidable opposition, and, since the constitutional point was unclear, Brandeis could give no formal legal reply to Lehman's objections. Instead he bombarded the other side with resounding slogans:

"There is no inconsistency between loyalty to America and loyalty to the Jewish spirit."

"Let no American imagine that Zionism is inconsistent with patriotism."

"Loyalty to America demands that each Jew become a Zionist."

Such phrases from so lofty a source had great effect. Brandeis was able to draw into the movement thousands of middle-class American Jews who previously had shunned it, and Zionism came to take on a less peripheral nature in American Jewish life as it lost its original conspiratorial character. Brandeis' standing in the nation, not merely in the Jewish community, was largely responsible for this transformation. Rumors were circulating that President

Wilson planned to name him to the Supreme Court, which had never had a Jewish member; certainly Brandeis had influence with the President, and that made Zionism respectable to the hesitant.

He used his influence in Washington carefully but effectively. In the spring of 1915, the Turkish wartime government tightened its restrictions on the Jewish community in Palestine and molested Zionist activists. Brandeis conferred with Secretary of State William Jennings Bryan, asking him to direct Ambassador Morgenthau to intervene at the Turkish court. Bryan wired Morgenthau at once, and the ambassador replied on May 2, "We have succeeded in suspending movement against Zionists."

Early in 1916 Wilson did indeed name Brandeis to the Supreme Court, telling the Senate, which had to confirm his nomination, "In every matter in which I have made test of his judgment and point of view, I have received from him counsel singularly enlightening, singularly clear-sighted and judicial, and, above all, full of moral stimulation." The struggle to obtain Senate confirmation was long and ugly. Many senators thought Brandeis excessively liberal, and some opposed him merely because he was a Jew. But on June 1, 1916, the appointment was at last confirmed and Associate Justice Brandeis joined the nation's highest court.

He could not now hold an executive post in a political organization, and so he resigned as chairman of the Provisional Zionist Committee. The resignation was purely a formality, however. Brandeis was instantly named honorary chairman, and behind that label he remained the silent leader of the committee, quietly directing its work day by day, hour by hour, from his offices in Washington.

There was much now to be done. In England, Weizmann had had remarkable success in winning the support of the British government for a Jewish homeland in Palestine after the war, but the promise was still tentative, and needed to be strengthened by the backing of President Wilson, backing that Brandeis was in the best position to obtain. And the United States, neutral in the war up to now, was drifting toward an involvement, despite Wilson's promises to the contrary in his successful campaign for re-election in 1916. By the beginning of 1917, Brandeis realized that his country might have a direct voice in the ultimate disposition of the territory at stake in the war—particularly that bit of Turkish territory known as Palestine.

THREE

Toward the Balfour Declaration

IN ENGLAND, during the last years before the First World War, Chaim Weizmann had patiently and deftly sought Gentile support for the Jewish homeland in Palestine. He was working in fertile ground, for many British Christians already had a hazy sympathy for Jewish aspirations, some because they held generally progressive and tolerant attitudes, some because of a vague conviction that the Bible predicted an eventual Jewish return to Zion, and some, Arnold Toynbee has suggested, because of a sense of guilt stemming from subconscious anti-Semitism.

Weizmann's first important convert was former Prime Minister Balfour, in 1906. But Balfour's political career was then in decline, and Weizmann had to look elsewhere. At a party in the autumn of 1914 he met by chance the influential editor of the Manchester *Guardian*, C. P. Scott, and quickly turned a general conversation on world problems into a specific discussion of Zionist aims. Scott, wishing to learn more of Weizmann's obsession with Palestine, invited him to meet with him again a few days later, and, after listening to a lengthy explication of Zionism, told Weizmann, "I would like to do something for you. I would like to bring you together with the Chancellor of the Exchequer, Lloyd George." And he added, "You know, you have a Jew in the government, Mr. Herbert Samuel."

"For God's sake, Mr. Scott, let's have nothing to do with this man," Weizmann blurted. Samuel, who had held several Cabinet posts in the government of Liberal Party Prime Minister Herbert Asquith, seemed to Weizmann to be "the type of Jew who by his very nature was opposed to us." In this Weizmann proved mistaken.

Before seeing Lloyd George, who was known for his support of the national rights of small countries, Weizmann provided Scott, who was arranging the interview, with maps and data on Palestine and educated him in Zionist history. Weizmann even dangled before Scott a bit of political bait to snare a Jewish homeland: "Should Palestine fall within the British sphere of influence, and should Britain encourage a Jewish settlement there, as a British dependency, we could have in twenty to thirty years a million Jews out there, perhaps more; they would develop the country, bring back civilization to it, and form a very effective guard for the Suez Canal."

Weizmann saw Lloyd George on December 3, 1914. Tense, overly conscious of the importance of the meeting, Weizmann was dismayed to find Herbert Samuel present, and at the outset felt too shy to speak. Lloyd George began to question him about Palestine, asking how many Jews were there now, how many the country could support, how secure the Zionist colonies were, and so on. Weizmann shrewdly described Palestine to Lloyd George as "a little mountainous country not unlike Wales," and won him instantly. Lloyd George suggested that Weizmann should confer with Balfour, who was once again the most powerful figure of the Conservative Party, and also that he see Prime Minister Asquith. At this point the supposedly non-Zionist Herbert Samuel astounded Weizmann by remarking that he was currently preparing a memorandum for Asquith recommending the establishment of a Jewish state in Palestine, when and if it was taken from the Turks.

Eleven days later Weizmann saw Balfour, who had forgotten neither his earlier meeting with Weizmann nor his sympathies for the Zionists. "I believe that when the guns stop firing you may get your Jerusalem," Balfour said now, and promised to do what he could for Weizmann, remarking, "It is a great cause you are working for."

Samuel presented his memorandum, "The Future of Palestine," to Prime Minister Asquith in January, 1915. Asquith reacted coolly, writing in his diary on January 28, "He [Samuel] thinks we might plant in this not very promising territory about three or four million European Jews and that this would have a good effect on those who are left behind. . . . I confess I am not attracted by this proposed addition to our responsibilities, but it is a curious

illustration of Dizzy's [Disraeli's] favorite maxim, 'Race is everything,' to find this almost lyrical outburst from the well-ordered
and methodical brain of Herbert Samuel." When the Samuel
memorandum was circulated among Asquith's ministers, strong
opposition to it came from Edwin Montagu, another Jewish member of the Asquith government, who regarded Zionism among
English Jews as treason to England. Montagu placed himself at the
head of a group of wealthy, assimilated English Jews who would
do all in their power to thwart the Zionist movement.

Weizmann now was involved with the British government in
his capacity as a chemist as well as a Zionist, and this gave him
additional leverage to further his campaign for the Jewish state.
He had long been working on a new method for making acetone,
which was used in the production of explosives and happened then
to be in short supply at British munitions plants. Weizmann's
interest in acetone was purely experimental and theoretical, and
he was astonished when in March, 1915, he was summoned to the
office of Winston Churchill—at the time the First Lord of the
Admiralty—and told, "Well, Dr. Weizmann, we need 30,000 tons
of acetone. Can you make it?"

Churchill gave Weizmann a staff and a plant, and he went to
work. Two months later a governmental shuffle produced a coalition Cabinet. Balfour replaced Churchill at the Admiralty and
Lloyd George became head of the Ministry of Munitions; Weizmann's proximity to these men in the course of his war work did
not injure his Zionist efforts, for now he was based in London and
meeting almost daily with high government officials. The chance
to toil a bit in the Zionist vineyard at these meetings was irresistible. His acetone project was successful—after the war Great
Britain would award him £ 10,000 as a token of gratitude—
and his prestige among the British leaders was greatly enhanced.

Throughout 1915, the English Zionists waged a largely successful propaganda campaign designed to make Asquith believe that
a majority of the world's Jews were Zionists—which was clearly
not the case. They also continued to stress the strategic importance of establishing, so close to the Suez Canal, a nation with ties
to Britain. This line of reasoning impressed many British leaders,
who were aware that France had designs on Syria and on as much
of the rest of the Turkish Near East as she could get; if Britain

helped to bring forth a Jewish state in Palestine, it could serve to block the French ambitions at least in part, since presumably the Jews would gratefully accept British hegemony.

There was a more immediate strategic consideration for a pro-Zionist British policy. The world's Jews were far from unanimous in their support for the Allies against Germany, Austria, and Turkey, the Central Powers. German Jews were aiding the German war effort both as soldiers and as scientists. The Jews of Russia, who detested the corrupt Tsarist regime, were welcoming the Germans as liberators and openly hoping for the collapse of Russia. The Jews of the United States shared the general neutrality of that country, but those who had escaped from Russian oppression only a few years before were by no means saddened by news of Russian losses in the war. It occurred to Sir Edward Grey, the British Foreign Secretary and one of Weizmann's newly persuaded Gentile Zionists, that an Allied statement in favor of Jewish settlement in Palestine might win the world's Jews to the Allied side. (Kaiser Wilhelm's government, which held a similar exaggerated view of the power of world Jewry to shape public opinion, was also considering a pro-Zionist declaration during the war, but nothing came of it.) In March, 1916, Grey actually sounded the Russian government out on the subject, and the Russians agreed that it might be a way to combat pro-German feeling among European Jewry.

But no declaration of support for a Jewish homeland emerged from Great Britain in 1916, despite the presence of Balfour, Grey, and Lloyd George in the Cabinet. Partly this was due to Asquith's indifference, and partly to the hostility expressed by the Montagu group of anti-Zionist Jews. But there was also a growing conviction among some British leaders that backing the Zionists might be a tactical error. Certain experts on the Near East, notably T. E. Lawrence ("Lawrence of Arabia"), pointed out that Britain could block France's ambitions in the Near East even more effectively by sponsoring an Arab state instead of a Jewish state. The government was divided, and never did arrive at a firm stand; all during the war it bought support on both sides by making promises of future nationhood to the Palestinian and Syrian Arabs as well as to the Zionists.

Late in 1916, though, Zionist sentiment among the British Cabinet ministers revived, and Weizmann suddenly became a figure of even greater importance to them. Several members of the Cabinet convinced themselves that support of Zionist ambitions by Britain might succeed in bringing the United States into the war on the Allied side. Justice Brandeis, the reasoning went, was a prominent American Zionist who exercised a special influence over President Wilson. Give Brandeis the hope of attaining Palestine for his people and he might be able to lead Wilson to ask for a declaration of war. And Weizmann, who as a Zionist leader was in regular contact with Brandeis, was the logical man to set in motion such a chain of events.

Weizmann did not believe for a moment that Brandeis had such power over Wilson or that the United States would join a world war merely because the pet project of an American Jewish leader received British blessing. But he had other reasons to think the time was propitious to ask the British government for a pro-Zionist statement. Another Cabinet upheaval in December, 1916, had made Lloyd George Prime Minister in place of Asquith. Balfour was now Foreign Secretary. The allies of the English Zionists now were in command.

Weizmann still had no official position in the World Zionist Organization; but at this point he assumed the presidency of the British Zionist Federation, and called a meeting of its leaders to prepare a memorandum of demands. They produced a document entitled, "Outline of Program for the Jewish Resettlement of Palestine in Accordance with the Aspirations of the Zionist Movement," which called for the "suzerain government" of Palestine, presumably Great Britain, to give official recognition after the war to a Jewish nation there, to grant free immigration into Palestine by the Jews of the world, and to give to the Jews of Palestine "every facility for immediate naturalization and for land purchase." Additional points dealt with the Jewish governing body of Palestine and the degree of autonomy it would enjoy.

In February, 1917, the Zionists showed their proposals to Sir Mark Sykes, a Cabinet minister who was an authority on Near Eastern affairs and who had come to favor a Jewish state. (In his memoirs, Weizmann describes Sykes as "not very consistent or logical in his thinking, but he was generous and warmhearted. He had conceived the idea of the liberation of the Jews, the Arabs, and the Armenians, whom he looked upon as the three downtrodden races *par excellence.*")

Sykes was in an odd position as he examined the Zionist document. The year before, he had negotiated a secret treaty with France, the Sykes-Picot Treaty, in which the entire Arab world north of the Sinai Peninsula was carved into French and British spheres of influence. The treaty awarded Lebanon, Syria, and northern Palestine—the fertile region from Acre to Tiberias—to France. What was left of Palestine would be "internationalized," which in practice would mean joint control by France and Great Britain as the two victorious powers in the war.

It was an arrangement highly unfavorable to Zionism, since it severed from Palestine some of its most valuable land, and placed the rest not under the control of Britain, with its sympathies toward the Jews, but under an unpredictable multinational body that might well lean toward the Arabs. However, the details of the treaty were known only to the inner circles of the British and French governments, as of February, 1917, and Sykes acted as though the treaty did not exist while conferring with Weizmann and his colleagues.

The Zionist program, said Sykes, seemed reasonable; but he warned that certain practical problems stood in the way of its fulfillment. The attitude of France was one. Delicately Sykes pointed out that the French were asking for Syria and a say in Palestinian affairs. The Zionists, he said, would have to discuss their plans "very frankly" with the French. At this suggestion the Zionists interrupted to say that they did not relish such negotiations, which they regarded as the business of the British government.

Sykes also observed that there might be trouble with the Arabs, who constituted the majority of the population of Palestine and who, on the verge of liberation from Turkish rule, were developing nationalistic thoughts of their own. Nevertheless he suggested that the Arabs would come to terms with the Zionists if they received Jewish support for their political demands in other parts of the Near East.

There was reason to hope that a Jewish homeland might yet emerge. But the next few months brought wild fluctuations in the outlook of Weizmann and his allies. It was a time when things were happening very quickly, and there was hardly opportunity to sort out the implications of one development when another erupted.

2.

The first of 1917's many upheavals was the overthrow of the Tsar in March. A spontaneous uprising of striking workers, crying, "Down with autocracy!" and "Down with the war!" turned almost unexpectedly into a revolution. Tsar Nicholas II and his family disappeared into captivity and before long were executed, and a socialist provisional government uncertainly and hesitantly took charge. Some members of this government were in favor of pulling out of the war at once and devoting full effort to the reconstruction of the fatherland; and the possibility that Russia's huge, if clumsy, military machine might be withdrawn from the conflict left the Allies in great alarm. Clutching at straws, the British government drew closer than ever to giving Weizmann his pro-Zionist declaration, in the hope that it would somehow induce the millions of Jews in Russia to exert a steadying influence on their chaos-riven land and keep it in the war.

From the point of view of Zionism, this was good news; but the possibility of Russia's withdrawal was dismaying to the Allies, who knew the war was far from won. A little later in March came battle news that dismayed the Zionists also. Their whole campaign was based on the assumption that the Allies would indeed capture Palestine; but when the British invasion of Palestine began, it went badly. Troops under Sir Archibald Murray came northward out of the Sinai Desert toward the two southern gateways of Palestine, Gaza on the Mediterranean and Beersheba 25 miles inland. On March 26 Murray attacked Gaza and had the town nearly surrounded by nightfall. Victory was at hand, but through failures in communication the British officers inexplicably ordered a withdrawal instead of making the final assault. When Murray launched a second Gaza offensive on April 17 he was thrown back by the Turks, who had greatly strengthened their fortifications in the interval. There could be no further chance to break through into Palestine until the autumn of 1917. Summer heat in the Sinai Desert was not considered a suitable environment for warfare.

While depressing events were going on in Palestine, the morale of the Allies was bolstered on April 6 by a long-awaited event: the entry of the United States into the war. German attacks on American shipping had made further neutralism impossible, and President Wilson, realizing his dream of bringing about a negotiated peace was illusory, called for a declaration of war. It would be many months before the American Expeditionary Force would be ready to take the field, but simply the symbolic gesture of the declaration was encouraging to the war-weary British and French.

For the Zionists it opened a whole new series of possibilities. No longer bound by the niceties of neutralism, President Wilson might feel free to take a public position on such matters as the dismemberment of the Turkish Empire. Pressed by Brandeis, Wilson might now call for a Jewish state in Palestine, by way of winning the support of American Jews for the war. Perhaps the United States would even participate in governing the conquered Turkish territories.

Even before the American entry, Weizmann had discussed this point with Foreign Secretary Balfour. Pondering the French coolness to Zionist ambitions—which conflicted directly with their own plan to establish a French-run protectorate in the Near East—Balfour had suggested on March 22, 1917, according to Weizmann's memoirs, that "if no agreement [on Palestine] could be reached between England and France, we should try to interest America, and work for an Anglo-American protectorate." Weizmann thought this "an attractive, if somewhat farfetched idea," and wrote to C. P. Scott, editor of the Manchester *Guardian*, "It is fraught with the danger that there always is with two masters, and we do not yet know how far the Americans would agree with the British on general principles of administration." Still, it was a matter to consider. But a simple declaration of American support for a British protectorate over a Jewish Palestine was preferable.

On April 8, two days after the United States had declared war, Weizmann said in one of his frequent letters to Brandeis, "The main difficulty seems to be the claims of the French. . . . We look forward here to a strengthening of our position, both by the American Government and American Jews. . . . An expression of opinion coming from yourself and perhaps from other gentlemen connected with the Government in favor of a Jewish Palestine under a British protectorate would greatly strengthen our hands."

While this letter was en route to the United States, Weizmann received stunning news from C. P. Scott. Scott had learned of the Sykes-Picot Treaty from sources in Paris, and told Weizmann about it on April 16. Startled to hear that his good friend Sykes had secretly promised the northern half of Palestine to the French and was willing to turn the rest over to an international body, Weizmann hurried to the Foreign Ministry to protest to Lord Robert Cecil, the assistant secretary for Foreign Affairs. (Foreign Secretary Balfour was on his way to America at the moment on a diplomatic mission.) Cecil heard Weizmann's objections to internationalization of Palestine and his fears of French interference with Zionist hopes; Weizmann did not actually mention the Sykes-Picot Treaty, but spoke only of "an arrangement which is supposed to exist."

It developed that the British government had been having second thoughts about Sykes-Picot. Sykes himself, who had been unable to tell Weizmann of the treaty's existence, had come to feel that it was unjust to the Jews. Cecil, agreeing that the Jews were morally entitled to a state in Palestine, and that such a state would have strategic value to Britain, was willing to help, but suggested to Weizmann that it would be useful if he were to mobilize Jewish opinion throughout the world in favor of a British protectorate there. This, of course, was what he had already begun to do; but now the chief burden had to shift to Brandeis in the United States.

Brandeis was one of the first men Balfour met when he arrived in the United States on April 20. The American Zionist jurist, speaking with the British Foreign Secretary at a White House party, assured Balfour that it was the desire of American Zionists to see a British administration in Palestine.

On May 6, Brandeis met with President Wilson for 45 minutes and explained the problem that had arisen between Britain and France over future possession of Palestine. Wilson replied that he was wholly sympathetic to the Zionist aims and would see what he could do to persuade the French to permit a Jewish state in Palestine. In due time, Wilson said, he would release a public statement calling for a Jewish homeland there, and would ask Brandeis to draft that statement for him; but he wanted to consult privately with France before issuing the declaration.

Brandeis reported to Balfour a few days later that Wilson would eventually commit himself openly to the Jewish state. This did much to ease Balfour's fears of trouble with France over support of Zionism, and he moved somewhat closer to a readiness to release the British government's long-promised statement of backing for a Jewish Palestine. On May 20, Weizmann confidently told a meeting of the English Zionist Federation that such a statement would be forthcoming, and called for unity among Jews as the great moment approached.

Predictably, the anti-Zionist English Jews opened a counter-attack four days later. Two of their leaders, David Alexander and Claude Montefiore, wrote a long letter to the London *Times*, calling on the British government to take no such position. The Jews are merely a religious community, they argued; they have no right to a national home. The most that the Palestinian Jews might ask was religious and civil liberty, "reasonable" immigration and colonization rights, and so on, with no trappings of statehood. The *Times* itself replied editorially, chiding these assimilated Jews for their selfish fears: "Only an imaginative nervousness suggests that the realization of territorial Zionism, in some form, would cause Christendom to turn round on the Jews and say, 'Now you have a land of your own, go to it.' "

Perturbed by the split among the Jews themselves, Balfour nevertheless asked the Zionists in June to supply him with the draft text of the statement they desired. On July 18, they gave him a three-paragraph formula that called for the recognition of Palestine as "the national home of the Jewish people" under British protection after the war, and committed the government to "the grant of internal autonomy to the Jewish nationality in Palestine, freedom of immigration for Jews, and the establishment of a Jewish National Colonizing Corporation for the re-establishment and economic development of the country."

Balfour approved the text. So did Lloyd George. But as it circulated among the Cabinet members, the most influential anti-Zionist Jews in England exerted great pressure for its rejection. Leading the campaign was Edwin Montagu, Secretary of State for India. It infuriated Weizmann that the only interference with the campaign for the Jewish homeland should come from Jews. Montagu's objections were so strident that Weizmann's strongest allies in the Cabinet hesitated once more.

Looking for reassurance, they turned toward Wilson. On September 4, 1917, Lord Robert Cecil cabled the President's adviser, Colonel House, "We are being pressed here for a declaration of sympathy with the Zionist movement and I should be very grateful if you felt able to ascertain unofficially if the President favours such a declaration." Three days later, House sent a memorandum to Wilson: "Have you made up your mind regarding what answer you will make to Cecil concerning the Zionist Movement? It seems to me that there are many dangers lurking in it and if I were the British I would be chary about going too definitely into that question."

Wilson was in a difficult spot. On the one hand, Justice Brandeis was pushing him to back Zionism. On the other, Colonel House was urging caution. (House's attitude toward Jews in general was an uneasy one. He had warned Wilson against letting Brandeis into the Cabinet in 1912, and five years later had opposed the appointment of Bernard Baruch as purchasing agent for war supplies, saying, "I believe Baruch is able and I believe he is honest, but I do not believe the country will take kindly to having a Hebrew Wall Street speculator given so much power. He is not the type that inspires confidence.") During September and early October, a number of meetings took place between Brandeis and House, Brandeis and Wilson, and House and Wilson, in an attempt to arrive at a satisfactory American policy toward Zionism. One man who took no part in these discussions, significantly, was Secretary of State Robert Lansing, who would normally have been involved in any planning involving the foreign policy of the United States. Wilson had not always consulted Lansing when making policy, but in this instance the President's omission had troublesome consequences for the Zionists later on, since Lansing was able to maintain that the State Department had never had any official role in formulating America's Palestine policy, and that the government could not be bound by the off-the-record talks of Colonel House and Justice Brandeis.

With Lansing (who was known to be hostile to Zionism) shut out, Brandeis gradually beat down House's reservations about a declaration for a Jewish homeland. On September 19, a cable from Weizmann to Brandeis gave a summary of the text of the declaration he was trying to get the British government to approve. Weizmann told Brandeis: "May expect opposition from assimilationist quarters. Would greatly help if President Wilson and yourself would support text. Matter most urgent."

Brandeis replied by cable a week later, "From talks I have had with the President and from expressions of opinion given to closest advisors I feel I can answer you that he is in entire sympathy with declaration quoted in yours of the nineteenth. . . . I of course heartily agree."

But this was the same kind of indirect expression of Wilson's backing that Brandeis had given Balfour in May. Weizmann desperately needed something more substantial, preferably a statement from Wilson himself. On September 18, Weizmann had discovered that Edwin Montagu's sharp protests had succeeded in getting the whole question of the Zionist issue dropped from the British Cabinet's agenda. Weizmann sought out Balfour and then Lloyd George, and managed to get the topic back on the agenda for October 4. When the Cabinet met that day, Montagu, close to tears, delivered an impassioned speech; the vehemence of his words and the implacability of his anti-Zionism amazed the assembled ministers. Lloyd George and Balfour felt they could not continue to withhold a pro-Zionist statement of some kind from the Weizmann faction, but the fury of Montagu's onslaught compelled them to abandon the July 18 formula that spoke of granting "internal autonomy" to the Jews of Palestine.

Instead, Balfour produced an emasculated compromise statement that said nothing at all about "recognizing Palestine as the national home of the Jewish people," as the July 18 wording had been. The new phrase was, "the establishment in Palestine of a national home for the Jewish race." That was quite a different thing; it could be interpreted almost any way at all, even to the extent of meaning that Great Britain was advocating nothing more than a Jewish colony within a Palestine run by Arabs.

Furthermore, the new text, the work of Leopold Amery, an assistant secretary to the Cabinet, included a specific guarantee of continued civil and religious rights for the non-Jewish inhabitants of Palestine, while omitting any reference to the Jewish National Colonizing Corporation that the Zionists had suggested as a quasi-governmental body there. Finally, as a gesture of conciliation to Montagu, Amery had thrown in a clause guaranteeing that nothing would be done to prejudice the rights of Jews of other countries "who are fully contented with their existing nationality and citizenship." This was to allay the fears of some assimilationists that they might be deported to the Jewish homeland the moment it came into being!

Several days passed while this next text was evolving. Weizmann, meanwhile, was making another attempt to get help from President Wilson. Late in September, Colonel House had replied on Wilson's behalf to Lord Robert Cecil's query of September 4,

Reconstruction of the Temple of Solomon, Jerusalem.
(Zionist Archives and Library)

A street scene in Jerusalem's Old City.
(Israel Information Services)

Theodor Herzl.
(Israel Information Services)

Louis D. Brandeis.
(Zionist Archives and Library)

Herzl greeting Max Nordau at the first Zionist Congress, 1897. (*Zionist Archives and Library*)

Recruits of the 3rd Contingent of the Jewish Battalion leaving a British recruiting station in New York, 1916.
(*Israel Information Services*)

Foreign Office,
November 2nd, 1917.

Dear Lord Rothschild,

I have much pleasure in conveying to you, on behalf of His Majesty's Government, the following declaration of sympathy with Jewish Zionist aspirations which has been submitted to, and approved by, the Cabinet.

"His Majesty's Government view with favour the establishment in Palestine of a national home for the Jewish people, and will use their best endeavours to facilitate the achievement of this object, it being clearly understood that nothing shall be done which may prejudice the civil and religious rights of existing non-Jewish communities in Palestine, or the rights and political status enjoyed by Jews in any other country"

I should be grateful if you would bring this declaration to the knowledge of the Zionist Federation.

The Balfour Declaration. (Zionist Archives and Library)

Balfour (with glasses and cane), Chaim Weizmann (seated, center), and Nahum Sokolow (right) in Paris, 1919. *(Zionist Archives and Library)*

Weizmann and Rabbi Stephen S. Wise (left). *(Zionist Archives and Library)*

David Ben-Gurion.
(Israel Information Services)

Golda Meir.
(Israel Information Services)

Rabbi Abba Hillel Silver addressing a rally in Madison Square Garden, New York, 1946. *(Zionist Archives and Library)*

A Zionist mass demonstration in New York City, July, 1947.
(Zionist Archives and Library)

Jewish immigrants bound for Palestine aboard a postwar refugee ship.
(Israel Information Services)

The *Exodus*, 1947. *(Zionist Archives and Library)*

Prime Minister Ben-Gurion reading the proclamation of Israel's establishment, May 14, 1948, in Tel Aviv. *(Zionist Archives and Library)*

Colonel David ("Mickey") Marcus.
(Zionist Archives and Library)

Moshe Dayan.
(Israel Information Services)

The founding of Tel-Aviv, 1908. *(Zionist Archives and Library)*

A view of modern Tel-Aviv. *(Israel Information Services)*

The port of Eilat. (*Israel Information Services*)

Israeli soldiers at the Wailing Wall after the conquest of Old Jerusalem in June, 1967. *(Israel Information Services)*

stating that the President did indeed favor a declaration backing the Zionists, but did not think the proper time for making the declaration had come.

Brandeis had not been able to push Wilson into a public commitment. The problem was that the United States, when it declared war on Germany, had not declared war on Turkey. Now, six months later, there still was no state of war between the United States and Turkey. It was Wilson's hope to detach Turkey peacefully from the Central Powers and persuade her to quit the war. If this came about, Wilson intended that the Turkish withdrawal be accompanied by the Turkish surrender of Arabia, Syria, Palestine, and Armenia, which would give Brandeis the Jewish national home he desired. But it was diplomatically unwise for Wilson to make statements about the disposition of the Turkish Empire while he was still engaged in his effort to get Turkey to withdraw, and while the United States and Turkey were at least in theory at peace.

On October 7, 1917, while waiting to receive Amery's amended text of the Palestine declaration, Weizmann wrote to Brandeis once more to say that the text would soon be available "and it would be most invaluable if the President would accept it without reservation and would recommend the granting of the declaration *now.*" After sending the letter, Weizmann finally got to see the actual text Balfour was offering. It was a painful moment. The flaws, ambiguities, and concessions to anti-Zionist Jews and pro-Arab British officials were all too evident. Weizmann and his colleagues, after an anguished discussion, decided to settle for the text as it now read.

"It is one of the ifs of history," he later wrote, "whether we should have been intransigent, and stood by our guns. Should we then have obtained a better statement? Or would the Government have become wearied of these internal Jewish divisions, and dropped the whole matter? Again, the result might have been such a long delay that the war would have ended before an agreement was reached, and then all the advantage of a timely decision would have been lost."

Weizmann cabled the new text to Brandeis on October 9 and requested yet again a statement of approval from Wilson, as well as an "enthusiastic message to us from American Zionists and also prominent non-Zionists." Brandeis and two other leaders of the

American Zionist movement, Jacob de Haas and Rabbi Stephen S. Wise, were distressed by the text and unhappy with the willingness of the British Zionists to accept it. But there was nothing that the Americans could do about that now.

The American Zionist leaders did propose some minor changes in wording when they met with Colonel House on October 15. The phrase about Jews "who are fully contented with their existing nationality and citizenship" seemed like too humiliating a concession to the assimilationists; they asked that it be stricken. Brandeis also requested that the phrase "Jewish people" be substituted for "Jewish race."

Colonel House had passed the text of the statement along to Wilson when it arrived on October 10. Three days later Wilson sent a note to House: "I find in my pocket the memorandum you gave me about the Zionist Movement. I am afraid that I did not say to you that I concurred in the formula suggested from the other side. I do, and would be obliged if you would let them know it." In this offhand way Wilson finally lent his support to the Zionist cause in a way that mattered. He still would not make a public statement, but he was at least willing to permit his confidant, House, to relay his expression of approval to the British government.

On October 16 House cabled London that Wilson had read the text of the Balfour statement and went along with it. He included the changes in wording requested by Brandeis, de Haas, and Rabbi Wise. This cable, Weizmann said afterward, "was one of the most important individual factors in breaking the deadlock created by the British Jewish anti-Zionists, and in deciding the British Government to issue its declaration." Brandeis' influence, then, proved vital in bringing about the first real step in the formation of the Jewish commonwealth in Palestine. His delicate prodding of House and Wilson, his carefully timed moves, produced in the end the commitment from the President that at last encouraged the British Cabinet to go forward.

And so, on November 2, 1917, the one-sentence document that became known as the Balfour Declaration was released. At Weizmann's suggestion, it was in the form of a letter addressed to Lord Rothschild, the nominal head of the British Jewish community and an active participant in the difficult negotiations that had led up to its issuance. It read:

Dear Lord Rothschild,

I have much pleasure in conveying to you, on behalf of His Majesty's Government, the following declaration of sympathy with Jewish Zionist aspirations which has been submitted to, and approved by, the Cabinet:

"His Majesty's Government view with favor the establishment in Palestine of a national home for the Jewish People, and will use their best endeavours to facilitate the achievement of this object, it being clearly understood that nothing shall be done which may prejudice the civil and religious rights of the existing non-Jewish communities in Palestine, or the rights and political status enjoyed by Jews in any other country."

I should be grateful if you would bring this declaration to the knowledge of the Zionist Federation.

Yours,
Arthur Balfour

3.

Historians have devoted much effort to an exploration of Great Britain's real motive in issuing the Balfour Declaration. Was it an attempt to forestall a German pro-Zionist propaganda coup? To reward Weizmann's services in making explosives for the war effort? To bribe the American Jews into supporting the war? To coax the Russian Jews away from backing the Bolsheviks who were about to pull Russia out of the war? To block French imperialism in the Near East, and gain for Britain a friendly outpost near the Suez Canal? It has been suggested that the Balfour Declaration was the gesture of naïve, sentimental men whose Sunday School lessons had left them stuffed with a mystical fondness for the idea of a restored Jewish nation in the Holy Land. It has also been suggested that the Balfour Declaration was the cynical deed of ruthless, amoral politicians who merely wanted to keep Weizmann and the other tiresome agitators happy, while simultaneously making secret and totally contradictory promises about Palestine to the French and the Arabs.

Some of all of this is true. The real genesis of the declaration probably lay in the sincere conviction of Balfour, Lloyd George, and the other British leaders that it was an act of moral grandeur to provide a homeland for the Jews. But a host of secondary factors —strategic considerations, gratitude toward Weizmann, a desire to influence the opinions of American and Russian Jewry, the need to forestall the Germans, and more—were also involved, and possibly each Cabinet minister had a different idea of what he thought he was doing when he voted to approve the declaration. There were elements both of sweeping humanitarianism and of short-range politicking in their decision.

The declaration, of course, was only a statement of British policy, not the key to the Holy Land. First Palestine had to be conquered. Then peace had to be negotiated. Finally Britain would have to persuade her allies to accept the Balfour promise. A great deal of diplomacy lay ahead for the Zionists and their adherents before any kind of Jewish state emerged. For Brandeis on one side of the Atlantic and Weizmann on the other, an ordeal of intricate campaigning still had to be endured.

The actual conquest of the Holy Land was settled within a few weeks after the declaration was issued. In July, 1917, the unsuccessful Sir Archibald Murray had been replaced as British commander in Palestine by Sir Edmund Allenby, who had distinguished himself in the fighting in France. Allenby began a bombardment of Gaza on October 20, seized Beersheba in a subsidiary thrust on October 31, and broke through into central Palestine by November 6. The Turks were forced into two groups, and Allenby kept them divided while he captured the port of Jaffa on November 14 and then began an inland march toward Jerusalem.

On December 9, 1917, the Holy City fell, and passed from Moslem control for the first time since Saladin had seized it from the Crusaders in 1187. Allenby led his men through a gate in the medieval wall of Old Jerusalem, and they prayed at the Wailing Wall, that stump of the Temple of Solomon, amid jubilant Jewish Jerusalemites. From the Zionist standpoint the war was over, though nearly a year of bloodshed remained before the agony in Europe ended.

Brandeis and his fellow American Zionists seized the occasion of the fall of Jerusalem to request from Wilson an American version of the Balfour Declaration. Wilson had continued to withhold any public statement on the subject on the grounds that no state of war existed between the United States and Turkey. This was something of a specious attitude now, since Turkey had lost Palestine and it would hardly make things worse if the United States offered a suggestion for the eventual disposition of the Holy Land. However, Wilson remained silent, and it was with great difficulty that Brandeis explained to Weizmann why no American declaration was forthcoming.

One reason for Wilson's silence was the attitude of his cautious Secretary of State, Robert Lansing, who wrote to the President on December 13, 1917:

My dear Mr. President:

There is being brought considerable pressure for the issuance of a declaration in regard to this government's attitude as to the disposition to be made of Palestine. This emanates naturally from the Zionist element of the Jews.

My judgment is that we should go very slowly in announcing a policy for three reasons:

First, we are not at war with Turkey and therefore should avoid any appearance of favoring taking territory from that Empire by force.

Second, the Jews are by no means a unit in the desire to reestablish their race as an independent people; to favor one or the other faction would seem to be unwise.

Third, many Christian sects and individuals would undoubtedly resent turning the Holy Land over to the absolute control of the race credited with the death of Christ.

For practical purposes I do not think we need go further than the first reason given since that is ample ground for declining to announce a policy in regard to the final disposition of Palestine.

Lansing's concern with the credit for the death of Christ probably had little impact on Wilson; but it was all too clear that the American Jews were "by no means a unit" in their attitude toward Palestine, and this was a powerful political consideration for the President.

The Zionist faction now was stronger than it ever had been. The prestige of Brandeis and the proclamation of the Balfour Declaration had made Zionism respectable, and by 1918 the Zionist Organization of America, as the Federation of American Zionists now was known, claimed 150,000 members, more than a tenfold increase since the beginning of the war. Thousands of other Jews joined the various labor Zionist parties or the religion-oriented Mizrachi Organization of America. But for most of these individuals, Zionist activities consisted of nothing more than the payment of nominal dues; and many of America's most articulate and influential Jews belonged to organizations that were either cool to Zionism or explicitly hostile to it.

The chief focal point of non-Zionist and anti-Zionist sentiment was the American Jewish Committee, an organization dominated by wealthy Jews with German and Reform backgrounds. While ecstatic Zionists paraded on New York's Fifth Avenue late in 1917 to celebrate the Balfour Declaration—it was the first Jewish parade ever held in the United States—the leaders of the American Jewish Committee were meeting to assess the declaration's possible dangerous implications.

The committee had been organized in 1906 in response to the Kishinev pogrom, the Dreyfus case, and other recent manifestations of resurgent anti-Semitism. A group of prominent American Jews, called to a gathering at the New York mansion of Jacob Schiff, the immensely wealthy banker and philanthropist, founded the committee to safeguard the rights and interests of Jews throughout the world. The organizers and early leaders included most of the country's best known Jews, an array of distinguished jurists, bankers, merchants, brokers, publishers, lawyers. Among them were such lawyers as Louis Marshall and Irving Lehman, the latter soon to become a judge; Adolph Ochs of *The New York Times;* Julius Rosenwald of Sears, Roebuck; Oscar Straus, a member of Theodore Roosevelt's Cabinet; and many members of the great Jewish banking families. (Brandeis was virtually the only American Jew of importance who was not involved with the committee. At the time of its founding he held himself apart from Jewish matters, and later his commitment to Zionism made him a natural enemy of the committee's leaders.)

Though from the outset the committee had East European and Orthodox members, it represented primarily the attitudes of the elite assimilated German-Jewish community. Its executive committee, consisting of a few dozen members, was drawn almost exclusively from that community, and exposed the committee to charges by the Jewish press that it was run by a "self-anointed, self-appointed, and self-perpetuated" clique, even though it liked to present itself as a broad-based lay body representing all American Jews.

Their outlook was humanistic and philanthropic; collectively they gave hundreds of millions of dollars to endow museums, seminaries, and hospitals, to send food and clothing to impoverished and persecuted Jewish communities in Europe and Asia, and to aid victims of the war. But they were not Zionists. They abhorred Zionism as a political movement, for they had the customary uneasiness of the wealthy assimilated Jew over the potential conflict of loyalties that a sovereign Jewish state might create. "Do not permit Zionism from over the seas to come among you," Jacob Schiff warned in a speech in 1915, and it was a phrase that any of his fellow American Jewish Committee associates might have uttered.

The power of the committee was exerted in other directions. In 1911 it succeeded in forcing the abrogation of a trade treaty with Russia, in retaliation for the refusal of the Tsarist government to honor an American passport if it was carried by a Jew. Three years later, when the onset of World War I sent hundreds of thousands of Polish and Baltic Jews into a panicky migration, the committee acted swiftly and generously to meet their needs.

The Jews of Palestine were in special difficulties, once Turkey had entered the war, for many of them were refugees from Russia and were regarded by the Turks as enemy aliens. In August, 1914, Ambassador Morgenthau cabled Jacob Schiff for funds to aid the Palestinian Jews, and the American Jewish Committee responded at once with $25,000, Schiff adding $12,500 more personally, and the Brandeis-led Provisional Zionist Committee supplying another $12,500.

A few months later, Schiff was instrumental in forming the American Jewish Relief Committee, a unified body that would coordinate the charitable efforts of all the numerous American Jewish groups during the war emergency. A month later this body set up the Joint Distribution Committee of American Funds for the Relief of Jewish War Sufferers to serve as its disbursing agency. The Joint Distribution Committee, originally an emergency group, is still in business, aiding Jews in many parts of the world and distributing millions of dollars a year.

This was splendid work, rising above all factionalism. But it was not Zionism. Militant Zionists recognized that it was necessary to feed the starving and clothe the naked, but they regarded the activities of the American Jewish Committee and even the Joint Distribution Committee as dilutions of the Zionist ideal. They felt that the money being used to feed Jews in Russia should rather be spent in transporting them to Palestine, and some extremists believed that it was actually harmful to aid the European war victims, since the more intense their sufferings were, the more powerful would be the moral pressure exerted to make Palestine a Jewish homeland. Behind the philanthropies of the committee, the Zionists suspected, lay a cunning plot to sidetrack the political aims of nationalistic Zionism.

The sniping of Zionists at the committee was sharp and fierce. When the brilliant European Zionist propagandist Shmarya Levin heard Jacob Schiff declare at a public meeting, "I am divided into three parts; I am an American, I am a German, and I am a Jew," Levin rose to ask exactly how Mr. Schiff divided himself. Was it horizontally or vertically? And, if horizontally, which part was it that he had left for the Jewish people? Schiff, before his death in 1920, actually came close to a Zionist outlook, but to Zionists he and the committee always remained anathema. The veteran American Zionist leader Louis Lipsky, writing about the committee in 1927, said, "We just could not abide its undemocratic constitution. It was a self-appointed body. It was contemptuous of public opinion, and invariably took the unpopular side. We, organizers of a free Jewish opinion, upon which Zionist success depended, felt that we had to fight the American Jewish Committee or be faithless as Zionists and Americans."

The committee confronted the issue of the Balfour Declaration at its executive session of February 2, 1918. Louis Marshall, the Syracuse-born lawyer who was a central figure both in the American Jewish Committee and the Joint Distribution Committee, read a newspaper report of a statement made by Professor Albert Bushnell Hart of Harvard. "The Jewish people must either fish or cut bait," Professor Hart had said. "They must either reject their American citizenship or renounce any such dangerous doctrine as Zionism. . . . There can be no justification for dual allegiance." In the debate that followed, Jacob Schiff advocated that the committee take no stand at all on the question of Zionism but continue to concern itself entirely with its philanthropic work—looking upon Palestine, as before, as simply one among many recipients for aid.

But in the end the committee, realizing it might isolate itself irretrievably from the majority of American Jews if it did not show at least some sympathy for the idea of a Jewish homeland, arrived at a position that backed spiritual and humanitarian Zionism while altogether avoiding political and nationalistic implications.

The dedicated anti-Zionists, unexpectedly deprived of the American Jewish Committee as a base of operations, continued their campaign privately. A Reform leader, Rabbi Julian H. Miller of Chattanooga, wrote to President Wilson, "Please do not take America from me. . . . My flag is Red, White, and Blue, how then can I have any other National Homeland." Henry Morgenthau, Sr., who had been ambassador to Turkey, called Zionism "the most stupendous fallacy in Jewish history. I assert that it is wrong in principle and impossible of realization; that it is unsound in its economics, fantastic in its politics, and sterile in its spiritual ideals." Morgenthau was one of 39 prominent Jews who signed an anti-Zionist petition that Congressman Julius Kahn, a Republican from San Francisco, presented to President Wilson on March 4, 1919. This lengthy document is perhaps the most forceful statement of the anti-Zionist Jewish position ever made.

The petitioners objected to "the organization of a Jewish State in Palestine" and to "the segregation of the Jews as a nationalistic unit in any country," asserting that "in so doing we are voicing the opinion of the majority of American Jews born in this country and of those foreign born who have lived here long enough to thoroughly assimilate American political and social conditions." They expressed sympathy with Zionist efforts "to secure for Jews at present living in lands of oppression a refuge in Palestine or elsewhere," but warned against awarding territorial sovereignty to those who sought such refuge.

"This demand," Morgenthau and the other petitioners said, "not only misinterprets the trend of the history of the Jews, who ceased to be a nation 2,000 years ago, but involves the limitation and possible annulment of the larger claims of Jews for full citizenship and human rights in all lands in which those rights are not yet secure." Also the rights of the Arab and Christian communities in Palestine had to be considered, they added. Any displacement of those communities by Jewish immigrants "would be a crime against the triumphs of their whole past history and against the lofty and world-embracing visions of their great prophets and leaders."

Lastly, to found a state on religious or racial grounds would be "contrary to the democratic principles for which the world war was waged. . . . To unite Church and State, in any form, as under the old Jewish hierarchy, would be a leap backward of two thousand years."

Wilson, locked in fierce struggle with Congress over his own domestic and international problems, did not respond to the petition; he had no wish to be drawn into a conflict among Jews.

4.

To the Zionists, these protests were an old story. Ignoring them, they concentrated on the work of transforming the Balfour promise into reality. The first move was to accept a British offer to send a Zionist commission to Palestine early in 1918 on an inspection tour. Chaim Weizmann was named chairman of this commission, and the other allied powers were invited to send representatives. Russia, deep in the chaos of its revolution, was unable to take part. The United States Zionists also declined to participate, apparently out of Brandeis's feeling—stimulated by strong pressure from Colonel House—that the absence of a state of war between the United States and Turkey precluded the visit of Americans in such a capacity to what was then still Turkish soil. Weizmann was greatly irritated by this overly precise legalism. In the end, his only colleagues on the commission were French and Italian Jews, and the delegate chosen by the French government was, perversely enough, a determined anti-Zionist.

The purpose of the commission was to collect information about what would be required to reconstruct the Palestinian economy; to provide a link between the British occupation forces and the Palestinian Jews; to coordinate the refugee resettlement program; to plan for the future Jewish commonwealth; to inquire into the possibilities of founding a Jewish university and similar institutions; and to establish friendly relations with the Arabs upon whom all this was to descend.

The commissioners entered Palestine by way of Egypt late in March, 1918, and gathered in Tel Aviv, then a town of about one hundred houses. The British military authorities, preoccupied by bad news coming from the European front, had little time for them; many of General Allenby's officers had never heard of the Balfour Declaration and had no interest in cooperating with Zionist visitors; and Arabs, already restless, were protesting that "the British have sent for the Jews to take over the country." The existing Palestinian Jewish community, disorganized and depleted, seemed uncertain of the commissioners' intentions or even of their good will. The Orthodox Jews appeared more concerned with the formalisms of their ritual observances, and whether those observances would be allowed to proceed unmolested under the new regime, than they were with the possible political realization of a Jewish state.

In June, 1918, the commissioners undertook their most delicate, and potentially most significant, task: an attempt to win support for the new Jewish homeland from Emir Faisal, commander-in-chief of the Arab army. At the suggestion of General Allenby they set out on a grueling journey toward the Arab leader's camp, hoping to create an understanding that would prevent friction between the Arabs and Jews of Palestine. Faisal was based in Amman, east of Jerusalem on the far side of the Jordan River. Because the Jordan Valley was still in Turkish hands, it was necessary for Weizmann and his colleagues to spend ten miserable days on a journey that should have lasted a few hours: by rail along the coast to Suez, then a harrowing sea journey around the tip of the Sinai Peninsula to Aqaba, and finally a grim desert treck north through the Negev Desert to Amman, where Faisal's officers greeted them with gifts of water and fruit.

Faisal was a member of the house of Hashem, a proud Arab dynasty that traced its ancestry to Mohammed himself. For centuries the Hashemites had held the hereditary post of Emir of Mecca, maintaining it even under Turkish rule. In 1916, T. E. Lawrence had persuaded Faisal's father, Emir Hussein, to cast off his allegiance to Turkey and join the Allied cause. Hussein, who dreamed of an Arab empire embracing Arabia, Iraq, Palestine (including the present kingdom of Jordan), and Syria (including what is now Lebanon), saw cooperation with the Allies as the best route toward gaining it. He provided an army of Arab guerrillas to be commanded by his son Faisal, with Lawrence as chief adviser. These irregulars won much attention by blowing up Turkish rail lines in Arabia and by capturing the port of Aqaba in the summer of 1917.

In return for this help, the British secretly promised Hussein that Faisal was to become king of a Damascus-based state comprising Syria and Palestine, and that Hussein's second son, Abdullah, would be made king of Iraq. (At the same time the British were party to the Sykes-Picot Treaty, which left the disposition of Syria and northern Palestine to France. They also were in the process of promising Palestine to the Zionists.)

Weizmann was warmly received when he came before Faisal.

The desert chieftain, an intelligent and far-seeing man, refused to regard Zionism as a threat to his family's dream of empire. In a two-hour conversation with Weizmann, he expressed a desire for harmony between Arabs and Jews in Palestine, and promised the full assistance of the Hashemites in implementing the Balfour Declaration. Difficult as it is to believe today, it seems that Faisal was altogether sincere; he saw no reason why his people and Weizmann's could not work together for mutual benefit, and, so long as the great powers permitted Hashemite rule over most of the Arab world, he would not begrudge some or all of Palestine to the Jews. But the intricacies of international politics upset the plans of the Hashemites for supremacy in the Near East, and choked off this promising beginning of a harmonious Arab-Jewish relationship almost at once.

Weizmann saw Faisal several times, coming to complete agreement on what was to be a stillborn treaty of cooperation. He also, in July, 1918, laid the foundation stones for the Hebrew University on Mount Scopus, overlooking the Old City of Jerusalem; and in October, he returned to London, both hopeful and troubled. The ambiguities in the Balfour Declaration were coming home to roost, for no one yet knew whether Palestine would become a sovereign Jewish state or merely a place where Jews might settle under Arab sufferance. An ominous warning had already come from Major W. G. Ormsby-Gore, the commission's liaison officer and a strong ally of the Zionists, who felt it was premature to talk of a Jewish state or commonwealth in Palestine and that any such expression of nationalistic sentiments by the Zionists only made the diplomatic task of the British government more difficult. The question of Sykes-Picot was still unresolved; the French plainly meant to keep Syria and as much of Palestine as they could get; they had no interest in Britain's promises to the Hashemites and even less in the claims of the Zionists.

The war ended with an armistice on November 11, and plans were drawn for a peace conference early in 1919 in Paris. To the Zionists, the need for a Jewish homeland was greater than ever, for Europe was in devastation and the Jews as a group had been hit harder than any other. The heavily Jewish sectors of Russia, Poland, Austria, and Hungary had been the scenes of some of the worst fighting, the most frequent conquests and reconquests, with pogroms an occasional by-product of the chaos of military conflict.

The inventory of calamity that emerged in the early postwar months served to convert many non-Zionist and even anti-Zionist Jews to the Zionist cause. Suddenly it seemed appropriate that these broken, homeless people should be allowed to emigrate to the Holy Land. But bitter differences within Jewry remained.

The Zionists themselves were split. There were quarrels over the proper method of colonizing and developing Palestine, and there were quarrels over a much more basic point, how to secure Palestine as the Jewish national home. Weizmann was beginning to emerge as a compromiser, a man of moderation, a practical politician who preferred taking one cautious step at a time. Increasingly, he would try to shape Zionist policies to what he considered a realistic view.

Arrayed against him were more impatient, more militant figures such as Jacob de Haas, Brandeis' mentor in Zionism and one of the dominant forces in the American movement. These militant Zionists insisted that national sovereignty be demanded at once for the Jewish commonwealth, followed by an immediate program of economic reconstruction in Palestine. They were infuriated by Weizmann's advocacy of a more "realistic" outlook. To this faction, acceptance of the Balfour Declaration itself had been an act of weakness; they felt Weizmann should have held out for the much more explicit guarantees of the statement's earlier text, and privately denounced him as a symbol of delay, timidity, and concession.

In February, 1919, a Zionist meeting in London was called to plan the movement's position at the peace conference. Some of the delegates, expecting that a Jewish state would come into being within a few months, showed up with lists of nominations for its cabinet; and Weizmann had to bring them down to earth by explaining how far they were from having the state they imagined.

The first session of the peace conference had met on January 18. More than thirty nations were represented. However, the four leading powers—France, Great Britain, the United States, and Italy—dominated the proceedings; two delegates from each of these nations, plus two from Japan, made up the Council of Ten that effectively held control. There was much to do: the organization of a League of Nations, the establishment of a host of new nations out of former Austro-Hungarian and German territory, the reconstruction of the shattered European economy, the prob-

lem of war reparations, and—somewhat low on the priority list—
the dismemberment of the empires of Germany and Turkey.

On February 23, the Council of Ten took up the question of
Palestine, and permitted five speakers to present the Jewish case.
The first four, all of them old Zionist stalwarts—Nahum Sokolow,
Weizmann, Menachem Ussishkin, and André Spire—briefly restated the nature of the Jewish claim to the Holy Land and presented a summary of Zionist requests. They called for recognition
of the right of Jews to reconstitute their national home in Palestine; for the fixing of boundaries for Palestine that ran from Aqaba
at the southern tip of the Sinai Peninsula to southern Lebanon, and
from the Mediterranean to the desert east of the Jordan River.
They also sought the encouragement of Jewish colonization in
Palestine; the award of a protectorate over Palestine to Great
Britain by mandate of the League of Nations; and the creation of
a Jewish quasi-governmental council in Palestine. The question of
political sovereignty for the Jewish homeland at some future date
was left untouched by design.

The fifth speaker was Sylvain Levi of France, who had been a
member of the Zionist Commission of 1918. He began by describing the virtues of Zionism as a moral force, but astoundingly
veered in mid-course to declare that it was unwise to award Palestine to the Jews, for they would unfairly dispossess the Arabs,
would create a new population of largely Russian extraction, and
Russians had "explosive" tendencies, and would pose problems of
dual allegiance for the rest of the world's Jews.

A panel that included Balfour, Premier Clemenceau of France,
and Secretary of State Lansing of the United States listened in
amazement to the unexpected tirade. Weizmann and his three
colleagues, aghast, wondered how they could get the floor again
for a refutation without seeming to transform the proceedings into
an undignified debate among Jews. They were saved, surprisingly,
by Lansing, who turned to Weizmann when Levi had finished and
asked, "What do you mean by a Jewish national home?" The
request for a clarification gave Weizmann a chance to make an
eloquent reply, which swayed the Council of Ten and brought a
statement by nightfall from the French members that France
would not oppose placing Palestine under British trusteeship, with
the formation of a Jewish state.

There still was reason to doubt the outcome. Syria's fate had not been settled, and the British were trapped in their mutually exclusive secret deals with the French and with the Hashemite Emir Hussein. If the French took control of Syria and the Hashemites were frozen out, the Zionist agreement with Faisal over the future of Palestine might be upset. How could the conflicting agreements be reconciled? Where would the boundaries, at present undefined, of "Syria" and "Palestine" be placed? Would the Jewish homeland somehow vanish during the negotiations? Among those who feared it would was Felix Frankfurter, the Vienna-born lawyer whom Brandeis had recruited for Zionism. Frankfurter, a former United States attorney, had served as an adviser to Wilson in the early days of his administration, then had joined the faculty of the Harvard Law School, and had returned to government service in 1917 in various advisory capacities. At the peace conference he played a double role, for he was counsel to President Wilson and also the representative of the American Zionist movement.

At this tense moment for Zionism, Faisal the Hashemite offered encouragement in a letter to Frankfurter on March 3, using terms that seem startling today:

"I want to take this opportunity of my first contact with American Zionists to tell you what I have often been able to say to Dr. Weizmann in Arabia and Europe:

"We feel that Arabs and Jews are cousins in race, having suffered similar oppressions at the hands of powers stronger than themselves, and by a happy coincidence have been able to take the first steps toward the attainment of their national ideals together.

"We Arabs, especially the educated among us, look with the deepest sympathy on the Zionist movement. Our deputation here in Paris is fully acquainted with the proposals submitted yesterday by the Zionist Organization to the Peace Conference [asking for a Jewish state]. We will do our best . . . to help them through: we will wish the Jews a most hearty welcome home."

Early in March, 1919, the peace conference decided to send a commission of inquiry to the Near East to make recommendations on the future of Syria and Palestine. Britain, France, and Italy all found it expedient to beg off, but the United States did not, and the commission ultimately consisted of just two members, both Americans: Henry C. King and Charles R. Crane. They had been carefully chosen by Colonel House and Secretary of State Lansing for their "impartiality" on the Jewish problem. To Felix Frank-furter this meant they were anti-Zionist. On March 26, Frank-furter, in some agitation, went to see Colonel House.

House's diary notes, "Felix Frankfurter was an excited after-noon caller. The Jews have it that the Inter-Allied Commission which is to be sent to Syria is about to cheat Jewry of Palestine. I assured him there was no such intention and gave him the real situation so he might take it to his fellow Hebrews." And again on April 29: "Frankfurter came again about his old trouble—'Palestine for the Jews.' He is afraid of the Syrian Commission. I advised him to go with them and keep in touch with the situation in that way."

Frankfurter's fears were not misplaced. The King-Crane Com-mission arrived in the Holy Land on June 10, 1919, and within ten days had reported to President Wilson that Moslem and Christian hostility would make establishment of Jewish sovereignty or even large-scale Jewish immigration unfeasible. In their final report, later that year, they quoted British officers in Palestine who be-lieved that the Zionist program could be carried out only by force of arms: "The officers generally thought that a force of not less than 50,000 soldiers would be required even to initiate the pro-gram." Though they expressed "a deep sense of sympathy for the Jewish cause," King and Crane observed that the Zionist claim "that they have a 'right to Palestine based on an occupation of two thousand years ago' can hardly be seriously considered," and recommended "that Jewish immigrants should be definitely limi-ted, and that the project for making Palestine distinctly a Jewish Commonwealth should be given up."

This appears to be the conclusion that House and Lansing had hoped to obtain when they chose King and Crane. But, by an-ticipating it, Frankfurter and Brandeis were able to negate it. They made Wilson aware that the King-Crane report was probably go-ing to be unacceptable to American Zionists, and when the Presi-dent finally received the report later in 1919 he was so dismayed by it that he ordered it pigeonholed instead of placing it before the peace conference.

Weizmann's group also felt pressure from the American Zionist leaders during the debate over Palestine in the summer of 1919. The Americans were urging that a harder line be taken at the peace conference; they insisted on asking for an immediate guarantee that Palestine was to become an autonomous Jewish commonwealth when the mandate authorities decided it was ready for self-government. Weizmann's cautious go-slow tactics bothered them, and when Brandeis and de Haas made a journey to Palestine in June, 1919, they stopped off briefly in London to make their position clear.

Weizmann was already aware of their feelings. He ascribed de Haas' unconcealed hostility to professional jealousy, an occupational hazard among Zionists. The English-born de Haas appeared to resent the great power Weizmann had attained in the movement while not actually holding office in the World Zionist Organization. As for Brandeis, he struck Weizmann as a Puritan, "upright, austere, of a scrupulous honesty and implacable logic. These qualities sometimes made him hard to work with; like Wilson he was apt to evolve theories, based on the highest principles, from his inner consciousness, and then expect the facts to fit in with them. If the facts failed to oblige, so much the worse for the facts." Privately Weizmann thought Brandeis a trifle naïve, insufficiently aware of the hard bargaining between England and France that would be needed to give the Jews their state. And it seemed to Weizmann that the American group had little grasp of the actual conditions in Palestine, a dilapidated country whose present Jewish population was, in the main, trained only for the study of the scriptures. "De Haas produced elaborate plans for the upbuilding of Palestine," Weizmann wrote, "which seemed to us both vague and fantastic. But we knew that much would depend on our American friends, and were anxious not to hurt their susceptibilities."

After an unsatisfactory meeting with Weizmann, Brandeis crossed to Paris, where he and Frankfurter conferred with Balfour. The British statesman spoke of himself as an "ardent Zionist" and praised the accomplishments of Jews—committing a minor faux pas, quickly corrected by Brandeis, when he credited Lenin with Jewish ancestry. Brandeis then presented the demands of the American Zionists. First, "that Palestine should be the Jewish Homeland, and not merely that there be a Jewish homeland in Palestine." This, he assumed, was the real commitment of the Balfour Declaration. Balfour did not contest the point. Second, Brandeis asked "economic elbow room for a Jewish Palestine," meaning "adequate boundaries, not merely a small garden within

Palestine." Specifically he meant the well-watered Galilee and as much of fertile Lebanon as could be wrested from the French. The eastern boundary of Palestine, said Brandeis, should be set as far east of the Jordan as Faisal would allow, perhaps all the way to the line of the Turkish railroad that Lawrence of Arabia's raiders had blown up. Balfour thought Faisal might agree with this. Finally, Brandeis urged that land purchase, under the British occupation of Palestine, should be permitted only to the state; he wanted no private land speculation, no private ownership at all.

In July the Brandeis party reached Palestine. For Brandeis it was his first visit to the Holy Land, and, like so many other travelers, he was deeply awed. The stark beauty of the Judaean hills, the glint of sunlight off the gilded dome of Jerusalem's great Mosque of Omar, the impact of discovering that there actually are such places as Bethlehem and Hebron and Beersheba and Nazareth, are irresistibly moving to any visitor, regardless of his religion or attitudes toward Zionism. Brandeis noticed also the marshes and swamps, the sand dunes, the lack of roads, the hopeless condition of so much of the land, but his innate optimism blotted these away in an instant. He was sure that the new British masters of Palestine, working in league with energetic Jewish leaders, would be able to obliterate within a few years the ruin caused by centuries of Turkish neglect. Palestine, he was convinced, would easily be ready to accommodate six million Jews in short order.

Brandeis assumed in this that the British administrators would, the instant the League of Nations had given them official charge of Palestine, begin draining marshes, clearing swamps, and building roads. But the outlook of the British military officials already in Palestine should have dampened some of this enthusiasm. When Brandeis arrived, he heard a number of disturbing complaints from the members of the Zionist Commission, the group that was preparing the way for the coming Jewish homeland. (The Zionist Commission was an outgrowth of the commission that Weizmann had headed in 1918. It had simply remained in Palestine, constituting itself as a permanent watchdog committee to provide liaison between the British occupation forces and the Jewish community in Palestine, after the three original commissioners had returned to Europe.) Dr. M. D. Eder, the acting chairman of the Zionist Commission, reported that Lieutenant Colonel Hubbard, the British governor in Jaffa, had said before witnesses, "If the Arabs will massacre the Jews in Jaffa I will not do anything to protect them; I will stand at the window, looking on, and laugh at them." Sir Ronald Storrs, the governor of the District of Jerusalem, had told the American Zionist Robert Szold, another member of the commission, that he had received no instructions from his government on implementation of the Balfour Declaration, and was ready to "go either way—the way of the Arabs or the way of the Jews." Many of the other British occupation officers were openly anti-Jewish, pro-Arab, or both.

Brandeis, checking into these charges, found that they were generally true, and when he returned to London in August, 1919, he informed Balfour of the situation. Angered, Balfour ordered a shake-up of the British administration in Palestine, starting with the man in command, General Sir Gilbert Clayton, who was replaced by a Zionist sympathizer, Colonel Richard Meinertzhagen. What Brandeis could not realize, however, is that most British officers greatly admired the Arabs, with whom they had fought against the Turks in the war, and were unlikely to display much willingness to cooperate with the incoming Zionists in any development program for Palestine that would involve displacing the Palestinian Arab community. The chances were good that the Balfour Declaration would be implemented, that the Jews would be let into Palestine. But, as Weizmann realized and the American Zionists failed to perceive, that did not automatically mean that a clear path to a viable Jewish state would at once be open.

FOUR

A Troubled Mandate

THE IMPATIENT, idealistic Americans had their way. Weizmann yielded to the extent of agreeing to let the Zionist representatives at the peace conference ask for all of Palestine as the Jewish national home. He also promised to demand that the ultimate aim of the British mandate would be the creation of a self-governing commonwealth. By the autumn of 1919 these proposals had received Balfour's blessing and were placed before the peace conference.

The first phase of that conference had by then come to an end with the drafting of the Treaty of Versailles, which brought an official close to the war and established the League of Nations. Under Article 22 of the League's covenant—included in the Treaty of Versailles—the former colonial possessions of Germany and Turkey would be allotted by League mandate to various Allied powers; the mandates were to be decreed at a conference to be held at San Remo, Italy, in the spring of 1920. The United States Senate refused to ratify the Treaty of Versailles, because it was unwilling to accept the loss of national sovereignty that it deemed was involved in joining the League of Nations; and so there could be no direct American participation in the parceling-out of mandated territories. But the United States insisted that as one of the major powers its consent was necessary for all mandate awards, and this was granted; each award would be submitted for American approval.

This was of great importance to the Zionist cause, for it was still possible that the Jewish homeland would be scuttled. An unofficial understanding already existed that France was to be given the mandate over Syria and that Great Britain would get the mandate for Palestine, and presumably the British mandatory officials would welcome Jews, in accordance with the Balfour Declaration. But there were grave difficulties over the boundary line between the two mandates. France was still clinging to the Sykes-Picot agreement, by which the watersheds of northern Palestine would be detached and made part of Syria, with somber economic consequences for Palestine.

In February, 1920, Brandeis went into action to prevent this. He cabled Balfour to say, "We are deeply concerned at information that it is proposed to carry out the Sykes-Picot Treaty to mutilate historic Palestine and render all future developments impossible." He also wired André Pierre Tardieu, France's representative at the peace conference, asking for "quick reassuring words." And on February 4 Brandeis wrote President Wilson to say that negotiations on the future of Palestine "have reached so critical a state . . . as to compel me to appeal to you." Reminding Wilson that Sykes-Picot was a secret treaty, a species that the President particularly detested, Brandeis said:

"The Balfour Declaration which you made possible was a public promise. I venture to suggest that it may be given to you at this time to move the statesmen of Christian nations to keep this solemn promise to Israel. Your word to Miller [David Hunter Miller, of the British delegation to the peace conference] and Lloyd George at this hour may be decisive."

Wilson at once cabled his ambassador in Paris, directing him to see the French and British delegates and express Wilson's support for the Zionist position.

Wilson's intervention helped in persuading the French to relinquish their claim to northern Palestine. With the creation of a Jewish homeland now beginning to seem possible, the Zionist Organization of America launched a drive to raise $10,000,000 in the United States "for the restoration of Palestine"—thus marking the beginning of the evolution of American Zionism from a wholly political movement to one that was greatly concerned with fund-raising as well.

By way of celebrating Jewish unity, Jacob H. Schiff was recruited for the advisory committee of the fund drive. A number

of important Gentile names went on the list of committee members too, including those of William Jennings Bryan, Governor
Alfred E. Smith of New York, James Cardinal Gibbons, President
Charles W. Eliot of Harvard, and three members of Wilson's cabinet. As Weizmann was discovering about this time the money that
was raised would go only a short distance to meet the needs of
restoring the homeland. He had assumed that the British government would make land available out of the public domain for the
new Jewish colonies in Palestine. But it had quickly become apparent, he wrote, "that this belief had no basis in fact, and that every
dunam [quarter-acre] of land needed for our colonization work
would have to be bought in the open market at fantastic prices
which rose ever higher as our work developed. Every improve-
ment we made raised the value of the remaining land in that
particular area, and the Arab landowners lost no time in cashing
in. We found we had to cover the soil of Palestine with Jewish
gold."

The San Remo conference opened on April 18, 1920. A week
later, the expected decision on the Near East was handed down:
Palestine to Great Britain (with the controversial watershed included), and Syria to France. The actual terms of the mandate
were still to be written and approved by the League of Nations,
but there was a clear understanding that the Jews were to have
their Zion at last. By way of underscoring that point, the British
government, after consulting with Weizmann, appointed a Jew,
Herbert Samuel, as the first high commissioner for Palestine.

The ghost of Sykes-Picot had been laid to rest; but now a new
obstacle arose. Would the Arabs permit the Jewish colonization of
Palestine?

True, Weizmann and Faisal had come to a friendly accord. In
his agreement with the Zionists, however, Faisal had stipulated,
"If the Arabs are established as I have asked in my manifesto of
January 4 [1919] addressed to the British Secretary of State for
Foreign Affairs, I will carry out what is written in this agreement.
If changes are made, I cannot be answerable for failing to carry out
this agreement." He meant the establishment of Hashemite rule
in Iraq, Syria, and Lebanon, in return for which he would allow
"all necessary measures" to be taken "to encourage and stimulate
immigration of Jews into Palestine on a large scale."

But by the middle of 1920 the Hashemites were in serious

trouble, and the prospects for harmony between Arab and Jew were thereby endangered.

The problems of the Hashemites had begun in their home territory of Arabia. Faisal's father, Emir Hussein, had been challenged by a rival prince, Abd-al-Aziz ibn Faisal Al Sa'ud, known outside Arabia simply as Ibn Saud. Since 1906 Ibn Saud had been the master of much of Arabia, excluding Hejaz and two other provinces under direct Turkish control. Hejaz was the center of Hussein's power. Then in 1919 the army of Ibn Saud annihilated that of Hussein, and thereafter Hejaz was completely surrounded by Saudi-held territory. The Hashemite grip on Hejaz became precarious. It appeared quite likely that the Hashemites would be driven from Arabia in another few years, and this in fact happened in 1924.

Meanwhile Hussein's son Faisal was attempting to take possession of Syria, which the British had promised him. In July, 1919, an Arab congress held at Damascus had elected Faisal king of Syria, and in March, 1920, another Arab meeting there had repeated the offer of the Syrian throne. Faisal arrived in Damascus soon afterward to begin his reign.

But at the end of April the League awarded the Syrian mandate to France, and the French wished to have no Arab kings to complicate their rule. In June they asserted their rights under the mandate, and the following month, after announcing the deposition of Faisal, they expelled him from Syria by force. They proceeded to split the coastal territory of Lebanon away from Syria as a separate state also under their mandate, and to set up a number of local governments that would offer no challenge to their authority.

The expulsion of Faisal and the French takeover of Syria aroused harsh feelings throughout the Arab world. The Arabs believed this series of events had been arranged with the connivance of the British, and such sentiment as had existed for allowing Jews to enter Palestine in accordance with British wishes instantly evaporated. Now, for the first time, voices of Arab hatred were heard, and violence followed.

The initial act of violence had not been specifically directed at the Jews. A condition of anarchy had developed in the northern Galilee, near the border between Palestine and what in early 1920 was still Syria. Bands of Arab marauders, who were loyal to Faisal and aware that he was being edged out of Syria by the French,

were roaming the border, harassing French soldiers and inciden-
tally making life difficult for five tiny Jewish settlements on the
frontier.

The Jewish leaders in Palestine sent a small band of defenders
north to protect these outposts. The leader of the defense group
was Joseph Trumpeldor, a militant Zionist from Russia. Before
settling in Palestine, Trumpeldor had served in the Russian army,
losing an arm in the Russo-Japanese War and subsequently being
named a warrant officer, the highest rank ever given a Jew by the
Tsarist regime. In February, 1920, while defending the isolated
northern settlement of Tel Hai, Trumpeldor and seven companions—two of them women—were killed by Arab raiders. They
were the first martyrs to Zionism, even though their deaths had
been an accident of Arab-French friction.

The next outbreak was no accident, and was aimed directly at
the Jews. In April, 1920, as the decision over the mandate was
approaching, nationalistic Arab instigators circulated rumors that
the Jews planned to desecrate the Moslem shrines in Jerusalem.
This whipped up powerful emotions and succeeded in touching
off a riot. An Arab mob armed with knives and clubs burst into the
Jewish quarter of the Old City. Five Jews were killed in the
pogrom and more than two hundred wounded in half an hour of
bloodletting. By the time the British occupation troops arrived,
everything was over.

Four Arabs also died in the riot. They were killed, not by the
defenseless religious Jews of the Old City, but by the prototypes
of today's Israelis: a dedicated band of armed Jews, able and ready
to meet force with force.

The guiding spirit of this movement was the fiery, dynamic
Vladimir Jabotinsky, whose zealous campaign to build Jewish military might cut him off from the main stream of the Zionist movement, and made him appear almost a diabolical figure to some of
its leaders. As a young man he was a brilliant, if undisciplined,
journalist and political agitator, who dreamed of organizing the
first Jewish army since the defeat of Bar-Kochba and using it to
wrest Zion from the Moslems.

At the start of World War I he conceived a subtle way to bring
this Jewish Legion into existence. He called on the commanding
officer of the British forces in Egypt and offered to form an army
of Jewish volunteers which, fighting under the Zionist flag, would

drive the Turks out of Palestine. Jabotinsky quietly planned that afterward this force would remain together and defend Zionist claims against possible Arab opposition. The British general was taken aback by the unorthodox proposal; he could hardly give authorization for the formation of a fighting unit that would issue its own battle orders. He countered by inviting Jabotinsky to organize a labor battalion, under the British flag but bearing a distinctively Jewish name—"Zion Mule Corps," perhaps.

Jabotinsky indignantly refused and went off to Italy. But his friend Trumpeldor took over the project and did create the Zion Mule Corps, which saw military action in Britain's disastrous Gallipoli campaign of 1915, and then was disbanded. Jabotinsky, meanwhile, had drifted on to London, where he was joined in 1916 by Trumpeldor and 120 veterans of the former Zion Mule Corps. Trumpeldor, Jabotinsky, and the 120 all enlisted in the British army and managed to stay together to form the 38th Battalion, Royal Fusiliers—a sub rosa Jewish Legion within His Majesty's armed force.

Quickly Jabotinsky sent Zionist recruiters to the New World, where they rounded up hundreds of Jews who had left Palestine to escape Turkish oppression during the war. These men hurried to Canada to volunteer for service, along with a surprising number of American Jews who preferred fighting for Zion in a British uniform to fighting for France in an American one.

"The Americans brought with them," Jabotinsky wrote, "a strong, often feverish interest in Palestine and everything Palestinian. . . . The Americans constituted the largest group in the Legion. Of our approximately 5,000 men, 1,720 (34 per cent) were from the U.S.; 30 per cent were Palestinians; 28 per cent came from Great Britain, 6 per cent from Canada, 1 per cent from the Argentine and 1 per cent from freed Turkish prisoners of war."

These new recruits became the 39th Battalion, Royal Fusiliers. Among them were Jacob Epstein, the sculptor, and a newspaperman named Gershon Agronsky, who would one day be mayor of Jerusalem. In the spring of 1918 the 38th Battalion sailed for Egypt, where it shortly was joined by the 39th. A 40th Battalion was created in Alexandria from liberated Turkish prisoners and other volunteers. After three years of scheming, Jabotinsky and Trumpeldor finally got their Jewish Legion into action in September, 1918, fording the Jordan near Jericho and occupying a Turkish post. A month later the Turks withdrew from the war.

Jabotinsky attempted to keep his Jewish Legion together as a Palestinian army after the war, to the considerable alarm of Weizmann and the other gradualist Zionist leaders. He went on recruiting, and had to be forcibly discharged from British service. But he had what he wanted: a nucleus of Jews who had been taught how to fight. When the Jerusalem riot of April, 1920, broke out, Jabotinsky's underground Jewish defense force rushed in to do battle. Afterward, he and 19 of his followers were arrested as troublemakers by the British. Jabotinsky was given a startling sentence of 15 years at hard labor, the others two or three years. Several Arab instigators were identified, and orders went out for their arrest too; but they took refuge in the desert east of the Jordan, and received sentences in absentia of up to 15 years.

Among these escaped instigators was a sinister figure named Haj Amin el-Husseini, a member of an influential Arab family of Jerusalem. Educated in Egypt, he was fiercely nationalistic, with a vision of a single Arab empire spanning the whole Near East and ruled, as in the grand days before the Turkish conquest, by a caliph, a dynastic successor to Mohammed. Inserting a Jewish commonwealth between Syria and Egypt was fatal to this dream of unity, and Haj Amin el-Husseini was willing to prevent the creation of that commonwealth in any way necessary, from political agitation to extermination of all Jewish settlers. Just as Jabotinsky and Trumpeldor represented the psychological ancestors of the modern Israeli, Haj Amin was the model for today's fanatical anti-Israeli Arab.

When Herbert Samuel became high commissioner for Palestine after the British assumed their mandate in July, 1920, one of his first acts was to decree an amnesty for those involved in the Jerusalem riot—both the Arab leaders of the outburst and the Jewish defenders. Jabotinsky went to London to have his sentence quashed altogether; Haj Amin returned to Jerusalem.

In March, 1921, Haj Amin's half-brother, the grand mufti of Jerusalem—spiritual leader of Jerusalem's Moslem community, and therefore a man of immense political power among the Palestinian Arabs—died. High Commissioner Samuel took the curious step of nominating the convicted conspirator, Haj Amin, to be the new grand mufti. He did this to neutralize the power of another Arab family, the Nashashabis, ancient rivals of the Husseinis. A

Nashashabi had just become mayor of Jerusalem, replacing a Husseini. Samuel thought it was a clever stroke to balance the elevation of a Nashashabi by keeping the muftiship in the Husseini family. But in the process he handed a position of enormous prestige to a man determined to work for the destruction of the Jewish commonwealth Samuel had been sent to Palestine to sponsor. With Haj Amin as grand mufti, new storms of Arab protest could be expected, and they swiftly materialized.

This time the trouble began in Jaffa on May 1, 1921. A small band of Jewish communists, much disliked by the majority of the Jewish immigrants and especially by those who were moderate socialists, was holding a May Day parade. The socialists were staging their own parade in nearby Tel Aviv. When the two Jewish processions collided near the Jaffa-Tel Aviv border, a fight broke out.

Arab onlookers, seeing the confusion, rushed to join it, and soon mob violence was unleashed. A frenzied Arab crowd stormed the Zionist Immigration Depot in Jaffa and killed 13 newly arrived Jews, while Jewish-owned shops were looted and destroyed. The rioting spread into Tel Aviv, where grim Jewish defenders held the Arabs off with sticks and stones, and during the next few days there was a general uprising against the Jews in many settlements. Arab attackers burned homes, despoiled orchards, carried away livestock.

The British proclaimed martial law, but made little attempt to intervene, and the burden of defense fell to the men trained by Jabotinsky. (These armed Jews occasionally "anticipated" Arab onslaughts during the disorders and made "preventive" raids; the Moslems were not the only aggressors, though the main guilt is theirs.) After a week of turmoil, 48 Arabs and 47 Jews were dead, hundreds on both sides were injured, and property losses were immense.

British authorities quite correctly attributed the 1921 troubles to Arab resentment over the pace of Jewish immigration, even though that immigration had been nowhere near as great as the Zionists had anticipated. Weizmann, addressing the peace conference in 1919, had envisioned 70,000 to 80,000 immigrants a year; Brandeis had expected a million Jews to enter Palestine in the first few years after the war. However, the quota announced by the high commissioner in August, 1920, covering the first year of the

mandate, was just 16,500 Jewish immigrants. By May of 1921 only
about 10,000 of these Jews had arrived in this third, or post-Balfour,
aliyah, most of them from Russia and Poland, but even this many
upset the Arabs. The newcomers settled on newly purchased land,
began to drain swamps, and were founding *kibbutzim*, or cooperative villages, along socialistic lines.

Reviewing the situation in June, 1921, High Commissioner
Samuel acted in a way that left Zionists appalled and made the
mufti rejoice. "I am distressed that the harmony between the
creeds and races of Palestine, which I have desired most earnestly
to promote, has not yet been attained," he said, and offered a
"clarification" of the Balfour Declaration concerning the meaning
of "a national home for the Jewish people." The British government, he said, had never intended that a Jewish government
would be set up in Palestine to rule the Moslem and Christian
majority, nor would the Jews be permitted to transform themselves by immigration into a majority themselves. It would be the
policy of the mandate, said Samuel, "that the Jews, a people that
are scattered throughout the world but whose hearts are always
turned to Palestine, should be enabled to found here their home,
and that some among them, within the limits that are fixed by the
numbers and interests of the present population, should come to
Palestine in order to help by their resources and efforts to develop
the country, to the advantage of all the inhabitants." Therefore
Samuel imposed sharp limits on future Jewish immigration. Jews
of independent means and those with a definite prospect of employment might continue to enter the country, "but the conditions of Palestine are such as do not permit anything in the nature
of a mass immigration."

Zionists everywhere raised cries of protest. There were demands for Samuel's removal. He tried to make it clear privately
that he was acting according to long-range plans: appease the
wrath of the Arabs now, keep them calm until they can come to
realize that the Jewish immigrants are no threat to them, and then
the building of Zion can resume. It was a crafty stratagem, and for
eight years it was successful. The new immigration restrictions
were never enforced to the letter, and Jews managed to trickle
into Palestine at a rate of a few hundred a month, with the numbers gradually increasing again once Arab suspicions had been
lulled. But two significant patterns had been exposed by the Brit-

ish response to the May, 1921, riots. One was that the Balfour Declaration stood revealed as a deliberately ambiguous document that could be interpreted to suit the needs of the moment. The other was that the British had no stomach for civil disorder in Palestine, and could be forced to reshape their policies by a few hundred howling rioters.

3.

The British were wrestling at the same time with another slippery matter: what to do about the Hashemites. Faisal, having been pushed out of Syria by the French, had angrily turned to his British allies, demanding compensation. His elder brother Abdullah, who had been promised the throne of Iraq, but who had never actually taken possession of it, was creating even greater difficulties by threatening to avenge the insult to his family through a holy war against France. In January, 1921, Abdullah marched north out of Arabia into the district of eastern Palestine known as Transjordan, and announced that he was going to continue on to Damascus and drive the French from Syria.

This tangle was now the problem of Britain's new Colonial Secretary, Winston Churchill, for all the mandated territories were the responsibilities of the Colonial Office. Since Churchill had had no previous involvement in Britain's Near East policies, one of his first acts was to call a conference at Cairo of all British senior officials in the Arab world. The Faisal situation seemed the most pressing, and the conference solved it by awarding him the throne of Iraq as king under the British mandate. An "election" in Iraq was hastily rigged, and by August of 1921 Faisal at last had a kingdom. But this removed from the Palestinian scene the only Arab leader who had shown sincere sympathy for the Zionist cause; and his Syrian experience had so embittered the moderate Faisal that within a few years he would be denying that he had ever made promises to the Jews at all.

It also left the British with an extra Hashemite prince, Abdullah, for whom no apparent kingdom was available. Abdullah had not yet made good his threat to march on Damascus, and was still camped in Amman in Transjordan, where the Arab population was hailing him as their ruler. But Transjordan was part of Palestine. Something had to be done quickly, for Abdullah had scarcely been pleased to see the British promote his younger brother to the

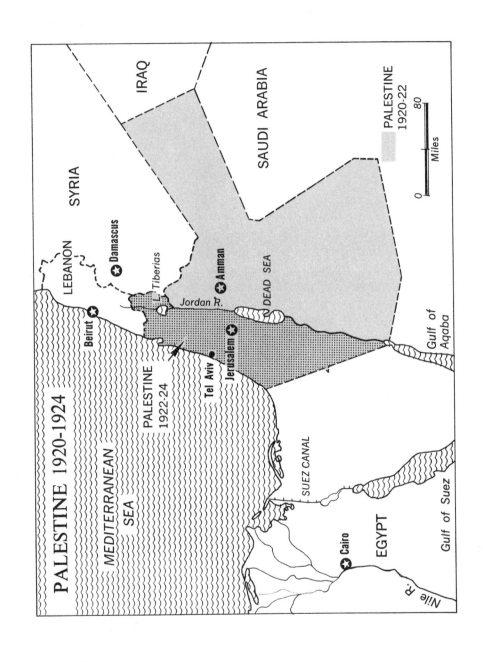

PALESTINE 1920-1924

MEDITERRANEAN SEA

LEBANON

SYRIA

Beirut

Damascus

L. Tiberias

PALESTINE 1922-24

Jordan R.

Amman

Tel Aviv

Jerusalem

DEAD SEA

IRAQ

SAUDI ARABIA

EGYPT

Cairo

SUEZ CANAL

Gulf of Suez

Gulf of Aqaba

Nile R.

PALESTINE 1920-22

0   Miles   80

Iraqi throne that they had earlier pledged to him. Late in March, 1921, Churchill went from Cairo to Jerusalem, where he met with Abdullah, High Commissioner Samuel, and Lawrence of Arabia, only a few weeks before the outbreak of the Arab riots. In half an hour the Abdullah crisis was ended: Churchill agreed to carve Transjordan free from Palestine and set it up as an autonomous kingdom under British protection and Abdullah's rule.

The Hashemites now were content. Palestine, though, had been diminished in size by 80 percent. The original mandated territory had covered about 45,000 square miles on both sides of the Jordan River, an area about the size of Pennsylvania. What remained after the subtraction of Transjordan was about 10,000 square miles, an area about that of Maryland. The Zionists had never shown any interest in Transjordan—the Jewish population of the entire huge tract had been two persons, in 1921—and what Abdullah had been given was mostly a barren wilderness, inhabited by wandering Bedouin tribesmen.

The deal with Abdullah, though, was not only "a serious whittling down of the Balfour Declaration," in Weizmann's words, which made much of the Holy Land inaccessible to Jews, but it created a situation of potential danger. A sparsely settled region had been turned into a political entity under the control of an Arabian dynasty that had had no previous claim to Palestinian soil; and that entity was so bleak, so far from viable, that there would surely be jealousy of Palestine, the neighbor to the west, with its seaports, its rivers, its growing cities, its orchards. The opportunity for friction between Arabs and Zionists was that much greater, now; the chance for harmony, that much less. Caught between British restrictiveness and the birth of an unexpected Arab kingdom on the east, the Jews of Palestine had reasons for anxiety. Their homeland had become a closet.

4.

Within the Zionist movement the events of 1920 and 1921 were creating uneasiness and apprehension; and the movement itself was developing serious fissures. The problem of financing the growth of the homeland was the main cause of dissension.

Enormous sums were needed. In 1919, Weizmann had met in Paris with Louis Marshall of the American Jewish Committee, who, although an assimilationist and not then connected with

Zionism, had—like many other non-Zionist Jews—come to look more sympathetically on the idea of the homeland since the war. After listening for a long while to Weizmann's discussion of the magnitude of the challenge in Palestine, Marshall burst out, "But, Dr. Weizmann, you'll need half a billion dollars to build up this country!"

"You'll need much more, Mr. Marshall," Weizmann replied. And he added, "The money is there, in the pockets of the American Jews. It's your business and my business to get at some of it."

In the spring of 1920, Herbert Samuel brought up the question of money in a letter to Weizmann, informing him that £2,000,000 would be needed for Palestine's railways and £300,000 for other public works. "It is very inadvisible," Samuel wrote, "that the administration for Palestine should have recourse to the British taxpayer for financial assistance." The World Zionist Organization had proposed forming the *Keren Hayesod*, or Palestine Foundation Fund, as a world-wide instrumentality for collecting money to rebuild Palestine. (The *Keren Kayemeth*, or Jewish National Fund, which was already in existence, was limited to the purchase of land in Palestine.) Samuel did not think that a fund-raising scheme that depended on voluntary contributions was secure enough a foundation for the Jewish homeland, and asked Weizmann to consider some other method at the forthcoming World Zionist Conference in London, which was to open on July 7, 1920.

The conference was not considered as important a gathering as a World Zionist Congress, of which there had been eleven between 1897 and 1913; but it was nevertheless the first meeting of the world's Zionists since the eleventh congress, seven years earlier, and was viewed as a necessary preliminary to a resumption of full-scale congresses.

Since the last congress the whole character of Zionism had changed, for the entry of Brandeis had imparted to it an American flavor, and the proclamation of the Balfour Declaration (aided in no small way by Brandeis' pressures on Wilson) had given it official governmental sponsorship. For the first time, a large delegation of American Jews took part in an international Zionist meeting. Brandeis headed the group, and Weizmann sought him out at once to tell him of the critical financial situation.

Brandeis objected to creating a fund-raising agency within the framework of the World Zionist Organization. The W.Z.O., as he saw it, was an agency for political agitation whose reason for existence had ended, essentially, with the Balfour Declaration. The Jews now had their homeland—or so it seemed in the summer of 1920—and what remained was purely an economic matter, a development program. To carry this out successfully, Brandeis argued, the financial cooperation of the rich non-Zionist Jews—the Schiffs, the Warburgs, the Lehmans, and such—was vital. These millionaire philanthropists would not come near any limb of the World Zionist Organization, which was tainted with politicking and aroused the old dual-allegiance question; but they would almost certainly contribute millions to a new, wholly non-political organization that was devoted to the building of Palestine but lay wholly outside the W.Z.O. Brandeis suggested that a committee of distinguished Jews, including many hitherto unconnected with Zionism, be named to handle the financing of the homeland. Through some failure of communication Brandeis came to think that Weizmann was giving his assent to this arrangement; but in fact Weizmann opposed it. When that became apparent at the next day's session Brandeis felt betrayed. To his associates he said bitterly, "Lloyd George might lie, but not to his Cabinet!"

An attempt by Brandeis to turn the whole Zionist movement to a nonpolitical orientation at the conference ended in failure. He argued for a change in policy that would "elicit the full cooperation of all the Jews, those who do not want to build up the Zionist Organization but who do want to share with the Zionist Organization in the upbuilding of Palestine." Weizmann, who had a much more accurate understanding of the real situation in Palestine, replied that the political work of Zionism "was far from finished; the Balfour Declaration and the San Remo decision were the beginning of a new era in the political struggle, and the Zionist Organization was our instrument of political action." After a sharp and often acrimonious debate, a majority of the delegates voted with Weizmann.

The size of the Zionist budget was another cause of dissension. Weizmann felt that Palestine would need something like $10,000,000 a year—most of which would have to come, of necessity, from the Jews of America. Brandeis and the other Americans were shocked, calling the figure "astronomical," and insisted that the most that American Jewry could provide was $500,000 a year. This led Weizmann to make one of his most injudicious remarks, telling Brandeis, "If this is all you can find in America, I will have to come over and try for myself." A pro-Weizmann faction within the American delegation urged him to do just that; but Brandeis was deeply stung by the challenge.

The unhappy conference ended by naming Weizmann president of the World Zionist Organization, giving him at last official recognition of the fact that he had led the movement for the past decade; Brandeis was tactfully awarded the title of honorary president. But he returned to the United States determined to continue the struggle against Weizmann for a depoliticization of Zionism.

Brandeis worked toward this goal even after the upheavals in the Near East in 1920 and early 1921 made it apparent that the political status of the Jewish homeland was far from secure. His insistence on ridding Zionism of any policy that might alienate previously non-Zionist Jews led to one of Zionism's great personal tragedies: Brandeis' dismissal by the movement he had done so much to build.

The pro-Weizmann group of American Zionists, led by Louis Lipsky, decided early in 1921 on the ouster of Brandeis and his closest collaborator, Federal Judge Julian Mack. Judge Mack had served for three years as president of the Zionist Organization of America. Brandeis had held the title of honorary president since his appointment to the Supreme Court in 1916. Their overthrow was set for the twenty-fourth annual convention of the Z.O.A., to open in Cleveland on June 5, 1921. The first tactical move of the Lipsky group was to arrange for Weizmann to come to the United States to proclaim the opening of the Palestine Foundation Fund as a purely Zionist enterprise. Weizmann had never visited the United States before.

He arrived by ship in New York Harbor on Saturday, April 2, 1921. It was the Jewish Sabbath, and so he could not go ashore until sunset. All afternoon Weizmann and his party (which included Albert Einstein) remained on the ship, bombarded by questions from newspapermen who came out by boat and wanted to find out what they could about Zionism and about the theory of relativity. When it finally became possible to land, Weizmann expected to go straight to his hotel and settle down to work.

But, he wrote, he had reckoned without his host, "which was, or seemed to be, the whole of New York Jewry. Long before the afternoon ended, delegations began to assemble on the quay and even on the docks. Pious Jews in their thousands came on foot [to ride on the Sabbath is forbidden] all the way from Brooklyn and the Bronx to welcome us. Then the cars arrived, all of them beflagged. Every car had its horn and every horn was put in action. By the time we reached the gangway the area about the quays was a pandemonium of people, cars, and mounted police. The car which we had thought would transport us quickly and quietly to our hotel fell in at the end of an enormous procession which wound its way through the entire Jewish section of New York. We reached the Commodore at about eleven-thirty, tired, hungry, thirsty and completely dazed."

While Weizmann was still on the ship, Judge Mack had handed him a printed memorandum setting forth the Brandeis-Mack position. It repeated the call to end the political lobbying of the Zionist Organization, and objected to the establishment of the Foundation Fund. Brandeis preferred "private investments" and "individual projects," operating outside the Zionist structure, to raise the needed money. To Weizmann it seemed like an ultimatum, and an ugly cleavage threatened. Samuel Untermeyer, a prominent Jewish lawyer of New York, sought without success to find a compromise between the Weizmann and Brandeis ideas.

At the beginning of May came the Jaffa riots, followed by High Commissioner Samuel's decree of limitations on Jewish immigration into Palestine. The timing for Brandeis was unfortunate, for now the need for further Zionist political work was evident. Sensing that the mass of American Zionists were with him, Weizmann declared the Palestine Foundation Fund to be established in the United States, by virtue of his authority as president of the World Zionist Organization. The break between him and Brandeis was complete.

When the Cleveland convention opened a few weeks later, in June, 1921, Felix Frankfurter delivered a strong indictment of the European Zionist leaders, and another Brandeis backer, Rabbi Stephen S. Wise, also spoke. After the Lipsky faction had stated its position, a vote of confidence in the Brandeis leadership was called, and it was defeated, 153-71. Judge Mack then resigned as president, and read a letter from Brandeis announcing his resignation as honorary president. The entire Brandeis group thereupon severed its connection with the Zionist Organization, and, until his death in 1941, Brandeis remained outside the movement that had rejected him, often delivering sharp criticisms of its policies. (He did not, however, lose interest in Palestine. He continued to work toward the economic rebirth of the Jewish homeland, and was one of the founders of the Palestine Economic Corporation—now the PEC Israel Economic Corporation—which, through investment of private American capital, has organized and financed business ventures in Palestine and Israel.)

When the Cleveland unpleasantness was over, Weizmann swung into a national fund-raising tour on behalf of the new Palestine Foundation Fund. Thus began a ritual that was to become the central feature of American Zionism: the fund drive. For months, on through the summer and into the autumn, the 47-year-old Weizmann pulled himself into every American city and town that had a sizable Jewish community. He endured breakfasts at the local city hall, speeches of welcome by the mayor, press conferences at which he almost invariably was questioned about his role in the invention of TNT. (He had had nothing to do with TNT.) Then came the formal luncheon with the most prosperous and prominent Jews of the city—"a long, grueling affair of many courses and speeches," he wrote, "and the arrangement always was that the guest of honor should speak last, lest the public should be tempted to leave, thus depriving some of the other speakers of their audience." In the late afternoon came the private meeting with the local Zionist workers—an important morale-builder, allowing fund-raisers of obscure position to get a brief but concentrated exposure to the charismatic one. Then there was dinner, "very like lunch, only more so," followed by a mass meeting at the city hall, and then, at last, an escape into the train that by morning would deposit him at the next stop on his route.

It was arduous work, and involved great resources of diplomacy. Most of Weizmann's listeners knew little or nothing about Palestine, other than that it was a place where Jews had lived in Biblical times, and they had to be educated in Zionist thinking from the beginning. Weizmann also had to give private interviews to "big donors"—anyone likely to contribute as much as $5,000—and some of these men, on the other hand, had quite definite ideas about Palestine. He wrote, "I would have to listen then to strange versions of the criticisms leveled at us by the Brandeis group, or by non-Zionists and anti-Zionists, to crank schemes for the overnight creation of a Jewish homeland, to paternal practical advice from successful businessmen, all of which had to be received attentively and courteously."

He found the American Jews "good, kindly, well-intentioned people, some of them intelligent and informed Zionists." But his endurance neared its limit as day after day he went through the same routine. Certain stereotypes began to emerge: the fluttery, giddy lady Zionist who was unable to understand the intricacies of Near Eastern politics, but wanted so much to help her downtrodden Jewish cousins overseas; the aggressive, status-conscious doctor or merchant who loudly and publicly pledged thousands to the cause, only to find some excuse for cutting his donation when check-writing time arrived; the big donor who would make his contribution conditional on having Weizmann accept an invitation to dinner, where he would be shown the donor's descendants unto the third or fourth generation; the operator who would offer a donation in return for some kind of commercial concession for his company in the new homeland; and so on. Any charitable cause has its comic side, and exposes the pretentions and foibles of the givers; yet the work had to be done. As David Ben-Gurion expressed it many years later, "A homeland is not created with applause."

5.

Exhausted, Weizmann returned to Europe in the autumn of 1921. He had managed to raise some $2,000,000—not as much as was needed, but four times what Brandeis had predicted American Jews would give. Judge Mack's rival fund drive, organized early in 1920 with all sorts of prestigious Gentile names on its letterhead, had never really managed to get under way, but Weizmann had found the proper technique for extracting dollars from the Jewish middle class.

"Despite the exhaustion and the discomfort and the occasional tedium," he wrote, "I felt an immense privilege in the work." He was able to convince thousands of American Jews, safe from pogroms and ghettos in the land of the free, that there was a reason for a Jewish homeland. It was time, he told them, for Jews to cease being international flotsam, vulnerable to changes in public sentiment, open to charges of parasitism, of a lack of patriotism. "The only man who is invited to dinner is the man who can have dinner at home if he likes," Weizmann said repeatedly. "If you want your position to be secure elsewhere, you must have a portion of Jewry which is at home, in its own country." They believed, and they gave.

He went straight from the United States to the Czechoslovakian spa of Carlsbad, where the Twelfth Zionist Congress—the first since 1913—had convened. The delegates heard about the split in the American movement and about the troubles with the Arabs in Palestine, but they also listened to exciting progress reports from the homeland. The *chalutzim*, the pioneers, had begun to dig wells, plant trees, drain marshes; the experiment of converting urbanized Jews to farmers seemed to be working.

The main challenge to Zionism now, despite Brandeis, was still political. The British government was preparing a draft of the actual text of the mandate—in essence, a constitution for Palestine —which the League of Nations would ratify. Zionists hoped that the terms of the mandate would make explicit what the Balfour Declaration had left vague; and to insure that Jewish rights would not be ignored, it was necessary to keep close watch over the British Foreign Office, which had the task of writing the text. Lord Curzon, now the Foreign Secretary, was not considered a friend of Zionism, and he was known to be disturbed by the Arab protests.

Lord Curzon's secretary, Eric Forbes-Adam, prepared the mandate's text. The Zionist representative who examined and discussed the emerging document with Forbes-Adam was a 28-year-old American, Benjamin V. Cohen, then at the outset of his distinguished career in public affairs. The Indiana-born Cohen had been Judge Mack's law clerk and an active supporter of Brandeis in the power struggle within the Zionist Organization of America, but he had remained in the movement after the walkout of most of the Brandeis-Mack faction. In later years he would serve in key advisory posts in the administration of Franklin D. Roosevelt, would become a familiar figure at the international conferences that shaped the postwar world, and would play an important role in the United States delegation to the United Nations. But here in 1921, five years out of law school, he was undertaking the most important work he had done thus far—helping to hammer out the shape of the new Jewish homeland's basic structure.

There were problems. Cohen wanted the preamble of the mandate to acknowledge "the historic rights of the Jews to Palestine," but Lord Curzon would not have it. "If you word it like that," Curzon said, "I can see Weizmann coming to me every other day and saying he has a *right* to do this, that, or the other in Palestine!" Balfour suggested referring to an "historical connection" rather than "rights," and in the final text the passage ran, "Recognition has thereby been given to the historical connection of the Jewish people with Palestine and to the grounds for reconstituting their national home in that country." Another change that followed the 1921 Arab riots was the insertion in the preamble that part of the Balfour Declaration concerning the establishment in Palestine of a national home for the Jewish people, "it being clearly understood that nothing should be done which might prejudice the civil and religious rights of existing non-Jewish communities in Palestine, or the rights and political status enjoyed by Jews in any other country." This guarantee had already been included in Article II of the mandate; placing it in the preamble as well stressed the point that Zionism would not be permitted to encroach on Arab interests in Palestine.

The final text of the mandate, completed early in 1922, carefully preserved many of the ambiguities of the Balfour Declaration, but the Jews could not seriously object to its terms. It approved "Jewish immigration under suitable conditions" and "close settlement by Jews on the land, including State lands and waste lands not required for public purposes." Hebrew, as well as Arabic and English, was to be an official Palestinian language. (This was a victory for that subgroup within Zionism that had argued for the revival of Hebrew as a secular language, after some twenty centuries in which it had been reserved for liturgical use only.) The mandatory power was directed, "so far as circumstances permit," to "encourage local autonomy." The critical Article IV set up the administrative machinery for an eventual Jewish government: "An appropriate Jewish agency shall be recognized as a public body for the purpose of advising and cooperating with the Administration of Palestine in such economic, social, and other matters as may affect the establishment of the Jewish national home and the interests of the Jewish population in Palestine, and, subject always to the control of the Administration, to assist and take part in the development of the country."

Here Weizmann registered a tremendous triumph over the

Brandeis adherents, for the mandate text went on to say, "The Zionist Organization, so long as its organization and constitution are in the opinion of the Mandatory appropriate, shall be recognized as such agency." There would be no removal of the Zionist Organization from politics; instead, it would be transformed from a pressure group into an organ of government!

The only important omission, from the Zionist standpoint, was a formula for the ultimate evolution of a self-governing Jewish state out of the mandate. Such a state was implied in the text, but no timetable for its birth was indicated, nor any hint of how the creation of such a state would be reconciled with the Arabs' own nationalistic claims. Still, Weizmann was satisfied, and he knew that he was not in a position at the moment to demand a more favorable text. An Arab delegation was currently in London to air grievances against the Zionists; some of the most influential British newspapers were denouncing the Jews for stealing Palestine from the Arabs and running distorted reports on Zionist "oppression" there; fiscal conservatives were calling Britain's involvement in Palestine a waste of the taxpayers' money, and loudly opposed the nonexistent British contributions to the upbuilding of the Jewish commonwealth; finally, reactionary members of the House of Lords had introduced a bill repealing the Balfour Declaration. The repeal bill actually passed in the Lords, and was defeated in the Commons only after heroic efforts by Churchill and Major Orms-by-Gore. Under this barrage, the Zionists could not ask for more than they had already received.

The Arabs, when they saw the text that Great Britain was about to present for League of Nations ratification, were so aroused that the British government found it necessary to issue a White Paper, or official statement of policy, as a gesture of reassurance. This was the first of several White Papers that Britain would issue on the subject of Palestine, and should not be confused with the stormy 1939 document that barred Jews from using Palestine as a refuge from Nazi persecution.

In their protest against the mandate text, the Arabs excavated a promise made to the old Hashemite Emir Hussein by Great Britain in 1915, defining an area in which "Great Britain is prepared to recognize and support the independence of the Arabs." Palestine, though not specifically mentioned in the grant of territory, was plainly included; the only area that the British specifically excluded was the part of Syria west of Damascus. All of this, of course, had been done long before Britain had become involved with the Zionists; the implied pledge of Palestine to the Arabs had been conveniently forgotten when the Balfour Declaration was issued. The Arabs now belatedly produced the six-year-old letter to Hussein and argued, with some justice, that it had been improper for the British subsequently to offer Palestine to the Jews. They demanded cancellation of the pro-Zionist clauses in the mandate text.

The British response came from the Colonial Office in the White Paper of June 30, 1922, signed by Winston Churchill but apparently written by Sir Herbert Samuel. It was a masterpiece of double talk. The White Paper admitted that there had been a pledge made on October 24, 1915, by Sir Henry MacMahon, then British high commissioner in Egypt, to Emir Hussein. But through some quick non sequiturs the White Paper "proved" that Palestine, which lies entirely south of Syria, was in fact covered by the clause about the territory west of Damascus, and so "The whole of Palestine was thus excluded from Sir Henry Mac-Mahon's pledge." Having slipped past this sticky point, the White Paper offered the Arabs a considerable consolation prize by specifying outright that the Balfour Declaration did not apply to the territories east of the Jordan. This amounted to a formal ratification of Churchill's creation of Transjordan as a kingdom for Abdullah.

The Arabs were further placated by a cunning paragraph which, though constructed almost entirely of phrases out of Zionist propaganda, succeeded in denying that there was any British intention to bring into being a sovereign Jewish state in Palestine. The passage deserves careful study. It is remarkable for its technique of wrapping an important promise to the Arabs in words that Jews could hardly resist applauding:

"When it is asked what is meant by the development of the Jewish National Home in Palestine, it may be answered that it is not the imposition of a Jewish nationality upon the inhabitants of Palestine as a whole, but the further development of the existing Jewish community with the assistance of Jews in other parts of the world, in order that it may become a centre in which the Jewish people as a whole may take, on grounds of religion and race, an interest and a pride. But in order that this community should have

the best prospect of free development and provide a full opportunity for the Jewish people to display its capacities, it is essential
that it should know that it is in Palestine as of right and not on
sufferance."

The same day that this Byzantinely complex White Paper was
released, the Congress of the United States was passing virtually
without opposition a naïve little resolution which, although trifling
and five years late, marked the first official recognition by the
United States of Jewish aspirations in Palestine. Its timing was
strange, for the big American oil companies were in the midst of
a campaign to get drilling concessions in Iraq, and opposed an
American commitment to Zionism on the grounds that it might
offend the Arabs and make obtaining the concessions more difficult. (President Wilson had felt some pressure from the oil companies in 1917, and this had evidently been one cause of his
vacillations over support for the Balfour Declaration and his unwillingness to anger the Turks. Standard Oil of New Jersey had
acquired oil concessions in the Negev Desert from Turkey.)

To the amazement of the oil men, Congress yielded to repeated
Zionist requests and approved a joint resolution on June 30, 1922,
which acknowledged that "the Jewish people have for many centuries believed in and yearned for the rebuilding of their ancient
homeland" and declared "that the United States of America favors
the establishment in Palestine of a national home for the Jewish
people, it being clearly understood that nothing shall be done
which may prejudice the civil and religious rights of Christian and
all other non-Jewish communities in Palestine, and that the holy
places and religious buildings and sites in Palestine shall be adequately protected." President Harding gave his signature to the
resolution, which in effect was an American restatement of the
Balfour Declaration. Its sponsors were the isolationist Senator
Henry Cabot Lodge of Massachusetts, who had done more than
any man to torpedo American membership in the League of Nations, and the conservative Representative Hamilton Fish of New
York. The power of organized American Jewry to influence
American foreign policy was becoming apparent.

6.

The League of Nations ratified the mandate text on July 24,
1922. A month later, at the annual World Zionist Conference at

Carlsbad, Weizmann had to face severe criticism from a faction of militant extremists who thought his acceptance of the mandate text was a sellout. He defended his actions on the grounds of realism and expediency; but the militants continued to argue that he should have insisted on a formal pledge of eventual Jewish autonomy. Vladimir Jabotinsky emerged as the leader of this group. In 1925, Jabotinsky would organize a Zionist party, the Revisionists, with the goal of "revising" the boundaries of Palestine back to their pre-White Paper lines, and incorporating Transjordan into a sovereign Jewish state. Ultimately the Revisionists would resort to terrorism to reach this goal, but for the present they contented themselves with making inflammatory speeches at Zionist meetings.

The mandate text had invited the World Zionist Organization to serve as the "appropriate Jewish agency" that would advise the British authorities in Palestine; and at the 1922 Carlsbad conference the W.Z.O. officially accepted, creating the instrumentality known simply as the Jewish Agency. At the outset the Jewish Agency was identical with the Zionist Organization, but Weizmann planned to use it as a device for bringing non-Zionist Jews into direct involvement with the growth of the Palestinian Jewish community. Where Brandeis had wanted to reconstitute the Zionist Organization itself so that its nature would be acceptable to the non-Zionists, Weizmann worked toward something much more subtle, a separate entity that the W.Z.O. would control, but which would allow the participation of the non-Zionist Jewish organizations with no loss of their identity. In this way he could channel toward Palestine the millions distributed by the great Jewish philanthropists, who gladly endowed Negro colleges, German museums and dental schools, Russian relief funds, and all sorts of other worthy causes, while keeping aloof from the needs of Palestine for fear of political complications.

To bring this about would not be easy, for there were many within Zionism itself who opposed giving the assimilationists any representation on the Jewish Agency. "If they want to cooperate," these Zionists said, "the doors of the organization are open to them. Let them become Zionists." Weizmann knew that that would never happen. And so in February, 1923, he persuaded the W.Z.O. leadership to approve a resolution making the Jewish Agency "responsible to a body representative of the Jewish people"—*all* the Jewish people, not merely the Zionists. Then he left for the United States to raise money and gather support.

Soon after his arrival in New York he was summoned to meet Felix Warburg, the head of the Joint Distribution Committee. Zionists were not fond of the Joint, which was contributing fortunes to the aid of the Jews of war-devastated Russia and Poland. The Zionists argued that instead of spending huge sums to rebuild the Jewish communities of these anti-Semitic lands, the Joint should devote its energy and almost limitless funds to getting those Jews out of Bolshevik hands and into Palestine. Warburg himself, a polished, highly cultured German-Jewish banker, the son-in-law of Jacob Schiff, was the epitome of the Reform-oriented non-Zionist upper-class American Jew, and Weizmann hoped that the invitation might indicate some birth of interest in Palestine on Warburg's part.

Instead, Warburg spent nearly an hour and a half denouncing the conduct of the Jewish settlers in Palestine. "A more fantastic rigmarole," Weizmann wrote, "I have, to be honest, never heard from a responsible quarter: bolshevism, immorality, waste of money, inaction, inefficiency, all of it based on nothing more than hearsay." When Warburg had finished, Weizmann dismissed all he had said as "tittle-tattle and backstairs gossip," and, feeling suddenly abashed, Warburg offered a contribution to the Palestine Foundation Fund. Weizmann refused it, suggesting that the only way Warburg could make amends was to go to Palestine and investigate conditions for himself. The financier unexpectedly agreed, and departed within a fortnight. Shortly Weizmann received a postcard from Warburg in Palestine, in which he wrote that he had gone up and down the country and felt like doffing his hat "to every man and tree" he saw. "I have seldom witnessed a more complete conversion," Weizmann wrote. Thereafter Warburg, while not exactly becoming a Zionist, contributed large sums to various projects in Palestine and served to narrow the gulf between the aristocrats of American Reform Judaism and the Zionists. By the fall of 1923, after his return from Palestine, Warburg was at work on a $500,000 fund for the Hebrew University that was then under construction in Jerusalem.

On the same American visit, Weizmann won strong backing from another prominent non-Zionist Jew, Louis Marshall of the American Jewish Committee. Weizmann recruited Marshall deftly and easily by stressing the spiritual and cultural values of rebuilding the Jewish homeland, and they appeared on the same platform on March 13, 1923, on behalf of the Palestine Foundation Fund.

The money was coming in, and a pattern of regular donations by American Jews was developing. Different cities responded in different ways. New York and Philadelphia were the chief Zionist bastions; Chicago was more difficult, because of the influence of the profoundly anti-Zionist philanthropist Julius Rosenwald. Cincinnati, where the Jewish community was of German origin and largely assimilated, was even worse. "Generally speaking," Weizmann wrote, "our difficulties increased as we moved westward. California was a different world, remote from the Jewish interests of the eastern states, and practically virgin soil from the Zionist point of view." Yet he managed to locate a cadre of Zionists almost everywhere, even in New Orleans, where he received generous contributions from the "Banana King," Samuel Zemurray of the United Fruit Corporation.

And the homeland was being built. By 1924, the postwar immigration total had passed 50,000, and the Jewish population of Palestine had risen above 100,000 for the first time since the destruction of the Second Temple. (There were 400,000 Arabs.) The restrictions on Jewish immigration imposed by High Commissioner Samuel after the 1921 disturbances had not proved to be an obstacle. Indeed, Jews were entering Palestine faster than the fledgling economy could support them, and unemployment was a serious problem as early as 1923.

The character of the immigrants began to change in 1924 as immigration regulations were altered. Israeli historians distinguish the influx of 1924–26 from that of 1919–23 by labeling it the fourth *aliyah*. The third *aliyah*, in the wake of the Balfour Declaration, had been essentially a continuation of the second, which had begun in 1904 and was interrupted by the war. It was made up mostly of energetic young Russian and Polish Jews, radical in ideology and dedicated to a return to farming life. The men and women of the second and third *aliyot* created the image of the Israel that was to come.

Then during the fourth *aliyah*, starting in 1924, the mandate officials agreed to permit the entry of "capitalists"—anyone who could prove possession of $2,500—over and above those Jews re-

ceiving entry visas as farmers and laborers. This was designed to
rescue thousands of Russian Jews of the bourgeoisie who had been
stranded in Poland after the war.

Ordinarily, these merchants and shopkeepers would probably
have emigrated to the United States, as so many like them had
done in the previous 40 years. But in 1924 the United States, for
the first time in its history, established a quota system for immigration, designed to keep the country from being flooded by refugees
from "undesirable" countries. The quotas prohibited the immigration of all Asians, who were deemed racially ineligible for citizenship, and made it almost impossible for immigrants from Southern
and Eastern Europe to get in. Citizens of Great Britain, Germany,
and Ireland were welcome to become Americans. Russians, Poles,
Italians, Greeks, and Hungarians were shut out, on the grounds
that they came from cultures differing too greatly in social attitudes from the prevailing mores of the United States. This de-
flected thousands of Eastern European Jews toward Palestine.

Old-line Zionists, schooled in the theory of strength through
agriculture, were uneasy about the fourth *aliyah*. Weizmann
wrote, "True, a considerable amount of capital was being brought
into the country by these small capitalists, but openings in industry, trade and commerce were as yet limited, and the numerous
small shops which seemed to spring up overnight in Tel Aviv and
Haifa caused me no little worry. These people were . . . not of the
chalutz [pioneer] type, and some of them were little disposed to
pull their weight in a new country. A few, in their struggle for
existence, showed antisocial tendencies; they seemed never to
have been Zionists, and saw no difference between Palestine as a
country of immigration and, for instance, the United States. Many
of them had no knowledge of Hebrew, and, it was soon being said,
rather ruefully, that at this rate Tel Aviv would soon be a Yiddish-
speaking town. Even to the casual observer, the new immigration
carried with it the atmosphere of the ghetto." The *chalutzim* did
not hide their distaste for the newcomers, some of whom were
dabbling in land speculation and other unsavory practices. The
friction between the two elements demonstrated once again something Gentiles found it hard to understand: Jews are no monolithic
people. Jews are quite capable of disliking other Jews, and even of
discriminating against them.

But there was forward movement, despite the cleavages within the Palestinian community, despite the feuding among the Zionists over the Revisionist aims, despite the possibility of renewed strife with the Arabs. Jewish villages grew into Jewish towns. The coastal plain of Palestine turned green again; orange groves sprouted where sand dunes had been. The Arabs were quiet. The Jewish settlers provided a market for their wares, introduced electricity, modern sanitation, and decent medical care for all, and created an atmosphere of progress without posing a threat of overwhelming the Arabs numerically. The Hebrew University on Mount Scopus had opened in 1925. That year, 34,386 Jews settled in Palestine—the peak year of the decade, for immigration between 1920 and 1929 would total only 100,000 all told.

There were setbacks amid the optimism; the great inflow of 1925 created such massive unemployment that Palestine experienced a sharp economic slump, and many Jews, disillusioned, departed again. Two Jews out of every ten that came to Palestine in the 1920's failed to stay. In 1927 there was actually a net outflow of Jews, and in 1928 the immigrants exceeded the number departing by a net of 10 persons. Meanwhile the Arab population, unfettered by immigration restrictions, was doubling during the decade to 800,000 by 1929. The Zionist dream began to look a bit faded; it seemed as though most of those Jews who wanted to go to Palestine had already gone there, and that they would always constitute a tiny minority among the multitude of Arabs. But at least they were there.

The failure of America's Jews to make the *aliyah*, though it should not have been surprising, was saddening. The number of American Jews who had settled in Palestine was at best a few dozen, and most of them gave up the pioneering life in weeks or months. Americans were sending their dollars—$15,000,000 between 1921 and 1930—but not their sons. "I honestly confess to one great sin that I have committed," Weizmann declared in 1928. "It is a sin of which all of us placed at the head of Zionist affairs have been guilty. We have abused America as a moneygiving machine. Under the pressure to which America has been subject, it has not developed an adequate, healthy, vigorous Zionism."

That might change. The important thing was that the homeland existed. And in the summer of 1929 Weizmann at last was able to bring into existence his expanded Jewish Agency, opening the way for non-Zionists to participate in Palestinian affairs.

Seven years of planning and negotiating had been necessary, for the non-Zionists did not want to come in, and many Zionists did not want to let them in. A typical Zionist attitude was that of Rabbi Stephen S. Wise, a former Zionist Organization of America president: "While their help was certainly both desirable and welcome, I felt that admitting them to a position of political leadership and responsibility meant a serious compromise with the basic principle of Zionism. . . . A philanthropic, economic, cultural, or spiritual interest in Palestine was laudable and helpful. But it was not Zionism."

The politics of necessity helped to overcome such objections. The Zionist movement was in trouble; it needed new recruits, especially wealthy ones. American Jewry—the only Jewish community in the world capable of bearing the financial burdens of supporting Palestine—had lost interest in Zionism. Fervor had ebbed after the ratification of the mandate, when it seemed as though the most important aims of the movement had been achieved. The Zionist Organization of America had 200,000 members within a year after the Balfour Declaration; a decade later, membership was less than one-fourth as high, and the organization showed a deficit of $150,000. Help was needed. For the sake of Palestine, Zionism had to abandon its ideological purity. The nation-builders, the political activists, would have to make room for those who were merely philanthropists.

But would the philanthropists join? The key man was Louis Marshall, the lawyer from upstate New York, who in the 1920's had emerged as the leader of the non-Zionist American Jewish community. Marshall was a man of ecumenical intentions—he was simultaneously president of the congregation of Temple Emanu-El, a Reform group, and of the Conservative Jewish Theological Seminary—and he responded eagerly to Weizmann's hints that he was the man to unite the Zionists and the non-Zionists, the Russian-American Jews and the German-American Jews, in one great endeavor. Weizmann pointed out to him that there were five times as many Arabs as Jews in Palestine, and thus no likelihood that the Jews would be anything but a minority there for many years to come. The sovereign state that the non-Zionists so deeply feared was nowhere near attainment. Reassured, Marshall agreed to put aside his reservations about the political and nationalistic implications of Zionism and lead the non-Zionists into the enlarged Jewish Agency, giving the movement their financial and moral support. In acknowledgment of the role American Jewry would have to play, Marshall was promised that 40 percent of the non-Zionist representation on the Jewish Agency would be American.

Weizmann pushed through the expansion of the agency at the Sixteenth World Zionist Congress at Zurich, in 1929. There would be 224 members in the agency's new governing body, half of them named by Zionists, half by various non-Zionist groups. Louis Marshall's American Jewish Committee received the largest single bloc of non-Zionist representatives: 44 seats. The congress adjourned on August 11, and on the same day the first meeting of the new Jewish Agency convened. On August 14, Zionists and non-Zionists signed a formal agreement of cooperation, labeled "the Pact of Glory." A galaxy of prominent Jews had assembled for the event: Albert Einstein, novelist Sholem Asch, French political leader Leon Blum, Sir Herbert Samuel, and, representing American Jewry, Louis Marshall and Felix Warburg. Marshall praised the rebirth of Jewish Palestine, declaring that it "has accomplished marvels in the last twenty-five years in stimulating Jewish thought among our youth throughout the world. It has brought about a renaissance of Jewish learning and scholarship which has once more made Hebrew a living language. It has given thousands of us, who at one time were indifferent to our history, something to live for and aspire for. Why should not such an ideal be regarded as belonging to all Jews?"

It was an exciting moment. The ideologues deplored the dilution of Zionism, and quietly made plans to undermine the new Jewish Agency. But to Weizmann and the other leaders it seemed at last to mark the emergence of world-wide unity among Jews on the vexed subject of the homeland. It was a unity of irreconcilables, of course, since one faction was committed to an independent Jewish nation and the other wanted nothing more concrete than a spiritual and cultural center; but for a brief while the "Pact of Glory" seemed authentically glorious.

The euphoria was short-lived. Only a few days after the signing of the pact, the Arabs, quiescent since 1921, burst once more into violence. Nationalist leaders such as the grand mufti had followed the news reports from Zurich, and were convinced that the Zionists had succeeded in hatching an international conspiracy that would pour hundreds of thousands of Jews into Palestine; and so they resorted to rioting as an act of political protest.

The pretext was a trivial dispute over the patch of ground in front of the Wailing Wall, the last remnant of the Temple of Solomon in Jerusalem. The wall lies along one side of the impressive platform on which the Temple once stood. That platform is now occupied by two great mosques, the Dome of the Rock and Al-Aqsa, and the whole precinct is sacred to Moslems. Under established custom Jews had free access to the wall—where it was traditional to mourn the destruction of the Temple—but were forbidden to make any structural changes in the area. Because Orthodox Jews disapprove of a mingling of the sexes in worship, a portable linen screen had usually been erected in front of the wall at times of prayer to separate male and female worshipers, but this practice had been discontinued after the 1921 riots. In September, 1928, at the urging of the pious, the screen was restored during the two days of Rosh Hashanah, the New Year's holiday,

The grand mufti seized on this excuse to claim that the screen was a structural change, a violation of the status quo, which portended a Jewish move to seize the entire Temple area—perhaps even to demolish the famed mosques and rebuild the Temple. Excited Arab youths, inflamed by this charge, petitioned the British governor of Jerusalem to have the screen banned. Some days later, the screen went up again for Yom Kippur, the Day of Atonement, the holiest day of the Jewish year. To prevent possible violence the governor asked that the screen be taken down; and when the worshipers at the wall refused, it was removed by British soldiers.

In the months that followed, the issue of the screen grew even more tense, and the inevitable explosion came on August 15, 1929, the somber holiday of Tishah B'ab, commemorating the destruction of the Temple. A band of Jabotinsky's Revisionists defiantly marched to the wall and posted a Zionist flag there. This was only a day after the signing of the Pact of Glory in Zurich; it seemed to the Arabs that the Jews were staking a claim to the Temple precinct, and the next day, urged on by the mufti, thousands of Arabs converged on the wall. Three elderly Jews were at prayer there; two were rescued by an Arab policeman, the third was badly beaten. The next day, a young Jewish boy was stabbed by Arabs. He died three days later, and his funeral procession turned into another riot, with the mourners driven off by Arabs.

Now a rumor circulated that the Jews, in retaliation, had destroyed the Dome of the Rock, and on Friday, August 23, a general Arab uprising began. Thousands of Arabs surged through the city with clubs and knives, attacking any Jews they encountered. The British police force, less than 300 men, was unable to cope with the outbreak. The underground Jewish defense corps organized by Jabotinsky, and now known as Haganah, "the defense," mobilized and took command of the Jewish sectors of the city. The fury spread to the villages near Jerusalem, and then to the ancient city of Hebron to the south, where 65 Jews were slain and 58 wounded. The bloodletting continued for nearly a week, and virtually every city was the scene of a massacre and an equally fierce Haganah counterattack. In all, 133 Jews and 116 Arabs perished. Palestine was at the brink of chaos.

Weizmann, who had gone on holiday to celebrate the enlargement of the Jewish Agency, hurried to London to confer with the British government. Lord Passfield, the new Colonial Secretary—better known as Sidney Webb, the socialist—did not seem to want to see him. Lady Passfield—Beatrice Webb—turned Weizmann away with the remark, "I can't understand why the Jews make such a fuss over a few dozen of their people killed in Palestine. As many are killed every week in London in traffic accidents, and no one pays any attention." Weizmann's old friends were out of office; the Labour Party now ruled, and to the Labourites Palestine was a distant land whose problems were irrelevant to those of the British working classes. The Arabs had rocked the boat, and the Labourites did not want to have to handle boats that rocked. It was easy to predict what their response would be. They would appoint a commission to investigate the troubles in Palestine; the commission would discover that the violence there was an outgrowth of Arab resentment over Jewish immigration; the government would decree that such immigration be sharply reduced, for the sake of law and order.

So it came to pass. In the fall of 1929, a government commission investigated, and placed the blame for the riots on the Arabs, but indicated that they had had some justification for attacking the Jews. Evidence that the uprising had been planned and incited by the grand mufti was ignored. The commission warned of the dangers of further Zionist expansion and suggested controls on

Jewish immigration, a formal statement on the rights of the non-Jewish community, and notice to the Jewish Agency that it was not entitled to take part in governing Palestine.

In the same dark season the New York Stock Exchange collapsed, heralding the onset of the long economic paralysis of the Great Depression, which would deprive the Zionist movement of its financial support. And Louis Marshall died in Zurich following emergency surgery, which took away a vital collaborator newly recruited to the cause. He had fallen ill immediately after signing the Pact of Glory.

FIVE

Toward the White Paper

THE CRISIS of the autumn of 1929 came at a time when Jews were more nearly united than they had been in decades, or would be again for many years to come. The non-Zionist organizations newly enfolded in the Jewish Agency joined the Zionist groups in denouncing the Arab attacks and the generally pro-Arab commission report that followed them. A Palestine Emergency Fund to aid the riot victims drew enthusiastic support from American Jews known for their previous antipathy toward Zionism: Herbert Lehman, Julius Rosenwald, Felix Warburg, Adolph Ochs. Within a few months the fund raised $2,100,000. The emergency even caused a reconciliation within the Zionist Organization of America; nearly all the Brandeis supporters returned to the fold except Brandeis himself, and Judge Mack accepted a post in the administration of the man who had ousted him from its presidency, Louis Lipsky.

On the political front, Zionist protests over the commission report led the British government to send a second commission to Palestine in May, 1930. But the findings of this commission were even more unpalatable to the Zionists than those of the last. The report of the commission, made public on October 21, 1930, held that Jewish colonization had displaced many Arabs. On the same day, the British government released its second White Paper on Palestine—the Passfield White Paper—which sharply criticized the activities of the Zionist pioneers in Palestine and proposed such severe limitations on further Jewish immigration that it was virtually a nullification of the Balfour Declaration.

Commotion followed. As a tactical move, Weizmann resigned

as president of the Jewish Agency. In Parliament, Lloyd George and other members of what was now the opposition party denounced the Passfield White Paper as a betrayal of Britain's promise to the Jews. Even the American Jewish Committee, still enjoying its honeymoon with Zionism, issued a statement "expressing its profound disappointment with the policy of the British Government as enunciated in the White Paper. . . ." Prime Minister Ramsay MacDonald bowed to pressure from many sides, and agreed, in February, 1931, that the restrictions proposed by the Passfield White Paper would not be put into effect. The attempt to retract the Balfour Declaration had failed; in the years just ahead, immigration of Jews to Palestine would reach levels undreamed of even by the militant Revisionists.

A sullen peace settled over Palestine. In a world buffeted by economic disasters, the Holy Land was a curious oasis of prosperity—a result of the heavy investment of American and British Jewish capital in the 1920's—and the boom provided employment for Arabs as well as Jews. Palestine had had its own depression in the mid-1920's, but now, with millions out of work in Europe and America, it was flourishing so satisfactorily that most Arabs were content with the state of affairs. The fanatics had not vanished, but they found it hard to agitate against Jews in the face of the prosperity that Jewish development projects had brought to the land.

If matters were going uncharacteristically well in Zion, they were characteristically troubled in Zionism. At the Seventeenth World Zionist Congress in Basel in July, 1931, Weizmann was overthrown by the Revisionists. The Jabotinsky faction, long opposed to Weizmann's gradualism, attacked him for having failed to respond with sufficient vigor to the Passfield White Paper. They were not satisfied with a mere promise from Britain that immigration could continue. The Revisionists wanted political control of Palestine at once, *all* of Palestine, including Transjordan. At the 1929 Congress Jabotinsky had openly assailed the use of the euphemisms "Jewish homeland" and "Jewish national home," which since Herzl's time the militant Zionists had defined one way and the more cautious another. "So far as I understand it," Jabotinsky said, "this word has simply one meaning for the soul of the Jewish people, and that is a National State with a preponderant Jewish majority, and in which the Jewish will must decide the form and the direction that the life of the community must follow. . . . What does the word Palestine mean? Palestine is a territory whose chief geographical feature is this: that the River Jordan does not delineate its frontier but flows through its center. What is the meaning of Zionism? Zionism does not mean some kind of endeavor to furnish suffering Jewish people throughout the world with a moral rallying point, a source of consolation, in Palestine. The word Zionism has always meant the practical solution of the political, economic, and cultural tragedy of many millions." Now Jabotinsky repeated his position and called for a vote of no confidence in Weizmann.

Most political movements eventually devour their leaders. In a roll-call vote, which Weizmann sat through to its end, the congress voted heavily in favor of the motion of no confidence. Then he left the hall, more saddened than embittered, remembering how Herzl had been broken by the Uganda controversy, remembering the downfall of Brandeis, even comparing himself to Moses, who came down from Mount Sinai bearing the tablets of the law and found the children of Israel worshiping a golden calf. At 57 Weizmann returned to chemistry, after an absence from the laboratory of 13 years, and soon he accepted the presidency of the British Zionist Federation, which he had had years before. Jabotinsky failed to secure control of the World Zionist Organization, however; after the delegates had removed Weizmann, they elected Weizmann's old colleague Nahum Sokolow in his place.

The movement toward unity in American Zionism, which Weizmann and Marshall had helped to launch so grandly in 1929, was also in disarray. In 1930, for the first time, Zionist and non-Zionist fund raisers joined in a single appeal, the Allied Jewish Campaign, with a goal of $6,000,000. Of this, seven-twelfths would be allotted to the non-Zionist relief and rescue organization, the Joint Distribution Committee, and five-twelfths would be channeled to Palestine. But the bleak economic conditions of 1930 did not encourage abundant giving, and the affiliation with the Zionists disturbed some of the Joint's biggest contributors. As a result, the combined drive took in less than a third of its quota, and in 1931 the two funds went their separate ways.

Nor was the expanded Jewish Agency working well. Every time the Revisionists fired another fusillade about immediate statehood, some of the non-Zionist members threatened to resign. Meanwhile, with Weizmann out of the picture, the militants were rapidly stacking the agency with a Zionist majority. Palestine, which still had a fairly large Orthodox community of non-Zionist Jews, was allotted 6 of the non-Zionist seats on the agency; but those seats all went to Palestinian Zionists who simply resigned from Zionist organizations in order to qualify as properly non-Zionist. The proportion of non-Zionists dwindled until after a few years the 20-man executive board of the agency consisted of 17 Zionists and 3 non-Zionists; eventually the Jewish Agency would be synonomous with the World Zionist Organization, as it had been when it was created in 1922.

2.

World events began to intersect the fate of the Jews again in 1933. In Germany, to which the Great Depression had brought enormous economic dislocations, a savior had arisen who intended to rescue the country from its anguish: Adolf Hitler, who on January 30, 1933, succeeded in being named Chancellor of the Reich. Hitler carried with him to power an assortment of ferocious demagogues, nearly all of whom shared with him the conviction that Germany's miseries were the work of the Jews.

In the spring and early summer of 1933, Hitler's National Socialist government set about remedying the situation by promulgating a series of laws that drastically limited Jewish participation in the professions, the arts, and commerce. There were not as yet any concentration camps, and the really repressive laws, those that relegated Jews to the lowest levels of German life, did not come into being until 1935. But it was immediately obvious to the large Jewish community of Germany that the troubles of 1933 were precursors of worse things, and soon after Hitler's accession a new exodus began. Doctors, scientists, philosophers, those who were quickest to sense that the barbarians had been unleashed again, flooded out of Germany, finding refuge in England, in the United States, in Switzerland—and in Palestine.

Net Jewish immigration into Palestine had picked up slightly since the years of little or no increase, 1927–28; but in 1931 only 4,075 Jews had settled there. In 1932 the figure doubled: 9,553. And in 1933 the total of Jewish immigrants was 30,327. Providentially, the restrictions of the Passfield White Paper were not in effect, and the British administration in Palestine saw to it that in their time of need the Jews were able to take full advantage of the existing immigration regulations. In 1934 there were 42,359 immigrants—the greatest influx of Jews into Palestine since the return from the Babylonian captivity. In 1935, when the infamous Nuremberg Laws were decreed, 61,854 immigrants reached the Holy Land. Palestine's Jewish population, which had been 200,000 in 1933, underwent nearly a twofold increase in those three years.

The newcomers were not all Germans. Actually, only one out of eight was a refugee from Hitler. Most of the scientists and artists then escaping from Germany were heading toward the urban centers of the West, not toward the orange groves of Zion. And many German Jews simply would not leave Germany until they were in mortal danger; that would not be until 1938. Nearly half of the immigrants of this fifth *aliyah*, the Hitler *aliyah*, came from Poland. These Eastern Europeans possessed an innate Zionism that German Jews had never had; and, looking across the border at what was happening in Germany, they chose to flee to the Jewish homeland while the route was still open. Strangely, there was heavy emigration from the United States to Palestine at this time: 3,693 people between 1933 and 1935, though not all of them were native Americans. There had never been any measurable flow of American Jews to Palestine before; but the economic advantages of life in the United States probably did not seem particularly compelling in those three years.

The new *aliyah* continued the urbanizing process that had begun with the invasion of Palestine by the "capitalists" of 1924. Those who came now were refugees, not pioneers, and nothing in their past lives had fitted them to be *chalutzim*. They were middle-class, middle-aged, to a great extent, with backgrounds as executives, professionals, or technicians; some had substantial capital. They could not readily go out to the collective farms of the Palestinian frontier. Weizmann, asked to deal with the problems of these immigrants, found a way of helping them to make use of their managerial or scientific skills without creating a troublesome expansion of the cities. He set up special suburban colonies, where the families could work at light agriculture while the heads of the households commuted to desk jobs in Tel Aviv, Jerusalem, or Haifa. The Zionist belief in a basically agrarian society was maintained, though with some difficulty.

As the breakdown of civilization in Germany sent the number of Jewish emigrants to Palestine mounting toward its 1935 peak, the Arabs began to see the fulfillment of their worst fear: if present trends continued, they would be outnumbered by Jews, and then they might be driven from the land. Even the most reasonable Arabs became convinced that the Western powers were parties to a conspiracy to dispossess them—for, at a time when the unfortunate upheavals in Europe were forcing thousands from their homes, countries such as the United States and Great Britain were quietly declining to accept more than a fraction of the refugees. And yet they were encouraging the dumping of the emigrés into the small, poor land of Palestine. Between 1932 and 1935, while Palestine was accepting nearly 145,000 Jews, a total of 3,000 had found refuge in Great Britain. In the same four years the United States, the wealthiest nation of all, had taken in just 14,202 Germans *of all faiths.* Was this not some sort of deliberate plot to fill Palestine with Jews? It was even said among Arabs—and not only by the fanatics—that Hitler himself was in collusion with the Zionists, working in his roundabout way to build the Jewish homeland by compelling reluctant Jews to leave Europe.

Hitler was no Zionist; and there was no formal conspiracy by the Western countries to take Palestine away from the Arabs. But certainly Great Britain and the United States in the middle 1930's regarded Palestine as a convenient warehouse for Europe's surplus of Jews. Denying their own responsibility to accept these homeless people, these two democracies gave little thought to the effect of their policies on the delicate balance of Arab and Jewish populations in Palestine. No attempt was made by these governments to open their own gates wider—not even after the early Nazi restrictions on Jews were replaced, in 1935, by savage laws closing nearly all occupations to Jews, even banning them from entire towns, and then by government-encouraged pogroms.

In October, 1933, the League of Nations had appointed an American expert on foreign affairs, James G. McDonald, as "High Commissioner for Refugees (Jewish or other) Coming from Germany." It was largely a token appointment, for the League was always hesitant to offend one of its members, and Germany still belonged; therefore McDonald was given an autonomous position outside the League's normal operations and, also, outside its financial structure. But he took his work seriously, devoting the next two years to a conscientious effort to find homes for the outcast victims of oppression. Realizing that Palestine could not possibly absorb all those who were in peril, he sought to obtain emergency liberalization of the immigration laws of the Western countries.

He failed. Few people, in or out of government, seemed willing even to believe that the Nazi persecutions were taking place. Great Britain, greatly concerned with avoiding friction with Hitler, acted as though admitting refugees would imply too sharp a criticism of the Reich's Jewish policies. The United States— vaguely humanitarian, but profoundly isolationist—simply wanted to keep from getting involved in Europe's troubles. The other world powers were equally eager to pretend that Hitler might go away if left alone. The Nuremberg Laws of September, 1935, depriving all of Germany's Jews of their citizenship and of the right to earn a living, were regarded as a purely internal matter; intervention by other nations would be in poor taste. Even when Hitler's troops moved across the Rhine six months later to occupy the demilitarized zone on Germany's border with France, nothing was said in protest. "After all, they are only going into their own back garden," one British statesman remarked. Such men as Lloyd George declared that Hitler was "the savior of Germany . . . a born leader of men, a magnetic dynamic personality. . . . The Germans have definitely made up their minds never to quarrel with us again." Jews continued to flee, usually compelled to leave all their possessions behind. The Jews? Let them go to Palestine!

In 1935 High Commissioner McDonald made two specific recommendations to relieve this misery: that Great Britain intercede with Germany to bring about an orderly evacuation of 100,-000 Jews over the next four or five years, the emigration to be financed wholly by Jewish organizations, and that the United States increase its immigration quota for German Jews. But the British government, after telling McDonald that his scheme "would be studied promptly and sympathetically," consulted with its embassy in Berlin, found that Hitler would regard such an intercession as a hostile act, and decided not to take action.

In the United States, the McDonald proposal was forwarded by Felix Warburg to Governor Herbert Lehman of New York, who passed it on to President Roosevelt. The State Department drafted a reply for Roosevelt saying that there was no quota for Jews as such, but that 25,957 Germans a year were eligible for admission to the United States without regard for their religious affiliations.

Only about 3,500 places on this quota had been taken annually in recent years, the State Department added. It did not explain the bureaucratic lunacies that kept the quotas from being filled.

For example, the Immigration Act of 1924 required applicants to file an assortment of documents from their countries of origin, such as a police certificate of good character and a record of military service. Jews fleeing Germany were scarcely likely to be able to collect the proper papers before they left. But if they had no documents, they could get no visa to enter the United States. Green H. Hackworth, a State Department legal adviser, commenting on the incongruity in 1933, loftily declared, "The mere fact that a Jew has been driven out of Germany into another country, or has found it desirable to flee from Germany to escape persecution, does not in and of itself excuse him from producing the documents required by Section 7(c) if it is reasonably possible for him to obtain such documents upon applying therefor to the appropriate German authorities." Nor could Jews stripped of their property by Nazi legislation meet the requirements for personal resources necessary for entry into the United States. And so, each year, 22,000 places on the quota for German immigration were going unfilled for lack of qualified applicants. What need was there to expand the quota? The only solution was to liberalize the visa-issuing procedures, perhaps by establishing a new category of "political refugees."

But McDonald got nowhere in this endeavor. A typical response was that of the American consul-general in Hamburg, who in May, 1936, cautioned the State Department about giving way to pressure from American Jews and their sympathizers on visa restrictions. If the restrictions are eased, he wrote, "It is entirely possible that the United States will find itself receiving nearly the full quota of 25,000 German Jews yearly, by 1937." The implication was that such an influx would be disastrous to the republic.

By then, High Commissioner McDonald had resigned in frustration and rage. He made his resignation known on January 1, 1936, with a bitter indictment of the Western world's inaction. "More than half a million persons," he wrote, "against whom no charge can be made except that they are not what the National Socialists choose to regard as 'Nordic,' are being crushed." He called on the League of Nations and its members to "move to avert the existing and impending tragedies."

It should be noted that relatively few Jewish voices were raised in the United States at this time in favor of liberalizing American immigration laws. Thomas A. Bailey's 1948 study of American public opinion and its effects on foreign policy, *The Man on the Street*, noted that a 1938 poll of American Jews showed that 70 percent favored greater admission of persecuted Jews, 5 percent had no opinion, and 25 percent *opposed* such a measure! Even among those who wished that some of Hitler's victims could be admitted to the United States, only a few dared to utter such wishes openly.

The era when minority groups could make demands upon the majority had not yet arrived in the United States. Despite the moral outrage they felt inwardly over the Nazi crimes, a good many American Jews were gripped by a paralysis born of insecurity when it came to asking their Gentile neighbors to let still more Jews into the country. The fear of creating an anti-Semitic backlash stifled the urge to attack restrictive immigration laws. Yet something had to be done to save the sufferers in Germany. Among American Jews, Zionism became a comforting substitute for the domestic political agitation in which they did not dare indulge. Harry Simonhoff, a veteran Zionist leader from Miami, declared in his reminiscences of the era:

"The reaction of the American Jew was sorrow, fear, anger, and compassion. Of course, the victims of Nazi savagery must be helped to leave their harsh, stepfather land. . . . What about this thing called Zionism? There might be something to the idea of a Jewish state in Palestine. If it is a matter of money, then here is a check."

And Samuel Halperin, a professor of political science who has made a searching study of the dynamics of American Zionism, explained:

"Probably at the core of some American Jews' pro-Palestine gestures at this time, though positive documentation is impossible, was the fear that Jewish refugee immigration into America, especially in the midst of an as yet unresolved economic crisis, would only aggravate American anti-Semitism. American Jews were eager to rescue fellow Jews from Hitler's reach, but not at the expense of their own security. Some alternative haven had to be found; and since only Palestine was ready to accept appreciable numbers of Jews, ideological objections to Zionism were submerged and reappraised."

Within the Zionist movement itself there were actually some

ultramilitants who argued that it was good strategy to make no attempt to liberalize the United States immigration laws. Those who held this position were extremists, virtually fanatics, to whom the building of a Jewish homeland in Palestine took priority over all other claims, even the claim of saving lives. The spokesman of this faction was the Revisionist Jabotinsky, who dreamed of signing treaties with the European dictators for the wholesale evacuation of their unwanted Jewish subjects to Palestine.

The rationale of the extremist position was the notion that the pool of refugees from Germany was an invaluable reservoir of political strength for the Zionist movement. If these sufferers could not find a nation in the West that would take them, they would have to go by default to Palestine; and if Hitler drove every Jew in Europe into exile, the end result would be a preponderant Jewish majority—and thereupon a sovereign Jewish state—in Palestine. To these Zionists, Hitler was indeed an unwitting collaborator in the cause. So, too, were the callous and indifferent bureaucrats of the United States, who blindly enforced idiotic regulations in a time of crisis. For Jews to attack those regulations, the militant minority insisted, would be unproductive from a Zionist standpoint. As the number of homeless Jews mounted, the Western countries would find it highly desirable to bring about their admission to Palestine regardless of Arab protests—for otherwise those Jews might have to be let into the Western countries.

Such a line of thought amounted to a cynical, calculating exploitation of a shocking situation, and most Zionists would have no part of twisted reasoning of this sort. If they failed to speak out against the American immigration laws, it was out of domestic considerations, not out of the desire to make Zionist capital from the Jewish tragedy in Germany. Nevertheless, there were Zionists who did reason this way.

An equally strange phenomenon of the times, another instance of the way conflict distorts the essence of thought, was the use made by the Nazis themselves of Zionist propaganda. The basic philosophy of Zionism had always been separatist, of course—the desire of Jews to withdraw from a hostile world—and now the Nazis began to quote from Zionist literature in a diabolically clever attempt to justify their expulsion of the Jews.

The philosopher Martin Buber had written in 1912, "Only there [in Asia] can we truly find ourselves again. Here [in Europe] we are like a wedge which Asia drove into Europe's structure, a thing of ferment and disturbance. We should return to Asia's bosom, and we will, at the same time, return to the true meaning of our mission, destiny, and existence." And the Jewish historian Simon Dubnow had said the same year, "A Jew . . . even if he happened to be born in France and still lives there, in spite of all these he remains a member of the Jewish nation, and whether he likes it or not, whether he is aware or unaware of it, he bears the seal of the historic evolution of the Jewish nation." And the Zionist philosopher Jacob Klatzkin, at the time of the Balfour Declaration: "We are not hyphenated Jews; we are Jews with no provision, qualification or reservation. We are simply aliens, we are a foreign people in your midst, and we emphasize, we wish to stay that way. There is a wide gap between you and us, so wide that no bridge can be laid across. Your spirit is alien to us; your myths, legends, habits, customs, traditions and holidays . . . they are all alien to us. The history of your triumphs and defeats, your war songs and battle hymns, your heroes and their mighty deeds, your religious and national shrines, your Sundays and holidays . . . they are all alien to us."

Thus the Nazis could say that they were thrusting from their midst a sinister, foreign Asiatic people, and thus the chief Jew-baiter of the Third Reich, Julius Streicher, could declare during his trial as a war criminal in 1946, "I always stood for the Zionist opinion. I will only mention here Theodor Herzl. . . . Like him, I advocated a national state for the Jews." And here were the Zionists seemingly agreeing, saying, yes, we are alien, yes, we are Asians, let us go back to our ancestral land, let us not become Americans or Englishmen or Frenchmen, for that is impossible, but let us be Jews in a Jewish state. It was a clever campaign, making use of quotations ripped from context and singling out Zionist rhetorical overstatements as though they were pronouncements of Jewish policy. What Streicher and his companions did not add, however, was that whatever separatist component existed in Zionism was the work of history's Streichers, who had pinned the Jews into ghettos, who had driven them from one nation to another, who had given them such a taste of Christian benevolence that they wanted nothing more dearly than a place to escape from it.

It was a difficult time, when words were losing their meanings and sanity was fleeing. Among those forced to cope with the new problems was Weizmann, who had been called back into office in 1935 as president of the World Zionist Organization and of the Jewish Agency. As always, he was a moderate, a gradualist, eager to see the Jewish population of Palestine grow but unwilling to encourage a sudden mass migration that could provoke Arab resistance. He remained ambivalent even on the critical point of whether there was ultimately to be a Jewish state, rather than just a "homeland."

But certainly Jabotinsky and his Revisionists saw the German atrocities as an opportunity to achieve an immediate Jewish majority—and Jewish sovereignty—in Palestine. To these men, even the 61,000 Jews who had come into Palestine in 1935 were far fewer than was desirable. The Revisionists had begun in 1934 to sponsor a secret *aliyah* of illegal immigrants, who entered Palestine without having obtained immigration certificates from the British. Perhaps 5,000 Jews a year found their way into Palestine in this fashion. The Revisionists were also smuggling arms into the country and turning Haganah, the underground militia, into an efficient and potent striking force, intended not merely for defense but as an activist army to bring about Jewish sovereignty.

The main stream of the Zionist Organization was also moving in an activist direction, despite Weizmann's hesitations. In 1935 David Ben-Gurion, the Russian-born Zionist with a strong socialist background, became chairman of the Jewish Agency's executive committee, and in effect a more powerful figure in the movement than Weizmann himself. Ben-Gurion quickly acted to strengthen Haganah and expand the illegal immigration.

Understandably, the Palestinian Arabs were alarmed. World events were sending a torrent of Jews into their land, and the Zionists were beginning to flex their muscles. The last hope of cooperation between Arabs and Jews failed early in 1936 when negotiations between Ben-Gurion and Arab leaders over formation of a political confederation of both peoples were broken off. An attempt to form a Palestinian legislative council with Arab, Jewish, and British representation had collapsed a short while before. As Jews continued to receive entry permits, the Arabs resorted to the device that had worked successfully in 1921 and 1929: rioting.

Under the tutelage of the grand mufti, a general strike of all

Palestinian Arabs began in April, 1936, with the aim of halting all Jewish immigration, preventing further sales of land to Jews, and establishing an Arab national government. The strike was accompanied by scattered violence, and then by raids on Jewish settlements and riots in Jewish urban districts. The British were the targets as much as the Jews; convinced that Britain meant to fill the land with Zionists, the Arabs assaulted British officials, blew up railroads, sabotaged oil pipelines. Retaliatory action by Haganah kept Jewish casualties low, but property losses were great, and the country was thrown into the kind of chaos that the British detested.

To Prime Minister Stanley Baldwin the uprising meant the deployment of British troops, difficult policy decisions, tiresome inquiries in Parliament. The reaction of his government was a mixture of hesitation, appeasement, and repression—followed, as usual, by the appointment of an official commission to investigate the Palestinian troubles. Zionists were apprehensive as the commissioners, headed by the distinguished statesman Lord Peel, departed for Palestine in November, 1936. For all except the militant Zionists, the growth of Palestinian Jewry in 1932–35 had been extraordinarily satisfactory; that was why the Arabs were rioting again. Any change in immigration regulations now, the Zionists reasoned, was likely to be a change for the worse.

3.

American Jews, meanwhile, had been demonstrating once again that Zionism in the United States thrives only in times of crisis. And so some Zionist leaders seized upon the horrifying rise of Hitlerism as a means of directing attention toward the goals of their organization and thus, perhaps, revitalizing it. In June, 1933, President Morris Rothenberg of the Zionist Organization of America declared that that group was "facing a new day in the history of the movement" and observed that the world-wide situation of the Jews made the creation of a Palestine homeland vital: "The events in Germany in particular call upon us for a rededication to our cause." In his report to the thirty-sixth annual convention of the Z.O.A. in Chicago in July, 1933, President Rothenberg said that "while the need for immediate relief to meet the dire conditions of Jews in Germany as in the lands to which many of them have made their escape was fully recognized," the Z.O.A.

leadership believed more strongly than ever "that a fundamental solution of the aggravated condition of Jewish homelessness had to be sought, and that Palestine offered the most promising hope in that direction."

Despite the emergency, the reawakening of American Zionism was slow in coming. In 1935, the Z.O.A. sponsored a "National Zionist Roll Call" aimed at getting 250,000 "registered sympathizers" to contribute $1 each. Less than 20,000 responded. An "Extension Fund" attempting to raise $100,000 brought in a net of $13,500. In 1933 and 1934, the non-Zionist Joint Distribution Committee and the Zionist Palestine Foundation Fund had once again cooperated in a single fund-raising campaign, but in October, 1935, the Joint pulled out of a proposed cooperative venture for 1936, fearing that its association with Zionism was hampering the fund-raising program.

By 1936, though, a revival of American Zionism was beginning. It came about partly from the realization that Nazism was far more evil than had earlier been seen, and partly because the Arabs, quiescent since 1929, were again violent in their opposition to Jewish immigration into Palestine. But there was a more immediate reason for American Jews to show new interest in a "foreign" movement like Zionism. Anti-Semitism, long an unimportant subterranean phenomenon in the United States, had abruptly surfaced.

Stimulated by direct encouragement from Berlin, an ugly collection of propagandists had begun to preach a gospel of hate. Jews had learned to live with the "acceptable" anti-Semitism of the day, the exclusive country club, the hotels that posted signs reading, "No dogs or Jews allowed," the restricted neighborhoods. That kind of thing—the unwillingness of the Gentile to mingle socially with the Jew—was contemptible and repugnant, but it was not really a menace, since few Jews were all that eager for the company of *goyim* anyway. But now came an anti-Semitism out of the Middle Ages, full of accusations that the Jews were draining the nation's wealth, that they had caused the Depression, that they were steering the country into war—everything, in fact, except the old accusations that they poisoned wells and sacrificed babies. It was the era of Gerald L. K. Smith, Father Charles E. Coughlin, the German-American Bund, the "Buy Christian!" campaign. The New Deal was labeled "the Jew Deal" because of the prominence of Felix Frankfurter, Benjamin V. Cohen, Samuel I. Rosenman, and other Jews in the Roosevelt administration. Roosevelt himself was branded an agent of a "Jewish-Zionist-Communist" conspiracy, and rumors of his Jewish ancestry were spread. A poll taken by *Fortune* in 1936 revealed that some 15 percent of the Americans questioned had answered "Yes" when asked, "Do you believe that in the long run Germany will be better off if it drives out the Jews?" Another 30 percent were so indifferent to the fate of Hitler's victims that they had no opinion about the question.

What was creeping into the open now was something darker and much more terrifying than the prejudice of the fastidious patrician who wanted to keep vulgar Jewish entrepreneurs out of his Anglo-Saxon environment. A Jew could be annoyed or even bitter over country-club anti-Semitism, but it did not frighten him; he could always start his own country club. But this Hitler-inspired Jew-hatred, spreading through all levels of society, was something different. Already there were cries for congressional investigation of Jewish influence in government, and wild whispers of the need to Do Something About the Jews. Whole nations could go insane. Germany was demonstrating that right now, and Jews needed few reminders of how Spain, England, France, Russia, and so many other countries had turned on them in the past when a certain critical temperature of anti-Semitism was reached. Could it happen in America? Yes, said the heirs to twenty centuries of persecution. Yes, even here.

The insecurities that these attitudes created led some American Jews to change their names and pass as Gentiles—the assimilationist escape, the donning of camouflage. Others, aware of how futile that way out had always been, enrolled in Zionism—as if seeking assurance that Palestine would be open to them if the fires now blazing in Germany broke loose in the United States.

Many who rushed into Zionism in the mid-1930's belonged to groups that in earlier years had been non-Zionist or even anti-Zionist. Most striking was the conversion of Reform Jews to Zionism. In the nineteenth century the Reform movement had assailed "Ziomania" and had implied that it verged on treason to the United States for an American Jew to support Zionism. The basic orientation of Reform Judaism toward acceptance by the Gentile world had always precluded sympathy for Jewish nationalism. The Pittsburgh Platform of 1885, in which the leaders of Reform declared, "We consider ourselves no longer a nation, but a religious community," had been an explicit repudiation of the Zionist idea at the very outset of the rebirth of Jewish nationalism. Through its official spokesman, the Central Conference of American Rabbis, Reform had continued to attack Zionism in the early years of the twentieth century, though there were a few influential Zionists such as Rabbi Stephen S. Wise within Reform ranks.

After the Balfour Declaration, Reform shifted from an anti-Zionist to a "non-Zionist" position that permitted it to work toward the economic, social, and spiritual development of the Jewish homeland in Palestine, while remaining aloof from Zionist "political machinations." Reform Jews were encouraged to direct their philanthropies toward Palestine, and the Reform layman Louis Marshall was able to lead his faction of Judaism into close cooperation with Weizmann and the Zionists when the Jewish Agency was enlarged in 1929. But only after Hitler came to power did Reform Judaism become deeply involved with Palestinian affairs. In 1935, in what amounted to a repeal of the Pittsburgh Platform, the Central Conference of American Rabbis passed a resolution making acceptance or rejection of Zionism a matter for individual conscience; the conference agreed to take no stand on Zionism itself, but to "continue to cooperate in the upbuilding of Palestine, and in the economic, cultural, and particular spiritual tasks confronting the growing and evolving Jewish community there." And in its 1937 meeting in Columbus, Ohio, the conference reacted to the strident new voices of anti-Semitism by proclaiming, "Judaism is the soul of which Israel is the body," and by asserting, "We affirm the obligation of all Jewry to aid in [Palestine's] upbuilding as a Jewish homeland." The same year the Union of American Hebrew Congregations, the main association of Reform laymen, backed the rabbinical group with its own resolution, urging all Jews "to give their financial and moral support to the work of rebuilding Palestine."

The anti-Zionists who once dominated Reform had been reduced by these resolutions to a minority position. Though they would continue to battle, sometimes vociferously, against emerging Jewish nationalism, they were doomed to see their remaining influence gradually ebb. But, as Ben-Gurion might have said, a homeland is not created with resolutions. The shift in the Reform position was accompanied by a dramatic increase in financial aid to Palestine by Reform Jews.

B'nai B'rith, originally a fraternal organization of Reform-minded German-American Jews, now became an important ally of Zionism. In part this was the result of the growth of B'nai B'rith's membership, which in the 1920's had come to include many Jews of Eastern European origin. After 1925 even the presidents of B'nai B'rith came from this group. When the Zionist Organization of America called a "non-partisan, non-political" National Conference for Palestine in January, 1935, B'nai B'rith enthusiastically took part.

B'nai B'rith had given sporadic aid to the Jews of Palestine since 1865, when $4,500 was contributed to a relief fund for victims of a cholera epidemic. Now its members provided hundreds of thousands of dollars to aid the resettlement of refugees from Nazi persecution—the first large-scale B'nai B'rith donation in a series that over the next 30 years would total many millions of dollars.

The lesson of 1936 was that American Jews of varying philosophies could be induced to support the development of Jewish Palestine, so long as the troublesome matter of political sovereignty was kept in the background. Of all the organizations of American Jews that had been traditionally hostile or indifferent to Zionism, only the American Jewish Committee, that oligarchic assembly made up primarily of wealthy German-American Jews, failed to draw closer to the movement during the 1936 crises of Nazi persecutions and Arab upheavals. With Louis Marshall gone, the committee's flirtation with Zionism had cooled; it retained its place on the Jewish Agency, but its leaders were uneasy, for they now had more reason than ever to think that the Zionists—contrary to their public statements of policy—were working toward establishment of a Jewish state, which the committee opposed.

In August, 1936, when a rumor circulated that the British were going to shut off Jewish immigration into Palestine in order to appease the Arab rioters, the acting president of the Zionist Organization of America asked the head of the American Jewish Committee, Cyrus Adler, to protest the rumored suspension to the State Department. Adler declined, explaining that it was the committee's policy to leave the problems of Palestine in the hands of the Jewish Agency. When a dozen or so protest delegations from Jewish groups descended on Washington that summer to support continued entry of refugees into the Holy Land, the committee was conspicuously absent.

But soon the committee's position within the American Jewish community became even more difficult. On July 7, 1937, the Peel Commission, sent by the British government to investigate the Arab riots in Palestine, released its report, and the report was a bombshell, for it recommended the creation of an independent Jewish state.

4.

No one had expected that. The six members of the Peel Commission were highly regarded men—three statesmen, two lawyers, and an Oxford scholar, all with deep experience in the problems the British had encountered in governing other peoples. The Zionists assumed that these wise and distinguished men had been sent to Palestine merely to find ways of comforting the angry Arabs. The Arabs assumed the same.

Several factors operated in the favor of the Jews, however. One was the revulsion created by the Nazi oppressions. Another was the good impression registered by an idealistic policy of *havlagah* ("self-restraint") enforced on the Jewish settlers in Palestine by the Jewish Agency. At the urging of Weizmann and others, the settlers were refraining from engaging in armed operations against the Arabs, except in genuine self-defense. This policy was monumentally unpopular among many Palestinian Jews, who yearned to retaliate against Arab provocations, but they reluctantly heeded the Jewish Agency's pleas for forbearance. Only the Revisionist firebrands, insisting that Jews had been a people of peace long enough, rejected *havlagah* entirely. In 1935 Jabotinsky had taken his party out of the World Zionist Organization altogether, and by 1937 he had split away from Haganah, the defense militia, to create a new underground terrorist force, the Irgun Zvai Leumi ("National Military Organization"). But the Irgun did not immediately make itself apparent. What the Peel Commission saw was a community of Jews admirably holding itself back from violence. The contrast with the Arabs, who were aiming their weapons at Jews and Britons alike, was powerful.

The commission collected information at 66 meetings in late 1936 and early 1937—first interrogating British officials, then Zionists, then Arabs. Weizmann, addressing the eighth meeting on November 25, 1936, delivered one of his most eloquent speeches. In an impromptu talk on the sufferings of his people through the ages, he said: "When one speaks of the Jewish people, one speaks of a people which is a minority everywhere, a majority nowhere, which is to some extent identified with the races among which it lives, but is still not quite identical. It is a disembodied ghost of a race, and it inspires suspicion, and suspicion breeds hatred. There should be one place in the world, in God's wide world, where we could live and express ourselves in accordance with our character, and make our contribution to civilization in our own way, and through our own channels." For three hours he traced the history of Zionism and the achievements of those Jews —a relative handful—who had been allowed to enter Palestine. But the most that Weizmann asked, at the end, was continued Jewish immigration, and self-government for Palestine under a legislative council made up of Arabs and Jews.

Other Zionist witnesses followed him, 40 in all, including most of those who were destined to be the first leaders of the state of Israel. Then came the Arab witnesses, led by the grand mufti. He listed the genuine grievances of his people, whose own national aspirations had gone unheard in the furor over Zionism, and cited the conflicting promises made by the British during the world war.

But soon he was making exaggerated references to the international power of the Jews, and speaking of "the Jews' ultimate aim" as "the reconstruction of the Temple of King Solomon on the ruins of . . . the al-Aqsa Mosque and the Holy Dome of the Rock." He demanded the termination of the mandate, establishment of an independent Palestine under Arab rule, and an end to further Jewish immigration and land purchase. And he insisted that the 400,000 Jews already in Palestine were more than that impoverished land could digest. When Lord Peel asked whether, in the independent Moslem Palestine that the grand mufti was advocating, some Jews might have to be removed "by a process kindly or painful as the case may be," the mufti merely replied, "We must leave all this to the future."

The hearings demonstrated the irreconcilability of Zionist and Arab ambitions. The mufti was plainly determined to subjugate the Jews; Weizmann was just as plainly resolved to maintain all that the Jews had won since the Balfour Declaration. And Jabotinsky, who testified before the Peel Commission in London (he had not set foot in Palestine since 1929) made it clear that there were at least some Jews as intransigeant as the mufti.

The commission's final report showed the hopelessness of the situation: "Almost a million Arabs are in strife, open or latent, with some 400,000 Jews. There is no common ground between them. The Arab community is predominantly Asiatic in character, the Jewish community predominantly European. They differ in religion and language. Their cultural and social life, their ways of thought and conduct, are as incompatible as their national aspirations."

There was one solution, however: partition of Palestine into two independent states, one Jewish, one Arab. The idea first had emerged at the session of January 8, 1937, a few days before the mufti had testified. It was a closed meeting, with Weizmann the only witness. Midway through it Professor Reginald Coupland, an Oxford don whose specialty was colonial history, unexpectedly asked Weizmann how he felt about a partition scheme: "If there were no other way out to peace, might it not be a final and peaceful settlement—to terminate the Mandate by agreement and split Palestine into two halves, the plain being an independent Jewish state, as independent as Belgium . . . and the rest of Palestine, plus Trans-Jordania, being an independent Arab state, as independent as Arabia."

Weizmann was stunned. "Let me think about it," he said.

He had managed to avoid, through all his years in Zionism, any solid commitment to Jewish sovereignty. That topic had always seemed too dangerous to approach, too likely to arouse hostility both within and without the Jewish world. At the peace conference in Paris in 1919, Weizmann had, it is true, incautiously remarked that he expected the Jewish national home to be "as Jewish as the French nation was French and the British nation British"—an unambiguous avowal of nationalism that was to be much quoted by anti-Zionists in years to come. Never again, though, had Weizmann spoken of a Jewish nation so explicitly, and he had taken some pains to occupy both sides of the nationalism question. But now that sovereignty was seemingly being thrust at him, he was compelled to decide where his own feelings lay. It was not a difficult decision. His emotions told him that independence was the goal toward which Zionism had really been working all along: "A small Jewish state, well organized, living in peace with its neighbors, a state on which would be lavished the love and devotion of the Jewish communities throughout the

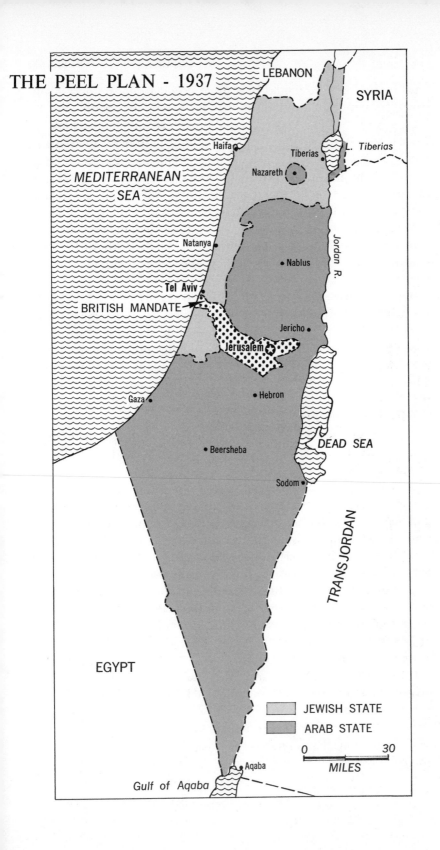

THE PEEL PLAN - 1937

LEBANON

SYRIA

Haifa

L. Tiberias

Tiberias

Nazareth

*MEDITERRANEAN
SEA*

Jordan R.

Natanya

• Nablus

Tel Aviv

BRITISH MANDATE

Jericho •

Jerusalem ✩

Gaza

• Hebron

DEAD SEA

• Beersheba

Sodom •

TRANSJORDAN

EGYPT

| | JEWISH STATE |
| | ARAB STATE |

0 ————— 30
MILES

Aqaba

Gulf of Aqaba

world—such a state would be a great credit to us and an equally great contribution to civilization," he wrote. It would also, he hoped, serve to allay Arab fears of Zionist territorial expansion: "A Jewish state with definite boundaries internationally guaranteed would be something final; the transgressing of these boundaries would be an act of war which the Jews would not commit, not merely because of its moral implications, but because it would arouse the whole world against them."

Weizmann privately informed the Peel Commission that he favored the partition idea, and during the early months of 1937 the commissioners drew up a tentative proposal for dividing the country.

The plan that emerged in July, 1937, was unlikely to delight the Zionists. The important ports of Acre, Haifa, and Jaffa were to remain in British hands. The mandate would also retain a corridor running inland through Lydda—where Palestine's only major airport was located—and taking in both Jerusalem and Bethlehem. The central plateau, from Nablus to Hebron, would be given to the Arabs and made part of Transjordan. The Arabs would also receive the entire Negev Desert and the two important towns on its fringes, Gaza and Beersheba. To the Jews would go the Galilee —minus the towns of Nazareth, Tiberias, and Safed, which were to stay in the mandate—and the coastal strip from a point just south of Haifa to the southern end of Tel Aviv; they would also get about one hundred square miles south of the Arab city of Jaffa, and were to have harbor privileges at Haifa. Altogether the Jewish state would contain about 20 percent of the land under the mandate. It would have nearly all of Palestine's fertile land—in return for which it would pay a yearly subsidy to its barren eastern neighbor, Transjordan. But it would be shorn of holy Jerusalem and most of Palestine's other metropolitan centers. Worse yet, the supposed "Jewish" state would come into being with a population of 258,000 Jews and 225,000 Arabs. The Jews would scarcely be a majority in their own country.

It was a sorry scheme, and Weizmann regretted that he had given its makers any encouragement. However, he felt obligated to support it at the Twentieth World Zionist Congress in August, 1937. He argued that the proposal was tentative, that it might be improved upon, that it offered the prospect of a Jewish nation that could absorb 100,000 immigrants a year and sustain a population of 3,000,000. Harsh opposition came from many sides. With great political skill—and amid the fury of his outmaneuvered opponents, who believed that Weizmann was selling Zionism out for a few scraps of land—he pushed through a resolution that called the partition scheme "unacceptable," but empowered the Jewish Agency's executive committee "to enter into negotiations with a view to ascertaining the precise terms of His Majesty's Government for the proposed establishment of a Jewish state."

The Arab leadership, aware that granting the Jews even 20 percent of Palestine might open the way to more ambitious Zionist demands, rejected the Peel plan entirely at a Pan-Arab Congress in Syria in September, 1937, and showed their grave disappointment with the commission's work by resuming their campaign of terrorism. Objections to partition were heard in the United States, too. While American Zionists denounced the miserliness of the offer of territory, American non-Zionists expressed shock at the sudden possibility that a Jewish state might be created. On January 16, 1938, the American Jewish Committee approved a resolution of unalterable opposition to the partition plan.

By the end of 1937, it was apparent that nothing was going to come of the Peel plan. The British government went through the motions of sending out another commission to determine methods of implementing partition, but the Jews were unwilling to settle for what had already been offered, and the Arabs were unwilling to yield even that much, so the development of a workable scheme was obviously impossible.

Sensing that terrorism was the route to political victory, the Arabs were now in virtual revolt against British authority in Palestine, and 1937 and 1938 were years of brutal bombings, ambushes, and assassinations. In October, 1937, the British outlawed the Arab Higher Committee, the pro-nationalist group that was running the revolt, and arrested five of its leaders, who were deported to the Seychelles Islands. But the grand mufti, head of the committee, escaped in disguise, fleeing to Iraq, from where he continued to direct the bloodshed.

The Jewish policy of self-restraint began to give way. Haganah now fought back fiercely, as did the underground Irgun Zvai Leumi, and casualties mounted on both sides. In 1938, 69 British were killed, 92 Jews, 486 Arab civilians—many of the last group victims of grudge-settling by the terrorists against their own people. About 1,000 of the Arab guerrillas were slain; 110 were hanged by the British. Deaths in all three groups between 1936 and early 1939 were close to 5,000. Anarchy seemed about to overwhelm the Holy Land; it was under siege from within.

One effect of the chaos was a sharp drop in Jewish immigration to Palestine. There had been 61,854 immigrants in 1935; the following year 29,727 entered, and in 1937 only 10,536. At the same time the number of Jews seeking to escape Nazi repression in Europe was increasing astronomically from month to month. German Jews, those that had not managed to flee earlier, had now been stripped of all rights and were in great peril. And the terror was spreading beyond Germany. On March 11, 1938, Hitler devoured Austria without effort, proclaiming it a province of the German Reich. Austria had 200,000 Jews, 180,000 of them in Vienna. A few days after the conquest, storm troopers led swastika-decked mobs on looting tours through the Jewish neighborhoods, shouting, "Out with the Jews!" Suicides among Viennese Jews averaged two hundred a day. In April, after stripping the Jews of Austria of their property by law, the Germans offered to let them leave the country. In the same month Hitler served notice on Czechoslovakia that he wished that portion of the country inhabited by ethnic Germans to be ceded to the Reich. The promise of another Nazi takeover sent Czech Jews into panic. But where were all the refugees to go?

Not to Palestine, it seemed. In July, 1937, Britain had put "temporary" limits on Jewish immigration into effect, "while the form of a scheme of partition is being worked out." A new government under Prime Minister Neville Chamberlain issued a White Paper decreeing that for the time being, only 12,000 Jews a year would be let into Palestine—this in the hope of getting the Arab terrorism to subside. Zionist efforts to have it rescinded failed. By the spring of 1938, 300,000 Jews were awaiting evacuation from Germany and Austria. That was enough to fill the Palestinian entry quotas for the next 25 years, unless the "temporary" limits were removed.

Where else could they go, then? To the United States, perhaps, the fabulously wealthy land that always had welcomed the victims of persecution? There was no welcome for homeless foreigners now. Some 10,000,000 Americans were out of work. Radical economic experimentation had failed to break the Depression; after some years of recovery, a new slide had begun in 1937. There was no disposition to help others at a time when things were so bad on the home front. Under the Immigration Act of 1924, a maximum annual immigration quota of 153,774 was in effect. More than half the available places—83,575—were assigned to Great Britain and Ireland. If these places were not used in any year (and the full British-Irish quota never was used), they could not be reallocated to other nationalities. The quota of Germans was 25,-957 a year; of Poles, about 6,000; of Rumanians, 300. And, as we have seen, State Department officials all through the 1930's manipulated the visa requirements in a way designed to allow as few of these quota places as possible to be filled. Thus the United States protected itself against an influx of jobless strangers at a time of general economic distress.

For example, in 1933, the number of aliens admitted to the United States under the immigration quotas was 8,220 while 145,-000 places went unfilled. In 1934, 12,483 came in; in 1935, 17,207; in 1936, 18,675. During the first four years of Nazi tyranny, therefore, the United States—which under its own existing quotas could have taken in more than 600,000 aliens—accepted about 55,000. About half of those came from Great Britain, Scandinavia, Italy, and other places where the need to escape was not notably urgent. During those same four years little Palestine managed to find room for more than 160,000 immigrants, three times as many as the United States. In sponsoring the Immigration Act of 1924, the House Committee on Immigration had declared, "This country thus serves notice that it can no longer be an asylum." But there had been no Nazi Reich in 1924.

The situation was outrageous, and there were many in the United States who spoke out against it—not all of them Jews. By the time of the rape of Austria, pressure was building up for an overhaul of our immigration laws. Despite the raw anti-Semitism loose in the land, despite the insistence of American isolationists and pacifists that the United States keep out of European affairs, despite the undercurrent of approval for much of what Hitler was doing, despite the feeling of millions of Americans that this country had taken in quite enough foreigners prior to 1924, a sufficient number of influential Americans did cry out that something had to be done to help the victims of Nazi crimes. Finally, the President of the United States felt that some action should be taken. And so, on March 22, 1938, President Roosevelt called for an international conference to discuss the plight of the refugees.

5.

Franklin Delano Roosevelt is perhaps the most enigmatic political figure involved in the struggle of American Jews to create a Jewish homeland in Palestine. To most American Jews he was a beloved figure, a warm and sympathetic man who had a profound understanding of human suffering, a deep loathing for bigotry and selfishness, and a powerful love of justice. When Roosevelt ran for President for the first time in 1932, he seemed an immensely more attractive figure to Jews than the aloof, uncommunicative Hoover. Weary of Presidents who—regardless of their private feelings— had seemed officially unconcerned with the less fortunate members of society, Jews cast off their last links to Republicanism and voted overwhelmingly for FDR. In Jewish neighborhoods of New York and Chicago he captured nearly 90 percent of the vote. In 1936, in 1940, in 1944, the Jewish vote for Roosevelt was close to unanimous. When he died in 1945, the outpouring of grief from the American Jewish community was extraordinarily intense. "The Jewish people lost an understanding friend, Zionism lost its avowed supporter," declared Dr. Israel Goldstein, then President of the Zionist Organization of America. From Rabbi Stephen S. Wise came the statement, "The Jewish people have never known a more understanding friend, who sorrowed over their oppression and misfortunes and who sought with all his strength to bring about a world where justice to Jews would be inevitable and the Jewish people would be restored in their ancient home." Similar comments came from other American Jewish leaders; and in the Jewish sections of Palestine flags flew at half mast.

Beyond doubt Roosevelt was a great leader and a great President. But was he really the "understanding friend" of the Jews and an "avowed supporter" of Zionism? Or did the Jews misplace the love and admiration they lavished on him?

Certainly Roosevelt vigorously prosecuted the war against Nazism, spoke out in bitter opposition to anti-Semitism at home and abroad, and gave active support to the campaign for a Jewish homeland. Yet the emerging record appears to show that Roosevelt's pro-Jewish feelings were superficial, donned for the sake of political effect, and that in truth the United States did little to aid the Jewish cause, and much to obstruct it, during his twelve years in office. As Jacques Torczyner, President of the Zionist Organization of America, put it in an interview in 1968, "When history will really be written, Roosevelt will be shown to have been not a friend of the Jews."

The reexamination of FDR's attitude toward Jewish problems began little more than a year after his death. The Zionist leader Rabbi Abba Hillel Silver—a Republican, it should be noted—told the Twenty-Seventh World Zionist Congress in December, 1946, that "throughout the Roosevelt Administration, the United States Government was determined to take no action whatsoever and to make no representations whatsoever to the British government either to open the doors of Palestine to Jewish immigration, or to live up to the other obligations which it had assumed under the mandate." The lawyer Bartley C. Crum—also a Republican at least in name, but chosen by President Truman as a member of the 1946 Anglo-American Commission of Inquiry on Palestine— asserted in 1947 that "Since September 15, 1938, each time a promise was made to American Jewry regarding Palestine, the State Department promptly sent messages to the Arab rulers discounting it and reassuring them; in effect, that, regardless of what was promised publicly to the Jews, nothing would be done to change the situation in Palestine." And David Niles, an administrative assistant to Presidents Roosevelt and Truman, remarked in 1962, "There are serious doubts in my mind that Israel would have come into being if Roosevelt had lived."

The complexities of Roosevelt's position on Jewish matters, the conflicts between image and reality, were unknown at the time of the 1938 refugee crisis. There was every reason to believe that his concern over the refugees was genuine, although he felt it would be more practical to admit them to the United States than to send them to Palestine. His relationship with the Jewish community in the United States had always been cordial, and he had shown interest in their problems, if no great depth of understanding.

By the summer of 1937 Roosevelt had been the recipient of more correspondence on the subject of Palestine than American Presidents were accustomed to receive on foreign matters in those isolationist days. Jews had asked him to support demands for their national homeland. Arab leaders had opposed those demands (the grand mufti had wired Roosevelt on June 21, 1937, "Arabs view with sadness and anxiety Jewish efforts to force U.S. to intervene against Arab rightful demands to live freely in their own country"). And American Christian educators had warned him against getting the United States involved in the Arab-Jewish controversy over Palestine, for fear of Arab reprisals against the numerous American Christian institutions of education and religion in the Holy Land.

Roosevelt knew little about Zionism or the Palestine issue in general. On July 7, 1937, he sent a memo to Cordell Hull, asking if the Secretary of State would "talk with me at your convenience in regard to the Palestine Mandate. . . . Is it true that the change in the present territorial boundaries and other matters requires the approval of the United States as a signatory to the Treaty setting up Palestine?"

The President was not likely to learn much about Palestine from his Secretary of State. Hull had had little contact with Jews or their problems, and regarded them, when he thought of them at all, as a baffling and alien species. He was a Tennesseean, a decade older than Roosevelt, who had seen action in the Spanish-American War and had served in both houses of Congress. Austere, something of a moralist, a strong opponent of injustice and aggression of all kinds, he had spent his life in the worlds of politics and international diplomacy, and was ill at ease outside the rarefied atmosphere of conference rooms. To the end of his life he never could grasp why it was that the Jews were so concerned about having Palestine.

Roosevelt still had acquired no mastery of Zionist tenets when he met, early in 1938, with Rabbi Wise, and spoke of "the urgent need to find an immediate sanctuary somewhere in the world for those homeless Jewish people." Wise declared, "My people will not go anywhere but Palestine. Sentiment, religion, history, principle move them." To which Roosevelt replied, "Stephen, the time is now. They can't wait for a land that is barren to be transformed." But in practice he did little in the prewar years to secure the admission of Jewish refugees either to Palestine or the United States.

On March 22, 1938—the day he called for an international conference on the refugee situation—Roosevelt was quick to add that he did not anticipate an increase in American immigration quotas, nor would any of the other nations invited "be expected or asked to receive a greater number of emigrants than is permitted by its existing legislation." Roosevelt might have pointed out that an increase in the American quotas was hardly necessary, since in 1937 the United States had let 126,000 places go unfilled in that year's quota of 153,774. There was no intention within the State Department even to liberalize the restrictions that kept the quotas from being filled, let alone to increase the quotas. When a group called the Jewish People's Committee for United Action Against Fascism and Anti-Semitism delivered to the White House, on June 7, 1938, a petition of 120,000 signatures calling for the utilization of unfilled quotas to admit refugees, presidential secretary Marvin McIntyre went through the ritual of accepting the petition, and then sent a memorandum to Undersecretary of State Sumner Welles that read, "Personally I do not see much necessity for any reply except that a more or less courteous but stereotyped answer signed by me may head off insistence in the future for a specific reply. What do you think." Welles agreed. Then as for many years to come, the State Department was more concerned with being able to "head off insistence" than with taking firm action.

The refugee conference opened at the French resort of Evian-les-Bains on July 6, 1938. The chief American delegate was Myron C. Taylor, former chairman of the United States Steel Corporation. His counsel was James G. McDonald, who had been the League of Nations high commissioner for refugee problems. Thirty-three nations had been included in Roosevelt's invitation: 20 Latin American countries, along with Great Britain, France, Italy, Belgium, Switzerland, Sweden, Norway, the Netherlands, Denmark, Canada, Australia, New Zealand, and South Africa.

Italy, newly allied to Germany, declined to take part. South Africa did not care to participate fully, but sent an observer. Observers also were sent by more than one hundred organizations representing persecuted minorities. Most of these were Jewish groups, but few of them were Zionist organizations, and the pressures that Jews intended to exert at Evian were not specifically Zionist pressures. They simply sought havens for oppressed Jews—havens in any part of the world, not only Palestine.

The question of Palestine, in fact, was not going to be permitted on the agenda. Perhaps as a result of his discussions earlier in the year with Rabbi Wise and other American Zionists, Roosevelt had remarked somewhat naïvely in June that one aim of the conference was to "manifest before the non-European world the urgency of emigration, chiefly to Palestine." The British government, then maintaining a low ceiling on Jewish admissions to Palestine in order to placate the Arabs, was alarmed at the prospect that the conference would turn into a pro-Zionist conclave, and privately asked Roosevelt to keep Palestine from coming under consideration. Roosevelt agreed that the conference would confine itself to finding homes for the refugees outside of Palestine. When American Jewish leaders asked that Chaim Weizmann be allowed to state the case for immigration to Palestine at the conference, the British delegation intervened, commenting that Weizmann's appearance before the conference would be unacceptable to their government; and the American representatives went to Evian under State Department instructions to keep away from the eloquent, persuasive Weizmann.

The exclusion of their leader did not greatly distress most Zionists. They realized that a conference whose primary purpose was to find alternatives to Jewish immigration to Palestine was not going to do their cause any good, and it would not be excessive to say that the truly dedicated Zionists hoped for the failure of the Evian talks. How disastrous it would be for Zionism if Australia, say, were to agree to admit a million Jews at once! They did not want a Jewish colony in Australia; they wanted Europe's suffering Jews to go only to Palestine, and if getting them there meant a prolongation of their suffering until the political climate was right, so be it. No better means of winning Palestine for Jews could be imagined than the existence of hundreds of thousands of displaced European Jews whom no other land would accept.

Therefore the organized Zionists remained indifferent, or even hostile, to the proceedings at Evian. For once there were no press releases, no petitions, no pamphlets from the active Zionist presses. In the memoirs of most Zionist leaders the Evian meeting gets no more than a contemptuous paragraph, at most; it was irrelevant to their aims. Weizmann's autobiography does not mention Evian at all. One historian of Zionism, Christopher Sykes, has commented, "This outlook and conception of policy, typical of the increasing narrowness of Zionist thinking, may seem horrifyingly party-minded and harsh. It was all that undoubtedly, but it was something more besides. It was not compassionless. The Zionists, both the more large-minded and the most narrow, had a constructive aim. The Zionists wanted to do something more for Jews than merely help them to escape danger. They wanted to help them to overcome their humiliation. They wanted to make them the object of respect, not the object of pity. They wanted to enable them to stop being pathetic, and they conceived that there was only one way to do this, to make them come to Palestine and undertake a fully national life. . . . That such was the basic Zionist idea is not a matter of opinion, but a fact abundantly provable by evidence. It was an idea in whose reality people outside could not usually believe at first, and which often shocked them when they recognized its existence. There can be no doubt that here again one is confronted with an idea which, even if judged as morally wrong, is such as could only be conceived by a great people."

In that special sense, Evian greatly aided the Zionist cause. Nation after nation politely explained why it could not take in Hitler's victims. Australia—an entire continent inhabited by less than ten million people—announced, "As we have no real racial problem, we are not desirous of importing one." Canada, Colombia, Uruguay, and Venezuela wanted only agricultural workers. Peru expressed fears of receiving too many lawyers and doctors. Nicaragua, Honduras, Costa Rica, and Panama jointly declared that they wanted no "traders or intellectuals." France, already burdened with 200,000 refugees, had no room for more. And so it went.

Denmark and the Netherlands, both overpopulated countries that had taken in many refugees from Germany, did offer accommodations for more until they could be settled elsewhere. Great Britain, in an echo of the old Uganda scheme, made available some odd corners of its empire, which resulted in the founding several years later of a small colony of urban Jews in the tropical jungles of British Guiana. Most amazingly, the Dominican Republic, which had not been noted for humanitarianism under the dictatorial rule of Rafael Trujillo, volunteered to accept 100,000 German and Austrian Jews if they were of respectable character and willing to undertake agricultural work. It was a noble offer—though it dismayed Zionists, who saw a host of potential Palestinian pioneers siphoned off to raise sugar in the West Indies—and a few hundred Jews actually did go there. But it was virtually the only constructive development at the conference. The best that the United States could propose as its own contribution was to agree to receive the full annual quota of 27,370 immigrants a year from Germany and Austria that was already set by law, and if possible to find room for a few thousand more above the quota. In 1939 the United States actually took in 33,515 German refugees; but only 21,520 came in in 1940, and the annual figure did not rise above 19,000 again until 1949.

The farcical proceedings at Evian were followed by several developments that greatly heightened the seriousness of the refugee problem. During the summer of 1938 Hitler had pressed his claim to the Sudetenland, as the section of Czechoslovakia inhabited by ethnic Germans was known. With German troops massed on the Czech border, Prime Minister Neville Chamberlain of Great Britain flew to Germany on September 15 to find some way of avoiding war. Chamberlain—son of Joseph Chamberlain, who had offered Uganda to Herzl in 1903—had become Prime Minister in May, 1937. Obsessed with a desire to maintain peace, he believed that a policy of appeasement was the best way to meet the demands of aggressors. It was Chamberlain who in 1937 tried to quiet the Palestinian Arabs by ordering "temporary" curbs on Jewish immigration pending the development of a workable partition plan; it was Chamberlain now in 1938 who agreed to let Hitler dismember Czechoslovakia in the hope that his territorial ambitions would halt there. After several meetings with the dictator, Chamberlain reached an understanding with him at Munich, on September 30, that Great Britain would not oppose the partition of Czechoslovakia. German troops occupied 11,000 square miles of the Sudetenland, and other segments of the country were awarded to Poland and Hungary. As Czechoslovakia began to vanish from the map, Czechoslovakia's Jews felt the earth opening under their feet.

Hitler dealt next with the Jews remaining within Germany. On October 28, 1938, he ordered the expulsion of thousands of Polish Jews who had lived in Germany for years. The move was carried out instantly and with exceptional brutality. On November 7 a young Polish refugee in Paris, learning of the hardships that his family was suffering, assassinated a minor German embassy official. Germany responded with a "spontaneous" pogrom on

November 10, the terrible *Kristallnacht,* the "night of broken glass," when 195 synagogues in Germany were burned, 7,500 Jewish-owned shops looted, more than 800 shops destroyed. *The New York Times* correspondent called it "a wave of destruction, looting and incendiarism unparalleled in Germany since the Thirty Years' War." The barbarities extended to Austria; all 21 of Vienna's synagogues were set afire, and 18 were wholly destroyed. Some 20,000 German Jews were arrested and placed in concentration camps "for their own protection." Those Jews who remained at liberty searched for ways to escape from Germany; and, seeing how coolly the great powers had let Hitler devour Czechoslovakia, the Jews of Germany's other neighbors began to think of fleeing.

The horrors of *Kristallnacht* served to draw the attention of world opinion to the intensification of the Nazi persecutions. Until then, an astonishingly large number of well-informed individuals had preferred to think of Hitler's Jewish policy as an internal German affair. But of course the world Jewish community had had no illusions about the Nazis since the day of Hitler's accession to power; and, with nearly all paths of escape closed to refugees by the bland obstinacy of most of the Evian nations, Palestine seemed the only hope left. Zionism, once the crusade of a relatively small band of idealists, received recruits from every faction of American Jewry as the dimensions of the approaching catastrophe became clear.

On October 10, 1938, a group of Jewish organizations—including the openly Zionist American Jewish Congress, Zionist Organization of America, Palestine Foundation Fund, Mizrachi, Hadassah, and Council of the Jewish Agency for Palestine, and such non-Zionist bodies as the American Jewish Committee, the Jewish War Veterans, and B'nai B'rith—petitioned Secretary of State Cordell Hull to "take suitable action to urge upon the British Government a reaffirmation and a fulfillment of its pledge to facilitate the establishment of the Jewish National Homeland and to assist and encourage immigration of European Jews into Palestine." On the same day a National Emergency Council on Palestine was formed by the Zionists to plan for mass public demonstrations; over 100 such demonstrations were held on October 23, and scores more on November 2, the anniversary of the Balfour Declaration. Zionist press releases, distributed to local newspapers, reaped a harvest of more than 150 favorable editorials in the month of October.

Roosevelt and Secretary of State Hull also experienced direct pressure from influential Jews. On October 12, Felix Frankfurter spoke by telephone to the President, urging him to intervene with Prime Minister Chamberlain on the Palestine question. Roosevelt suggested that Frankfurter compose a note that he could send to Chamberlain, and the next day Benjamin V. Cohen forwarded this text, which Frankfurter had drafted, to Roosevelt:

"With increased pressure on the Jews in Central Europe the tasks of sheer humanity we set for ourselves at the Evian Conference have become even more difficult of fulfillment. Apart from mere numbers in Palestine is a significant symbol of hope to Jewry. Therefore I earnestly urge that no decision may be made which would close the gates of Palestine to the Jews. Shutting the gates of Palestine to Jews would greatly embarrass efforts towards genuine appeasement because it would be interpreted as a disturbing symbol of anti-Semitism."

On October 14, Cordell Hull was visited by a delegation of Jewish leaders: Louis Lipsky, Stephen Wise, Solomon Goldman —the current president of the Zionist Organization of America— and Henry Monsky, the president of B'nai B'rith. Monsky read Hull a statement reminding him that by a treaty between the United States and Great Britain signed in 1924, Britain agreed to make no modification in the terms of the Palestine mandate without the consent of the United States. The purpose of this treaty had been to safeguard American commercial interests in the Holy Land. But, as Monsky pointed out, it could also be construed to give the United States a voice in the mandate's policy toward Jewish immigration. Any attempt to ban or severely limit Jewish immigration on a permanent basis, as the Chamberlain government was rumored to be considering as a means of appeasing the Arabs, might be interpreted as a modification in the terms of the mandate.

Hull offered a diplomatic reply to the effect that the State Department "would take all necessary measures to protect American rights and interests in the Holy Land," which was not exactly responsive to Monsky's point. Later that same day, Justice Brandeis visited President Roosevelt, and spent more than an hour with him to urge keeping Palestine open to Jewish refugees. It was the first overt move of a Zionist nature Brandeis had made in many years.

The petitions, the interventions, the delegations, were all in vain. The letter Frankfurter had drafted was never sent. Secretary of State Hull released a statement a few days afterward saying that "the American government and people have watched with the keenest sympathy the development in Palestine of the [Jewish] National Home," but that the United States was powerless to influence British immigration regulations. And on October 19, President Roosevelt himself declared, "I understand that under the terms of our Convention with Great Britain regarding the Palestine Mandate, we are unable to prevent modifications in the Mandate. The most we can do is to decline to accept as applicable to American interests any modifications affecting such interests unless we have given our assent to them."

On November 15, Roosevelt soothed the sting of this refusal by issuing a public condemnation—his first, amazingly enough, after almost six years of Hitler's regime—of the Nazi policies. "The news of the past few days from Germany has deeply shocked public opinion in the United States," FDR declared. "I myself could scarcely believe that such things could occur in a twentieth century civilization. With a view to gaining a firsthand picture of the situation in Germany I have asked the Secretary of State to order our Ambassador in Berlin to return at once for report and consultation." In the context of American politics in 1938, this mild, myopic statement was deemed a radical departure from the customary noninterventionism of the United States. But in the press conference that followed, the President gave a negative reply to a question on the possibility of a liberalization of American immigration laws to admit more refugees. The United States would deplore what the Reich was doing, but would not take action to give succor to its victims.

Two days later, Great Britain made an odd proposal designed primarily to keep the awkward question of Jews and Palestine from arising. Sir Ronald Lindsay, the British ambassador to the United States, suggested to Undersecretary of State Sumner Welles that Britain would gladly relinquish some of her 65,000 places in the American immigration quota so that they could be awarded to German refugees. In 1937 some 63,000 of the British places had gone unused for lack of applicants. It was a curious form of generosity on Britain's part—like denying a starving man a crust of bread, but expressing a willingness to be cosigner with him on a bank loan. All the same, it was a way of saving thousands of people. Welles replied that such an arrangement would be highly irregular, presenting formidable legal problems, since the quotas had been set by Congress and could not be made transferable by the nations to whom they were granted. He gratuitously added the amazing comment that it was his "very strong impression that the responsible leaders among American Jews would be the first to urge that no change in the present quota for German Jews be made."

An even more grotesque revelation of our real attitude toward the refugee problem unfolded in the first half of 1939. Early in January, Senator Robert F. Wagner of New York and Representative Edith Nourse Rogers of Massachusetts—neither of them Jewish—introduced bills in Congress that would permit the entry of 10,000 refugee children under the age of 14 into the United States in 1939, and 10,000 more in 1940, in addition to the regular German quota. A Quaker group had volunteered to assume all responsibility for selecting, transporting, and finding foster homes for the children. Four thousand families of all faiths were already willing to adopt them; and, to reassure the labor unions, the Wagner-Rogers Bill specified that none of the rescued babes would be allowed to seek jobs in the United States, depriving American workingmen of their wages. The bill had the strong support of Mrs. Roosevelt, who then as always was a genuine friend of the oppressed. Naturally, it also had the backing of the American Jewish community.

However, President Roosevelt himself took no immediate position on this seemingly innocuous proposal. On January 12, one well-known American Jew, the comedian Eddie Cantor, wrote to presidential secretary Marvin McIntyre, asking that FDR speak out: "If these boys and girls were permitted entry into this country, they would look upon our leader as a saint—they would bless the name of Franklin D. Roosevelt." McIntyre replied that despite the obvious merits of the bill there were fears in the White House "that it would be inadvisable to raise the question of increasing quotas or radical changes in our immigration laws during the present Congress." The President was in the midst of a delicate effort to pry $500,000,000 loose from Congress to expand the air force and build naval bases. He did not want to confuse matters now by asking for the admission of 20,000 refugee children as well.

This was not exactly heartlessness, but rather a matter of practical politics. Since practical politics also demanded a settlement of the refugee problem, Roosevelt cabled Myron Taylor in London on January 14, asking him to confer with Prime Minister Chamberlain about the chances of finding homes for the unwanted Jews in Africa. Roosevelt suggested that Chamberlain might be able to persuade Portugal, long a British ally, to open her colony of Angola to the exiles. But the British Foreign Office noted that Portugal was "sensitive" about her colonies, and the subject was dropped.

On January 30, 1939, Hitler declared in a speech that "Should international Jewry, inside and outside Europe, succeed once more in plunging the nations into war, the result will be . . . the annihilation of the Jewish race in Europe." Six weeks later, despite or perhaps because of Chamberlain's surrender at Munich, Germany invaded what was left of Czechoslovakia, cutting it into several puppet states and imperiling hundreds of thousands of frightened Jews. Hungary (445,000 Jews) made its own anti-Semitic laws, established by the pro-Nazi group that had long ruled it, more severe. Rumania (900,000 Jews) did the same, and similar restrictions were expected imminently in Poland (3,500,-000 Jews). And in April, 1939, with the refugee crisis growing more agonizing each week, the Congress of the United States opened hearings on the proposal to admit 20,000 Jewish children from Germany.

Former President Hoover, former presidential candidate Alf Landon, the American Federation of Labor, and the Congress of Industrial Organizations all declared their support. So did the Quakers, the Unitarians, Cardinal Mundelein of Chicago, the YMCA, the Federal Council of the Churches of Christ, and, of course, various Jewish groups, though as usual they were circumspect, almost self-effacing, when supporting pro-Jewish legislation.

But Secretary of State Hull pointed out that to grant these extra visas might encourage even greater departures from the quota system, and also would require hiring new clerical personnel. An American Legion spokesman warned that if the bill passed, it might lead next to the importation of 20,000 Chinese children;

"certainly they are being persecuted too." Francis H. Kinnicutt of the Allied Patriotic Societies—a lobbying group representing the Society of Mayflower Descendants, Daughters of the American Revolution, Sons of the American Revolution, United Daughters of the Confederacy, and 26 other patriotic groups—testified that "we must recognize that this is just part of a drive to break down the whole quota system—to go back to the condition when we were flooded with foreigners who tried to run the country on different lines from those laid down by the old stock. . . ." After a number of other hostile patriots had been heard, the sessions adjourned until late May. In the month-long interval, the Quakers and other supporters of the bill carried out a desperate campaign for it; but propaganda came from the other side, too, as when on May 4 the American Legion attacked the Wagner-Rogers bill because "it was traditional American policy that home life should be preserved" and the bill would take young children away from their parents.

The hearings resumed on May 24. Representative A. Leonard Allen of Louisiana questioned comedian Joe E. Brown, a supporter of the bill. Allen demanded, "Would the gentleman advocate bringing the hordes of Europeans here, when the record shows we have thousands and thousands of poor people in this country who are in want?" A speaker from the Defenders of the Constitution expressed the fear that the rescue of the children "will tend to create more opposition to the Jews, and we don't want to do that, because they're nice people."

On June 1 the hearings were concluded. President Roosevelt had made no recommendation whatever on the bill. When it left the House Committee on Immigration a month later, it had undergone one significant amendment: the 20,000 children would be admitted *within* the German quota, not in addition to it. This made a mockery of the entire proposal, since the already slender number of adult refugees able to secure quota places would have to be trimmed sharply if the children were admitted on this basis, and Senator Wagner withdrew the bill altogether. There would be no horde of young Europeans to serve, as one witness had put it, as "potential leaders of a revolt against our American form of government."

The rejected children would not find a haven in Palestine, either. On May 17, 1939—during the recess between the first and second hearings on the Wagner-Rogers Bill—the British government had released a new White Paper on Palestine. This was *the* White Paper, the document that negated the Balfour Declaration and the terms of the League of Nations mandate by cutting off Jewish immigration to the Holy Land, thereby slamming the last door in the face of Europe's hopeless multitude of victims.

6.

At the beginning of 1939 the British government had still been searching, at least in theory, for a solution to the insoluble problem of dividing Palestine between Arabs and Jews. Actually, the Chamberlain regime had already reached the view that the realities of the world crisis required an end to British sympathy for Zionism. It was apparent that the Arabs, attracted by Germany's anti-Jewish policies, were moving steadily closer to an alliance with the Axis powers. The grand mufti was known to be in contact with Hitler. It seemed highly likely that the Arab world, embittered by Zionist successes, would join forces with Germany.

Chamberlain was not primarily worried by the prospect that the inexhaustible oil fields of the Arab countries would serve to fuel the Axis war machine; he still was confident that his policy of appeasement would prevent war between Great Britain and Germany. But he felt great concern over the likelihood that a general Arab uprising against Britain throughout the Near East would seriously undermine the stability of British imperial interests there. A revolt against the British administrative presence in Egypt, for example, would be a grave matter, threatening Britain's control of the vital Suez Canal. Since the Arabs would not yield on the issue of Zionism, Chamberlain proposed to buy their continued favor by repudiating the Balfour Declaration.

He had already taken the first step by placing "temporary" limitations on Jewish immigration to Palestine in 1937. Now he prepared the way for a complete surrender to the Arabs by calling a meeting of Arabs and Jews in London in February, 1939. Ostensibly this was designed as one more attempt to end the deadlock over partition; in fact it was a final empty gesture, doomed in advance.

The Jewish Agency and the Palestinian Arabs both sent representatives. And, by way of stressing his eagerness to woo the whole Arab world, Chamberlain also invited delegates from

Egypt, Saudi Arabia, Iraq, Yemen, and Transjordan. Colonial Secretary Malcolm MacDonald met separately with the Jewish and Arab delegations and once more presented the Peel Commission's partition plans. The Arabs, as before, insisted on a halt to Jewish immigration and land purchase, and rejected any establishment of a Jewish state. The Jews, as before, protested that the territory offered by Lord Peel was inadequate. Neither side showed interest in the idea of a single independent state ruled jointly by Arabs and Jews, a possibility that the British hopefully raised several times.

On March 15, MacDonald presented a series of final proposals; both sides turned them down. That same day German troops occupied Czechoslovakia, and as they moved into Prague, Prime Minister Chamberlain observed that Britain could hardly risk war for the sake of "a far-away country of which we know very little and whose language we don't understand." If Czechoslovakia seemed so remote to him, how could he show much interest in Palestine?

Weizmann and the other Zionist delegates in London knew now that they could hope for nothing from Great Britain; there had already been ample clues that Chamberlain intended to offer Palestine to the Arabs as a bribe meant to keep them away from Hitler. Confirmation came by accident, shortly before the close of the conference on March 17. Through a clerical error, a letter from the Colonial Office meant only for the Arab delegates was delivered to Weizmann. It contained suggestions for closing Palestine to Jews—the outline of the future White Paper—that amounted to a death sentence for Zionism. Weizmann demanded an explanation from Colonial Secretary MacDonald, who insisted that the document did not represent "the final view of His Majesty's Government, that it was only a basis for discussion, that everything could still be changed." But MacDonald's words carried no conviction. On May 17 the White Paper was issued.

The White Paper declared that there was to be no partition of Palestine, and that it had never been Britain's intention to turn Palestine either into a Jewish state or an Arab state. Rather, Britain felt a "desire to see established ultimately an independent Palestine State," which it was hoped could be founded within ten years. At that time Britain would relinquish the mandate.

Jews were to have a role in governing the proposed independent

Palestine, but the White Paper laid down regulations designed to make them permanently a minority. Jewish immigration would be restricted to 10,000 a year for the next five years, plus 25,000 refugees who would be immediately admitted. After the admission of these 75,000 Jews in a five-year span, there would be no further Jewish immigration "unless the Arabs of Palestine are prepared to acquiesce in it." Purchase of land by Jews in Palestine was forbidden except in certain districts amounting to 5.2 percent of the area under the mandate, where such purchases could be made with consent of the mandatory high commissioner.

The White Paper created an uproar in Parliament. Winston Churchill denounced it with all the passion at his command, and Herbert Morrison of the Labour Party warned that if Labour ever came into power, it would not consider itself bound by its terms. Even so, Parliament approved the White Paper by a vote of 268 to 179, with 110 members—most of them members of Chamberlain's Conservative Party—abstaining.

In the United States, 15 of the 22 members of the House Committee on Foreign Affairs filed objections to the White Paper, calling it "a clear repudiation" of the Balfour Declaration, the mandate of the League of Nations, and the 1924 agreement between Great Britain and the United States. They requested the State Department to notify the British government that if the White Paper were put into effect, it would be regarded "as a violation of the British-American Convention [of 1924] and will be viewed with disfavor by the American people." At the same time, 28 members of the Senate issued a similar statement calling the defense of Jewish interests in Palestine "a moral obligation of the United States."

President Roosevelt himself evidently thought that the White Paper had been unwise, although whether he deplored the content of the decree or merely its timing is difficult to tell. At any rate, among the Roosevelt papers at Hyde Park is a memorandum from the President to Cordell Hull and Sumner Welles, dated May 10, 1939—a week before the White Paper was made public—which says, "I still believe that any announcement about Palestine at this time by the British Government is a mistake, and I think we should tell them that." The next day, responding to a letter from Justice Louis Brandeis attacking the still unissued White Paper, Roosevelt said that "in regard to the Palestine situation, I want again to assure you that everything possible is being done to forward the matter." However, no record of an actual attempt by the United States government to prevent issuance of the White Paper can be found.

The World Zionist Congress of 1939 angrily spurned the White Paper, terming it illegal, a breach of Britain's obligations under the mandate. Nor did the Arabs greet it with the expected enthusiasm. They found the provision allowing 75,000 more Jews into Palestine to be offensive, and one Arab leader who spoke in favor of accepting the new arrangement was assassinated by the mufti's terrorists.

Even the Permanent Mandates Commission of the League of Nations, not noted for independence of action, rejected the White Paper, calling it an unacceptable reinterpretation of Britain's responsibilities and a violation of the principles of the mandate. But the League had no way of preventing Britain from shaping her own Palestine policies. Attempts by American Zionists to persuade President Roosevelt to intervene also failed. The President wrote apologetic letters to Brandeis, Frankfurter, and his other Zionist friends, explaining that he was unable to meddle in the decisions of the British government.

And so, on the eve of the most terrible campaign of extermination ever directed at the Jewish people, the White Paper took effect, and the only remaining place of refuge was barred. "It is in the darkest hour of Jewish history," said the Jewish Agency, "that the British Government proposes to deprive the Jews of their last hope and to close their road back to their homeland. It is a cruel blow, doubly cruel because it comes from the Government of a great nation which has extended a helping hand to the Jews and whose position in the world rests upon foundations of moral authority and international good faith."

There would be no sovereign Jewish state, now. There would only be a Jewish ghetto in Palestine.

SIX

Zionism at War

ON SEPTEMBER 1, 1939, German tanks moved into Poland, and the Second World War began. Hitler had secured his position the previous month by signing a nonaggression pact with the Soviet Union, the only major power that remained in the way of his ambitions. Great Britain and France had thus far indicated a willingness to let Hitler do as he pleased; and the United States remained invisible behind a barrier of neutrality and isolationism.

The failure of the appeasement policy was evident now, and, after Germany ignored a British ultimatum to withdraw from Poland, Great Britain declared war on September 3. The French declaration came five hours later. There was no immediate clash between the German army and those of France and Great Britain, nor would there be for many months, but naval battles began at once, and full-scale hostilities seemed inevitable. Chamberlain, a dismal, depleted figure, brought Winston Churchill into his Cabinet as First Lord of the Admiralty, and disappeared into the background of his administration.

What Churchill called a "sinister trance" prevailed on the European front until the spring of 1940. Then, on April 9, Germany invaded and seized Norway and Denmark. On May 10, German divisions smashed into Holland, Belgium, and Luxembourg. That evening Churchill replaced Chamberlain as Prime Minister, taking over at a bleak moment when it seemed that the Nazi steamroller must inevitably crush Great Britain and France as well. An attempt to push the Germans back from Belgium led to the bottling up of 350,000 Allied troops at the port of Dunkirk, from which they were evacuated on May 26; in June, France collapsed, signing an armistice with Germany on June 22, and London began to crumble under German bombing raids. Italy was in the war, now, striking in North Africa. By the summer of 1940 Britain stood alone in Europe against the barbarian tide.

There was painful irony in this for the Jews. Hardly had they begun denouncing British perfidy over Palestine than they found themselves compelled to rally behind Britain as the last defender of European civilization. In contrast to World War I this new war was sparked by a fanaticism that went beyond mere territorial ambitions; it was a genetic crusade aimed at "purifying" the world by eliminating such strange breeds as Jews and gypsies, and Jews everywhere saw the Nazis as their common enemy. Despite the White Paper, there could be no conflict of loyalties for a Jew; with Britain all that stood between the Nazis and the total conquest of Europe, the Jews would support Great Britain. "We shall fight the war as if there were no White Paper," David Ben-Gurion said—though he added, "And we shall fight the White Paper as if there were no war."

The situation of the Palestinian Jews was particularly critical. Their survival was directly connected with the defeat of the Axis, for the Arabs were openly pro-Hitler, and were making no secret of their intention to massacre the Jews if the British were driven out of the Near East by the Germans. Within a few days after the outbreak of the war, therefore, more than 130,000 of Palestine's 450,000 Jews registered for combat service with the British armed forces. Arab volunteers could be counted in the hundreds.

The idea of a Jewish Legion—an army of Jews fighting against the Axis under their own flag—soon came under discussion. In World War I, when Jabotinsky and Trumpeldor had proposed such an army, the more moderate Zionist leaders had been uncomfortable about it; but now the World Zionist Organization itself favored the concept. The coming of the war, the ferocity of the Nazi persecutions, the indifference of the Western countries to the plight of the refugees, the unconcealed hostility of the Arab world, and the British betrayal implicit in the White Paper, all had collectively transformed the moderate Zionists into full-fledged Jewish nationalists. For years they had clung to the polite fiction of a "Jewish homeland," which could be defined, if political considerations made it expedient to do so, as nothing more than a retirement colony or an experimental agricultural station. The

delegates to the World Zionist Congress of 1931, at which Weizmann had been deposed for being too moderate, had nevertheless
voted 121 to 57 to put aside a Jabotinsky motion that would have
defined the aim of Zionism as the establishment of a Jewish state.
Now, realizing how desperate their position was, they dropped all
masks and plainly declared that they would settle for nothing less
than a sovereign Jewish nation in Palestine—for which a Jewish
army was the prime requisite.

Late in August, 1939, with war inevitable, Weizmann wrote to
Prime Minister Chamberlain offering the services of the Jewish
Agency in recruiting "Jewish manpower, technical ability, resources, etc.," in case of war. Chamberlain replied in vaguely
courteous terms; but when General Sir Edmund Ironside, chief of
the Imperial General Staff, tried to form a Jewish Legion the
following month, he was overruled by Chamberlain's Cabinet. It
was not the purpose of the White Paper, he was told, to encourage
the Jews to take up arms. That fall 43 Palestinian Jews were
arrested and given long prison sentences for drilling in secret,
although they claimed they were training themselves for service
in the war, not for anti-Arab or antimandate terrorism.

The Zionists of Europe and Palestine continued to press for a
Jewish Legion, and at the same time aggressively stated their new
activist position on sovereignty. In December, 1939, Weizmann
called on Churchill—then First Lord of the Admiralty—and discussed various Zionist issues, adding that after the war he expected
to see a state of three or four million Jews established in Palestine.
"Yes, indeed, I quite agree with that," Churchill said. When
Churchill became Prime Minister six months later, there was hope
that the Jewish Legion would be formed. Indeed in September,
1940, the British government informed Weizmann that it had
"decided to proceed with the organization of a Jewish army. . . .
Its size, to begin with, would be 10,000 including 4,000 from
Palestine. They would be trained and organized in England and
then dispatched to the Middle East."

Weizmann, elated, declared, "It is almost as great a day as the
Balfour Declaration." Shortly came word from Churchill that he
meant to repudiate the 1939 White Paper as well. But pro-Arab
factions within the Churchill government blocked both moves.
There still was reason to believe that the Arab states, officially
neutral, might be weaned from their Axis sympathies; but this

could never be accomplished if Britain suddenly showered favors on the Jews. The reasoning was cruel but logical: the Jews would continue to back the Allies in any event, for they had no choice but to oppose Hitler. On the other hand the Arabs, a far more numerous group, could go either way, and thus must be coddled and appeased. Churchill yielded. The White Paper remained in force, and the Jewish Legion was "temporarily" postponed, and then postponed again. It eventually materialized in an extremely modest incarnation only in the final months of the war.

Though the Jewish Legion scheme came to very little, it was symbolic of the changed outlook of the World Zionist Organization. No longer would its leaders bow and scrape on demand, and explain in soft voices that the terms "Jewish homeland" and "Jewish state" were by no means synonymous. Such semantic jugglery had always been necessary so that the movement would not alienate the assimilated Jews, so that it would not unduly alarm the Turks, British, or Arabs, so that the most cautious members of the Zionist Organization itself would not be upset. But the early Zionist Max Nordau had confessed long ago that he had urged adoption of the term "homeland" at the First Zionist Congress in 1897 as "a circumlocution that would express all we meant, but would say it in a way so as to avoid provoking the Turkish rulers of the coveted land. . . . It was equivocal, but we all understood what it meant."

The time for circumlocutions and equivocations was over. The World Zionist Organization, now based in Palestine and dominated by Ben-Gurion and other activists, had adopted much of the militance of Jabotinsky's Revisionists. Through the Jewish Agency it sponsored Haganah as the clandestine army of the nation-to-be. It set up the Mossad le Aliyah Bet, the "Committee for Illegal Immigration," to smuggle Jewish refugees into Palestine in defiance of the White Paper. And it laid plans for transforming the Jewish Agency, after the war, into the government of an independent Jewish Palestine. The years 1939 and 1940, dark as they were for free men everywhere, were vigorous years of reawakening for the international Zionist movement.

2.

In the United States it was all quite different. The American Zionists had drifted out of contact with the parent W.Z.O. and did not share its militance. Not only the Zionists but virtually every Jewish faction seemed suddenly to have lost its voice. As a result of the crises of recent years, more American Jews than ever now accepted the Zionist idea; possibly even a majority of them had come to think that there should be some sort of Jewish homeland (though not necessarily a sovereign state) in Palestine. There was a widespread feeling that the United States should be doing more to persuade the British to revoke the White Paper. There was nearly universal belief, except among the diehard extremist Zionists, that the United States certainly should be taking in more refugees itself. And there was almost unanimous belief within the Jewish community that the abominations of the Hitler regime had to be halted, if not by direct American involvement in the war then at least through shipments of munitions and supplies to the British.

But scarcely anything was heard in public from American Jews about these four issues of Jewish concern. Paradoxically, it was Gentiles who spoke up most vigorously against the White Paper, as when William Green of the A.F.L. forwarded to Roosevelt in the spring of 1939 an urgent anti-White Paper telegram from Goldie Meyerson of the Palestine Labor Federation—who later became better known as Golda Meir, Foreign Minister and more recently Prime Minister of the State of Israel—and added his own strong endorsement of her protest. (The White House replied to Green with a letter expressing Roosevelt's "sympathy in the idea of establishing a National Home for the Jews in Palestine" but repeating the State Department's 1938 opinion that the United States had no right by treaty to prevent the issuance of the White Paper.) Zionist organizations and officials occasionally sent wistful letters to the President, asking him once more to speak with the British about the White Paper, and now and then there was a more vigorous attempt at pressure; there was also a scattering of mail on the subject of admitting refugees to the United States. Mostly, though, the Jewish community maintained a judicious silence on anything that had to do with the war, Palestine, Hitler, or the refugees. At the moment, the temper of the times seemed to require this kind of caution.

It is difficult now to recreate or even to comprehend the American mood during the 27 months between the invasion of Poland and the Japanese attack on Pearl Harbor. There was an absolute fear of discussing or thinking about the war that raged in Europe. Ostrichlike, millions of Americans waited for the unpleasantness to go away. Men in the highest levels of government felt no moral imperative to support Great Britain, and regarded as subversive suggestions that the United States prepare itself for direct involvement in the war. The Neutrality Act of 1937, which forbade the export of arms and ammunitions to "belligerents," had passed by a vote of 377 to 12 in the House of Representatives, 41 to 15 in the Senate, and remained in effect just as though all the "belligerents" of 1939–40 were equally unworthy of our aid. The Selective Service Act of September, 1940, the first major step in rebuilding our demobilized armed forces, passed in the House by the margin of a single vote. Other pro-British or pro-rearmament bills became law only after delicate maneuvering.

President Roosevelt himself was determined to stand by Great Britain and, if necessary, to join her in the war; but he felt it necessary to engage in an elaborate ballet of political gyrations each time he moved away from a position of strict neutrality. He sensed that the mood of the nation was profoundly isolationist— despite the agitations of New York liberal intellectuals and other atypical groups—and he was compelled to cloak each action in a multitude of reassurances aimed at the uneasy isolationists west of the Hudson River. Thus he moved with extreme care—excessive care, his critics later would insist. With the clarity of hindsight we see that Hitler was a unique monster whose depredations demanded reprisals from all of humanity. But that was not at all so clear to Americans in 1939 and 1940. So long as there was no direct threat to American interests, Europe's catastrophes seemed irrelevant.

Retrospect makes some of Roosevelt's caution look unnecessary, even obscene. His failure to speak out in favor of the harmless Wagner-Rogers proposal for bringing 20,000 refugee children to the United States, for example—even though his wife had strongly urged him to support the measure—seems like a needless capitulation to the superpatriots. But Roosevelt, however he may have felt about saving the lives of 20,000 children, was also concerned with getting a major rearmament program through a hostile Congress, and chose not to antagonize the isolationist bloc over a handful of refugees. His eye was on the larger picture, the possibility that America would be drawn into the war while still unready; and he was looking also toward the presidential election of 1940. He did not want to be pushed from office on the eve of a world war by an electorate that could be made to think he was under the control of the much-condemned "international Jewish conspiracy."

American Jewry, Zionist and non-Zionist, was trapped by the same kind of fears. Every Jew in the United States loathed Hitler, of course. Every Jew privately believed that something should be done to stop the Nazis. But how could American Jews ask the United States to go to war merely to save Europe's Jews? "See," the isolationists would cry, "the Jews are dragging us into the war! The Jews want American boys to die for them!" And then all the old anti-Semitic accusations would pour forth. The Jews would be portrayed as stateless schemers, manipulating the countries in which they happened to live for the sake of their oppressed brethren. It was hopeless to expect people to realize that the Nazis were waging war against all humanity. It even seemed risky to talk about the White Paper or the American immigration laws. It went against the whole psychological orientation of American Jews to call attention to themselves in that way. They had learned long ago that it was safest to remain inconspicuous when surrounded by vast numbers of Gentiles.

Weizmann, visiting the United States early in 1940, was dismayed by the climate there. "One had to be extremely careful of one's utterances," he wrote. "As I said in one of my addresses: 'I am not sure whether mentioning the Ten Commandments will not be considered a statement of policy, since one of them says: Thou shalt not kill.' " Frustrated in his attempt to mobilize American public opinion, he was even more distressed to receive word from well-informed sources in Switzerland of the still-secret German plans for mass extermination of the Jews. "It was like a nightmare which was all the more oppressive because one had to maintain silence," he said. "To speak of such things in public was 'propaganda.' "

In February, 1940, he saw Roosevelt and sounded him out on American support for a postwar Jewish state in Palestine. The President seemed friendly, Weizmann declared, "but the discussion remained theoretical." Weizmann was glad to escape from the "artificial atmosphere" of America, where realities were being denied at all levels and the nation was, "so to speak, violently neutral, and making an extraordinary effort to live in the ordinary way."

Another visitor at about this time was Vladimir Jabotinsky, the militant Revisionist Zionist, who was trying to organize a Jewish army, wholly independent of the one the World Zionist Organization was trying to form. Jabotinsky was not interested in forming an all-Jewish combat force within the British army, as he had tried to do in World War I. What he wanted now was a Jewish army unaffiliated with the army of any of the world's recognized nations, one that would fight alongside the Allies as the soldiery of the as yet unborn Jewish state. The core of it would be Palestinian —his own clandestine terrorist group, the Irgun Zvai Leumi, was intended to be the nucleus—but he hoped to recruit American Jews. Under existing United States law, he knew, it was illegal to solicit volunteers for any of the present belligerent armies, but he imagined that it would be possible to sign up men for the army of a nonexistent nation.

Arriving in the United States in March, 1940, he discovered that Jews and non-Jews alike were trying hard to ignore the war. "People here," he wrote, "have simply stopped taking the war seriously; war news appears on the second page of the newspapers. Accordingly, the Jewish mood is also not at all 'on the eve.' " The Jews, in fact, were displaying a timidity that amazed him: "Jews are still shy of saying any decisive word lest they be charged with warmongering. (I have never seen American Jewry so scared of local anti-Semitism as they are now that the danger seems really tangible and widespread.)"

On March 19 he held a rally at New York's Manhattan Center, attended by 5,000 people. "I challenge the Jews, wherever they are still free, to demand the right of fighting the giant rattlesnake not just under British or French or Polish labels, but as a Jewish army," he cried. "Some shout that we only want others to fight, some whimper that a Jew only makes a good soldier when squeezed in between Gentile comrades. I challenge the Jewish youth to give them the lie."

His zeal and personal magnetism struck a sympathetic response in the United States, as it had in World War I. Newspapers all over the country commented favorably, and many Americans, Jewish and Gentile, offered to join Jabotinsky's army; they included many experienced soldiers, including aviators and radio operators.

There was no outcry among the isolationists, since Jabotinsky was not advocating any official involvement by the United States in the war. Even the British ambassador to the United States, Lord Lothian, was cooperative, agreeing to send a representative to a second Jabotinsky rally on June 19 "to show his sincere appreciation of the Jews' desire to help at this crisis."

Nevertheless, the project frightened the American Zionist establishment, which wanted no part of the flamboyant Jabotinsky. A few days before the rally, four Zionist leaders—Louis Lipsky, Rabbi Wise, Eliezer Kaplan, and Solomon Goldman—called on Lord Lothian in Washington and announced that "responsible Zionist quarters disassociated themselves from Jabotinsky's adventurous scheme." Lord Lothian found it prudent not to be represented at the rally; and in the June 21 issue of *New Palestine,* the official organ of the Zionist Organization of America, support was given to the Jewish Agency's plan for a Jewish army, which, it was said, would consist merely of "four divisions of Jewish soldiers in Palestine for the defense of Palestine and the Near East, plus eventually recruits from neutral lands who are living as refugees in those lands."

Jabotinsky's plan for an army of freebooters miscarried, and his quixotic career was ended by death in August, 1940. His project for a Jewish army, however, was continued by a young Palestinian named Hillel Kook, who used the pseudonym of "Peter Bergson" to avoid embarrassment to his uncle, the revered and saintly chief rabbi of Palestine. He opened an office in New York and began a recruiting campaign in the spring of 1941, but it met with little success.

In the spring of 1940, Jewish Agency leader David Ben-Gurion had set out on a journey to Britain and the United States. Before he left Palestine, two of his colleagues told him of the attitudes of the American Jews, whom they had recently visited. Moshe Shertok said, "There are millions of active and well-organized Jews in America, and their position in life enables them to be most dynamic and influential. They live in the nerve-centers of the country, and hold important positions in politics, trade, journalism, the theater and the radio. They could influence public opinion, but their strength is not felt, since it is not harnessed and directed at the right target. The Zionist Organization of America is at a low ebb. It is rent by internal dissension and disrupted by personal and

factional rivalries. The Jewish masses show deep feeling and a
basic natural loyalty for our cause, but this feeling is not utilized
and put to practical ends. . . . Whatever hopes are aroused [con-
cerning Palestine] . . . from time to time are based on somebody's
personal acquaintance with Roosevelt or some other political
figure. We have never yet got as far as the application of strong
public pressure in America, by using means which count in modern politics."

Eliahu Golomb, even more pessimistic, told Ben-Gurion,
"Were I to tell you all I saw in Jewish and Zionist circles in
America, I would paint a rather dismal picture. Moshe [Shertok]
spoke of our hopes about America and of the Jewish strength that
exists there. . . . I must say that this strength today is neither
willing nor able to fight for Zionism. This does not mean that
American Jewry is devoid of Zionist feelings. On the contrary,
Zionist feelings are much stronger among them than it would
appear from the condition of the Zionist Organization of America.
A force can be crystallized from among American Jews for political action and practical aid for our cause. But so far it does not
actually exist—it is only a potential force. To bring it into being
much work needs to be done.

"The American Jew thinks of himself first and foremost as an
American citizen. This is a fact, whether we like it or not. When
the Jew—and the Zionist—goes to vote in American elections, it
is not the candidate's attitude to Zionism which will determine his
choice. . . . Loyalty to America is now the supreme watchword."
Golomb saw only a slender hope "that we will find in American
Jewry the support that our position demands."

Ben-Gurion arrived in New York in October, 1940. He talked
with a great many Jews, both Zionist and non-Zionist. Among
them was a leading member of the American Jewish Committee
with whom Ben-Gurion had formed a warm friendship, though
the man was a convinced anti-Zionist. They discussed the problems Britain was facing in the war, and the need she had for
American aid. "He agreed with all I said," Ben-Gurion wrote,
"but argued that he could do nothing in public, since he might
injure the Jews of America. I asked him: 'Which are you first, a
Jew or an American?' To my surprise he replied: 'A Jew. We are
a minority here. If I stand up and demand American aid for Britain, people will say after the war that the dirty Jews got us into it, that it was a Jewish war, that it was for their sakes that our

sons died in battle.' This fear I found in almost all Zionist circles."

The strength and growth of the women's group, Hadassah, impressed Ben-Gurion greatly, although, since Hadassah's orientation was mainly philanthropic, he found more to discuss with the leaders of the frankly political Zionist Organization of America. He also attended meetings of the emergency committee that the chief leaders of American Zionism had formed, and talked with old Brandeis, who admitted that he had been wrong to split with Weizmann in 1920. But when he left the United States early in 1941, Ben-Gurion still was troubled about the condition of the American movement: "Not only were there personal animosities and a lack of cohesion, but the movement was still very far from grasping the full gravity of the White Paper policy, the terrible and tragic situation of European Jewry, and the fearful danger that Nazi Germany presented to the entire world. But though confused, the community was imbued with a deep feeling of Jewish solidarity and was always ready to listen to the message from Palestine. There was, furthermore, a sincere desire to overcome ideological inertia and discard the tradition of philanthropic Zionism."

By early 1941 American Jewry was beginning at last to stir. Some Zionist leaders were calling upon the American movement to catch up with the activist world organization and embrace "Maximal Herzlian Zionism," which is to say, advocacy of a Jewish national state in Palestine. The first move in this direction came not from any of the avowedly political Zionist groups, such as the Zionist Organization of America, but from a fund-raising entity, the National Conference for Palestine, which met on January 25 and 26, 1941. David Ben-Gurion, who had been visiting the United States at that time (and who was considerably disgusted by the prevailing neutralism and pacifism in the American Jewish community), was the guest of honor. He spoke in support of the Jewish Agency's plan for a Jewish Legion within the British army. "We need a Jewish army to help Britain," he declared. "There is no more sacred task at the moment than the defeat of Hitler." The delegates applauded that, and cheered a resolution once again condemning Britain for the White Paper; and then Rabbi Abba Hillel Silver, who was emerging as the most militant of the American Zionists, delivered an undisguised appeal to Jewish nationalism:

"What are all our efforts for? What are we aiming at? We have no new aims. We accept no substitute aims. Ours is the historic and millennially unsurrendered and uncompromised aim of rebuilding Israel's national life in Israel's historic national home. Our aim is a Jewish Commonwealth. Such a Jewish Commonwealth was the clear intent of both the letter and the spirit of the Balfour Declaration. Two decades of legal hairsplitting and sundry White Papers have not succeeded in whittling down the clear, full-orbed intent of that historic document or in giving moral sanction to any deviation from it."

Silver amazed the 1,500 delegates by quoting to them the slogans of Ireland's national liberator, Daniel O'Connell—"Agitate! Agitate! Agitate!" and the French revolutionary leader, Danton— "Boldness! More Boldness! And always Boldness!" America's Jews had been silent long enough. It was time to insist on an end to the White Paper, the opening of Palestine to Europe's refugees, and a guarantee of independence for Jewish Palestine after the war. The weight of the American Jewish community had to be brought to bear on the Roosevelt administration, so that that administration in turn would exert pressure on Great Britain, in whose hands the fate of Palestine lay. The fear of "embarrassing" the President by making such demands, the fear of an anti-Semitic backlash in America aroused by daring to call for aid to oppressed Jews overseas, the fear of provoking accusations of dual loyalty by calling for creation of a Jewish nation—all these fears must be put aside in the face of the emergency created by the war.

That was the first full-fledged public expression of what was, within a few years, to become the position of a majority of American Jews: a demand for a Jewish nation in Palestine. Up till then, such a goal had been mentioned only within organized Zionism,* and not even by a majority of Zionists; many American Zionists had often disavowed the goal of nationhood, some sincerely, some for tactical reasons. But the commitment of American Jewry to "political" or "maximal" Zionism was soon to spread beyond the original minority of supporters and extend to most—though not all—members of the Jewish community in this country; and without that commitment, the creation of the State of Israel would certainly have been delayed, perhaps greatly.

*The Z.O.A. had 43,295 members in 1940. Some 171,000 American Jews—out of about 5,000,000—belonged to one Zionist group or another that year.

Rabbi Silver's outburst of January, 1941, was not followed by any immediate declarations of support for political Zionism from other Zionist leaders. At the moment Silver stood alone. The 47-year-old Rabbi Silver, Lithuanian-born but reared in the American Midwest, was something of an outsider in the Zionist movement at that time, noted for his vocal criticisms of the more hesitant men. As the leader of Cleveland's main Reform temple, Silver had had to struggle against anti-Zionism within the Reform movement, and had moved on after that battle to confront the often sluggish Zionist organization itself. He was impatient and aggressive; he had lost his faith in the policies of conciliation and caution that had governed Zionism for so many years. Since the White Paper, he had begun to feel that it was a waste of time to try to curry favor with Presidents and Prime Ministers; what was needed, he maintained, was fewer pro-Zionist statements wrung from canny politicians, and more pro-Zionist action brought about through the pressure of public opinion. Quiet diplomacy had failed; it was a time for mass meetings and demonstrations, for firm declarations of purpose, for petitions, for agitation.

Slowly—very slowly—the Zionist Organization of America moved in the direction Rabbi Silver was urging. One step was the organization of a new propaganda unit, the American Emergency Committee for Zionist Affairs, later called the American Zionist Emergency Council (AZEC). Established in 1939 in response to the White Paper, it served for a year and a half as nothing more than a coordinating body linking four Zionist groups—the Z.O.A.; the Mizrachi or Orthodox Zionist organization; Hadassah, the Women's Zionist Organization of America; and Poale Zion, the Labor Zionist organization. Not until January, 1941, when Emanuel Neumann, an energetic and skillful leader, took charge of its Department of Public Relations and Political Action, did it begin really to function.

One of Neumann's first projects was to revive the American Palestine Committee, an organization of pro-Zionist Christians that had been founded, and almost immediately allowed to lapse, in 1932. It came back into being on April 30, 1941, with a membership that included three Cabinet members, 22 governors, 68 United States senators, 200 members of the House of Representatives, and hundreds of other prominent citizens. Some of these joined because they were profoundly sympathetic to the Zionist

cause; others let their names be used simply because it was politically expedient to do so. (The number of Arab voters in the United
States was insignificant, so there was nothing to lose and perhaps
a good deal to gain by offering lip service to Zionism.) Regardless
of motive, the presence of so many distinguished Christian names
on the roster of the American Palestine Committee was a powerful propaganda weapon, which Neumann exploited adeptly to
create the impression of American unanimity on the subject of a
Jewish homeland.

For example, on November 2, 1942—the twenty-fifth anniversary of the Balfour Declaration—the American Palestine Committee issued a statement entitled "The Common Purpose of
Civilized Mankind," which proclaimed itself to be a reaffirmation
of the "traditional American policy" of support for a Jewish national home. It was signed by 68 senators and 194 members of the
House, including some of the most powerful leaders on Capitol
Hill. This widely distributed document served to foster the quite
inaccurate impression that the United States had accepted some
legal or moral obligation to work for the establishment of a Jewish
state. Later there would be even more nearly unanimous congressional support for Zionist aims, and much of this was due to the
skillful exploitation of the endorsements of the Christian sympathizers of Zionism.

Getting past Congress to the State Department—where foreign
policy was shaped and carried out—was a much more difficult task
for the Zionist propagandists. The highest officials of the State
Department, men like Cordell Hull and Sumner Welles, were
willing to receive Jewish delegations and acknowledge Zionist
petitions. It was necessary for them to do so, for they were highly
visible members of an administration that projected an image of
warm humanitarian concern for minorities. But the middle levels
of the State Department were staffed by anonymous, faceless
bureaucrats, most of whom were anti-Zionist or even anti-Semitic.
They were a remarkably homogeneous group: a background of
wealth and Protestantism, education at Princeton, Yale, or Harvard, membership in the proper clubs. Most of them had had little
or no contact with Jews, but felt a vague distaste for them, charac-
terizing them as pushy, coarse, aggressive. Some had served in the
Near East and were designated as "experts" on the Arab world;
and, like their British counterparts, they had been captivated by
the Bedouin mystique. If they thought of all Jews as cigar-chewing

garment manufacturers, they thought of all Arabs as romantic, hard-riding, noble desert sheikhs. Thus the State Department was packed with men who lacked any understanding of the Jewish situation and who regarded Zionism merely as an ugly land-grabbing scheme. Such men assumed—perhaps with some justice—that whatever pro-Zionist promises their chiefs made had been issued simply to keep the Jewish voters happy; and, as we will see, they did much to sabotage the attempts of the Zionist leaders to influence American policy.

In fairness, it should be added that the State Department's hostility to Zionism was not entirely, or even primarily, a result of an antipathy to Jews. There was a genuine feeling that any official American support for a Jewish homeland in Palestine would greatly complicate Britain's military situation by tipping the entire Arab world from its posture of neutrality into an overt alliance with the Axis. Preventing such a catastrophe was of overriding strategic concern within the State Department. Its members were wholly unable to comprehend the emotional forces motivating the Zionists. Zionism struck most State Department men as a quaint sentimental obsession, which simply could not be humored at such a critical moment.

Thus when the American Palestine Committee was being revived in the spring of 1941, the State Department received immediate protests from the British over this show of seemingly official backing for Zionism. Britain was horrified to find so many governors, senators, congressmen, jurists, and civic leaders—more than 700—on its list of members. Early in April, 1941, Neville Butler of the British embassy in Washington called on the head of the State Department's Division of Near Eastern Affairs, Wallace Murray, to tell him that the formation of this committee was, from the British viewpoint, "particularly unfortunate at this time." Butler feared that "it would be broadcast by the Germans and Italians throughout the Arab world and would serve further to stir up difficulties with the British in Iraq and other Arab countries."

Murray reported this to his superiors—Secretary of State Hull, Undersecretary Welles, and Assistant Secretary Adolph A. Berle, Jr. Berle passed it along to the White House with the suggestion that it would be best if President Roosevelt changed his mind about sending a message of greeting to a major dinner of the American Palestine Committee to be held on April 30. Later in the month there were several other British attempts to interfere with the dinner, perhaps even to have it canceled, but these ended when Secretary Hull admitted that "it would be difficult to deal with the matter."

There were several meetings in April, 1941, between State Department officials and Zionist leaders. Weizmann was in the United States again that spring—he was the main speaker at the American Palestine Committee's dinner—and he spoke with Sumner Welles, who impressed him as "well informed and well disposed toward us." But then Weizmann met with Wallace Murray of the Division of Near Eastern Affairs, who, he quickly discovered, "was an avowed anti-Zionist and an outspoken pro-Arab." This, according to Weizmann, "naturally affected the attitude of his subordinates and associates." Murray was correct but cool toward the Zionist leader, and stressed the importance of doing nothing that might drive the Arabs into open allegiance to Hitler. In fact he implied that it might be best for the Jews to abandon Palestine altogether for the sake of the war effort.

Assistant Secretary Berle made this point more explicit a few days later when he met with Emanuel Neumann of the American Zionist Emergency Council. Berle thought it probable that the Axis would soon launch a successful invasion of Palestine, and proposed that the Palestinian Jewish community be immediately evacuated to—of all places—Saudi Arabia, to avoid a massacre. He believed that King Ibn Saud, whose financial position was said to be "desperate," would accept the Palestinian Jews in return for American economic aid. Another possibility, Berle told the amazed Neumann, was evacuation to Kenya. In any case it was preferable that the Zionists promptly renounce their political claim to Palestine. "In return, and by way of compensation for our renunciation," Neumann later said, "we might get a kind of 'Vatican City' in Palestine after the war, and a real territory for building a Jewish nation, elsewhere—in the highlands of Abyssinia, which was good country for white settlers." Neumann observed that Abyssinia was at present in Axis hands, having been conquered in the 1930's by Italy.

"Of course," Berle replied, "but it will be in Allied hands if we win the war."

"Quite true," said Neumann, "but in that case, so will Palestine, too, be in Allied hands—and, if, God forbid, we lose the war, there will be neither Palestine nor Abyssinia."

Nothing more was heard of the evacuation scheme.

The State Department continued to insist that Zionism had best be laid to rest for the duration in order to keep the Arabs pacified. The American minister in Cairo, Alexander C. Kirk, wired Secretary Hull on May 23, 1941, to express his surprise "that the responsible heads of world Jewry have not apparently been brought to realize the great contribution which they could render not only to the cause of democracy but also to their coreligionists" by giving up "the noble sentiments" of Zionism. "The maintenance of present concepts in respect of Zionism," Kirk said, "constitutes a major obstacle to the successful prosecution of the war in this area." Murray forwarded this to the White House. On June 28, Kirk again asked that pressure be brought on the Zionists to "revise their views," and recommended that the United States make "a declaration of policy in respect of the Arab people."

In July, Sumner Welles rejected both suggestions, the first because it was idle to think that the Zionists would yield, the second because the United States "can hardly be expected to adopt an attitude or policy which is more pro-Arab than the British."

The State Department's fear of exacerbating the sensitivities of the Arabs extended into some remarkably peripheral areas. For instance, Secretary of State Hull found it necessary to warn President Roosevelt against granting the Jewish National Fund's request that he send a message of greeting "which would convey a word of encouragement to the defenders and builders of the Jewish National Home in Palestine" to a Zionist meeting to be held in Detroit, since the Jewish National Fund's stated aim was "to redeem the soil of Palestine as the inalienable property of the Jewish people," and Hull did not want the President to appear to be endorsing this aim. And when a Jewish symphonic group in Palestine asked permission to name a new musical amphitheater after Roosevelt, Hull cautioned that "in view of the situation in the Near East . . . where there is a strong feeling against Zionism among the Arab peoples . . . it is suggested for your consideration that the matter be deferred for the time being." What troubled him was the goal of the Palestinian musical group, as given in its letter to Roosevelt, "to colonize in Palestine Jewish artists uprooted in the strife-torn lands of the world."

Later in 1941, Neumann won what seemed to be a considerable victory for Zionism over the State Department. He persuaded Welles to promise that the State Department would request Great Britain not to take any action regarding the future of Palestine without prior consultation with the United States, and that in the event of such consultation, the Zionist leadership would be kept informed of all developments. To the Zionists it appeared that Welles was granting them a certain official standing in any Palestine decisions. But it was simply another instance of the State Department's habit of seeking ways to head off conflict with troublesome pressure groups. Welles wrote Wallace Murray on October 3 that he had made the promise because "for reasons of policy as well as for reasons of expediency I consider it . . . important that everything be done by this Government to prevent Jewish groups within the United States from adding in any way to the obstacles already confronted by the British Government in the Near East."

In nine more weeks these fine calculations were to become obsolete. Japanese bombs fell on the American naval base at Pearl Harbor; the United States declared war on Japan with only a single dissenting vote in Congress, and three days later declared war on Germany by a unanimous congressional vote. By December 11, 1941, neutrality was dead and isolationism was treason; it suddenly became permissible to declare openly that the Axis powers had to be destroyed. All the absurd and degrading hesitations, diplomatic niceties, and self-censorships of the neutralist era were discarded.

From the Jewish point of view, the entry of the United States into the war made possible the unleashing of the Zionist movement. Now as never before, American Jews felt justified in exerting political pressure on their government; and, for the first time, they began to call with unabashed fervor for a Jewish state in Palestine as the only answer to the horrors of Nazism.

3.

The new voice of American Jewry was evident in a "Call to American Zionists" issued on February 10, 1942, by the Zionist Organization of America, speaking in favor of a Jewish army:

As self-respecting Jews, we must insist that the Jewish people, rising to national stature in Palestine, be permitted both to exercise the elementary right of self-defense and to make their full contribution to the defeat of Hitler. As loyal Americans and lovers of freedom, we must insist, with all the emphasis at our command, that the vital front in the Near East be strengthened by every man that can be thrown into the struggle.

We must speak out. He who lets fear stifle his voice or indifference dull his ardor falls short of the performance of his full duty to the cause of freedom and democracy, to America, to the Jewish people and the Jewish Homeland. . . . Fellow-Zionists! Assume the responsibility which world events impose upon you. . . .

If we stand up now as men and women, as Americans and as Jews, we can make certain that the Star of David will be carried to the inevitable victory of the Allied cause, along with the banner of our Republic and the flags of all the free peoples of the world.

The ringing rhetoric of this statement, the casual assumption that American Jews had obligations of duty to "the Jewish homeland," the implied contempt for the fearful or the indifferent Jew, marked a striking departure from previous declarations, which had been almost apologetic in tone. While the mood of militance still boiled, those who had helped to create it hastily arranged for an official ratification of the change in policy. An "Extraordinary Zionist Conference" was held from May 6 to 11, 1942, at the Biltmore Hotel in New York. More than six hundred delegates representing the four main American Zionist groups—the Z.O.A., Mizrachi, Hadassah, and Poale Zion—gathered to discuss, virtually for the first time, the true aim of the Zionist movement.

A number of visiting European and Palestinian Zionists attended, among them Chaim Weizmann and David Ben-Gurion. Their positions were quite different, and the subtle tensions between these two veteran Zionist champions polarized the conference. Weizmann, now 68, was in poor health, and his eyesight was failing. And he was broken by sorrow after the death three months earlier of his eldest son, an officer in the Royal Air Force. His innate caution and moderation had deepened with the years, and now this cosmopolitan scientist, this suave high tactician who had been the embodiment of Zionism for thirty years, called for a retreat from the recent impulsiveness. Yes, he said, he favored a Jewish state in Palestine as deeply as anyone; but he counseled against any resolution demanding independence on Zionist terms at this time. Such agitation struck him as immature and premature, and not a little arrogant. Suddenly the whole American movement seemed to have converted to Revisionism. Weizmann begged the conference to reconsider, saying it would be damaging to the British war effort to do anything now that would enrage the Arabs.

To the delegates Weizmann seemed a voice out of the past, uttering unacceptable homilies more appropriate to a State Department man than to the president of the World Zionist Organization and the Jewish Agency. They turned instead to Ben-Gurion, 14 years Weizmann's junior, a short, implausibly vigorous man who exhorted them to reaffirm what he claimed was the original intent of the Balfour Declaration—a "Jewish commonwealth" in Palestine. The little Russian-born labor leader was tanned by the sun of the Holy Land; he had actually lived there, striving to build Zion while Weizmann, based in London, engaged in behind-the-scenes negotiations with the world's leaders. As the head of the Jewish Agency's executive committee, Ben-Gurion had been in daily conflict with the British mandate officials who were enforcing the White Paper, and now he let all his frustrations and zeal and fire pour out.

Indeed he went too far, shocking the delegates by the violence of his attack on the revered Weizmann. Though they thought Ben-Gurion's behavior was unseemly, they accepted his ideas. Guided by Abba Hillel Silver, who was seeking vindication of his own militant policies, they voted overwhelmingly for an eight-point platform that soon became known as the Biltmore Program —a document that committed the American Zionist movement to a Zionism more nationalistic than that of the Zionists in Palestine itself.

The Biltmore Program demanded that the White Paper be rescinded and that the Balfour Declaration be recognized as having promised the Jews a "commonwealth" in Palestine. It called for "a Jewish military force fighting under its own flag and under the high command of the United Nations." And in its concluding plank it made the first outright request for Jewish rule of Palestine that had ever come from any broad-based Zionist group:

"The new world order cannot be established on foundations of peace, justice and equality unless the problem of Jewish homelessness is finally solved. The Conference urges that the gates of

Palestine be opened; that the Jewish Agency be vested with control of immigration into Palestine and with the necessary authority for upbuilding the country, including the development of its unoccupied and uncultivated lands; *and that Palestine be established as a Jewish Commonwealth integrated in the structure of the new democratic world.*" (Emphasis added.)

American Zionism had found its destined role. The timidity of 1939–40 had given way to the dynamic, enthusiastic nationalism of 1942. One by one, the Zionist organizations of the United States gave their approval to the Biltmore Program. Hereafter, the Jews of America would be the most insistent and the most persistent supporters of the drive to create a Jewish state. Leaders of government on all levels from city mayors to the President would be bombarded with Zionist propaganda; endless petitions would circulate and mass meetings would be held; millions of dollars would be contributed to the cause.

Older Zionists would regard the demands of the Americans as naïve and even a little irresponsible—the rash belligerence of latecomers newly inflamed with zeal. Weizmann and others of his generation would mildly object that the clarion calls for Jewish statehood emanating from the United States were unaccompanied by practical plans for implementing an orderly end to the mandate, nor was anything concrete being said about the real and aching problem of how to find room for a million Palestinian Arabs in a Jewish nation.

In Palestine substantial numbers of Jewish settlers were taken aback by the Biltmore stand, which struck them as poorly timed and likely to antagonize the British into forcing some sort of undesirable partition plan upon them. Ben-Gurion, when he returned to Palestine late in 1942, had to work hard to persuade the executive committee of the Jewish Agency to give its formal blessing to the Biltmore Program, which it finally did by a vote of 21 to 4.

Despite the opposition, the new activism became an official part of American Zionist policies. "The day of appeasement is past," declared *New Palestine,* the Z.O.A. organ, a week after the Biltmore Conference. "Zionism must recover the missionary zeal of its early years. To convert non-Zionists and even anti-Zionists to our cause must be the task to which every one of us addresses himself."

4.

Zionism was making deep inroads even into ostensibly non-Zionist regions of the American Jewish community, such as the Reform movement. Reform, as we have seen, had moved away from its original anti-Zionism in the 1930's, through a series of resolutions commending the achievements of Palestine's Jews and encouraging American philanthropy toward Palestine. But Reform had taken great care not to endorse anything that might imply support for Zionism's controversial nationalistic aims.

By 1942, though, Edward L. Israel, a member of the executive committee of the Zionist Organization of America, was also executive secretary of the Union of American Hebrew Congregations, the powerful association of Reform laymen; and another Z.O.A. official, Rabbi James G. Heller, was president of the Central Conference of American Rabbis, the Reform rabbinical body. Other Zionist sympathizers were in lesser positions of power in both groups, and at the 1942 meeting of the CCAR 33 rabbis presented a resolution supporting the formation of a Jewish military force fighting under a Jewish flag. This was clearly a motion in favor of Jewish nationalism, and many of the Reform rabbis were scandalized by it. Yet it passed, after bitter debate, by a vote of 64-38.

The reaction to this was intense among those Jews who had always loathed "Jewish national chauvinism." They felt that they were at the mercy of the Zionists and that the whole American Jewish community was being stampeded into an intolerable conflict of allegiances. Their alarm resulted in the creation of the first and only Jewish organization dedicated to a repudiation of the Zionist idea: the American Council for Judaism.

Dismayed Reform rabbis held a series of strategy-planning sessions culminating in a general conference of non-Zionist rabbis in Atlantic City on June 1, 1942. The invitation to this gathering amounted to a manifesto of the non-Zionist Jews:

"We like-minded men have appeased the Zionists with consent, assent and co-operation from Convention to Convention, until their victories through the years have been so cumulative that they now know no bounds. The day had to come when we must cry 'halt.' The conditioning of American Jewry by a Jewish flag and a Jewish Army and a state in Palestine and a dual citizenship in

America, is more than we can accept. . . . We refuse any longer
to be religious acrobats. We cannot pact with the untenable position in society which nationalism as a creed imposes on us."

There was real anguish in their feelings. Most Gentiles and
younger Jews today assume that the American Jewish community
was always overwhelmingly Zionist in sympathy; the gallantry
and determination of the Israelis have such irresistible emotional
appeal that it is difficult to imagine how any American Jews except
members of some perverse splinter group could have failed to
support the Zionist movement from its earliest days. But when
Israel was still unborn many American Jews looked upon Zionism
as a threat to their status as loyal citizens of the United States.
There was deep feeling in the misgivings expressed by the 1942
manifesto:

"We have been watching with anxiety the secularistic tendencies in American-Jewish life, the absorption of large numbers in
Jewish nationalistic endeavors, the intrusion of the Palestine issue
as an irritating factor in intracommunity relations, the persistent
public expression of extremists who presume to speak for all
American Jewry, *the efforts to cultivate and promote a sense of psychological difference between American Jews and their fellow Americans
which plays into the hands of our enemies, the unremitting efforts of
certain groups to put American Jews behind programs of international
political pressure*, the reduction to secondary importance of the
traditional religious basis of Jewish life. . . . "(Emphasis added.)

At the same time, no Jew could altogether repudiate the Palestinian community, especially in the bleak days of 1942. Therefore,
in the "Statement of Principles by Non-Zionist Rabbis" issued by
the Atlantic City conclave, the Reform leaders declared, "Realizing how dear Palestine is to the Jewish soul, and how important
Palestinian rehabilitation is toward relieving the pressing problems of our distressed people, we stand ready to render unstinted
aid to our brethren in their economic, cultural and spiritual endeavors in that country. But . . . we are unable to subscribe to or
support the political emphasis now paramount in the Zionistic
program. We cannot but believe that Jewish nationalism tends to
confuse our fellow-men about our place and function in society
and also diverts our attention from our historic role to live as a
religious community wherever we may dwell."

The rabbis now turned to the lay non-Zionist community. In

November, 1942, they recruited a Polish-born journalist and public relations consultant, Sidney Wallach, who since 1933 had been
executive director of the American Jewish Committee—itself an
organization that had little sympathy for militant Zionism. Wallach gathered the support of a number of wealthy and influential
Jewish laymen, most of them drawn from the ranks of the American Jewish Committee, for a new and explicitly anti-Zionist organization. Rabbi Morris S. Lazaron of Georgia, a man of
distinguished Sephardic ancestry and emphatic anti-Zionist beliefs, coined its name: the American Council for Judaism.

Early in 1943 the council incorporated itself and obtained tax-
deductible status from the federal government. Its first president
was Lessing J. Rosenwald of Philadelphia, the retired chairman of
the board of Sears, Roebuck and Co. Rosenwald had put his vast
financial resources behind the council's work. However, at Sidney
Wallach's suggestion that it would look better if the council drew
its highest officer from the rabbinate, the post of executive director
was given to a 35-year-old Ohio-born rabbi, Elmer Berger. Berger
would serve as the organization's chief spokesman for the next
quarter of a century. By August 31, 1943, the council was a going
concern. Among its other early sponsors were Arthur Hays Sulzberger, publisher of *The New York Times;* Rabbi Jonah Wise, executive director of the Joint Distribution Committee; Rabbi Julian
Morgenstern, president of Hebrew Union College; and a number
of other Jewish businessmen, educators, and jurists.

The council's main thesis was, "The basis of unity among Jews
is religion. Jews consider themselves nationals of those countries
in which they live, and those lands their homelands." It opposed
an attempt to establish a national Jewish state in Palestine "or
anywhere else," terming it "a philosophy of defeatism, and one
which does not offer a practical solution of the Jewish problem. We
dissent from all those related doctrines that stress the racialism, the
nationalism and the theoretical homelessness of Jews."

It won no wide following in American Jewry at the outset, and
is more than ever a minority group today. The largest membership
it claimed at any time was 15,000—about one-third the size of the
Zionist Organization of America in 1942—and its Zionist foes
insist that its enrollment was really never greater than 8,000. Since
the founding of the State of Israel the position of the American
Council for Judaism has become increasingly awkward, and most

American Jews of the present day, if they have heard of it at all, dismiss it as a fringe group of diehard extremists. But at the time it was organized the council spoke for a large, generally inarticulate segment of the American Jewish population.

Its activities were and are confined chiefly to propaganda: the publication of books, periodicals, and press releases intended to explain the anti-Zionist position, and occasional appearances before governmental groups shaping American foreign policy. The heart of its argument was what it conceived as the menace of dual loyalty; as Rabbi Louis Wolsey, one of its founders, told the House Committee on Foreign Affairs in 1944, creation of a Jewish state would mean that "I am looked upon as a member of a nation whose headquarters is in Palestine, and that I am subject to suspicion, alienism, and perhaps worse." It assailed Zionists as "Palestinians first and Americans second" and asserted that money donated to Zionist charities would be used for "foreign governmental purposes." A triumph of Zionism, it warned, might mean that all American Jews would someday be expected to move to Palestine, or else to "ghettoize" themselves in the United States. The council also expressed fears for the welfare of the Moslem and Christian inhabitants of Palestine. In short, this group—whose officers and membership came mainly from the upper economic levels and had a German-Jewish background—crystallized all the viewpoints that assimilated American Jews had taken on the issue of a homeland in Palestine since the middle of the nineteenth century.

Organized Zionism was severely shaken by the establishment of the council—not because there was any chance that it would win mass support in the American Jewish community, but because it threatened to shatter the image of Jewish unity that was Zionism's chief public relations tool. How could the Zionists successfully exert pressure on the President and Congress if the council caused it to appear that many Jews in America opposed creation of a Jewish state in Palestine? What leverage would Zionism have if it were made to seem the minority movement that it once had been?

A Zionist Organization of America memo circulated to district and regional chairmen in December, 1942, signaled the counterattack: "For the first time in decades the Zionist movement faces formal and organized opposition from within Jewish ranks. A group of Reform Rabbis selected this, the most critical hour in Jewish history, to attack the whole Zionist structure and to challenge the validity of our Zionist program. . . . The enemies of Zionism have declared war upon us. They have set out to undermine and discredit the Zionist ideal before the American Public and Government."

The Zionists fought back by forming a Committee on Unity for Palestine, organized by the distinguished Reform Rabbi Arthur J. Lelyveld. The Committee on Unity flooded the country with propaganda denouncing the council under such titles as, "They Sharpened the Dagger," "A Stab in the Back," "Anti-Zionism, a Fear Psychosis," and "The American Council for Judaism: A Current and Timely Study in Frustration and Aggression." The council's members were accused of wishing to deny their Jewish heritage, of trying to slip into the background of American life, of showing personal cowardice, even of being anti-Semitic.

The psychologist Kurt Lewin—who happened to be an ardent Zionist—became the chief ideologue of the Zionist counterattack. His 1941 book *Resolving Social Conflicts* had dealt in detail with the phenomenon of Jewish anti-Zionism even before there had been an American Council for Judaism, and pertinent sections now were widely quoted and distributed. Lewin introduced the theory of "Jewish self-hatred"—the desire of the Jew who seeks status and security to disown his origins. "Having achieved a relatively satisfactory status among non-Jews," he wrote, "these individuals are chiefly concerned with maintaining the status quo and so try to soft-pedal any action which might arouse the attention of the non-Jew. . . . They are so accustomed to viewing Jewish events with the eyes of the anti-Semite that they are afraid of the accusation of double-loyalty in the case of any outspoken Jewish action. If there is 'danger' of a Jew's being appointed to the Supreme Court, they will not hesitate to warn the President against such an action. . . ."

Through an intensive campaign of this sort, the Zionists were able to isolate and discredit the council, forcing it into a defensive position that ultimately led it to adopt extraordinarily extreme stands. Its zealous efforts to block an American involvement with Palestine often resulted in statements of policy that struck most uncommitted Jews as strangely pro-Arab, and cost it much support. More than ninety Reform rabbis had signed the Atlantic City manifesto that had brought the council into existence; but by September, 1943, a month after its incorporation, more than half of these had withdrawn from active membership, and less than a dozen rabbis remained in the council by 1946. Rabbi Louis Wolsey himself, a founder and officer of the council, resigned in a conspicuous way in 1946 to protest the organization's attempts to thwart the entry of Jewish refugees into Palestine. His disillusioned statement, "Why I Withdrew from the American Council for Judaism," became a keystone in the continuing Zionist attack on the organization.

Nevertheless the council was a major irritant for Zionism in the war years, and seemed for a while to pose a real threat to the movement. Though it has had little influence in recent years, it continues to refine and clarify its case against Zionism, and enjoys the services of several eloquent and sophisticated propagandists. One of them, Michael Selzer, even succeeded in turning the concept of "Jewish self-hatred" against the Zionists themselves. Selzer —writing in 1967—argued that Israel is a secularized state of farmers and soldiers that has deliberately shed the whole of traditional Jewish culture out of repugnance for every aspect of that culture. He quotes the enlightened and assimilated nineteenth-century Jews who had harshly criticized the medievalism and obscurantism of *shtetl* life: "You have justified the insults and the curses of your foes," wrote one. "Jewish life is a dog's life that evokes disgust," said another. The Jews, according to a third, are "not a nation, not a people, not human," and a fourth calls them "gypsies —filthy dogs, inhuman." These Jewish anti-Semites, Selzer asserts, were the spiritual ancestors of the Zionists, for, in the wake of declarations that the Jews of Eastern Europe should "de-Judaize" themselves, "once it was agreed that the Jews should attempt to renounce all that was unique about them, it only required a short additional step to conclude that the 'normalization' of the Jewish people would not be accomplished completely until the Jews, like most other nations in the world, acquired their own territory and sovereign independence."

In the new Zionist commonwealth, long beards and the study of Biblical commentaries gave way to planting orange trees and building highways; and Judaism, Selzer declares, was deliberately rejected by the Zionists for the sake of bowing to the Gentile contempt for the "parasitic" *shtetl* culture. The vigor, the worldliness, the military might of Israel, are all examples of this surrender to "Jewish self-hatred," and must, Selzer insists, be opposed by those who value the age-old traditions of Judaism. The intricacy, at least, of this line of reasoning must be admired. Selzer himself, interestingly, is no aged Orthodox Talmudic scholar, but a Reform Jew born in 1940 and educated at Oxford.

5.

During the war years when organized anti-Zionism was first mounting its attack, the Zionists were exposed to heavy fire from another quarter entirely. The Revisionists—the Zionist extremists who had no patience with tactics of compromise—unexpectedly and disturbingly emerged as a highly visible and powerful force.

The Palestinian calling himself "Peter Bergson," who had taken command of the Revisionist cause after Jabotinsky's death in 1940, had acquired a valuable ally: Ben Hecht, the hard-boiled newspaperman-turned-playwright, a man whose passions were ideally suited to the conspiratorial and inflammatory movement that was Revisionism. Hecht, born in the Russian-Jewish ghetto of New York in 1894, had grown up in Wisconsin, where he was only dimly aware of what it might mean to be a Jew. Not until 1939, in fact, did he feel any identification with his heritage. He wrote, "I had before then been only related to Jews. In that year I became a Jew and looked on the world with Jewish eyes. The German mass murder of the Jews, recently begun, had brought my Jewishness to the surface. I felt no grief or vicarious pain. I felt only a violence toward the German killers. I saw the Germans as murderers with red hands. Their fat necks and round, boneless faces became the visages of beasts."

He was outraged that "a people to whom I belonged, who had produced my mother, father and all the relatives I had loved, was being turned into an exterminator's quarry, and there was no outcry against the deed. No statesmen or journalists spoke out. Art was also silent. Was the Jew so despised that he could be murdered en masse without protest from onlookers, or was humanity so despicable that it could witness the German crime without moral wince?"

Hecht joined an organization called Fight for Freedom—highly unpopular at the time—whose aim was to bring the United States into the war against Germany. He wrote propaganda speeches and a pageant called *Fun to be Free*, which the impresario Billy Rose staged in New York's Madison Square Garden. And he began a column in the liberal New York newspaper *P.M.* in which he attacked American Jewish political, social, and literary figures who "were reluctant to speak out as Jews under attack" against German atrocities but "preferred to conduct themselves as neutral Americans."

The heads of the Hollywood film companies, most of them Jewish, objected to Hecht's articles. He learned from them of a meeting between Joseph Kennedy, the American ambassador to Great Britain, and a group of Jewish studio executives, in which Kennedy "had told them sternly that they must not protest as Jews, and that they must keep their Jewish rage against the Germans out of print. Any Jewish outcries, Kennedy explained, would impede victory over the Germans. It would make the world feel that a 'Jewish War' was going on."

Infuriated, Hecht wrote a column in April, 1941, headed "My Tribe Is Called Israel," in which he declared, "My way of defending myself is to answer as a Jew. . . . My angry critics all write that they are proud of being Americans and of wearing carnations, and that they are sick to death of such efforts as mine to Judaize them and increase generally the Jew-consciousness of the world." A few days later he received a letter from Peter Bergson, about whom he knew nothing, inviting him to meet him in New York. Hecht agreed to see Bergson and another Palestinian at the 21 Club.

Bergson, who was in his thirties and spoke with an English accent "and a voice inclined to squeak under excitement," praised Hecht's outspoken attitude and asked him if he had ever heard of the work of a man named Vladimir Jabotinsky. No, Hecht said. Bergson asked Hecht what his feelings were about Palestine. Hecht replied "that as a Jew I had no interest in Palestine and I felt that its problems confused the issue." His main concern was "the cowardly silence of America's influential Jews toward the massacre of Jews started in Europe." The two Palestinians smiled politely and left after asking permission to call on Hecht at his hotel.

A few days later Bergson and three companions appeared at Hecht's room in the Algonquin Hotel. They informed him that he had been chosen to lead a drive to raise millions of dollars for Palestine. Hecht tried to refuse. "I disliked causes," he wrote. "I disliked public speaking. . . . I had . . . always bolted any conversation about a Jewish homeland. Finally, there was nothing more socially distasteful to me than getting involved in a money-raising campaign."

But his visitors were persuasive, and shortly Hecht found himself affiliated with a group known as the Committee for a Jewish Army of Stateless and Palestinian Jews. It was the old Jewish Legion project—an army under a flag that bore the Star of David. The World Zionist Organization's independent effort to bring such an army into being was stalled in the British bureaucracy. Bergson meant to create the force in the United States with the help of the baffled Hecht, who found the concepts of a Jewish army, a Jewish nation, a Jewish flag, wholly incomprehensible.

They gave him a quick course in Revisionist Zionist theory, which was based on the notion that the British were sworn enemies of the Jews of Palestine and were secretly fomenting anti-Jewish riots and terrorism there. Furthermore, they added, without an independent Jewish state the Jews of all nations were eventually doomed to meet the fate of the Jews of Germany. Hecht had his doubts about that, but he was disturbed by the evidence they produced of British crimes, direct and indirect, against the Palestinian Jews. Bergson also denounced the Zionist regime of the Jewish Agency for its policy of *havlagah,* self-restraint. "They have pledged themselves to turn over to the British authorities any Jew who carries a gun," he said. "The Zionists have been of great help to the British in informing against us."

"Us" meant the Irgun Zvai Leumi, the clandestine terrorist group, some three hundred men and women dedicated to the expulsion of the British from Palestine—by force, if necessary— and the "pacification" of the Arabs. "The Jews could run the Arabs out of Palestine in a week if they wished to," Bergson said. "But they don't wish to. The Jews have promised the British not to disturb the peace by hitting back at any Arab attacks." The only Jewish reprisals, he said, had been the work of the Irgun, which had a policy of killing two Arabs for every murdered Jew.

Hecht was exposed to a detailed history of Jabotinsky's futile crusade and the "treachery" of the organized Zionists, who had collaborated with the British in keeping Jewish immigration into Palestine down. Bergson particularly excoriated Weizmann, whom he bitterly called "the King of the Jews," adding, "The respect which the Jews of the world feel for him is only equaled by the harm he has done them. Even the Jews of Poland who are now being exterminated still respect the man who persuaded them to stay in their homes and be killed—instead of going to Palestine to live." Such men as Weizmann were not exactly traitors, said one of the Palestinians; merely "respectable people who are afraid of offending anybody—even their enemies."

"I don't see much difference between traitors and cowards," Hecht said. His conversion was complete.

The Irgun, he discovered, was represented in the United States by six men and a girl; this was to be the nucleus of the future Jewish Legion. Hecht was asked to launch a publicity campaign in the press, favoring the creation of a Jewish army, and then to carry the fight to Congress and the White House. He was caught by Bergson's vision of Jewish soldiers liberating North Africa, moving on to Palestine to open its ports to refugees, taking command of the Holy Land away from the British. A little to his own surprise, Hecht found himself early in 1942 canvassing Hollywood for support for the Irgun.

Plans for a mass meeting were drawn. A thousand telegrams of invitation went out over Hecht's signature. As the day of the rally neared, Hecht sought backing from twenty of the most powerful Jewish movie executives, but they all were horrified by the scheme. A few Hollywood figures, Jewish and Gentile, did get aboard: David O. Selznick, Burgess Meredith, Hedda Hopper. Hecht's name was enough to get hundreds of movie people to the rally. Senator Claude Pepper of Florida had been persuaded to speak. Also on the program was Colonel John H. Patterson, who had commanded the Jewish troops assembled by Jabotinsky and Trumpeldor in the closing days of World War I. Many members of the audience walked out in shock when they realized the nature of the cause Hecht had asked them to support. But those that remained pledged donations of $130,000.

Only $9,000 of this ever actually was contributed, but it was enough to carry the campaign to Washington. Bergson went to the capital with another of his converts, the industrialist and advertising executive Alfred Strelsin, and together they managed to make the Revisionists look less like an underground band of guerrillas and more like a broad-based Zionist movement, at least as respectable in standing as the Zionist Organization of America.

Zionism was politically fashionable in 1942. Bergson and Strelsin signed up as supporters a group of dignitaries who were eager to do the right thing for the downtrodden Jews, and who had no idea at all of the fierce ideological infighting within the Zionist camp. Thus Chief Justice Harlan Stone responded, "It's a wonderful idea! . . . I wish your program for a Jewish army in Palestine all necessary success." A young Navy Department official named Adlai Stevenson was won over, and introduced Bergson to Secretary of the Navy Knox, who expressed his support also. Under Secretary of War Patterson spent two hours with Bergson and offered him a group of military experts to help plan the new army. Some fifteen hundred public figures—including a third of the Senate—signed a Revisionist petition in December, 1942. Congressman Andrew Somers introduced a resolution in the House calling for the formation of the Jewish army Bergson advocated.

The State Department was perturbed; on June 2, 1942, Wallace Murray of the Division of Near Eastern Affairs told President Roosevelt that "the agitation for the formation of a Jewish army in Palestine is having alarming effects in the Near and Middle East." In India, he said, where "the only worthwhile fighting material . . . is drawn from the large minority group of 80 million Moslems," hostility to the Allied cause was growing, "due to the fear that their fellow Moslems in Palestine will be overridden. As the result of continuous agitation by the Zionists of their ambitions in Palestine, the Axis propagandists have been broadcasting, with good effect from their viewpoint, that the United States intends to turn Palestine over to the Jews despite the opposition of the Moslem majority in that country." Murray asked once again for an unequivocal American declaration opposing the political aims of Zionism. The President shrewdly declined, replying on July 7, "The more I think of it, the more I feel that we should say nothing about the Near East or Palestine or the Arabs at this time. If we pat either group on the back, we automatically stir up trouble at a critical moment."

Zionists of a more conventional stripe than Bergson's were perturbed, too. When Bergson tried to get Felix Frankfurter, who had replaced his mentor Brandeis on the Supreme Court, to sign his petition, Frankfurter crisply replied, "It would be improper for a Supreme Court Justice to express an opinion on this issue." He had an opinion, though, and it was the same as that held by Rabbi

Stephen Wise, who led a delegation of Zionist Organization of America members to Washington to protest Bergson's maneuvers. Hecht was astounded to see Wise enlist the aid of Representative Sol Bloom of New York in putting an end to the War Department's tentative agreement to aid Bergson. Wise explained that the proposed Jewish army seemed imprudent and objectionable to the majority of American Jews, and it ended there. Hecht was surprised that a Jew, and a Zionist at that, would kill the project that other Jews had worked so hard to nurture.

"It's not a matter of what the Zionists believe," one of the Irgun men explained. "They fought the project not because they are against it, but because they are against us. Stephen Wise will not tolerate any other Jewish organization working for Palestine and stealing honors and publicity from him."

The true explanation was somewhat more complex. Certainly Wise disliked the Revisionists and was unwilling to stand by while they lobbied unhindered in Washington. But he objected to them for ideological reasons, not out of a hunger for glory. Wise spoke for the moderate, conciliatory wing of Zionism—unlike his far more fiery colleague, Abba Hillel Silver—and he regarded the Irgun as a dangerous group of belligerents who, through their terrorist activities, might wreck the whole Zionist cause by damaging its moral stature. They were little more than hoodlums in his eyes, and the fact that they were dedicated hoodlums, pledged to the same sacred cause he served, did not matter. Perhaps there would be a Jewish army someday, Wise thought, but when it came into existence it must not be a Revisionist army.

6.

Amid all these obstacles and rivalries the regular Zionist movement proceeded with its own political campaign to create a Jewish state. As its main propaganda weapons it had two focal points for moral outrage: the British policy toward "illegal" immigration to Palestine, and the growing awareness that the Nazis intended not merely to oppress the Jews of Europe but to exterminate them.

The illegal-immigration theme was easy to exploit, because it involved the seemingly heartless behavior of America's closest ally. Since 1934 Zionists had been engaged in thwarting British immigration limits by smuggling Jews into Palestine by sea. This practice was begun by the Revisionists but soon adopted, in a sub rosa way, by the quasi-governmental Jewish Agency. It involved assembling a large number of refugees at some Mediterranean port and loading them aboard some old freighter that had been purchased in the maritime black market. The ship then headed for Haifa, and, if all went well, five hundred or more Jews could be slipped ashore there at night. The British were on guard for these dismal, overloaded "coffin ships," and intercepted some; but even that was a victory of sorts for Zionism, since the turning away of hapless refugees by the British at the very gate to the Holy Land greatly aided the Zionists in their propaganda efforts.

There were tragic moments. In 1940 an unseaworthy ship called the *Salvador*, laden with refugees from Bulgaria, sought to land at Istanbul for refueling. Turkish harbor officials refused to let the ship in, because none of its passengers carried valid visas to any country; the *Salvador* turned toward Palestine instead, struck a rock in the Sea of Marmara before it had gone any great distance, and was wrecked. Of its 350 passengers, 231 were drowned. The Turks picked up the rest, but sent 59 of them back to Nazi-ruled Bulgaria; the remaining 70, for some reason, were allowed to go on to Palestine.

On November 11, 1940, two forlorn Haifa-bound refugee ships, the *Pacific* and the *Milos*, were intercepted by the British navy on the coast of Palestine and brought into Haifa. The 1,700 refugees they bore were not permitted to land, and the mandate officials announced that they would be deported to Mauritius, a British colony in the Indian Ocean, aboard a merchant vessel named *La Patria*. When the Jewish Agency protested, the mandate issued a statement of policy that declared, "His Majesty's Government are not lacking in sympathy for refugees from territories under German control. But they are responsible for the administration of Palestine and are bound to see to it that the laws of the country are not openly flouted." Since "a revival of illegal Jewish immigration at the present juncture" would be "likely to affect the local situation most adversely, and to prove a serious menace to British interests in the Middle East," the refugees could not be allowed to enter.

The refugees were placed aboard the *Patria*. While this was going on a third ship carrying another 300 refugees, the *Atlantic*, was brought into Haifa. The British intended to transfer the new-comers to the *Patria* as well. But on the morning of November 25, before it could be done, there was an explosion aboard the *Patria*, and in less than 90 minutes she sank. Two hundred and forty refugees and 12 policemen perished in the explosion or from drowning. The Jewish Agency announced that the passengers, despondent at being sent away, had scuttled the ship in an attempt at mass suicide. Later investigation showed that the explosion was actually the work of Haganah, working under Jewish Agency instructions to disable the ship so that its cargo of refugees could not be taken from Haifa. The dynamite crew miscalculated, blowing up not just the engines but the ship itself, which made the mass-suicide story necessary. (As a result of Weizmann's intervention with the British Foreign Secretary, Lord Halifax, the *Patria* survivors were allowed to remain in Palestine.)

The most widely publicized sinking was that of the *Struma*, in February, 1942. This was a 180-ton craft intended to carry about 100 passengers; she held 769 refugees when she set out from the Rumanian port of Constanza on December 16, 1941, heading for Haifa. Developing leaks and engine troubles, the *Struma* tried to put in for repairs at Istanbul, but again the Turks refused to allow anyone to land who did not have a legitimate entry certificate for Palestine. No one aboard did, and the British refused to issue any, insisting that that year's quota of Jews under the White Paper restrictions was already full. For ten weeks the *Struma* remained at anchor, unfit to go to sea, while the Jewish Agency attempted to obtain certificates for her people; they were fed meanwhile by means of a $10,000 grant from the (non-Zionist) Joint Distribution Committee, which also pleaded with the British to relax its regulations. The British announced, "The High Commissioner fears that admission of these Jews into Palestine would provoke tension in our relations with the Arabs and most particularly with the Arabs of Iraq," where British troops had been employed a few months before to crush a pro-Axis coup d'etat.

The Turks lost patience and on February 24 towed the *Struma* to sea; her passengers unveiled a banner reading, "SAVE US!" and her captain, knowing the ship could never make it to Palestine, tried to return to Rumania. Six miles out the *Struma* sank. It is not known if she struck a mine, capsized in a storm, or was hit by a torpedo. Of her 769 passengers, 2 survived. After the disaster word arrived that the British had belatedly agreed to grant Palestine certificates to the 70 children on board.

Zionists made political capital out of these tragedies. They portrayed the British mandatory officials as brutal, callous men carrying out inhuman laws in an inhuman way. In truth they were simply plodding, unimaginative bureaucrats who privately felt unhappy about sending all those Jews away; but rules were rules, and if one began to admit even a few boatloads of refugees, there would shortly be half a million sufferers waiting to come ashore at Haifa, and the Arabs would be up in arms from Cairo to Baghdad.

But in the United States, where the delicacies of the British position were hard to appreciate, the cruelty of the White Paper became obvious to a great many Gentile citizens. They had no clear idea of what Zionism was all about, but they did know that the Jews of Europe were in a bad way; and if some of these unhappy victims were able to get all the way to Palestine, why couldn't they be let in? Why were the British so eager to please the Arabs anyway, when the Arabs seemed so fond of Hitler? The *Struma* sinking in particular created a widespread impression in the United States that President Roosevelt really ought to say a word or two to Prime Minister Churchill about the Palestine situation.

A far more terrifying means of arousing consciences became available to the Zionists later in 1942. News trickled out of Europe that the Germans had formulated plans for a "final solution to the Jewish problem"—the mass extermination of Europe's entire Jewish population. These Jews had already been stripped of all civil rights and property and had been herded into concentration camps, where many of then—perhaps as many as a million—had perished by 1941 from starvation, disease, or torture. A number of Nazi officers had indulged in wholesale executions as private ventures. But not until the middle of the war did the formal Nazi policy of genocide emerge, with its fantastic and nightmarish apparatus of slaughter, the death camps, the gas chambers, the giant crematoria. It was in 1942 and early 1943 that the contracts for this machinery of murder were being let and the plans were drawn for the "processing" of five million victims.

The full devilish artistry of the "final solution" did not become apparent to the outside world until after the war. Many Americans, including some high governmental officials, had gone on doubting that crimes of such magnitude had ever been committed even by the Nazis until they saw the terrible newsreel sequences showing the colossal boneheaps and the elaborate execution facilities at such places as Auschwitz and Dachau. But such proof should not have been necessary. The details had been available long before.

In August, 1942, Gerhart Riegner of the Geneva office of the World Jewish Congress—an international organization with close ties to Zionism—learned from a German industrialist who was visiting Switzerland that Hitler had ordered the obliteration of European Jewry in specially designed gas chambers. Riegner already had received authoritative reports of the slaughter of hundreds of thousands of Polish Jews in mobile gas vans, and the shooting of vast numbers of Russian Jews by special Nazi murder units that had followed the Nazi invasion troops into Russia after Hitler had broken his nonaggression pact with Stalin. But the scope and ingenuity of this new plan went far beyond these early experiments in extermination.

Riegner collected as much documentation as he could and reported what he knew to Howard Elting, Jr., the American vice-consul in Geneva, instructing him to notify the United States government. Riegner also asked Elting to pass the information to Rabbi Stephen Wise, using diplomatic channels to insure privacy and the safe arrival of the message. As a precaution Riegner gave the same information to the British consulate, again requesting that it be forwarded to Rabbi Wise.

According to State Department documents now available for consultation at the National Archives, members of the State Department's Division of European Affairs decided to suppress Riegner's story because of the "fantastic nature of the allegations," and chose not to inform Rabbi Wise "in view of the apparently unsubstantiated nature of the information." However, the British Foreign Office had no such qualms, and routinely relayed to Wise the duplicate message that Riegner had sent via London. It reached him on August 28, and Wise at once got in touch with Undersecretary of State Sumner Welles, who had concurred in the decision to take no action on the Riegner cable. Welles begged Wise not to make a public statement until the facts could be verified, and Wise agreed.

There followed several months of procrastination, during which the State Department gathered a good deal of verification, from reliable sources in neutral countries, from Polish and Czech escapees in Switzerland, from anti-Nazi German officers who smug-

gled out secret documents describing the factories for processing
Jewish corpses into soap, glue, and oils. Yet the men of State,
skeptical of the motives of those who revealed these monstrosities,
found themselves unable to believe any of the stories—even when
Hitler himself, on September 30, 1942, made public announcement of his intentions. Not until November did Welles inform the
by now exasperated Wise that the horrifying reports were indeed
correct. Wise was released from his vow of silence, and on November 25 the American public finally learned of the German plans
for the most monstrous crime in modern history.

The Jews of the world named December 2 as a day of mourning
for those who had already perished—believed to be at least two
million by then. Surely now the gates of Palestine would be
thrown wide to let in as many Jews as could still be snatched from
destruction; perhaps even the United States (which had accepted
36,220 quota immigrants in 1941 and 14,597 in 1942, mostly from
Great Britain and Scandinavia) might find itself willing to take in
some of the doomed. Hundreds of thousands of European Jews,
possibly several million, were still outside Hitler's immediate
grasp. Many had fled to overcrowded neutral countries, and many
more were under the control of German puppets in places like
Rumania and Bulgaria, where the local authorities were willing to
let their Jews be evacuated in return for bribes. Now, surely,
President Roosevelt would issue an executive order creating a
haven for these Jews in the United States. Now, maybe, he would
also suggest to his friend Winston that the time had come to
rescind the White Paper. But the President was silent.

The first attempt to spur the President into action came from
Rabbi Stephen S. Wise, who had emerged as the spokesman for
American Zionism and, indeed, for American Jewry, in the early
1940's. Wise, born in Budapest in 1894, brought to the United
States in infancy, educated at the City College of New York and
Columbia University, had been a major force in leading Reform
Jews toward Zionism. Articulate, compassionate, a careful planner
who had no love for militant extremism, a resonant orator, he put
forth his views from the pulpit of New York's Free Synagogue—
which he had founded in 1907—and through the medium of the
innumerable Jewish and Zionist organizations of which he was an
officer.

On December 2, the day of mourning, Rabbi Wise sent FDR
a letter headed "Dear Boss," reminding the President "that the

most overwhelming disaster of Jewish history has befallen Jews in the form of the Hitler massacres" and expressing the hope "that you will speak a word which may bring solace and hope to millions of Jews." Wise asked permission to lead a delegation to the White House made up of representatives of B'nai B'rith, the American Jewish Committee, and the American Jewish Congress. (The last was a group that had been organized in 1917 as a Zionist rival to the American Jewish Committee, then strongly non-Zionist. The policies of the congress, which Rabbi Wise had headed since 1925, were essentially indistinguishable from those of the Zionist Organization of America.) "It would be gravely misunderstood," Wise warned, "if . . . you did not make it possible to receive our delegation and to utter what I am sure will be your heartening and consoling reply."

Roosevelt received the delegation on December 8. Wise presented a memorandum calling on Roosevelt to "raise your voice —in behalf of the Jews of Europe. We ask you once again to warn the Nazis that they will be held to strict accountability for their crimes." But the somber document, which contained a stark indictment of the Nazi plans, had been worded in a manner designed not to offend any Jewish faction, and so it did not mention Palestine or the White Paper at all, and said nothing even about immigration quotas. When the memorandum appealed to the President to "Speak the word! Institute the action!" it was asking for nothing more concrete than the creation of an American commission "to receive and examine all evidence of Nazi barbarities against civilian populations, and to submit that evidence to the bar of public opinion and to the conscience of the world." It was a pointless request, since the United States and Great Britain had announced joint sponsorship of a War Crimes Commission two months earlier. Jewish activists, including those of the Revisionist persuasion and a good many of Wise's own colleagues, felt that Wise had missed an opportunity; his impressive-sounding memorandum had begged the real questions and amounted to nothing. He was accused of having wished to avoid putting his friend the President on the spot.

But soon an outcry against the Nazi crimes arose on many sides. Yiddish newspapers published editions bordered in black; New York's Mayor Fiorello La Guardia called for city-wide prayers; half a million Jewish workers in the New York area staged a ten-minute work stoppage by way of protest. There were public meetings and demonstrations. Petitions were circulated. Jewish organizations issued statements of policy. Louis Lipsky thundered, "Greater trials the Jewish people have never suffered in the long history of martyrdom. The story of today is incredible; but the incredible has become real. . . . The homelessness of the Jewish people must come to an end. . . . We must assemble all our strength and force the Gates of Justice; standing there as a united people until justice is done. Or we shall be doomed for generations to an ignoble existence and ultimate disappearance."

Thousands of letters and telegrams poured into Washington, demanding an end to American immigration quotas and visa restrictions, an end to the White Paper, an Allied appeal to the Axis for the release of the remaining Jews. The Joint Distribution Committee offered to supply funds for the support of refugees in neutral countries until some permanent shelter could be found for them. And the Joint asked the government to use its influence to persuade the neutrals (particularly Spain, Portugal, Switzerland, Sweden, and Ireland) to accept more refugees. These proposals were routed to the State Department, which promised to "study" them.

Four Jewish luminaries of show business, Ben Hecht, Moss Hart, Kurt Weill, and Billy Rose, undertook to produce a pageant called *We Will Never Die* as a "Memorial to the Two Million Jewish Dead of Europe," intended to keep public opinion aroused. Hecht's Irgun friends had formed an Emergency Committee to Save the Jewish People of Europe, which offered to sponsor the pageant, but Hecht felt that the propaganda effort would be more successful if it had a broader base in the Jewish community. Thereupon he rented a hotel suite and summoned officers from 33 Jewish organizations in the New York area. Hecht read excerpts from his text, and Weill played the accompaniments on a piano. Then Hecht asked his guests for support—no money, no work, no ticket-selling, merely the names of their organizations on the publicity releases.

Quickly he learned why Jewish leaders were forever calling for "unity." He tells in his autobiography, *A Child of the Century,* how "the representative of the American Jewish Congress stood up, pointed a finger and cried out, 'As an organization, we refuse to work with Morris Goldfarb! Never will the American Jewish Congress join up with anything in which the *Arbeiterring* [an

association of Jewish labor socialists] is involved!' A man, possibly
Morris Goldfarb, was on his feet yelling back, 'And we will never
work with the American Jewish Congress in a thousand years.'*
Other voices arose. English and Yiddish outcries filled the room.
Within five minutes a free-for-all, bitter as a Kentucky feud, was
in full swing. The thirty-two Jewish organizations were denouncing each other as Socialists, as Fascists, as Christians, as undesira-
bles of every stripe. The door opened and the thirty-third
representative—he who had taken the wrong subway—entered.
He understood instantly what was going on and began yelling
without taking his hat off."

Hecht and his friends put the pageant on with the aid of no
organization but Peter Bergson's. In February, 1943, Hecht began
auditions, and found enough volunteers to make up ten companies. "Each evening our rehearsal hall filled up with thousands of
frostbitten applicants," he wrote. "They were like strange soldiers
come from the moon to help the Jews." He signed up stagehands,
public relations men, a platoon of rabbis and cantors, and dozens
of famous actors and singers.

In the midst of the rehearsals Rabbi Wise called, to say that he
disapproved of Hecht's script and wished that the pageant be
canceled. Hecht refused. A short while later Billy Rose called
Governor Thomas E. Dewey of New York, asking him to declare
the day of the pageant an official day of mourning for New York
State in memory of the murdered Jews. Dewey agreed. The next
day Rabbi Wise journeyed to Albany to tell the governor that the
Jewish voters of New York were likely to turn against him if he
failed to break with the "dangerous and irresponsible racketeers
who are bringing terrible disgrace on our already harassed people." Dewey, who had presidential aspirations for 1944, spent two
days trying to fathom the Byzantine intricacies of the Jewish
community, and then decided to declare the day of mourning
anyway.

We Will Never Die gave two performances in a single night.
Each show had a capacity audience of more than twenty thousand,
and another twenty thousand in the streets outside listened over
loudspeakers. Subsequently it toured the nation; and, Hecht
claimed, "The news and pictures of our pageant in the press were

*Leaders of the American Jewish Congress, it should be noted, regard this story as
apocryphal.

the first American newspaper reports on the Jewish massacre in Europe."

That was an exaggeration. But it is true that relatively little was getting into print about the Nazi crimes, and in early 1943 the Jewish organizations intensified the pressure of their publicity campaign. The Zionist groups, naturally Palestine-oriented, hammered at the White Paper; the other organizations begged havens for the remaining Jews anywhere. Suggestions for saving them arose daily and were just as frequently shot down, as when Secretary of the Interior Harold Ickes, writing to Roosevelt in response to Rabbi Wise's suggestion that refugees be settled in the Virgin Islands for the duration of the war, observed that "in view of the depressed economic condition of the islands, and the difficulties of supply arising out of the shipping shortage," the idea was impractical. So many other ideas were deemed impractical that the not very militant Wise caused the American Jewish Congress to sponsor its own Madison Square Garden rally on March 1, 1943, at which 75,000 people struggled for the 21,000 seats. Chaim Weizmann, the featured speaker, delivered a harsh indictment of Allied policies:

"The world can no longer plead that the ghastly facts are unknown and unconfirmed. At this moment expressions of sympathy without accompanying attempts to launch acts of rescue became a hollow mockery in the ears of the dying. The democracies have a clear duty before them. Let them negotiate with Germany through the neutral countries concerning the possible release of the Jews in the occupied countries. Let havens be designated in the vast territories of the United Nations which will give sanctuary to those fleeing from imminent murder. Let the gates of Palestine be opened. . . . The Jewish community of Palestine will welcome with joy and thanksgiving all delivered from Nazi hands."

On March 4, Wise submitted a summary of the rally's requests to Roosevelt, saying, "I beg you, dear Mr. President, as the recognized leader of the forces of democracy and humanity, to initiate the action which . . . may yet save that people from utter extinction."

The President replied nineteen days later in the usual courteous but abstract way, acknowledging the rally proposals and declaring, "The whole history of our country in extending refuge and offering succor to suffering peoples is substantial testimony to the spirit of humanity prevailing among our citizens. In that tradition this Government has moved and continues to move, so far as the burden of war permits, to help the victims of the Nazi doctrines of racial, religious, and political oppression."

The cries of the dying were being drowned out by polite and noble statements—unaccompanied by action.

The one concrete action the United States did take in 1943 was to stage an Anglo-American conference in Bermuda to survey the refugee situation. That situation was growing ever more critical. Myron Taylor, President Roosevelt's representative at the Vatican —who had tried in vain to persuade Pope Pius XII to condemn the Nazi crimes against civilians—cabled the State Department on March 26, 1943, that Bulgarian and Rumanian Jews were now vanishing into the death camps. "European Jewry disappearing while no single organized rescue measure yet taken," Taylor declared, thinking that his words would be heeded when the agenda was drawn for the following month's Bermuda Conference.

However, the State Department had also heard from the British government, which had earnestly requested that the troublesome subject of Palestine be kept off the agenda, as it had been at the abortive Evian Conference of 1938. Indeed, the British wished that the conferees could avoid talking about Jews altogether. Thus the announced intent of the meeting was to study methods of dealing with the problem of "political refugees . . . not confined to persons of any particular race or creed."

The American delegates to the conference—Representative Sol Bloom of New York, Senator Scott Lucas of Illinois, and Dr. Harold Willis Dodds, president of Princeton University—were sent to Bermuda under orders not to raise religious issues and not to mention either Palestine or the American immigration quotas. Jewish organizations were denied the right to attend the conference as observers. Representative Bloom, an Orthodox Jew who was chairman of the House Foreign Affairs Committee, underlined that by announcing that the conference would ignore any proposal put forth by Jewish "pressure groups."

Though he was a Zionist of sorts, Bloom had long been a cause of discomfort to many Jews, who found his behavior embarrassingly coarse. He had aroused more amusement than enmity, but now he was the target of severe criticism. *Zionews,* a Revisionist organ, declared, "As so often happened, fate chose a *Jew* to be the spokesman of the concerted effort to liquidate Zionism and thus condemn Europe's Jewry to annihilation."

The Bermuda Conference, foredoomed, was grimly farcical. Both the British and American delegations issued statements even before it began, deploring the fate of the refugees but remarking that not much could be done for them. Dr. Dodds of Princeton declared, "The problem is too great for solution by the two governments here represented." Palestine was not mentioned as a possible shelter for the refugees, though Angola and several other exotic spots in the tropics were briefly discussed. All of these were dismissed because of the scarcity of Allied shipping space. Palestine was accessible by land from neutral Turkey via Syria, and several thousand refugees had actually taken that route to safety in the last several years.

The British chief delegate, Richard Kidston Law, turned down the idea of a direct appeal to the Germans, and expressed opposition to exchanging prisoners of war for refugees. Law feared that "dumping" large numbers of refugees into Allied countries would allow a great many Axis sympathizers or even disguised spies to come in. The State Department representative at the meeting, Robert Borden Reams, killed several other possible means of refugee aid with similar arguments. When Sol Bloom unexpectedly blurted that it might be helpful if the United States and Great Britain were to take in a large number of refugees themselves, he was cut off by Dr. Dodds with a reminder that the conference had no power to shape such policies. Later, Bloom even brought up the forbidden topic of Palestine, and was silenced again.

The Bermuda Conference produced just one tangible recommendation: that 21,000 refugees in Spain, two-thirds of them French citizens who had fled the German occupation, be transferred to North Africa. All other projects were rejected, to the relief of Secretary of State Hull, who wrote President Roosevelt early in May that "the unknown cost of moving an undetermined number of persons from an undisclosed place to an unknown destination, a scheme advocated by certain pressure groups, is, of course, out of the question."

The World Jewish Congress branded the Bermuda Conference as "a monument of moral callousness and inertia." On the floor of the House of Representatives, Representative Emanuel Celler of New York—a Jew whose Zionist feelings had awakened only after the Nazi horror had begun—declared on May 3: "The delegates to the Bermuda Conference say: 'Victory is the solution.' The trouble is that by that time there will be no refugees. The number of exterminated Jews have now reached the two-million mark; when victory comes, the refugee problem will be resolved. Victory is not the only solution—what about Palestine? Is the White Paper so sacrosanct that it cannot be lifted?"

7.

Nothing apparently was going to be done about the White Paper—which, under the terms of its five-year limit, would in effect completely ban Jewish immigration into Palestine after March 31, 1944. (The existing annual quota of 10,000 Jews would then be replaced by a quota to be set by the Palestinian Arabs, whose attitude was easy to predict.) President Roosevelt, who claimed to regard the White Paper as unjust, continued to avoid raising the subject with Prime Minister Churchill, whose distaste for the White Paper was also a matter of public record, but who had not made any formal effort to have it rescinded. Both men, though they probably were sincere in their disapproval of the document, were evidently too deeply preoccupied with the larger events of the war to want to become entangled in the complexities of Jewish nationalism. Not only would lifting the White Paper restrictions cause disturbances among the still theoretically neutral Arabs, but it would create an insurrection among the pro-Arab middle-echelon men of the Foreign Office and the State Department. From the point of view of the Allied leaders in 1943, it was simplest to stay out of the entire business and merely issue soothing, reassuring statements whenever the angry rabbis came calling.

The angry rabbis grew angrier, for Jews were dying and nothing was being done to save them. They had heard all about the delicate political considerations that made it necessary to leave Europe's Jews to Hitler's mercies, but they were becoming convinced now that the entire United States government, except for the President himself, was involved in a conspiracy to allow Hitler to eradicate their people. If they had been able to see some of the governmental correspondence that was released from secrecy after the war, they would surely have cried out to the heavens.

On April 26, 1943, for example, Admiral William D. Leahy of the Joint Chiefs-of-Staff protested the inclusion of some 5,000 Jews in the group of 21,000 refugees that the Bermuda Conference had recommended moving from Spain to North Africa. "The influx of a considerable group of Jewish refugees to North Africa," he told the President, "might cause such resentment on the part of the Arab population, as to necessitate military action to maintain order." It would also place "added and unwarranted administrative responsibility on the Supreme Commander in North Africa."

About the same time, Sweden, which had already taken in 35,000 Jews, offered to request Germany to release 20,000 more, whom the Swedes would house until the end of the war. The Swedish government asked if Great Britain and the United States would share the cost of food and medicine for the new refugees —all children—and would allow these supplies to get through the naval blockade surrounding Europe. The Foreign Office approved the scheme, and referred it to the State Department on May 19, 1943. The State Department "studied" the request until October 11, when, after repeated British prodding for a decision, it replied that limiting the rescue program to Jewish children might antagonize the Germans. The plan was changed to include some non-Jewish Norwegian children, and finally was resubmitted to Sweden in January, 1944. By then the political circumstances had changed; the Swedes no longer felt able to ask Germany for release of refugees; the children perished.

On February 12, 1943, a *New York Times* correspondent reported that the fascist puppet government of Rumania was interested in releasing 70,000 Jews, including 10,000 children under the age of 12, upon payment of $600,000 to cover evacuation expenses. The refugees would be shipped to Palestine aboard Rumanian ships which would display the insignia of the Vatican to insure safe passage. In making this offer, the Rumanian government hoped to obtain gentle treatment for itself in the increasingly likely event that the Allies would be victorious in Europe. But there was little time to waste, for the Nazis would soon be coming into Rumania in full force and then, the Rumanians said, the Jews would undoubtedly be slaughtered.

In March, confirmation of the Rumanian offer came from several reliable sources. The State Department took no action until May 25, when—after queries by Rabbi Wise, bitter newspaper ads sponsored by Hecht and the Revisionists, and pressures from various other Jewish quarters—a cable was sent to the United States minister in Switzerland, requesting him to obtain more details. (Since the Arabs had shown some agitation over the prospect of having 70,000 Rumanian Jews sent to Palestine, the State Department also sent a confidential message to King Ibn Saud of Saudi Arabia on May 26, promising him that nothing would be done to change the status quo in Palestine "without full consultation with both Arabs and Jews." This note was not made public until 1947.)

From Switzerland came precise instructions on how the rescue was to be carried out—beginning with the deposit of the $600,000 ransom in a special Swiss bank account. Jewish organizations in the United States immediately pledged to supply the funds. All that was needed now was a license for the transfer of the money from the United States to Switzerland; under wartime regulations such transfers had to be approved both by the Treasury Department and the State Department. In July, the Treasury Department granted its approval. State did nothing.

On July 22 Rabbi Wise visited Roosevelt and mentioned the matter. The President asked the State Department what was going on. Only after incensed Treasury Department officials did some pushing did State decide, on September 28, that it could approve the fund transfer. Assistant Secretary of State Breckinridge Long received a memo from Robert Borden Reams of his department protesting the decision, asserting that it would "incense the British" and that "we are granting to a special group of enemy aliens relief measures which we have in the past denied to Allied peoples." Long consoled him by writing, "As a matter of probability, these transactions will not be completed. There is no available, presently known method for the people for whom the funds are intended to leave the jurisdiction of the enemy."

And so it came to pass. The British, who had been remarkably slow in entering the discussion, belatedly discovered that all these Rumanian Jews were intended for Palestine, and raised the matter of the White Paper. On December 15, 1943, the British Ministry of Economic Warfare expressed concern "with the difficulties of disposing of any considerable number of Jews should they be rescued." The Palestine quota was filled—forever, if the White

Paper stayed in effect. No European nation, Allied or neutral, had room for 70,000 new refugees. The United States, which had admitted 23,725 immigrants in 1943 (4,705 of them Jewish refugees), was not likely to take them in. Where, then, was the haven? There was no haven. When 1943 ended only 48,000 of the 70,000 remained alive, and they were still in a Rumanian concentration camp, waiting for the executioners to arrive.

The American Jewish leadership had no clear idea of the extent of the obstructionism practiced within the State Department in these and a number of other instances. But it was clear enough that greater militance—and a more convincing show of unity—were required to break through a wall of governmental indifference. The old ideological conflicts between the Zionists and the non-Zionists had to be resolved in some way, particularly in the matter of reopening Palestine to Jews, for that was now in the most literal sense a matter of life or death.

The unity movement had its origin at a meeting in a New York hotel room in June, 1942. Chaim Weizmann, Louis Lipsky, Stephen Wise, and several other veteran leaders of the Zionist movement were there. So, too, was Henry Monsky, the president of B'nai B'rith and a natural focus for any drive toward unity, since he was the avowedly Zionist head of a large non-Zionist organization. To Weizmann, Monsky seemed an ideal intermediary between the old-line Zionists on one hand and the elitist, non-Zionist American Jewish Committee, which was gravely alarmed by the openly nationalistic talk of most Zionists during the war years. Weizmann suggested that Monsky sponsor a new ecumenical Jewish organization that would mobilize the entire American Jewish community on behalf of a Jewish Palestine.

The split in Jewish ranks deepened in the six months that followed. The latter half of 1942 saw the revolt of the anti-Zionist Reform rabbis that led to the formation of the American Council for Judaism; and there was a sharp turn away from cooperation with Zionism within the American Jewish Committee. The committee, since the days of Louis Marshall, had maintained a tense and wary affiliation with the Zionists, taking care to stress that its interest in Palestine was purely cultural, spiritual, and philanthropic, not at all political or nationalistic.

Typical of the committee's outlook was that of Joseph M. Proskauer, a distinguished Alabama-born attorney who had practiced law in New York since 1899, and who had been a judge of the New York State Supreme Court from 1923 to 1930. Judge Proskauer, a man of powerful connections in the legal, political, and academic worlds, regarded a Jewish state as a "Jewish catastrophe" and had declared that the committee's cooperation with the Zionists was a "tragic error." When Proskauer was mentioned prominently as a candidate for the presidency of the committee in 1942, Zionists moved to head off an expected rupture by issuing a number of reassuring statements, such as this one on April 16 from David Ben-Gurion, then visiting New York:

"No Zionist questions that American Jews owe their allegiance to America on exactly the same basis as all other Americans. Whatever view they hold on the nature of the ties which bind together Jews of different countries, it in no way impairs the allegiance of American Jews to America."

But a month later Ben-Gurion helped put the explicitly nationalistic Biltmore Program across at the "Extraordinary Zionist Conference" in New York. Reassuring statements were useless now. In the summer of 1942 Proskauer and his supporters threatened to secede from the American Jewish Committee and enter the group that was to become the American Council for Judaism unless the committee at once took an anti-Zionist position. The committee's leaders capitulated, and late in 1942 it was arranged that Proskauer would be chosen as the committee's new president at its annual meeting on January 31, 1943.

Anticipating trouble, Henry Monsky hurriedly set in motion plans for the gathering of all Jewish organizations that Weizmann had requested him to call. Without taking time to consult the other leaders of B'nai B'rith, Monsky sent out invitations on January 6, 1943, to a meeting in Pittsburgh, sponsored by B'nai B'rith, designed to bring about "some agreement on the part of the American Jewish community . . . with respect to the postwar status of Jews and the upbuilding of a Jewish Palestine."

The American Jewish Committee and one other group ignored the invitation; but 78 delegates representing organizations with about 1,000,000 members were present on January 23 and 24. Robert P. Goldman, a member of the non-Zionist Union of American Hebrew Congregations, set the tone for the gathering when he said, "We all want Palestine. There is not a person in this country, I think, who does not want Palestine for Jews, and it is just a question of defining terms. . . . If we can sit down together and change a word here and a word there, and compromise on this statement and that statement, as statesmen must do, we will come to a common conclusion."

The delegates voted to call an American Jewish Assembly for the summer of 1943—a representative body of 500 members, 125 named by the national Jewish organizations and 375 elected through popular vote of local or regional Jewish communities. Only once before had such an assembly been called: in 1917, when at the behest of such Zionist leaders as Brandeis, Wise, Lipsky, Mack, and Frankfurter, the original American Jewish Congress had been organized, consisting of 300 delegates chosen by 335,000 voters. (It met only to deal with the effects of the war on the Jewish world, and was not then intended as a permanent body. The mass-membership American Jewish Congress that exists today, though it grew out of the original congress, is a different kind of group altogether.)

Proskauer, as expected, assumed the presidency of the American Jewish Committee a week after the Pittsburgh meeting. (He had also been offered the presidency of the American Council for Judaism, but declined it so he would be free to head the more influential committee.) When he took office, surprisingly, he told the pro-Zionist members of the committee that he wished "to hold out the hand of friendship and fellowship to the most ardent Zionist."

That same day—January 31, 1943—the committee adopted a statement of views on Palestine that was rather less hostile to Zionism that most of Proskauer's prior declarations. It noted, "We affirm our deep sympathy with and our desire to cooperate with those Jews who wish to settle in Palestine," while commenting that "settlement in Palestine, although an important factor, cannot alone furnish and should not be expected to furnish the solution of the problem of post-war Jewish rehabilitation." It endorsed a policy "of friendship and cooperation between Jews and Arabs in Palestine," and hoped that the country would become, "within a reasonable period of years, a self-governing commonwealth." Nothing was said about its becoming a *Jewish* commonwealth; and the statement stressed that "there can be no political identification of Jews outside of Palestine with whatever government may there be instituted."

Proskauer continued his efforts toward unity by agreeing, somewhat hesitantly, to let the committee take part in Monsky's proposed American Jewish Assembly. On behalf of the committee, Proskauer did propose several face-saving provisos, though: that the meeting be renamed the American Jewish Conference, to avoid allowing it to seem "a quasi-political 'Assembly' that would consider itself empowered to speak for and act in this country for Jews no matter to what extent they might hold varying beliefs," and so forth. A conference, unlike an assembly, could not take binding votes. It could merely discuss the issues and try to reach a consensus.

After much negotiation, the Zionists agreed to the change in name, and Proskauer agreed to send a committee delegation to the conference. The Zionist press did not hide its glee at having "trapped" the mighty men of the committee into attending a Zionist-dominated gathering by so simple a ruse as a change of name. Quite openly the Zionist organs predicted that the committee would find itself unable to protest when the conference did, after all, call for a binding vote on the subject of a Jewish state in Palestine.

Final preparations for the conference began at the end of April, 1943. After much wrangling, 65 national organizations were selected to choose the 125 organizational delegates—wholly philanthropic groups such as the Joint Distribution Committee and the Hebrew Immigrant Aid Society (HIAS) were excluded—and a mechanism for local election of the 375 community delegates was devised. Each community was allowed 1 delegate per 10,000 Jewish inhabitants, but an elaborate cumulative-voting scheme of proportional representation was imposed to insure a Zionist majority.

Sophisticated political maneuvering had been a basic part of the atmosphere of Zionism from the very beginning; but now the stakes were higher than usual, for the American Jewish Conference had been summoned into existence as a way to concentrate the power of the entire American Jewish community against the White Paper. Its aim was to *seem* democratic while actually representing only the position of America's Zionist Jews; successfully carried off, the stacking of the conference might lead to an appearance of power that could have great impact on the Roosevelt administration, and at last induce the President to take steps to have Jews admitted again to Palestine. Only the American Jewish community now was capable of bringing the necessary political pressures to bear. Weizmann, old and ill, no longer headed a real constituency, since most of the European members of the World Zionist Organization were in Nazi concentration camps, and many had perished. At a time like this, the American Zionists did not feel they could afford the luxury of an unrigged election.

Last-minute adjustments resulted in the selection of 379 local delegates and 123 organizational delegates. A panel of 22,500 electors, representing more than 2,000,000 American Jews from 8,486 localities, chose the local delegates from among 968 candidates. Of the winners, 240, or 63 percent, were members of the Zionist Organization of America. More than 100 others were affiliated with Mizrachi, the Orthodox Zionist group, or Poale Zion, the Labor Zionists. The organizational delegates, since they were not all drawn from Zionist groups, included a few who were not in sympathy with the goal of the conference, but Zionists would be in an overwhelming majority and there was no doubt that their wishes would prevail. *New Palestine*, a Zionist magazine, remarked that "for appearance's sake" it might have been better to elect a few more non-Zionists.

The loading of the conference with Zionists was apparent even in Washington, where word had penetrated that the Jews were about to stage some sort of convention that would be potent propaganda for the Zionist cause. Some State Department officials conferred with their British counterparts on the advisability of issuing a public statement calling on Jews to avoid discussion of "extreme" Zionist goals during the war as a matter of patriotic duty. Surreptitious efforts were made to get the conference postponed or to have its demands diluted. They were futile. On August 29, 1943, the American Jewish Conference's first session convened in New York's Waldorf-Astoria Hotel with 501 of the 502 elected delegates present and its outcome predetermined.

For greater maneuverability a steering committee had grouped the delegates in nine blocs. Each bloc would select speakers and committee members. When all overlappings were accounted for, the General Zionists—the Z.O.A., Hadassah, and the Order of the Sons of Zion—had the biggest bloc, 116 delegates. The next largest was designated the American Jewish Congress bloc, made up of 111 delegates of 10 organizations with Zionist orientations. The B'nai B'rith bloc had 63 members; that of Mizrachi and other

Orthodox groups, 61 members; the Labor Zionist bloc, 49 members; Reform Judaism, 21 members; Conservative Judaism, 19 members; a different Labor Zionist bloc unwilling to be lumped with the other, 16 members. Three delegates refused to join any bloc at all; and the American Jewish Committee, surrounded and outnumbered, found its handful of delegates included in a "Non-Partisan" bloc of 42 members, along with the Jewish War Veterans and the National Council of Jewish Women.

Henry Monsky opened the meeting by congratulating the conference for consisting of "leadership democratically chosen from the ranks of American Israel," and declared, "Our people's salvation depends upon a united front. With magnificent fortitude have the Jews in the stricken lands manifested once again the will of Israel to survive. Their fight is our fight. Their struggle is our struggle. Their ultimate fate may in large measure determine our fate. The doctrine of isolation in matters of Jewish interest is fatal to our cause. We are an integral group, call it what you will— religious or national—it matters not, for we do have a common inheritance, a common history, a common religion, common traditions and a common cause, and we must strive for a common basis of action."

Joseph Proskauer, speaking for the American Jewish Committee, pointed out that the "unity of Jewish action" that the conference was seeking should not compel anyone to sacrifice his principles. Compromise was necessary; areas of disagreement should be skirted and areas of agreement discussed. One area of agreement, he said, was recognition of "the superb achievement made by our people in Palestine," an achievement in which "Jews throughout the world . . . regardless of their ideologies, have been glad and proud to help. . . . I do not believe we would ever have a difference in adopting a formula along the lines . . . of keeping the gates of Palestine open."

The note of cautious compromise had been sounded a short while before Proskauer spoke when Rabbi Stephen Wise, in urging the conference to denounce the White Paper, avoided any mention of the strongly nationalistic Biltmore Program of the previous May.

There was, in fact, a quiet agreement among the moderate Zionist leaders that they were not going to push the issue of political Zionism too far at this session of the conference. Instead they intended to concentrate on the relatively noncontroversial topic of reopening Palestine to Jewish refugees.

In line with this strategy of not raising the question of national independence for a Jewish Palestine, no speaking time had been allotted to the nationalistic firebrand Abba Hillel Silver. When the conference held its "Palestine Night," only the moderates would speak, and they would promote the compromise by which the Zionists would put aside their demand for a Jewish common-wealth—at least for the present—in return for non-Zionist backing for unlimited Jewish immigration into Palestine. But Silver wrecked this plan through a parliamentary maneuver that brought him to the rostrum as a speaker on behalf of the American Jewish Congress, Wise's own group, with which Silver had never been affiliated. Swiftly he transformed the conference from a compro-mising body to a militant body by crying out that the only solution for the plight of the Jews "is to normalize the political status of the Jewish people by giving it a national basis in its national and historic home."

Silver retraced the history of the Balfour Declaration, interpret-ing it not as "an immigrant aid scheme" but as a promise of Jewish sovereignty. "Why," he demanded, "has there arisen among us today this mortal fear of the term 'Jewish Commonwealth,' which both British and American statesmen took in their stride, as it were, and which our own fellow-Jews . . . endorsed a quarter of a century ago? Why are anti-Zionists, or non-Zionists or neutrals —why are they determined to excise that phrase and, I suspect in some instances at least, the hopes?"

The Zionist goal of Jewish statehood was no mere matter of ideology, Silver said. It was essential for the "salvation of a people fighting for its very life." He rejected compromise and scorned mere rescue and relief schemes:

"We cannot truly rescue the Jews of Europe unless we have free immigration into Palestine. We cannot have free immigration into Palestine unless our political rights are recognized there. Our political rights cannot be recognized there unless our historic con-nection with the country is acknowledged and our right to rebuild our national home is reaffirmed. These are inseparable links in the chain. The whole chain breaks if one of the links is missing."

While the Zionist architects of the intended compromise with the non-Zionists looked on with stony faces, Silver declared, "A strange thing has occurred here. We are asked not to relinquish our convictions but at the same time not to express them. . . . Is this Jewish statesmanship? Is this Jewish vision, courage, faith? Or, are we to declare in this great assembly . . . that we stand by those who have given their tears and their blood and their sweat to build for them and for us and for the future generations, at long last after the weary centuries, a home, a national home, a Jewish Commonwealth, where the spirit of our people can finally be at rest, as well as the body of many of our persecuted people?"

It was magnificent rhetoric. Silver had voiced beliefs which nearly everyone in the hall shared, but which their leaders had told them to suppress. Now the demand for Jewish nationhood was in the open, and there was no masking it with bland words. Cheers and shouts of praise arose; the delegates began to sing "Hatikvah," the Zionist anthem; many wept; minutes passed before the demonstration subsided. Silver was in full command of the conference from that point on. Presiding over the 67-member Committee on Palestine, he worked to shape the conference's resolution on Palestine to fit his own beliefs.

Three draft resolutions were submitted. One, sponsored by pro-Zionist blocs representing 337 of the 501 delegates, called bluntly for "re-creation of the Jewish Commonwealth." The Reform bloc called merely for "all Jews . . . to unite their efforts toward the establishment of . . . a Jewish homeland in Palestine." Three delegates without bloc affiliation submitted an even more limited proposal.

In the committee debate that followed, Rabbi James G. Heller of the Reform rabbinical organization noted that the American and British governments were considering issuing a statement that would "place for the duration of the war, as a matter of patriotic duty, a quietus on the discussion of Zionism in this country," and therefore "extreme demands" by the Zionists would seem "inadvisable" at the present. He called for a committee to "formulate further statements to be brought as recommendations to further meetings." Other moderate Zionist leaders took the same approach. It seemed to such leaders that they stood a better chance of getting what they wanted if they adopted a program calculated to stir no excitement among the Arabs or the British.

Proskauer, naturally, supported the moderates and termed the practice of making huge demands in the hope of getting partial fulfillment "a very dangerous doctrine." He said, "All the people hostile to Jewry are just waiting for the urging of these maximum demands in order to cement the opposition to the legitimate building up of Palestine itself." Remarking that he had "spoken to Washington" that very afternoon, he said that "sources which he could not disclose" had warned him that "it would be a tragedy to put forth this maximal demand." If the "maximal" position were adopted, Proskauer cautioned, he would have to give serious consideration to the possibility that the American Jewish Committee would "exercise our right to dissent and withdraw" from the conference. He concluded, "Nobody expects a Jewish State now; nobody wants it now. . . . There are those who are not identified with Zionists, but who want to help in the building of Palestine, yet they believe that it is a grievous error to ask for statehood now."

M. J. Slonim, a delegate from St. Louis, responded with an argument that showed shrewd insight into the pattern that postwar international politics was going to take. All the other peoples of the world, he said, were "asking for the maximum" in their postwar peace plans. Why should Jews alone be different and ask for the minimum? In the new world order that was coming, power would flow to those who made the most aggressive demands; the meek would be shouldered aside.

The most extreme views came from the Religious National Orthodox bloc, which subscribed to the political theories of the Revisionists, though having little else in common with the belligerent and secularized followers of Jabotinsky. Gedaliah Bublick, the leader of this Orthodox bloc, regarded the Jewish commonwealth resolution as a mere minimum. What he really wanted was "a Jewish State on both sides of the Jordan, and a Jewish army led by a Jewish general."

Silver, who presented himself as a mediator, beat back objections by the moderates and kept the fierce quasi-Revisionists of Bublick's bloc under control. At the fifth committee meeting he offered a new draft resolution on Palestine embodying ideas drawn from all three suggested texts. It called for the fulfillment of the Balfour Declaration, and reconstitution of Palestine as the Jewish Commonwealth. The White Paper must be abrogated. Palestine must be opened to Jewish immigration.

On the night of August 31, Proskauer and two other members

of the American Jewish Committee met privately with Rabbis Wise and Silver and Nahum Goldmann of the Jewish Agency in an attempt to prevent this resolution from coming to a vote. Silver refused to yield, and Goldmann observed that "in view of the tremendous pro-Zionist emotion generated throughout the country we would be torn limb from limb if we were now to defer action on the Palestine resolution."

The next day Silver's resolution was offered to the full American Jewish Conference. Monsky seconded it, and Rabbi Wise called for a vote. Four delegates, three of them members of the American Jewish Committee, were opposed. The remaining 497 delegates excitedly cast affirmative votes. Another frantic demonstration followed. When the meeting was calm again, Proskauer rose and sadly said, "We regretfully dissent from concurrence with these resolutions," though he expressed the hope that some cooperation still was possible between the American Jewish Committee and the Zionists.

Silver had triumphed. In its issue of September 24, 1943, *New Palestine* jubilantly declared, "The Zionist position is now the position of American Jewry. The Conference has served to crystallize Jewish opinion in our own country. This marks the end of long discussion and debate. . . . The time has come for action."

8.

The new unity was more symbolic than real. Rabbi Silver's soaring rhetoric had worked the overnight conversion of many influential American Jews to political Zionism. But many others remained opposed. Predictably, the American Council for Judaism took the position that the vote at the conference meant merely that 497 individual Jews had announced their support for the Biltmore Program. Such traditionally neutral organizations as B'nai B'rith and the Central Conference of American Rabbis declined to pass supporting resolutions of their own in favor of a Jewish state, although they did condemn the White Paper. The lay Reform group, the Union of American Hebrew Congregations, was presented at its meeting of October 4, 1943, with a resolution drawn up by anti-Zionist rabbis insisting that the union refuse to take part in further sessions of the American Jewish Conference. The quarrel was patched over by Silver.

The American Jewish Committee also felt injured by the conference's vote, and on October 24 announced its decision to withdraw from the conference, which brought immediate tirades from the Zionist press. One Yiddish newspaper called it "an act of national sabotage in the most critical moment of Jewish history."

But no one had ever expected Jewish unanimity on a question that carried such an emotional charge. The very multiplicity of Jewish organizations, the confusing welter of congresses and committees and conferences and councils, was proof of the Jewish love for disputation. What the American Jewish Conference of the summer of 1943 had accomplished was a *relative* unity of organized American Jewry. The Biltmore Program of 1942 had been the work of Zionists exclusively; the 1943 meeting had drawn in a host of neutral organizations, whose leaders had recorded their votes in favor of a Jewish state in Palestine, and it was no longer necessary to defer to the sensitivities of those few non-Zionists who had voted the other way. The American Jewish Committee, like the American Council for Judaism, could now be ignored.

On September 18, 1943, a delegation of American Jewish Conference leaders called on Secretary of State Cordell Hull to tell him that the Palestine resolution represented the unmistakable will of the American Jewish community. Less than a week later, Rabbi Israel Goldstein, the new president of the Zionist Organization of America, declared that American Zionism's task thenceforward was to "win the wholehearted approval of the *American Government* and people for the Zionist program with respect to Palestine, which now has become the program of the whole of American Jewry represented through the democratically elected American Jewish Conference."

Goldstein, along with Rabbi Wise and Henry Monsky, were named cochairmen of the new Interim Committee of the American Jewish Conference. The 52 members of this committee were given the responsibility of mobilizing American public opinion in favor of the Zionist aims. Actual day-by-day propaganda activity was the province of the American Zionist Emergency Council (AZEC), now headed by Abba Hillel Silver. AZEC, originally the political action wing of the four major American Zionist organizations, had been an effective pressure group under the leadership of Emanuel Neumann in 1941 and 1942; but Neumann had resigned at the end of 1942 in despair over "recurrent factional and personal differences" and "vacillation in policy and in action." The steamroller of the American Jewish Conference had flattened factional differences and ended vacillations of policy; a few days after the adjournment of the conference a new AZEC, greatly expanded to make it more representative of the Zionist movement, was in operation. Officially, Silver and Wise were cochairmen. This gave the Zionists the best of both worlds, since Wise, a New Deal Democrat, had access to President Roosevelt that was denied to the Republican Silver. But it was Silver, the high-riding militant, who dictated AZEC's tactics, often over the objections of the gentler, more conciliatory Rabbi Wise.

AZEC's budget of more than $500,000 a year was underwritten by the Jewish National Fund and the Palestine Foundation Fund, which in theory were supposed to use their money for, respectively, the purchase of land in Palestine and the economic development of Palestine. Contributions donated for use in Palestine thus were diverted to an organization devoted to spreading Zionist political propaganda in the United States, which caused particular distress to the non-Zionists and anti-Zionists.

What made the situation all the more thorny was the fact that since 1939 a single fund-raising body, the United Jewish Appeal, had handled charitable collections both for Zionist and non-Zionist causes. This had been tried in the early 1930's without much success, but the plan of a combined collection was revived in 1939 after the horrors of the *Kristallnacht* pogrom. Moved by Rabbi Silver's words, "You can no longer separate the problems of Palestine and Europe," the non-Zionist Joint Distribution Committee had joined with the United Palestine Appeal to create the United Jewish Appeal, which thereafter would allocate a stated portion of its yearly intake to Zionist projects. In 1943, 34.6 percent of the UJA's receipts were awarded to the Zionists. The use of a portion of this money to pay the expenses of AZEC meant that non-Zionist donors were being asked to pick up part of the check for a propaganda campaign of which they disapproved. But there was nothing they could do about it except grumble; the merging of the fund-raising bodies was inextricably permanent by then.

Under Silver, AZEC opened a full-time lobbying office in Washington and established 14 professionally staffed committees to deal with such things as labor relations, contact with the Christian clergy, news dissemination, postwar planning, and community liaison. Local Jewish leaders were drawn into the work through the formation of more than 400 district Zionist Emergency Committees of 8 to 12 persons. These little groups were composed not just of Zionist activists, but of members of B'nai B'rith, synagogue brotherhoods and sisterhoods, congregational leaders, and so forth. The idea was to make involvement in Zionist propaganda as widespread as possible.

From AZEC headquarters in Washington flowed a stream of directives to these local committees. They were told to make contact with their congressmen, either through visits to the capital or, more desirably, by inviting the legislators to "small functions" when they were visiting their home districts. According to a confidential AZEC memorandum, the purpose was "to produce in this country what already exists in the British House of Commons, a group of national legislators who are familiar with the details of the Palestine situation and can discuss it intelligently."

The local Zionists were also advised "to cultivate the local political leader, who is often a close friend of the Congressman or Senator. That person might be talked to and persuaded to throw the weight of his political influence and power behind our cause. If the officeholder happens to be a member of one party, the other political party should not be neglected. If your present Congressman is a Republican, or vice versa, he may be opposed in the next election by a Democrat. The latter prospective candidate should be cultivated."

Silver always stressed the importance to Zionism of a nonpartisan approach, and not merely because he himself supported the party then in national disfavor. Although the Democrats were considered to be more deeply concerned with the rights of ethnic minorities, it would, he felt, be disastrous to court them exclusively while ignoring the Republicans. The fact that Jews in the United States now voted overwhelmingly Democratic was a powerful political weapon for the Zionists, since it gave them not only leverage over the Democrats—who were eager to retain all those votes—but over the Republicans, who were just as eager to win them away. So long as Zionism remained utterly nonpartisan, it could play one political party off against the other to maximum advantage. And 1944 was a presidential election year.

The national office of AZEC distributed instructions to the local committees in holding mass meetings and demonstrations, in creating news, in obtaining favorable editorials and interviews. It told how to stage "educational" seminars, how to get Zionist speakers into public halls, how to arouse the interest and support of the Gentile majority. In addition AZEC set up "vigilance committees" to monitor anti-Zionist activities on the part of Arab or British agents in the United States (as well as anti-Zionist Jews), and purchased radio time to further the propaganda effort.

Above all AZEC welded the Jewish community, by way of the local emergency committees, into an instrument for registering mass opinion on subjects of vital concern to Zionism. AZEC instructions to local committeemen declared:

"On certain occasions it will become necessary to produce a dramatic demonstration of . . . American public opinion. That means deluging public officials, Congressmen and Senators, with letters and telegrams. *You must* be prepared at quick notice . . . to go into action to organize *letter-writing and telegram campaigns*. . . . Those who have the responsibility for formulating American foreign policy must be made to feel that the Jews of America are aroused on the question of the White Paper; that they want it abrogated; and that this is the sentiment of millions of Jews throughout the United States."

The White Paper was the prime target of this newly created apparatus for political agitation. Despite periodic protests dating back to 1939, the Roosevelt administration had carefully avoided raising the subject of the White Paper with the British, out of respect for the British feeling that a shift in the official Palestine policy would lead to a troublesome Arab uprising, drawing men and materiel away from the war effort. Instead, Roosevelt sought to find some alternate haven for the remaining refugees—a haven which, for political reasons now difficult to comprehend, had to lie outside the United States. As late as September 27, 1943, he told a member of his staff that he "was still working on the possibility of at least a certain number of [refugees] being settled in the trans-Andean portion of Colombia in South America."

A few days later Abba Hillel Silver began turning on the pressure, pledging that AZEC would "mobilize all the energies of American Jewry during the next seven months to prevent the greatest miscarriage of Justice in our days and the most brazen repudiation of the sanctity of convenants." On September 30 there was a mass Zionist protest meeting in New York. On October 2 and 3, eleven senators—five Republicans, six Democrats—

issued statements calling for an end to the White Paper's immigration restrictions. Several also endorsed the idea of a Jewish state. On October 3, AZEC formally called upon the United States government to secure abrogation of the White Paper, which, it said, had been illegal, since it altered the status of Palestine without the consent of the United States, required under the treaty of 1924. On October 6, 500 rabbis marched on the Capitol in a group and, amid much emotional display, presented a petition of Zionist demands to Vice-President Henry A. Wallace. On October 24 there were mass meetings in some 30 cities. On November 2, the anniversary of the Balfour Declaration, 119 rallies were held across the nation; more than 15,000 were turned away from the one in New York's Carnegie Hall, which was filled to capacity.

These stratagems bore the mark of Rabbi Silver. Rabbi Wise, whom he had displaced as the leader of American Zionism, had relied on his friendship with Roosevelt, and hoped that he could influence American policy through frequent visits to the White House by small delegations of distinguished Zionists. Silver—as he declared early in 1944 in a letter to Chaim Weizmann—was "definitely not of the opinion that quiet diplomacy will alone bring about the desired results or that we should pin our hopes entirely upon the good will of one or two people . . . our good friends here, upon whom we have been relying so much [the reference is to Roosevelt] will not move on their own accord, inspired by the moral righteousness of our cause. Nor will the intercession of a few powerful people achieve the desired results. Our friends might be inspired to move and take some definite action as a result of the pressure of five million Jews in a critical election year." Later in 1944, Silver emphasized his policy: "We must build upon the broad and secure base of public sentiment, the approval of public opinion which in the final analysis determines the attitude and action of governments in democratic society." Quoting one of the Psalms, he said, " *'Put not your trust in princes. . . .'* Put not the future of our movement in the sole keeping of individuals, however friendly, however great . . . talk to the whole of America."

From Portsmouth, New Hampshire, came 11,000 letters opposing the White Paper. From Detroit, Michigan, came 22,000 postal cards and 19,000 letters. Leominster, Massachusetts, sent 1,000 telegrams. South Bend, Indiana, forwarded a petition with 60,000 signatures.* The AZEC-led campaign was burying Washington under tons of paper.

The outcry was heard, and an election-conscious Congress responded. On January 27, 1944, Representatives James A. Wright, Democrat of Pennsylvania, and Ranult Compton, Republican of Connecticut, introduced a pair of identical resolutions in the House that restated the text of the 1922 congressional resolution supporting "the establishment in Palestine of a national home for the Jewish people," and added:

Whereas the ruthless persecution of the Jewish people in Europe has clearly demonstrated the need for a Jewish homeland as a haven for the large numbers who have become homeless as a result of this persecution: therefore be it

Resolved, That the United States shall use its good offices and take appropriate measures to the end that the doors of Palestine shall be opened for free entry of Jews into that country, and that there shall be full opportunity for colonization, so that the Jewish people may ultimately reconstitute Palestine as a free and democratic Jewish commonwealth.

On February 1 the same resolution was introduced in the Senate, jointly sponsored by Senators Robert F. Wagner, Democrat of New York, and Robert A. Taft, Republican of Ohio.

In the House the Wright-Compton resolutions fell into the domain of Representative Sol Bloom, the head of the Committee on Foreign Affairs. He hoped to win House approval for the resolutions without the formality of a public hearing; but the American Council for Judaism set up a clamor for open discussion of the measures, and Bloom was forced to call a hearing for February 8. Zionists, non-Zionists, and anti-Zionists all hurried to Washington to make their views known.

Bloom opened the hearing by distributing to members of his committee a pamphlet he had prepared, which he said would give them "full information with reference to the legislation . . . under consideration." It consisted of a 100-page summary of the Zionist position, concluding with a 19-page attack on the White Paper released by the Jewish Agency; there was no discussion of pos-

---

*There were not, of course, 60,000 Jews in South Bend, which then had a total population of about 100,000. The AZEC campaign was reaching far beyond the Jewish community.

sible Arab objections to creation of a Jewish homeland in Palestine.

This initial display of the committee chairman's position was followed by a stream of Zionist testimony from Abba Hillel Silver, Louis Lipsky, Rabbi James G. Heller, and others. Emanuel Neumann, seeking to reassure committee members disturbed by the one-sidedness of Chairman Bloom's presentation, insisted that "the Arab citizens of the Jewish Commonwealth will be as favorably situated as are the French-speaking citizens of the British Dominion of Canada. . . . All shall be eligible to public office, even the highest." Neumann emphasized that Zionism did not intend any evacuation of the Arabs then living in Palestine, but rather would attain a Jewish majority there through mass immigration. And—allaying fears of a different sort—he declared that "no one suggests an American expeditionary force to maintain order in Palestine."

Opposition to the Wright-Compton resolutions came almost entirely from the anti-Zionist Jews of the American Council for Judaism. Although many Gentiles had testified in favor of the resolution, only three non-Jews spoke against it: two naturalized American citizens of Arab descent, and one native American with some background in Near Eastern affairs. One of these Arab spokesmen, Professor Philip K. Hitti of Princeton University, went straight to America's most vulnerable point when he remarked that Arabs could not see "why the Jewish problem, which is not of their making, should be solved at their expense. . . . They fail to understand .why American legislators, so solicitous for the welfare of the European Jews, should not lift the bars of immigration and admit Jewish refugees [to the United States]."

Much more severe criticisms came from the Jewish anti-Zionists. Rabbi Louis Wolsey of Philadelphia raised the specter of dual allegiance, claiming that with a Jewish state in Palestine, the loyalty of American Jews to the United States would be forever suspect. He felt that nothing stood in the way of returning the Jews of Europe to their countries of origin after the war. Lessing J. Rosenwald, the president of the American Council for Judaism, insisted that the idea of a Jewish nation was identical with "the concept of a racial state—the Hitlerian concept," and therefore was "repugnant to the civilized world." Louis Lipsky found it advisable to point out to the House Committee on Foreign Affairs that the American Council for Judaism spoke for a mere 2,500

Jews, while the American Jewish Conference was the voice of 2,500,000 Jews who desired a Jewish Palestine.

As the hearings proceeded, the preponderance of pro-Zionist testimony and the obvious sympathy of a majority of committee members made it appear certain that the committee would report the resolutions favorably to the House, where approval seemed sure. There was anguish in the Arab world, and the distress was nearly as great in some branches of the British and American governments. The war was not going particularly well for the Allies in early 1944, and trouble with the Arabs was less desirable than ever just then—particularly since critical negotiations over an oil pipeline across Saudi Arabia were taking place. The State Department quietly suggested to certain members of the House of Representatives that the phrase "Jewish commonwealth" be deleted from the resolutions; but on February 27 Representative Wright made this attempt at dilution public and said he intended to fight it.

Protests over the resolution continued to come from the Arab capitals. On March 4, the grand mufti delivered a broadcast in which he cried, "Arabs! Rise as one and fight for your sacred rights. Kill the Jews wherever you find them. This pleases God, history, and religion. This saves your honor. God is with you." An American monitoring service picked up the broadcast and relayed its text to Washington.

That same day, at the Senate hearings on the parallel Wagner-Taft resolution, Army Chief of Staff George C. Marshall said that he would not be responsible for the military complications in the Moslem world if the pro-Zionist resolutions passed in Congress, and Secretary of State Cordell Hull told the senators that conflict in the Arab world, endangering American troops and requiring the diversion of soldiers from the main war fronts, would not only be troublesome in itself but might disrupt the negotiations with Ibn Saud over the oil pipeline, and could even lead "other special interests" to press for the introduction of similar resolutions dealing with controversial territorial issues in areas such as Poland and Italy.

Hull suggested to President Roosevelt that he should be prepared to intervene if the dangerous resolutions seemed to be nearing passage. A similar warning came from Speaker of the House Sam Rayburn, who wrote to the President on March 7 that "it will really lead to danger, I believe, if we are not careful." Rayburn added, though, "I think we have it in hand in the House." Roosevelt replied on March 9 that he was "glad" things were under control in Rayburn's domain. "The volume of protests," he said, "merely illustrated what happens if delicate international situations get into party politics."

However, the President himself had certain domestic political commitments that year. On March 3, Senator Robert Wagner— a Catholic, but also a candidate for re-election in the state that had the greatest concentration of Jews in the country and in the world —mentioned the size of the AZEC letter-writing campaign against the White Paper to Roosevelt, telling him "how the Jews of America felt about the situation." The President replied, "You know, Bob, where I stand on Palestine; my heart is still in the right place." Whereupon Wagner suggested, "Why don't you call leaders of American Zionism, and tell them that?" And so on March 9—the same day that he was expressing his relief to Sam Rayburn that the Wright-Compton resolutions were unlikely to pass—Roosevelt allowed Rabbis Wise and Silver to call on him.

The Zionist leaders told him bluntly that he would have to make a statement about Palestine. Otherwise, they said, it would undermine their own position; the Jews of America knew that they were going to the White House, and would not forgive them if they came away empty-handed.

"What shall I say?" Roosevelt asked.

Wise and Silver had brought a draft statement. The President made a few changes in it out of deference to Churchill's political position, and it was released to the newspapers that afternoon. It was cast in the form of a statement not by Roosevelt but by the two rabbis:

> The President has authorized us to say that the American Government has never given its approval to the White Paper of 1939. The President expressed his conviction that when future decisions are reached, full justice will be done to those who seek a Jewish National Home, for which our Government and the American people have always had the deepest sympathy, today more than ever in view of the tragic plight of hundreds of thousands of homeless Jewish refugees.

Zionists hailed the statement as a great victory for their cause. Never before, they pointed out, had the President given even this much public assurance of his support for a Jewish Palestine.

But a close analysis of the text shows that no Zionist rejoicing was called for. Roosevelt, the consummate political craftsman, had edited the Wise-Silver draft in a way that robbed it of all meaning. He was willing to say that the United States had "never given its approval to the White Paper," which was undeniably true; but the corollary that the President was thereby *disapproving* of the White Paper existed only in the minds of Zionists, not in the text. The clause about "full justice will be done to those who seek a Jewish National Home" was superbly ambiguous. And the President's "deepest sympathy" for "the tragic plight of . . . homeless Jewish refugees" was something that he had been regularly expressing since 1938, without, however, taking any real step to alleviate that plight.

On March 17—nine days after this Zionist "victory"—the Wright-Compton resolutions met a quick death. Secretary of War Henry L. Stimson had sent a note to Representative Bloom, explaining that "it is the considered judgment of the War Department that without reference to the merits of these resolutions, further action on them at this time would be prejudicial to the successful prosecution of the war."

By a vote of 11-3, Bloom's committee decided that "action upon the resolutions at this time would be unwise." At the same time, similar War Department intervention killed the Wagner-Taft resolution in the Senate. The baffled Zionists were left with their resounding statement of March 9, but without the expected congressional underpinning for it.

The Arabs, however, still needed to be pacified. On March 11, Ambassador Alexander E. Kirk in Cairo told the State Department that the Egyptian Prime Minister had asked him in great consternation if President Roosevelt had really authorized the Wise-Silver statement of March 9. On March 14, Imam Yahya of Yemen, acting through the Egyptian legation in Washington, had expressed "his and his people's dissatisfaction and disapproval of the Resolution of the American House of Representatives purporting to create a National Home for the Jews in Palestine." The imam reaffirmed "the traditional and firm friendship of the Arabs for the Anglo-Saxon allies, and, therefore, deems it unfair and unjust to usurp the long-established rights of the Arabs in the Holy Places." Other protests came in from Emir Abdullah of Transjordan and from the governments of Iraq, Lebanon, Syria, and Saudi Arabia.

To each of these the State Department gave a careful (and secret) reply, pointing out the ambiguities in the March 9 statement and assuring the Arabs that no matter what the President had *seemed* to say, he had not really pledged anything to the Zionists at all. Typical of these confidential messages was the one for Abdullah, dated March 23, which said, "In so far as Palestine is concerned, I am glad to convey to you the assurance that in the view of the Government of the United States no decision altering the basic situation of Palestine should be reached without full consultation with both Arabs and Jews."

Since these documents would have had explosive political effects in the United States, they were, of course, not made public either by senders or recipients, and they remained unknown until after President Roosevelt's death. Only by accident were they revealed during the course of a postwar Anglo-American investigation of the Palestine situation. Sir John Singleton, a British member of the postwar investigating committee, commented tellingly after seeing the secret State Department file, "It appears that Great Britain is not the only power who promises the same thing to two different groups."

9.

AZEC's first experiment in political agitation thus ended disastrously, with a misleading pseudo-pledge from the White House, an abortive congressional resolution, and secret State Department promises to the Arabs that the status quo would be maintained in Palestine. It later developed that during this Zionist pressure campaign the Roosevelt administration had—for the first and apparently only time—actually made a pale attempt to get the British to lift the White Paper restrictions. A "memorandum of conversation" between Secretary of State Hull and Lord Halifax, the British ambassador, not made public by the State Department until 1964, quotes Hull as saying that "the President and myself, and other officials of this Government, in the light of our international interest in the Jewish situation, based primarily on the residence and citizenship of some five million Jews in this country, are in earnest sympathy with the proposal of the Jews that the immigration provisions be extended by the British government beyond March 31. . . . We could not help but be thoroughly sympathetic with the Jewish request not to terminate the immigration provisions of the White Paper on March 31. . . ." But Hull immediately added that he was searching for some way to "define the attitude of this Government publicly without seriously embarrassing the British in dealing with the military situation." Hull's search was fruitless. The British did nothing to help him and the whole black comedy of the congressional resolutions followed. On March 31, 1944, the most restrictive aspects of the White Paper went into effect on schedule, and all legal Jewish immigration into Palestine was thereafter forbidden.

The only consolation for Jews at this time was not one that served the aims of Zionism. Some steps at last were being taken to rescue the refugees, although not primarily to send them to Palestine. Late in 1943, Secretary of the Treasury Henry Morgenthau, Jr.—Jewish, but no Zionist—had become aware that the State Department appeared to be systematically sabotaging every attempt to save Europe's Jews from Hitler's death squads. The absurd months of bureaucratic delay over the Swedish offer to accept refugee children and the Rumanian offer to put up surplus Jews for ransom convinced Morgenthau and other Treasury officials that an investigation of State Department policies was in order. Randolph Paul, the Treasury Department's general counsel, was assigned the task of preparing documentation of State's obstructionism to be placed before President Roosevelt. Paul's assistant, Josiah E. DuBois, Jr., did most of the actual research, with the aid of John Pehle, the Treasury man who had conducted the agonizing negotiations with the State Department over a license for transfer of the Rumanian ransom money to Switzerland. Neither Paul, DuBois, nor Pehle were Jews.

In January, 1944, Paul gave Secretary Morgenthau his findings, headed "Report to the Secretary on the Acquiescence of This Government in the Murder of the Jews." The 18-page report began by saying that State Department officials "have not only failed to use the Government machinery at their disposal to rescue Jews from Hitler, but have even gone so far as to use this Government machinery to prevent the rescue of these Jews." Morgenthau abridged it by half and deleted its inflammatory title, but it remained a startling exposé when he, Paul, and Pehle gave it to the President on January 16. Roosevelt read it in their presence. He was shaken by the implication that more than mere incompetence was involved. The report said that "responsible people and organizations" had come to see "plain anti-Semitism motivating the actions of these State Department officials and . . . it will require little more in the way of proof for this suspicion to explode into a nasty scandal."

Six days later, Roosevelt created the War Refugee Board by executive order, with John Pehle in charge. Its function was "to take action for the immediate rescue from the Nazis of as many as possible of the persecuted minorities of Europe—racial, religious, or political—all certain victims of enemy savagery." Unbelievably, this was the first time a government agency in the United States had been charged with the responsibility of aiding these victims, despite all the proclamations of sympathy and outrage that had emanated from Washington all through the war years. In the ten years since Hitler had come to power, the United States had admitted 476,930 aliens, though the quotas set up by the highly restrictive Immigration Act of 1924 would have permitted the entry of 1,537,740 aliens in that decade. Of those who managed to come in, 165,756 were Jews, and about 138,000 of those were refugees from persecution. By its own laws the United States could have saved more than a million additional victims through June 30, 1943.

The establishment of the War Refugee Board did not mean any change in American immigration policies—in all of 1944, only 9,394 quota immigrants would manage to get in, many of them British or Scandinavian. But at least an official American agency would be working to get refugees out of German-occupied and satellite countries and into temporary havens. Between February and October, 1944, a War Refugee Board official in Turkey was able to rescue more than 6,000 Jews and get them into Palestine under terms of a special agreement with the British, who undertook to accept in Palestine any Eastern European Jew who reached neutral Turkey. (The agreement was revoked in October when the War Refugee Board proved too successful in finding candidates for admission.) In the spring of 1944, 600 Jews of Spanish origin were shipped from German-occupied Greece to neutral Spain, and later to a refugee camp in North Africa. Here and there, in groups of a few hundred or a few thousand, human beings were spared from the gas chambers. However, for every one that was saved, hundreds were engulfed by the "final solution to the Jewish problem."

Pehle was hampered by the unwillingness of most nations to accept the refugees his agents rescued. Palestine was, in effect, closed. Australia, South Africa, Canada, and other large, sparsely populated countries outside the war zone made excuses, as they had done at Evian in 1938. The Soviet Union was not even considered as a home for refugees. Russia was under direct German attack, with many Russian Jews already slaughtered. And in any case the Jews of Russia had long been a persecuted minority trying to get out; Russia was no place to send Jews *to*. The Latin American countries were indifferent or even hostile to the suggestion that they should admit refugees. (The Dominican Republic, which actually had accepted a small number of Jews after Evian, took no more now.) The United States itself set a poor example. When Samuel Grafton, a columnist for the *New York Post*, suggested in April, 1944, that this country should establish "free ports"—essentially, reservations—where refugees could temporarily be held without violating immigration laws, the War Refugee Board urged the President to approve the idea. And so, in July, 1944, 984 Jewish and non-Jewish refugees were transferred from a refugee camp in Allied-held southern Italy to Fort Ontario, an abandoned army base in upstate New York. There they were confined behind barbed wire. This "concentration camp" near Oswego was the only "free port" established, and these were the only refugees admitted to the United States under the emergency provisions.

Where it could, the State Department continued to practice its murderous habits of delay. Early in 1944, the War Refugee Board attempted to secure the freedom of 238 Polish Jews, almost all of them rabbis, who were being held in an internment camp in German-occupied France. These 238 had managed to buy passports from profiteering Latin American consuls in Europe, and so were officially considered eligible for entry into the countries whose passports they held. Although Peru, Costa Rica, Ecuador, and the other nations involved had not permitted entry to holders of these passports, the Germans were keeping them alive against the possibility that they could be exchanged for German nationals. in Latin America. By 1944 this possibility looked dim, and the Germans proposed to deport the 238 Poles to the Auschwitz death camp. Quickly the War Refugee Board arranged for them to be released in exchange for 238 disabled German prisoners of war in

Texas. But the swap had to be approved by the State Department, which took no action from February 21 to April 7. In the meantime the rabbis were sent to Auschwitz, where they died.

10.

The War Refugee Board, created too late and strangled by State Department red tape, was unable to make real inroads on the refugee problem despite the dedication and, in some cases, the physical heroism of its officials. By the summer of 1944 it was clear that the Board, like the punctured congressional resolutions of the winter, had been intended mostly as a means of keeping the disgruntled Jewish community at peace with the government. To the Zionists, the only real solution to the refugee problem, more so now than ever, was Palestine; and as the presidential campaign season approached they intensified their pressure.

Franklin Delano Roosevelt was seeking an unpredecented fourth term in the White House. He had become gaunt and haggard and old during the war years, and many of his intimates privately doubted that he could live through another four years as President. He was in some mild political trouble, too. Although he had won reelection in 1940 by a one-sided electoral vote of 449 to 82, he had drawn 54.7 percent of the popular vote, sharply down from his astonishing 1936 figure of 60.2 percent. Furthermore, his Republican opponent, Wendell Willkie, had carried ten states, more than the Republicans had taken against Roosevelt in the 1932 and 1936 elections combined.

In the congressional elections of 1942, the Republicans had picked up 10 seats in the Senate and 47 in the House, and since then a coalition of Republicans and southern Democrats had been able to block much of FDR's legislative program. If the big states that had gone Republican in 1942—California, New York, Massachusetts, Ohio, Michigan, Pennsylvania, Minnesota, and Illinois—voted for the Republican presidential candidate in 1944, they would give him 207 electoral votes. Another 72 electoral votes from smaller states seemed safely Republican. In 1944 it took 303 votes to elect a President. By holding onto all the states they had won in 1942, and picking up just 14 electoral votes elsewhere in the nation, the Republicans could put their man in the White House in 1944.

There were many Republican volunteers for the assignment of

dethroning Roosevelt. Among them was Wendell Willkie, the 1940 candidate; but he was deemed too unpredictable by party regulars. The favorite of the extreme right was General Douglas MacArthur, the hero of the Pacific war. However, he was unable to seek the post openly. Governor John W. Bricker of Ohio had the backing of his fellow Ohioan, the powerful Senator Robert Taft. Young Harold E. Stassen, the governor of Minnesota, also had presidential hopes.

It was generally agreed that the leading candidate was the dapper, efficient, youthful Thomas E. Dewey, 41 years old, who had become famous in the 1930's for his sensational prosecution of organized crime in New York, and who in 1942 had been elected governor of that state. Among Dewey's many advantages as a candidate was his chance of carrying New York, his home state, which controlled the largest single bloc of electoral votes.

Dewey almost certainly could not win the election unless he won in New York. And Dewey could not carry New York without winning the support of its millions of Jewish residents. But the only way to lure the Jews of New York away from their allegiance to Roosevelt was by promising something that most of them seemed desperately to want: a Jewish homeland in Palestine. So, for the first time, a blatant bid to capture the Jewish vote became a feature of an American presidential election.

The Republicans held their nominating convention in Chicago late in June, 1944. As expected, Dewey was chosen to run. Governor Bricker of Ohio received the vice-presidential nomination. The party platform included, by unanimous decision, a Palestine plank, which stated:

"In order to give refuge to millions of distressed Jewish men, women, and children driven from their homes by tyranny, we call for the opening of Palestine to their unrestricted immigration and land ownership, so that in accordance with the full intent and purpose of the Balfour Declaration of 1917 and the resolution of a Republican Congress in 1922, Palestine may be constituted as a free and democratic Commonwealth. We condemn the failure of the President to insist that the mandatory of Palestine carry out the provision of the Balfour Declaration and of the mandate while he pretends to support it."

Cairo newspapers instantly denounced this plank. One labeled it quite accurately a means "of obtaining Jewish votes in the

United States," while another called it "an outrage against a small and friendly nation" and suggested returning the displaced Jewish refugees to their native countries after the war, rather than shipping them to Palestine.

The Zionists were thrown into embarrassing confusion. Abba Hillel Silver recommended that AZEC express its satisfaction at the Republican endorsement of Zionist aims; but his motives were suspect, for he was a loyal Republican himself, and though he insisted that it was simply good political sense for the Zionists to show pleasure at the plank, other Zionist leaders who were staunch Democrats objected. Henry Monsky of B'nai B'rith called the criticism of President Roosevelt in the final sentence "obviously wrong," and Rabbi Wise termed it an "unjust aspersion" on the President. Even an amended proposal that would have limited the expression of satisfaction to the "positive" portion of the Republican plank failed by a narrow margin to pass in the AZEC governing committee.

The New Zionist Organization—as the Revisionists now were known—jumped into the picture with full-page newspaper advertisements intended to goad the Democrats into issuing an even stronger Zionist plank at their convention. On July 18, the eve of the Democratic convention, the *New York Post* carried this ad:

Delegates to the Democratic Convention! *Yours is the responsibility!* Yours is the party which has brought this administration to power and which is fighting to maintain it in power for the next four years. Yours is the responsibility for everything that has been done or left undone in the past, and for what will or will not be undertaken *tomorrow.*

The Republican Party has strongly declared itself for a firm stand by the United States on this issue. An opposition party can do no more than to *proclaim* a policy which it intends to pursue. A party in power can *carry out* a policy which it finds desirable. The Democratic Party must therefore see to it that the Government takes immediate and effective action on behalf of a Jewish Palestine.

The Democratic Party would not go that far, but it did match the Republican plank with one of its own:

"We favor the opening of Palestine to unrestricted Jewish immigration and colonization, and such a policy as to result in the establishment there of a free and democratic Jewish commonwealth."

The convention renominated President Roosevelt without op-position, though there were private misgivings over the alarming deterioration in his health. The misgivings over renominating the incumbent Vice-President, Henry A. Wallace, were not at all private. Wallace was considered a political liability, too far to the left, a dangerous man to have on the ticket with Roosevelt's future so uncertain. As one Democratic leader had put it in the spring of 1944—not where the President could hear it—"You are not nominating a Vice-President of the United States, but a Presi-dent." Over Roosevelt's objections, therefore, Wallace was dropped, and the convention chose as Roosevelt's running mate an obscure and unspectacular Missouri senator, Harry S Truman.

The presence of Zionist planks in the platforms of both major parties upset the American Council for Judaism, which deplored "the injection of the Palestine issue into American partisan poli-tics" and condemned this attempt to bid for the votes of American Jews. The Arabs, too, were upset, and after the government of Iraq had lodged a protest over the planks, Secretary of State Hull told FDR on July 26 that it would be advisable for leaders of the two parties to avoid making campaign statements likely "to arouse the Arabs or upset the precarious balance of forces in Palestine."

But AZEC's propaganda machine could not now be halted. The Zionists solicited statements of support from every member of Congress and from every state legislature in the country. Since the United States in 1944 had a total of about one hundred thousand residents of Arab origin, and more than five million Jews, politi-cians had a great deal to gain and nothing to lose by endorsing the AZEC program. Congressmen with large Jewish constituencies naturally fell in line, and even those from districts where Jews were scarce preferred to join the movement for the sake of sup-porting a humanitarian cause.

By the time the election campaign was at its peak, 411 of the 531 members of the 78th Congress were on record in favor of immedi-ate American action to bring about a Jewish commonwealth in Palestine. Congressmen from every state in the Union—86 per-cent of the Senate and 75 percent of the House—had also an-nounced that they favored the Jewish right to settle in Palestine unhindered by the White Paper restrictions. And 19 state legisla-tures, representing more than 60 percent of the population of the United States, had passed pro-Zionist resolutions. That figure would have been even higher if all state legislatures had had sessions scheduled for 1944. By 1945, 39 legislatures, covering 85 percent of the country's population, had passed such resolutions.

These were easy symbolic victories. On August 24, several congressmen trying to ride this wave of seeming popular support for Zionism introduced resolutions calling on the President and the Secretary of State "to use their good offices with a view to the establishment in Palestine of emergency shelters" for Jewish refugees then leaving Hungary. Secretary of State Hull, alarmed, quickly suggested to Representative Sol Bloom that this was a matter best left to the War Refugee Board, and warned the President of "the effect that these resolutions will undoubtedly have upon the political situation in the Near East." The resolutions were allowed to die.

The campaign was nearly dead, too. Dewey was trying to wage an aggressive struggle, but, since he was in sympathy with most of the social legislation of the New Deal, he had only one real issue: that "tired old men" were running the government. Roosevelt, who did not enter the campaign until late in September, was an infuriatingly elusive target, and Dewey was forced to take harder swings. He charged that "Mr. Roosevelt, to perpetuate himself in office for sixteen years, has put his party on the auction block— for sale to the highest bidder," and claimed that the Democratic Party had been captured by "the forces of communism." In the 1944 campaign "communism" was Republican shorthand for "Jewish labor leaders." Though most of the labor leaders working for FDR were hostile to communism, many of them were undeniably foreign-born, and seemed frighteningly alien to the native-born Americans making up the core of the Republican strength. The Russian-born Sidney Hillman of the Amalgamated Clothing Workers of America was a special target. Republican spokesmen made sinister references to his "rabbinical education" and approved campaign posters that said:

IT'S YOUR COUNTRY. . . .
WHY LET SIDNEY HILLMAN RUN IT?
VOTE FOR DEWEY AND BRICKER

This, though, was hardly the kind of tactic likely to win the admiration of the Jewish voters whom the Republicans had tried to woo with their Palestine campaign plank. And as Roosevelt began his counterattack, mocking Dewey's flailings before huge audiences, the Republican strategists remembered the Zionism issue. On October 12, Dewey issued a statement restating his party's Zionist plank and declaring his support "for the reconstitution of Palestine as a free and democratic Jewish commonwealth."

Roosevelt quickly neutralized this ploy. Three days later, Senator Robert Wagner rose before the annual convention of the Zionist Organization of America to read a letter from the President that quoted the Democratic Palestine plank and promised, "Efforts will be made to find appropriate ways and means of effectuating this policy as soon as practicable. I know how long and ardently the Jewish people have worked and prayed for the establishment of Palestine as a free and democratic Jewish commonwealth. I am convinced that the American people give their support to this aim and if reelected I shall help to bring about its realization."

The New Zionist (Revisionist) Organization shot back an open letter to the President on November 2, calling his statement on Palestine "not satisfactory" because it included the indefinite phrase "as soon as practicable." How soon would that be? Since the war was almost over, since the strategic considerations that had earlier been the excuse for delay no longer mattered, why wait even one day longer? Why not now, before the election, take whatever steps were necessary to make Great Britain rescind the White Paper?

But for the 472,000 Jewish Americans who were members of other Zionist groups in 1944, and for the millions of Jewish Americans who were not, the President's promise of October 15 settled the matter of Palestine as a campaign issue. He had declared that he would work for a Jewish state in Palestine if re-elected, and that was enough. Even those who felt that his refugee policy had been cynical and evasive, those who had the uncomfortable feeling that behind the image of warmth and concern there hid an unusually crafty and calculating politician, were swayed. On November 7, Roosevelt won another overwhelming victory. He had 25,600,000 popular votes and 432 electoral votes. Dewey had 22,000,000 popular votes, 99 electoral votes. FDR's share of the popular vote had dropped from 54.7 percent in 1940 to 53.7 percent in 1944, and

Dewey had carried a dozen states. But there was no doubt of the wishes of the electorate.

Many voters of German, Irish, and Italian stock had deserted him—the German-Americans and Italian-Americans for obvious reasons, and the Irish-Americans because Ireland was neutral and Ireland's great enemy, Britain, had had such strong support from Roosevelt. Protestant voters had been lukewarm; only 31 percent of the Congregationalists, 40 percent of the Presbyterians, and 44 percent of the Episcopalians went Democratic. The Catholic voters were 72 percent for Roosevelt.

But he captured 92 percent of the Jewish vote. In a heavily Jewish precinct of Chicago's Ward 49, Roosevelt drew 89.6 percent of the votes cast; in an adjoining precinct of Christian residents he took only 39.4 percent. New York's 47 electoral votes went to Roosevelt by a plurality of 316,000 out of 6,316,000 votes cast. The almost unanimous Democratic vote by that state's Jews was decisive in defeating Dewey in his home territory. Of the fourteen states that contained more than 90 percent of American Jewry, Dewey had carried only one, Ohio. In Michigan, a state that had voted Republican in 1940 and had a large Jewish community, Dewey lost by 22,476 votes. The Jewish vote may not have defeated Dewey, but it certainly prevented him from winning.

To politicians of both parties, the analysis of the returns from Jewish districts proved that it was good business to come out in favor of a Jewish state in Palestine. To Arab leaders, Roosevelt's promise to help fulfill the dream of Zionism seemed like an omen of trouble ahead. To Zionists it appeared as though the bitter struggle was nearly over, for they had a binding commitment from the President of the United States, and no voice would speak more potently than his in the shaping of the new postwar world. Under the circumstances, the weeks after the election seemed like an auspicious time for the Zionists to press for immediate implementation of the presidential campaign pledge.

But the time was not really auspicious at all.

SEVEN
Agitation and Agony

THE PRESIDENT had said he would work toward a realization of the Zionist dream. The Congress, which was on record on an individual basis in favor of fulfillment of that dream, could now perhaps push the President into action by passing a pro-Zionist resolution. In the closing weeks of 1944 debate began again on the shelved Wright-Compton and Wagner-Taft resolutions.

The revival of the debate was stimulated by a cloudy letter from Secretary of War Stimson to Senator Taft dated October 10, 1944 —at the height of the election campaign. Stimson had killed the resolutions the previous March on the grounds that "further action on them at this time would be prejudicial to the successful prosecution of the war." Now the Secretary of War had reviewed the situation, and had found "that there is still strong feeling on the part of many officers in my department that the passage of such a resolution would interfere with our military effort. However, I do feel that the military considerations which led to my previous action in opposing the passage of this resolution are not as strong a factor as they were then. In my judgment, political considerations now outweigh the military, and the issue should be determined upon the political rather than the military basis."

Did Stimson mean by "political considerations" the domestic tug-of-war over the Jewish vote in the forthcoming election? Did he mean the politics of Arab versus Jew in the Holy Land? Or, perhaps, the diplomatic-political complications of having Congress take a position on what was, really, an internal affair of the British government? Stimson did not clarify. But his letter indicated that the Pentagon, at least, would not again interfere. On the strength of that, the House and Senate resumed hearings on the resolutions. The House Foreign Affairs Committee acted quickly, sending the Wright-Compton measure along to the full House with only two minor changes, and recommending its adoption.

But the State Department moved firmly to spike the Senate version. Early in December the new Secretary of State, Edward R. Stettinius testified at a session of the Senate Foreign Relations Committee. (Following the elections Cordell Hull had retired, after 12 years of service.) Passage of the Wagner-Taft resolution "at the present time," Stettinius said, "would be unwise from the standpoint of the general international situation." On December 9, Stettinius told the President of the position he had taken; Roosevelt replied that it was "just right." The Senate committee, aware that the 44-year-old Secretary of State would not have opposed the resolution without direct instructions from the White House, acquiesced, voting 12 to 8 to postpone action on it indefinitely. Four days later, 12 committee members—7 Democrats and 5 Republicans—made individual announcements that they personally had approved of the resolution. Zionists were becoming all too familiar with this sort of maneuver: a statement of warm personal regard from a high political figure, coupled with an absence of binding formal action.

The tabling of the Senate resolution amounted to a second death for the measure, and touched off an explosion within the Zionist high command. Rabbi Abba Hillel Silver had been responsible for pressing for renewed consideration of the pro-Zionist resolutions. His great rival, Rabbi Stephen Wise, had argued that it was rash to try to bring the issue before Congress again without first getting the approval of the President and the State Department. Wise and Silver had both known that such approval would not be available, for on November 21 Roosevelt had forwarded to them the texts of a number of anti-Zionist resolutions that had lately been adopted by the Arab Union Society, the Higher Committee for the Defense of Palestine, the Young Men's Moslem Association, and other such groups. The implication was that this was a poor time to antagonize the Arabs further by congressional action.

Wise agreed. He felt that the recent presidential pledge of support for a Jewish Palestine was enough of a Zionist victory for the moment; he feared angering and alienating his friend Roosevelt by putting too constant a pressure on him. But Silver, no friend of the President, still heard the resonant phrases of the presidential campaign promises. He wanted those promises redeemed, and saw a strong Zionist vote in Congress as the best way of reminding Roosevelt that he had not forgotten the rhetoric of October. And so, through AZEC, Silver urged the House and Senate to take action on the resolutions, despite Wise's warning that the prospects were poor and that the Zionist movement would suffer a loss of prestige in the event of a defeat.

The defeat came; and in the post mortem of December, 1944, Silver discovered that he had been undercut by his own colleagues. For while Silver had been pushing for passage of the resolutions, Rabbi Wise had notified his friends in Washington that the Zionist Organization of America was not in sympathy with Silver's tactics and would not go against the President's wishes in the matter of immediate congressional action. On December 21, Roosevelt wrote Wise, thanking him for his "considerate attitude."

Silver's position had also been undermined by the parent Zionist instrumentality, the World Zionist Organization, through its executive arm, the Jewish Agency. Previously absent from the American political scene, the Palestine-based Jewish Agency had set up an office in Washington in the summer of 1943 under the direction of Nahum Goldmann, assisted by Louis Lipsky. Goldmann was a Polish-born Zionist who had been the Jewish Agency's representative at the League of Nations from 1935 to 1939, and had been a cofounder of the World Jewish Congress in 1936. In Washington, Goldmann at once came into conflict with the volatile Rabbi Silver, who believed that his AZEC ought to be the only Zionist pressure group in the capital. Emanuel Neumann, who had rejoined AZEC, declared on Silver's behalf in September, 1944, that "the interests of the Zionist Movement are jeopardized by the existence in this country of two political agencies." Neumann tried to arrange a division of responsibility, whereby AZEC would handle all matters pertaining to the dissemination of Zionist propaganda in the United States, and the Jewish Agency office would handle dealings with foreign governments. Although Goldmann agreed with this plan, the Jewish Agency office frequently poached in Silver's territory—and in the events of late 1944 Goldmann sided with Rabbi Wise against Rabbi Silver on the issue of pressing for the congressional resolutions.

The Zionist Organization of America's executive committee, discussing the defeat of the resolutions at its meeting of December 19, 1944, heard Goldmann declare that President Roosevelt "was antagonized for no good reason. . . . He requested that this problem be left in his hands for a little while longer." Goldmann said that "the political effect of the deferment of the resolution on Palestine . . . is grave indeed. Antagonizing the President of the United States is a serious matter. . . . The policies of the Zionist Emergency Committee [AZEC] during the last month were contrary to Zionist policy as conceived and carried out during the last twenty years." Silver's recent actions seemed almost comparable, in Goldmann's view, to the tactics of the detested Revisionists: "Jabotinsky was a great Zionist but his policies of antagonizing the powers that be—even though they were often unjust to Jewish people—would have led to a catastrophe. . . . If this fight against the President and this policy of attacking the Administration is continued, it will lead us—and I choose my words very carefully —to complete political disaster."

Silver was found guilty of the cardinal sin of traditional Zionism: he had asked for too much, too soon. His failure to get the approval of Congress for the pro-Zionist resolutions brought him down, and he was forced to resign as cochairman of AZEC and chairman of the executive committee of the Zionist Organization of America. As 1945 began, the moderate Wise faction was in command. However, the moderates had misjudged the temper of the American Jewish public. Upon Silver's dismissal, the controversy over tactics spread from the inner councils of Zionism to synagogues and community centers all across the nation, and soon a pattern of broad support for Silver's hard-line approach became evident. The demand for his return to Zionist high office culminated in an agreement in July, 1945, by which he regained the two positions he had lost seven months before. By that time, Roosevelt was dead, the war in Europe was over, and the world had become a very different place.

2.

The first order of business for President Roosevelt, as he began his fourth term in 1945, was a three-power conference to determine the shape of the postwar world. In January, it became known that he would meet at the Black Sea resort of Yalta with Prime Minister Churchill and Soviet Premier Joseph Stalin the following month to discuss, among other things, coordination of the final Allied offensive against Germany; the division of defeated Germany into zones of occupation; the status of Poland, Rumania, Bulgaria, and other liberated states; the structure of the future world organization, the United Nations; and certain territorial matters in the Far East.

Rabbi Wise, for the moment the unchallenged leader of the American Zionist movement, wanted one other item added to the Yalta agenda. On January 12, 1945, he wrote the President, "My associates of the American Zionist Emergency Council and I feel that before you leave for the Conference, a small delegation of us who, it is needless to say, stand gratefully and loyally at your side, ought to have some time in which to present the case of Palestine. . . ."

The problem of the Soviet attitude toward Zionism was something the Jews hoped Roosevelt could handle. Even before the Russian Revolution, the Bolsheviks had attacked Zionism as a bourgeois delusion, a diversion of energies away from the true struggles of the working class. Once the Tsarist regime fell, the Soviet authorities outlawed Zionism as an undesirable cult, and forbade the emigration of Russian Jews. Except for a brief period in the 1920's, that prohibition had remained in effect; the Jews of Russia were locked into their country, bound by restrictive laws as harsh as those of the Tsars.

Under Stalin, Zionism had been opposed not only for ideological reasons—as a nationalistic phenomenon injurious to the solidarity of the international brotherhood of man—but as a tactical matter. To Stalin, the Zionists seemed to be the allies of the British in maintaining an imperialist grasp over the Palestinian segment of the Arab world. So long as the Arabs were in a rebellious ferment over the attempts of the British to impose some sort of Jewish entity in Palestine, the Soviet Union saw advantage for itself in encouraging that ferment through denunciations of Zionism. And so, while continuing to suppress and persecute Jews at home, the Russians also worked against the emergence of a Jewish national state abroad. But perhaps the war had worked some change in Stalin's views, especially since the situation in Palestine had changed: now it was the Jews who rebelled against British authority and the Arabs who preferred the status quo of the mandate.

Meanwhile, the American Palestine Council, the AZEC-sponsored organization of Christian Zionists, sent a memorandum to its 15,000 members, calling on them to "take a few minutes right now to write or wire President Roosevelt" concerning "the tragic problem of the uprooted Jews of Europe. The doors of Palestine must be opened wide to Jewish immigration. . . ." The effects of this campaign had not yet begun to show when Rabbi Wise and his colleagues called on Roosevelt on January 22. Wise brought with him an eight-point AZEC policy statement that opened with the words, "The Jewish people are entitled to a national homeland of their own." It argued that this demand had been internationally recognized until the 1939 White Paper, which "proposed to convert Palestine into an Arab State in which the Jews would be a fixed and permanent minority. The attempt to sacrifice the Jewish National Home to Arab demands is warranted neither by justice nor expediency."

The Arabs, AZEC's paper said, could live elsewhere if they so chose. The Jews had no other place in which to build their needed homeland. "The only answer to continued Arab opposition is the creation with all possible speed of the accomplished fact of a Jewish majority in Palestine." To effect this, an international program for transporting Jews to Palestine should be initiated without delay. By way of a *quid pro quo* to the Arabs, the United Nations could undertake large-scale development schemes in the sparsely populated and backward Arab countries.

"Any proposal for partitioning Palestine," the statement went on, "must be rejected. Apart from other considerations, the separation of the water resources of the north from the undeveloped land areas of the south will render impossible the establishment of a viable Jewish state capable of absorbing large numbers of immigrants. The Jewish Commonwealth must comprise an undiminished and undivided Palestine." And, the statement added prophetically, "the Jews of Palestine have every confidence in their ability . . . to defend themselves within the structure of any international organization which may be set up to maintain peace and order in the world."

Roosevelt had heard all these arguments before. Now, exhausted and worn, he listened again, and made his customary expressions of sympathy for the Jewish struggle—and offered a few practical objections to the Zionist aims. Could a poor land like Palestine really absorb so many refugees? How could the Zionists give assurance to the Arabs that once the Jews had a territorial foot-hold in Palestine they would not try to extend their power into neighboring Arab countries? What about the possibility that the Soviet Union might oppose the establishment of a Jewish state, by way of winning favor for itself with the Arabs? Roosevelt was aware of Stalin's long hostility to Zionism.

In all his previous meetings with Roosevelt, Wise had heard only mild criticisms of Zionism based on broad and general matters of wartime strategy. Now the President seemed to be getting down to cases, and the President's questions were ominous. Two days after the meeting, Wise tried to salvage things in a long letter to FDR, dealing categorically with all the presidential objections. Yes, said Wise, Palestine could support millions of immigrants, especially if a Jordan Valley Authority reclamation plan were put into effect patterned after the New Deal's own Tennessee Valley Authority redevelopment scheme. Wise quoted David Lilienthal of the TVA to the effect that the Jordan idea "is an eminently practical and desirable one." And of course, Wise said, "the Jews have not the slightest desire or intention to colonize the Arab lands outside Palestine." He asserted that he wished to put that on record "in the most unequivocal way." The effect of creating a Jewish state would be the opposite: to draw Jews out of the Arab countries and into Palestine. As for the problem of possible Russian opposition, Wise said that he had learned of a recent conversation on the subject of Palestine between Stalin and President Benes of Czechoslovakia, "who is a convinced Zionist of long standing." According to Benes, Stalin would raise no objections to the establishment of a Jewish commonwealth in Palestine.

Nevertheless, Wise was apprehensive about the depth of Roosevelt's commitment to Zionism on the eve of the President's departure for Yalta. As it turned out, the Yalta Conference, which lasted from February 4 to 11, 1945, did not touch on Palestine at all. Chiefly it was concerned with Russia's postwar claims. Stalin, confident and aggressive, marked off huge areas of the world as Soviet spheres of influence, and wrung agreement from a tired Churchill and a mortally weary Roosevelt.

Roosevelt did intend to discuss Palestine while he was abroad, however, but not with the British, and not in any manner that was likely to please his friend Rabbi Wise. On the last night of the conference, the President let it be known that he intended to stop in Cairo on his way home from Yalta and would confer there with King Farouk of Egypt, King Ibn Saud of Saudi Arabia, and Emperor Haile Selassie of Ethiopia. When Churchill asked presidential assistant Harry Hopkins later that evening about the subject of Roosevelt's talk with Ibn Saud, Hopkins said merely that it would be "the Palestine situation."

Roosevelt met with Ibn Saud aboard an American warship in the Suez Canal in mid-February. No official account of their conversation was ever made public, but the essence of their discussion was indirectly revealed during the Truman administration, and in 1954, a pro-Arab group, American Friends of the Middle East, published a detailed report on the encounter by William A. Eddy, who had served as the interpreter. According to Eddy, Roosevelt had told Ibn Saud that he felt a personal responsibility toward the victims of Nazi persecution and regarded himself committed to help them. He asked the Arabian monarch for suggestions. Ibn Saud promptly replied, "Give them and their descendants the choicest lands and homes of the Germans who had oppressed them."

Roosevelt pointed out that few German Jews were eager to return to the land that had caused them such torment, even under those conditions; they seemed to have "a sentimental desire" to settle in Palestine. Perhaps, the President suggested, traditional Arab hospitality could be invoked to make the Jewish refugees welcome in Palestine.

Ibn Saud held firm. "Make the enemy and the oppressor pay! That is how we Arabs wage war. Amends should be made by the criminal, not by the innocent bystander. What injury have the Arabs done to the Jews of Europe? It is the 'Christian' Germans who stole their homes and lives. Let the Germans pay."

When Roosevelt indicated that this was not a satisfactory proposal, Ibn Saud produced an even less palatable one, telling the President "that it is Arab custom to distribute survivors and victims of battle among the victorious tribes in accordance with their number and their supplies of food and water." Little Palestine had already absorbed more than her fair share of refugees. Why not take the rest into the vast and fertile lands of the Allies? This suggestion, of course, Roosevelt was not prepared to endorse.

As the conversation proceeded, it turned into a monologue in which Ibn Saud made it quite clear that the Arabs would resist a Jewish intrusion into the Near East with all their strength. The towering desert king made a strong impression on the President, who came away from the meeting convinced that the Zionist cause was hopeless, that a Jewish state in Palestine could be established and maintained only by military force.

On March 1, 1945, having returned to the United States, Roosevelt delivered his official report to Congress on the Yalta meeting. The hand of death seemed visibly to rest on him. He spoke in a fumbling, hesitant way and the fatigue his efforts caused him was startlingly apparent. During his speech he inserted a number of rambling ad-lib comments that struck his listeners as irrelevant or incomprehensible. Among his unexpected interpolations was this remark on his visit to Egypt:

"Of the problems of Arabia I learned more about that whole problem, the Moslem problem, the Jewish problem, by talking with Ibn Saud for five minutes than I could have learned in an exchange of two or three dozen letters."

That sentence drew more comment than any other part of the whole unhappy speech. Senator Edwin Johnson, Democrat of Colorado, a strong Zionist supporter, said, "With all due respect to the President and King Ibn Saud, I must say that the choice of the desert king as expert on the Jewish question is nothing short of amazing. . . . I imagine that even Fala [Roosevelt's dog] would be more of an expert. . . ." Judge Samuel I. Rosenman, a close friend of the President, described Roosevelt's remark as "almost bordering on the ridiculous" and "a thought that must have popped in his head at just that moment."

Rabbi Wise was also agitated. On March 4 he sent Roosevelt a lengthy telegram in which he declared, "It would be less than frank if I failed to tell you that the absence in your statement to Congress of any reference to the tragedy which has overwhelmed the Jewish people and of any hope or comfort for them has caused deepest concern and disquiet nor were these relieved by your passing allusion to the Jewish problem, in connection with your conversation with Ibn Saud."

Now Roosevelt had to repair his standing with the Jewish community, and on March 16 he allowed Wise a 45-minute conference at the White House, in which he insisted that he still favored unrestricted immigration into an independent Jewish common-wealth in Palestine. After the meeting Wise released a statement quoting the President as having said, "I made my position on Zionism clear in October. That position I have not changed and shall continue to seek to bring about its earliest realization." Ac-cording to a confidential report on Wise's White House visit made public by David Ben-Gurion in 1964, Roosevelt had also told Wise that "the Big Three [Roosevelt, Churchill, and Stalin] had decided that Palestine should be given to the Jews and immigration should continue," and that he "had been disappointed by Ibn Saud." Roosevelt supposedly said to Wise, furthermore, that Churchill had requested him "not to expect a formal withdrawal of the White Paper: this was not the way things were done in England."

What Rabbi Wise did not discover on March 16 is that Roosevelt had, at the conclusion of his meeting with Ibn Saud, reiterated the policy that the State Department had set forth to various Arab leaders many times since 1938: that the United States would not countenance any change in the status of Palestine that was objec-tionable to the Arabs. Thus Roosevelt had become snared in the same trap that had caught the British in World War I; he was committing his country to a pair of mutually exclusive Palestine policies, and was making promises to the Zionists that directly contradicted his promises to the Arabs.

The word that suggests itself for this sort of maneuvering is *duplicity.* That Roosevelt was engaged in double-dealing on the Palestine issue is beyond any question. What is harder to deter-mine is his motive for such double-dealing. Was it simply that as an old man contemplating the imminence of death he was simply stalling, making these insincere promises as a way of leaving the impossible decision on this insoluble problem to his successor? Or had he genuinely meant his pro-Zionist pledge of October, 1944, and was now hoping to extricate himself from it, somehow, after having had a glimpse at the harsh realities of the Arab stand? Or, perhaps, he felt that Palestine was really no concern of the United States, and that in time the whole thing would be settled without his involvement. In that case it was merely good politics to stay on friendly terms with both sides as long as possible.

The most charitable interpretation of Roosevelt's actions, and possibly the one closest to the truth, is that he saw no future for Palestine except as a state ruled jointly by Arabs and Jews. He was therefore trying to keep all options open until some reconciliation of the two conflicting nationalistic drives became feasible. The Jews would never accept an Arab-ruled Palestine; the Arabs, Ibn Saud had just made clear, would never accept a Jewish-ruled Palestine; and since neither side was willing even to think about partition, Roosevelt may have hoped that ultimately a binational Palestine might emerge.

If he had any such long-range goal in mind, he was saying nothing about it to anyone in 1945, and his Yalta performance brought him under attack from an expected foe—Abba Hillel Silver—and from some close friends as well. Silver, still officially in limbo after his overthrow a few months earlier, came before a Zionist policy-making meeting on March 21, 1945, to call for an even greater campaign for mass support: "Let the American people speak up—its ministers and educators, its writers and journalists, its leaders of capital and labor, its State Legislators, its Congressmen and Senators, of both political parties, Republicans and Democrats alike. . . . Let them make known their will to our Government and to our Chief Executive. . . . Let a mighty chorus of voices rise to the ears of the men whom destiny has chosen for great decisions." And Silver spoke bitterly of world leaders who "wagged their heads in sympathy and then proceeded to speak in the barren legalism of constricted hearts, of their inability to intervene in the domestic affairs of other nations and of their own inviolate immigration laws."

Bernard Baruch, the venerable counselor to Presidents, called on Roosevelt to protest his involvement with Ibn Saud. Although Jewish, Baruch had never been openly active in Jewish organizations or philanthropies, and had been described by Louis Brandeis as "a foul-weather Jew," one who would defend Jewish causes only in a time of emergency. This was evidently such an emergency. But after his White House visit Baruch said—according to Ben Hecht, whose passionate partisanship makes him not the most reliable of witnesses—"I have had a two-hour talk with President Roosevelt about the Jews and the Jewish problem. I have spoken also to Governor Dewey on the same subject. I can only tell you as a result of these talks that, despite my having been a lifelong

Democrat, I would rather trust my American Jewishness in Mr. Dewey's hands than in Mr. Roosevelt's."

But the most scathing words came from the Brooklyn congressman Emanuel Celler, a member of the inner circle of Democrats in the House of Representatives. On March 18, 1945, he reacted to the latest Wise announcement of Rooseveltian sympathy for Zionism with this speech at a Zionist dinner in New York:

"And what of our great President and beloved President? What of his mighty promise to reopen the doors of Palestine, a promise he made when he campaigned for re-election—a promise that garnered many votes? We are told that once for want of a nail a shoe was lost, and for want of a shoe a horse was lost, and for want of a horse a rider was lost, and for want of a rider a battle was lost, and for want of a battle a kingdom was lost. Well, were it not for his overwhelming vote in my own Congressional district (wherein in some precincts 1,400 votes were cast for Roosevelt as against 4 for Dewey), were it not for that vote in my district, Brooklyn in turn, where over one million Jews reside, would have been lost to Roosevelt; without Brooklyn, New York City would have been lost, and without New York City, New York State would have been lost to Roosevelt. And without New York State, the nation might have been lost to Roosevelt because similarly Jews held the balance of power in many metropolitan areas. They tipped the scales in favor of Roosevelt. They now look to Roosevelt with bewilderment. Why his silence? They cannot understand his retreat from fulfillment of his mighty promise.

"A bit from *Alice in Wonderland* is particularly apt: 'Take some more tea,' the March Hare very earnestly said to Alice. Alice in an offended tone replied, 'I have nothing yet, so I can't take more.' 'You mean you can't take less; it is very easy to take more than nothing.' Just so the Jews are given more and more promises, but nothing when it comes to performances."

Roosevelt made no further public statements on the subject of Palestine. However, he privately reiterated commitments he had made to the Arabs. In March and early April, 1945, letters bearing his signature went out to the King of Saudi Arabia, the Regent of Iraq, the Prime Minister of Lebanon, the Prime Minister of Egypt, the Emir of Transjordan, and other Arab leaders, offering reaffirmations of his earlier promises to them. This is the letter to Ibn Saud, dated April 5, 1945:

I have received the communication which Your Majesty sent me under date of March 10, 1945, in which you refer to the question of Palestine and to the continuing interest of the Arabs in current developments affecting that country.

I am gratified that Your Majesty took this occasion to bring your views on this question to my attention and I have given the most careful attention to the statements which you make in your letter. I am also mindful of the memorable conversation which we had not so long ago and in the course of which I had an opportunity to obtain so vivid an impression of Your Majesty's sentiments on this question.

Your Majesty will recall that on previous occasions I communicated to you the attitude of the American Government toward Palestine and made clear our desire that no decision be taken with respect to the basic situation in that country without full consultation with both Arabs and Jews. Your Majesty will also doubtless recall that during our recent conversation, I assured you that I would take no action, in my capacity as Chief of the Executive Branch of this Government, which might prove hostile to the Arab people.

It gives me pleasure to renew to Your Majesty the assurances which you have previously received regarding the attitude of my Government and my own, as Chief Executive, with regard to the question of Palestine and to inform you that the policy of this Government in this respect is unchanged. . . .

And on April 12, 1945, this letter went from the White House to Prince Abd-ul-Ilah, the Regent of Iraq:

I have received the letter which you sent me under date of March 10 and in which you outline the attitude of the Arabs toward the question of Palestine.

I take this opportunity to express to you my appreciation for this statement of the Arab position. . . . I desire, in this connection, to renew to you the assurances which have been previously communicated to the Iraqi Government to the effect that in the view of the Government of the United States no decision affecting the basic situation in Palestine should be reached without full consultation with both Arabs and Jews.

I am looking forward to meeting Your Highness on the occasion of your forthcoming visit to the United States. . . .

The meeting between President Roosevelt and Prince Abd-ul-Ilah did not take place. On the same day that his staff was sending the letter to the Regent of Iraq, the President suffered a fatal cerebral hemorrhage at his vacation retreat in Georgia, and by evening Vice-President Harry S Truman had been sworn into office as President. Who, the world wondered, is Harry S Truman? And what, the Zionists added, is his position on Palestine?

3.

The new President was altogether unlike his predecessor. Roosevelt had been a patrician, sophisticated and sleek, gifted to the point of deviousness in the arts of government. Truman was a Missouri farm boy with no college education, who had been a bank clerk, a lieutenant in the First World War, a haberdasher in Kansas City, and, after the dismal failure of his clothing store, a small-time politician in the Prendergast Democratic machine that ruled Missouri. Loyalty to the Prendergast operation carried Truman steadily higher, in a casual and unplanned way, from a county highway commission to a county court to the United States Senate. His personal honesty, his devotion to his responsibilities, and his simple, straightforward, blunt approach to complex problems enabled him to survive the collapse of the Prendergast machine and the jailing of most of its leaders in 1938; re-elected to the Senate in 1940, he reached national prominence as head of a "watchdog" committee investigating graft and waste in the national rearmament program, and when political considerations made necessary the dumping of Henry A. Wallace from the Democratic ticket in 1944, Truman was pushed forward by a coalition of big-city bosses as a substitute candidate for Vice-President. He was deemed ideal ballast for the ticket, since he was midwestern, upright, vigorous, a loyal party man, and a liberal of a sober, middle-of-the-road sort. Whether he was capable of handling the presidency does not seem to have been taken into consideration, which seems strange, considering that the Democratic leadership was aware of Roosevelt's poor health.

Roosevelt himself took no steps to prepare his Vice-President for eventual succession to power. In the five months between the election and Roosevelt's death there was scarcely any consultation between President and Vice-President. Truman was left out of all planning of major domestic and foreign programs, and knew nothing of the complex and delicate political juggling acts that his exceedingly complicated predecessor had been engaged in. Even the existence of the atomic bomb—due to have its first test explosion in the summer of 1945—was unknown to Truman until he entered the White House. To a man of limited experience and modest abilities, then, went the immense job of leading the world's most powerful nation into the era of change that was to follow history's most devastating war.

America's Jews reacted with dismay to the transfer of power. They wept for Roosevelt as they would have wept for a lost father, and they looked with suspicion at the new man with the rural twang in his voice. Roosevelt, they said, understood the problems of the Jews; he loved the weak and the dispossessed. They believed he would have eventually triumphed over British obstinacy and Arab hostility and turned Palestine into the longed-for Zion. But what would this Truman do? How could a man of the dusty plains comprehend the anguish of an urban people? How could he ever take Roosevelt's place?

In the intensely emotional period immediately after the President's death, even those Jews who had most harshly denounced Roosevelt's apparent capitulation to Ibn Saud now mourned the loss of a powerful ally. Only a few, such as the irrepressible Ben Hecht, seemed aware that Roosevelt's aid to the Jews had taken the form of noble words, not deeds. "No humanitarian hero was lying dead for me," Hecht wrote. "A bold and fretful man, an arrogant and lusty man, but a stranger to love and goodness, had died for me. A man with the gift of making himself unreasonably loved, a man who had discovered the poor, like some happy political explorer come upon a hidden continent of voters, was being wept over, and all his great fine deeds acclaimed. In my mind his chief monument remained—the dead Jews of Europe."

Only in years to come, as secret evidence emerged, would the Jews of America discover what Ben Hecht already knew: that they had greatly overestimated Franklin D. Roosevelt. And also in years to come they would make a second unexpected discovery: that they had greatly underestimated Harry S Truman.

There was no reason for much optimism about Truman's Palestine policy as he assumed office. His only public statement on Palestine had been made in 1944 during the debate in the Senate Committee on Foreign Relations over the Wagner-Taft resolution: "My sympathy, of course, is with the Jewish people and I am of the opinion that a resolution such as this should be very circumspectly handled until we know just exactly where we are going and why. . . . I don't want to throw any bricks to upset the applecart, although when the right time comes I am willing to help make the fight for a Jewish Homeland in Palestine." It was the sort of lukewarm, hesitant comment that might have been made by any man who had a good heart but no real knowledge of the issues at stake.

Truman was aware, though, of the intensity of public feeling about creation of a Jewish homeland, and he realized too that the impending end of the war in Europe would leave millions of homeless survivors of the conflict—many of them Jewish—in need of shelter and resettlement. Finding a home for these "displaced persons" would, Truman knew, be a matter of high priority. What Zionists wondered, however, was whether the down-to-earth little man from Missouri would be able to understand the compelling, almost mystic reasons why the Jewish war victims should be allowed to settle in Palestine, or whether in the interests of expediency he would try to arrange their relocation in South America, Australia, Africa, or some other equally unacceptable place. They decided to commence the new President's education in Zionist theory at once.

Secretary of State Stettinius anticipated that. Five days after Truman was sworn in, Stettinius sent him a memorandum that warned, "It is very likely that efforts will be made by some of the Zionist leaders to obtain from you at an early date some commitments in favor of the Zionist program which is pressing for unlimited Jewish immigration into Palestine and the establishment there of a Jewish state. As you are aware, the Government and people of the United States have every sympathy for the persecuted Jews of Europe and are doing all in their power to relieve their suffering. The question of Palestine is, however, a highly complex one and involves questions which go far beyond the plight of the Jews in Europe." Stettinius spoke of the "continual tenseness" in the Near East and added a phrase that indicated the changed nature of the relationship of the United States to the rest of the world: "As we have interests in that area which are vital to the United States, we feel that this whole subject is one that should be handled with the greatest care and with a view to the long-range interests of the country."

Prior to World War II, the United States had never considered itself to have "interests" in the Near East other than the protection of American tourists and Christian missionaries there. But the war

had made the United States a nation with "interests" everywhere;
the strategic importance of the Near East as a gateway to Asia
suddenly had to be taken into account in American planning, and
also the discovery that the Arab sheikhs were sitting atop a pool
of oil amounting to two-thirds of the world's known supply. As
President Truman would shortly learn, many powerful members
of his administration were strongly opposed to any pro-Jewish
Palestine policy simply because they did not want to endanger
access to Arab oil.

Stettinius offered to give Truman a complete briefing on the
Palestine problem. The new President was already submerged
under a host of issues whose existence he had never suspected: the
partition of Germany into equitable occupation zones, the rapacity
of Russia in demanding control of the former Nazi empire, the
problems of Chiang Kai-shek's China, a treaty with Mexico over
water rights, the progress of the atomic bomb. However, Truman
found time on April 19 to glance through the State Department's
Palestine file and President Roosevelt's declarations of Palestine
policy, as well as to refresh his knowledge of the Balfour Declaration and other relevant documents.

What he found in the files was muddled and contradictory. The
President's 1944 campaign pledge and his various communications to Rabbi Wise indicated genuine sympathy for a Jewish
Palestine; but there was no indication that anyone in the State
Department felt the same way. As Truman wrote years later, "I
was skeptical, as I read over the whole record up to date, about
some of the views and attitudes assumed by the 'striped-pants
boys' in the State Department. It seemed to me that they didn't
care enough about what happened to the thousands of displaced
persons who were involved. It was my feeling that it would be
possible for us to watch out for the long-range interests of our
country while at the same time helping these unfortunate victims
of persecution to find a home."

Truman's education in Zionism entered its next phase on the
morning of April 20—the beginning of his second week as President—when Rabbi Wise arrived to discuss with him the problem
of resettling the Jewish refugees. To Wise, this problem was inextricably linked with the birth of a Jewish state in Palestine, and he
told the President as much. Truman agreed. After his visit, Wise
released an authorized statement declaring that the new President

was "carrying out the policies of President Roosevelt and that he knew what President Roosevelt's policy regarding Palestine had been."

But Truman had a two-dimensional view of Roosevelt's Palestine policy. At the beginning of May, while Secretary of State Stettinius was in San Francisco at the conference organizing the United Nations, Acting Secretary of State Joseph C. Grew supplied the third dimension in a memorandum informing Truman that "although President Roosevelt at times gave expression to views sympathetic to certain Zionist aims, he also gave certain assurances to the Arabs which they regard as definite commitments on our part." Grew submitted a précis of Roosevelt's conversation with Ibn Saud, a copy of the April 5 letter to the Arabian king, and a summary of the frequent promises to Arab rulers to the effect that "there should be no decision altering the basic situation in Palestine without full consultation with both Arabs and Jews."

Truman now realized that he had been too hasty when he blithely told Wise he would carry on Roosevelt's Palestine policy; he made the uncomfortable discovery that Roosevelt had left him bound by irreconcilable pledges to the Arabs and to the Zionists. In fact, the United States had no coherent Palestine policy at all.

Truman felt he would have to improvise. For guidance he had several not too closely related tenets. One was his belief in the urgency of doing something about Europe's displaced persons. Another was his reverence for what he called "the noble policies of Woodrow Wilson, especially the principle of self-determination," which gave him a sympathy for Jewish nationalistic aspirations in Palestine. (It is not clear how Truman applied Wilsonian principles to the nationalistic aspirations of the Arabs who, after all, had constituted a majority of the people of Palestine at the time of its liberation from Turkish rule.) Third was Truman's naïve belief that the Arabs and the Zionists would ultimately grow more flexible and come to some reasonable accommodation with one another over sharing the Holy Land. Fourth was his desire to avoid involving the United States too deeply in the troubles of Palestine.

Somehow Truman hoped to generate a workable solution out of these principles. In the end he achieved at least partial success, but not without finding it necessary to take part in the same tortuous intrigue, the same game of encouraging both sides, that had typified Roosevelt's approach.

4.

The first Palestinian crisis of Truman's presidency erupted during the San Francisco Conference at which the United Nations was born. The first step toward the formation of a new world organization had been taken on January 1, 1942, when 26 nations that were engaged in war with the Axis powers had signed a declaration of agreement. Planning the future organization continued throughout the war, and the number of signatory nations increased as more nations entered the hostilities. By early 1945, 50 "states" were eligible to attend the San Francisco meeting—including some, like Egypt, India, and the Philippines, that had not yet attained full political independence.

The presence of these nonsovereign states had led Zionists to demand that a Jewish delegation be seated at San Francisco also. This suggestion had come first from the Revisionists, in 1942, and at that time had been attacked by more conservative Zionist groups as irresponsible. But by 1945 there was widespread feeling among Jews in the United States that a Jewish delegation be allowed to participate—particularly after Egypt, Syria, Saudi Arabia, and Lebanon had made themselves eligible to go to San Francisco by issuing token declarations of war against the Axis in 1945. (A fifth Arab state, Iraq, had declared war in 1943 and would also be represented at San Francisco.) In his meeting with Roosevelt on March 16, 1945, Rabbi Wise had brought up the matter of a Jewish voice at San Francisco on issues involving Palestine, and the President had promised to refer the subject to Secretary of State Stettinius; but, according to Stettinius, he never did.

Nor did 88 mass rallies sponsored by AZEC and the American Jewish Conference succeed in accomplishing anything. The largest of these, held in New York on April 29, attracted more than sixty thousand people. By then the San Francisco Conference was four days old. The Arabs, who had not fought against Hitler, were represented by five delegations. The Jews, Hitler's chief victims, had none. "There is one reason for this," observed David Ben-Gurion. "We are a people without a state, and therefore a people without credentials, without recognition, without representation, without the privileges of a nation, without the means of self-defense, and without any say in our fate." Israel Goldstein, head of the Z.O.A., called it "a vicious circle. They [the Jewish people] had no status there, therefore they could get no status."

Two Jewish groups—the American Jewish Conference, which was strongly pro-Zionist, and the American Jewish Committee, which was not—did receive from the United States the semiofficial status of "consultants," along with 40 other American organizations not concerned with Jewish affairs. Many other Jewish organizations, Zionist, non-Zionist, and anti-Zionist, were present at San Francisco without even this much recognition. Yet a 9-man AZEC team, aided by the 11 representatives of the American Jewish Conference, managed to distribute more than 40 separate propaganda releases in 3 languages to the assembled delegates and the press.

The aim of the Zionists was to have the old League of Nations Mandate for Palestine dissolved without, however, imperiling the promise implicit in it to create a Jewish commonwealth. AZEC and other groups in the main stream of Zionism were in favor of an international trusteeship for Palestine under the United Nations. As successor to the mandate, this international trusteeship would continue to grant the Jewish Agency quasi-governmental powers and would ultimately propose a plan for independence under Jewish administration. The radical Revisionists, of course, had their own program, also calling for United Nations trusteeship in place of the mandate, but asking that "Palestine, in its historic and natural borders, must be treated internationally as the Jewish Homeland"—that is, that Transjordan be included. The Revisionist program also called for Palestinian independence under Jewish rule "on the basis of a democratic constitution guaranteeing equal rights to all citizens" in no more than five years. All the Zionist groups were agreed on the importance of opening Palestine to Jewish immigration again during the period of trusteeship.

The Arab states had different ideas. They wanted the San Francisco Conference to declare Palestine an Arab state, or at the very least to word the UN charter's section on trusteeship in such a way as to end the special status of the Jewish Agency that the mandate had granted. With the United States government still paralyzed by the shock of Roosevelt's death, and Great Britain as eager to gratify Arab wishes now as she had been in 1939, it seemed likely that the Arabs would have their way. When the Jewish Agency was refused observer status at the meetings of the trusteeship committee, the prospects of Arab victory looked even better. Executives of American oil companies ostentatiously played host to the Arab delegates, conducting the picturesquely robed sheikhs on tours of San Francisco and assuring them that the outcome of the conference would not disappoint them.

But it did. The Zionist attendees, well schooled in the techniques of propaganda by this time, tirelessly presented their case to the delegates, talking now to the Prime Minister of New Zealand, now to the Minister for Foreign Affairs of the Netherlands, now to Foreign Minister Masaryk of Czechoslovakia, always stressing their strongest point, the need of a place of refuge for the displaced persons and the heartlessness of the prevailing White Paper restrictions.

Although the Zionists could not extract at San Francisco any guarantee of an eventual Jewish state in Palestine, they did thwart the Arab attempt to undo the Balfour Declaration. On May 15, the trusteeship committee produced a preliminary draft that declared that nothing in the trusteeship system "should be construed in and of itself to alter in any manner the rights of any state or any peoples in any territory." This was sufficient to safeguard the position of the Jewish Agency in Palestine.

The Arab states at once sought to amend this clause. On May 24 the Egyptian delegation proposed to change the text to speak of "the rights of the *people* of any territory," by which was meant the indigenous people, not any immigrants who happened to have arrived in a given territory in the past twenty or thirty years. Harold Stassen, a member of the American delegation, led the fight against this small but significant emendation two days later, and the Egyptian motion was rejected by a vote of 25–5, only the Arab states voting in its favor. The final text of the trusteeship chapter of the United Nations Charter contained an even more definite rebuff to the Arabs than the original version:

"Except as may be agreed upon in individual trusteeship agreements . . . placing each territory under the trusteeship system, and until such agreements have been concluded, nothing in this Chapter shall be construed in or of itself to alter in any manner the rights whatsoever of any states or any peoples or the terms of existing international instruments to which members of the

United Nations may respectively be parties."

With these dry legalisms the Zionists were assured that the new world organization would not hand Palestine over outright to the Arabs. That was some small comfort, at any rate. The Truman administration and the State Department took comfort from a different aspect of the dispute: the way it had been settled without the need of an official statement of policy from the United States. The hope arose that the United Nations, by collective action, would relieve the United States of the need to make irksome decisions in troublesome foreign disputes. That hope was short-lived, however.

5.

The war in Europe ended on May 7, 1945. The continent lay in rubble; millions of people were homeless, lost in the chaos the Third Reich had left as its sole heritage. Within the German concentration camps were hundreds of thousands of survivors, gaunt walking skeletons whom the Nazis had not had time to expose to the "final solution." Outside the death camps the situation of a vast population was not much better. There was no shelter for them, and famine and disease stalked the shattered cities. Of all the problems that faced the leaders of the postwar world, the problem of the displaced persons was the most immediate and the most intense. Many of them were Jews; and one did not need to be a Zionist to feel that it was proper to let these uprooted Jews find new homes for themselves in Palestine. All during his first few months in office President Truman was bombarded with letters and telegrams urging him to work toward having the White Paper rescinded.

The President's State Department advisers continued to tell him that the Arabs would never permit renewed Jewish immigration into Palestine and that any pressure exerted on that score by the United States would gravely injure American interests in the Near East. Let the United Nations handle the problem, they argued. Truman, although he suspected that some of the State Department people were more concerned with the niceties of diplomacy than they were with the sufferings of the displaced persons, did not yet have a firm grasp on the intricacies of the situation, and decided to play for time. On June 22, 1945, he sent Earl G. Harrison, the dean of the University of Pennsylvania Law

School and a former United States commissioner of immigration, on a fact-finding mission to Europe. Harrison was instructed to visit the displaced-persons camps, especially in Germany and Austria, and to gather information on the living conditions of the refugees, their needs, and "the views of the possibly non-repatriable persons as to their future destination"—that is, whether there really was such a general eagerness to go to Palestine.

About the same time, in response to a letter of inquiry from the Prime Minister of Egypt, Truman authorized the sending of another of those statements that said that "no decision should be taken regarding the basic situation in Palestine without full consultation with both Arabs and Jews." Similar letters went to other Arab leaders. Telling them such things would avoid unnecessary friction in this difficult time; and in any case Truman genuinely believed that both Arabs and Jews should be consulted in any settlement of the Palestine issue.

Harrison's report on the refugee camps was due in August. In July, Truman was to meet at Potsdam, Germany, with Churchill and Stalin. He hoped there to get from Churchill some of the background behind the issuance and continued enforcement of the White Paper. By autumn, then, Truman expected to have a much deeper understanding of the entire Palestine dilemma.

The Potsdam meeting opened on July 17. A week later, Truman informed Churchill in writing that he wished to discuss Palestine with him; and, even in advance of Harrison's report, the President had evidently come to some conclusions about the displaced persons, for he told Churchill, "There is a great interest in America in the Palestine problem. The drastic restrictions imposed on Jewish immigration by the British White Paper . . . continue to provoke passionate protest from Americans. . . . Knowing your deep and sympathetic interest in Jewish settlement in Palestine, I venture to express to you the hope that the British government may find it possible without delay to lift the restrictions of the White Paper on Jewish immigration into Palestine. . . ." Truman conceded "the difficulties of reaching a definite and satisfactory settlement," but requested Churchill's preliminary thoughts.

However, Churchill had no chance to reply. The next day, July 25, he flew back to Great Britain to await the results of his country's first Parliamentary election since 1935. The Labour Party, advocating socialization of much of British life, had waged a strong campaign against Britain's wartime hero, but still it came as a surprise and a shock when, by noon on July 26, it became clear that Churchill and his Conservative Party had been thrust from power. Labour had taken 393 seats in Parliament, the Conservatives only 189. Under the British system, Churchill was immediately replaced as Prime Minister by Clement Attlee, the leader of the Labour Party, who set out to Potsdam at once.

To Zionists the stunning electoral upheaval seemed like a clear gain. Churchill, like Roosevelt, had turned out to be a friend of Zionism in word but not in deed, deploring the White Paper but doing nothing while in office to abrogate it. The Labour Party, on the other hand, had formally pledged itself to Zionism by a party resolution of December, 1944: "The Arabs have many wide territories of their own; they must not claim to exclude the Jews from the small area of Palestine, less than the size of Wales. Indeed, we should examine also the possibility of extending the present Palestinian boundaries, by agreement with Egypt, Syria, and Transjordan." This had been followed by a statement from Hugh Dalton, one of the leaders of the Labour Party, on the eve of the 1945 election: "We consider Jewish immigration into Palestine should be permitted without the present limitations which obstruct it." Dalton went on, more cautiously, "We have also stated very clearly that this is not a matter which should be regarded as one for which the British government alone should take responsibility. . . . Steps should be taken in consultation with the American and Soviet governments to see whether we cannot get common support for a policy which will give us a happy, a free, and a prosperous Jewish state in Palestine." With Labour coming in, the White Paper seemed doomed.

Truman could not press Attlee for immediate action, though. He knew from his own experience what it was like to be catapulted into high office without adequate preparation, and he was content when the new Prime Minister, replying on July 31 to Truman's note to Churchill, simply promised that the points Truman had raised would receive attention. After his return to the United States, the President held a press conference on August 10 in which he said, "The American view on Palestine is that we want to let as many of the Jews into Palestine as it is possible to let into that country. Then the matter will have to be worked out diplomatically with the British and the Arabs, so that if a state can

be set up there they may be able to set it up on a peaceful basis."
He asserted that he had informed both Churchill and Attlee of
these views.

Truman was still no Zionist, and certainly not a political Zionist.
He accepted it as axiomatic that no sovereign Jewish state could
be set up in Palestine except by force of arms, and in his August
10 press conference he remarked, "I have no desire to send 500,000
American soldiers there to make peace in Palestine." He saw
Palestine only as a solution to the refugee problem, and would
very much have preferred some arrangement whereby the displaced persons could resume their lives in the European countries
from which Hitler had ripped them. Shortly after the press conference he told Representative Adolph Sabath of Illinois that he was
trying to secure such humane treatment for Europe's Jews that
they would not *need* to migrate to Palestine.

But on August 24 Truman received the initial report from Earl
Harrison, his emissary to Europe. It spoke of "Jewish displaced
persons ... living under guard behind barbed-wire fences in camps
of several descriptions ... amid crowded, frequently unsanitary
and generally grim conditions, in complete idleness, with no opportunity, except surreptitiously, to communicate with the outside world, waiting, hoping for some encouragement and action
in their behalf. . . . The desire to leave Germany is an urgent one.
. . . They want to be evacuated to Palestine now. . . ."

For some of the European Jews, Harrison wrote, "There is no
acceptable or even decent solution for their future other than
Palestine. This is said on a purely humanitarian basis with no
reference to ideological or political considerations so far as Palestine is concerned." He felt that "some reasonable extension or
modification" of the White Paper should be possible "without too
serious repercussions" if indeed there existed "any genuine sympathy for what these survivors have endured." Actually the British
had granted a few entry certificates to Palestine in 1945 for Jewish
immigrants, despite the supposed White Paper cutoff in 1944, but
this additional quota was just about exhausted by August. "To
anyone who has visited the concentration camps and who has
talked with the despairing survivors," said Harrison, "it is nothing
short of calamitous to contemplate that the gates of Palestine
should be soon closed."

The Jewish Agency had recently submitted a memorandum to the British government, calling for the immediate admission of 100,000 Jewish refugees to Palestine. Some 1,500,000 European Jews had survived the war. Over 250,000 of them were in displaced-persons camps, and hundreds more arrived at the camps every day. Truman, deeply moved by the Harrison report, now chose to support the Jewish Agency's request. On August 31, 1945, he forwarded a copy of Harrison's report to Prime Minister Attlee, with an accompanying letter that said:

It appears that the available certificates for immigration to Palestine will be exhausted in the near future. It is suggested that the granting of an additional one hundred thousand of such certificates would contribute greatly to a sound solution for the future of Jews still in Germany and Austria, and for other Jewish refugees who do not wish to remain where they are or who for understandable reasons do not desire to return to their countries of origin.

. . . I concur in the belief that no other single matter is so important for those who have known the horrors of concentration camps for over a decade as is the future of immigration possibilities into Palestine. . . . As I said to you in Potsdam, the American people, as a whole, firmly believe that immigration into Palestine should not be closed and that a reasonable number of Europe's persecuted Jews should, in accordance with their wishes, be permitted to resettle there. . . .

The main solution appears to lie in the quick evacuation of as many as possible of the non-repatriable Jews, who wish it, to Palestine. If it is to be effective, such action should not be long delayed.

Thus began the affair of the 100,000 refugees, which was to absorb an improbable amount of President Truman's attention and energy over the next two and a half years, to place a severe strain on Anglo-American relations, and, by drawing the United States more deeply than ever before into a direct involvement in the future of Palestine, to lead in a roundabout way to the birth of the State of Israel.

6.

The political situation in Palestine itself had never been anything less than highly complex since the arrival of large numbers of Zionist immigrants after World War I. During World War II it had become almost impossible. Though untouched by the war itself, Palestine was now a battleground in a many-sided struggle among contentious nationalistic groups.

The war against Hitler had turned many young Palestinian Jews into trained fighters. Some thirty thousand Jewish volunteers from Palestine were accepted into the British armed forces, and many of these gained combat experience that served them well when they returned to their homeland. About five thousand of these men were included in the Jewish Brigade Group, the miniature version of the hoped-for Jewish Legion, that finally was permitted to come into existence at the end of 1944. Carrying its own banner bearing the Star of David, the Jewish Brigade was formed too late to play a meaningful role in the destruction of the Third Reich, but it did participate in engagements late in the war in western Egypt, North Africa, and Italy.

There was also Haganah, the Zionist militia, whose status grew more ambiguous than ever during the war. The Zionists themselves had always been divided in their attitude toward Haganah. Activists wanted it to become a national army capable of holding Palestine against any opposition; the more cautious ones viewed it merely as a "fire brigade" to be employed in quelling unusual and abnormal disturbances, such as Arab riots. The Jewish Agency, nervous about Haganah at first, had accepted its existence in the 1930's and, under Ben-Gurion's leadership, had even given Haganah a sort of official status within the central Zionist structure. But no one in the Jewish Agency or among the British officials of the mandate was ever quite certain whether to regard Haganah as illegal or not.

The British confusion over Haganah can be seen in the use made of this Jewish armed force during the war. Officially Haganah was banned; from time to time its leaders were arrested and imprisoned by the British. But when it appeared as if Palestine might be in danger of Axis invasion, the British set up a home guard called the Jewish Settlement Police, made up entirely of Haganah men and staffed by Haganah officers under nominal British supervision. Jews nicknamed it "the legal Haganah," and the mandate authorities pretended to ignore the fact that it was recruited, staffed, and run by the forbidden underground army.

Britain also used Haganah members for dangerous espionage work on other fronts. In 1940, Arabic-speaking Haganah men created an intelligence network for the Allies in Syria and Lebanon, which were then held by the Nazi-dominated Vichy government of France. When the Allies invaded Syria a year later, 43 Haganah officers who had been imprisoned by the mandate at Acre were released so they could lead British soldiers through the mountain passes north of Palestine. Haganah teams disseminated anti-Axis propaganda throughout the Arab world and Haganah saboteurs harassed Axis installations. In May, 1941, 23 Haganah commandos under a British officer raided Tripoli with the intent of destroying oil refineries. All perished in the attempt. Haganah parachutists—including a number of girls—were dropped into German-occupied Europe, where they made contact with underground resistance forces and helped to smuggle escaped Allied prisoners of war (and Jewish refugees) to safety.

By this cooperation in the British war effort, Haganah intended no implied approval of British policies in Palestine. It was strictly an alliance of convenience; Hitler was Haganah's enemy as well as Britain's. Besides, what Haganah learned while carrying out secret missions for the British could be put to practical use in the coming struggle against the Arabs for possession of Palestine. Similarly, those Palestinian Jews unable to take part in actual combat were willing workers in the new war factories that sprang up all over their land. They learned how to produce parts for rifles and machine guns, how to repair tanks, aircraft, and military trucks, how to make ammunition and service battle equipment. These would be useful skills on the home front someday; and a small but steady percentage of what the war factories produced was siphoned off into the secret Haganah munitions caches.

Independent of Haganah was the Irgun Zvai Leumi, the clandestine supernationalistic army that refused to acknowledge the authority of the Jewish Agency. The Irgun, a pragmatic group, worked with the Jewish Agency when that seemed desirable, and even collaborated occasionally with the British. (An Irgun commando team was sent by the British into Iraq in 1941 in an unsuccessful attempt to capture the grand mufti, who was directing the pro-Axis movement in the Moslem world from his place of exile in Baghdad.)

Although the Irgun was careful to do nothing that might hamper the British war effort, its main goal was to replace the mandate by Jewish sovereignty in Palestine. During the early war years the

Irgun's activities centered on abetting the illegal immigration of refugees into Palestine, and on a campaign of civil disobedience and sabotage directed at the mandate. But by late 1944 it was engaged in open terrorism designed to make continued occupation of Palestine by the British more trouble than it was worth.

Through no coincidence, this change in policy occurred at a time when the implacable Menachem Beigin was taking control of the organization. Beigin, a Polish Jew who had undertaken a hazardous odyssey through Russia and Iran at the outbreak of the war, had reached Transjordan in 1942 and enrolled in the Allied forces there, only to desert soon afterward and slip surreptitiously into Palestine. Ferociously anti-British and militantly Zionist, he found a spiritual home in the Irgun and shortly was its commanding officer. A harsh, almost fanatical man, Beigin detested everything about the mandate and detested even more passionately the Jewish Agency "appeasers" who were willing to collaborate with British officials. He attacked Ben-Gurion and the other Zionists in terms a rabid anti-Semite might hesitate to use, and declared war on the mandate and on any Arabs who happened to get in the way of the drive toward Jewish independence.

An attempt by Beigin in 1944 to work out an alliance with Ben-Gurion came to nothing. Ben-Gurion sent a Haganah leader to confer with Beigin, who refused to renounce terrorism. One stormy meeting between Beigin and the top Haganah commander ended with the Haganah man telling the Irgun chief, "We shall step in and finish you." By 1945, Beigin and the Irgun were conducting terrorist operations throughout Palestine, to the dismay of the Jewish Agency.

Yet the Irgun was serenely moderate compared with the third of Palestine's underground Jewish armies, the Stern Gang. This outfit of true fanatics had been founded by Abraham Stern, a brilliant, romantic, somewhat unstable young Jew whose extreme devotion to political Zionism amounted to an obsession. Stern repudiated all compromise and all delay. Those Jews who preferred the path of caution were as much the enemies of Zion in his eyes as was the grand mufti. His followers called him "the Illuminator" and looked upon him as a prophet.

In January, 1942, the Stern Gang killed two officials of Histadrut, the Palestinian Jewish labor federation; a month later the mandatory police rounded up 20 of the gang's members, and Stern himself was killed. The death of "the Illuminator" inspired the tiny band of terrorists to new bombings and assassinations. While the Irgun blew up police stations and the offices of the mandate's civil service, the Stern Gang shot British officials and also a good many Jews.

The highest placed of its victims was Lord Moyne, the British minister of state in Cairo, who was killed by two Sternists in the Egyptian capital on November 6, 1944. Moyne had been suspected of opposing Jewish immigration to Palestine, though in fact he was not particularly hostile to Zionism. His assassination was of little if any tactical value, and did considerable harm by alienating supporters of the Zionist cause, such as Winston Churchill, who rose in the House of Commons to declare upon news of Moyne's death, "If our dreams for Zionism are to end in the smoke of assassins' pistols and our labors for its future are to produce a new set of gangsters worthy of Nazi Germany, many like myself will have to reconsider the position we have maintained so consistently and so long in the past."

The Jewish Agency was prompt to disassociate itself from the murder in Cairo, and gave orders to Haganah to round up as many terrorists as possible for deportation. By the spring of 1945, 279 Sternists and Irgunists had thus been expelled from Palestine.

Among Jews outside Palestine, the acts of the terrorists and the Moyne assassination in particular produced reactions of horror, for violence had never been part of the Jewish tradition, and not even the White Paper seemed sufficient cause for political murder. But there were some who admired the Irgun and even the Stern Gang for taking up arms in a holy cause. Ben Hecht, the chief propagandist for militant Zionism in the United States, called the Sternists "as valorous and nobly inspired a group of human beings as I have ever met in history," and praised the Irgun as "Jews finally fighting for their own honor. . . . The great fact was that here were Jews with a new soul, or, possibly, an old one returned. They did not dream of victory as a thing to be won by a tearful parade of their virtues. . . . Here were Jews who did not believe in the Jewish master plan of submitting always to injustice and then patiently removing it as one removes burrs from a dog's body."

Hecht told how "news of every gun it [the Irgun] fired, every barrel of dynamite it exploded, of every arsenal it looted and railroad train it tipped over was brought to me in secret communiqués, some of them hidden in cigarette packages. I never read news with a more pounding heart."

The main effect of the Jewish terrorism was to force the mandate officials into a clearly pro-Arab position. Regardless of official British policy, the average British administrator in Palestine had always inclined more toward the Arab side than the Jewish, and this was even more true of the average British soldier or policeman in Palestine. The abstract niceties of Zionist theory mattered less, to them, than the partly justifiable Arab claim that the Jews were trying to take away land that belonged to Arabs. The British generally felt that the large Arab majority in Palestine was being victimized by the aggressive Zionist minority, and they found the Arabs easier to get along with in most matters than the thorny, argumentative Jewish pioneers.

During the late 1930's, when the mufti-inspired Arabs were in a state of more or less continuous insurrection against both the Jews and the British mandate, the sympathies of the British in Palestine had turned definitely toward the Zionists. But this rapprochement lasted only a few years. By 1943, the terrorist activities of the Irgun and the Stern Gang and even the milder activities of the Jewish Agency-backed Haganah had convinced the mandate officials and soldiers that the Jews were their enemies. Heavy sentences were meted out to Jewish terrorists and arms smugglers, and harsh treatment was given to the few British soldiers who were found guilty of selling ammunition and weapons to the Jews. The sub rosa collaboration between British military officials and the Jewish underground did not prevent the British civil authorities from taking strict suppressive measures against the Jewish community, so that by 1945 there was virtually an undeclared war between the British and the Jews in Palestine.

The British had no real reason to favor the Arabs at this time, however. The neutral Arab states had been centers of Axis propaganda and espionage, while in Palestine only 8,745 men out of an Arab population of 1,000,000 had volunteered for service in the Allied army; less than half as many Palestinian Jews had supplied four times as many troops. The Arabs throughout the Near East had looked upon the Axis as liberators who would rid them of the British and the French. So it was not out of any fondness for Arabs that Great Britain ordered a crackdown on Zionist activities in Palestine as the war neared its end. Nevertheless, one could not oppose Zionists without by implication supporting Arabs; and the feeling among the Jews of Palestine that the British under the mandate favored the Arabs contributed to the collapse of communications and the drift toward chaos that Palestine experienced in 1945 and 1946.

7.

When, in late 1945, President Truman asked Prime Minister Attlee to admit 100,000 Jewish refugees to Palestine, he had no idea that he was requesting a major shift of balance in a region already tottering on the brink of anarchy. But he soon learned how complicated the Palestine problem really was.

Attlee had heard a good deal about Palestine by then from the British experts on the Near East whom he consulted after his sudden rise to power. They told him with great unanimity that the White Paper must be maintained. A typical report came from the Cairo Study Group of the Royal Institute of International Affairs, which informed the Prime Minister that the White Paper was "the only possible compromise. . . . The Zionists would never accept the White Paper officially but many of them would acquiesce if it were carried out firmly. The Arabs would certainly revolt with the assistance of the Arab states if a Jewish state were established but if the White Paper were carried out they would lose their fear both of Zionism and of the British government's intentions. . . ."

Therefore, in his reply to Truman's August 31 letter about the 100,000 Jewish refugees, Attlee reminded the President that Churchill and Roosevelt had repeatedly told the Arabs that no major changes in Palestine policy would be made against their will, and that any other course would "set aflame the whole Middle East." Attlee asked for more time to arrive at his own policy toward Palestine. Nevertheless, Britain agreed to relax its restrictions to the extent of admitting a maximum of 1,500 Jews a month to Palestine.

Abba Hillel Silver, now restored to the Zionist posts he had lost at the end of 1944, released a statement on September 23, 1945, in which he and his AZEC cochairman, Rabbi Wise, rejected the British offer as wholly inadequate. Silver and Wise called on Truman to take steps to prevent a "shameful injustice." Four days later, AZEC bought advertising space in 50 newspapers to publish an open letter to Attlee which warned that Zionist patience was exhausted, and that the only acceptable solution now was the opening of Palestine to unrestricted immigration and the proclamation of a Jewish state. The two rabbis called at the White House on September 29 to press these demands, but they must have received little satisfaction from the President, for they declined to comment in any way on their discussion with him. It seemed likely that Truman criticized them for interjecting the question of Jewish sovereignty into the refugee issue. That same day a delegation of the American Jewish Committee—which did not want a sovereign Jewish state in Palestine or anywhere else—got a much more cordial hearing from the President, who at that time evidently shared the committee's belief that Palestine should be looked upon solely as an emergency haven for the displaced persons. Truman listened to their careful explication of the difference between seeking a haven and seeking a Jewish state, and assured them that he was doing all in his power to arrange for the issuance of a "substantial number of certificates" for immigration to Palestine.

Between the Zionists and their goal stood the chunky figure of Ernest Bevin, the new Foreign Secretary of the Labour government. In the lexicon of Zionism, Bevin is discussed in terms only slightly less corrosive than those reserved for Hitler himself, and indeed he did go to great lengths to keep Jews out of the Holy Land. But perhaps he was more a victim of circumstances than a villain. Hardly the anti-Semite he was made to seem, he was rather a tradition-minded man of limited experience in international politics, who sought simple solutions in an awesomely complicated era, and clung to those solutions desperately despite all the evidence of their failure.

Bevin was an old trade-union man who had not particularly wanted to be Foreign Secretary, and who had no particular aptitude for the job. He was no intellectual, and quite vividly disliked the cadre of intellectuals in the Labour Party. Yet he did recognize that the war had brought great changes to world politics, and he saw as his mission the necessity of adapting British policies to those changes. Britain now was sapped and battered by the war, and her empire had already begun to slip away from her. It was apparent to Bevin that Russia, though also gravely injured by the war, was emerging as the new imperialist force in the world. Bevin felt the desperate need to protect British oil interests in the

Near East against Russian expansionism, for if the oil were cut off, Britain's industries would wither.

Thus he sought to maintain Britain's alliances with Egypt, Iraq, and Transjordan, and to secure a few permanent British bases in the Near East that would assure an unbroken flow of oil from Iraq and the Persian Gulf to Great Britain. He was willing to ignore the Arabs' wartime fondness for Hitler in order to keep open that oil lifeline. If this meant repudiating Labour's 1944 pledge to support the Zionist goal, so be it. Much was clear in 1945 that had not been apparent to Labour's top men the year before, and Bevin shrank from taking any step that might alienate the Arabs now that he was in office.

Of course, there was the problem of the Jewish refugees. Simple humanity demanded that something be done about them. Bevin wished that the United States would take them all in itself, but the United States was not about to do that, and so Bevin agreed in September, 1945, to let 1,500 Jews a month into Palestine. It seemed to him that the Arabs might tolerate this trickle of immigration, though they certainly would not go along with the proposal to let in 100,000 Jews, which first had been made by Moshe Shertok of the Jewish Agency in June, 1945, and now had been taken up by President Truman.

After all, Bevin reasoned, he was offering the Zionists 18,000 immigrants a year, which was more than they had had in the last two pre-White Paper years, and certainly more than had been envisioned by the framers of the White Paper. It seemed quite a fair offer to him, and he was surprised and angered by the intensity with which the Zionists turned it down. Thereafter his attitude moved quickly from a take-it-or-leave-it outlook to one of open hostility to Zionism; he had a great deal more to think about than Palestine, and, as he put it in one of his more unfortunate phrases, the Jews were not "at the head of the queue" in his order of priorities.

The more vigorously the Zionists pushed for their program, then, the more stubbornly Bevin fought back, until he had convinced himself that the Zionists were part of some world-wide conspiracy to tip the Near East to the Russians by angering the Arabs. Still, even at his most irascible, Bevin was more anti-Zionist than anti-Semitic. He had played an important role in the quashing of the anti-Zionist Passfield White Paper of 1930, and he thought that that and his offer of 18,000 new immigrants a year should have earned him the cooperation of Zionism. But when he failed to get it he turned bitter, and chose to become the defender of the simple, victimized Arabs against the aggressive, ungrateful Zionists. In any case he had no real understanding of Zionism. "There's only a Jewish religion, not a Jewish nation," he once said, when warned that the Jews of Palestine would fight to the death for their independence. Ben-Gurion said of him "that he was a very forceful character indeed, very strong-willed, bubbling with self-confidence and with considerable powers of leadership," but criticized "his closed mind, his lack of sensitivity, and his absence of a sense of history. He also showed the weakness of a man who is afraid to reverse himself lest he appear weak." When Truman turned to Great Britain to ask for admission of the 100,000 to Palestine, it was Bevin who blocked the way.

Within the State Department the old fear of upsetting the Arabs was as strong as ever. As Truman put it, State "continued to be more concerned about the Arab reaction than the sufferings of the Jews." An Arab spokesman said late in September, 1945, that he "would like to remind [Truman] of one of the last promises made by President Roosevelt," in which he had assured Ibn Saud that "he would not support the Jews in Palestine."

However, in a press conference on September 26, Truman gave an unequivocal "no" to a reporter's question as to whether Roosevelt had indeed made any such commitment to the Arabian king. This distressed the State Department. And on October 12, the situation grew worse when four Arab states—Egypt, Syria, Iraq, and Lebanon—officially notified the new Secretary of State, James F. Byrnes, that they would go to war if any attempt were made to found a Jewish state in Palestine. Byrnes suggested that Truman make public Roosevelt's letter of April 5 to Ibn Saud, and also issue a new statement of his own reaffirming Roosevelt's position. These two acts, said Byrnes, would show a token of friendship to the Arabs and make clear in this country that the President was not pledged to a policy of unilateral Zionism.

"I decided it would be well for the American people to under-stand that we wished to maintain friendship with the Arabs as well as with the Jews," Truman wrote, explaining why he authorized Byrnes to release the text of Roosevelt's letter. But the President declined to make any statement of his own. He left that job to

Byrnes. On October 18, the Secretary of State announced that President Truman was still discussing with Prime Minister Attlee "ways and means of alleviating the situation of the displaced Jews in Europe, including consideration of Palestine as a possible haven for some of these homeless Jews." But, Byrnes said, it had always been the policy of the United States "that this Government would not support a final decision which in its opinion would affect the basic situation in Palestine without full consultation with both Jews and Arabs."

By way of demonstrating that this had been Roosevelt's policy as well as Truman's, Byrnes went on to quote the text of the April 5 letter to Ibn Saud. It was the first time that one of the many letters vowing that the Arabs would have a voice in determining the future of Palestine had been made known to the American public. The State Department underscored this stand by sending cables to five Arab capitals on October 23, admitting that Palestine was under consideration as a refugee haven, but insisting that "there has been no change in this government's previously announced attitude on Palestine."

While Truman and Byrnes were engaged in these tortuous maneuvers, Attlee and Bevin had been meditating about Palestine, reaching the conclusion that the only safe thing to do was to stall. So on October 19 the British produced a proposal calling for an Anglo-American Committee of Inquiry that would examine the whole problem of the Jewish refugees, with an eye toward finding havens for them that did not necessarily include Palestine. The Committee of Inquiry first would tour British- and American-occupied Europe to study the conditions in the refugee camps, and then would try to locate countries willing to accept quantities of displaced persons. Palestine, the British said, would have to be peripheral to the main investigation, since there seemed to be no way of bringing large numbers of Jews into that country without provoking civil disturbances.

"The fact has to be faced," the British note declared, "that there is no common ground between the Arabs and the Jews. They differ in religion and in language; their cultural and social life, their ways of thought and conduct, are as difficult to reconcile as are their national aspirations." The Committee of Inquiry, therefore, would consult with the Arabs in the hope of finding a solution to the Palestine question, and meanwhile Jewish immigration there would continue at the proposed rate of 1,500 a month. The admission of refugees en masse would be pigeonholed pending detailed exploration of the situation.

American Zionists were staggered for the second time in two days. Byrnes' October 18 announcement had shaken them severely, for it revealed what they had not previously suspected, that despite Roosevelt's lofty proclamations of support for Zionist aims, he had been capable at the close of his life of sending a secret communication to the Arabs denying that he meant any such thing. They did not yet know, and probably would not have believed, that *every* promise Roosevelt had made to American Jewry about Palestine since 1938 had been accompanied by such a secret message of denial to the Arab rulers; they thought that the letter to Ibn Saud had merely been a sick old man's aberration, but that was bad enough. On October 23, AZEC presented a strong memorandum to the State Department denouncing the April 5 letter and the October 18 Byrnes statement as unexpected departures from an "unbroken chain of pro-Zionist acts, promises and pronouncements" by which the United States had previously committed itself to support for a Jewish state. The Zionists were due for a bitter surprise on that count.

But the news of a new study commission was devastating. Rabbis Wise and Silver wired Truman on October 30 to protest that the Harrison report surely provided all the information that was necessary. "What is called for is a policy not a further inquiry," they said. "Based on bitter experience over many years, we venture to affirm that the setting up of the proposed commission will bring the solution not one step nearer. It will, on the contrary, further complicate the situation, make for interminable delays and lead to confusion worse confounded." Reciting the sad history of the Evian and Bermuda conferences and the War Refugee Board, they argued that Palestine, then and now, offered the only real refuge for the war victims, and urged immediate admission of the 100,000 Jews, as well as abandonment of the White Paper and implementation of "the original purpose and underlying intent" of the Balfour Declaration, by which they meant creation of a Jewish state.

Truman reacted peevishly to the lengthy telegram from the Zionist spokesmen. "In my own mind," he wrote, "the aims and goals of the Zionists at this stage to set up a Jewish state were secondary to the more immediate problem of finding means to relieve the human misery of the displaced persons." Since "Palestine was not ours to dispose of," Zionist intransigeance was complicating his negotiations with the British. Though he felt that "America could not stand by while the victims of Hitler's racial madness were denied the opportunities to build new lives," neither did he desire "a political structure imposed on the Near East that would result in conflict. My basic approach was that the long-range fate of Palestine was the kind of problem we had the U.N. for. For the immediate future, however, some aid was needed for the Jews in Europe to find a place to live in decency."

The impatient Rabbi Silver was particularly thorny for Truman. In August, at the World Zionist Conference in London, Silver had hinted that virtue might lie in violence, and had declared that it might be "the height of statesmanship to be unstatesmanlike." In the months that followed he had issued a whole series of jabbing statements urging independence for Jewish Palestine, and the more frequently he insisted that Truman fulfill a demand that was not in the President's power to fulfill, the more irritated Truman grew.

The upsurge of Jewish terrorism in Palestine was also hampering Truman's unquestionably sincere campaign in favor of admission of the 100,000 Jews to Palestine. Haganah, abandoning its policy of self-restraint, had announced a willingness to cooperate with the Irgun and the Stern Gang in anti-British activities. On September 23, 1945, the Haganah commander sent a wire to London (where Weizmann, Ben-Gurion, Moshe Shertok, and other Jewish Agency leaders were conferring with Bevin) to ask permission to cause "one serious incident. We would then publish a declaration to the effect that it is only a warning and an indication of much more serious incidents that would threaten the safety of all British interests in the country, should the government decide against us. . . ." This wire was intercepted by the British secret service, with immediate effects on Bevin's attitude. When Weizmann rejected the offer of 1,500 immigrants a month, Bevin burst out, "What do you mean by refusing? . . . Are you trying to force my hand? If you want a fight you can have it!"

Bevin got his fight. In October, the underground Jewish radio Kol Israel proclaimed a Jewish resistance movement. Members of the Palmach, an elite Haganah commando group, liberated the illegal immigrants confined in a prison camp at Atlit on the Palestinian coast. Some sixty thousand Jews wearing concentration-camp uniforms from Belsen and Buchenwald demonstrated outside Tel Aviv. And on October 31 the "one serious incident" took place. That night Palmach troops sank three small naval craft and blew up railway lines in fifty different places; the Irgun attacked the rail yards at Lydda, midway between Tel Aviv and Jerusalem, and the Stern Gang damaged the oil refinery at Haifa. It was a skillful, well-planned strike, carried out with little loss of life and to devastating economic effect, but it hardly made Bevin's outlook on Zionism more mellow. Britain hastily sent a contingent of her Sixth Airborne Division to Palestine to restore order. According to a British public opinion poll, the country favored a strong policy against the Zionist terrorists.

Though convinced that the Zionists were their own worst enemies, Truman persevered in his efforts to get Jewish refugees into Palestine. The British proposal for a new study committee struck him as a transparent attempt to create delay, and as a camouflaged rejection of his request for the 100,000 entry permits. He knew that he could not force Bevin to abandon the idea of a committee altogether, but he exerted pressure to limit the committee's scope to an examination of the suitability of Palestine for the refugees, and to require it to render its report within 120 days. In November, when Attlee was in Washington, Truman repeated his firmness on these points, and Attlee yielded. On November 13 the formation of the committee was officially announced. It would have six British and six American members, and its tasks would be "to examine political, economic and social conditions in Palestine as they bear upon the problem of Jewish immigration and settlement therein and the well-being of the peoples now living therein"; "to examine the position of the Jews in those countries in Europe where they have been the victims of Nazi and Fascist persecution . . ."; and "to consult representative Arabs and Jews on the problems of Palestine. . . ." By focusing the committee's attention almost entirely on Palestine, Truman had won a small victory over the British, who would have preferred not to link Palestine with the refugee issue at all. But Bevin had won four more months of delay.

8.

Few American Jews were enthusiastic about the establishment of the Anglo-American Committee of Inquiry. The American Council for Judaism endorsed it; the American Jewish Committee found it unobjectionable, but called for immediate entry of the 100,000 to Palestine on humanitarian grounds while the investigation proceeded. AZEC charged, though, that President Truman had "fallen in a carefully prepared trap," and the New Zionist (Revisionist) Organization of America urged Jews to have no dealings with the committee. Even the conciliatory Rabbi Wise, when he agreed to testify before the committee, said that he was doing so only with "very great reluctance."

There was no doubt now about where the American Jewish community stood on the Palestine question. There was almost total agreement, barring only some members of the American Council for Judaism, that large numbers of refugees should be admitted to Palestine at once; and there was nearly the same degree of support for full Jewish sovereignty in Palestine. The effects of the vigorous AZEC propaganda campaign, coupled with the shocked realization of the true impact of Nazism on European Jewry, had created a remarkable transformation: what had been the position only of a minority of activist American Zionists before the war now was the accepted belief of almost all American Jews. Thus an articulate and energetic pressure group had been created in the American Jewish community, unified and vocal enough to ensure that the Truman administration would pay heed to their demands.

The degree of American Jewish unity was indicated by a poll taken by the Elmo Roper organization and released by Senators Robert Taft and Robert Wagner on November 16, 1945. A cross-section of American Jews was asked for expressions of opinion on two conflicting statements:

1) A Jewish state in Palestine is a good thing for the Jews, and every possible effort should be made to establish Palestine as a Jewish state, or commonwealth, for those who want to settle there.

2) Jews are a religious group only and not a nation, and it would be bad for the Jews to try to set up a Jewish state in Palestine or anywhere else.

Of those interviewed, 80.1 percent declared themselves in favor of a Jewish state, 10.5 percent were opposed, and 9.4 percent had no opinion. The Roper pollers commented that the percentage of undecided respondents was unusually low, and that nearly all of those who took pro-Zionist or anti-Zionist positions spoke firmly and quickly, as though they had given the issue long thought and had their minds made up.

Support for a Jewish state was higher among those Jews who attended religious services (86.6 percent) than among those who did not (70.1 percent); it was higher among those over 50 (82.9 percent) than among those under 35 (77.9 percent); it was higher among those who spoke English poorly (84.3 percent) than among those who spoke it well (78.9 percent). The far West showed the greatest support for Zionism (83.2 percent) and the South the least (67.0 percent). Wealthy Jews backed a Jewish state less consistently (73.9 percent) than Jews of the lower middle class (84.1 percent). Despite these statistical variations, the poll plainly showed that anti-Zionism and even non-Zionism were not viable forces in American Jewry.

The strength of Zionist feeling in the United States undoubtedly led to the third and ultimately successful attempt to get a pro-Zionist resolution through Congress, in late 1945. On October 26, 1945, Senators Taft and Wagner, the sponsors of the ill-fated 1944 resolutions, introduced a new measure asking that the United States support unrestricted Jewish immigration into Palestine in order to bring about the creation of "a free and democratic commonwealth in which all men, regardless of race or creed, shall enjoy equal rights." Three days later the Republican House leader, Joseph W. Martin of Massachusetts, introduced an identical resolution in the lower chamber. To avoid a repetition of the 1944 fiasco, the Zionists had secured the approval both of President Truman and Secretary of State Byrnes before permitting the resolutions to be revived.

On November 29 President Truman astonished everyone by revealing, at a press conference, that he no longer favored the resolutions, since he believed no official recommendations on Palestine should come from Congress until the Anglo-American Committee of Inquiry had made its report. The following week a clarification of Truman's change of heart came from David Stern, publisher of the Philadelphia *Record* and a Democratic

Party leader in Pennsylvania. The President, said Stern, was in favor of a "free Palestine" as a haven for refugees, but he disliked the concept of a Jewish state. "As a true American," according to Stern, Truman did not think any government should be organized along religious or racial lines.

Taft and Wagner defended their bill on December 6 by denying that the Zionists intended to found a "theocratic" state or one that would practice racial or religious discrimination. A Jewish state, they said, was simply a state in which Jews constituted the majority.

Despite the presidential intervention, the Senate Committee on Foreign Relations voted 17–1 on December 12 to adopt the resolution, although it amended the text slightly to take into account the status of the Palestinian Arabs. Now it called upon the United States to "use its good offices with the Mandatory Power to the end that Palestine shall be opened for the free entry of Jews . . . so that they may freely proceed with the upbuilding of Palestine as the Jewish National Home, and, in association with all elements of the population, establish Palestine as a democratic commonwealth in which all men, regardless of race or creed, shall have equal rights."

The House Foreign Relations Committee gave its approval, and on December 17 and 19, 1945, the Senate and House of Representatives adopted the resolutions by overwhelming voice vote. A presidential signature was not required, which spared both the Zionists and the President the embarrassment that a veto would have caused. At last Congress was on record in support of Zionism, for what that might be worth. It proved to be worth very little, except as a symbolic victory. No real decisions were to be made until the Anglo-American Committee had made its report, many months hence.

On December 10, nine days before the House gave final approval to the resolution, President Truman announced the names of the American members of the committee. Judge Joseph C. Hutcheson of the Fifth Circuit Federal Court of Houston, an old friend of Truman's who had crusaded against the Ku Klux Klan in Texas, was designated the American chairman. The other members included James G. McDonald, the former League of Nations high commissioner for German refugees; Frank W. Buxton, editor of the Boston *Herald*; Dr. Frank Aydelotte, director of

Princeton's Institute for Advanced Study; and William Phillips, a career diplomat, former United States ambassador to Italy.

The sixth place on the panel was originally listed as going to O. Max Gardner, former governor of North Carolina. Actually, Truman had chosen a Republican lawyer from California, Bartley Crum, but the State Department had rejected him as too liberal. Crum had been involved in a variety of liberal causes, both as special counsel for the President's Committee on Fair Employment Practices and in private life; he was particularly concerned with the employment problems of Negroes and with the plight of the anti-Franco refugees from Spain. Truman repeatedly proposed his name, and the State Department just as repeatedly refused. But at the last minute the President insisted, and Governor Gardner withdrew to make room for Crum on the committee.

The six American committeemen included no Jews and no one who, as a holder of elective office, might be unduly subjected to political pressures. Aside from McDonald, there were no members of the delegation who had had any connection with Jewish refugee problems or any familiarity with Zionist theory. As Crum admitted in his valuable book on the Anglo-American Committee, "When I began, I had the usual American ignorance of Palestine. The word had had its magical connotations through my youth. It was the Holy Land, of course. But when I thought of it, it was in terms of stained glass windows and pilgrimages. I had a vague idea that Great Britain had done something rather reprehensible in issuing a White Paper in 1939, but I had no definite knowledge as to the terms of this document."

The British delegation was headed by Sir John Singleton, a judge of the King's bench. Among its members were a banker, Wilfrid Crick; Sir Frederick Leggett, a labor mediator; Lord Robert Morrison, a former union leader who had served in the House of Commons before being raised to the peerage; Richard H. S. Crossman, a Labour member of Parliament and a leading left-wing intellectual; and Major Reginald Manningham-Buller, a Conservative member of Parliament.

The twelve men gathered in Washington in the closing days of 1945. When they paid an official call on President Truman, he told them that never before had the White House received so great a volume of mail as it was getting now on the problem of the displaced persons. And soon the committee members were getting mail and offers of advice too, from Zionist groups, the Institute for Arab-American Affairs, the British Information Service, the American Red Cross, and dozens of other organizations. "Jewish and Arab groups of every persuasion," Bartley Crum wrote, "were prepared to explain the issues to me in from 1,000 to 100,-000 words. Letters, telegrams, speeches, books, and even prayers began to descend upon me. . . . But it was not until I met Loy Henderson, Chief of the Near East Division of the State Department, that I received my sharpest and clearest briefing. He took me aside and told me, 'There is one fact facing both the United States and Great Britain, Mr. Crum. That is the Soviet Union. It would be wise to bear that in mind when you consider the Palestine problem." Henderson meant that a pro-Zionist committee report might drive the Arab states into the Communist camp.

The hearings began on January 4, 1946. Earl Harrison was the first witness, testifying that it was impossible for the displaced persons to go back to Germany or Poland. Even now, their lives were not safe there, and Palestine held the only hope for them. Joseph Schwartz of the Joint Distribution Committee followed, saying the same thing. Of the 1,250,000 European Jews who had survived the war, those of Western Europe would be able to reintegrate themselves in their former countries, but the Jews of Germany and Eastern Europe had no property, no prospects of settlement, not even any legal status. Two American economists finished the day's session by reporting that Palestine was economically able to absorb 100,000 refugees within six to nine months and perhaps 1,000,000 over the next decade.

Then came the spokesmen for the Jewish organizations. Rabbi Wise sketched the history of Zionism in the United States, stressing the role played by Justice Brandeis and President Wilson. Emanuel Neumann presented the legal case for Zionism, basing his arguments on the pledges inherent in the Balfour Declaration and the mandate text. When Major Manningham-Buller asked him if establishment of a Jewish state might entail the eviction of the Palestinian Arabs, Neumann replied, "The Zionist movement has never suggested the displacement of a single Arab from Palestine."

Henry Monsky of B'nai B'rith spoke on behalf of the American Jewish Conference, that quasi-representative assembly first called in 1943 and then in its third session. He devoted his time to an attack on the White Paper. Judge Joseph Proskauer represented the American Jewish Committee, making it clear that his group was "not identified with the Zionist movement." He spoke against establishment of a Jewish state, but argued for the immediate emptying of the refugee camps into Palestine, "the only place where they [the refugees] can go immediately." Sir John Singleton asked why it was impossible to arrange for them to go to some other country. "If you can do it, then God be with you," Proskauer replied. "But . . . I don't believe that the world can force these people to go where they do not want to go and where they would be strangers in a strange land."

Professor Philip Hitti of Princeton, a Christian Arab, presented the case for the other side. Palestine, he said, had been the home of the Arabs for many centuries; a Jewish state could be founded there only by force. Even if the Jews abandoned their nationalistic ideas, said Hitti, the Arabs would not accept large-scale Jewish immigration, which "seems to us an attenuated form of conquest." Another American Arab scholar, Dr. John Hazam of the College of the City of New York, raised objections to the industrialization that Zionist pioneers had brought to Palestine, turning the country into a "combination of Pittsburgh and Coney Island." And Dr. Frank W. Notestein, a Princeton population expert brought along by Professor Hitti, testified that it would never be possible to maintain a Jewish majority in Palestine, since the Arab birth rate was twice as high as that of the Jews. The implication was that the Jews could keep their proposed state "pure" only by expelling the Arabs.

Lessing Rosenwald, speaking for the American Council for Judaism, raised a stir (and split his organization) by coming out against any attempt to create such a "pure" state through refugee immigration or other means. He attacked the idea of a Jewish state as a "Hitlerian concept," and warned of the dangers of "Jewish nationalism" in a way that startled the committee members, who had not realized that Jews could be so vehemently anti-Zionist. Another much-publicized witness was Dr. Albert Einstein, probably the most famous of all the refugees from Hitlerism, who calmly asserted that all the difficulties in Palestine "are artificially created by the English. I believe if there would be a really honest government for the people there, which would get the Arabs and Jews together, there would be nothing to fear." His attack on

"British colonial rule" amazed the British committeemen.

The second phase of the Anglo-American Committee's investigations took place in London. Aboard the *Queen Elizabeth*, en route to Gerat Britain, Evan Wilson, a State Department liaison man, warned the committee not to reach a decision that seemed too favorable to the Jews, for then "an aroused Arab world might turn to the Soviet Union for support." Harold Beeley, an expert on the Near East from the British Foreign Office, spoke on the same theme. According to Crum, Beeley asked that Palestine be viewed "in the framework of strong Soviet expansionism. The Soviet planned to move down into the Middle East. The United States, therefore, would do well to join Britain in establishing a *cordon sanitaire* of Arab states. If Palestine were declared an Arab state, it would be a strong link in this chain." Soon it became evident that a majority of the British representatives shared these feelings; the Americans were much less worried about the perils of Russian influence in the Near East.

In its desire to impress on the American committee members the importance of keeping Arab interests in mind, the State Department made a critical blunder by turning over to them its secret file of confidential communications with the Arab leaders—seventeen cables, letters, and memoranda of conversations, dating from 1938 to 1945, in which the State Department had systematically negated all of President Roosevelt's public statements of support for Zionism. Bartley Crum was so shocked by this record of double-dealing that his first impulse was to resign from the committee. Instead, he chose to stay on and work to remedy what he regarded as his country's questionable conduct. Subsequently he made public a summary of the secret file. (When he challenged Undersecretary of State Dean Acheson in 1946 to release the actual texts of the letters, Acheson refused; but eventually the contents of the file were declassified by the State Department, and Crum's accusations were confirmed.)

Judge Hutcheson shared Crum's dismay over the secret file. William Phillips and James McDonald were less upset, for McDonald had had extensive contact with the State Department and Phillips, as a career diplomat, was part of it, so the revelations came as no surprise. The British delegates were generally amused at the naïveté that had allowed the Roosevelt administration to carry on the same kind of untenable double policy that their own government had tried to maintain thirty years before. Richard Crossman remarked, "I must say it pleases me to find the British and the Americans are in the same boat."

As the voyage continued, several of the British delegates voiced open hostility to Zionism. One referred to it as "Jewish Fascism," another repeatedly referred to Lessing Rosenwald's phrase, "the danger of Jewish nationalism," and a third termed Zionism "Communism in disguise," observing that "hundreds of thousands of these Jews have been behind the Russian lines for years. We simply cannot afford to have the Middle East go communistic." They spoke out strongly against the illegal immigration into Palestine, the terrorist activities of Haganah, the Irgun, and the Stern Gang, and the governmental authority that the Jewish Agency had assumed. Crum felt uncomfortable at what seemed to him to be prejudgment of the case. He had already come himself to feel that the unilateral White Paper had been illegal, but he was "determined to see the picture whole and judge it whole."

In London there were more hearings at which Zionists made their demands and Arabs opposed them. The American committeemen in particular worked hard to grasp the realities of the problem, with which most of them were still quite unfamiliar. When Nathan Jackson of the Jewish Socialist Labour Party of Great Britain testified, Judge Hutcheson asked him, "What do you mean by a Jewish state," adding, "I couldn't justly say to an American that because I am of Scotch descent, I want a Scottish state in Texas. Why do the Jews have to do that in Arabia when I can't do it in Texas?" Jackson replied, "Gentlemen, nowhere has the Jew control of his own identity as a group—nowhere in the world. Other peoples have." And when a Labour Party member of Parliament was asked about his party's unequivocal 1944 platform pledge to support Zionism, he answered plainly that the pledge had been "hurried through. . . . These resolutions were put forward and accepted because nobody objected, as far as I can remember." Campaign promises evidently meant no more in Great Britain than they did in the United States.

Tensions were beginning to build among the members of the committee. Crum asserted that "we, the Americans, began with the assumption that the nations of the world must cooperate. . . . Yet, I sensed that the British felt they must never compromise Britain's position as a great world power. Thus not only our points of view on Palestine differed radically from each other, but our national approaches to international problems." Cleavages developed until "some of us were scarcely speaking to each other." The Americans were generally pro-Zionist and the British were anti-Zionist, but neither side displayed real unity. Among the Americans, Buxton was openly pro-Zionist and Crum and McDonald sympathetic. Aydelotte and Phillips usually leaned toward the British view. Judge Hutcheson maintained judicious impartiality. On the British side, Manningham-Buller was strongly anti-Zionist, but Crossman frequently took a firm stand in favor of the Jews.

While in London the committeemen met Foreign Secretary Bevin, who had already emerged as the *bête noire* of Zionism, thanks to a series of undiplomatic remarks in the final months of 1945. His clumsiest comment had been a warning to the Jews not to let themselves look too greedy for Palestine: "I am very anxious that Jews shall not in Europe over-emphasize their racial position. . . . I want the suppression of racial warfare, and therefore if the Jews, with all their sufferings, want to get too much at the head of the queue, you have the danger of another anti-Semitic reaction through it all." With such maladroitness Bevin acquired a reputation, probably not deserved at that time, as an opponent of Jewish aspirations. When he addressed the committee, he expressed the belief that "racial states could no longer exist," but pledged that he would abide by whatever recommendation the committee made. According to Crossman, Bevin promised that if the committee turned in a unanimous report, he would "do everything in his power to put it into effect."

The committee now split into four groups to visit Poland, Czechoslovakia, Germany, and Austria, in order to ascertain the conditions in the displaced-persons camps. In Germany, Crum learned that the United Nations Relief and Rehabilitation Administration had taken a poll of 18,311 refugees. Thirteen had said they wished to remain in Europe. Of the other 18,298, Palestine was the chosen destination of 17,712. The inmates of the camps paraded before the committeemen waving banners reading, "Open the Gates of Palestine!" Sir Frederick Leggett was disturbed by the sight of a group of children singing the Zionist anthem "Hatikvah." "That is nationalism implanted even in the hearts of the very young, after the Nazi fashion," he said to Crum, who replied, "Would you feel the same way if you saw a group of

British youngsters singing 'God Save the King?' " In a camp in Austria, Richard Crossman had a chilling conversation with a 16-year-old boy whose mother had managed to reach America. "I have cut her off, root and branch," the boy said stonily. "She has betrayed the destiny of my nation. She has sold out to the *goy*. She has run away to America. It is the destiny of my nation to be the lords of Palestine. It is written in the Balfour Declaration."

Such episodes were repeated again and again. A child in one camp tugged at Crum's coat and said, "Mr. America, Mr. America, when are you going to let us out of here?" In Warsaw, the committee members found an urn waiting for them in their hotel room, with a note attached: "This urn contains the ashes of a Jew burned to death at Maidenek. For God's sake, let the living go!" At the refugee center on the site of the Bergen-Belsen death camp, the committeemen heard a steady, monotonous refrain: *"Wir wollen nach Palästina"*—"We want to go to Palestine." Some of the British members thought that the urn had been in poor taste and that the chants and banners in the camps reflected a deliberate attempt to sway them, organized by Zionist propagandists, which Crum believed was probably the case.

Yet even the most anti-Zionist committeemen, stunned by the sight of these terrible camps and the gaunt survivors, were beginning to think less about the need to please the Arabs and more about the need to get the war victims to the one land they desired. There seemed no hope whatever of restoring them to citizenship in their native countries. Anti-Semitism still was strong among the defeated peoples, and even among some of the Allied officers who now ruled them. A British officer in charge of displaced persons in the British zone of Austria told Crum and Crossman, "Frankly, I'm an anti-Semite. I honestly hate the Jew bastards. I wish they'd all been burned to death." The auxiliary bishop of Vienna said to Judge Hutcheson, "We do not hate the Jews, we hate only the Jewish spirit. We believe the best solution to the Jewish problem would be to change this Jewish spirit into a Christian spirit. The Jews should become Christians." It was quite clear that there was little eagerness in the occupied countries to welcome back the outcasts.

In February, 1946, the committeemen reunited in Vienna and went on to Cairo to hear the viewpoint of the Arab leaders. The content of these sessions was predictable enough, but there was one memorable and telling moment. It had always been a tenet of Zionism that there need be no enmity between Arab and Jew, for both were children of Abraham, cousins of the same desert heritage, sundered only by an accident of history. Indeed, relations between Arabs and Jews in the Near East had generally—with some conspicuous exceptions—been quite harmonious. There were large and ancient Jewish communities in every Arab city, and Jews had frequently risen to positions of high secular power in Moslem governments. This had begun to change only after the first successes of Zionism in the early twentieth century; the present hostility between Arab and Jew in Palestine was very much a modern phenomenon. During the Cairo hearings an eloquent explanation for this was offered by Abdur Rahman Azzam Pasha, the secretary-general of the recently formed Arab League, the latest attempt at a union of states in the Arab world:

Our brother has gone to Europe and the West and come back something else. He has come back a Russified Jew, a Polish Jew, a German Jew, an English Jew. He has come back with a totally different conception of things, Western and not Eastern. That does not mean that we are necessarily quarrelling with anyone who comes from the West. But the Jew, our old cousin, coming back with imperialistic ideas, with materialistic ideas, with reactionary or revolutionary ideas and trying to implement them first by British pressure and then by American pressure, and then by terrorism on his own part—he is not the old cousin and we do not extend to him a very good welcome. The Zionist, the new Jew, wants to dominate, and he pretends that he has got a particular civilizing mission with which he returns to a backward, degenerate race in order to put the elements of progress into an area which has no progress. Well, that has been the pretension of every power that wanted to colonize and aimed at domination. The excuse always has been that the people are backward and he has got a human mission to put them forward. The Arabs simply say "No." . . . We are not going to allow ourselves to be controlled either by great nations or small nations or dispersed nations.

Azzam Pasha's statement ignored the mystic component of Zionism—the need to return to a beloved ancient homeland—and also its special political nature—the wish to transform a scattered people into a sovereign entity. But it clarified the difference between Arab anti-Zionism and the kinds of anti-Semitism practiced elsewhere. In Europe anti-Semitism had been motivated partly by jealousy ("the Jews have all the money") and partly by superstition ("the Jews killed Christ"). In the United States anti-Semitism was most frequently a matter of snobbery ("the Jews are too pushy"). But the Arabs opposed Zionism because they saw it as a species of western imperialism aimed at inserting in their midst a culture alien to their own.

Underlying their hostility to Zionism was the fear that the industrial Western world, having thrust them out of Palestine, would go on to colonize Egypt, Syria, Iraq, and the rest of their region. Hatred of Jews as Jews was not a significant motivating force for them. They wanted the Zionists kept out of Palestine in the same way that they wanted the British to withdraw from Egypt, Transjordan, and Iraq, and the French to get out of Syria and Lebanon. Only a handful of Islamic fanatics—their violent prejudices carefully nurtured by the grand mufti—looked upon anti-Zionism as a war against enemies of their faith.

From Cairo the committee journeyed to Jerusalem, 600 miles away, arriving on March 6. They found Jerusalem an armed camp. "Barbed wire in great coils was everywhere," Crum wrote, "tanks could be seen at various intersections, special pill boxes had been put above the entrance of the [King David] hotel, and on the roofs and on the lawn of the imposing YMCA building across the street, soldiers manning machine guns surveyed all avenues of approach."

Jewish terrorism was becoming uncontrollable throughout Palestine. In Tel Aviv, British-owned shops had been looted and British official buildings burned. On December 27, the Irgun had raided two police headquarters and an arms dump, killing nine British soldiers. Jewish children were taught to spit at the British troops, calling them "Gestapo" and "English bastards" in an attempt to provoke incidents.

On January 28, the new mandatory high commissioner, Sir Alan Cunningham, had promulgated severe laws decreeing death as a penalty not only for taking part in terrorists raids but even for belonging to a terrorist society. At the same time he had permitted the exiled grand mufti's cousin to return to Palestine, where he immediately organized a general strike to protest the monthly Jewish immigration quota of 1,500. Sabotage and assassinations continued through February at a rising pace.

The first Jewish witness to come before the committee in

Jerusalem was Chaim Weizmann, now 72, still the president of the
World Zionist Organization and its alter ego, the Jewish Agency
for Palestine. Drained of vitality by the unspeakable catastrophe
that had befallen his people in the war, Weizmann said wearily,
"We are an ancient people. We have contributed to the world. We
have suffered. We have a right to live—a right to survive under
normal conditions. We are as good as anyone else, and as bad as
anyone else." Discussing anti-Semitism, he said, "One of its fundamental causes is that the Jews exist. The growth of anti-Semitism
is proportionate to the number of Jews per square kilometer. We
carry the germs of anti-Semitism in our knapsack on our backs."
It was the old Herzl thesis, so unpalatable to assimilated Jewish
anti-Zionists: Jews are different, Jews are alien, Jews can never be
fully accepted in the Gentile world, Jews must for safety's sake
segregate themselves in a land of their own. They could no longer
remain in Europe, said Weizmann. Europe was sick, and the presence of Jews there might aggravate the sickness. But he insisted
that he favored a binational Palestine from which no Arabs would
be displaced. "In the future Jewish state," he said, "Arabs would
have complete freedom of culture and language. The Jews have no
desire to dominate the Arabs. At best, the Jewish state will be an
island in an Arab sea."

Next came Ben-Gurion, an altogether different personality,
forceful, stubborn, determined. Weizmann had seemed withered
by age and sorrow. Ben-Gurion spoke with vigor and confidence
as he talked of Jewish independence—"Jewish soil, labor, agriculture, industry. We mean Jewish language, schools, culture. We
mean Jewish safety and security—complete independence as for
any other free people." The hearings took on a farcical note when
the matter of Jewish terrorism came up. "I am against violence,"
said Ben-Gurion, but he smiled. Asked if he would say anything
about Haganah, he replied that there was a Hebrew word, *haganah*, meaning "defense," and that he had heard it might also be the
name of some organization, although he was unable to say whether
it was a philanthropic society or perhaps an insurance company.

After calling Arab witnesses who asked that Palestine be made
an Arab state in which the rights of Jews would be safeguarded,
the committee went on to tour the country. Crum was surprised
to find that so many of the Jewish children he saw were blond and
blue-eyed, quite unlike the dark-haired, dark-eyed people he had

seen in the refugee camps. "One might almost assert," he wrote, "that a new Jewish folk is being created in Palestine: the vast majority almost a head taller than their parents, a sturdy people more a throwback to the farmers and fishermen of Jesus' day than products of the sons and daughters of the cities of eastern and central Europe."

Crum was offended by the aggressive commercialism of the Arab tourist guides in such places as Bethlehem and Nazareth; he was impressed by the orange groves near the coast, the vineyards and dairies in the hills, the growing industrialization around Haifa; he was awed to follow Jesus' final journey through the winding streets of Old Jerusalem, and equally awed by the prosperous modern city of Tel Aviv that the Zionists had built beside Jaffa's picturesque squalor. He toured the Hadassah Hospital just outside Jerusalem, built with the contributions of American women Zionists; he saw the fine Hebrew University; he attended a Hebrew play in Tel Aviv's Habima theater, and talked to the actor who was going to play Hamlet in Hebrew the following week.

Then the committee members visited the *kibbutzim*, the communal farming villages where private property was virtually unknown and a unique utopian societal structure seemed to be emerging. They inspected the Jordan Valley to see if it held the resources to support a larger population. They went into Arab towns to learn how the people, not the leaders, felt about Zionism. They spoke with Jewish terrorists who calmly vowed to fight to the death if the committee turned in an anti-Zionist report, and they spoke with the British military commander in Palestine, who said that if British troops were withdrawn, "the Haganah would take over all of Palestine tomorrow," and would "hold it against the entire Arab world."

Bartley Crum concluded from his Palestinian tour that a binational state would be possible: "The basic truth of Arab-Jewish life in Palestine is that political conflict on high levels does not affect the relations among the men on the street." Other committee members who made side trips to Iraq, Syria, Lebanon, and Saudi Arabia were not so certain of that. Sharp divisions sundered the twelve men as they gathered in Switzerland at the end of March, 1946, to write their report. Some felt that the Balfour Declaration had been an immoral transgression on the rights of the Arab population of Palestine, and that Zionism was a racist movement not too different in its basic outlook from Hitlerism. Others believed that the Jews were entitled to a national home in Palestine, but that they had already attained it; no further immigration was necessary. And others wanted to bypass the political questions entirely and consider only the hardships of the people in the refugee camps.

Slowly, bitterly, in sessions lasting 12 to 16 hours a day, an attempt was made to reconcile these differences, with Judge Hutcheson the chief advocate of unity and harmony. It was Hutcheson who produced the memorandum that was the basis of the committee's final unanimous position. On April 20, 1946, the committee submitted its report, and it was made public ten days later. These were its main points:

——The White Paper had been a mistake and its restrictions on Jewish immigration and land purchase should be lifted.

——Though Palestine alone could not meet the immigration needs of the Jewish war victims, no other home for them seemed available at this time.

——100,000 certificates for the admission of Jewish refugees into Palestine should be authorized at once, and actual immigration "be pushed forward as rapidly as conditions will permit."

——Proposals to transform Palestine into an Arab-ruled state or a Jewish-ruled state should be rejected as undesirable and unworkable solutions: "Jew shall not dominate Arab and Arab shall not dominate Jew in Palestine."

——Partition of Palestine between Arabs and Jews was likewise unacceptable.

——Britain should continue to govern Palestine under the terms of the mandate, pending execution of a United Nations trusteeship agreement that would lead to some long-range settlement of the Palestine problem.

The committee members were reasonably satisfied with their work, since they had provided a home for the refugees without bogging down in the more intricate and perhaps insoluble political questions. Pleased by their own unanimity and fairmindedness, they were certain that their findings would be immediately translated into action. The sole hesitant note was sounded by Sir John Singleton, who, as the committee was winding up its work, remarked, "You know, Crum, these are only recommendations."

9.

The Anglo-American Committee's report did not delight the Arabs, who thought that admission of the 100,000 refugees would be a large step toward creation of a Jewish state. Nor did the report please the Zionists, who saw themselves again denied Jewish sovereignty.

In the United States, AZEC prepared a blistering statement attacking the report for its rejection of Jewish nationalism, but Bartley Crum talked the Zionist leadership out of releasing it, knowing that it would infuriate the President. Instead, Crum persuaded Truman to announce on April 30 that he was "very happy" that the committee had endorsed the request for admission of the 100,000, and then persuaded AZEC to reply the same day with a statement terming the President's aid on the refugee question "most gratifying." In this tactful way AZEC agreed for the moment to overlook the committee's sidestepping of the political aspects of Zionism, but only for the moment. Within a few days AZEC had a new statement out that criticized the report for its denial of "Jewish rights and aspirations" and calling it unacceptable except for its refugee provision. The American Jewish Conference also rejected all but that one section of the report, as did a revisionist group, the Hebrew Committee of National Liberation. The American Jewish Committee, of course, gave the report a warm reception, and the American Council for Judaism found that it could approve the admission of the 100,000 on humanitarian grounds.

But would any part of the report be implemented? Britain was in an uproar over the ever more deadly Jewish terrorism; on April 25 the Stern Gang had killed seven British soldiers in Tel Aviv, which led to the first serious reprisal the following night, when angry British troops wrecked a dozen houses and injured a great many innocent Jews. Palestine was sliding into anarchy and to Bevin the admission of 100,000 more Jews would serve to grease the slide. When the British committee members returned home, Bevin in his anger refused at first to see them, then had a harsh interview with Crossman, accusing him of having "let us down." On May 1, Bevin told Parliament that there could be no thought of admitting any large quantity of refugees to Palestine until the "illegal armies" were disbanded. His promise of giving assent to the committee's findings, so long as they were unanimous, was a casualty of his rage. And, since nothing could ever induce Haganah to disband, an impasse was in the making.

Zionists now protested that their accusation of six months earlier—that the Anglo-American Committee had been nothing more than a British stalling device—was being vindicated. Prime Minister Attlee gave them more ammunition for this charge later in May. On May 8, Truman wrote Attlee to say that "the first thing to be done is to initiate consultations with Jews and Arabs to which both our governments are committed," and appended a long list of Jewish and Arab organizations that he felt should be invited to the talks. Two days later Attlee replied that his government felt that several weeks, or better yet a month, would be needed to plan the conference. And so the 100,000 certificates of entry went unissued through May, nor was there any sign in June that the refugees might soon be leaving the camps.

Repeated requests by Truman for some action on the 100,000 met with new British delays. The British now raised the question of who was going to pay for the transfer of the refugees, and also asked the United States whether it planned to offer military assistance in the event of an uprising by Palestine's angry Arabs. Neither of these points had previously been given much consideration by President Truman, who now realized that Britain, nearly bankrupted by the war, was in no position to pay the costs of resettling the refugees or of maintaining an increased military force in Palestine.

The resettlement costs did not seem a serious problem. Jewish philanthropic groups in the United States could probably handle them. But the military matter was something else. Truman wrote, "The country was neither disposed nor prepared to assume risks and obligations that might require us to use military force." He requested the opinion of the Joint Chiefs of Staff, who replied that not only was the demobilized United States unable to spare troops for Palestine, but that "the political shock attending the reappearance of U.S. armed forces in the Middle East would unnecessarily risk serious disturbances throughout the area far out of proportion to any local Palestine difficulties." The nation's military leaders, Truman wrote, "were primarily concerned about Middle East oil and in long-range terms about the danger that the Arabs, antagonized by Western action in Palestine, would make common cause with Russia."

Thus Truman had no way of demanding that the British honor the Anglo-American Committee's report. He continued to request admission of the 100,000 to Palestine, but he was in effect cheering the Zionists on from the sidelines, and so he was unable to insist convincingly that the British undertake a project for which the United States would give no material support.

Bevin felt victimized. On the one hand he was under pressure from Truman, who, Bevin was convinced, had taken up the cause of the refugees only for his own political advantage. On the other hand, Bevin was being attacked by irate Zionists, who were painting him as another Hitler because he would not authorize the 100,000 entry certificates. The 100,000 now were taking on a symbolic importance; but Bevin was less concerned with symbols than what he saw as the necessity to maintain order in Palestine and in the Moslem world generally. When Harold Laski, the chairman of Bevin's own Labour Party, accused him of sacrificing "the Jews who escaped from the tortures of Hitlerism to the Arab leaders," Bevin fought back wildly, declaring on June 12 that it would cost Britain another army division and £200,000,000 to admit the 100,000 to Palestine. In blind rage he cried, "Regarding the agitation in the United States, and particularly in New York, for 100,000 to be put into Palestine, I hope it will not be misunderstood in America if I say, with the purest of motives, that - that was because they do not want too many of them in New York."

This half-truth particularly pained President Truman, because he was then deep in a struggle with his own State Department to increase the number of refugees entering the United States. Beyond much doubt there had been a conscious effort among State Department bureaucrats for many years to keep the immigration quotas from being filled. This policy existed in part because of the prewar high unemployment rate in the United States and in part, apparently, out of sheer distaste for foreigners. The last year when the quotas had been even nearly filled was 1930, when 141,497 immigrants had come in out of a quota of 153,714. From 1936 to 1945, actual quota immigration had averaged just 28,425 a year. In the years 1942–45, only enough entry visas were issued to fill 8 percent of the quota places.

President Truman had attempted to remedy this bizarre, uncharitable situation by a directive of December 22, 1945, in which he said, "This period of unspeakable human distress is not the time

for us to close or narrow our gates." He did not call for an increase
in existing quotas, nor did he propose that unfilled quotas be made
cumulative from year to year; he merely requested that 39,000
quota places theoretically intended for emigrants from Central
and Eastern European countries be awarded at once to displaced
persons in the refugee camps of the American zones of occupation
in Germany and Austria. Even this limited objective was sabotaged by the bureaucracy. By the time of Bevin's June 12 blast,
only some 3,000 immigrants had come in under the Truman directive, and indeed it would take almost two years for the 39,000
places to be filled. Still, this was not Truman's fault, and he resented the assertion that he was using the refugees in a cheap and
cynical political ploy.

Yet Truman felt helpless to compel the British to admit the
100,000 to Palestine. With each new terrorist act in Palestine,
Bevin's position was hardening. On June 16 nine bridges were
blown up, including four railway bridges and the Allenby Bridge
across the Jordan near Jericho, and a Stern Gang team destroyed
the railroad workshops at Haifa. Ten days of minor incidents
followed, capped by a British order on June 29 for the arrest not
only of suspected terrorists but of the Jewish Agency leaders.
Some 2,600 men were rounded up on the Sabbath, among them
Moshe Shertok. Ben-Gurion would have been arrested too had he
not been in Paris. Retaliation for the arrests came in mid-July
when the Irgun, acting with Haganah's blessing if not overt cooperation, blew up a wing of Jerusalem's King David Hotel, the
headquarters of the British occupation forces. There were 91 fatalities, including British, Arabs, and Jews. Forty-five people were
injured.

This monstrous act cost the Zionists much sympathy throughout the world. But the British, so remarkably maladroit at public
relations, quickly restored the balance when their commanding
officer in Palestine, Sir Evelyn Barker, vented a violently anti-
Semitic outburst in which he urged "punishing the Jews in a way
the race dislikes—by striking at their pockets." Zionist propagandists gave Sir Evelyn's tasteless remarks world-wide publicity, and
were able to dramatize once again the Jewish people's need to
escape from this kind of reflexive hatred into a homeland of their
own.

Against so dismal a background of British-Zionist enmity, Truman had only one means of leverage to get the 100,000 into Palestine, and he hesitated to use it. Late in 1945, Britain had asked the United States for a loan of 5 or 6 billion dollars for 50 years at no interest, in order to stave off the financial collapse that would otherwise be inevitable. This was more than the United States was willing or able to give, but after lengthy negotiations President Truman approved a loan of $3,750,000,000 at an interest rate of 1.63 percent. Congressional ratification of the loan was necessary, and the bill was working its way through Congress in the spring of 1946 while the Palestine situation was reaching a crisis.

At the urging of Abba Hillel Silver, American Jews began to bombard the President and the Congress with letters and telegrams demanding that approval of the loan be held up until the 100,000 were on their way to Palestine. Silver declared at a mass rally in New York on June 12, "in view of the shocking record of broken pledges . . . American citizens have the right to turn to their representatives . . . and inquire whether the Government of the United States can afford to make a loan to a government whose pledged word seems to be worthless. They should also inquire whether American money, including that of the Jewish citizens of the United States . . . should be used to back up a government whose Foreign Secretary has repeatedly given evidence of a virulent anti-Jewish bias." Former Mayor Fiorello LaGuardia of New York echoed this: "If Britain wants credit, the best way to get it is the indication that the borrower knows how to keep his word." The British loan might have been in serious trouble in Congress had Rabbi Wise not broken the Zionist ranks by announcing that he felt that the loan was "imperatively needed," even though it was "very difficult for me as an American Jew and Zionist" to support it.

The anti-loan campaign caused serious uneasiness in London, although Truman had given no sign that he was ready to use a sort of blackmail to get his wishes on the refugee question. To avoid jeopardizing the loan, the Attlee government continued to express a willingness to discuss Palestine with the United States, and in June it was agreed that there would be yet another Anglo-American conference on the subject. President Truman designated his ambassador to Great Britain, Henry Grady, as the head of a three-man American delegation that would meet in London with a

British team led by Herbert Morrison, the leader of the Labour majority in Parliament.

On July 15, 1946, Congress backed the loan to Britain over strong Republican opposition, and President Truman signed the bill into law the same day. Six days later the Morrison-Grady talks began, and by July 25 this Anglo-American Committee of Experts (whose American representatives were not experts on Palestine at all) produced its recommendations. What the committee had come up with, essentially, was a revival of the Peel partition plan that had instantly been dismissed in 1937 by both sides as unacceptable.

The Morrison-Grady plan called for dividing Palestine into three parts, all three to remain under a British trusteeship. Out of Palestine's 10,000 square miles, 1,500 would be designated as a "Jewish province." This was a stripped-down version of the 2,600-square-mile Jewish state offered by the Peel Report, and was to take in most of the coastal plain, some inland territory, and the eastern Galilee. Great Britain would maintain direct control over Jerusalem, Bethlehem, and the Negev Desert. The rest of the country would become an Arab state. The central government, in British hands, would exercise authority over the semiautonomous Jewish and Arab states, and would continue to hold the responsibility for defense, police, foreign relations, prisons, the courts, the post office, and most other civil functions; it would also retain final authority over immigration, though the provincial governments would have the right of appeal to the United Nations Trusteeship Council. The "Jewish province" would have a large Arab minority, whose rights would be safeguarded by law so that the Arabs "will be freed once and for all from any fear of Jewish domination."

Morrison-Grady permitted the 100,000 refugees to be admitted to Palestine, the catch being that they could not come in until twelve months after implementation of the partition plan. The United States was required to accept "sole responsibility" for their transfer from Europe to Palestine, and for feeding them during their first two months in Palestine. (President Truman had agreed to this at the beginning of July in a letter to the Jewish Agency.) The United States would also be expected to make a "substantial grant"—amounting to $50,000,000—to aid the Palestinian Arabs, and was to establish an economic development program for the entire Arab world.

A less palatable set of proposals would have been hard to imagine. Admission of the 100,000 refugees had now been made contingent on Arab and Jewish acceptance of a partition plan that had been discarded almost a decade before, and in a dozen ways the new recommendations undid even the mild and cautious suggestions of the Anglo-American Committee of Inquiry.

The only ones who could be satisfied by Morrison-Grady were the British, who knew that by putting forth an obviously impossible plan they had won another few months of delay. Indeed, the entire scheme seems to have been the work of the British, and was accepted by Ambassador Grady only over the vehement protests of his own advisers and fellow conferees.

Somewhat naïvely, Truman was willing at first to approve Morrison-Grady. It seemed to him the quickest way to get the 100,000 into Palestine, and he completely misjudged the temper of the Zionist leaders, thinking they would accept the partition for the sake of having the refugees admitted. He was growing tired of listening to Jewish nationalist demands, anyway. More pressing problems were on his mind, for his administration was in a shambles; the country was bedeviled by strikes, a rampant postwar inflation, and other uncontrollable economic troubles, the Soviet Union was posing what then looked like an immediate threat to begin World War III, and Truman's own blunt approach to delicate dilemmas had made him a national laughingstock, a bungling figure whose policies were sure to be repudiated in the 1946 congressional elections. Those who could not forgive him for not being Franklin Delano Roosevelt were openly speaking of his presidency as one of the most disastrous in American history. Understandably, he wanted to disentangle himself from the Zionists and get down to issues of more immediate domestic concern.

When the Morrison-Grady plan was officially announced on July 30, Truman indicated his approval. Immediately Emanuel Celler and eight other New York congressmen, all with a strong electoral stake in supporting Zionism, went to the White House to protest. Truman paid little attention, shuffling papers on his desk while Celler read a prepared statement. Finally the President broke in to say that he had no time to listen, that he knew enough about the subject, and was working on broad plans to bring hundreds of thousands of displaced persons into South America, the British Empire, and the United States. The displaced persons, not the Jewish state in Palestine, were what mattered to him. Truman suggested that the congressmen had come to see him only because they were up for re-election that fall, and blurted that he had had his fill of people coming to him with foreign problems. Why did people not concentrate on United States problems, for a change? Then he dismissed his visitors curtly. "It was rough," a member of the delegation said afterward.

Senator Robert Wagner also called on the President, accompanied by James McDonald of the defunct Anglo-American Committee of Inquiry. They called Morrison-Grady "the negation, not the fulfillment, of the Anglo-American Committee's basic program to facilitate Jewish settlement in Palestine." McDonald asked permission to read a one-page memorandum on his position, but Truman was so angry that he refused to hear McDonald speak.

The Zionists too turned on the pressure. Telegrams poured into the White House, among them one from Henry Monsky on July 31, saying that "the very consideration of this proposal destroys the confidence of the American Jewish community in Anglo-American negotiations on Palestine." The following day Abba Hillel Silver called a press conference to attack Morrison-Grady and to stimulate Jewish intervention.

Within a few days Truman found himself under massive pressure from the entire spectrum of American Jewry—the Revisionists at one extreme to the American Council for Judaism at the other. The Hebrew Committee of National Liberation declared that "the Hebrew people do not propose to be relegated to a shameful existence in a British-dominated ghetto." The American Jewish Committee called it "wholly unrealistic" to make admission of the 100,000 contingent on a partition plan. Rabbi Silver, speaking for AZEC, called Morrison-Grady a "conscienceless act of treachery." The American Council for Judaism was "deeply disturbed" at the retreat from implementation of the refugee plan.

The issue became tied to the fall congressional elections when Senator Robert A. Taft termed the plan "cynical," saying that it would bring "complete frustration" to the Jews in Palestine and "deep despair" for the surviving Jews in Europe. David Niles and Samuel Rosenman, two of President Truman's closest advisers and both Jewish, warned the President privately that Governor Dewey of New York was about to issue a strong pro-Zionist statement, and that unless Truman repudiated Morrison-Grady it could have a devastating effect on the chances of New York's Democratic congressmen in the election.

The President, wavering, asked the six American members of the former Anglo-American Committee to prepare some comments on Morrison-Grady and present them to a State Department group that included Ambassador Grady and Acting Secretary of State Dean Acheson. On August 9 the six committee members announced their unanimous opposition to the Morrison-Grady scheme. Judge Hutcheson, no Zionist, called it "a complete sell-out: a very pretty—even a grandiose—sell-out, but a sell-out nevertheless," which would create a "ghetto in attenuated form." The same day Postmaster General Robert E. Hannegan conveyed these conclusions to Truman. Also on August 9 such top Zionists as Rabbi Silver, Monsky, Emanuel Neumann, and Nahum Goldmann were circulating in the capital, expressing their viewpoints to several Cabinet members.

Truman yielded. In his memoirs he relates that he "studied the proposed plan with care. But I was unable to see that anything could come out of it except more unrest. . . . It seemed a retreat from the fine recommendations that had been made by the Anglo-American Committee of Inquiry earlier in the year." On August 12 he informed Attlee that "the opposition in this country to the plan has become so intense" that he could not support it, and four days later the White House officially announced American rejection of the Morrison-Grady formula. The political might of American Jewry had spiked an unsatisfactory solution to the Palestine problem. But no alternate solution now seemed in sight, and the displaced persons remained in their dismal camps.

10.

Unexpectedly, the scrapping of Morrison-Grady was followed by a conciliatory move from an unlikely quarter: the Jewish Agency. Ben-Gurion and the other Jewish Agency leaders who had avoided the June 29 British roundup of Palestinian Zionists announced from Paris in August, 1946, that they were willing to accept a partition plan after all. This was a definite retreat from the position that international Zionism had officially embraced since the Biltmore Program of 1942, which had called for a Jewish state embracing the whole of Palestine. But it represented a pragmatic assessment of the feasible Zionist options. The Jewish Agency now asked for a Jewish state of some 7,500 square miles, similar in outline to the Israel that later emerged, although not including the central triangle reaching to Jerusalem. President Truman's approval was sought and quickly was given; then, with Weizmann as the chief negotiator, the Jewish Agency attempted to persuade Ernest Bevin to support and enforce the new partition plan.

Weizmann and Bevin talked, on and off, all through September, and apparently the talks were going well and nearing some sort of accommodation. But the fragile accord was shattered by developments growing out of the American election campaign. Once more the threat had been raised that Governor Dewey, running for re-election in New York, was going to come out with some lavishly pro-Zionist statement, and his Democratic opponent, James Mead, called on Truman to neutralize it with a new declaration of his own. Also asking for help was the Democratic candidate for the Senate in New York, Herbert H. Lehman. Lehman had been governor of New York from 1933 to 1942, always winning election by large margins. But, although Jewish, he had never been identified with Zionist causes; he belonged to the old German-Jewish elite that opposed all manifestations of Jewish nationalism, and his considerable activities on behalf of the Jewish refugees (he had headed the United Nations Relief and Rehabilitation Administration since 1943) had not included any effort to create a Jewish state in Palestine to receive them. With New York's Jewish population now caught up in a frantic fervor of Zionism, Lehman was in trouble among his own people.

Against his better judgment, then, Truman broke a silence of several months on Palestine with an announcement on October 4, 1946, the eve of Yom Kippur, the holy Day of Atonement. Having given advance notice to Attlee and Bevin (who asked him not to speak out at this time) the President restated his request of the previous year for the admission of 100,000 refugees to Palestine. He promised to ask Congress for a program of economic assistance to that country. He took aim at America's most embarrassing liability in the whole discussion by advocating "that the immigration laws of other countries, including the United States, should be liberalized with a view to the admission of displaced persons." Finally, he praised the Jewish Agency for having "proposed a solution of the Palestine problem by means of the creation of a

viable Jewish State in control of its own immigration and economic policies in an adequate area of Palestine instead of in the
whole of Palestine. . . . To such a solution our Government could
give its support."

Why Truman released this statement just then is not entirely
clear. James Forrestal, who was serving as Secretary of the Navy
at the time, believed it was a purely political maneuver, and in his
diary quoted Secretary of State James F. Byrnes to the effect that
the step had been taken at the urging of Presidential advisers
David K. Niles and Samuel Rosenman. To Forrestal, it was simply
a case of Truman's yielding to Jewish pressures out of fear of losing
Jewish votes. Truman himself devoted half a page in his memoirs
to an expression of outrage over such an attribution: "The timing
was nothing unusual," he wrote, "and what I had said was simply
a restatement of my position; namely, that I wanted to see one
hundred thousand Jews admitted to Palestine." Support for this
position later came from Dean Acheson, Truman's Undersecretary of State in 1946, who wrote, "The statement was attacked
then and has been since as a blatant play for the Jewish vote. . . .
Plainly it could be so interpreted, but I do not believe that it had
any such purpose. When President Truman engaged in a political
maneuver, he never disguised his undiluted pleasure in it. . . . But
he never took or refused to take a step in our foreign relations to
benefit his or his party's fortunes. This he would have regarded as
false to the great office that he venerated and held in sacred trust."

The Yom Kippur statement got Truman into trouble everywhere. The Arab countries reacted loudly, threatening to withhold important pipeline transit concessions and air rights; Ibn
Saud accused Truman of breaking earlier American promises to
the Arabs and of condoning "Jewish aggression." An irate Bevin
broke off his negotiations with Weizmann, on the pretext that
Truman's ill-timed intervention had upset the Arabs and killed
any chance of an agreement. "In international affairs," he said
bitterly, "I cannot settle things if my problem is made the subject
of local elections."

Even the American Zionists were angered. Silver and other
militants were already up in arms over the Jewish Agency's abandonment of the Biltmore Program; they wanted no partition of
Palestine and were hardly likely to applaud President Truman for
endorsing one. At the opening of the 49th Annual Convention of

the Zionist Organization of America, on October 26, Z.O.A. President Silver declared, "I reject with contempt all those who unctuously and mendaciously suggested to governments or to the public press that those Zionists who do not favor partition are dangerous extremists, and that partition must be accepted lest the movement fall into their hands." He argued that the Jewish Agency had no right to enter into negotiations for partition without the approval of a World Zionist Congress. A furious debate followed, in which moderates like Louis Lipsky asserted that no Zionist liked partition, but that it was the only way out of the impasse. Shouts of "appeasement!" came from the floor. In the end the convention approved a resolution reaffirming "the legally established rights of the Jewish people . . . to the whole of mandated Palestine, undivided and unlimited."

At about the same time Dewey outbid Truman by asking that "several hundred thousand" refugees be admitted to Palestine; he said nothing on the dangerous topic of partition. In the election, New York's voters re-elected Dewey and sent the Republican, Irving Ives, to the Senate; the Jews of New York turned away from Ives' opponent Lehman in great numbers, feeling that he was insufficiently committed to Zionism. Across the nation the voters were also going Republican, although for many reasons other than the Palestine issue. For the first time since before the Depression, control of both houses of Congress went to the Republicans, and President Truman, clearly repudiated, looked like an isolated and impotent figure as he began the final two years of what seemed certain to be his only term in the White House.

II.

Foreign Secretary Bevin's belief that the Jews of New York dictated the foreign policy of the United States grew stronger when he visited this country in November, 1946. The New York longshoremen, who are given to expressing their political views in the most direct way possible, refused to handle his baggage. A Revisionist advertisement in the *New York Post* told him that "many Americans, irrespective of race and creed, and above all, the overwhelming majority of American Jews . . . do not believe that he is entitled to the traditional hospitality of this great city of New York. We believe he deserves to be told the plain truth: 'If anyone is not wanted here, thou art the man.' " Several times his safety was jeopardized by demonstrations.

Bevin reacted with equal hostility, issuing a flurry of anti-Zionist statements. He would not mind letting refugees into Palestine, he said, if it were only a humanitarian matter. "Unfortunately, that is not the position," he went on. "From the Zionist point of view, the 100,000 is only a beginning, and the Jewish Agency talk in terms of millions." And he demanded brusquely, "Why should an external Agency, largely financed from America, determine how many people should come into Palestine and interfere with the economy of the Arabs, who have been there for 2,000 years?" He enraged many congressmen with the painful accuracy of his charge that some of the most enthusiastically pro-Zionist members of Congress were equally enthusiastic advocates of limiting immigration into the United States.

One did not have to be a secret anti-Semite to oppose bringing refugees into the United States. Some of the most dedicated Jewish Zionists were against liberalization of American immigration practices, on the grounds that the Jewish claim on Palestine would be weakened if the refugees were absorbed by other countries. The non-Zionist Jewish lawyer Morris Ernst, asked by President Roosevelt to plan a postwar project for world-wide resettlement of the refugees, wrote that he was amazed "when active Jewish leaders decried, sneered and then attacked me as if I were a traitor. At one dinner party I was openly accused of furthering this plan of freer immigration in order to undermine political Zionism. . . . I could see why . . . the leaders of these movements should feel that their pet thesis was endangered by the generosity and humanity of the F.D.R. program."

Ernst later wrote that he found many Zionist leaders displayed "a deep, genuine, often fanatically emotional vested interest in putting over the Palestinian movement" even if it were necessary, in order to do so, to block refugee movements into other lands. He called such Zionists men "who are little concerned about human blood if it is not their own."

The same point was raised by the historian Arnold Toynbee, who, in an unsympathetic discussion of Zionism in his *A Study of History*, commented on the lack of interest among Zionists in the resettlement of European Jews anywhere but in Palestine. Noting, for example, how coolly Zionists had reacted to a United Nations resolution of December 15, 1946, that urged member

states to accept as many refugees as possible, Toynbee remarked
that "the makers of Zionist policy" may have been motivated in
part "by a callous determination to turn the personal tribulations
of European Jewry to account for the promotion of Zionist political aims in Palestine. Whatever the mixture of Jewish motives may
have been, Jewry made it clear that it had set its heart on a Jewish
national state in Palestine as an asylum for the remnant of the
European diaspora. . . ."

The accusation that Zionists were cool toward any but a Zionist
solution of the refugee problem has frequently been dismissed as
a calumny invented by anti-Zionist Jews or anti-Semitic Gentiles.
Yet ample evidence exists that the Zionist movement valued the
pressure created by Europe's mass of refugees and that many
Zionists did not want that pressure dissipated by emigration to
lands outside Palestine. One wartime Z.O.A. president had declared, "Are we again, in moments of desperation, going to confuse Zionism with refugeeism, *which is likely to defeat Zionism?**
. . . Zionism is not a refugee movement. It is not a product of the
second World War, nor of the first. Were there no displaced Jews
in Europe, and were there free opportunities for Jewish immigration in other parts of the world at this time, Zionism would still
be an imperative necessity."

It is a matter of record that Zionists were conspicuously absent
from hearings held in 1947 by the 80th Congress on a bill introduced by Representative William G. Stratton of Illinois, which
would have allowed up to 400,000 European refugees into the
United States. The transcript of the 11-day hearing covers 693
pages of testimony, of which just 11 pages were contributed by
Jewish organizations. Senator Herbert Lehman of New York was
the only witness who appeared on behalf of the major organizations. The national commander of the Jewish War Veterans offered a brief statement in favor of the bill, and a similar resolution
from the Jewish Community Councils of Washington Heights and
Inwood in New York City was read into the record. The rest was
silence; no Zionist witness or statement whatever came before the
House. By contrast, Zionist groups had supplied nearly 500 pages
of testimony in 1944, when hearings on the Wright-Compton
resolution calling for a Jewish homeland were held in Congress.

The combative nature of the Zionists was evident also in Basel

*Emphasis added—R.S.

in December, 1946, when the 22nd World Zionist Congress—the first since 1939—convened. The Jewish Agency was on the defensive for its willingness to talk partition with Great Britain. The British government, influenced by the new pro-Zionist Colonial Secretary Arthur Creech Jones, had asked that the partition discussions be reopened; Shertok and the other detained Jewish Agency leaders had been freed as a gesture of good will, and 2,800 illegal immigrants confined in a camp on the island of Cyprus had been allowed into Palestine. Weizmann, the elder statesman of Zionism, came before the 22nd Congress to ask for a vote of confidence in the policy of negotiating with Britain. He attacked the American militants, Silver and Neumann, for having offered tacit encouragement to a Jewish revolt in Palestine, a revolt to which, they had said, American Jews would give "full political and moral support." Weizmann declared, "Moral and political support is very little when you send other people to the barricades to face tanks and guns. The eleven new [Zionist] settlements in the Negev have, in my deepest conviction, a far greater weight than a hundred speeches about resistance—especially when the speeches are made in New York while the proposed resistance is to be made in Tel Aviv and Jerusalem."

Once again the moderates and the radicals in Zionism were at war. The radicals had cast Weizmann down in 1931; now they did it again. Hitler had so decimated the European Zionists that of the 385 delegates at the 22nd Congress, 121 were from the United States, and the 56 Z.O.A. delegates were the largest single bloc in the hall. Most of them followed the leadership of Silver and Neumann. When Weizmann halted, Neumann cried out, "Demagogue!" The old man, his eyesight so dim he could not see his accuser, peered slowly about, and finally said:

"Somebody has called me a demagogue. I do not know who. I hope that I never learn the man's name. I—a demagogue! I who have borne all the ills and travails of this movement. The person who flung that word in my face ought to know that in every house and stable in Nahalal, in every little workshop in Tel Aviv or Haifa there is a drop of my blood. You know that I am telling you the truth. Some people do not like to hear it, but you will hear me. I warn you against bogus palliatives, against short cuts, against false prophets, against facile generalizations, against distortion of historic facts. If you think of bringing the redemption nearer by un-Jewish methods, if you lose faith in hard work and better days, then you commit idolatry and endanger what we have built. Would that I had a tongue of flame, the strength of prophets, to warn you against the paths of Babylon and Egypt. 'Zion shall be redeemed in Judgment'—and not by any other means."

It was a magnificent moment for the venerable Zionist chieftain, an outcry worthy of an outraged Moses, an angry Isaiah. The delegates, all of them, rose humbly, awed, to applaud as Weizmann groped his way down the aisle and toward the door.

But eloquence was not enough; this was a time of impatient men. Silver and Neumann called for a vote on a resolution that favored "establishing Palestine as a Jewish Commonwealth" and declaring that "in the existing circumstances the Zionist movement cannot participate in the London conference." It drew 171 votes. A counterresolution sponsored by Weizmann and Wise, asking for a resumption of negotiations, received only 154 votes. This made the customary re-election of Weizmann as president of the World Zionist Organization impossible; out of respect for him, no president at all was elected, but that hardly softened his defeat. The congress also established a six-member American section of the Jewish Agency, with Rabbi Silver as its chairman. The militants were in full control of the movement.

12.

The main thrust of Zionism now was coming from the United States—a situation that would have seemed incredible as recently as 1940. American Jews by the hundreds of thousands now were engaged in pro-Zionist political agitation, were donating huge sums to the Zionist cause, were even working directly to supply guns and ammunition to the Jewish insurgents in Palestine.

Organized American Zionism was showing tremendous growth. The membership of the Zionist Organization of America was up from 43,000 in 1940 to 217,000 in 1947. Hadassah's roster had climbed from 73,000 to 198,000 in the same time, and the smaller Zionist groups had shown similar increases. Nearly a million American Jews now paid dues to the World Zionist Organization or one of its affiliates.

But the enthusiasm was more than a matter of paying dues, as is shown by the impressive rise in American Jewish financial support for Jewish Palestine. Sophisticated fund-raising techniques encouraged ever-mounting charitable quotas in Jewish communities. From 1901 to 1929, American remittances to Palestine had totaled $14,000,000. From 1930 to 1939 they were $8,000,000. But between 1939 and 1948 American Jewry donated over $200,000,-000 for Zionism.

The United Jewish Appeal drive of 1939–40 had raised $14,-500,000, of which only 24.1 percent was allocated for Palestine. UJA took in $35,000,000 in 1945, $103,000,000 in 1946, $118,-000,000 in 1947; and in those years about 40 percent of the money raised went to Palestine. The UJA collection in 1948, drawn from a potential contributing public of about five million Americans, exceeded the entire national collections of the American Red Cross by 400 percent and those of the American Cancer Society by nearly 1200 percent.

In addition to the main unified appeal, which transmitted funds only to the Palestine Foundation Fund and the land-buying Jewish National Fund, separate fund drives were undertaken by a host of organizations with special beneficiaries in mind. Thus the women's group, Hadassah, contributed $6,300,000 in 1947, chiefly for its hospital in Jerusalem; the American Technion Society raised $211,000 for support of the scientific university in Haifa; the American Friends of the Hebrew University donated $771,000; the National Labor Committee for Palestine provided $1,926,000; and so on. Uncountable millions of dollars went to Palestine as private gifts from individuals, families, and foundations, and as investments in the stock of Palestinian corporations. The supposedly non-Zionist Joint Distribution Committee, which had expended about $20,000,000 in Palestine from 1914 to 1946, gave $6,879,000 in 1947 alone, and more than twice as much the following year.

While no one could denounce philanthropy, American participation in the clandestine Zionist military operations in Palestine was highly controversial in the postwar years. This participation had begun during the war with the involvement of Ben Hecht and other entertainment-world figures in raising money for the Irgun Zvai Leumi. But, while Hecht's vociferous propaganda attracted most of the attention in 1946 and 1947, many American Jews who had no admiration whatever for the Irgun's methods were quietly aiding Haganah, which they deemed a more respectable underground force. Ben-Gurion had recruited this support on a visit to the United States in the summer of 1945.

"Arms meant money, and we had none," Ben-Gurion wrote. "I did not expect to get arms from the United States but I did expect to get money to finance purchases which might be effected elsewhere. And for this I turned to a good friend, Henry Montor, who had directed with such success the United Jewish Appeal. . . . I asked him for a list of about twenty wealthy Jews whose devotion to the security of Palestinian Jewry was wholehearted, and I asked another friend, Rudolph Sonneborn, to offer his house for a meeting on a subject of great importance. Both responded willingly without asking any questions. The result of the meeting was several million dollars with which we could begin to 'shop' for machinery and equipment to set up a proper arms industry."

Yaacov Dori, Haganah's chief of staff, who was also in the United States at that time, discovered that a good deal of American surplus war materiel was for sale—though not for military purposes. Hayim Slavin, the head of the underground arms industry in Palestine, hurried to the United States to inspect what was available; he saw that it would be useful, and bought it. "Machines and equipment were dismantled," Ben-Gurion wrote, "the parts shipped separately to Palestine as industrial machinery, and despite the strict watch kept on imports by the Mandatory authorities, and the frequent searches they carried out in Jewish settlements and urban quarters, every part reached its destination. None fell into the wrong hands." In this surreptitious way the future State of Israel began to arm itself, a process that would reach a crescendo in 1948.

Hecht, meanwhile, was sparking the Irgun's fund-raising campaign in the United States with a series of fiery newspaper advertisements and noisy mass meetings. His home in Nyack, north of New York City, became a command post: "Around me in Nyack the Palestinian underground crackled constantly. Russian and British spies pattered through the house and eavesdropped at the swimming pools where the Irgun captains were wont to gather for disputation." Organized Zionism assailed Hecht as that contradiction in terms, a bloodthirsty Jew, and labeled him a wild man, an irresponsible fanatic. In the summer of 1946 *The New York Times* refused to run a Hecht-authored advertisement for Peter Bergson's Revisionist group, which now was called the American League for a Free Palestine. *Times* publisher Arthur Hays Sulzberger, an anti-Zionist and an American Jewish Committee stalwart, had in the past been willing to run Zionist ads, but he rejected this one because of the league's suspected connection with the Irgun terrorists, and because he did not feel that the charges of British crimes against the Palestinian Jews were correct. "We happen to believe that the British are acting in good faith and not in bad faith," Sulzberger said. "From our standpoint, therefore, your advertisement is not true." Hecht responded with new salvos of accusations against Jews who thwarted Jewish aspirations.

Hecht dramatized and glamorized the Irgun leadership. His heroes were the grim Menachem Beigin, the Irgun commander, and Abrasha Stavsky, the coordinator of the Revisionists' program for smuggling Jews into Palestine. He turned them into Palestinian equivalents of George Washington or Simon Bolivar. In 1946 the Irgun and the Stern Gang claimed to have killed 373 people in Palestine, 300 of them civilians; when the British threatened to begin hanging terrorists, Beigin announced over the underground radio a policy of "an eye for an eye, a tooth for a tooth. An English soldier on the gallows for every Jewish soldier who is hanged." Hecht seized on that for his propaganda campaign. A Jewish terrorist was arrested in 1946 in connection with the murder of a policeman, and when in January, 1947, he was sentenced to be hanged, Hecht hailed him as a martyr condemned to death for the crime of having been a soldier of his country. The Irgun promptly kidnaped a British judge and a civilian in Tel Aviv, as hostages for the terrorist's safety. A stay of execution was granted and the hostages were returned, but after three months the terrorist was hanged anyway. He was the first member of the Jewish underground to be executed by the British in Palestine.

As a result of this skillful portrayal of underground heroism, a substantial sector of American Jewry ignored the warnings of the moderate Zionist leaders and aided the terrorist cause. Hecht wrote, "I watched with awe as they rose out of the stores and workshops and came to our side. Jewish clerks and salesladies, garage workers, plasterers, elevator boys, Yeshiva students, policemen, garment workers, prize fighters, housewives; Jewish soldiers and sailors still in American uniforms, Jews from night clubs, tenements, farm lands, synagogues and even penthouses came boldly to the Irgun banner. . . . They poured their dollar bills and five-dollar bills into the Irgun coffers and the coffers swelled with millions. They crowded our rallies and theaters. They cheered with joy and there was no more fear in them than in any other group of humans whooping for victory. They were all Americans with no desire to settle anywhere else, but they stormed the [League for a Free Palestine's] offices demanding to be ferried to Palestine into the ranks of the Irgun."

Among the Irgun's benefactors was Mickey Cohen, the California gambling overlord, who called on Hecht in Hollywood and asked what he could do to help the Jews fighting in Palestine. This led to a strange fund-raising dinner called by Cohen in a Los Angeles café, a grotesque parody of the sort of functions at which prosperous middle-class Jews vie with one another for status by making public pledges of cash for Zionism. Hecht wrote, "I addressed a thousand bookies, ex-prize fighters, gamblers, jockeys, touts and all sorts of lawless and semi-lawless characters; and their womenfolk. At the finish of my oratory, Madam Frankie Spitz took over the hat passing. There was no welching. Each of the bookies, toughies and fancy Dans stood up and called out firmly his contribution.

"I stood against the back wall with Mickey. He struck me a stinging blow on the arm and said, 'Make another speech and hit 'em again.' "

Hecht begged off, saying he had just left the hospital and could not speak again. So Cohen pushed his bodyguard, Mr. Howard, forward. "You tell 'em," Cohen ordered. "Tell 'em they're a lot o'cheap crumbs and they gotta give double." Hecht wrote, "Mr. Howard roared inarticulately over the microphone for a spell. When he had done, Mickey came to the edge of the stage and stood in the floodlights. He said nothing. Man by man, the 'underworld' stood up and doubled the ante for the Irgun." The meeting raised $200,000 for, in Cohen's phrase, "Jews ready to knock hell out of all the bums in the world who don't like them."

Hecht's next publicity triumph came on May 15, 1947, when fifteen newspapers, including the New York *Herald Tribune*, published an advertisement he had written, "Letter to the Terrorists of Palestine." Hundreds of other newspapers picked the ad up as news, reprinting lengthy excerpts from it. It was addressed to "My Brave Friends," and began:

You may not believe what I write you, for there is a lot of fertilizer in the air at the moment.

But, on my word as an old reporter, what I write is true.

The Jews of America are for you. You are their champions. You are the grin they wear. You are the feather in their hats.

In the past fifteen hundred years every nation of Europe has taken a crack at the Jews. This time the British are at bat.

You are the first answer that makes sense—to the New World.

Every time you blow up a British arsenal, or wreck a British jail, or send a British railroad train sky high, or rob a British bank, or let go with your guns and bombs at the British betrayers and invaders of your homeland, the Jews of America make a little holiday in their hearts.

Not all the Jews of America were for the terrorists, of course, Hecht continued. A small percentage opposed them; and, "unfortunately, this small percentage includes practically all the rich Jews of America, all the important and influential ones, all the heads of nearly all the Jewish organizations whom the American newspapers call 'The Jewish Leaders.' They're all against.

"Every time you throw a punch at the British betrayers of your homeland, nearly all these Jews have a collective conniption fit.

"They rush in waving white handkerchiefs and alibis. They didn't do it—not they!

"Respectable people don't fight. They gabble."

Comparing the terrorists to the American Revolutionary Army under George Washington—"The respectable and wealthy American colonists preferred British admiration to liberty and freedom," Hecht wrote—the advertisement promised that the Irgun's cause would ultimately triumph despite all opposition:

For a change, the Jews of America hear more than Jewish groans to solace.

We hear Hebrew courage.

We hear brave men fighting on despite torture, calumny, low supplies and overwhelming odds!

We're out to raise millions for you.

Hang on, brave friends, our money is on its way.

Four days after the advertisement was published, *The New York Times* (which had not run it) carried a report from its Washington correspondent, James Reston, on the protest filed with the State

Department by the British ambassador to the United States:
". . . in the view of his Government an advertisement published
in a New York paper amounted to an incitement to murder British
officials and soldiers in the Holy Land. The British Government
apparently made it clear that it was not asking for the suppression
of this kind of advertising or of any other, but it evidently stated
that it did not understand why American citizens should contribute funds to carry on a war against the citizens of a friendly
nation."

But many Americans, and nearly all American Jews, had ceased
to regard Great Britain as "a friendly nation." The Palestine situation had so inflamed Anglo-American relations that the British
were regarded in some quarters as successors in crime to the
Nazis. In March, 1947, one Revisionist group had called for a
boycott of British goods, taking an advertisement in the liberal
New York newspaper *P.M.* to advocate "economic resistance of
all freedom-loving Americans" to "British atrocities in Palestine
. . . by means of organized boycott of British goods and services
. . . shipping, insurance, airlines, tourist travel, etc." Anti-British
stickers began to appear on lampposts and in subway stations all
over New York. A Revisionist-sponsored "Sons of Liberty Boycott Committee" in New York published a 16-page list of goods
and services to avoid. "Don't be a party to murder—don't buy
British goods," was the slogan. The boycott movement spread
even to the mainstream of Zionism when the Z.O.A. considered
giving an official blessing to it. (In the end it decided not to,
because of possible British retaliation against Jewish Palestine's
economy.) Though its chief effect on Britain was psychological,
the 1947–48 boycott campaign undoubtedly played a part in the
eventual British decision to get out of Palestine altogether.

The biggest single weapon of the Zionist propagandists was the
aliyah bet, the illegal immigration. This had been going on since
long before the war, but by 1945 had become a systematic enterprise, in which a network of Jewish Agency operatives collected
refugees in the European displaced-persons camps, slipped them
out via well-planned escape routes to Mediterranean ports, and put
them aboard ships bound for Palestine. Many of these ships were
intercepted by British patrols and their passengers prevented from
entering the Holy Land. Either way the Zionists benefited: if they
got new immigrants into Palestine, that was excellent, and if the

refugees were caught by the British, the interceptions gave world-wide publicity to the Jews' poignant struggle to reach their destined homeland.

In the three years from the end of World War II to the birth of the State of Israel, 84,000 Jews were removed from camps in seven European countries and embarked from 24 secret points for Palestine aboard 63 different ships, most of them virtually unseaworthy. Nearly all of these vessels were stopped by the British and the passengers dumped into a prison camp on Cyprus.

There was a good deal of American involvement in this traffic. Members of the U.S. armed services in Europe were part of the operation that got the refugees out of the detention camps; other Americans served as crewmen on the ships, and plenty of American money went into buying and equipping them. Even the austere Joint Distribution Committee knowingly channeled funds into the *aliyah bet*, though it was careful to avoid any direct connection with it.

A team of Haganah leaders came to New York late in 1945 to organize the postwar illegal immigration. They set up a legitimate-looking shipping company that purchased a pair of old Canadian corvettes in Panama and hired seamen for them. By the spring of 1946 the ships, the *Josiah Wedgwood* and the *Haganah*, were ready to set out. Their 45 crew members consisted mainly of American Zionists eager to reach Palestine themselves. The two vessels took on their human cargo in Europe, and on June 26, 1946 the *Josiah Wedgwood* delivered 1,290 refugees to Palestine; the *Haganah* brought in 2,678 more on July 29.

Other ships were added to the fleet—the *Gerilah*, the *Chaim Arlosoroff*, the *Atzmaut*, and half a dozen more. Most of them had American crewmen, 329 of whom settled in Palestine. A little office in New York was the recruiting center. It called itself the Palestine Vocational Service, and ostensibly supplied information and aid to prospective settlers in Palestine, but in fact it was conducting a quest for engineers, navigators, deck officers, stewards, radio operators, and able-bodied seamen, with or without experience. It functioned by word of mouth and by placing unobtrusive advertisements in maritime journals and newspapers that listed only a post office box number.

This Haganah-run operation had the support of the Jewish Agency. There was also an ultra-illegal immigration enterprise run by the Irgun; the Jewish Agency disapproved of this mainly because its leader was Abrasha Stavsky. (Most Zionists of the Jewish Agency faction regarded Stavsky as guilty of the 1933 assassination in Tel Aviv of Chaim Arlosoroff, a young associate of Weizmann's, although Stavsky had been acquitted of the crime in a disputed trial.) Since the 1930's Stavsky had been bringing Jews to Palestine in dismal, leaking tubs, sometimes even on rafts; in 1946 the American League for a Free Palestine attempted to raise money so that his operation could be expanded from "the present trickle to a mass exodus," as Ben Hecht put it.

Hecht called openly for American money to finance the illegal immigration; he, Louis Bromfield, and Will Rogers, Jr., constituted a Repatriation Advisory Board that issued the periodic calls for funds. "It costs $250 to move one concentration camp victim from Europe to Palestine," they announced in one ad. "The number who will reach Palestine next week depends on you." On November 11, 1946, the Repatriation Board claimed that "since last month, more than $250,000 has been sent to Europe to finance the emigration of Jews to Palestine." However, only one ship was purchased and outfitted under this program: the S.S. *Abril*, renamed the *Ben Hecht*, which the British intercepted near Haifa on March, 8, 1947. There were 599 "illegals" on board, all of whom were taken to Cyprus for internment. The next day a League for a Free Palestine spokesman hinted that 300 additional passengers had been safely landed in Haifa before the arrest: "The *Ben Hecht* left Europe with over 900 Hebrew repatriates aboard. News reports say that the ship was picked up with 600 passengers. Those 300 Hebrews unaccounted for did not disappear into thin air or into the Mediterranean. Let the British try to find them."

The widespread public support for the *aliyah bet* disturbed and embarrassed the British government, which was being made to look arbitrary and tyrannical when it turned away homeless Jews within sight of the Holy Land. Several times the British attempted to cut this traffic off at what they imagined was its place of origin. A British official charged in August, 1946, that "American financial sources" were responsible for "encouraging and directing" the illegal immigration. He would not name specific individuals or organizations, but cited "the many advertisements in United States newspapers appealing for money to aid European Jews to get to Palestine by illegal means," and mentioned one advertisement headed "American Dollars Pitted Against British Arms." The only group advertising, though, was Hecht's; the Haganah enterprise was completely clandestine.

The British also asked the State Department to cooperate in choking off the illegal transport of refugees, but there was little that the State Department was able to do. In the spring of 1947 Britain again protested the open solicitation of funds for the *aliyah bet*, this time expressing the exaggerated belief "that already this year between twenty-five and thirty million dollars have been received for the purpose of encouraging illegal immigration, buying guns, and openly advocating support of the terrorists who are shooting down British soldiers." American contributions to underground activities in Palestine did not amount to a tenth as much. But by the spring of 1947 the British were so bedeviled by the Palestine mess that they were having great difficulty in distinguishing fact from delusion.

The main instrument of torment for the British just then was a 4,000-ton steamer formerly known as the *President Warfield*, which once had carried vacationers about in Chesapeake Bay, and later had served to transport Allied troops from Britain to France during World War II. She had been sold to scrap dealers by the United States in 1946 for $8,000, but an agent of Haganah spotted her in Baltimore and acquired her for $40,000 cash, no questions asked. (Much of the money for the purchase came quietly from the Joint Distribution Committee.) A 24-year-old merchant seaman from Cincinnati, Bernard Marks, took command of the antiquated three-deck vessel, which was renamed *Yeziat Eiropa 1947* ("Exodus from Europe 1947") and usually called simply the *Exodus.* She was the thirty-fourth and largest ship to join the postwar *aliyah bet* fleet.

Captain Marks assembled a crew of 69, most of them Americans, and set out into the Atlantic on February 25, 1947. The *Exodus*, still officially traveling under the name of the *President Warfield*, carried papers listing China as her destination. But the British were not deceived. When the ship stopped for refueling in the Azores, Britain attempted to prevent the Portuguese officials there from supplying her with oil. The Portuguese would not be pressured, and on April 30 the ship arrived at the Italian port of La Spezia, followed by several British vessels and a team of British intelligence men.

All during May and June the *President Warfield* remained at La Spezia, taking on supplies under British surveillance. At the same time thousands of Jewish refugees were mysteriously arriving in Marseilles, where Haganah men supplied them with valid French passports stamped with visas for Colombia. (By this time the underground had become adept at producing documents of all sorts.) By night these refugees were whisked out of Marseilles and taken to villas in the little French harbor of Sète, midway between La Spezia and Marseilles.

On July 4, 1947, the *President Warfield* appeared at Sète and began to take on passengers, a job that required six days. French port officials blandly permitted the refugees to embark, since their papers were in order. The British government, meanwhile, was frantically exerting pressure in Paris to halt the ship's departure, insisting that she was obviously bound not for South America but for Palestine. Unable to decide what to do, the French in the end did nothing either to aid the *President Warfield*'s sailing or to hinder it. Captain Marks left harbor on July 10 without even the assistance of a harbor pilot. His vessel, bearing 4,530 passengers, went aground once, freed herself, and headed into the open Mediterranean. When she was at sea the *President Warfield* officially transformed herself, by means of a huge banner, into the Haganah vessel *Exodus.*

In torrid summer weather the *Exodus* headed eastward through the Mediterranean. The sweltering passengers lived in mounting discomfort for seven days and seven nights, tolerating the ghastly conditions on the overcrowded ship because each moment brought them closer to Palestine. A woman died in childbirth; the sanitation system broke down; many of the older refugees became ill. Off the coast of Palestine a British patrol fleet closed in, and at 10 in the evening on July 17 the underground radio in Palestine broadcast a message from the *Exodus,* spoken in English by a young American Episcopalian clergyman on board, John S. Grauel:

"This is the refugee ship *Exodus 1947.* Before dawn today we were attacked by five British destroyers and a cruiser at a distance 17 miles from the shores of Palestine, in international waters. The assailants immediately opened fire, threw gas bombs, and rammed our ship from three directions. On our deck there are one dead, five dying, and 120 wounded. The resistance continued for three hours. Owing to the severe losses and the condition of the ship, which is in danger of sinking, we were compelled to sail in the direction of Haifa and so save the refugees on board from drowning."

The dead man was Hirsch Yakubovitch, 16, whose parents had perished in the Nazi gas chambers. Two others later died of the injuries they had suffered during the capture of the ship. One was a refugee, the other the 23-year-old first mate, William Bernstein of San Francisco. But they had not died as victims of any sudden wanton attack. Father Grauel, who was covering the voyage for a church newspaper, had carefully worded his broadcast to give the impression that the British had ruthlessly and brutally pounced on the defenseless vessel; but that was merely the first phase of the propaganda campaign that the Zionists were about to shape around the voyage of the *Exodus*.

In fact, the shots fired by the British ships had been the traditional warning shots telling Captain Marks he was surrounded and had better halt; the ramming had been fairly gentle, more a hint than an assault; and the battle aboard the ship had been touched off by its crew and passengers, not by the unhappy, reluctant British seamen who went aboard to take possession. Young Yakubovitch had been killed when he attacked the boarding party with a hatchet. Bernstein had died of a concussion. The boarding party had been more concerned with self-defense than with attack; some of its members had been captured and locked in a boiler room.

The British cooperated beautifully, if unintentionally, in the Zionist publicity campaign, contributing some extraordinary blunders that helped transform the *Exodus* case into a *cause célèbre*. When the battered ship was towed into Haifa, the sick and wounded passengers were hospitalized, but the others were forced to spend a day in wire cages erected on the docks, while furious Jewish demonstrators who had come out from the city shouted curses at the British from the far side of barricades, and an army of foreign journalists watched. Then the captured refugees were hustled aboard three British transports, which presumably were to take them to the internment camps on Cyprus, where they could await openings in the 1,500-per-month immigration quota. However, the transports bypassed Cyprus and headed up the Mediterranean toward France. Bevin, it seemed, had been particularly maddened by this latest illegal voyage, and wished to make an example of its passengers. They had departed improperly from France; therefore they would go *back* to France.

As the three transports slowly moved westward, Jewish propagandists extracted a maximum of newspaper space from the event, mobilizing world opinion against the British. Emanuel Neumann, that year's Z.O.A. president, called Britain's actions "piracy" and "murder," and the American Jewish Conference, terming it a violation of freedom of the seas, asked President Truman to protest the "illegal" British blockade of Palestine. The American Jewish Committee asked Foreign Secretary Bevin to admit the *Exodus* people to Palestine; and late in July there were demands both in the Senate and the House of Representatives that the United States take steps to secure the admission of these refugees to the Holy Land.

If the British had reconsidered at that point and sent the transports back to Haifa, they would have robbed Zionism of a powerful focus for agitation. As though to insure that no British change of heart would take place, however, the Irgun contrived to stage an atrocity of its own just as the *Exodus* passengers were nearing France. In May, 1947, Irgun commandos had blown up the prison in Acre, releasing 41 Jewish terrorists (and more than 200 ordinary criminals). Three Irgun men captured in this operation had been sentenced to death; the Irgun thereupon captured two British sergeants and said that they would die if the three terrorists did. On July 29, the *Exodus* refugees arrived at the harbour of Port de Bouc, near Marseilles. On the same day the three Irgun men were executed, and later that day the Irgun announced that it had carried out its own sentence on the British sergeants. Two days later their bodies were found hanging and boobytrapped near Tel Aviv. Tensions had reached the point of hysteria. Some British soldiers and policemen staged an instant reprisal, running amok in Tel Aviv and shooting five innocent people to death. There was no chance now that Bevin could change his mind about the passengers from the *Exodus*.

As the transports waited in harbor, the French proceeded to announce that they would not accept any of the refugees except those who would go ashore voluntarily; they were not going to permit Britain to dump thousands of unwilling deportees on them. This was quite explicitly a pro-Zionist move, for the French government and people both were in strong sympathy with Zionism and had little liking for the British Palestine policies.

Of those aboard the transports only a handful, nearly all seriously ill, announced a willingness to land. The rest stayed put. Haganah agents circled the transports in launches, telling the refugees over loudspeakers to hold firm; the refugees responded by hanging Union Jacks decorated with swastikas out the portholes. For three weeks the transport ships lay at anchor off Port de Bouc. The health of the refugees deteriorated in the heat and the crowded conditions, but they refused to budge, and the French continued to insist that they would not let the refugees be unloaded by force. Since Britain denied responsibility for feeding the 4,400 Jews remaining on board, Jewish organizations took over the task; the Joint Distribution Committee sent 150 tons of food, clothing, medicine, and school supplies. In the United States political leaders in both parties deplored the *Exodus* affair, and on August 2 British consulates throughout the country were painted with swastikas as the anti-British fervor reached a peak.

Events in Palestine grew more violent, forcing the Attlee government into an ever more one-sided stance. There now were Arab terrorist groups too, which operated with the tacit compliance of the British; in virtually every way the British had become the allies of the Palestinian Arabs against the Jewish underground. The Irgun blew up a troop train and announced that it planned to destroy the entire Palestinian railway system. A battle between Arabs and Jews began in the dreary no man's land between Tel Aviv and Jaffa, and raged murderously for a week while the British cheered the Arabs on. And through all this the continued presence of the *Exodus* at Port de Bouc left Britain open to charges of inhumanity and anti-Semitism. Bevin sought desperately for a way to end the disastrous affair. He could not get the refugees into France; it was unthinkable to admit them to Palestine; to send them to Cyprus would mean further loss of face; Colombia had branded their visas as forgeries; the United States had not offered to take them in, nor were they interested in going there. Ultimately Bevin found a solution that was a masterstroke of negative public relations for Great Britain. On August 21 the *Exodus* refugees were told that if they did not disembark within 24 hours, they would be transferred, by force if necessary, to internment camps in Germany.

It was an act of glorious folly. The refugees remained on ship, and shortly an astonished world learned that the British were sending these thousands of homeless Jews, who had come so close to the gates of Palestine, back to the country of the gas chambers and the storm troopers, back to the land they detested so bitterly that they could barely stand the sound of its language. On September 8, 1947, the first of the three transports docked at Hamburg. The refugees had warned their British guards (with whom they had actually become quite friendly during the weeks at Port de Bouc) that they would have to stage demonstrations upon landing, not in any personal way but merely for the sake of publicity; and there was a token disturbance as the human cargo was unloaded. But on September 9, during the disembarking of the 1,485 passengers of the third ship, a violent riot broke out; the British had to call for reinforcements who, armed with clubs, ax handles, and fire hoses, injured many of the passengers before they regained control.

The blood that flowed that day was worth more to Zionism than a hundred fund-raising dinners. For by this time the exasperated British had decided to shrug off the whole thorny Palestine issue. They had handed the entire problem to the United Nations. The future of the troubled land now depended on how well the Zionists and their Arab foes were able to present their respective cases to the world; everything had come down now to persuasion and propaganda.

EIGHT

The Making of a State

FOR SEVERAL years the British had been considering getting out of Palestine. The subject had been raised periodically in Parliament during the war, and was more frequently heard there in 1945 and 1946 as the Holy Land's descent into anarchy began.

The British were troubled most by the posture of the United States, which offered lofty advice about the refugee problem but did nothing to alleviate Britain's troubles with the Arabs. Thus Lord Altrincham, an opponent of continued British presence in Palestine, told the House of Lords on October 30, 1946, "I am bound to say that if the United States continues to claim to dictate a policy for immigration into Palestine regardless of the facts while we bear the brunt, then the only course for us is to return the Mandate to the United Nations and to ask them to take action upon it."

And three months later, Churchill declared that "we should definitely give notice that, unless the United States come in with us shoulder to shoulder on a fifty-fifty basis, to take a half and half share of the bloodshed, odium, trouble, expense, and worry, we will lay our Mandate at the feet of the United Nations Organization."

Foreign Secretary Bevin, too, was aware of the failure of Britain's Palestine policy and increasingly irate over the way his campaign against Jewish terrorism was making him look like some Hitlerian monster before the eyes of the world. He made a last attempt to resolve the Palestine question in January, 1947, by calling a conference of Arab and Jewish leaders in London. The Jewish Agency boycotted the meeting, and the Arab delegates were as stubbornly anti-Zionist as ever.

On February 7 Bevin put forth a compromise plan involving a partition of Palestine along the Morrison-Grady lines, plus a guarantee of entry permits for 96,000 Jews at a rate of 4,000 a month for two years, after which the Arabs would have veto power over further Jewish immigration. Both sides instantly rejected this arrangement, and on February 14, in an I-wash-my-hands-of-it mood, Bevin announced that he would refer the matter of Palestine to the United Nations. There would be new investigations, a new round of debate. "After two thousand years of conflict," he said a few days later, "another twelve months will not be considered a long delay."

He could not do so, though, without first denouncing the role of the United States in undermining his authority. Addressing the House of Commons on February 25, Bevin said, "We might have been able to do more for the Jews . . . if the bitterness of feeling which surrounds this problem of immigration had not been increased by American pressure for the immediate admission of 100,000. I do not desire to create any ill feeling with the United States, in fact, I have done all I can to promote the best possible relations with them . . . but I should have been happier if they had had regard to the fact that we were the Mandatory Power, and that we were carrying the responsibility—and if they had waited to ask us what we were doing." But, he went on, the political future of Palestine had become entangled with the political futures of President Truman and Governor Dewey, and rash statements by American politicians trying to curry favor with American Jewish voters had destroyed Bevin's bargaining position with the Arabs.

President Truman went into one of his celebrated rages over this charge, but the White House's only official reaction was a taut statement on February 26 that "the impression . . . that America's interest in Palestine and the settlement of Jews there is motivated by partisan and local politics is most unfortunate and misleading." However, Senator Owen Brewster, a Republican from Maine, called Bevin's words "the workings of a deeply distressed conscience," and Abba Hillel Silver, branding as a "mischievous distortion" Bevin's claim that Truman's interventions had caused a breakdown in Palestine negotiations, labeled Bevin's speech "as mendacious, misleading, and insulting a statement as ever issued from the lips of a British Foreign Secretary."

When the clamor died down, though, one essential fact remained: the British were ready to admit defeat in Palestine.

2.

On April 2, 1947, the British delegation at the UN asked Secretary-General Trygve Lie to add Palestine to the agenda of the regular fall session of the General Assembly. Lie was also requested to "summon, as soon as possible, a special session of the General Assembly for the purpose of constituting and instructing a special committee" that would report on its findings later in the year. In making this request, Britain attempted to maintain a pretense that it was seeking advice from the UN, rather than looking for a way out. "We are not going to the United Nations to surrender the Mandate," said Colonial Secretary Creech Jones in Parliament. "We are . . . asking for their advice as to how the Mandate can be administered. If the Mandate cannot be administered in its present form, we are asking how it can be amended."

A majority of the UN's members quickly agreed to the special session of the General Assembly, and it opened on April 28. Promptly it was submerged in a torrent of oratory over an Arab proposal to make the subject of the fall debate "The termination of the Mandate over Palestine and the declaration of its independence." The British felt it premature to talk about independence for Palestine before the special committee had made its report, and the United States agreed. The Arab motion was defeated on May 1 by a vote of 24–15, with 10 abstentions.

The next battle came over whether to allow Jewish representation at the fall General Assembly session. The Jewish Agency had asked permission, as a matter of "simple justice," to speak on behalf of the Jewish people. The Communist bloc gave immediate support to this application. (The Soviet Union at this time was starting to shake off its long-standing enmity for Zionism. Motivated by a desire to ease the British out of the Near East as quickly as possible, it was in the process of executing a 180° turn toward support for Jewish national aims.) Poland, therefore, proposed a resolution inviting the Jewish Agency to speak at the General Assembly meeting. The chief United States delegate, Warren R. Austin, objected, saying that the United Nations Charter did not provide for the presence of nongovernmental bodies in UN debates, and that if the Jewish Agency were allowed to come in, other Jewish or non-Jewish organizations might demand the same privilege. However, Austin conceded that since the Arabs were so well represented in the UN, it might be "useful" to hear the Jewish side, and so he suggested that the Jewish Agency be recognized as having "a unique status in international law" and that it be permitted to address the UN. But, Austin said, it should appear at the preliminary committee meetings now going on, not at the full assembly in the fall; and it should be made clear that the UN did not look upon the Jewish Agency as spokesman for all the Jews of the world. The Polish resolution was defeated and Austin's was passed.

After a great many more maneuvers of this sort, the special session of the General Assembly voted to establish the United Nations Special Committee on Palestine, known as UNSCOP, which was to spend the summer of 1947 gathering information and to make recommendations in the fall to the General Assembly. At the insistence of the United States and Great Britain, nations who were represented on the Security Council were excluded from participation in UNSCOP. The ostensible purpose of this was to produce an unbiased panel, but it also served to keep the Soviet Union off the investigating committee, and thus to deprive Russia of a voice in shaping the future of the Near East.

The eleven members of UNSCOP were carefully chosen in accordance with the existing UN power blocs: Sweden and the Netherlands from Western Europe; Canada and Australia from the British Commonwealth; Peru, Guatemala, and Uruguay from Latin America; Czechoslovakia and Yugoslavia from Eastern Europe; and India and Iran from Asia. It was assumed that the Latin American countries would speak for the position of the United States, that Canada, Australia, and the Western European countries would follow the British line, that the Eastern European representatives would pay heed to Russia's views, and that the Asian delegates would support the Arabs.

The great unknown in this neat equation was the United States. President Truman had spoken out often enough on the subject of admitting Jewish refugees to Palestine, but he had never taken a clear or consistent position on the *political* future of the Holy Land. In theory, the United States was bound by the declarations of Presidents Wilson and Roosevelt in favor of establishing a Jewish homeland there; however, that ambiguous phrase was empty of definite meaning.

As UNSCOP began its deliberations in New York City on May 26, 1947, the Truman administration maintained its silence. On July 31, a delegation of Democratic members of Congress, headed by Senator James E. Murray of Montana and Representative Emanuel Celler of New York, called on Secretary of State George C. Marshall to press for a clarification of American policy. "Unless the United States takes a stand and offers leadership," said Senator Murray, "the United Nations possibly will not be inclined to take a stand." Marshall assured his visitors that he was giving the problem his earnest consideration, and sent them away feeling that they had accomplished something. The diaries of Secretary of Defense James Forrestal note, however, that when the subject of Palestine came up at the Cabinet meeting of August 8, "The President interjected . . . that he proposed to make no announcements or statements upon the Palestine situation until after [the] United Nations had made its finding. He said he had stuck his neck out on this delicate question once, and he did not propose to do it again."

3.

UNSCOP took testimony for three months, in the United States, in Europe, and in Palestine. The chief Jewish spokesmen who came before it were Abba Hillel Silver, in his capacity as head of the American branch of the Jewish Agency, and Moshe Shertok, the chief of the Jewish Agency's Political Department. The venerable Weizmann also spoke, reminding his listeners of how he had appeared in a similar role before the League of Nations a quarter of a century earlier to explain why the Jews felt they needed a homeland.

On August 31, 1947, UNSCOP published its findings. There were two plans, both calling for a termination of the British mandate. The minority report, signed by India, Iran, and Yugoslavia, favored an independent federal state in Palestine, consisting of Jewish and Arab states subordinate to a central government. There would be two legislative bodies, one giving equal representation to Arabs and Jews, the other elected on the basis of proportional representation by all the inhabitants of Palestine, and hence dominated by the Arab majority. Jewish immigration into the

Jewish state would be allowed for three years, under quotas regu-
lated by the United Nations, and thereafter immigration would be
controlled by the Palestinian federal government.

The majority report was signed by Canada, Czechoslovakia,
Guatemala, Netherlands, Peru, Sweden, and Uruguay. (Australia
chose to support neither proposal.) It specified the partition of
Palestine into sovereign Arab and Jewish states, linked only by an
economic union providing for currency, customs, transportation,
and joint economic development. Each of these states was to be
democratic in character, with a constitution safeguarding the civil
and religious rights of minorities. Jerusalem would be set apart as
an internationalized territory under United Nations administration; the Arab state would include the western Galilee with the
towns of Acre and Nazareth, the inland districts of Samaria and
Judaea centering on Nablus and Hebron, and a coastal strip running from Ashdod, south of Tel Aviv, to the Egyptian border; the
Jewish state would take in the rest of the coast, the eastern Galilee,
the Negev, and an inland plain.

These two states and the internationalized territory of Jerusalem
were to come into being by September 1, 1949, with the British
maintaining control meanwhile under United Nations jurisdiction. During the transitional period, 150,000 Jewish immigrants
were to be admitted to the Jewish sector, and additional restrictions on Zionist land purchases were to be abolished. If the transitional period were to last more than two years, 60,000 Jewish
immigrants would be admitted in each following year until the
partition took effect. Thereafter, the independent Jewish state
would set its own immigration policies.

A meeting of leaders of the World Zionist Organization was in
progress in Zurich when these conclusions were released. The
minority plan, which was no better than the Morrison-Grady
scheme, was dismissed at once as "wholly unacceptable." The
reaction to the majority plan was more complex. The W.Z.O.
expressed pleasure that most members of UNSCOP had "recommended the early establishment of a sovereign state," but yet the
territory that was being offered comprised "a minor part of the
territory originally promised to the Jewish people on the basis of
it historic rights and does not include areas of the utmost importance." It constituted only 6,000 square miles (the original territory of Palestine, before the creation of Transjordan, had been

more than seven times as large), and most of that was desert. The Jewish "state" would really be little more than a ribbon of land following the Jordan River southward to a point below the Sea of Galilee and snaking westward to run down the coast from Haifa to Tel Aviv. Jerusalem, Zion itself, would be completely surrounded by Arab territory.

Even so, most of the Zionist leaders were disposed to accept the UNSCOP verdict as the best that they were likely to get, and some favored an enthusiastic show of approval for the plan. Apparently even the militant Rabbi Silver and Emanuel Neumann took some sort of "positive attitude," according to David Horowitz of the Jewish Agency. But there was nothing positive in the unreconstructedly Revisionist statement that Silver made in an interview in the New York Jewish *Day* on September 3, 1947. The boundaries drawn by UNSCOP, he said, were "a great blow and we must fight against this; I still maintain my previous position that we must demand all of Palestine and wait for such an offer on the part of the United Nations Assembly as will prove acceptable to us."

At Silver's instructions, AZEC sent memoranda of warning to all of its local committees: "If the impression is created that the Jewish people regard the majority report as being in their favor, the efforts of our enemies within the U.N. further to whittle down pro-Jewish recommendations will be greatly facilitated. . . . *We urge local Zionist leaders and spokesmen, as well as the local Jewish press, to refrain from making favorable comments on the* [UNSCOP] *recommendations and to be guided by the official attitude of our movement, which we will rush to you as soon as it has been formulated.*"

But, for the first time, Silver had misgauged the mood of his constituency. Most American Jews immediately and happily hailed the partition plan as the only feasible and satisfactory solution to the Palestine issue that was likely to emerge. One-seventh of a loaf seemed better than none. The terrorism, the bizarre *Exodus* episode, the threat of warfare in the Holy Land, had dampened everyone's militance, and few shared Silver's view that Zionism should continue to hold out for more. Take what's available, people were saying. Accept the partition plan, for the next one may be even worse.

Silver, an adroit politician, sensed the isolated nature of his position and began to prepare a strategic retreat so that he, too, could come out for partition after his long years of opposing it. He started to develop the theme that the Jews, for the sake of the unhappy refugees, would have to yield and make one more great sacrifice by swallowing the partition plan. He had no choice, for time was short and the need for Jewish unity was great. The General Assembly meeting was due to convene on September 16. The debate on Palestine would probably begin in October, and no one doubted that its outcome would be some sort of settlement. The moment for the final propaganda campaign was at hand, therefore. Not merely public opinion, but the opinions of governments themselves, now had to be won if the Zionists were to have any sort of state at all.

As the opening of the UN debate neared, it became apparent that Great Britain would oppose the UNSCOP report. The Arabs, of course, resisted giving even one square inch of Palestine to the Jews. The Soviet position was unclear. Russia had for many years denounced Zionism, but in recent months had been showing signs of moving away from its outlook.

Nor was it possible to predict what line the United States would take. Public opinion in the United States was strongly in favor of the partition plan, which only a few weeks after its announcement had become universally regarded as beneficial to the Jews. In September, such figures as Sumner Welles, Eleanor Roosevelt, and Bartley Crum spoke for partition. Governor Thomas E. Dewey declared that UNSCOP's majority report "does not give the Jews all that was promised by the nations, but a partition which gives the Jews in Palestine an independent commonwealth and an opportunity for a large immigration can be accepted as a statesmanlike solution." Speaker of the House Joseph Martin commented that a solution for "the tragic problem of Jewish national homelessness had been delayed entirely too long" and was "never more urgent than today." Another Republican, Senator Taft, asked President Truman to put the United States "definitely on record" in favor of the majority report.

The White House was deluged by mail and telegrams from citizens, some spontaneous, much stimulated by Zionist organizations' requests. The Harry S Truman Library in Missouri has in its files a partial sampling of this correspondence, amounting to 62,850 postal cards, 1,100 letters, and 1,400 telegrams on Palestine for the third quarter of 1947 alone. The Palestine mail had been abnormally heavy since the beginning of 1946, much of it at first supporting the President's campaign to admit 100,000 Jewish refugees to the Holy Land. Now it centered almost wholly on the partition plan. In this quarter, as all through the 1946–48 period, more than 75 percent of the mail came from the New England, Middle Atlantic, and East North Central regions of the United States, where 86 percent of the Jewish population (and 50 percent of the population as a whole) resided. Form letters predominated, such as this one circulated in May, 1947, by a Zionist group in Brooklyn:

SAMPLES OF LETTERS.....
　　　TO BE MAILED IMMEDIATELY.....
　　WRITE THEM IN YOUR OWN HANDWRITING......
President Harry S. Truman
White House
Washington, D.C.
Dear Mr. President:
I look to you as our leader to instruct our delegates to the U.N. to take a firm stand on the Palestine question along the lines of the Mandate, resolutions in Congress and your public statements.

Law and humanity requires that those unfortunate Jews be given an opportunity to once again become members of the human race.
　　　　　　　　　　　　　Sincerely yours,
　　　　　　　　　　　　　　[Signature]

Although the American people, Jewish and Gentile, were overwhelmingly in favor of partition, the government itself was divided and confused. President Truman himself had never fully understood the Zionist demand for political sovereignty and was uncertain of the attitude he should take toward it. He was willing to back partition if it would help get refugees into Palestine, but the State Department was warning him, as it had so many times before, that any support for Jewish nationalism would gravely offend the Arab world and injure the American position in the Near East. Truman's contempt for the "striped-pants boys" of the State Department had led him to dismiss these warnings as the panicky outbursts of upper-class diplomats who disliked Jews; but now the President began to hear objections to Zionism from a man whose counsel he valued greatly and could not so easily dismiss: Secretary of Defense James Forrestal.

4.

Secretary of Defense Forrestal's attempt to intervene in the making of American policy toward Palestine was, as were most of his other actions in high office, misinterpreted; and in some Jewish quarters he earned a reputation as an anti-Semite second only to Ernest Bevin. Hatred for this strange, intense, and ultimately tragic man still runs high among Zionists. But the nature of his conduct indicates that his anti-Zionism stemmed from no hatred of Jews nor love of Arabs, only from his dedication to the welfare and security of the United States.

Forrestal, the son of an Irish carpenter who had built a substantial construction business in New York State, was a quick-witted, hard-working, humorless and ambitious man who after a brief stay at Princeton turned to Wall Street. He was so successful a bond salesman that by 1923 he became, at 31, a partner in the investment banking house of Dillon, Read and Company. Fifteen years later he became president of Dillon, Read, but after two years in that post he resigned, in June, 1940, to become a special administrative assistant to President Roosevelt.

Forrestal felt that the United States would inevitably be drawn into the war. And he believed correctly that his position in the financial world (where loathing for Roosevelt was almost unanimous) would make him useful in Roosevelt's program for rearming the country. By August, 1940, he held the newly created post of Undersecretary of the Navy, and during the war years he played an instrumental role in the gigantic procurement program by which the navy was rebuilt. When Secretary of the Navy Frank Knox died in the spring of 1944, Forrestal replaced him in what was then a Cabinet position. After the postwar consolidation of the armed forces into the new Department of Defense, Forrestal became, on July 26, 1947, the first Secretary of Defense.

He had been concerned over the Near East for some time by then. Forrestal was one of the first to view that area not in terms of the conflicting nationalisms of Arabs and Jews, but as a vital strategic zone in the postwar rivalry between the United States and the Soviet Union. During the war, the Near East had been of high importance because of its position along the supply route to our ally, Russia. When friendship between the United States and Russia cooled at the end of the war, it began to seem desirable for the United States to maintain bases in the Near East for the purpose of "containing" Russia by controlling that supply route. Since the old British hegemony over the Near East was clearly in collapse, Forrestal and others in the military establishment saw it as essential that the United States replace Britain as the dominant factor in the region, lest the Soviet Union move in to fill the vacuum the British withdrawal was creating.

Forrestal was worried about oil. As early as 1920 American oil companies had looked toward the still unmeasured oil pool beneath the Near East; with governmental aid these companies shortly obtained a 23.75 percent share in the Iraq Petroleum Company. Later, American oil companies obtained drilling concessions in the Arabian sheikhdoms of Kuwait and Bahrein, and in Saudi Arabia, where a joint venture of Texaco and Standard Oil of California operated under the name of The Arabian-American Oil Company (ARAMCO). The Saudi Arabian oil field alone contained proven reserves of six to seven billion barrels of oil, with the possibility of another forty billion. By contrast, the proven oil reserves of the entire United States in 1947 totaled about twenty billion barrels, and the rate of discovery of new reserves seemed to be falling off, suggesting that the wells might soon be dry. (American production of oil was then running at slightly under two billion barrels a year.) The United States might be able to get along for another fifteen or twenty years on her existing oil, but her allies in Western Europe were dependent almost wholly for their energy supplies on oil from the Near East. The Soviet Union, though, was self-sufficient in oil. In the coming world struggle that Forrestal predicted, the United States and her military partners would be able to meet the Russian threat only with the aid of Arab oil. To alienate the Arabs over the question of a Jewish state in Palestine seemed, to Forrestal, suicidally foolish.

Forrestal therefore regarded the attempts of American Jews to swing the support of the United States behind the Zionist cause as dangerous to this country's long-range strategic position. As early as July 26, 1946, following a Cabinet discussion of Palestine, Forrestal had noted in his diaries that "Jews are injecting vigorous and active propaganda to force the President's hand with reference to the immediate immigration of Jews into Palestine." His concern with the political power of American Jewry grew considerably over the succeeding twelve months, and as the debate over the partition plan began in the fall of 1947 Forrestal made it his responsibility to combat this power wherever he could.

At a Cabinet lunch meeting on September 4, 1947, Postmaster General Hannegan brought up the subject of President Truman's making a new statement of policy on Palestine—not so much on the partition issue as on the matter of getting the "150,000" (sic) refugees admitted. According to Forrestal, Hannegan "said he didn't want to press for a decision one way or the other but simply wanted to point out that such a statement would have a very great influence and great effect on the raising of funds for the Democratic National Committee." Hannegan went on to point out that the Democrats had received large sums from Jewish contributors in the 1946 election campaign, "and that they would be influenced in either giving or withholding by what the President did on Palestine."

Forrestal then observed that Truman's Yom Kippur Palestine statement of October, 1946, had done nothing to help the Democrats in the 1946 New York elections, but had done a good deal to anger the British and harm Anglo-American relations. Truman himself, still sizzling over the furor his 1946 Palestine statement had aroused, declined to make any new statement now, and the General Assembly session opened twelve days later without any announcement of an American position on Palestine.

Forrestal's ally in the State Department in this campaign against Zionism was Loy W. Henderson, head of the State Department's Division of Near Eastern and African Affairs, and another of the villains of Zionist demonology. Through the comings and goings of Secretaries of State—Hull, Stettinius, Byrnes, Marshall—Henderson's authority in the department had steadily risen, and Henderson believed that the security of the United States was tied to maintaining the friendship of the Arab nations. James McDonald, who did not share this belief, described Henderson as "intelligent, vigorous and autocratic . . . prone to consider the Middle East as a personal province and himself as its benign overseer." Another friend of Zionism, Bartley Crum, told the American Christian Palestine Committee on August 21, 1947, that "some State Department officials are captives of the British social lobby" in Washington, and when asked to name them merely replied, "It would be a salutary thing if Mr. Loy W. Henderson's resignation was requested." As Henderson's role in shaping American foreign policy emerged, feeling against him grew, until some months later the *New York Post*—with a large Jewish readership—called him a "loyal ally of the British Colonial Office and ardent friend of the anti-Semitic dictators of the Arabian League, including Hitler's ex-pal and untried war criminal the Grand Mufti."

In truth Henderson was neither a friend to Nazis nor an anti-Semite. He simply believed, quite sincerely, that Arab oil was of greater importance to the United States than Jewish national aspirations. The events of the following two decades showed that the fears of Henderson, Forrestal, and others of their school of thought were needless, for the Arabs would go on selling oil to the United States regardless of the degree of American support for Zionism. But it was impossible to know that in 1947, and in 1947 the chances of an immediate outbreak of World War III seemed great. One could not risk antagonizing the oil sheikhs in such precarious times, Henderson argued.

The same attitudes were held by many other State Department men, though with proper professional style they did not allow their private beliefs to interfere with their execution of the President's orders. Typical of this group was Dean Acheson, who, as Undersecretary of State from August, 1945, to June, 1947, had the administrative responsibility for implementing most of Truman's critical Palestine decisions. In his memoirs, *Present at the Creation*, published in 1969, Acheson declared, "I did not share the President's views on the Palestine solution to the pressing and desperate plight of great numbers of displaced Jews in Eastern Europe. . . . The number that could be absorbed by Arab Palestine without creating a grave political problem would be inadequate, and to transform the country into a Jewish state capable of receiving a million or more immigrants would vastly exacerbate the political problem and imperil not only American but all Western interests in the Near East. From Justice Brandeis, whom I revered, and from Felix Frankfurter, my intimate friend, I had learned to understand, but not to share, the mystical emotion of the Jews to return to Palestine and end the Diaspora. In urging Zionism as an American governmental policy they had allowed, so I thought, their emotion to obscure the totality of American interests. . . . Despite my own views, I did my best loyally to see that the President's wishes were understood and carried out. . . . "

With Henderson and Forrestal tugging him one way, and the

Zionists and the Republican leadership pulling him the other, President Truman continued to avoid committing the United States to any firm position on Jewish statehood. Secretary of State Marshall, in his opening address to the General Assembly on September 17, 1947, made what seemed to be a pro-partition pledge by saying that the United States "gives great weight" to the recommendations of UNSCOP and particularly to "those which have been approved by the majority of that committee," which brought cheers from the American Jewish Congress. However, six days later Marshall lunched with the Arab delegates to the UN to tell them that the United States was still keeping "an open mind" on Palestine.

On October 6, Postmaster General Hannegan—who had also been national chairman of the Democratic Party, and who was beginning to worry about the 1948 presidential election—brought up Palestine again at a Cabinet lunch. Forrestal tells us that Hannegan "said many people who had contributed to the Democratic campaign fund in 1944 were pressing hard for assurances from the administration of definitive support for the Jewish position in Palestine. The President said that if they would keep quiet he thought that everything would be all right, but that if they persisted in the endeavor to go beyond the report of the United Nations Commission there was grave danger of wrecking all prospects for settlement. Hannegan tried to press him on this matter but he was adamant."

Forrestal, dismayed by the repeated attempts of the American Jews to place the government under political pressure on behalf of Zionism, privately began to search for some way to get Palestine out of American domestic politics altogether—a quixotic notion, as he was to find. He also continued to advocate close American ties with the Arabs. On October 9, a Senate committee called him in to ask why, in view of the severe domestic steel shortage, he had licensed the export of 20,000 tons of steel to build an oil pipeline in Saudi Arabia. Forrestal replied that "because of the rapid depletion of American oil reserves and an equally rapidly rising curve of consumption we would have to develop resources outside the country. The greatest field of untapped oil in the world is in the Middle East. . . . Pipe for the Arabian pipeline should have precedence over pipe for similar projects in this country."

That same day President Truman received word from the State

Department that the Arab League members were preparing to move troops close to the borders of Palestine, and were ready to go to war if the United Nations attempted to impose the partition plan. This seemed to underscore the Forrestal-Henderson suspicions that it would be risky for the United States to back partition.

But President Truman's reaction was unexpected. He sent word to the State Department to issue a public statement in favor of partition, and on October 11 Herschel V. Johnson of the United States delegation to the UN astonished the General Assembly by declaring that the United States "supports . . . the majority plan which provides for partition and immigration," although asking "certain geographical modifications," such as transferring the predominantly Arab town of Jaffa to the territory of the proposed Arab state. Two days later Soviet delegate Semyon K. Tsarapkin announced that Russia also supported the partition plan. "Those damned Jews!" one anti-Semite supposedly commented. "They even bring America and Russia together when they want something."

5.

On October 6, President Truman had been "adamant" in his refusal to make a pro-Zionist statement. On October 9, he told the State Department to support partition, despite known Arab wrath. Why the swift change of heart? Only one explanation seems probable: that the United States, receiving some advance word that the Russians were going to come out in favor of partition, chose to make the first move. There need be no fear of driving the Arabs into the Russian camp if the Russians too were anathematized as Zionists.

Under Stalin, of course, Zionism had always been regarded as a sinister international conspiracy, and the emigration of Russian Jews to Palestine had generally been thwarted by official policy. All through 1946 the Russians had kept up their traditional attacks on Zionism, which was termed an effort to secure a capitalist-imperialist beachhead in the Near East. A typical comment was that of Radio Moscow when the Anglo-American Committee's report, favoring admission of the 100,000 to Palestine, was made public: "Foreign observers discern a desire of the American rulers to satisfy Zionist circles in the United States, and also to win the sympathy of the Jews in Palestine and make them supporters of America."

But the desire to push Britain out of the Near East became paramount in Soviet planning in 1947, and the Jews looked like useful pawns. Stalin's tested tactic of war-by-proxy guided Soviet decisions now. It seemed possible to evict the British, provided the Soviet Union joined the United States in sponsoring some Zionist solution to the Palestine issue. And so, as early as May, 1947, Russia's Andrei Gromyko had told the UN that a partition of Palestine might be acceptable to his country. From that point until the actual creation of Israel, Russia, the old enemy of Zionism, would be Zionism's most committed advocate at the United Nations. To replace the British presence in Palestine with two tiny, helpless sovereign states, one Arab and one Jewish, would serve Russian policy admirably, opening the way for Soviet penetration of the entire area. There would be time later for the Russians to repair their relations with the Arabs.

The reaction in Great Britain to the American and Soviet moves was one of shock; the partition of Palestine seemed certain now that both superpowers backed it, and the British felt betrayed. The Arab states, too, were in disarray. The October 11 American statement produced an immediate charge from Cairo that "the United States is conspiring with the Zionists against the Arabs for pure imperialistic purposes, utilizing the Jewish problem as a screen behind which to hide this conspiracy. The United States today is an imperialist power of the first degree. . . ." And on October 15, Camille Chamoun of Lebanon told the UN that by advocating the cession of Arab territory to the Zionists, the United States had "destroyed at one fell swoop the fine idealism which was the only real source of the prestige of the American nation in the world. . . . Whatever the explanation the United States delegate may give for his attitude, he will never prevent public opinion from believing that it depends on two principal factors: (1) considerations of domestic electoral policy and the United States administration's need to appease the Jewish voters. Indeed, the creation of a Jewish state has become a classic theme on the eve of each legislative or Presidential election in the United States. (2) A desire for political penetration in the Middle East dictated by a pitiless capitalism, with Zionism in the van."

By then the Russian announcement of support for partition had also come, though. Chamoun denounced that too, though not so violently. But the Arabs knew they had been outflanked. It was clear now that the Jews would have at least part of Palestine.

There still was much to discuss. Implementation of partition seemed doubtful at best, for only the Jews had accepted the idea even in principle. ("If heavy sacrifice is the inescapable condition of a final solution," Abba Hillel Silver announced, "if it makes possible the immediate re-establishment of the Jewish State, the ideal for which a people has ceaselessly striven, then the Jewish Agency is prepared to recommend acceptance of the partition solution.") The Arab states had unanimously rejected it with such terms as "unjust and inequitable" (Lebanon) and "illegal and unworkable" (Yemen). It appeared likely that any attempt by the Zionists to claim the territory awarded them by the United Nations would result in war. Who would take the responsibility for enforcing partition?

Many UN delegates thought that the United States, which was emerging as the strongest advocate of a Jewish state, should do it. They argued that the October 11 American announcement of backing for partition had committed this country to send troops, if necessary, to Palestine; the critical phrase in that statement was an expression of America's willingness "to participate in a United Nations program to assist the parties involved in the establishment of a workable political settlement in Palestine."

Within the Truman administration a few advisers believed that the United States should make a definite commitment of troops, on the theory that the mere promise of American military intervention would discourage the Arabs from going to war. But a majority of American strategists in the Pentagon and in Congress were flatly against any kind of American involvement. The October 11 statement had raised one possible means of maintaining peace there: "The problem of internal law and order during the transitional period . . . might require the establishment of a special constabulary or police force recruited on a volunteer basis by the United Nations." There was no necessary implication in this that the United States intended to volunteer for this "police force," and by the middle of October authoritative reports were circulating that President Truman opposed any deployment of American troops in Palestine, even under UN command. By the end of the month the United States had even withdrawn its suggestion for a UN volunteer peacekeeping force. Several presidential advisers had noted that if such a force came into existence, the Soviet Union would probably demand representation on it, thereby gaining a military foothold in the Near East. And so on October 31, the United States delegation asked the Palestine subcommittee of the General Assembly to rule that Great Britain, as the mandatory power, should retain responsibility for maintaining order in Palestine until July 1, 1948, when that responsibility would be transferred to the new Jewish and Arab states, each of whom thereafter would look after its own security.

This request was a mixture of naïveté and cynicism, always a bad combination. Great Britain was already doing a conspicuously poor job of keeping order in the Holy Land, despite the presence of 80,000 men there; nothing in Britain's current attitude indicated a desire to impose tighter restrictions on the contending Arab and Zionist factions. The proposal to leave the partitioned states to their own devices as of July 1, 1948, simply ignored the vehement Arab promise to go to war. By abdicating responsibility, the United States was guaranteeing a brief period of chaos in Palestine under an indifferent Britain, followed by an indefinite period of even greater chaos once British troops departed. But political realities at home and in the Cold War hemmed in American policymakers. They did not dare commit American soldiers to Palestine, nor did they want the Soviet Union to step in, and so they advocated the creation of a power vacuum, hoping that the Zionists would be able to live up to their claim of being able to take care of any Arab threat.

On November 3, the Soviet Union proposed a slightly different plan involving a commission, appointed by the Security Council, to supervise the military forces of the new Jewish and Arab states. The Russian proposal called for a British withdrawal on January 1, 1948, six months ahead of the American-suggested date. Out of this came an American-Russian compromise that specified that British troops would leave Palestine on May 1, 1948, with the Arab and Jewish states coming into existence no later than July 1, 1948; thus there would be a transitional period of up to three months. During this time a United Nations commission of three to five members would administer the country and would attempt to prepare the two new states for full independence. This commission would be selected by the General Assembly from among the smaller nations who favored the partition plan, and would be subject to the instructions of the Security Council. There was unusual harmony and good nature among the American and Soviet delegates as they worked out this agreement.

Great Britain introduced a discordant note by objecting that the United Nations had no authority under its own charter to assume administrative responsibility in Palestine during the transitional period. The United States rejected this as a legalistic quibble. Britain also said it would have no part in implementing a plan that did not have the full approval of both peoples of Palestine, to which American delegate Herschel Johnson retorted, "I think there is no delegation here which does not know that no plan has ever been presented, either to this Assembly or to the mandatory government during its long years of tenure, or in any other place, which would meet with the acceptance of both the Arabs and the Jews. . . . Neither the Jews nor the Arabs will ever be completely satisfied with anything we do, and it is just as well to bear that in mind."

Johnson brushed aside the Arab threat to resist partition by force, saying that the United States "refuses to believe that any members of the United Nations, whatever may be their opinions on this highly controversial and bitter question, will attempt to defy the decision which may be taken by this organization." It was a brave but unrealistic assertion.

Thus the decision was taken, by Russo-American fiat, to cut Palestine in two, stand back, and leave the Arabs and Jews to their own devices. Thus the Gordian knot was severed, and anarchy let loose. But the only alternative would have been to replace the British mandate with a permanent United Nations occupation force, and that hardly seemed desirable.

The United Nations also struggled in October and November of 1947 to remedy the serious flaws in the UNSCOP partition plan itself; the two states the plan would have created looked like weird serpents, writhing about one another in a deathgrip, neither one having the appearance of a viable nation. Some rearrangement of the allotments seemed necessary.

The trouble was that most UN members felt that the Jews had been awarded too much territory—60 percent of Palestine—while the Jewish Agency felt that the Jews were receiving too little.

Though the agency had accepted the partition, it was hardly content with its initial terms. In particular the Zionists were asking for the western Galilee, a fertile and well-watered district that would also be a useful strategic buffer along the Lebanese border. The Jewish Agency offered to surrender a strip of territory in the Negev, including the town of Beersheba, in return for the western Galilee. But the United States opposed the trade, which would have added some 200,000 acres to the Jewish state and stripped the Arab state of its only adequate port, Acre, and its only good farmland.

The United States was more concerned with making adjustments in the other direction, believing that only through liberal concessions to the Arabs could war be avoided. One American goal was to reduce the size of the Arab minority in the Jewish State. UNSCOP's plan would have left 416,000 Arabs under Jewish rule; by transferring predominantly Arab Jaffa to the Arab state, some of the potential friction in this arrangement could be avoided. Over Jewish Agency protests, the UN Palestine subcommittee approved the transfer.

Another American proposal intended to mollify the Arabs involved the Negev, the wasteland that begins at Palestine's middle and runs down to the Gulf of Aqaba, which gives access to the Red Sea. Though formidably bleak and dry, the Negev held great possibilities for development. Twenty centuries earlier, a cunning people called the Nabataeans had farmed it quite successfully by means of extraordinarily clever irrigation schemes, and there was no reason why modern equivalents of those resourceful schemes could not make the Negev bloom again. There was also a possibility, however slight, that oil might lie beneath the sands of the Negev. More immediately, Aqaba could be turned by means of some dredging into an excellent harbor, providing a maritime route from Palestine to the ports of the Indian Ocean. The UNSCOP partition plan had awarded most of the Negev, including the critical Gulf of Aqaba outlet, to the Jews. But early in November the United States announced that in the interest of equity it favored giving the whole southern half of the Negev, from the Gulf of Aqaba northward, to the Arabs.

It was a signal for the Zionist propaganda machine, which had been relatively inactive for a number of weeks, to swing back into action.

6.

As soon as the Negev crisis erupted, AZEC wired its hundreds of local emergency committees, requesting that "large numbers of telegrams be sent immediately" to President Truman and Acting Secretary of State Robert A. Lovett. This suggested text was provided:

We are distressed to learn that United States delegation to United Nations is pressing for exclusion of the large and important area of Negev from the Jewish State, contrary to UNSCOP majority recommendations which our government has endorsed. Such revision would sharply reduce Jewish area, thus curtailing ability of Jewish State to absorb immigrants. It would also reduce the possibility for future economic development and render the Jewish State unviable. We must protest most vigorously against this unwarranted stand by United States Delegation which is particularly shocking in view of the fact that it follows our government's forthright support of UNSCOP majority plan which evoked general praise and satisfaction. Furthermore the present United States position endangers the unity which has thus far prevailed in United Nations on Palestine issue. We appeal to you to intervene immediately so that this injustice shall not be done.

On November 19, Chaim Weizmann called on President Truman to discuss the fate of the Negev. He spoke of its potential value in agriculture—a potential that could be realized only if it were awarded to the Jews, for the Arabs had never shown that they were capable of the intensive farming needed to bring the Negev to life. He pointed out how a port could be built at the Gulf of Aqaba only through Jewish initiative. "I pleaded further with the President," Weizmann wrote, "that if the Egyptians choose to be hostile to the Jewish State, which I hope will not be the case, they can close navigation to us through the Suez Canal when this becomes their property, as it will in a few years." The Gulf of Aqaba would provide the Jewish state with an alternate sea route to the Orient in this eventuality. Truman quickly grasped the significance of the Negev to the Zionists, and promised to communicate at once with the American delegation at the United Nations.

At three that afternoon, Herschel Johnson of the American delegation was due to meet with Moshe Shertok of the Jewish Agency to outline the United States position on the Negev. No

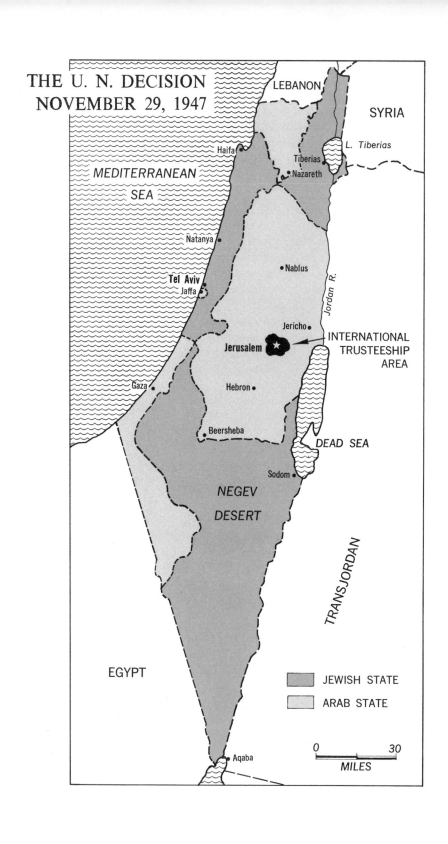

THE U. N. DECISION
NOVEMBER 29, 1947

LEBANON

SYRIA

MEDITERRANEAN
SEA

Haifa

L. Tiberias

Tiberias

Nazareth

Nâtânya

Nablus

Jordan R.

Tel Aviv
Jaffa

Jericho

INTERNATIONAL
TRUSTEESHIP
AREA

Jerusalem

Gaza

Hebron

Beersheba

DEAD SEA

Sodom

NEGEV
DESERT

TRANSJORDAN

EGYPT

JEWISH STATE

ARAB STATE

0   30

Aqaba

MILES

new instructions had come through from Washington, and so as the meeting began Johnson started to tell Shertok that the Negev would have to go to the Arabs. Shertok grew excited and upset. A telephone call came for Johnson, but he would not break off his conversation with Shertok until an aide whispered to him, "The President, sir." Quickly Johnson went to a phone, and spent twenty minutes conferring with Truman; when he returned to the agitated Shertok, he bore new instructions. Weizmann had saved the Negev for the Jews. They could keep the desert's southern half after all. By way of compensation to the Arabs, though, they were to surrender some five hundred square miles of territory around Beersheba in the upper Negev and along the border between the Negev and the Egyptian-administered Sinai Peninsula. To this Shertok agreed.

A quick defensive maneuver had prevented the loss to the Jews of the vital Negev, but the main battle was yet to be won: securing General Assembly approval of the partition plan itself. A two-thirds majority was required. The United Nations now had 56 members. Six of these were Arab states, and several others, with large Moslem populations, might be expected to vote against partition. A preliminary tally late in November showed that the outcome would be close and that partition might fail, destroying all the work of the last five months, unless a number of undecided countries could be won to the Zionist side.

The Zionists undertook a desperate last-minute lobbying campaign, striving to line up the necessary General Assembly votes. David Horowitz of the Jewish Agency tells how "the telephones rang madly. Cablegrams sped to all parts of the world. People were dragged from their beds at midnight and sent on peculiar errands. And, wonder of it all, not an influential Jew, Zionist or non-Zionist, refused to give us his assistance at any time. Everyone pulled his weight, little or great. . . . In one day we met with tens of delegations."

The chief target of this effort was the United States, which the Zionists believed was not working hard enough to swing friendly countries into line. Liberia, Greece, the Philippines, China, and Haiti all were nations that the Zionists deemed American "satellites," and yet all had shown opposition to partition. The United States had only recently given the Philippines its independence, was underwriting the weak and shaky regimes in China and Haiti, was pouring hundreds of millions of dollars into Greece under the Truman Doctrine reconstruction program, and had long been regarded as the protector of Liberia. Why, the Zionist leaders asked, since the United States favored partition itself, was it not instructing these client states to do the same? And why was no word being passed to the Latin American countries, which everyone knew were under the sway of the United States?

The underlying assumptions of this kind of thinking greatly bothered President Truman. He later wrote, "Not only were there pressure movements around the United Nations unlike anything that had been seen there before but . . . the White House, too, was subjected to a constant barrage. I do not think I ever had as much pressure and propaganda aimed at the White House as I had in this instance. The persistence of a few of the extreme Zionist leaders—actuated by political motives and engaging in political threats—disturbed and annoyed me. Some were even suggesting that we pressure sovereign nations into favorable votes in the General Assembly. I have never approved of the practice of the strong imposing their will on the weak, whether among men or among nations. . . . No American policy worthy of the name will ever treat any other nation as a satellite."

As the week of the final debate approached, Zionist leaders also asked congressmen to communicate directly with the governments of the uncommitted countries, and made the same requests of such State Department men as Undersecretary Robert Lovett and Loy Henderson. Lovett told James Forrestal shortly afterward that "he had never in his life been subject to as much pressure as he had been in the three days" immediately preceding the General Assembly's vote. The Firestone Tire and Rubber Company, which had a concession in Liberia, informed the State Department that Zionists had asked it to direct its representative in Liberia to bring pressure on the Liberian government in favor of partition. Felix Frankfurter and his Supreme Court colleague, Justice Frank Murphy, reportedly intervened directly on behalf of partition with the government of the Philippines.

Forrestal had been brooding all month about a way of neutralizing the political power of American Jewry. On November 6 he had spoken to Senator J. Howard McGrath of Rhode Island, the Democratic Party's national chairman, and told him, "No group in this country should be permitted to influence our policy to the point where it could endanger our national security." McGrath responded by saying "that there were two or three pivotal states which could not be carried without the support of people who were deeply interested in the Palestine question." Forrestal retorted, "I would rather lose those states in a national election than run the risks which I feel might develop in our handling of the Palestine question."

On November 26, just as the climax to the UN debate was about to begin, Forrestal had lunch with McGrath after letting him read a secret CIA report on Palestine. Once again Forrestal stressed the dangers of allowing domestic politics to shape foreign policy. But McGrath still took a less lofty approach. He noted that a substantial percentage of the contributions to the Democratic National Committee came from Jews, and many of these contributions were made "with a distinct idea on the part of the givers that they will have an opportunity to express their views and have them seriously considered on such questions as the present Palestine question." There was a feeling among the Jews, McGrath went on, that the United States was not doing all it could be doing to solicit pro-partition votes at the UN. To which Forrestal replied that such solicitation was "precisely what the State Department wanted to avoid; . . . we had gone a very long way indeed in supporting partition and . . . proselytizing for votes and support would add to the already serious alienation of Arabian good will."

Practical politics, in the end, triumphed. Irritated as he was by the Zionist lobbying, President Truman bowed to the pressure and permitted the American delegation at the UN to aid in collecting votes for partition. According to a report in *The New York Times* for November 28, 1947, "Since Saturday [November 22] the United States delegation has been making personal contact with other delegations to obtain votes for partition." Although it was denied by the President, many Zionist leaders have asserted that Truman himself took part in this effort in the final hours before the vote. Supposedly a group of senators visited him on the morning of Thanksgiving Day, Thursday, November 27, to urge greater activity on behalf of partition, and, as soon as he returned from Thanksgiving services, the President called Secretary of State Marshall and instructed him to make personal contact with the ambassadors of the noncommitted countries, in order to gain pledges of support for partition.

On Saturday, November 29, the General Assembly prepared to take the vote on partition. The outcome was still uncertain, for three days earlier the UN's Palestine committee had voted to send the measure to the full assembly by a margin of 25 to 13, one vote less than the two-thirds majority that was required by the assembly. If the same proportion held on the final vote, the measure would fail. No one knew whether the frantic last-minute lobbying had really accomplished any changes of position.

On the day the General Assembly was to meet at Lake Success for the historic vote some ten thousand people sought passes to the small visitors' gallery. Ticket holders had to fight their way through the crush when more than a thousand people milled before the single entrance of the visitors' gallery. The glassed-in radio, television, and motion-picture booths were backed with extra guests. In the aisles of the General Assembly chamber itself stood UN officials who had left their offices to witness the balloting.

Just as the roll call was about to begin, the Arabs attempted a desperate diversionary stratagem. The Lebanese delegate requested that the General Assembly first vote on what he maintained was a new proposal for a federation of Arab and Jewish areas. Herschel V. Johnson of the United States rose to object that the Lebanese proposal was identical to the UNSCOP minority report, and need not be considered again. There was a whispered discussion between Secretary-General Trygve Lie and Dr. Oswaldo Aranha of Brazil, the president of the General Assembly for that session. Aranha then ruled Lebanon out of order and called for the vote on partition.

The measure now decreed, "The Mandate for Palestine shall terminate as soon as possible, but in any case not later than August 1, 1948. . . . Independent Arab and Jewish States, and the specific international regime for the City of Jerusalem . . . shall come into existence in Palestine two months after the evacuation of the armed forces of the Mandatory Power has been completed, but in any case no later than October 1, 1948."

The vote was in alphabetical order. Afghanistan voted against partition; Argentina abstained; Australia, Belgium, Bolivia, Brazil, Byelorussia, and Canada all cast favorable votes. And so it went, taking only three minutes. Costa Rica, Czechoslovakia, Denmark, the Dominican Republic, Ecuador, France, Guatemala, Haiti, Iceland, Liberia, Luxembourg, the Netherlands, New Zealand, Nicaragua, Norway, Panama, Paraguay, Peru, the Philippines, Poland, Sweden, the Ukraine, South Africa, Uruguay, the USSR, the United States, and Venezuela voted for partition. Cuba, Egypt, Greece, India, Iran, Iraq, Lebanon, Pakistan, Saudi Arabia, Syria, Turkey, and Yemen were opposed. The remaining nations —Chile, China, Colombia, El Salvador, Ethiopia, Honduras, Mexico, the United Kingdom, and Yugoslavia—abstained; Thailand was absent. The vote, 33 to 13, provided the necessary two-thirds majority.

In the visitors' gallery a woman cried, "We've got it! We've got it! We've won!" A rabbi shouted, "This is the day the Lord hath made! Let us rejoice in it and be glad!"

Dov Joseph, a Canadian-born official of the Jewish Agency, wrote, "Pandemonium broke loose in the halls the moment that President Aranha declared the result of the voting. . . . Applause rolled round the walls. Men embraced each other sobbing with joy; women were almost hysterical with gladness. The face of the British delegate was grim and set, and the Arab representatives sat white with a fury which was to express itself, in a few short hours, in a wave of disorder, murder and sabotage throughout Palestine. But for the brief spell, it was our moment. The President knocked good-humoredly for order with his gavel, but the hubbub continued to mount. The meeting was adjourned; the delegates streamed into the lobby; the galleries emptied and the Jewish observers who were present were left to savor the sweet fulfillment of that moment of destiny."

At the Jewish Agency's office on East 66th Street there was an impromptu celebration. Moshe Shertok and a few others made short speeches. Several blocks to the west, five thousand New Yorkers crowded into the St. Nicholas Arena, a dilapidated boxing hall, to hear Chaim Weizmann hail in Yiddish the birth of the Jewish state. And as the news spread to the millions of Jews in the city, a holiday hysteria took hold.

Herzl's dream had been fulfilled. The assembled nations of the world had voted to let the Jewish people enjoy sovereign statehood once again, after a lapse of twenty centuries. All that remained now was to persuade the Arabs to ratify that decision.

7.

On November 30, 1947, one day after the General Assembly's vote, the first shots were fired in a war that is still going on, more than twenty years later. Arab snipers attacked an ambulance on its way to the Hadassah Hospital on Mount Scopus, near Jerusalem. On the same day three Arabs fired on a Jerusalem-bound bus near Lod Airfield, killing five Jews. Seven Jews were killed in an Arab ambush in Tel Aviv. There were other incidents in Haifa, Safed, and in the Negev. In Jerusalem the next day the consulates of Poland and Sweden, which had voted for partition, were attacked, and threats were made against the Czechoslovak consulate. An Arab mob swept through a Jewish shopping district in the newer part of Jerusalem, led by an armored car manned by British police. Haganah forces blocked the mob's advance and dispersed it with warning shots.

Within two days of the partition vote, bombings, snipings, and ambushes erupted throughout Palestine. Arabs who lived in predominantly Jewish quarters began to move out; so did Jews living in Arab sectors. A synagogue was set afire. A bus was blown up by a land mine. The Arab Higher Committee proclaimed a three-day nation-wide strike to begin on Tuesday, December 2. Instant chaos was engulfing Palestine.

The British officials of the mandate announced that the situation was not serious. But the British could afford to be casual now; six more months and they would be rid of their Palestinian albatross forever. On December 11, Colonial Secretary Creech Jones announced that the mandate would be terminated and all British troops withdrawn on May 15, 1948. The toll in the disturbances that week was 71 Arab fatalities, 74 Jews, 9 British. The action at this point consisted of relatively disorganized attacks by Palestinian Arabs against the Zionists, almost invariably followed by fierce Jewish reprisals; but by the end of December the character of what was taking place began to change, quickly becoming an international war, with armed bands from several Arab states converging on the Jewish communities of Palestine. Some eight hundred Arab volunteers entered from Syria on January 9. They were prevented by British troops from attacking two Jewish border settlements, and Britain lodged a formal protest with Syria over the violation. But these were empty maneuvers, for the Arab raiders remained in Palestine, and were joined a few days later by a larger Syrian band commanded by regular officers of the Syrian army.

At about the same time soldiers of Transjordan's formidable Arab Legion, trained by the famous British officer Sir John Glubb (Glubb Pasha), moved across the Jordan to occupy the region around Nablus in the northern part of the district known as the West Bank, which the partition plan had awarded to the Arabs. Egyptian troops massed on Palestine's southwestern border near Gaza. And on January 25, the commander-in-chief of what now is called the Arab Liberation Army began operations in Palestine. He was a brigand named Fawzi el Kawakji, who had fought for the Turks against the British in World War I, had led Arab rioters in the 1936–39 troubles in Palestine, and had spent the years of World War II in Germany.

The Jewish Agency had reacted to this many-fronted menace by calling up all men between 17 and 25 for national defense. Haganah was going into full mobilization.

In New York, far from the scene of strife, the United Nations was innocently taking steps toward the peaceful implementation of its partition resolution of November 29. The five member nations of the commission that was to supervise Palestine's transition to independence were selected: Bolivia, Czechoslovakia, Denmark, Panama, and the Philippines. This Committee of Five, later known as the "Five Lonely Pilgrims," was instructed to proceed to Palestine and begin working with the mandate officials toward the transfer of power the following May.

However, Prime Minister Attlee, while stressing Great Britain's "loyal acceptance" of the will of the United Nations, announced that it would be impossible for his country to cooperate in any decision not satisfactory to the whole of Palestine's population. Since partition was obviously unsatisfactory to Palestine's Arabs, therefore, Britain would not admit the members of the Committee of Five to Palestine before the termination of the mandate, would not open a port for the entry of the 150,000 Jewish immigrants prescribed under the UN resolution, and would not permit the creation of an official Jewish militia, as the UN had directed, for the defense of the Jewish sector. Instead, the British said, they themselves would retain all responsibility for governing Palestine until their withdrawal four months hence. Almost simul-

taneously—on January 12, 1948—the British Foreign Office revealed that it had authorized a shipment of weapons to Egypt, Iraq,
and Transjordan "in fulfillment of treaty obligations" with those
states.

The casualties in Palestine's undeclared war totalled, by January
18, 720 dead and 1,552 wounded since the partition vote.

The official policy of the United States at this time was one of
keeping hands off. In marshaling support for partition, the Truman administration had clearly indicated that no American troops
were going to be sent to separate the Arabs and the Jews if a war
broke out, and, when the war did break out without delay, the
administration adhered to that policy. The administration further
established its neutrality by the arms embargo of December 5,
1947, by which the United States discontinued "for the present"
the licensing of arms shipments to all Near Eastern countries. This
ban applied equally to both Jewish and Arab arms purchases, but
the cruelty of its seeming impartiality became evident a few weeks
later when the British arms sales to the Arab countries were revealed.

The arms embargo brought the Truman administration under
heavy fire from American Jews and their supporters in Congress.
On January 27, 1948, Representative Jacob Javits of New York
attacked the embargo in the House, and Representative Arthur G.
Klein of New York called on Secretary of State Marshall to lift the
embargo or to modify it "so as to permit shipment or transfer of
selected police and militia weapons and ammunition for Jewish
defense purposes." But the next day the Secretary of State responded that no relaxation of the embargo was presently planned.

The Forrestal-Henderson policies were, for the moment, dominant in Washington. Forrestal had reacted bitterly to the government's support for partition, telling his fellow Cabinet members
on December 1 that he "thought the decision was fraught with
great danger for the future security of this country." Two days
later the Secretary of Defense complained to former Secretary of
State Byrnes that "it was a most disastrous and regrettable fact that
the foreign policy of this country was determined by the contributions a particular bloc of special interests might make to the party
funds." Forrestal still was worrying about Arab oil; when he break-
fasted early in the new year with B. Brewster Jennings, the president of the Socony Vacuum Oil Company, the Secretary of

Defense declared gloomily that "unless we had access to Middle East oil, American motorcar companies would have to design a four-cylinder motorcar sometime within the next five years." And the next day, at the regular Cabinet meeting, Forrestal argued that without Arab oil we could neither fight a war nor sustain our peacetime economy, and would have to convert to four-cylinder cars "within ten years."

Having seen an "adamant" President Truman give way under pressure from American Zionists, Forrestal feared that in the stress of the 1948 presidential campaign the Zionists might push the President into sending American troops to protect Jewish Palestine, which Forrestal regarded as an ultimate disaster. He tried to head off this calamity by reaching across party lines and obtaining pledges from leading Republican figures that they would not make Palestine a campaign issue in 1948. James Byrnes warned him not to bother seeing Senator Taft, since Taft followed Abba Hillel Silver on Palestinian affairs.

On December 10, Forrestal called on the powerful Republican Senator Arthur H. Vandenberg, head of the Senate Foreign Relations Committee, to win his support for a nonpartisan Palestine policy. But Vandenberg told him that most Republicans felt that the Democrats had made political capital out of Palestine, and that they were entitled to do the same. He quoted Harold Stassen's remark: "If Republicans are to cooperate on foreign policy they will have to be in on the take-off as well as in the crash landing."

On December 13 Forrestal tried again, drawing Governor Dewey aside at a dinner and posing "the question of getting nonpartisan action on this question, which I said was a matter of the deepest concern to me in terms of the security of the nation. The Governor said he agreed in principle but that it was a difficult matter to get results on because of the intemperate attitude of the Jewish people who had taken Palestine as the emotional symbol, because the Democratic Party would not be willing to relinquish the advantages of the Jewish vote." When Dewey asked Forrestal what he thought the next developments in the Palestinian crisis would be, Forrestal answered that "there would inevitably be two things coming up: (1) the arming of the Jews to fight the Arabs (2) unilateral action by the U.S. to enforce the decision of the General Assembly." Senator Vandenberg, who was standing nearby, broke in to say that he was unequivocably against unilateral American action "because it would breed . . . a wave of violent anti-Semitism in this country." At the same dinner, Justice Frankfurter approached Undersecretary of State Robert Lovett to discuss aid to the Jews in Palestine. Lovett replied curtly that he had had enough of Palestine for a time and did not want to hear of it again, which angered Frankfurter greatly.

Most members of the Truman administration, in fact, had had enough of Palestine for a time. Unremitting Zionist pressures had made almost everyone, from the President down, hostile to further action on behalf of the unborn Jewish state. Thus, while he had no luck luring Republicans into renouncing Palestine as a political issue, Forrestal was able to make his views prevail among the leaders of his own party, at least in the opening weeks of 1948. On January 21, Forrestal gave Undersecretary of State Lovett a position paper on Palestine that he had written. "It is doubtful if there is any segment of our foreign relations of greater importance or of greater danger in its broad implications to the security of the United States than our relations in the Middle East." The Forrestal paper termed it "stupid" to let the situation develop in such a way as either to do "permanent injury to our relations with the Moslem world" or to end in a "stumble into war." It was disturbing, Forrestal went on, that pro-Zionist contributors to the Democratic Party were able to ask for "a lien upon this part of our national policy," and he urged Secretary of State Marshall to take up this matter with the President before the pressures of the coming presidential election campaign forced the United States into a unilateral action in Palestine.

Lovett agreed with all that Forrestal had said, and showed him a policy statement just drafted in the State Department, which concluded that the partition plan was "not workable" and that the United States was not bound to support it if it could not be made to work without the use of force.

Almost obsessively, Forrestal discussed Palestine with anyone who would listen, now. On January 24 he talked about it with General Alfred Gruenther of the Joint Chiefs of Staff. On the 28th he discussed it with Herbert Feis of Princeton's Institute for Advanced Study, a former economic adviser to the State Department. Forrestal brought up "the impressions I had of schisms among the Jewish people themselves on the wisdom of projecting the United States into the politics of the Middle East." But Feis, a Jew, reminded Forrestal that "the desire for a national Jewish state was a matter of deep and emotional concern to the Jewish community in the United States," and said he "felt sure that a policy of firmness by the United Nations would dispose of Arab resistance."

The next evening, Forrestal met with Loy Henderson and other State Department men, including a future Secretary of State, Dean Rusk, then director of State's Office of Special Political Affairs. Henderson suggested that the General Assembly's partition vote had merely been a recommendation, which could be discarded if it proved unworkable—as it now was proving to be. This opinion bolstered Forrestal when he met on February 3 with Franklin D. Roosevelt, Jr., who came in to advocate greater American support for partition and the Jewish state. Forrestal repeated to the former President's son the Henderson argument that the partition vote had merely been a tentative recommendation, "that any implementation of this 'decision' by the United States would probably result in the need for a partial mobilization, and that I thought the methods that had been used by people outside the Executive branch of the government to bring coercion and duress on other nations in the General Assembly bordered closely on scandal."

Roosevelt did not care to discuss these ideas, but made it clear that Zionist "zealots" were out to upset the government's current neutralist policy. Forrestal replied that he "had no power to make policy but that I thought I would be derelict in my duty if I did not point out what I thought would be the consequences of any particular policy which would endanger the security of this country." When Roosevelt observed that this might hurt the Democrats politically, the Secretary of Defense cited a prediction of Senator McGrath that "our failure to go along with the Zionists might lose the states of New York, Pennsylvania, and California." Then Forrestal added that he thought "it was about time that somebody should pay some consideration to whether we might not lose the United States."

It is evident from these diary extracts that Forrestal had fastened on Palestine with a terrible intensity, greatly magnifying the risks that creation of a Jewish state involved for the United States. Perhaps the obsessive nature of his fixation on Zionism was an early symptom of the mental breakdown that was to force his resignation from office in March, 1949 and to lead to his suicide two months later. Yet he was utterly sincere and altogether irreproachable, if misguided, in his fanatic anti-Zionism; despite the charges of his enemies, anti-Semitism did not enter into his calculations. The passion with which he pressed his viewpoint undoubtedly had much to do with the policies of the United States toward Palestine in January and February of 1948.

Many of Forrestal's fellow Democrats felt that the arms embargo worked a grave injustice on the embattled Palestinian Jews, who by February, 1948, were in serious danger of defeat. The Arabs had seized commanding positions overlooking highways and roads, and were threatening to cut off Jerusalem, with a Jewish population of 100,000, from contact with Tel Aviv. The British had still not allowed the UN committee to enter Palestine; and their technique of "maintaining order" under the dying mandate seemed to involve giving guns to the Arabs and arresting the Jewish defenders. Within the State Department a minority faction had begun to argue in favor of legalizing the shipment of guns to Haganah. But the leaders of the State and Defense Departments prevailed. Even after Senator Owen Brewster of Maine showed that under existing law the arms embargo was illegal as presently constituted (he called it "a high-handed, arbitrary and wholly unwarranted usurpation of legal authority") the embargo remained.

The White House mailroom bulged with expressions of protest from the citizenry. In 1946, Americans had urged the President to work for the admission of refugees to Palestine. In 1947, they had backed the partition plan. In the first quarter of 1948 they called for arms for the Zionists, and the volume of mail was two to three times as great as ever before. The Truman Library has 214,000 postcards, 17,200 telegrams, and 27,600 letters on file for those three months. This mail came from individuals and groups, from Jews and Gentiles, but a good deal of it represented an organized campaign. Typical material employed in this campaign is the flyer below, distributed by a Zionist group in New York to Jewish parochial-school children:

TO ALL PUPILS IN JEWISH SCHOOLS

A. Send a letter to the President of the United States, or a post card, similar to the following. Re-write it in your own words.

Dear President Truman:

I am a student in the ____(name)____ Hebrew School in __(place)_____. I am _____ years of age. Please help the Jewish boys and girls in Palestine so that they can win their battle for freedom. The Arabs are attacking them and they cannot defend themselves. We are told that their brothers and fathers do not have enough guns to defend themselves because they have no place to buy them. Why can't the United States furnish them with guns just like we did to England and France? The United States promised to help the new Jewish State. As an American child, I feel sure our country will make good its promise.

B.   Take this home and ask your father or mother to write to the President, a letter similar to the following:

Dear President Truman:

We are proud of the U.S.A. and of your administration for having done so much to make possible the U.N. decision regarding a Jewish State in Palestine. But we are in great anxiety because evil men are trying to annul that glorious promise; to the deep hurt of the United Nations, the renewed suffering of the Jews, and the everlasting shame of our beloved country. What happens to the setting up of the new Jewish State will be a barometer of faith or lack of faith in the efforts made to create a more united and better world.

We respectfully beg of you, Mr. President, to use your powerful influence that—

1. The United States should take the lead in the Security Council to send an international force to Palestine; and to give an immediate allotment of arms to equip the Jewish militia.

2. The United States should urge that the Palestine Commission of the United States proceed to Palestine at once.

3. The United States, together with other members of the United Nations, should halt threatened aggression of Arab states.

4. The United States should immediately modify the existing embargo so that arms may be sent without delay to those who are defending the United Nations decision and withheld from those who are attacking it.

5. The United States should protest to the United Kingdom against its failure to discharge its responsibilities for law and order and against its persistent obstruction to the United Nations decision.

The increasingly more strident clamor for the United Nations peacekeeping force in Palestine disturbed the President nearly as much as it did Forrestal. On January 15, 1948, the Jewish Agency had appealed to the United Nations to establish an international peace force to put partition into effect. A month later, the United Nations Commission on Palestine backed this request, warning that it would be unable to maintain law and order unless adequate military forces were made available. Meanwhile Forrestal had consulted General Dwight D. Eisenhower, who told him on February 6 that "effective U.S. participation in a Palestine police force would involve about one division [about 15,000 men] with appropriate supporting units." This was unacceptable to the President, who, learning that the Arabs planned to start full-scale military operations in late March, could do no more than publish an appeal asking them "to preserve the peace and practice moderation."

At the United Nations, American delegate Warren Austin submitted a vague resolution on February 25 which appealed "to all governments and peoples, particularly in and around Palestine, to take all possible action to prevent or reduce such disorders as are now occurring in Palestine." The Security Council passed it by an 8–0 vote on March 5, but it did nothing to halt the slaughter, which by the end of February had claimed 2,500 lives on both sides.

All proposals to set up an international police force were shunted aside; Austin told the Security Council on February 24 that "the charter of the United Nations does not empower the Security Council to enforce a political settlement. . . . The Council, in other words, is directed to keeping the peace and not to enforcing partition." Secretary of State Marshall remarked the same month that no discussion of ways to enforce partition should begin until the Security Council had received and studied the report of the Committee of Five, which had not yet then been able even to enter Palestine, let alone to write a report. Nor was President Truman inclined to be helpful.

At the request of the Jewish Agency, Weizmann came to the United States on February 4 to persuade Truman to give stronger support to partition, but the President would not even see him. Truman was heartily tired of Zionists and Zionism. As he wrote years later, "Individuals and groups asked me, usually in rather quarrelsome and emotional ways, to stop the Arabs, to keep the British from supporting the Arabs, to furnish American soldiers, to do this, that, and the other. I think I can say that I kept my faith in the rightness of my policy in spite of some of the Jews. When I say 'the Jews,' I mean, of course, the extreme Zionists. I know that most Americans of Jewish faith, while they hoped for the restoration of Jewish homeland, are and always have been Americans first and foremost.

"As the pressure mounted, I found it necessary to give instructions that I did not want to be approached by any more spokesmen for the Zionist cause."

In those dark late winter days of 1948 the Zionists once again had reason to recall the Biblical phrase Abba Hillel Silver had quoted in 1944: *"Put not your trust in princes. . . ."* They had gone about as far as possible through political action and the marshaling of public opinion. If a homeland really were going to come into being now, it would be only by force of arms.

8.

The Jewish population of Palestine at the beginning of 1948 was about 650,000. Some 54,000 of these were enrolled in Haganah, but 9,500 of Haganah's members were adolescents without military experience, and 32,000 were men in middle age unfit for combat. The real fighting strength of Haganah on the eve of independence was about 12,500, of which 3,000 comprised the elite Palmach commando corps and 9,500 the regular defense force. In addition, the Irgun had perhaps a thousand guerrillas and the Stern Gang a few hundred. Arrayed against this tiny force was an Arab army that could draw on nations with an aggregate population of more than 50,000,000.

The weapons of the Jewish army consisted of an improvised hodgepodge of homemade mortars, stolen British guns, antiquated surplus items, and smuggled arms from friends overseas. Haganah's total arsenal amounted to 10,500 rifles, many of them dating from World War I; 3,500 submachine guns; 775 light machine guns; 160 medium machine guns; 672 one-inch mortars; and a "heavy artillery" of 84 three-inch guns.

There was also a Jewish air force of sorts, assembled largely through the efforts of Americans. It stemmed from a scheme conceived early in 1947 by two California Jews, Leo Gardner and Sam Lewis, to transport clandestine immigrants to Palestine by air. Gardner and Lewis, both active Los Angeles Zionists, had been pilots in the United States Air Force during the war. Upon their return to civilian life they thought of persuading the Jewish Agency to buy a few war surplus planes, which they would repair and recondition for use by the *aliyah bet*. A Curtis C-46 Commando was selling for about $5,000 then, and a Constellation for $15,000—a fraction of their original cost.

The Jewish Agency approved the idea. Three more former air force pilots were drawn into the project: Al Schwimmer, who now worked for Trans World Airlines, Ray Selk, and William Sosnov. In October, 1947, after Ben-Gurion had given the idea his blessing, Haganah procurement agent Yehuda Arazi met with Schwimmer in New York and provided him with funds to buy ten C-46's and three Constellations. The planes were in storage in California; the conspirators had them towed to an airport near Burbank, California, where the newly founded Schwimmer Aviation Company set about making them fit for flight. While the planes were being overhauled, Gardner and Lewis were recruiting and training Jewish American war veterans as pilots. A wealthy Jewish girl named Eleanor Rudnick arranged to lend the training crews several of her own crop-spraying planes so they could sharpen their old skills in the air. The next recruit was Irvin ("Swifty") Shindler, who ran a small private airline in New York called Service Airways, Incorporated. Schwimmer Aviation bought his firm to use as a front organization; the plan was to pretend to be an ordinary commercial freight line.

All the Americans involved in the enterprise still believed that they were going to be transporting refugees. But early in 1948 the Haganah man, Yehuda Arazi, broke the news that the planes would actually serve as the nucleus of the air force of the Jewish state, and that one of their first tasks would be to transport arms for Haganah. A shipment of weapons, Arazi said, was now waiting in Honolulu, having been assembled by a Jew who lived in Hawaii; would Schwimmer Aviation please get someone out there at once to pick up the merchandise?

It was an order.

The situation was awkward, for, whereas smuggling immigrants merely violated the dictates of the British White Paper, smuggling arms to Palestine had been prohibited by the State Department embargo of December 5, 1947, and violators were subject to prosecution. Indeed, at the beginning of February six men were arrested in New Jersey for attempting to ship 60,000 pounds of TNT to Palestine; they were caught when a crate of the explosives accidentally broke open on a Jersey City pier. But the anxiety of the Gardner-Lewis-Schwimmer group dissolved when Federal Judge Sylvester Ryan heard the New Jersey case on February 17. "You were endeavoring to provide means of defense to an otherwise helpless people," Judge Ryan said. "I do not regard you men as criminals and therefore will not impose any jail sentence. I likewise feel that it will serve no useful purpose to impose a fine." He placed the six on probation for one year. The case seemed to set a pattern for judicial handling of the unpopular arms-running restrictions.

However, for tactical reasons it was deemed wisest not to use an actual member of Schwimmer Aviation to ship the weapons, since if anything went wrong the whole group might be implicated. So Gardner and several others flew to Las Vegas and approached the colorful Hank Greenspun, a radio-station and newspaper proprietor of considerable local fame. When he heard the story, Greenspun dropped everything and went at once to Honolulu, where he found 400 0.50-caliber aerial machine guns and spare parts waiting, packed as "aircraft engines," along with 45 genuine aircraft engines. He arranged to have these shipped to Los Angeles; since the crates had come from Hawaii, they entered the United States without customs inspection.

The machine guns were unpacked and passed along to various warehouses whose owners were Zionist sympathizers. The 45 aircraft engines were taken to Schwimmer Aviation's headquarters at Burbank. Two days later, FBI agents, tipped about the Honolulu cargo, raided the Schwimmer base. They found only aircraft engines, legitimate enough equipment for an airline company to have, and left disappointed.

It seemed best to find a new base of operations, though, now that the FBI had been alerted. A friend of Swifty Shindler's learned that the Republic of Panama had an underutilized airport and was trying to find a company to start air service there. The Zionist group promptly rented hangar space and created Lineas Aereas de Panama (LAPSA) as its new cover organization. Now the hiring of personnel and the transfer of aircraft out of the United States could proceed unimpeded.

The war in Palestine had entered its worst phase, when defeat of the Jews looked imminent. A Haganah Air Service was already in action, transporting supplies and arms to Jewish units cut off in various parts of the beleaguered country. It consisted at the moment of a few Piper Cubs and some British trainers that had been salvaged from junkheaps, although a fast-talking Haganah man had succeeded in buying some surplus light planes from the British themselves, who did not realize the real identity of the purchaser. Other Haganah agents were roving Europe, picking up surplus planes on behalf of fictitious airlines, or posing as wealthy young playboys planning to do some traveling in planes of their own.

By March, 1948, the first of the planes collected in California by Schwimmer Aviation were ready to go to Palestine. A dozen flight crews had been recruited under the auspices of the cover outfits, Service Airways and LAPSA. The old surplus aircraft now appeared to have been transformed into cargo carriers, to get around the problems of the arms embargo, and LAPSA had acquired export licenses from the State Department permitting the shipment of a C-46 to Italy and a Constellation to Panama.

The C-46 crossed the United States, passed customs inspection at a New Jersey airfield on March 6, and took off for Europe with refueling stops at Labrador, Greenland, Iceland, Shannon, and Geneva. On March 9 the plane landed at Perugia, Italy, where its journey halted for several weeks while plans were drawn to get it to Palestine without attracting the attention of American intelligence agents, who were devotedly searching out violators of the arms embargo, everywhere. The only action the plane saw was a day's flight over the Adriatic in search of a freighter carrying ammunition and 6,000 Czech-made guns destined for Syria; but the freighter had not yet left port, it turned out, and a Haganah team sank it by riveting a time bomb to its hull. (Later, when the Syrians chartered an Italian ship to salvage the cargo of arms, Israelis intercepted the ship and brought the weapons to Israel.) The C-46 remained at Perugia well into April.

On April 9, four more C-46's were ready to leave the United States. The flight leader of the group was former Lieutenant Commander Hal Auerbach of the United States Navy, a Distinguished Flying Cross holder who after the war had become an inspector for the Civil Aeronautics Administration until resigning to fly for Haganah. The first destination of the planes was Panama, where

Sam Lewis had already delivered one Constellation; but U.S. customs officials, suspecting that LAPSA was involved in arms traffic with Palestine, refused to grant permission for the C-46's to leave an airfield near Philadelphia. After complicated wrangling and some menacing noises from LAPSA's lawyer in New York, take-off permission was grudgingly granted and the planes flew to Panama by way of Jamaica.

Two days later, five more C-46's set out from Los Angeles to Panama. One, overloaded with weapons, crashed in Mexico, killing its pilot, William Gerson. The remaining planes reached Panama safely, and after some difficulties with the Panamanians —who had been warned by the FBI that LAPSA was a suspected Haganah front—the planes were transferred one by one to Italy, and then were slipped into Palestine to be turned once more into warplanes.

"Little by little, by using ingenuity, we succeeded in building up the armament of our planes," wrote Benjamin Kagan, an officer in the Haganah Air Service. "We assembled an assortment of equipment to be adapted to the wings and fuselage for carrying and launching bombs. With a few changes, a small transport or pleasure plane could be made capable of carrying six 155-pound bombs, four under the fuselage and two under the wings."

This haphazardly constructed air force drew pilots from all over the world—Swedes, South Africans, Frenchmen, even some British volunteers who opposed their country's policies toward Zionism. "But, for sheer picturesqueness, no group could compare with the Americans," wrote the Russian-born Colonel Kagan. "Among them were dedicated volunteers, mercenaries, and adventurers out for anything. No two were alike. Almost all of them had to their credit a past history that would make the most imaginative novelist pale with envy. The majority were American Jews, some professed the convictions of ardent Zionists; others were indifferent to our problems, but that did not prevent them from fighting passionately for our cause. They felt that they were Americans first of all, and they remained that way throughout everything. However, each time that the existence of the Jewish people was threatened, we could count on them; we would find them ready to fight, and in the front lines."

Fighting for Jewish Palestine became, for a good many American Jews, a much more satisfactory kind of Zionist activity than writing checks, sending telegrams to the President, or even smuggling guns. The majority of them had seen action in World War II and had acquired specialized skills that Haganah badly needed: they were engineers, pilots, communications experts, aircraft mechanics, tank commanders, radar technicians, munitions maintenance men, bombardiers, master gunners. The best known of them, Colonel David (Mickey) Marcus of Brooklyn, became a high officer in the Israeli army; others fought and died in the ranks beside lifelong Palestinians.

Most of them served in the brigade known as Mahal, short for Mitnadvei Hutz-la-Aretz, "Overseas Volunteer Brigade." Haganah announced the formation of this group in the fall of 1947. P. E. Lapide's *A Century of U.S. Aliya,* published in Jerusalem in 1961, declares, "The response amongst U.S. army veterans exceeded availability of military equipment or even swift means of transportation to the far-off battlefields. Many volunteers paid their own way, some even brought their own arms. . . . Mahal numbered some 5,300 volunteers, whose largest single contingent was made up of roughly 1,770 Americans. . . . [They] fought on all fronts in all three arms of Israel's Defense Forces. Several Israel Army units were made up almost exclusively of English-speaking [American and British] volunteers, particularly in the Air Force, where English remained for many years the *lingua franca* of command. One brigade alone suffered seventy-two battle casualties, with the abnormally high rate of 30% of all her officers wounded or killed in action."

A poll taken by the American members of Mahal showed that 98 percent of the American volunteers were veterans of World War II; 95 percent had had no Zionist-organization affiliations; 90 percent had known no Hebrew when they arrived in Palestine; 85 percent had no knowledge of Yiddish either; 83 percent were American-born; and only 3 percent intended to settle in the Holy Land. Despite this last figure, 370 of the Americans—21 percent of the group—settled in Israel after the war.

In 1963 Harold Isaacs, a professor of political science at the Massachusetts Institute of Technology, interviewed a number of these Americans who fought for Palestine and remained as citizens of Israel. Some spoke of having come from families with a long tradition of Zionism, but that was not necessarily an incentive for them. One said, "My family was Zionist. This gave it a negative value for me when I was younger. I didn't become Zionist or even particularly Jewish until the [second world] war. . . . We began to hear what was happening to the Jews in Europe. By the time I was out of the service and had gone to Columbia to get a Ph.D., what was happening in Europe was affecting me greatly. I could have finished in 1948 and gotten an assistant professorship, but when the war broke out in Israel I decided to come and help build this state." Another, born in the Bronx, had served in the American merchant marine during the war: "There was nothing Zionist in my life, no Zionist youth movement, nothing. When I got out in 1946, I began to read about the situation. When I heard about the call for volunteers for the illegal immigration ships, I decided to find out about it. I asked only one question: was it for pay or for no pay. They said it was for no pay, and I said, OK, I'll go. If people were going to be paid, they could find better-qualified people than me, and I wasn't interested. But if it's a volunteer deal, I said, OK, I'd go. That was the beginning of my Zionism. Why? How do we know? There was what happened in Europe and what didn't happen. It's what the Nazis did and what the democratic countries didn't do. I'm a Jew, maybe I ought to put that first in explaining why. . . . Then there's the fact that I was brought up in the American tradition, whatever that is. To me it means you're for the underdog, and these Jews were really the underdogs." Another who came in 1948 said, "I was disappointed in the non-Jewish world, in the view it took of the Jewish plight. I came to feel my Jewishness more than my Americanism."

The United Nations Security Council, in a resolution introduced by Great Britain, called on all governments to discourage their citizens from volunteering for military service in the Near East. Ostensibly this was aimed at Arabs as well as Jews, but France and the United States succeeded in attaching amendments that would permit the immigration of men of military age into Jewish-held Palestine. However, the State Department adopted policies of its own designed to keep Americans from volunteering for service with Haganah. On January 30, 1948, the United States Consulate General in Jerusalem issued this decree:

The United States Government has informed the American Consulate General in Jerusalem that it has noted press statements indicating that some American veterans who were studying in Palestine under the G.I.

Bill of Rights, have identified themselves with armed groups in the country and have participated in fighting and other activities related to the present disturbances in Palestine. Three American citizens have been reported killed in such activities.

The American Consulate General has been instructed to announce the view of the United States Government that American passports are not granted to American citizens for the purpose of proceeding abroad to enter foreign military service . . . [and] to take up the passports of these American citizens who are serving in a military capacity in Palestine and, in addition, to state that while engaged in such service Americans will not be regarded as entitled to recognition as citizens.

Once it became clear that volunteers for Palestine might be stripped of their American citizenship, Representatives Andrew L. Somers of New Jersey and Abraham J. Multer of New York introduced a House resolution on March 9 which would have assured any person who joined an armed force pledged to uphold the UN's partition of Palestine that he would not "lose his status as a citizen of the United States" by serving in such a group. But the bill never got out of committee, and on March 30 the State Department announced that it would refuse to issue passports to American citizens seeking to join fighting forces on either side in Palestine.

The target of these rulings was not particularly Mahal, whose recruiting was taking place quietly, but rather the George Washington Legion, a project of Ben Hecht and the American League for a Free Palestine. On March 30 the legion held a mass rally in New York at which the speakers were Barney Ross, the former boxing champion and a marine corps hero, and Major Samuel Weiser, formerly of the British army. Weiser told the crowd that a country that did not fight for its survival did not deserve to survive. Ross said that he did not want to lose his American citizenship, "but I certainly want the right to fight for a cause that is just. . . . All I've got left is my heart and two good hands to talk for me." Three hundred young men signed up at the rally. By May, the George Washington Legion was claiming 5,000 members, although only a few of them actually got to Palestine.

The State Department continued to regard any American who donned the uniform of the Israeli army (or any other foreign army) as having lost his citizenship; even to vote in a foreign election was deemed grounds for loss of citizenship. These policies remained in effect until May 29, 1967, when the United States Supreme Court, ruling on the case of an American citizen who had lost his citizenship for voting in an Israeli election, declared that Congress did not have the power to pass laws depriving Americans of their nationality without their consent. (The remarkably apt timing of the ruling, though unintentional, was a factor in the unusually large number of Americans who attempted to volunteer for service in Israel in the war that broke out the following week.)

A number of Americans who did not go to fight in Palestine in 1948 were active in the United States or Europe in the vast, loosely organized program to smuggle arms and ammunition. The Schwimmer Aviation group, which sent so many reconditioned planes to Haganah's air force, was one of many such enterprises. There was considerable harassment by enforcers of the arms embargo, and a good many arrests were made.

On April 27, 1948, New York police entered a loft occupied by an export-import firm and found a large cache of rifles, revolvers, hand grenades, and ammunition concealed in bales of food and clothing destined for Palestine. Two young men, who admitted membership in the Zionist Youth Movement, were arrested on the premises: Joseph Untermeyer, the 19-year-old son of poet Louis Untermeyer, and Isaiah Warshaw. They were charged with violation of New York's Sullivan Law, which prohibits the possession of guns.

Young Untermeyer's mother, who was the treasurer of the American League for a Free Palestine, called in a lawyer named Paul O'Dwyer to handle the case. O'Dwyer, the younger brother of Mayor William O'Dwyer of New York City, had grown up in Ireland, where he saw the British suppress the nationalistic rebellions of the Irish Republican Army. Paul O'Dwyer had come to regard Zionism as a movement not very different in spirit from the kind of underground activity he had seen in County Mayo. In 1946, one of Ben Hecht's advertisements for the American League for a Free Palestine—the American arm of the Irgun—had drawn him to join, and for the next two years he worked to raise money for the Jewish terrorists and spent time in Europe helping to smuggle immigrants to Palestine.

When Untermeyer and Warshaw came up for trial, O'Dwyer told the court that the Sullivan Law had been enacted "to prevent gangsterism," while "these guns were to be sent to Palestine to

protect people in their homes." The defendants asserted that they
knew nothing about the hidden weapons and had merely been
packing food and clothing for the needy. But O'Dwyer argued
that even if they had been actively engaged in sending arms to
Palestine, "it would have been a worthwhile act." The presiding
magistrate dismissed the case, ruling that the prosecution had not
proved "knowledge or possession."

Soon afterward, four rabbinical students from Brooklyn were
arrested for firing guns at tin cans in the New Jersey meadows
near Elizabeth. They explained that they had bought the guns as
legitimate war souvenirs from World War II veterans, and had
come to New Jersey to fire them in celebration of a Jewish holiday, Lag B'Omer. When asked if they were not testing the guns
prior to shipping them to Palestine, the students replied that they
did indeed hope to donate the weapons to the Haganah once the
arms embargo was lifted. Accepting all this at face value, the judge
fined them $25 apiece, then suspended the fines.

On November 24, 1948, five young men were caught in New
York as they loaded two crates of arms and ammunition aboard a
truck. When they came to trial in Felony Court the following
month, Paul O'Dwyer was again the defense attorney. He gave
the same arguments he had used in the Untermeyer-Warshaw
case, and called for dismissal of the case, adding, "If there is any
conspiracy at all, that conspiracy exists with the State Department, and —" The magistrate broke in to say, "Case dismissed."

(O'Dwyer's activities on behalf of the Irgun and in defense of
arrested gun-runners figured oddly in the 1968 senatorial election.
Running for the seat held by Jacob Javits of New York, O'Dwyer
cited his long association with these and other Zionist causes to
prove that he was more worthy 'of receiving the votes of New
York's Jews than the Jewish Senator Javits, whom he termed a
lukewarm supporter of Israel. But Javits easily won re-election.)

9.

Three months had passed since the United Nations had voted
for partition. On May 15, or within another three months, the
British would withdraw from the Holy Land. By that time, a
complete vacuum would exist and the Jews could set up their own
nation in Palestine. But by March of 1948 it appeared the Zionist
dream had foundered. The infiltrating Arab forces were cutting

the country apart by seizing strategic outposts on the highways, and although not one Jewish village or town had actually been conquered by the Arabs, many were isolated and under heavy siege. Those in the Negev no longer had any contact with the rest of the country, except when the Haganah Air Service could get a plane through to them. And Jerusalem, surrounded by Arab troops, was running short of food and water, while Haganah relief parties found it impossible to traverse the blockaded road that ran to the capital from Tel Aviv.

The Jews of Palestine were hanging on, but all their energies were being expended in defense; they could not push the Arabs back. And everyone in Palestine knew that the Arabs had committed only a fraction of their available manpower to the struggle. The real Arab armies had not yet even crossed into Palestine. There was talk among some of the Jewish leaders of a new Masada, with death again preferable to surrender.

At this most dismal of times for the Zionist cause, a new problem emerged: rumors spread that the United States was going to abandon the partition plan as unworkable and propose to the United Nations that some kind of trusteeship scheme be developed to replace the mandate. If that were true, the unborn Jewish state would become one of history's abortions, since any return to a one-Palestine concept would have to be a capitulation to the belligerence of the Arabs.

On February 11, President Truman had declared that the United States supported partition as strongly as ever. But Ambassador Austin's statements at the United Nations later that month cast strong doubts on that. Austin had opposed creation of a UN peacekeeping force, and had also put forth the weird resolution of February 25, directing the Security Council to consult with Britain in order to find out whether the situation in Palestine "is a threat to international peace." If the British said it was not, the United Nations should not even consider taking further action. Since the British had already made it clear that they were not going to admit that a state of war existed in Palestine, the Austin resolution seemed to imply that the United States was willing to let chaos reign.

In truth the Truman administration was badly divided. A few of the men around the President were in favor of military intervention by the United States, unilaterally or through the United

Nations, to restore order in Palestine. One member of this faction was Dean Rusk, who advocated American intervention in Palestine in 1948 in almost precisely the terms he would use, a decade and a half later, to support American intervention in South Vietnam. Forrestal's diary quotes Rusk as telling one meeting of government planners, "If we did nothing, it is likely that the Russians could and would take definite steps toward gaining control in Palestine through the infiltration of specially trained immigrants, or by otherwise capitalizing on the widespread, violent civil war that would be likely to break out." But most presidential advisers had come to believe that the partition plan should be abandoned.

They were troubled about oil. The Arab League had announced in mid-February that American oil companies would not be permitted to lay pipelines across the territory of any member country until the United States changed its views on partition. Syria thereupon voided a signed contract for a pipeline through her territory. King Ibn Saud was under pressure from fellow Arab rulers to take punitive measures against the Arabian-American Oil Company. Vice-Admiral Robert B. Carney, deputy chief of naval operations, told the House Armed Services Committee that "in the event of serious disturbance in the Middle East, there is cause for grave concern for the fortunes of American oil facilities throughout that area, and to those who might desire to deny the oil of the Middle East to us [the reference is to the Soviet Union] such disturbance could afford nice opportunities for interference." Despite a series of confusing and contradictory statements by American officials, it was evident by the beginning of March that the United States was backing away from partition. As one Soviet delegate told the UN on March 11, "Everyone is acquainted with the ambiguous role of the United States regarding Palestine. We are all aware of pressures that American oil interests are exercising on the American government in this instance."

To Zionist leaders it seemed that the only way to prevent the United States from touching off a repudiation of partition at the UN was to make a direct appeal to President Truman, and that the only man who could sway Truman effectively was Chaim Weizmann. Truman had been greatly impressed by Weizmann at their one meeting, in November, 1947, and had readily given the venerable Zionist leader his aid on the Negev question. But now, three months later, Truman was still irritated by the Zionist propaganda barrage that had surrounded the General Assembly's debate over partition, and all during the winter of 1947–48 he had angrily kept the doors of the White House closed to Zionist spokesmen. Weizmann had been waiting for a month in New York for word that the President would receive him.

American Jewish leaders resorted to an elaborate device in order to bring Weizmann and Truman together. They reached out to Kansas City, Missouri, for an old friend of Truman's named Eddie Jacobson, and asked him to request of the President—as a personal favor—that he let Weizmann call on him.

Jacobson and Truman had served in the artillery together in World War I. After the war, Jacobson had been Truman's partner in the ill-starred haberdashery venture—Jacobson the buyer, Truman the salesman—and they had remained in touch over the years. Though Jewish, Jacobson had never been interested in Zionism; he was deeply concerned with the problem of the displaced persons, however, and several times before and after Truman had assumed the presidency had spoken to him to obtain relief for some specific hardship cases that had been called to his attention.

A group of Kansas City Jews, aware of Jacobson's closeness to Truman and the potential that that held for shaping American policy on Palestine, had begun to convert Jacobson to Zionism almost as soon as Truman entered the White House. A key figure in the project was Mrs. Ernest E. Peiser, a leader of Hadassah in Missouri, whose husband's business partner had been in the same battalion as Truman and Jacobson during the First World War. Through this partner, Herman Rosenberg, Mrs. Peiser was able to meet Jacobson, give him Zionist literature, and introduce him to visiting Zionist dignitaries. However, Jacobson, a Reform Jew, remained under the influence of the rabbi of his congregation, a man who was still not certain of the desirability of creating a Jewish state.

But in June, 1945, Rabbi Arthur J. Lelyveld, then director of the Committee on Unity for Palestine of the Z.O.A., came to Kansas City to address non-Zionists in parlor meetings and home gatherings, for the purpose of counteracting the statements of the American Council for Judaism. At one such meeting at the Peiser home the articulate, persuasive Lelyveld met Jacobson and, in a discussion lasting well past midnight, set forth the Zionist case. Jacob-

son's sympathies at last were captured; he met several times privately with Lelyveld in the following days, and finally Jacobson
invited the rabbi to go with him to Washington to explain the
Zionist position to the President.

On June 26, 1945, Jacobson brought Lelyveld and another Zion-
ist, Charles Kaplan, vice-president of the Shirtcraft Corporation of
New York, to the White House for a one-hour meeting with
Truman. Lelyveld provided the President with a full briefing on
Zionism, and attempted to soothe the sense of annoyance that
Truman had already begun to feel over the pressures being
brought to bear on him by "that New York rabbi"—Abba Hillel
Silver. Truman listened attentively. When the three visitors
emerged from the meeting, Jacobson explained to reporters that
Rabbi Lelyveld had wanted "to clear up several things" with the
President regarding Palestine, adding, "Kaplan sells shirts, I sell
furnishings, and the rabbi sells notions."

But it was too early, at this time, for Truman to adopt the sort
of policy toward Palestine that Jacobson had hoped to inspire.
Jacobson returned to Kansas City and for the next two years
played little role in the increasingly complex struggle to sway the
President's feelings. It was only when the problem of arranging
a Weizmann-Truman meeting arose that Jewish leaders thought of
making use of Jacobson's friendship with Truman a second time.

Jacobson was a member of the Kansas City lodge of B'nai B'rith,
and had met some of the national leaders of that organization,
including the long-time executive vice-president, Maurice Bisgyer, during the celebration of his lodge's seventy-fifth anniversary in the fall of 1947. In February, 1948, Bisgyer explained the
Weizmann situation to Jacobson, who responded by sending this
wire to his old friend on February 21:

"Mr. President I know that you have very excellent reasons for
not wanting to see Dr. Chaim Weizmann. No one realizes more
than I the amount of pressure that is being thrown on you during
these critical days, but as you once told me this gentleman is the
greatest statesman and finest leader that my people have. He is
very old and heartbroken that he could not get to see you. Mr.
President I have asked you for very little in the way of favors
during all our years of friendship, but am begging of you to see
Dr. Weizmann as soon as possible. I can assure you I would not
plead to you for any other of our leaders."

Six days later Truman replied that "there wasn't anything he [Weizmann] could say to me that I didn't already know, anyway," and added, "The situation has been a headache to me for two and a half years. The Jews are so emotional, and the Arabs are so difficult to talk with that it is almost impossible to get anything done. The British, of course, have been exceedingly noncooperative in arriving at a conclusion. The Zionists, of course, have expected a big stick approach on our part, and naturally have been disappointed when we can't do that."

Jacobson persisted. He traveled to Washington and presented himself at the White House on March 13, without an appointment. Presidential Secretary Matt Connelly greeted him and agreed to let him see Truman, though asking Jacobson not to bring up the subject of Palestine. Jacobson told Connelly that that was exactly what he had come to discuss, and entered Truman's office.

They exchanged gossip for a few minutes. Then Jacobson mentioned Palestine, and, according to the account he gave a Kansas City newspaper years later, the President "immediately became tense and grim, abrupt in speech and very bitter in the words he was throwing my way. In all the years of our friendship he never talked to me in this manner." Seeing Weizmann, Truman felt, "would only result in more wrong interpretation." He told Jacobson "that he didn't want to discuss Palestine or the Jews or the Arabs or the British; that he was satisfied to let these subjects take their course through the United Nations." And, Jacobson's account continues, Truman spoke of "how disrespectful and how mean certain Jewish leaders had been to him. I suddenly found myself thinking that my dear friend, the President of the United States, was at that moment as close to being an anti-Semite as a man could possibly be."

Suddenly Jacobson pointed to a small statue of Andrew Jackson in the President's office. "He's been your hero all your life, hasn't he?" Jacobson asked. "You have probably read every book there is on Jackson. . . . I have never met the man who has been my hero all my life, but I have studied his past like you have studied Jackson's. He is the greatest Jew alive, perhaps the greatest Jew who ever lived. You yourself have told me that he is a great statesman and a fine gentleman. I am talking about Dr. Chaim Weizmann. He is an old man and a very sick man. He has traveled thousands of miles to see you, and now you are putting off seeing him. That isn't like you."

Truman peered out the window for a long moment. Then he turned to Jacobson and said, "All right, you bald-headed son of a bitch, you win. Tell Matt [Connelly] to invite Dr. Weizmann here."

Weizmann saw the President on March 18. He was smuggled secretly into the White House through a side gate, and there was no public announcement of his visit. They spoke for some forty-five minutes. Truman's account relates that Weizmann "talked about the possibilities of development in Palestine, about the scientific work that he and his assistants had done that would someday be translated into industrial activity in the Jewish state that he envisaged. He spoke of the need for land if the future immigrants were to be cared for, and he impressed on me the importance of the Negev area in the south to any future Jewish state. . . .

"I told him, as plainly as I could, why I had at first put off seeing him. He understood. I explained to him what the basis of my interest in the Jewish problem was and that my primary concern was to see justice done without bloodshed. And when he left my office I felt that he had reached a full understanding of my policy and that I knew what it was he wanted."*

Weizmann left the White House in an optimistic mood. According to one of Truman's biographers, Jonathan Daniels, the President had told Weizmann, "You can bank on us. I am for partition."

The next day, March 19, Ambassador Warren Austin announced at the United Nations that his government now believed the partition plan could never be put peacefully into effect. The chief United States delegate called for a General Assembly meeting in order to establish a "temporary trusteeship for Palestine. . . . without prejudice to the rights, claims or position of the parties concerned or to the character of the eventual political settlement. . . . " In the meanwhile, Austin said, "We believe that the Security Council should instruct the Palestine Commission to

---

*Abba Hillel Silver always tried to minimize the significance of this episode. In 1963, six months before his death, Silver said, "It was American Jewry, rising magnificently to the challenge of the hour, which was responsible for the victories in Washington and Lake Success—not the intervention of someone who was smuggled into the White House through a back door, and who by the magic of his personality won over the President of the United States, and presto, it was all done."

suspend its efforts to implement the proposed partition plan."

10.

Zionist leaders were astounded by the March 19 reversal of American policy, coming less than twenty-four hours after Weizmann's meeting with Truman. Had the President lied to Weizmann? Or had the State Department begun to make policy behind the President's back? Either way, the implications were shocking: if Truman were not personally dishonest, then he was unable to control his own administration. At the United Nations, says *The New York Times* account of March 20, Zionist representatives were "stunned, some seemed near tears," while Arab delegates "indicated openly that they thought partition was dead and the victory theirs."

The Jewish Agency expressed sorrow "that a revision of an international judgment, maturely arrived at after prolonged and objective investigation, can be extorted by threats and armed defiance." Dr. Emanuel Neumann, speaking for the Zionist Organization of America, called on President Truman "to shake himself loose from this conspiracy fostered by oil profiteers." The American Jewish Committee—now only dimly non-Zionist and greatly in favor of partition—deplored the shift and suggested that it "has resulted in a loss in international prestige by the United States and has been a blow to the United Nations." Secretary-General Trygve Lie shared that feeling. In his autobiography he tells how he went to Austin the day after the speech to reveal his "sense of shock and of almost personal grievance." Lie viewed Austin as the innocent spokesman of a policy dictated by Washington, a policy that he told Austin was "an attack on the sincerity of your devotion to the United Nations cause, as well as mine," and he proposed that they both resign "as a measure of protest . . . and as a means of arousing popular opinion." Austin declined.

The storm over the American abandonment of partition grew more violent in the days that followed. The *Times* said on March 21, "It comes as a climax to a series of moves which has seldom been matched for ineptness, in the handling of any international issue by an American administration. . . . Somewhere along the line there has been a shocking lack of liaison and of common purposes between the American State Department and the American delegation in the United Nations, with the White

House itself apparently utterly at sea. . . . We have played a shabby trick on the Jewish community in Palestine, which put its faith in our promise." The Chicago *Sun* commented, "Our government has finally dropped the pretense that it still favored partition—the solution which our delegates so vigorously pushed through the U.N. General Assembly last fall." Eleanor Roosevelt was reported to be so upset by the reversal that she had asked to resign as an American UN delegate in order to be free to speak out against it. The Chicago *Sun* asserted that Truman and Secretary of State Marshall had told her she could criticize the decision as much as she cared to, but need not resign.

White House mail, predictably, was heavy, and so was the State Department's. Hundreds of thousands of postcards, letters, and telegrams came in. The State Department alone received 30,000 protests the day after Ambassador Austin's speech. In a single weekend later in the spring the White House and the State Department received 200,000 communications on Palestine, about half of them aimed at the abandonment of partition.

The Synagogue Council of America, an organization that represented rabbinical and lay groups of all three Jewish factions—Orthodox, Conservative, and Reform—asked that April 8 be a day of prayer "to give expression to the shocked conscience of America at the inexplicable action of our Administration in reversing its Palestine policy" and "to demand the fulfillment of the plighted word of this country and of the nations of the world. . . . " On March 24, 600 Jews from Brooklyn picketed the White House. A week later the American Trade Union Council for Histadrut—the American affiliate of Histadrut, the Palestinian labor federation—called for a half-day work stoppage in New York on April 14, and a demonstration meeting at Yankee Stadium. The New York Central Trades and Labor Council, representing all A.F.L. unions in New York City, approved the strike, as did the New York State C.I.O. Council. It was the first time in the history of the American trade union movement that an officially endorsed strike had been called for a political purpose. Some 250,000 workers in New York City stayed away from their jobs on April 14, and 30,000 attended the Yankee Stadium meeting despite a heavy rain.

Why had the March 19 policy shift come about? Had President Truman been deceiving Weizmann the day before, or had the

President been unaware of what the State Department was about to do?

The evidence of Truman's own memoirs is contradictory. He makes a valiant effort to insist that the March 19 Austin statement was really consistent with his assurances to Weizmann: "This was not a rejection of partition but rather an effort to postpone its effective date until proper conditions for the establishment of self-government in the two parts might be established. My policy with regard to Palestine was not a commitment to any set of dates or circumstances; it was dedication to the twin deal of international obligations and the relieving of human misery. *In this sense, the State Department's trusteeship proposal was not contrary to my policy.*" (Italics added.)

The key phrase is "the State Department's trusteeship proposal." Truman had not authorized it and knew nothing about it until it had been made public. In the same section of his book he speaks of "the Department of State's specialists on the Near East [who] were, almost without exception, unfriendly to the idea of a Jewish state," and says, "There were some men in the State Department who held the view that the Balfour Declaration could not be carried out without offense to the Arabs. Like most of the British diplomats, some of our diplomats also thought that the Arabs, on account of their numbers and because of the fact that they controlled such immense oil resources, should be appeased. I am sorry to say that there were some among them who were also inclined to be anti-Semitic." It was this faction of State—encouraged by Forrestal at the Defense Department—that maneuvered to bring about the March 19 pro-trusteeship statement. Truman's annoyance with the move is hinted at when he says, "Anybody in the State Department should have known—and I am sure that some individual officials actually expected—that the Jews would read this proposal as a complete abandonment of the partition plan on which they so heavily counted. . . . In this sense, the trusteeship idea was at odds with my attitude and the policy I had laid down."

When we turn from the official memoirs to the accounts of other men who were on the scene, the real story becomes evident. The North Carolina newspaperman Jonathan Daniels, a close observer of Washington events for many years, asserts that Truman first learned of the Austin speech and the new policy by reading the morning newspapers on March 20. At 7:30 that morning, Daniels

says, Truman called his special counsel Clark Clifford, asking him
to come to the White House: "There's a story in the papers on
Palestine and I don't understand what has happened."

When Clifford arrived, he found Truman as disturbed as he had
ever seen him. The President asked, "How could this have happened? I assured Chaim Weizmann that we were for partition and
would stick to it. He must think I am a plain liar." Clifford phoned
Secretary of State Marshall, who was in San Francisco, and Undersecretary Lovett, who was in Florida; both were as amazed by
the trusteeship proposal as Truman. After some investigation it
developed that there had been a State Department memorandum
to the effect that if partition proved unworkable, trusteeship
should be put forth to prevent a vacuum. Marshall had initialed this
memorandum, and State Department men who had opposed partition all along took advantage of Marshall's absence to send Ambassador Austin the instruction for the March 19 speech. The
result, as Clifford put it, was that "every Jew thought that Truman
was a no-good."

Patching up this scandalous rift in the administration was a
ticklish business. Truman at once sent word privately to Weizmann, via Judge Samuel Rosenman, that "there was not and
would not be any change in the long policy he and I had talked
about." Weizmann accepted this pledge and he alone among Jewish leaders took no part in the denunciation of Truman that followed the Austin speech. Publicly, though, Truman could not
easily repudiate his UN ambassador's declaration without expos-
ing the chaotic state of his administration. It was impossible for
him to admit that anonymous middle-echelon men in the State
Department had on their own initiative given the United States
an altogether new Palestine policy while their superiors were
looking the other way.

Therefore on March 20 Secretary of State Marshall hurriedly
called a press conference in California at which he announced that
the new policy had been adopted when it "appeared to me after
most careful consideration to be the wisest course to follow, and
after President Truman approved my recommendation." He insisted that it did not necessarily mean permanent shelving of the
idea of partition.

On March 25—while the uproar over the Austin speech was at
its peak—Truman, at his regular press conference, continued the

pretense that he had countenanced the policy shift, saying that it "had become clear that the partition plan cannot be carried out at this time by peaceful means. We could not undertake to impose this solution on the people of Palestine by the use of American troops, both on Charter grounds and as a matter of national policy. . . . Trusteeship was proposed only after we had exhausted every effort to find a way to carry out partition by peaceful means. . . . Trusteeship is not proposed as a substitute for the partition plan but as an effort to fill the vacuum soon to be created by the termination of the mandate on May 15." When a reporter asked, "You are still in favor of partition at some future date?" Truman replied that he was trying to say that as plainly as he could.

The bombardment of criticism continued. Senator Murray of Montana, a Democrat, called the situation "one of the most shocking retreats in the history of our foreign relations," and Senator Wherry of Nebraska, a Republican, said the President was "only shifting from one foot to another" and that "he might as well have stuck with the partitioning decision in the first place." Truman quietly proceeded with the job of extricating himself from the mess the State Department had created for him. On March 30, Ambassador Austin introduced two new resolutions at the Security Council. One called for a truce in Palestine, and the other asked a "special session of the General Assembly to consider further the question of the future government of Palestine." Trusteeship was not mentioned. On April 1, the Security Council approved both proposals by 9–0 votes, Russia and the Ukraine abstaining. Austin then invited all Security Council members to an informal discussion of the trusteeship idea on April 5; only Russia and the Ukraine did not attend. At this meeting Austin presented a 15-point outline of a trusteeship plan under which a governor-general appointed by the United Nations would rule Palestine with the aid of a locally recruited police force. The plan was vague and loose, and Austin made a point of mentioning that the United States itself had no special commitment to it. What he was doing, in effect, was simply going through the motions of talking about trusteeship, so that his March 19 proposal would not look utterly foolish. It was purely a tactical maneuver designed to allow the United States gradually to grope its way back to its original position in favor of a Jewish state.

In fact the United States now was more firmly resolved on the creation of a Jewish state than ever before. The chief result of the State Department's March 19 coup had been to turn the infuriated President Truman, for the first time, into a staunch Zionist. He felt that he had been undermined, betrayed, deceived, and mocked by members of his own government. He took it as a personal affront. Hereafter he would pay no heed to the appeasers of the Arabs, the worriers over oil, the frenetic anti-Communists, and the subtle anti-Semites in the Departments of State and Defense. His legendary temper had been aroused; he was determined to have his revenge on the career men who had tried to dictate policy behind his back; he resolved that the Jews were going to have their state, at once, with the official blessing of the United States.

II.

On March 23 the Jewish authorities in Palestine announced that they would oppose any United Nations move to postpone or block the implementation of partition. They rejected the trusteeship proposal that the United States had so unexpectedly raised four days earlier, and called for the United Nations Palestine Commission to enter the Holy Land at last and take charge during the waning weeks of the mandate. The proclamation also declared that a Jewish state would be formed under a provisional government no later than May 16—the day after the scheduled British withdrawal.

The tide of the war in Palestine was definitely turning. By early April, the Jewish position no longer seemed precarious. Arab morale was buffeted by a series of defeats.

One major operation began on March 31, immediately after Haganah had received a large consignment of arms purchased in Czechoslovakia. (The Czech munitions-makers were doing business with both sides in the war.) In order to open the blockaded road from Tel Aviv to Jerusalem, the Jewish army launched an attack on the hilltop village of Castel, five miles west of Jerusalem, which was held by a tough Arab force under the command of the grand mufti's cousin, Abd el-Kader el-Husseini. The battle lasted ten days, and Castel changed hands several times. But when Abd el-Kader was killed on the last day of the conflict the Arabs lost their will to fight, and an important section of the road came under Jewish control.

Arab forces still dominated a stretch of the road farther west, at

Latrun, but on April 13 a convoy of 178 trucks carrying 550 tons of food was able to get through to the besieged Jewish population of Jerusalem. Another convoy reached the encircled city on the fifteenth, and two days later a six-mile-long convoy, 300 trucks strong, got through. On April 20 Ben-Gurion himself entered Jerusalem with a fourth convoy, greatly buoying the morale of its defenders. But the struggle continued in Jerusalem, much of which remained in Arab hands.

Elsewhere, the brigand chieftain Fawzi el Kawakji mounted an assault on April 4 against the Jewish settlement of Mishmar ha-Emek, between Haifa and Tel Aviv, in an attempt to block the road linking these two important cities. But within ten days Palmach units had forced Kawakji into a disorderly, humiliating retreat, and as the Arabs fled Haganah was able to sweep the enemy out of several nearby villages.

While the battles of Castel and Mishmar ha-Emek were going on, a somber event occurred at the Arab town of Deir Yassin, near Castel. On April 8, soldiers of the Irgun and the Stern Gang seized Deir Yassin despite Haganah's advice that the place was of little strategic value. After overcoming the resistance of a band of Arab soldiers, the Jewish terrorists entered the town and carried out a savage massacre; a Red Cross representative who visited Deir Yassin on April 10 found 254 civilians, men, women, and children, dead. Haganah men ordered the terrorists out, but the damage was done, and the Jewish moral position irreparably stained by the crime.

A correspondingly ghastly Arab reprisal followed on April 12 on the outskirts of Jerusalem. A convoy of buses traveling under Red Cross badges was making its way to Mount Scopus, the site of the Hebrew University and the Hadassah Hospital. Jewish troops were stationed on Scopus, and quite likely the convoy was bringing food and relief personnel for this garrison, but its main purpose was to transport hospital and university people. As the buses passed near an Arab district of Jerusalem they were ambushed, and in the seven-hour battle that followed, 77 Jewish doctors, nurses, university teachers, and students were killed, while British troops in a military post 200 yards away refused to intervene.

But the crime of April 12 did not cancel the crime of April 8; and the news of the Deir Yassin massacre, as it spread through the

Arab populace of Palestine, had a profound and historically significant effect. It inspired such panic that a mass exodus of frightened
Arabs began, drastically and permanently changing the population balance of Palestine. Fear of Jewish vengeance sent thousands
of Arabs a day across the borders into Syria, Lebanon, or Transjordan. On April 10, 6,000 Arabs lived in Tiberias, by the Sea of
Galilee; by April 18 they were all gone. Haifa, which fell to Haganah on April 22, had had an Arab population of 62,000; all but 5,000
fled within hours after the Jews took it. The effect of the flight was
cumulative. The more Arabs who departed, the more there were
that decided to flee. Arab Palestine, which had numbered over
700,000 at the beginning of 1948, simply melted away, building
up a vast refugee population in the neighboring lands; in the second half of April alone, more than 150,000 Arabs left the country.

It had not originally been the intention of the Jewish Agency
to drive the Arabs out of the future Jewish state. Zionist planning
had always reckoned on the presence of a large Arab minority.
Only the extremists of the terrorist groups had looked forward
eagerly to eviction of the Arabs. The migrations, when they began, came as a surprise to the Jews, and there were attempts by
at least some Jewish leaders to persuade the Arabs to stay. Haifa's
mayor, Shabetai Levy, made strenuous efforts to prevent the flight
of his city's Arabs. But the exodus continued, and before long it
became Haganah policy to encourage it, usually through psychological warfare rather than by force. Though at first only the most
vindictive and ruthless of the Jewish leaders wished to expel the
Arabs from what was to be Jewish-governed territory, the advantages of such an expulsion soon came to seem overwhelming even
to the moderates. And so the Jews began to give publicity in radio
and press to episodes of looting and murder committed against the
Arab civilian population by Jewish terrorists, and they said nothing to contradict the wild rumors, usually spread by the tense
Arabs themselves, that the entry of Jewish forces into an Arab
district would be followed by a wholesale massacre of noncom-
batants. In some areas, Haganah sound trucks rolled through Arab
quarters, blaring dire warnings of the fate that would befall any
who lingered until the main army of the Jews arrived. Many Arabs
accepted these hints at face value and fled. Actual cases of forcible
ejection were relatively few, as a result, and subsequent Arab
charges of widespread Jewish atrocities were described by United

Nations mediator Bernadotte in September, 1948, as "greatly exaggerated." (To save face, the Arab leaders later attempted to claim that they had organized the flight themselves, in order to clear the land and allow Arab invasion armies to move with complete freedom. An Arab statement of 1949 declared that they "Proudly asked for the evacuation of the Arabs and their removal to the neighboring Arab countries. We are very glad to state that the Arabs guarded their honor and traditions with pride and greatness." This self-defeating boast merely gave the Zionists a way of avoiding responsibility for the hundreds of thousands of Arab refugees who now huddled in hideous "temporary" refugee camps.)

The snowballing demoralization of the Arab civilians—and to some extent of the Arab soldiers—did not mean that the Jews had won the war. The real war had not yet even begun. But it did turn vast tracts of Palestine into wholly Jewish territory, easing the military task of Haganah and providing assurance that the Zionist state would be able to come into existence upon the expiration of the mandate. Jerusalem still was ringed by Arabs, and much of the territory between Jerusalem and Tel Aviv remained under Arab control. But in the north, as the stampede of civilians continued, Acre and then Safed became Jewish cities, and Jewish authority was beginning to extend into regions that the partition plan had set aside for the proposed Arab state.

The Zionists now started to give some thought to the provisional government of the Jewish commonwealth. On April 6, a meeting of the Jewish leaders opened in Tel Aviv. It was decided to form a 37-member National Council made up of executives of the Jewish Agency, the Jewish National Council in Palestine, and other public bodies. Provision was made to grant representation to the Arabs who might remain in Jewish territory, and plans were drawn to take over such governmental functions as postal service, tax collection, and public utilities. The British, with less than six weeks remaining to their mandate, were already beginning to let those function lapse; the Jews knew they would inherit a government in chaos. It seemed impossible to pull everything together in time for the intended declaration of independence on May 15. No one was certain what boundaries to claim for the new state, or where to place its capital (Jerusalem was the sentimental choice, but Jerusalem was still under siege), or even what to call the country. During all the years of Zionist dreaming and planning, it had been sufficient to speak merely of "the homeland" or "the national home," but that would not do now.

Another important question concerned the international status of the new nation. In view of the talk of trusteeship now being heard at the United Nations, would the Jewish state be able to gain recognition as a sovereign entity? Or would it be regarded by the rest of the world as an outlaw that had proclaimed its own independence in defiance of the UN?

The position of the United States could be decisive. On April 9, Weizmann wrote to Truman to say, "The choice for our people, Mr. President, is between statehood and extermination." Warning against adoption of a trusteeship plan, Weizmann said, "I tremble to think of the wave of violence and repression which would sweep Palestine if the conditions and auspices of the recent unhappy years were to be continued under British or indeed under any foreign rule. I also know how passionately the British people desire the end of this troubled chapter. Should your administration, despite all this, press for any prolongation of British tenure, it would mean a responsibility for terrible events." Pointing out that "Jews and Arabs are both mature for independence, and are already obedient in a large degree to their own institutions, while the central British administration is in virtual collapse," Weizmann insisted that "the clock cannot be put back to the situation which existed before November 29. I would also draw attention to the psychological effects of promising Jewish independence in November and attempting to cancel it in March. . . ."

Truman agreed with every word of this, but the realities of politics forced him to keep silent for a while; he was not yet ready to repudiate the trusteeship idea that he detested, nor did he want to touch off a battle with the anti-Zionists within his administration. And so when the special session of the General Assembly summoned by the Austin resolution of March 30 convened on April 16, the United States delegation offered a new and expanded trusteeship plan, now in 47 sections but just as vague as before, and clearly labeled only a working paper, not an official American proposal.

Most of the other delegates were puzzled by the purpose of the move, and only Nationalist China showed any interest in supporting it. *The New York Times* commented editorially on April 21 that it "seems likely to arouse fresh doubts about the ultimate American position." This was precisely Truman's intention. He was going to allow his UN delegates to lobby halfheartedly for a trusteeship in place of partition, meanwhile letting time run out on the mandate; on May 15 partition would be a *fait accompli* and trusteeship would be dead without the necessity of the United States having to swallow its own misbegotten scheme in public. Because the President was keeping his own counsel, neither the United Nations nor the State Department perceived his ultimate goal. But Truman had made his aims clear to the one man who needed to know the truth. On April 23, the eve of Passover, just as Chaim Weizmann was about to leave his New York hotel room to attend a *seder* service, he received an urgent message to go to the apartment of President Truman's close friend, Judge Samuel Rosenman. Weizmann called on Rosenman, got to the *seder* late, and, according to his biographer, Israeli diplomat Abba Eban, sat through the service "in a mood of faraway abstraction, and left early." Rosenman had told Weizmann, at the President's request, about a conversation that Truman and Rosenman had had not long before. Truman had opened that conversation by saying, "I have Dr. Weizmann on my conscience." He had gone on to speak to Rosenman about the March 19 muddle and the attempts he had made to pull the United States back from its unauthorized commitment to trusteeship. If he could succeed in doing this, the President said through Rosenman, and if a Jewish state then came into being, he would recognize it immediately. The only condition he made was that he would deal with just one Jewish representative: Weizmann.

Weizmann had probably done more than anyone else to bring about the age-old dream of a Jewish state in the Holy Land. Now he knew on the eve of the holiday that commemorates the deliverance of the Jews from their bondage in Egypt that this dream would finally come true.*

At the United Nations, though, the United States continued to give lip service to trusteeship. After its April 16 plan sank from sight, it proposed on April 28 an odd new plan that would have put off any UN decision until the fall, meanwhile leaving the Arabs and Jews to govern the respective areas of Palestine in

---

*Truman's promise of recognition for the Jewish state remained a secret among Weizmann and his closest associates, and was not made public until 1962, a decade after Weizmann's death.

which they had already seized control. This proposal quickly died, and on May 3 the British Colonial Secretary, Arthur Creech Jones, told the General Assembly that it was best to drop the trusteeship notion altogether and appoint a "neutral authority" to oversee the Holy Land until some permanent solution emerged. This was seen as an acceptance of the existing partition of the country that had been achieved by military force.

Now even the State Department diehards saw that there was no way to prevent the partition of Palestine, although as late as May 13—just 31 hours before the expiration of the mandate—the United States delegation at the UN was still struggling to compose a resolution calling for a single administration over all of Palestine. However, the realists within the State Department understood that partition was already a fact, and would be openly acknowledged as such within minutes after the official end of British responsibility for Palestine.

If the Zionists carried out their pledge of March 23 to proclaim a Jewish state at the moment of British withdrawal, though, the Arab nations would almost certainly issue declarations of war against that state. Since the end of November, 1947, the fighting in Palestine had been carried on by clandestine Arab infiltrators, numbering less than ten thousand. But what would happen there once the governments of Egypt, Syria, Lebanon, Iraq, Transjordan, and the other Arab states felt free to send in their troops? They had held off this long only because Palestine was still theoretically under British rule, but once that pretense was abandoned on May 15 they would have no inhibitions about invading. The State Department planners gloomily predicted the need to send an international army into Palestine to defend the Jewish population from what looked like certain massacre.

The only hope seemed to lie in getting the Zionists to refrain from proclaiming their state until a truce could be arranged. Jorge Garcia Granados, who had been Guatemala's representative on UNSCOP, wrote that "in a number of private talks at Lake Success, New York and Washington, representatives of the United States State Department exerted the strongest possible pressure on Jewish leaders in an effort to persuade them not to proclaim a state. Veiled threats of possible American disfavor, even of severe economic sanctions, were expressed." Zeev Sharef, a member of Israel's first government, explained in his 1962 book, *Three Days,* that these threats were made informally, "not necessarily voiced directly to the official representatives of the Jewish Agency." Sharef reported that the chief threat was, " 'We shall not permit the Jews to use our dollars in order to wage a war we don't want.' There was no express threat of sanctions on fund-raising in America, but of an embargo against dollar remittances to Palestine which could be imposed on both the Jews and Arabs. Dollar payments from America to any outside territory could be halted by the simple device of requiring that they must have prior approval." The State Department men also threatened to make public "certain documents" dealing with terrorism, illicit arms purchases, and illegal refugee immigration, apparently in the naïve hope that these revelations would shock the American Jews out of their by now almost unanimous support of Zionism.

The only State Department proposal that emerged into the open was one made by Dean Rusk, then Assistant Secretary of State, on May 3. He called for an immediate cease-fire for ten days beginning May 5, and an extension of the mandate for ten days to May 25, while representatives of the Jewish Agency and the Arab states met in Jerusalem or some other Near Eastern city to negotiate a lasting truce. Rusk volunteered the use of the presidential plane, *The Sacred Cow*, to transport the Jewish representatives from New York to Palestine.

Several of the Jewish Agency's leaders in New York were in favor of accepting the cease-fire proposal, although not the extension of the mandate, but after a bitter meeting at which Emanuel Neumann, Abba Hillel Silver, and Mrs. Rose Halprin of Hadassah fought against making any concessions, the whole Rusk proposal was turned down.

On May 8 Moshe Shertok, representing the Jewish Agency, flew from New York to Washington to meet with Secretary of State Marshall and Undersecretary Lovett. Shertok wrote, "Both spoke with great earnestness about the truce, and they showed complete sincerity when they depicted the situation as disastrous and capable of developing into a danger to world peace. In their view they were bound to do everything in their power to avert such a calamity. They uttered no threats; they merely warned what the Jewish people must expect when faced by the Arab regular armies: if the Jews persisted in their course, they must not seek the help of the United States in the event of an invasion."

In his reply, Shertok expressed some confusion over the true purpose of the United States. Did it genuinely want to see a Jewish state come into being, or were these maneuvers over a truce part of a plan to postpone the birth of that state indefinitely? The United States, said Shertok, had helped the Jews to obtain their state through its actions at the United Nations in the partition debate; but its aid had been purely political. It had refused to sell arms to the Palestinian Jews or even to provide military guidance. What the Jews had obtained in Palestine they had won by their own means, Shertok declared, and so they could not regard themselves as bound in any way by the wishes of the United States.

Shertok then flew to Tel Aviv to discuss this meeting with the other Jewish leaders. He found himself suddenly hesitant, wondering if Marshall and Lovett had not been right that it would be best to postpone the declaration of independence, or perhaps merely to proclaim a "government" rather than a "state" on May 15. But he discovered most of his colleagues inflexibly set on independence. Two of the military leaders, Haganah commander Israel Galili and Haganah officer Yigael Yadin, thought that a postponement of the declaration might be in order simply to give the army more time to get prepared for full-scale war. But they were overruled. The vote was for independence, at once.

The end of the mandate was now at hand.

The British withdrawal had been going on for weeks. Early in April, British military headquarters had been moved from Jerusalem to Haifa, the port of departure. By April 15, many British officials and several thousand troops were on their way home. On April 20 the British closed their military court in Jerusalem, and six days later shut down their postal system. Each withdrawal was followed by a Jewish seizure of the abandoned offices; at no time was there any formal transfer of authority from the British to their successors. The British were simply walking out, making no provision for the orderly continuation of governmental functions.

On Friday, May 14, 1948—the last day of the mandate's life— the skeleton crew running the remaining British administration announced that Sir Alan Cunningham, the British high commissioner, was not going to wait for the official end of the mandate at midnight; he would leave Jerusalem that morning. And at nine in the morning on May 14 Sir Alan's bulletproof car drove out of the capital, taking him to Haifa to begin his homeward voyage.

The rest of the British civilians and troops followed him out. The headquarters of the mandate had been in New Jerusalem, the western section that had begun to develop in the nineteenth century. This part of the city was now under Jewish control, although the picturesque walled Old City was still besieged by the Arabs. Haganah men waited near the British offices; the moment the evacuation was complete, Jewish forces took command of them.

In Tel Aviv, meanwhile, David Ben-Gurion was putting the finishing touches on the Jewish state's declaration of independence. He was going to make the proclamation at four that afternoon, Palestine time, so that the new state would come into being instantly at midnight when the mandate died. Out of deference to devout Jews he could not issue the proclamation later in the day, for at sundown the Sabbath would begin, and all temporal affairs were supposed to halt.

The proclamation had been drafted by Moshe Shertok, but Ben-Gurion revised it to make its prose more taut and Biblical, less legalistic. He cut it to 979 Hebrew words, pruning it by about one-fourth its original length. A fierce debate broke out in the final hours over the phrase "Almighty God" in Shertok's draft; several Marxist Jews were offended by this religious reference, and in the end Ben-Gurion substituted the ambiguous expression *Tsur Yisrael*, "Rock of Israel." The name of the new state also was settled at the last moment, not because there was any disagreement about it, but simply because in the rush of events there had been little opportunity to think about it. But the choice of the name proved remarkably easy. There was only one possibility, obvious and unavoidable: Israel, which had been the name of the kingdom ruled by David and Solomon.

At four that afternoon several hundred people gathered in the Tel Aviv Museum, a low white concrete building once the home of Tel Aviv's first mayor, Meir Dizengoff. Only 25 of the 37 members of the provisional National Council were present. The rest were in Jerusalem, unable to make the short journey to the coastal city because the Arabs again controlled a vital point on the road. But several hundred invited guests were on hand—Zionist leaders, foreign visitors, and members of the press—and the long room was crowded as Ben-Gurion rose to speak. Above his head hung a portrait of the man who had dreamed of this moment: Theodor Herzl.

In a controlled, powerful, impressive voice Ben-Gurion read:

"We, the members of the National Council, representing the Jewish people in Palestine, and the World Zionist Movement, are met together in solemn assembly today, the day of termination of the British Mandate for Palestine; and by virtue of the natural and historic right of the Jewish people and of the Resolution of the General Assembly of the United Nations,

"We hereby proclaim the establishment of the Jewish State in Palestine, to be called *Medinat Yisrael* (the State of Israel).

"We hereby declare that, as from the termination of the Mandate at midnight, the 14–15th May, 1948, and pending the setting up of the duly elected bodies of the State in accordance with a Constitution, to be drawn up by the Constituent Assembly not later than the 1st October, 1948, the National Council shall act as the Provisional State Council, and that the National Administration shall constitute the Provisional Government of the Jewish State, which shall be known as Israel.

"The State of Israel will be open to the immigration of Jews from all countries of their dispersion; will promote the development of the country for the benefit of all its inhabitants; will be based on the principles of liberty, justice and peace as conceived by the Prophets of Israel; will uphold the full social and political equality of all its citizens, without distinction of religion, race or sex; will guarantee freedom of religion, conscience, education and culture; will safeguard the Holy Places of all religions; and will loyally uphold the principles of the United Nations Charter. ...

"We extend our hand in peace and neighborliness to all the neighboring states and their peoples, and invite them to cooperate with the independent Jewish nation for the common good of all. The State of Israel is prepared to make its contribution to the progress of the Middle East as a whole.

"Our call goes out to the Jewish people all over the world to rally to our side in the task of immigration and development and to stand by us in the great struggle for the fulfillment of the dream of generations for the redemption of Israel.

"With trust in the Rock of Israel, we set our hand to this Declaration, at this Session of the Provisional State Council, on the soil of the Homeland, in the city of Tel Aviv, on this Sabbath eve, the fifth day of Iyar, 5708, the fourteenth day of May, 1948."

The reading took seventeen minutes. When it was concluded a

rabbi pronounced a blessing, and the Palestine Philharmonic Orchestra played "Hatikvah," the Zionist song that by the next morning would be a national anthem. Ben-Gurion dismissed the meeting.

At midnight the mandate for Palestine perished, without a single mourner. And when the sun's rays came westward across the Jordan the following dawn, they touched the soil of an independent, fully sovereign Jewish state for the first time since the legions of Rome had marched into Palestine in 63 B.C.

NINE

Medinat Yisrael

PRESIDENT TRUMAN had had advance word of what the Zionists were going to do, but only by a matter of a few hours. On the morning of May 14, Chaim Weizmann's secretary appeared at the White House bearing a letter to the President from Weizmann. It thanked Truman for his "very great contributions ... toward a definitive and just settlement of the long and troublesome Palestine situation," declaring that "the leadership which the American Government took under your inspiration made possible the establishment of a Jewish State." That state, said Weizmann, was due to begin its existence immediately upon termination of the mandate, and the Zionist leader expressed the hope "that the United States ... will promptly recognize the Provisional Government of the New Jewish State. The world, I think, will regard it as especially appropriate that the greatest living democracy should be the first to welcome the newest into the family of nations."

In the early afternoon, Truman summoned Secretary of State Marshall, Undersecretary Lovett, and two members of the White House staff, Clark Clifford and David Niles, to discuss an appropriate response. Tel Aviv lies seven time zones east of Washington. Ben-Gurion had already read his proclamation, and the mandate's last night had begun. The President said that he intended to recognize the Jewish nation. Marshall thought it would be inadvisable to do so. Clifford pointed out that Truman was already on record in favor of an independent Jewish state, and that it would be unrealistic to withhold recognition now. Marshall took this to mean that Clifford, the politically sophisticated presidential adviser, wanted Truman to keep in mind the importance of the Jewish vote in the coming presidential election. Angrily, the Secretary of State said, "Mr. President, this is not a matter to be determined on the basis of politics. Unless politics were involved, Mr. Clifford would not even be at this conference. This is a serious matter of foreign policy determination, and the question of politics and political opinion does not enter into it."

The discussion veered back and forth several times between recognition and nonrecognition, and when it became apparent that Truman was going to insist on recognition, the State Department men attempted to persuade him to wait at least a few days. The President refused to consider any delay. "I was well aware," he wrote, "that some of the State Department 'experts' would want to block recognition of a Jewish state. . . . I was told that to some of the career men of the State Department this announcement [of recognition] came as a surprise. It should not have been if these men had faithfully supported my policy. The difficulty with many career officials in the government is that they regard themselves as the men who really make policy and run the government. They look upon the elected officials as just temporary occupants."

A momentary problem arose over the mechanics of according recognition. Up till now Truman's dealings with the Jewish Agency had been via Weizmann. But Weizmann held no official post in the Zionist movement at this time, nor was he even a resident of Palestine. A White House aide hurriedly summoned the Jewish Agency's official representative in Washington, Eliahu Epstein. (In accordance with Israeli custom, he has since Hebraicized his name to Eliahu Elath.) Clark Clifford told Epstein of the impending recognition and asked him to draft a formal letter requesting such recognition.

Epstein immediately began work on it, assisted by three aides —David Ginsburg, Oscar Gass, and Robert Nathan. They produced a brief statement with one significant omission: the name of the new nation, which Epstein had not yet received from Tel Aviv. By three in the afternoon the name still had not come through. Epstein left blank spaces for it in his letter, which he gave to his press officer, an American-born Palestinian newspaperman named Harry Zinder, to take to the White House. Almost immediately afterward Epstein learned by radio that the new state was to be called Israel. He sent out a messenger who overtook Zinder's cab and gave him the information. Filling in the name by hand, Zinder continued on to the White House. At five o'clock the letter was on President Truman's desk. Epstein had written:

"I have the honor to notify you that the State of Israel has been proclaimed an independent republic within frontiers approved by the General Assembly of the United Nations in its Resolution of November 29, 1947, and that a provisional government has been charged to assume the rights and duties of government. . . . The act of independence will become effective at one minute after 6 o'clock on the evening of May 14, 1948, Washington time. . . . I have been authorized by the provisional government of the new State to tender this message and to express the hope that your government will recognize and will welcome Israel into the community of nations."

Truman offered a two-sentence reply:

"This Government has been informed that a Jewish state has been proclaimed in Palestine and recognition has been requested by the provisional government thereof.

"The United States recognizes the provisional government as the *de facto* authority of the new State of Israel."

The recognition statement was issued at 6:11 P.M. Eastern Daylight Time, on May 14, 1948. In the severed land that had been Palestine midnight had already come, and the State of Israel was eleven minutes old. At the Jewish Agency's Massachusetts Avenue building in Washington, the blue-and-white Israeli flag had been flying since the stroke of six.

The United Nations had convened at 5 P.M. The meeting had been under way a short while when a newsman whispered to Guatemala's Jorge Garcia Granados that an American declaration of recognition was on its way. Garcia Granados, a strong supporter of the Zionists, passed the word around in delight. A *New York Times* account the next day characterized the general reaction as "anger, incredulity, and shock, mixed finally with relief. . . . Delegates, officials and the small crowd of visitors were dumbfounded . . . and few believed it at first. . . . The first reaction was that someone was making a terrible joke, and some diplomats broke into skeptical laughs. . . . Most of the remarks heard around the corridors were too caustic to be attributed to the authors. One delegate asked another for the United States position on Palestine and was told by another diplomat that he did not know because he had not seen an announcement for twenty minutes.... Sir Carl Berendsen of New Zealand remarked tartly that he was 'Just dizzy, that's all, just dizzy.'... There was considerable resentment among many of the delegations over the way the United States has pushed so vigorously for a trusteeship agreement in United Nations debates while apparently intending all the time to approve partition by recognizing the new state of Israel.

"This feeling soon began to give way in some delegations to one of relief that the United States had at last come out firmly after what many of them believed was a long display of indecision."

At about 6:20, the news of the recognition came over the International News Service teletype, for Truman's press secretary had given the story out the moment recognition was proclaimed. The Jewish Agency's press officer at the UN tore the bulletin from the machine and took it to Abba Hillel Silver, who cried, "This is marvelous! This is what we've been waiting for."

The White House had also sent word to Ambassador Austin. But the American delegates at the UN were unable to believe what they heard, and kept an embarrassed silence while Austin checked the accuracy of the report. A Colombian delegate advanced to the rostrum and demanded to know if the United States had indeed recognized the Zionist state. "I regret that we have no official information," one of the American delegates replied. A few minutes later, Dr. Philip C. Jessup of the American delegation entered the hall, looking stunned and bewildered. It was Jessup who only a day and a half earlier had submitted a draft of a new resolution that would have postponed partition. Now, badly shaken, he read Truman's two sentences of recognition.

In the corridor some time later, Garcia Granados encountered an aide to the American delegation and mentioned the statement. "That is White House language, not State Department," the aide said sharply.

Andrei Gromyko of Russia shortly was denouncing the irresponsibility of American policy on Palestine, calling it "completely devoid of principle," and arguing that United States efforts to undermine the partition plan had helped to bring on the present chaos in the Holy Land. He made it clear that the Soviet Union would also offer quick recognition to Israel, in keeping with its belated (and cynical) conversion to Zionism. "The Jewish State is in existence," Gromyko said. And so it was. Russia granted recognition on May 17; Guatemala had done so the day before.

Most Americans hailed the birth of the new state. Hundreds of newspapers across the nation offered congratulations. A B'nai B'rith survey later showed that 64 percent of the editorials were favorable, 32 percent noncommittal, only 4 percent questioned the wisdom of creating a Jewish republic. On May 15, some 500 telegrams reached the White House, nearly all of them praising the President for having offered such swift recognition. That evening, a group called the Committee of Jewish Writers and Artists held a celebration at the Polo Grounds, one of New York's baseball stadiums; and on Sunday the sixteenth, the American Zionist Emergency Council staged its own "Salute to the Jewish State" in Madison Square Garden, with 19,000 people in attendance and 6,000 more standing outside in a steady rain to listen over loudspeakers. Another 75,000 had been turned away.

Sunday's *New York Times* devoted a column to a close analysis of President Truman's reasons for extending recognition to Israel. One motive, it said, was the President's awareness that no trusteeship arrangement could be contrived. Another was the march of events in Palestine, including the Jewish military successes, which demonstrated that the United Nations could do nothing to alter the division of the Holy Land between Jews and Arabs. The abrupt British withdrawal had created a vacuum that the President had felt it necessary to fill by recognizing Israel. Third, the *Times* said, "New York City Democratic leaders, in particular Edward J. Flynn, national committeeman, insisted that in an election year it was essential to take some action to propitiate Zionist supporters, who were turning against the Truman Administration because of its previous reversal on partition." The New York City politicians, the *Times* went on, had exerted particularly strong pressure in the final days of the mandate and had attacked the State Department for its politically risky anti-Zionist stand.

Beyond much doubt the President did have domestic political considerations on his mind when he recognized Israel. Truman was going to need all the votes he could attract in November, for he was under fire from every side; liberal northerners thought he was too rigidly anti-Communist, conservative southerners thought he was too liberal and much too kind to Negroes, and there had already been a movement to dump him from the 1948 Democratic ticket, replacing him by the popular war hero Dwight D. Eisenhower. General Eisenhower had spiked that movement early in 1948 by declaring he was not a candidate, and by spring it was certain that Truman would have the nomination. But it was equally certain that he would be beaten by the probable Republican nominee, Thomas E. Dewey of New York. A strong bid to the Jewish voters could do Truman no harm, and might strengthen his slim chance to retain the presidency.

But he would not have let such a purely political aim shape his foreign policy if he really believed the dire predictions of the State Department, the Defense Department, and the Pentagon that any pro-Zionist move would bring catastrophic Arab retaliation against American oil interests in the Near East. Truman was too independent-minded a man to have placed partisan interests above national security. If his main interest had been to please the Jewish voters, he could have done it far more effectively by announcing open support for the Zionist program long before the spring of 1948.

Truman's virtually singlehanded recognition of Israel, which undercut his whole administration, was in fact a daring gamble that paid off. He guessed that the Arab threat of reprisals against the United States for any aid to Zionism was an empty bluff; he was right. He suspected that the Russians would recognize Israel with great speed, and therefore that it would benefit the United States to move even faster; he was right. He believed that the new Jewish state would be able to sustain its existence; he was right. In this way he became convinced that it was proper and desirable to defy his own advisers in the matter of Palestine. Although he had not at first been sympathetic to the creation of a Jewish state, he had come to feel intuitively by the spring of 1948 that such a state should be allowed to exist. Almost certainly his meetings with Weizmann in November, 1947, and March, 1948, were instrumental in his conversion to Zionism, for he saw in Weizmann a kindred spirit, tough, crafty, patient. As the prototype of all underdogs—the little ex-haberdasher from Missouri who had been catapulted into the world's most demanding job—Truman perhaps came to identify with the Palestinian Jews, who against improbable odds were prepared to claim and defend a homeland. The salty, blunt-spoken President, uneasy in the presence of the slick "striped-pants boys" who ran his foreign policy, chose for once to ignore their cautious warnings and their fastidious concern for Arab opinion, and, in his characteristically straightforward and undevious way, offered his hand to Israel.

2.

The banner headline on the front page of the May 15 issue of *The New York Times* declared:

ZIONISTS PROCLAIM NEW STATE OF ISRAEL
TRUMAN RECOGNIZES IT AND HOPES FOR PEACE
TEL AVIV IS BOMBED; EGYPT ORDERS INVASION

At one in the morning on Israel's first day of existence, David Ben-Gurion was awakened to learn that the United States had granted recognition. Ben-Gurion—who had just become Prime Minister—expressed his pleasure and went back to sleep. Several hours later he was awakened again, and was told, as he later put it, "that our people in the United States demand that I broadcast to them." Putting a coat over his pajamas, he drove to the Tel Aviv radio station at the shore near the present site of the Sheraton Hotel and went on the air shortly after 5 A.M.—11 P.M. of the previous day in the eastern United States—to declare his gratitude. At 5:25 A.M. a loud explosion interrupted his speech. Ben-Gurion paused a moment; then his listeners heard him say, "A bomb has just fallen on this city from enemy aircraft flying overhead."

A shadowy war had been going on in Palestine since the General Assembly's partition vote; but now the real war, what Israelis call the War of Liberation, was beginning. Five Arab states—Egypt, Transjordan, Syria, Lebanon, and Iraq—had declared war on Israel. Their armies—bolstered by contingents from Saudi Arabia and Yemen—were crossing the borders of the new state. The Secretary-General of the Arab League declared, "This will be another war of extermination which will be talked about like the Mongol massacres and the Crusades."

In theory, at least, the Jewish defenders were outnumbered beyond calculation. The Egyptians claimed to have a fighting force of 200,000 men; Syria was making similar claims; the Premier of Iraq talked of unleashing 2 or 3 million of his people to obliterate the Zionists. The real figures were less overwhelming but still formidable. The Arab allies were able to put some 120,000 men in the field. The Egyptian army, swollen by recent volunteers, totalled 40,000; Lebanon had 10,000 men in arms, Syria 20,000. Transjordan could offer its impressive British-trained Arab Legion, 40,000 soldiers strong. Iraq, which did not border on Israel, was sending an expeditionary force of 5,000 and 5,000 more were on their way from the two Arabian countries. Of all these, 24,000 troops were actually moving into combat on Israel's northern, eastern, and southern borders. They were supported by modern bombers and fighter planes, tanks, armored cars, and heavy artillery. Against them Israel could send an army only half as large and miserably equipped; but behind the Haganah forces stood a citizen army that included every able-bodied Israeli man, woman, and child.

In the north, a small but well-trained Lebanese force was trying to break through onto the coastal road leading down to Haifa. On the east, a strong Syrian army was attacking the settlements near the Sea of Galilee that guarded the approach to the city of Tiberias. Transjordan's Arab Legion was occupying the interior of the country, the West Bank region, which under the partition plan had been destined to become the Arab state, and also had taken a firm grip on Old Jerusalem. The Iraqi troops had seized the Arab-populated region around Nablus and were only ten miles from Israel's coastal strip. In the south, 10,000 Egyptians, aided by Saudi Arabians and Yemenites, were in action along Israel's Sinai frontier; they were moving rapidly up the coast to Gaza, in an effort to sever the whole of the northern Negev from Israel.

The first reports to reach the outer world were dismaying. A correspondent for the British *Daily Telegraph* reported on May 17, "Lydda airfield taken. Fall of Beersheba. Armies of five Arab states are advancing into Palestine on three fronts; the Iraqis have crossed the Jordan; the Lebanese are pushing south on the coastal road; the Syrians are advancing on Lake Tiberias [the Sea of Galilee]; the Egyptians are driving inland." But the real situation was less ominous. Lydda (Lod) and Beersheba had been in Arab hands prior to the invasion; the troops of Iraq and Transjordan were moving through territory that Israel did not claim; the Syrians were still on their own soil as they marched toward the Sea of Galilee; and the Egyptian thrust, while serious, had not come anywhere near the heart of Israel's territory. The battleground was a tiny one. Although the enemy might be no more than ten miles away here, twenty miles there, the Israelis did not feel that they had the Arabs in their midst.

The Jews put up a desperate resistance, all the while going through the new and instantly cherished routines of sovereignty. Amid the chaos of battle the National Council met to elect Chaim Weizmann the first President of Israel—a purely ceremonial post, under the parliamentary scheme of government that was planned. President Weizmann, in New York, received word of his election on May 17. President Truman at once invited him to make a state visit to Washington, and he traveled to the capital aboard a special train, to be escorted down a Pennsylvania Avenue that was decked with the flags of Israel and the United States.

Another bit of official business for the new government was to make its army legal. By a decree of May 28, Haganah, the Irgun, and the Stern Gang were dissolved as separate units and merged into the new Israel Defense Force, Zva Haganah Le-Yisrael, called by an acronym, in Hebrew fashion, simply Zahal.

The tiny army fought valiantly on all fronts. The Lebanese were contained fairly easily, for Lebanon, a mercantile nation with a large Christian population, had never been passionately opposed to Zionism and was merely making a *pro forma* appearance in the war. Around the Sea of Galilee, a few hundred Israeli defenders at the villages of Degania, Mishmar Hayarden, and Ein Gev blocked the Syrian thrust, while at the town of Gesher, farther south, a small Israeli unit kept the Syrians and the Iraqi troops from joining. In the northern Negev the frontier outposts of Yad Mordechai and Nitzanim held off huge Egyptian forces, and though they both eventually were engulfed, they created enough delay to permit the regular Israeli army to dig in behind them. The Egyptian advance was stopped at Ashdod, on the Mediterranean coast some twenty miles south of Tel Aviv.

The only real triumph for the Arabs in the early weeks of the war—and it was a bitter one for Israel to accept—was the final capture of the Old City of Jerusalem. Jewish forces within the medieval walled town had held out for months while the Arab Legion tightened its grip; but in the end only 35 Israelis fit to fight remained inside the city, and there was no way of getting reinforcements through the Arab blockade. Confusion and dissension among the Israeli commanders forced the surrender of the Old

City on May 28. The remaining Jewish civilians were allowed peacefully to withdraw into the Israeli-occupied New City, and for the first time since the Babylonian captivity no Jews dwelled in the true Jerusalem. The Wailing Wall, the ancient Jewish cemetery on the slopes of the Mount of Olives, the many synagogues of the Old City, now disappeared behind the barricades of no man's land, and would remain gallingly unattainable, symbols of frustration for Israel, for the next 19 years.

On May 20 the United Nations had responded to the outbreak of full-scale war by naming a mediator for Palestine: Count Folke Bernadotte, a member of the Swedish royal family and the head of his country's Red Cross. Bernadotte at once attempted to arrange a truce. For several weeks, while their troops were advancing toward Israeli territory, the Arabs ignored his calls for a cease-fire. But when the strength of the Israeli defense became apparent, the invaders changed their minds. A truce now seemed a convenient way to bring in reinforcements and build up the deployment of guns and tanks. The Israelis felt the same way; they wanted a breathing spell.

On June 11, both sides agreed to a four-week cease-fire. Under its terms, movement of military material was forbidden, as was the reinforcement of armies already in the field. But little attention was paid to these restrictions. The Arabs made use of the truce period to double their forces, bringing them to 50,000, including volunteers from North Africa and the Sudan. Israel, too, looked to her friends overseas for aid: men, guns, planes, dollars, anything that was offered.

3.

One of the most valuable of Israel's military officers during the first phase of the War of Liberation was an American, David (Mickey) Marcus. Born in Brooklyn, a small Jewish boy growing up in a tough neighborhood, Marcus had turned himself into an outstanding athlete and, partly on the strength of his record in high school sports, had won appointment to the U.S. Military Academy at West Point in 1921. A few years after his graduation he resigned his army commission to enter law school, and when he had his degree he became first a Treasury Department lawyer, then a member of the staff of the U.S. attorney for New York, where he specialized in prosecuting prohibition-era gangsters. In

1934 Mayor Fiorello LaGuardia of New York asked Marcus to serve as first deputy commissioner of correction. For the next five years he tackled corruption in New York's vast and archaic prison-administration system, and in 1940 he became commissioner of correction, a post which he held only a short while.

When Marcus' Army Reserve unit was activated later in 1940, he became a lieutenant colonel and judge advocate of the 27th Infantry Division. Although his services to the army were sup-posed to be purely in legal matters, Marcus managed to acquire some battle training by leading his division on maneuvers in Loui-siana in the summer of 1941. After the war broke out he followed his unit to the Pacific, but saw no action there, since he was assigned to command a training school in Hawaii that prepared men for jungle warfare.

In 1943 Colonel Marcus was transferred back to Washington as a member of the army's Civil Affairs Division, a desk post involv-ing policy planning; he was present at the 1943 meetings of world leaders in Cairo and Teheran, getting his first view of Palestine on a side trip. (He knew little of Zionism and claimed later never even to have heard of Theodor Herzl.) His love of adventure led him to wangle a place in the invasion of France on D-Day, June 6, 1944, parachuting into Normandy although he had never jumped before, and finally tasting combat in an engagement with a Ger-man machine-gun emplacement.

He was present also at the Yalta Conference of 1945, and after the war was shifted to Germany, where he saw the Dachau death camp a few days after its liberation. For the first time he under-stood what the war had done to Europe's Jews, and the plight of the survivors at once became of the highest importance to him. In Germany Marcus had many planning responsibilities, including a stint organizing the mammoth war-crimes trials at Nuremberg.

Finally, in the spring of 1947, he applied for his discharge and at the age of 45 returned to enter private law practice. Later that year he was visited by a certain Major Shamir from Palestine, who asked his advice. Shamir had been sent to recruit a few American military experts to help Haganah, and thought that Colonel Mar-cus might be able to recommend some of the men he had served with. Marcus sounded out a few of his wartime colleagues, but without success. In the process, he discovered from Shamir that the Jewish army was badly understaffed and underequipped, and was in need of intensive reorganization if it hoped to win a real war. By January, 1948, Marcus still had not been able to persuade any of his friends to take on the assignment. It did not come as any great surprise when Shamir and Moshe Shertok asked him to go himself. And with little hesitation he accepted.

Marcus arrived in Palestine during the tense days of February, 1948, when Arab guerrilla actions seemed destined to cut the Jewish territory apart. From Tel Aviv he wrote his wife, on February 16, "The task seems so gigantic. No one man can do this job; were there 50 men here trained at staff level, perhaps that would be enough." The Palestinians, he said, were "physically and mentally a new breed of men. Yes, a different kind of Jew is being born; and if the baby is not to perish, all the help that America can give, must be given NOW. The problem is difficult only because the needed support is denied to them."

Speaking no Hebrew, only hazily acquainted with the outlines of the Zionist struggle, Marcus plunged jauntily into his assignment, getting to know the Haganah commanders, learning the structure of the Jewish army, probing for its weaknesses and its strengths. He toured the country, taking notes, observing the fighting already going on, shaking his head bitterly over the casualties and the assaults on the civilian population.

His informal approach won him the quick support of the Haganah men, who themselves were informal and unconventional in their outlook. The rigidities, the pomposities, the concern with protocol, so much a part of an officer's attitude in any conventional army, were absent. Perhaps the Jewish officers would develop an interest in titles, ribbons, and other perquisites of rank later on, but there was no time for such amusements now. Nor were they so jealous of their status that they would not take advice from the brash American; they knew that he had a great deal to offer them.

Marcus was on hand during the final months of the mandate, when the British abdicated all responsibility and gave the Arabs carte blanche to strike at the Jews. His letters to his wife are full of resentment over British one-sidedness. "It is frightening to watch the Arabs being armed under Treaty," he wrote on March 15, "and to watch the admission of the invaders: trained battalions of non-Palestinian Arabs, dressed in civil attire, fully British-armed and equipped and trained, with German and Polish officers. It seems we are under the influence of Neutral Britain. The British manage every day to search our convoys and confiscate our arms. They have yet, to my knowledge, to hold up one Arab convoy."

He did what he could to reshape the Jewish guerrillas into a modern army ready to fight a full-scale war, writing a 280-page training manual that set down the essence of his ideas. He proposed to combine the flexibility and informality of the Haganah's traditional tactics with the more orthodox military methods of a larger army.

His ideas met with an eager reception. Ben-Gurion, writing to Moshe Shertok, said, "The expert who came with Shlomo [Shamir] has been a blessing to us. His conclusions show a marvelous grasp of the present situation, both on its good and bad sides (and the bad are neither few nor slight)."

In April, 1948, the illness of Marcus' wife forced him to return suddenly to New York, but he could permit himself only a short visit with her. At the end of the month, Shertok asked him to go back to Palestine, and Marcus agreed, promising his distressed wife that he would be with her again by the end of June.

He arrived in Palestine a few weeks before independence, and found that Haganah had taken control of nearly the entire northern part of the country from Haifa east to Tiberias. But the Jewish desert outposts of the Negev were being cut off, and the center of the country was split by the Arabs' command of the vital road linking Jerusalem and Tel Aviv. When the war began in earnest on May 15, Haganah's tasks were multiplied tenfold. Now Marcus attempted to work out new deployments of the Israeli army that would be able to handle the thrusts of invasion on every front. He journeyed into the Negev to put together a striking force handling newly purchased weapons; then, as the Negev troops held the Egyptians back, Marcus shifted his base of operations to the tortured, isolated capital, Jerusalem. The cream of the Arab troops—Transjordan's elite Arab Legion—was engaged in the struggle to deny Jerusalem to the Jews. The British general Glubb Pasha directed the Arab Legion, and nearly forty other British officers were serving in it, leading the artillery campaign against the Jewish quarters of the city.

When Marcus reached Jerusalem, about May 25, the Old City was already certain to fall to the Arabs, and the sprawling, populous New City was under heavy Arab attack. The key to the situation was the Tel Aviv-Jerusalem road, the only supply route for the Jews; and that road was choked midway by an Arab bastion holding the hill town of Latrun. All attempts at dislodging the Arabs from Latrun had failed, with severe Israeli losses. A new effort on May 26, following a strategy suggested by Marcus, also failed. The novice warriors of Israel were simply no match for the heavy guns of the superb Arab Legion garrison and its British-trained officers. The Israelis fell back to consider alternatives.

In the next few days, the surrender of Old Jerusalem took place, and Marcus acquired for the first time an official place in the Israeli army. On May 28, a decree signed by Ben-Gurion named "Brigadier General Stone"—Marcus' pseudonym while in Israel—as "Commander of the Jerusalem Front, with command over the Etzioni, Har-El, and 7th Brigades. General Stone is authorized to select officers and noncoms from the aforementioned three brigades to form his staff."

Immediately Marcus drew a new and more ambitious plan to take Latrun, involving a feint toward the town's police station and a quick infantry movement while the Arab Legion's attention was distracted. On paper it was a classic maneuver, but in practice the Israelis were unable to achieve the precise timing necessary to carry it off. An essential infantry column went awry, and 137 Israelis died, with Latrun remaining in Arab hands. Marcus cabled Haganah's Yigael Yadin, "I was there and saw the battle. Plan good. Artillery good. Armor excellent. Infantry disgraceful."

It had been a near miss, though, and the Arabs were greatly alarmed at the contributions that the new Israeli strategist had made. The British, bowing to United Nations pressure, had on May 30 withdrawn all of their officers on duty with the Arab Legion, except for Glubb himself; the news that an American colonel was directing Israeli troops, therefore, was doubly dismaying.

Marcus now abandoned hope of seizing Latrun and improvised an alternate measure: construction of a back road to Jerusalem that would avoid the Arab gun emplacements on the Latrun heights. Since the middle of May, Haganah trucks had been using a dirt track south of the highway and parallel to it, shielded by a ridge of hills from the Arab artillery.

On May 31, Marcus toured this track and gave orders for it to be transformed into a permanent highway. Israeli engineers told him it would be impossible to cut a road there, because of the steep grades and the plunging ravines. But Marcus went ahead. He radioed Ben-Gurion, "Can build road if you give me the equipment. Need bulldozers, compressors, stonecutters and builders—but top priority for bulldozers."

Hundreds of laborers were sent to the site, and earthmoving equipment was brought in from several points. In some places along the construction line, Arab patrols were only 500 yards away. But the work went on, twenty-four hours a day, blasting and bulldozing and quarrying, until within five days the rough track was wide enough for heavy-duty trucks. By June 9, the road was ready. Tel Aviv and Jerusalem again were linked; and the Latrun bypass that Mickey Marcus had built saved New Jerusalem for Israel. It was to remain the main highway across the waist of the country until the war of June, 1967, when Israel achieved full control over the Latrun road at last.

The Marcus Road was Mickey Marcus' final contribution to the State of Israel. On the night of June 9 he took up quarters in the magnificent monastery of the town of Abu Ghosh, a few miles outside Jerusalem. The United Nations truce was due to go into effect a day and a half later, and Marcus hoped to use the interval without combat to develop strategies for the inevitable next phase of the war. On June 10 he drafted plans for the defense of the new road and a possible renewed assault on Latrun, and late that night, restless, he left his cot to stroll in the monastery courtyard. Wrapped in his bedsheet to ward off the chill of the hilltop town's night air Marcus slipped past a fence and wandered off into the darkness.

Since Arab troops—commanded, despite the orders of their government, by British officers—were camped nearby, Israeli sentries had been posted around the monastery to guard against a sudden raid. At about 3:35 A.M., one of these sentries, a man who had come from Eastern Europe only a few weeks before, heard sounds in the underbrush to the north of the monastery. Suddenly he caught sight of a figure clad in white, moving toward him. The sentry readied his rifle and called out in Hebrew, "Who goes there?" Marcus, returning from his stroll, gave the password. The sentry was not sure if he had been addressed in English, or in English-accented Hebrew. But either way something seemed amiss, and he began to think that some Arab Legion officer was making a reconnaissance mission. He fired a warning shot into the air. The man in white continued to advance, one hand raised, perhaps in salute, perhaps to hurl a grenade. The sentry fired again, and Marcus fell, slain by one of his own men. He was the last Israeli casualty before the June 11 truce became effective, six hours and ten minutes later.

His body was flown back to the United States on June 30, so that he did, as he promised, get home by the end of June. After a funeral service at a Brooklyn temple, a 60-car procession journeyed to New York City Hall, where Mayor William O'Dwyer led a brief ceremony of tribute. Then the mourners began the long journey to the cemetery of the Military Academy at West Point, north of the city. Governor Thomas E. Dewey attended the interment, as did former Secretary of the Treasury Morgenthau; and two Haganah men were among the ten pallbearers: Yosef Hamburger, who had served aboard the *Exodus,* and a tough young officer named Moshe Dayan. Of the more than three thousand men who lie buried at West Point, David Marcus is the only one who was killed while fighting under a foreign flag.

4.

A war tragedy of a very different sort also occurred in June, 1948.

The unification of the two terrorist groups with Haganah on May 28 had been more apparent than real. Some members of the Irgun and the Stern Gang had refused to accept the authority of Haganah at all, while others, giving lip service to their new commanders, continued to plan and execute their own operations. In the United States, Peter Bergson's American League for a Free Palestine went on functioning outside the established Haganah arms-smuggling channels.

About the time of American recognition of Israel, Bergson had purchased a ship that he named the *Altalena,* after one of Jabotinsky's pen names. It was to sail from New York to France, pick up a load of munitions, and proceed to Israel. (Despite recognition, the United States still had not lifted the arms embargo. Weizmann, visiting President Truman on May 25, had said it was urgent to end the embargo, and at a press conference two days later Truman declared that such a move was "under consideration," but the embargo remained in effect.)

The *Altalena* was commanded by an American, Monroe Fein,

and when it left the United States it carried a thousand volunteer soldiers for Israel. Also on board were Menachem Beigin, the Irgun commander-in-chief, and Abrasha Stavsky, the coordinator of the Irgun's immigrant-smuggling program. Stavsky, one of the most passionate of the Revisionists, had not set foot in the Holy Land for many years, having left it after his trial for the murder of Chaim Arlosoroff of the Jewish Agency. (Though convicted and sentenced to death, Stavsky raised a technicality in his appeal and won acquittal.) Now that Israel existed, he was going home.

At a French port the *Altalena* took on a cargo that Ben Hecht claimed cost $5,000,000: 5,000 rifles, 250 submachine guns, some tanks, bazookas, and cannons, and 4,000,000 rounds of ammunition. According to Hecht, 20 percent of this cargo was going to be turned over to the Irgunists in Jerusalem, who were still fighting as a separate force, and the rest would be offered to the Haganah-led Israel Defense Force, Zahal. The thousand volunteers would be allowed to enter whichever army they wished, Zahal or the Irgun, since, as Hecht put it, "it was all the same now."

The Israeli government, however, feared that its own authority would be bypassed and that everything on board the *Altalena* would go straight to Irgunist dissidents who were taking no orders from Tel Aviv. The presence of such ominous figures as Beigin and Stavsky on the ship increased the worries of the Ben-Gurion government, for Beigin was regarded as an unpredictable outlaw and Stavsky as a dangerous criminal. As an extra complication, the June 11 truce had gone into effect, and UN observers were patrolling the coast to prevent just such shipments of arms and men. The arrival of a conspicuous vessel like the *Altalena* would be a major embarrassment to Israel.

As the *Altalena* neared the Israeli coast on June 22, government officials ordered her captain to surrender his cargo immediately upon landing. The order was ignored. The *Altalena* made an unsuccessful attempt to land at the resort town of Natanya, just up the coast from Tel Aviv, and then dropped anchor off a hotel beach in Tel Aviv itself. A UN observer plane had sighted it, and by the time it reached Tel Aviv a large crowd was on the beach: Irgun men, UN people, newspapermen, a detachment of the regular Israel Defense Force, and assorted spectators.

What happened next is a matter for sharp disagreement. This

is the account of Dov Joseph of the Jewish Agency, the Israeli military governor of Jerusalem, who was in Tel Aviv that morning to obtain supplies for his city:

"Tel Aviv was then weakly garrisoned, most of the men being at or near the front, and the Etzel [the acronym for the Irgun] quickly seized control of a small section of the beach and began unloading in a small lighter. Reinforcements were hurried in by the Israel government, and in a sharp engagement six Etzel members were killed and eighteen wounded, while the Israel Army lost two men killed and six wounded. The *Altalena* itself was shelled by a warning cannon shot after the Etzel men had begun firing at Israeli Army positions with antitank guns and other heavy weapons from the poop of the ship. A second warning shot hit the vessel, causing an explosion, and the ship burst into flames. Its crew abandoned it and began to swim ashore. According to the Israeli government account the Army tried to rescue some of the swimmers; according to the U.N. observers, fire was directed at the men in the water. Certainly there was crossfire between the Israel Army forces and the Etzel men on the beach and in the streets which led to the scene. In all, fourteen Etzel men lost their lives and sixty-nine were wounded in the attempt."

Ben Hecht offered this version:

"A little late but in fine order the Jewish government of the new state of Israel appeared on the beach. Jewish soldiers with cannon and machine guns came marching toward the harbor of Tel Aviv. The blue-starred flag of Israel was over their heads. They opened fire on the *Altalena.*

"It was easy target practice—an anchored ship at a hundred yards. Shells struck the *Altalena* as if someone were intent on ringing up a big score in a shooting gallery. A rifle volley killed six men on its decks and wounded twenty. A second volley killed four and wounded fifteen. A third killed four more and wounded thirty.

"Stavsky remained standing where he was. But he turned his back to the shooting. . . .

"Others jumped. Machine guns turned on the swimmers. The Haganah accuracy had improved. Forty swimmers were hit. Six of these drowned.

"Below decks on the burning ship Irgun men were having an argument with their commander in chief. Menachem Beigin, like

Stavsky, refused to abandon ship. He would remain where he was, said Beigin, and die when the ship exploded.

"Beigin was a brave and dedicated man. But he weighed too little. He was easily lifted out of his cabin and carried off to safety by his men.

"Stavsky, with his back still turned to the firing squads with the Hebrew flag over their heads, watched the *Altalena* burning. He had seen bonfires on the sea before. A special volley was trained on the tall figure still standing with its back turned to the Jews. He went down full of Jewish bullets.

"When Stavsky was dead, politician Ben-Gurion issued a statement to the world.

" 'Blessed be the bullets that killed these enemies of Israel,' he said. 'The cannon that destroyed the *Altalena* is a holy gun and should be placed in the temple.' "

Hecht was a man with axes to grind, and his account seems less reliable than that of the dispassionate Joseph, but whatever contradictions exist, it is painfully clear that there was warfare between Jew and Jew on the Tel Aviv beach that day, and that many Jews died at the hands of their brothers. (Stavsky fell at almost the very spot where Arlosoroff had been assassinated fifteen years before.) Joseph's summary of the incident makes the motives of the Israeli government clear: "For a body of citizens to attempt to enforce a decision on a lawfully constituted government by force of arms is treason and rebellion, and it had to be dealt with as such. It was not simply a question of preventing a violation of the truce. There was also the need, at the very outset, not only to show our enemies that Israel was master in its own house, but also to serve notice on dissident revolutionary elements within our community that they would not be allowed to take control of the state except by the ordinary means of democratic persuasion."

Most of the heavy material aboard the *Altalena* was destroyed when the ship burned. But some of the cargo had been unloaded during the earlier and abortive landing attempt at Natanya, and this was seized by the Israel Defense Force in a brief struggle. While the regular Israeli soldiers were rounding up the Irgunists at Natanya, the UN observers were kept away from the scene for several hours by an Israeli colonel, who said that it would violate national security to let the observers see Israeli battle tactics or weapons. Most of the volunteer soldiers who had sailed on the

Altalena succeeded in escaping into Israel, and ultimately enrolled in regular army units.

5.

The airplane-smuggling operation that was conducted in the United States under the name of the Schwimmer Aviation Company was still very much in action after the founding of Israel. Word had come from the Israeli air force leaders that medium bombers now were needed, rather than the fighting planes obtained earlier. "If we wanted to win the war and win it quickly," Colonel Benjamin Kagan wrote, "we had to have bombers in order to be able to hit the enemy's airfields, to destroy his aircraft on the ground and, if necessary, bomb his cities. We did not, of course, believe in massacring the civilian population, but we well knew that, even without causing serious damage, a bomb dropped on Damascus or Cairo could more surely pave the way to victory than any local military success. The weapon of psychology has always been an essential one."

Al Schwimmer, who was in charge of procuring the bombers, found four surplus B-17's, two in Florida, one in Oklahoma, and one in California, which he bought for $20,000 apiece through a dummy corporation. All but the Oklahoma plane were in flying condition. He also bought, for $6,000 apiece, four A-20 bombers in Oklahoma that needed a good deal of work before they could be used.

The California B-17 was taken to Miami to join the other two, and on June 12, 1948, the 3 bombers took off for Puerto Rico on the first leg of their journey to Israel. They were to fly from Puerto Rico to the Azores, then to a Czechoslovakian airfield whose use Israel had been able to obtain, and from there to Israel. In order to deceive the FBI—which was spreading a world-wide net to intercept violators of the arms embargo—the airport authorities in the Azores were to be told that the final destination of the planes was Ajaccio, Corsica. Arrangements were made for Ajaccio to send word to the Azores that the planes had landed safely there.

A few days later newspapers reported the disappearance of 3 B-17's off the Azores. Portuguese rescue ships were searching the ocean for wreckage. Schwimmer, checking hurriedly with Czechoslovakia, learned that the 3 planes had arrived there on schedule. But somehow the Ajaccio people had failed to send the false confirmation to the Azores, and the Azores airport had issued an alarm. The FBI, suspecting what had really happened, moved into the case, and shortly made an arrest. Two of the B-17's had been sold to Schwimmer by Charles Winters, a non-Jewish American flier who also had volunteered to pilot one of the planes to Europe. On his return to the United States the FBI picked him up for embargo violation. He refused to name the other parties in the transaction, even when he was accused of giving aid to the Russians, at that time a serious charge in the United States, which then was panicky over the perils of Communism. Winters was tried and found guilty, and on February 4, 1949, he was sentenced to an 18-month prison term and a $5,000 fine for his aid to Israel.

The B-17 affair led the State Department to mount an intensified attack on American munitions smugglers, since their acts not only broke the United States arms embargo but, as of June 11, 1948, defied the terms of the United Nations Palestine truce. Word went out to American embassies everywhere that all planes of American origin in foreign airports that seemed destined to be shipped to Israel were to be confiscated, and the passports of American air crews believed to be engaged in plane-smuggling were to be withdrawn.

On June 27, Belgian, French, and Dutch authorities, acting at the request of the United States, seized several Israel-bound airplanes that had not yet departed for the Holy Land. American and British agents also attempted to shut down the Israeli operation in Czechoslovakia, but that country, which had just come under Communist rule, offered no cooperation to the investigators. (The aid given to Israel by Communist Czechoslovakia at that time was particularly distressing to the State Department; some State Department men began to imagine that Israel was about to become a Communist satellite.)

Meanwhile Schwimmer and his associates were trying to get the fourth B-17 and the four rebuilt A-20's out of the United States. A private airport operator in Westchester County, New York, agreed to handle the B-17 on a no-questions-asked basis. It arrived at his field on July 11, 1948, a Sunday, at six in the morning. After receiving 2,500 gallons of gasoline and 100 gallons of oil, it took off with a crew of eight under Captain Irvin Shindler. For the record, Shindler announced that his destination was California and the purpose of the journey was "flight training," but the plane headed north instead, toward an airfield in Newfoundland. Bad weather forced Shindler to land at another field in Canada, where he explained that he belonged to the "Overseas Air Training Corps" and had been forced into Canadian territory by foul weather. He might have pulled off this bluff if a Canadian customs official had not found a cargo of weapons aboard; suspicious, the Canadians decided to impound the plane and its crew pending an investigation.

When informed of the case, the State Department immediately asked that the plane be returned to the United States. Although Shindler and his crew stoutly denied that they had been planning to fly to Israel, they were fined $100 for illegal passage through Canadian air space. On July 14 they were released—with just enough fuel to get them back to the United States. To make sure they went nowhere else, a Royal Canadian Air Force fighter plane was assigned to escort them part of the way. By promising to head directly for Boston, Shindler persuaded the Canadians to cancel the escort, and on July 17 the plane took off. Sympathetic maintenance men at the Canadian field quietly filled its fuel tanks beyond the decreed level, and the B-17 flew nonstop to the Azores, landing twelve hours later. The exhausted crew chose to rest there for a few hours instead of refueling immediately and going on to Czechoslovakia, which proved to be an error, for the State Department used the interval to get the Portuguese authorities to seize the plane and its crew.

By July 25, Shindler and his eight men were back in the United States. FBI agents met them at the airport. Though Shindler went to prison, two other crew members who were not American citizens were sent to Ellis Island for deportation. Shindler's trial began on March 10, 1949. The prosecution asked for penalties similar to those that had recently been imposed on Charles Winters, but the judge, ruling that "manifestly the accused is not one of those people who are determined to break the laws of their country," dismissed the case. The B-17, though, remained in the Azores and eventually was broken up for scrap.*

*In 1949, nine members of the Schwimmer group were indicted for violations of the Neutrality Act and the Export Control Law. Several of the nine voluntarily came back from Israel to stand trial. After a four-month hearing, Al Schwimmer, Leo Gardner, and Ray Selk each were fined $10,000, but given no prison sentences. The other six were acquitted.

6.

The United Nations truce was due to expire on July 9, 1948. During the lull in the fighting, the UN mediator, Count Bernadotte, had proposed a political settlement that called upon Israel to surrender the Negev, most of the Galilee, and Jewish-held Jerusalem. This was obviously unacceptable, and the Israeli government rejected it outright. (The Stern Gang, accusing Bernadotte of fronting for British and Arab interests, warned him to get out of the country at once.) Israel was, however, willing to extend the truce while some other settlement was sought. The truce had been highly valuable to Israel, which had been able to bring in heavy weapons from Czechoslovakia and elsewhere, and to train enough men to get the army's strength up to 30,000.

The Arabs also rejected the Bernadotte plan, for they, too, had regrouped and strengthened themselves during the truce, and now they felt they would be able to smash Israel. The Egyptians ended the truce a day early by attacking the Jewish settlement of Beer Tuvia on July 8; this opened the "ten days' war," a notable episode in Israel's history. Rested, confident, far more professionally equipped, the Israelis beat back the Arabs on every front and went on to seize great tracts of territory they had not held before. The towns of Lydda and Ramleh, lying between Jerusalem and Tel Aviv, fell into Jewish hands for the first time. In the Galilee, Israeli forces took Nazareth and established control over almost the whole region except for a 300-square-mile section along the Lebanese border.

The conquest of territory was accompanied by eviction of Arab civilians, which now became an official Israeli policy. "The situation in Palestine," Ben-Gurion had said on June 16, "will be settled by military power." When asked about the flight of Arabs from Jaffa after its capture by Israel on May 12, he replied, "War is war. We did not want war. Tel Aviv did not attack Jaffa. Jaffa attacked Tel Aviv and this must not occur again. Jaffa will be a Jewish town. The repatriation of Arabs to Jaffa is not justice but folly. Those who declared war on us will have to bear the result after they have been defeated." The Israeli army interpreted this as an order, and indulged, when fighting resumed after the truce, in a practice euphemistically called "encouraging" the Arabs to leave. On July 9, a number of Arab villages east of Tel Aviv were "encouraged" to evacuate. Rather severe encouragement was applied to the wholly Arab towns of Lydda and Ramleh when they fell on July 12; hardly any Arabs remained in them the next day. Only in Nazareth, where a strong Arab mayor was able to keep his people together, was there no disruption of population. Nazareth's Arabs did not flee, and after the war were granted Israeli citizenship. Nazareth still contains the largest and most prosperous Arab community in Israel.*

The Jewish forces triumphed everywhere but in the south, where the Egyptians remained firmly dug in at Gaza and across the Negev. On July 14, Al Schwimmer's three B-17's took off from Czechoslovakia for a raid on the Egyptian positions. One flew to Cairo and dropped two tons of bombs near King Farouk's palace, greatly demoralizing the population; another bombed the base at Gaza; the third, after an unsuccessful attempt to find the Sinai town of El Arish, also bombed Gaza. The three planes landed in Israel on July 15, taking off several hours later for another raid on El Arish. Over the next few days they bombed the Egyptians repeatedly, and might have ousted them from the Negev but for the sudden imposition of a new cease-fire. The Jewish victories in the "ten days' war" had been so great and so swiftly attained that the astonished Arabs accepted on July 18 the truce they had spurned on July 8. Israel, quite content with her ten days' work, also accepted a renewal of the truce, and relative peace came to the Holy Land once again. The pattern of June was repeated, with both sides making use of the opportunity to bring in men and supplies.

Czechoslovakia remained Israel's chief source of planes and munitions. In mid-July, American planes flew over the Israeli base in Czechoslovakia, photographing the aircraft ready to leave. The State Department threatened to bring Czechoslovakia's truce violations before the United Nations, and simultaneously promised that certain measures restricting the export of American goods to Czechoslovakia might be eased if the Czechs ceased giving aid to Israel. As a result of this interference, the Czechs notified Israel on August 12 that she could no longer use her base on their territory. The United States had also learned that LAPSA, supposedly an airline operating out of Panama, was a pro-Israeli front. The American ambassador in Panama notified that country's govern-

*Excluding territories conquered in the war of June, 1967.

ment that LAPSA was "actually dedicated to illegal operations of transport and bombing, with bases in Czechoslovakia and Palestine, and transported bombs, airplane parts, and arms of various types," and on September 18 Panama canceled LAPSA's registration, greatly hindering the international movements of its planes.

During the summer Count Bernadotte continued to work on a plan for a peaceful division of Palestine. But his task was much harder now, since Israel had conquered so much additional territory in July. Bernadotte could devise nothing that did not involve the yielding of land won with Israeli blood, so that Israel interpreted every proposal this well-meaning diplomat made as a pro-Arab move. Criticism of Bernadotte in Israel grew intense, and on September 17 a Stern Gang team shocked the world by assassinating him in Jerusalem. Prime Minister Ben-Gurion angrily denounced the murder of the UN mediator. But the search for his killers was carried out with no great fervor, and they were never discovered. Ralph Bunche of the United States replaced Bernadotte as mediator.

7.

The United States, at this time, was preparing to hold the election that would send Thomas E. Dewey to the White House in Harry Truman's place. No one, except perhaps the man from Missouri, expected to see Truman returned to office. When the Republican nominating convention had convened on June 19, the opening speakers had jeered mercilessly at him, Clare Boothe Luce calling him "a gone goose" whose "time is short and whose situation is hopeless." Dewey was nominated on the third ballot, with Governor Earl Warren of California as the vice-presidential candidate.

Two weeks later, the gloomy Democrats met to choose Truman as their nominee. The convention picked Senator Alben Barkley of Kentucky as his running mate. Barkley, who was 74, had been deemed too old to run for Vice-President in 1944, but that scarcely mattered now, since the Republicans were going to win the election.

The only excitement at the Democratic convention came when a group of northern liberals led by the ebullient young mayor of Minneapolis, Hubert Humphrey, succeeded in writing a strong civil rights plank into the platform. This unprecedented move, a break from past caution on the awkward question of handling America's submerged black minority, caused the Mississippi delegates and half of those from Alabama to walk out of the convention, amid threats by southerners to bolt the party in the election.

A few days later, on July 17, leading southern conservatives met in Alabama to found the States' Rights Democratic Party, with Governor J. Strom Thurmond of South Carolina as its presidential candidate. This segregationist party succeeded in getting on the ballot in only 15 states, but 13 of these states were in the south and their electoral votes in the past had almost automatically gone to the Democrats. Deprived of them, Truman seemed to have no chance at all to win election.

His troubles increased on July 22 with a revolt on the left. A group of liberals and radicals organized the Progressive Party, naming former Vice-President Henry A. Wallace as its presidential candidate. Wallace, who got on the ballot in 45 states, could be expected to draw the votes of normally Democratic liberals who felt that Truman's foreign policy was too sternly anti-Communist and his domestic policies were lacking imagination.

The Democrats, then, had split into three independent parties; the Republicans were united. Long before the actual campaigning began, Dewey was starting to choose members of his prospective Cabinet.

But there had to be a campaign nevertheless, and Palestine was among the important issues. Truman's recognition of Israel was one of the few acts of his regime that had won wide approval in the United States; the Republicans attempted to neutralize this by adopting a platform plank on June 23 that criticized the "vacillation" of the Truman administration on Palestine. They pledged to Israel "full recognition, with its boundaries as sanctioned by the United Nations, and aid in developing the country." The Republicans' Israel plank was adopted unanimously. It received more applause than any other section of the platform when it was read on the convention floor.

The advantage still lay with the Democrats, though. It was Truman, after all, who had led the world in giving *de facto* recognition to Israel in May. On June 22, he had extended this by announcing the establishment of diplomatic relations between the United States and Israel. Since recognition *de jure*—full recognition accepting the government of Israel as a legally constituted entity—had not yet been granted, no exchange of ambassadors was possible, but agreement was reached whereby Israel and the United States were to set up "missions" on each other's soil and to exchange "special representatives." This was seen as an important step toward full recognition.

Israel chose Eliahu Epstein as the head of its mission in the United States. Truman was under heavy pressure from certain politically unsophisticated Zionists to select some prominent Jew as the United States special representative in Israel, but more knowledgeable Jewish leaders such as Rabbi Wise and Eddie Jacobson opposed the move. It would be improper, they felt, to turn this quasi-ambassadorial post into a Jewish political fief; and it would be demeaning toward Israel as well, a form of religious segregationism, to send a Jew as special representative. These enlightened Zionists felt that Israel, although a Jewish land, was nevertheless a nation like all other nations, and should not be accorded such a simple-minded form of special treatment.

Truman also grasped the importance of sending a Christian as his special representative to Israel, and named James G. McDonald to the post. McDonald had been actively concerned in Jewish affairs since 1933, when he had become the League of Nations commissioner for refugees. He was well acquainted with the American Zionist leadership and eminently acceptable to them for the job in Israel. (He was less acceptable to the State Department, which would have preferred sending a career Foreign Service man to Tel Aviv.)

In various ways in the summer of 1948 Truman took pro-Israeli stands. He spoke several times of lifting the arms embargo; he hinted that the United States might soon grant *de jure* recognition to Israel; he sent a message on July 3 to the Zionist Organization of America's convention in Pittsburgh, saying that Israel "must find its rightful place in the United Nations." On July 14 the Democratic National Convention adopted a lengthy Israel plank embodying all of these promises:

President Truman, by granting immediate recognition to Israel, led the world in extending friendship and welcome to a people who have long sought and justly deserve freedom and independence.

We pledge full recognition to the State of Israel. We affirm our pride that the United States, under the leadership of President Truman, played a leading role in the adoption of the resolution of Nov. 29, 1947, by the United Nations General Assembly for the creation of a Jewish State.

We approve the claim of the State of Israel to the boundaries set forth in the United Nations' resolution of Nov. 29 and consider that modifications thereof should be made only if fully acceptable to the State of Israel.

We look forward to the admission of the State of Israel to the United Nations and its full participation in the international community of nations. We pledge appropriate aid to the State of Israel in developing its economy and resources.

We favor the revision of the arms embargo to accord to the State of Israel the right of self-defense. We pledge ourselves to work for the modification of any resolution of the United Nations to the extent that it may prevent any such revision.

We continue to support, within the framework of the United Nations, the internationalization of Jerusalem and the protection of the Holy Places in Palestine.

The leaders of American Jewry were unimpressed by this list of promises. They did not understand why the Democrats bothered to speak of "pledging" full recognition or "favoring" a revision of the arms embargo. They were still running the country. If they felt Israel should have full recognition, all they had to do was grant it. As for the arms embargo, the Democrats had imposed it in the first place; surely they could lift it as well. The gulf between Democratic promises and Democratic performance was embarrassingly wide, and the platform plank did more harm than good.

The problem of *de jure* recognition, though, was not as simple as the Jewish leaders believed. Truman was unable to award it as easily as he had given *de facto* recognition. His statement of May 14 had granted unconditional American recognition of the existence of the State of Israel, but only tentative recognition of Israel's provisional government. Before the United States could move to the next step—*de jure* recognition—Israel would have to satisfy certain requirements that the State Department regarded as essential. Special Representative McDonald, who discussed this point with Undersecretary of State Robert Lovett before departing for Israel in July, 1948, wrote that Lovett "spoke of those conditions which precedent traditionally regarded as essential to recognition, especially a stable government, willing to honor its international obligations, and in effective control of a recognized territory. He

slowly began to embroider on the theme; the present Provisional
Government of Israel must prove that it was not a junta. A constitutional assembly must be set up; elections must be held. He was
concerned about the Jewish terrorists—the Irgun Zvai Leumi and
the Sternists. . . . They were still recalcitrant, he said; they made
their own proclamations and in other ways indicated their potential or active hostility to the Provisional Government."

McDonald felt that President Truman wanted to give *de jure*
recognition to Israel at the earliest possible moment, but was
unwilling to get into another battle with the State Department.
Therefore Truman would withhold such recognition until after
Israel had held her first elections which were expected to take
place in October, 1948. On September 8, Secretary of State Marshall told a press conference that the United States expected to
grant full diplomatic status to Israel within a few weeks. But the
chaotic conditions in the Holy Land did not permit so early a vote,
and the elections were postponed. So, too, was *de jure* recognition.
On October 17, Rabbi Stephen Wise gave Truman an angry 15-
page protest from the American Jewish Congress, which asserted
that "*de jure* recognition of Israel by the United States cannot be
any longer delayed without playing fast and loose with accepted
principles and practices" of American diplomacy. "Nothing in
our diplomatic practice of the past several years can any longer
justify withholding full recognition."

It must have been tempting to the President to yield to the
Zionists, with the American election little more than two weeks
away. But he held firm. Israel would not have full American recognition until she had replaced her original self-appointed government with a more democratically chosen body.

The arms embargo caused more political trouble for Truman.
It had been decreed in December, 1947, during his period of pique
over excessive Zionist lobbying. But now he was stuck with it, for
it had been built into the United Nations truce arrangements. He
could not announce that the United States would no longer take
steps to prevent the shipment of arms to the Near East, when such
shipments were expressly prohibited by the UN. He could only
say from time to time that the embargo would end whenever the
United Nations policy changed. Meanwhile, American agents
were acting with extraordinary zeal to enforce the embargo all
over the world, and each seizure of an Israel-bound plane, each

arrest of arms smugglers, each State Department protest against such friends of Israel as Czechoslovakia, made Truman's pro-Zionist statements seem all the more insincere.

The question of an American loan to Israel cast additional doubts on the Truman adminstration's sincerity. At his meeting with Truman on May 25, 1948, President Weizmann of Israel had asked for a grant of $90,000,000 to $100,000,000, "first of all for military purposes." At a news conference afterward Weizmann said he believed that "my plea for a loan was not in vain." But the United States was not about to lend Israel money for guns, or, so it appeared, any other purpose. All during the spring and summer of 1948 the loan request wandered through bureaucratic mazes in Washington. If Truman had really been interested in buying Jewish votes, he probably could have cut through the red tape, but the first grant of American funds to Israel was in fact not authorized until two months after the presidential election.

An additional vexation for Zionists was the American handling of the European refugee camps. The termination of the mandate had meant the end of the White Paper restrictions, of course, and since May 15 Israel had been open to unlimited Jewish immigration—with healthy men of military age preferred, naturally. A joyful flow of displaced persons into Israel began at once. But in the summer of 1948, Count Bernadotte asked the Allied powers to suspend the exit of Jewish displaced persons from the camps until he could work out a system of "proportional admission" creating a balance between the number of young Jewish men entering Israel and the number of Arabs of military age entering the rest of Palestine.

The American administrators of the refugee camps in the United States occupation zones in Germany and Austria immediately announced compliance with the UN mediator's request, halting the departure for Israel of all Jewish displaced persons between the ages of 18 and 45. In disbelief, Israel's special representative in Washington protested "the apparent willingness of the United States to collaborate in the implementation of a policy designed to check the emigration of Jewish displaced persons to Israel," and on September 4 the State Department agreed to let the outflow from the camps resume, except in the case of trained fighting personnel.

Despite the President's own feelings and the promises of the

Democratic platform, then, the Truman administration did very little in the spring and summer of 1948 to curry favor among Jewish voters. Truman's attention seems to have drifted away from the Palestine problem after his May 14 recognition decree, thus allowing the hard-line men of the State Department to make policy once more. He had begun his desperate campaign to win election in early June, with intensive cross-country journeys and daily speeches, and as he concentrated on that formidable challenge he apparently paid little heed to the many governmental acts of omission and commission that could be interpreted as anti-Israeli. Abba Hillel Silver summed up Jewish discontent with recent Democratic policies in a press conference held on September 8, after his return from a visit to Israel:

> There is a growing feeling among the people in the State of Israel that our State Department is again collaborating with Mr. Bevin. They feel that our State Department has put every obstacle in the way of the full recognition of Israel. It has blocked a United States loan to the new state. It has interfered with the free movement of refugees to Israel from the American occupation zones on the basis of unwarranted interpretation of the terms of the truce.
>
> The American Government has thus placed itself in line with the British Government, which, contrary to all law, has kept 13,000 Jewish refugees of military age in detention camps in Cyprus, and has prohibited them from emigrating to Israel.

The most serious breach between the Truman administration and the American Jewish community in 1948 came over American support for the Bernadotte partition proposals. In the spring, the UN mediator had suggested a realignment of territory that, for Israel, represented a huge step backward even from the relatively unsatisfactory 1947 partition plan. His final report, released posthumously on September 20, would have severed still more land from Israel, and would have forced the Jewish state into federal union with Transjordan, an obviously impossible arrangement.

The day after the final Bernadotte report was released, Secretary of State Marshall—evidently without consulting President Truman—told the United Nations, meeting in Paris, that Bernadotte's proposals "offer a generally fair basis for settlement of the Palestine question. My government is of the opinion that the conclusions are sound, and strongly urges the parties and the General Assembly to accept them in their entirety as the best possible basis for bringing peace to a distracted land." On September 22, Foreign Secretary Bevin announced in the House of Commons that Britain would give "wholehearted and unqualified support" to the Bernadotte plan and would "insist emphatically" that it be put into operation.

American Zionists regarded this as a keeping of strange bedfellows, and AZEC took full-page advertisements headed, "Mr. Truman: Where do you stand on this issue?" Truman was aboard his campaign train while the storm over Marshall's backing of the Bernadotte plan was blowing up; he finally found out what was happening on September 28, in Oklahoma City.

Truman did not like the Bernadotte plan, which, he said in his memoirs, "looked to me like a fast reshuffle" handing too much important territory to the Arabs. Once again he found it necessary to disassociate himself from an anti-Zionist posture forced on him by the State Department. Aboard the campaign train Truman conferred worriedly with his staff. "It was clear to me," he wrote, "that the Bernadotte plan was so different from the original partition plan that it could not be accepted without a change in policy. I told my staff, therefore, that I would issue a statement reaffirming the Israel plank of the Democratic platform. . . . I would use it in an early speech, after consultation with Marshall or Lovett."

Marshall returned from Paris on October 9, and faced some sharp presidential questioning. He insisted, says Truman, "that his comment on the Bernadotte plan had been intended primarily to encourage negotiation between the Arabs and the Jews so as to say, in effect, that the partition plan was not completely rigid."

How satisfactory this explanation was to Truman is hard to say; but the President did not want the ambiguities and contradictions of American policy on Palestine to be drawn into the election campaign, and so he decided not to issue the planned statement reaffirming the platform plank.

He wrote, "I was satisfied that the Secretary [Marshall] understood my position and, in turn, I had no desire to display publicly any differences about specific points as long as there was agreement on the general policy." A few days later, when Great Britain and China introduced a new General Assembly resolution that was sharply anti-Israel in tone, a wary Truman warned the State

Department that he wanted no comment at all on it, pro or con, from the American delegation in Paris.

However, his hope of keeping Palestine out of the political arena was doomed. A story began to circulate in October that the United States not only had supported the Bernadotte plan but was actually responsible for it. Representative Emanuel Celler, returning from a four-week tour of Israel, said that he had learned there that a Foreign Office man and a State Department man had visited Bernadotte four days before the mediator's death. They had told him, Celler claimed, that Great Britain and the United States would not support his proposal before the General Assembly unless it were changed to show greater favor to the Arabs, and Bernadotte had yielded to this pressure.

A spokesman for Ralph Bunche, who had worked with Bernadotte in drafting the final partition plan, called Celler's charge "utterly untrue," though he admitted that the visit to Bernadotte had taken place. Its purpose, however, had been a discussion of the Arab refugee problem. On October 20 and 21, several New York newspapers carried corroborating reports that the Bernadotte plan had indeed been redrawn at the insistence of British and American diplomats.

Thomas Dewey, serenely moving toward his inevitable election, chose to take political advantage of this controversy. On October 22 he issued a brief statement that reiterated the Republican campaign plank on Israel and implied that the Democrats had gone back on their own campaign promises to defend Israel's territorial integrity.

Truman interpreted this as an attack on his own integrity, and vowed to fight back. On October 24, as he boarded his campaign train for his final swing through the country, he said, "The Republican candidate for President has seen fit to release a statement with reference to Palestine. ... I had hoped our foreign affairs could continue to be handled on a non-partisan basis without being injected into the Presidential campaign." Truman then said that he stood "squarely" on the Democratic platform plank and would countenance no revision in the 1947 UN partition plan that was unacceptable to the state of Israel.

On October 28 Truman addressed a Madison Square Garden rally of New York's Liberal Party. This was a party that had been organized primarily by Jewish labor leaders, had a predominantly

Jewish membership, and almost always awarded its nominations to Democratic Party candidates. He gave his audience of 16,000 the statement on Palestine that had been drawn up aboard the campaign train in Oklahoma a month earlier and had remained unissued:

"The subject of Israel ... must not be resolved as a matter of politics in a political campaign. I have refused consistently to play politics with that question. I have refused, first, because it is my responsibility to see that our policy in Israel fits in with our foreign policy throughout the world; second, it is my desire to help build in Palestine a strong, prosperous, free, and independent democratic state."

He was playing politics with Palestine now, and doing it superbly:

"I have never changed my position on Palestine or Israel. As I have previously announced, I have stood, still stand, on the present Democratic platform of 1948. The platform of 1944 had provisions in it under which I have been trying to act. The platform of 1948 reiterates those provisions and goes a little further. And I'm glad it did go a little further."

The voters went to the polls on November 2. Early results, curiously, showed Truman ahead; but these returns were coming from the Democratic strongholds in the eastern cities. Once the rural vote began to come in, the totals would be quite different. An early edition of the Chicago *Tribune* bore the headline, "DEWEY DEFEATS TRUMAN," and the New York *Daily Mirror*'s early edition talked of "a possible electoral vote landslide" for the Republicans. But when dawn came Truman was still ahead. He had taken 28 states, with 303 electoral votes. Dewey had 16 states and 189 electoral votes. Thurmond, the segregationist candidate, had won four southern states and 38 electoral votes. (He got one more later when a Truman-pledged Tennessee elector voted for him.) Wallace's Progressive Party had not captured any states, although it did get 1,100,000 votes, 500,000 of them in New York. Thanks to New York's heavy Wallace vote, Dewey had taken that state's 47 electoral votes. If Wallace had not been on the ballot, Truman would have beaten Dewey in his own state.

Dewey's overconfidence had cost him the presidency; Truman's courageous and desperate campaign had won him the sympathies of millions of voters who had felt only scorn for him a few months before, and in the end he was able to surmount the splintering of his party to attain a White House term in his own right.

An analysis of the astonishing election showed that for all the reversals and intricacies of his administration's Palestine policies, Truman had been able to hold most of the Jewish vote, running nearly as well in Jewish neighborhoods as had Franklin Delano Roosevelt. Where Truman had lost Jewish votes, he had lost them to the ultraliberal Henry Wallace, not to Dewey; districts that had customarily given 90 percent of their vote to Roosevelt gave 75 percent of it in 1948 to Truman, 15 percent to Wallace. The determining factors that caused Jewish voters to shift to Wallace had nothing to do with Palestine. They centered primarily on domestic economic programs and on the nature of the American relationship with the Soviet Union. In the long run, the Jews had made their choices on the basis of who could do more for the United States, not who could do more for Israel.

To the Republicans the lesson was clear. Regardless of the myths about the Jewish vote, it was not something that could be won merely by standing up for Israel. Jews would not forsake the Democrats except under extraordinary circumstances. The Republicans kept that in mind when they finally did attain the White House in 1952.

8.

During the summer and early autumn of 1948, while the United States went through the rituals of its presidential campaign and the United Nations wrestled with the Bernadotte plan, a truce prevailed in the Holy Land. The Arabs, badly jolted by their defeats of July, were willing to let the truce continue indefinitely in the hope that the United Nations would find some way of taking back from the Jews the territory they had lost. Israel, though, was ready to go to war again, and—mindful of world opinion—was merely waiting for some plausible pretext to resume hostilities.

Israel was unwilling to allow the July 18 truce lines to become the permanent boundaries of divided Palestine, for at the time of the July 18 truce most of the Negev, vital to Israel's economic development, was still under Egyptian control. In the months of the truce Israel had succeeded, despite embargoes and blockades, in greatly enhancing her military strength. By early October she

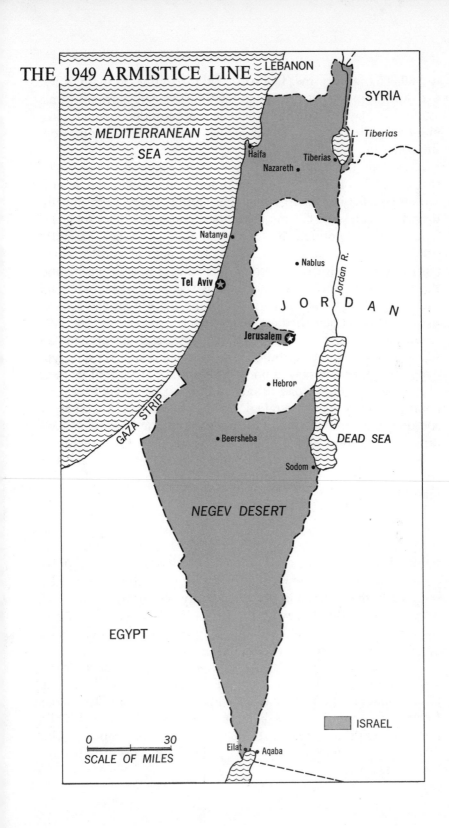

THE 1949 ARMISTICE LINE

LEBANON

SYRIA

MEDITERRANEAN
SEA

L. Tiberias

Haifa

Tiberias

Nazareth

Natanya

Nablus

J O R D A N

Jordan R.

Tel Aviv

Jerusalem

Hebron

Beersheba

DEAD SEA

Sodom

NEGEV DESERT

GAZA STRIP

EGYPT

0   30
SCALE OF MILES

ISRAEL

Eilat   Aqaba

had 80,000 men in arms. The army had three times as many rifles, five times as many machine guns, ten times as many antitank guns, as on the day of Israel's proclamation of independence, five months before. That day Israel had had just four heavy guns; now she had 250.

Under the truce agreement, Egypt was required to permit Israel to send convoys bearing food and medicine to the Jewish settlements behind the Egyptian lines in the Negev. Occasionally there had been some harassment of these convoys. On October 15, Israel formally notified the United Nations observers that a 16-truck convoy was about to depart. As the trucks neared Egyptian positions, they came under attack; one vehicle was set on fire and the others were forced to retreat. This was precisely what Israel had hoped the enemy would do. Claiming that Egypt had broken the truce, Israel launched an all-out attack.

On the evening of October 15 the motley Israeli air force raided El Arish, Gaza, and three other Arab emplacements. Many Egyptian planes were destroyed on the ground at El Arish. The next day, ground troops broke through Egyptian positions at several points in the Negev. A strategic intersection fell on October 19 and on October 20 the Jews took Beersheba. The Egyptians were driven out of most of the Negev by the sudden thrust, retaining only their strongholds at Gaza and Faluja. Meanwhile, another Israeli force swept toward Bethlehem and Hebron under the command of Moshe Dayan.

United Nations mediator Ralph Bunche succeeded in imposing another cease-fire on October 22, before Israel could take the valuable Bethlehem-Hebron district. On November 4, Britain attempted to get the Security Council to order Israel to withdraw to the lines held on October 14, but the move failed. During the new truce, the Egyptians evacuated many of the troops that had been cut off in the Negev by the Israeli breakthrough, but 2,500 men remained isolated at Faluja, among them a young intelligence officer, Major Gamal Abdel Nasser.

In the north, the July 18 truce had remained unbroken after the Negev fighting had begun anew. The uneasy peace there was briefly punctured on October 28 when Fawzi el Kawakji's Arab Liberation Army raided a kibbutz in the Galilee. The Israelis retaliated with a 60-hour operation in which they captured the whole of the Galilee and seized a number of villages in Lebanon.

Once again, a foolish Arab move had given the Jews a pretext for expanding their territory.

The fighting continued in this start-and-stop manner through the closing months of 1948: a truce violation, an Israeli retaliation, a shift in the boundary lines. By the end of the year Israel held all the territory that had been awarded to her by the partition vote of November 29, 1947, and a good deal more besides. On December 27 Israel drove the Egyptians out of El Auja, a bastion on the border between the Negev and the Sinai Peninsula, and the next day Israeli troops pushed into the Sinai. Now they were fighting on Egyptian territory. The Egyptian army, demoralized, simply crumbled; by December 30 the Israelis were outside El Arish, the main Egyptian base in the Sinai, ready to take it. But then came a message from Tel Aviv to the Israeli commanders, Yigal Allon and Yitzhak Rabin, telling them to pull out of the Sinai within 24 hours. Strong protests had come through from London and Washington over Israel's incursion into Egyptian territory, and Ben-Gurion had decided that things might be going a little too far.

Egypt saw the shape of things to come, however. On January 6, 1949, the Cairo government announced that it was willing to let Ralph Bunche negotiate an Egyptian-Israeli armistice. The next day the war between Egypt and Israel came to an end. An armistice was signed on February 24, under which all of the Negev except the coastal strip from Gaza south remained in Israel's possession. (The Gaza Strip had been marked in the UN partition plan of 1947 as part of the patchwork independent Arab state of Palestine.) The trapped Egyptian brigade at Faluja was allowed to withdraw. No Egyptian troops now remained on what had become Israeli soil.

The situation with regard to Israel's other major frontier, that facing Transjordan, was more complicated. There had been little fighting between Israel and Transjordan since the fall of 1948, thanks in good measure to the shrewdness of Transjordan's king, the old Hashemite Emir Abdullah. But Transjordan was still in possession of a good deal of territory that Israel wanted. The Arab Legion held the eastern half of Jerusalem, including the Old City with its holy sites; that, however, the Israelis realized was beyond their capacity to seize. There was also, though, a token Transjordanian force at the southern tip of the Negev, occupying the area around the Gulf of Aqaba that was deemed so vital to Israel's

maritime interests. And the central part of Palestine, the West
Bank region, was held by Iraqi troops. Iraq, while declining to sign
an armistice on the grounds that she had no common frontier with
Israel, had announced that she was going to withdraw her troops
from the West Bank on March 13, and Transjordan was planning
to send the Arab Legion in to replace them.

Israel had to have the Gulf of Aqaba, and certain hawkish members of her government wanted to have the West Bank too. The
first of these prizes was easily attained. While Israeli diplomats
filibustered the armistice talks with Transjordan in early March,
a strong Israeli army headed through the Negev toward the Gulf
of Aqaba. On March 10 Israel told Mediator Bunche that she was
claiming the territory on the gulf that had been allotted her by the
United Nations partition plan. Transjordan wisely withdrew her
troops without a battle, and the boundary between the two countries was adjusted so that each of them had an outlet on the Gulf
of Aqaba—Transjordan keeping the town of Aqaba, her only port,
and Israel taking over the nearby Palestinian police post of Umm
Rash Rash, which became the Israeli port of Eilat.

The West Bank problem was more difficult, for it involved a
major tract of land. Israel probably could have captured it, for her
army now numbered over 100,000, but it could be done only with
a full-scale military effort that would undoubtedly brand the Jewish state as an aggressor. Negotiations seemed more desirable.
King Abdullah met with an Israeli delegation in his winter palace
near the Dead Sea, and an agreement was reached whereby certain strategic hills in the West Bank went to Israel and the rest
remained in Arab hands. The Iraqi troops finally made their promised withdrawal on April 3, Transjordanian troops moved into the
West Bank in their place, and that same day Israel and Transjordan
signed an armistice. The final armistice, between Israel and Syria,
was signed on July 29, 1949; the delay was caused by governmental upheavals within Syria.

The spring of 1949, then, saw the end of the struggle to divide
Palestine. A Zionist state had successfully proclaimed and defended its existence, and the hostile Arab world had grudgingly
conceded that existence—although the supposedly temporary ar-
mistices of 1949 never were followed by the expected permanent
peace treaties that were to establish normal political relations between Israel and her neighbors.

The new Jewish nation covered 8,000 square miles. As a result of the opportunities created by the Arabs at each breaking of the 1948 truces, it had seized a great deal of territory in the north (the Galilee) and in the south (the Negev) that would not have belonged to it had the Arabs simply acquiesced in the United Nations partition plan of November 29, 1947. The long, narrow outlines of the state were awkward and seemingly unmanageable; the Israel that emerged in 1949 had a 600-mile land frontier to defend from north to south, but at its widest east-west point was only 69 miles in breadth. In the populous middle section of the country the width ranged from 9.5 to 16 miles; a quick westward thrust by Arab armies there could cut the nation in half.

The independent Arab state that the United Nations had hoped to create never was born. Its central district, comprising nearly one-fifth of the old Palestine, would have been the West Bank region, which Transjordan had swallowed. (Since Transjordan now occupied land on both sides of the Jordan River, its name was a misnomer, and it soon was calling itself the Hashemite Kingdom of Jordan.) Egypt held the 135-mile Gaza Strip; Israel herself had taken much of the prospective Arab state's territory in the Galilee and a healthy slice of it in the Negev.

The United Nations plan was thwarted in another way; for Jerusalem, the holy of holies, did not become the international city the UN had decreed. Jordan annexed the eastern half and closed its sacred places to Jews; the Wailing Wall became surrounded by the shacks of Arab squatters, the synagogues of the Old City's Jewish quarter were desecrated, and the Jewish cemetery on the Mount of Olives was subjected to worse defilements.

Israel, also defying the United Nations, annexed the newer western half of Jerusalem and designated it as her capital. (The United States and many other countries refused to accept the annexation as legal and kept their embassies in Tel Aviv, which they insisted was Israel's proper capital.) A hideous wall of barbed wire divided the two Jerusalems. Jews were totally forbidden to pass from west to east, while tourists who wished to cross from Jordanian Jerusalem to Israeli Jerusalem had to submit to the bureaucratic rituals of the Mandelbaum Gate. No one but diplomats, church officials, and United Nations representatives could cross in the other direction. Jordan would not permit the entry of tourists whose passports carried the visa of the State of

Israel, which to Jordan was known as "Israeli-occupied Palestine."

In this precarious way, surrounded by beaten but vindictive foes, Israel took her place in the family of nations. On January 25, 1949, she held her first elections, choosing the 120 members of her parliament, the Knesset. The factionalism of Zionism was reflected in the fragmentation of Israel's political parties; 24 parties competed on the ballot and, under a system of proportional representation, 16 managed to elect one or more candidates. Mapai, Ben-Gurion's party, had the biggest bloc—48 members—but the roster of parties included a cluster of socialist and communist groups, two Orthodox parties devoted to upholding Judaism in Israel, a party led by the Irgun, a party led by Sternists, a businessman's party, a women's party, and more. Several Israeli Arabs were elected to the Knesset; despite military "encouragement," some 167,000 Arabs remained in Israel at the end of the War of Liberation, out of the 700,000 that had lived in future Israeli territory at the beginning of 1948. When the Knesset held its first session on February 15, 1949, it confirmed Ben-Gurion as Prime Minister and formally elected Weizmann, by unanimous vote, as President of Israel, a post that he held until his death at the age of 78 in 1952.

As promised, the United States gave full recognition to Israel immediately after the Knesset elections. President Truman made the announcement on January 31, 1949; among those present when he signed the decree was his Kansas City friend, Eddie Jacobson. Most other nations, except in the Arab world, had either granted recognition to Israel already or swiftly gave it now. Even Great Britain, whose government had worked so hard to prevent the birth of Israel, joined the move toward recognition, after some prodding by Richard Crossman, former Prime Minister Churchill, and others. Churchill had pointed out in December, 1948, that Foreign Secretary Bevin's continued disdain for Israel was unrealistic and was greatly harming Anglo-American relations. On January 26, 1949, Parliament debated the point at length. Churchill again said that British recognition of Israel was necessary and in Britain's own interest.

The role that the United States had played in aiding the creation of Israel came under attack in the debate. Crossman, replying to the opponents of recognition, declared, "It is easy to make jibes about the votes in New York and to insult the President of a great

Republic. But if we had had a million Jews in this country, our Cabinet might have been slightly more careful to keep their election pledges. Do not let us attack American politicians for what we ourselves would have done. . . . Anyone who thinks that it was just the Jewish vote in New York that made Mr. Truman a sincere and ardent Zionist, must be very badly informed. . . . America could have nothing but a Zionist policy in Palestine. Politicians have to face the facts, and we ought to have faced the fact that America could not be persuaded to condone the destruction of Israel, or its overrunning by the Arabs, or anything of that sort."

Great Britain gave *de facto* recognition to Israel on January 29.

Shortly Israel also won admission to the United Nations. Encouraged by the United States and the Soviet Union, she had submitted a formal application for membership on November 29, 1948, the anniversary of the historic partition vote.

The application was considered on December 17. Five of the eleven Security Council members were in favor of admission, and only one, Syria, was opposed. But Great Britain and four other members abstained, and the application failed of the necessary seven affirmative votes. Israel resubmitted her application on February 28, 1949, and in a new vote on March 7, nine members were in favor, one—Egypt—opposed, and Great Britain again abstained. The General Assembly approved the application on May 11 by a vote of 33–11, with 13 abstentions, and Israel became the fifty-ninth member of the United Nations, taking her place among the sovereign states of the world at last.

9.

The existence of Israel as a legally constituted nation posed certain complex problems for the American Zionist movement. Since the late nineteenth century it had worked toward the creation of this state, against formidable odds. Now the state was a reality. Did American Zionism as a political movement have a continued reason for existence, or should it, its great goal fulfilled, simply wither away? If American Zionism continued, what would be the status of American citizens of the Jewish faith who involved themselves in the affairs of what was, after all, a foreign state?

Bureaucracies do not of their own volition wither away, and by 1949 American Zionism had created an immense bureaucratic structure that sprawled over a host of organizations. A million

Americans belonged to these organizations. The major groups had large full-time professional staffs, and officers who derived considerable prestige within the Jewish community from their positions. A good many people depended for their livelihoods on the continued existence of the Zionist movement. Zionism had attained so much momentum that, even if the new State of Israel were totally self-sufficient at birth, it would have been painfully difficult for the movement to dismantle itself.

However, no American Zionist believed that Israel's triumphs of 1948 and 1949 made dissolution of the world Zionist movement appropriate or even possible. Zionism now would have to shift some of its aims, of course. There was no need now to battle for political sovereignty for the Jews of Palestine; the struggle against the mandate and the White Paper, the campaign in the United Nations, and all the rest of the recent political conflicts now receded into history. Israel existed.

She existed, though, on the brink of an abyss. She was a small country, half of it an almost uninhabited desert, with little in the way of natural resources. All about her were hostile neighbors who made no secret of their intention to destroy her as soon as they had the necessary strength. The need to maintain an immense army of defense would be a permanent drain on Israel's slender resources.

Israel's immigration policy was also designed, seemingly, to insure national bankruptcy. This policy—formally set forth in 1950 as the Law of Return—guaranteed Israeli citizenship to every Jew in the world who asked for it, without restriction. Other countries had devised selective immigration laws that screened out the lame, the halt, the blind, and those who were likely to become public charges; those were precisely the people that Israel had been founded to receive. Israel underwent a selective immigration in reverse. Out of the refugee camps of Europe poured thousands of war victims—the aged, the young, the feeble, the dazed. Some had spent their whole lives in internment; they had no skills and little education. All were suffering in some degree from the shock of their experiences. They had no capital and no prospects. Half of them were under 14 or over 45, so they could make little or no productive contribution to their adopted nation.

Also there began to come to Israel Jews from the Arab lands, from Morocco and Yemen and Algeria and Iraq, who had lived in medieval squalor and almost inconceivable poverty. For centuries these "Oriental" Jews, as Israelis of European origin called them, had been indistinguishable from the Arabs except in religion. Now these strange people, most of them destitute, chronically diseased, and wholly unfamiliar with the world of the twentieth century, flooded into tidy, up-to-date Israel, creating enormous problems of adaptation and absorption. The little country teemed with newcomers. The healthy and self-supporting Jews of the Western world remained where they were; the poor, the sick, the rootless ones went to Israel. Under the mandate, Jewish immigration to Palestine had exceeded 40,000 a year only twice, in 1934, when 42,000 Jews entered, and in 1935, when the figure was 61,000. But in the first 35 weeks of Israel's existence—from May to December, 1948—an influx of 101,000 immigrants was sustained. Jewish immigration in all of 1948–49 came to 340,000. Israel absorbed 700,000 immigrants in her first four years—more than the total Jewish population of the country on the day independence was attained. All through the countryside rose the tents and tin-roofed shacks of the newcomers, living on a government dole and looking in vain for housing and employment in a land that had not really been ready to accept them.

Israel needed financial help in order to feed and clothe and heal all those Jews who had flocked to her, and to develop industry and agriculture so that a skyrocketing population could become self-sustaining. Giving financial aid was something that the prosperous Jews of America were uniquely fitted to do. Much of the energy that had previously gone into political agitation on behalf of Palestinian Jewry now went into fund-raising for Israel.

A good deal of the emergency money came through the Joint Distribution Committee, which had always been dedicated to helping needy Jews everywhere and never had been involved in the political struggles of Zionism. In 1949, the Joint spent $54,-000,000 to transport 210,000 Jews to Israel, bringing them from North Africa, the Near East, India, China, Cyprus, and the European displaced-persons camps, which were finally empty at the end of the year. In 1950 the Joint helped 162,000 more Jews reach Israel: 23,000 from Iraq, 10,000 from Persia, 1,085 from Shanghai, 50,000 from Rumania, and 48,000 from Yemen—the whole of the ancient Yemenite Jewish community, whisked across the desert by air in a project dubbed Operation Magic Carpet. The Joint also spent large sums for the care of these immigrants within Israel. The American Jewish fraternal groups, such as B'nai B'rith, provided additional heavy contributions for the struggling new nation; this, too, was philanthropy without political implications. But such Zionist entities as Mizrachi, Hadassah, the Zionist Organization of America, and Poale Zion, which had always been openly political in orientation, now found a justification for continued existence by diverting more and more energy into philanthropy. Expanding their long-established fund-raising programs, they channeled millions of dollars into Israel.

American Zionists also regarded it as essential to carry on their political activities after the birth of Israel. They had seen the American government's Palestine policy waver frequently and change course many times. From 1948 on they constituted themselves as a lobbying group devoted to pleading Israel's case in Washington. They worked to bring about generous grants to Israel under the American foreign aid programs; they urged the government to make arms available to Israel; they attempted to elicit from the government a promise that the United States would defend Israel from attack if necessary; and, whenever some Israeli retaliation against an Arab provocation made Israel look excessively aggressive or militaristic, the Zionist spokesmen in the United States offered explanations and clarifications designed to strengthen Israel's position in the world community. All of these activities had to be handled with the greatest tact and delicacy, of course, since, by acting as lobbyists for a foreign nation, the American Zionists knew they were moving into a forest of ambiguities. It was necessary for them to invoke loyalty to a supranational "Jewish people," while affirming their undivided allegiance to the United States and denying that their activities in Israel's behalf conflicted with that allegiance. Thus, as Jacques Torczyner of the Zionist Organization of America expressed it in 1968, "We believe that what is important to maintain is the unity of the Jewish people, and this unity you can only maintain if you have the State of Israel and a movement that links the Jews of the world to that state."

The financial and political problems of Israel, the unity of the Jewish people, and the unwillingness of a bureaucracy to abolish itself were not the only things that kept American Zionism alive and flourishing after 1948. Powerful psychological and emotional factors were at work. For many Jews, Zionism had become a cherished social activity; for some it had become virtually a substitute religion, a surrogate for Judaism.

The tendency for American Jews to fall away from Judaism, to make some social or cultural or political or financial activity of a Jewish nature take the place of actual religious worship, has been a source of concern to the rabbinate for several generations. Judaism is an abstract religion that foregoes many of the techniques used by other creeds to keep the faithful enrolled. It offers no threat of damnation and hellfire for apostates; it has no confessional, no communion, not even—since the destruction of the Second Temple—a true priesthood. Few Jews feel that God is peering down at them, keeping a tally of their sins and good deeds; it is easy for a Jew to think of God as a remote and dim figure, someone who may have spoken with Abraham and Moses long ago, but who certainly has not been heard from lately. Many quite devout Jews carry on a thoroughly Orthodox Jewish life without developing any relationship with the Deity at all; they obey the ethical precepts of Judaism, observe the dietary laws, visit the synagogue regularly, celebrate the prescribed holidays, and give no thought whatever to the possible existence of supernatural powers.

A powerful factor in holding this religion together so long was persecution. Condemned for their strangeness, mocked on the streets, forced to huddle together in ghettos, Jews defiantly clung to their creed and triumphantly preserved every syllable of its teachings as a way of resisting the mindless cruelty of the Gentile world. But as the persecution ebbed, so did the religious impulse. The nineteenth century, in which Jews in Western Europe and the United States attained an unprecedented degree of freedom from anti-Semitism, saw the appearance and striking success of Reform Judaism, a movement that sought to strip the religion of nearly its whole burden of dogma and ritual.

In the twentieth century, when Jews won still greater freedom from oppression, they discovered other ways to express their Jewishness. They could join B'nai B'rith or some other fraternal order; they could plunge into philanthropy by working for the Joint Distribution Committee; they could delve in the political maze of Zionism. One did not have to be religious in order to be a Zionist. Indeed, some of the most dedicated and militant Zionists were also militant atheists, who wanted a Jewish homeland simply as a place where they could get away from the sneers of the *goyim.*

Of course, most Zionists, like those who were involved in the other Jewish organizational activities, did believe in showing up at the synagogue now and then, whether for the sake of sentiment or to keep up appearances in the community. Nearly every American Jew still goes to the synagogue for the High Holy Days of Rosh Hashanah and Yom Kippur; most take part in the ceremony of Passover; a good number are present each week for the Sabbath services. But Judaism as such, the consideration of the relationship of God to man and man to God, plays a small part in the life of such people, and they constitute a majority of American Jews. What concerns them is the fund-raising drive, the election at the fraternal lodge, the schedule of forthcoming concerts at the community's Jewish center, the latest Israeli victory over the Arabs, and so forth.

Not all Jewish leaders deplore this outlook. Early in this century Dr. Mordecai M. Kaplan, the leader of a movement called Reconstructionism, declared that a Jew can live his Judaism in many ways outside the synagogue and still be an authentic Jew. And, in fact, most American Jews still live their Judaism inside the synagogue, even if what they do there has no real religious content, but rather a largely social meaning. Synagogue attendance is higher than ever in suburban Jewish America, not because affluent Jews feel any great impulse toward prayer, but because the synagogue is a convenient and pleasant place for them to gather.

Zionism has much the same appeal. It provides a social framework, allowing Jews to come in contact with people who share their background, community position, and political views. It gratifies the urge toward power by creating an organizational structure within which one can rise. It yields prestige by making possible the public and conspicuous donation of money for Israel. And it satisfies the conscience, for it is a Jewish thing to do, and aids deserving people far away. It is in short, an attractive way of being Jewish in an era when passionate religious commitment no longer seems relevant.

The essentially secular nature of Zionism was apparent long ago. A sociological analysis of a typical American Jewish community made in 1938 by Samuel Koenig offered these remarks about Zionism:

"Most of the gatherings inspired by the movement are largely devoted to fund raising, and consist of tea, bridge, and theater parties, luncheons, dinners, concerts, etc. This is particularly true of the women's organizations which are the strongest numerically and the most active. Reports and informative and inspirational talks by local and out-of-town speakers, whereby the interest in the Zionist cause is sought to be aroused, are, as a rule, part of these gatherings, but their general character is mainly social. Individuals belong to those organizations chiefly because it is the thing to do, because they offer social opportunities, and because they serve a 'good cause.'"

Zionism in the United States could not have withered away after the birth of Israel, then, because it was too important a pastime for too many people. What did begin to dwindle, to some extent, was *organized* Zionism. Membership in overtly Zionist organizations has been declining steadily since the 1948 peak. Only Hadassah, the women's group, which is strongly philanthropic in outlook and provides a rich social and cultural life for its members, has shown an increase. The Z.O.A. and other primarily political groups, which led the way in the battle of petitions and manifestos that helped to create Israel out of Palestine, are shrinking. American Zionist groups today have less than half as many members, all told, as in 1948, and some 60 percent of these are in Hadassah.

But this is deceptive. Zionism has merely undergone a change in the United States, becoming more diffuse, less highly organized. Such groups as B'nai B'rith, the Union of American Hebrew Congregations, and the American Jewish Committee, which once were considered non-Zionist or anti-Zionist, now regularly adopt pro-Israel positions that surely would have startled their members of thirty or forty years ago. All of American Jewry has been Zionized in some degree. The average American Jew, while he probably does not consider himself a Zionist, is nevertheless a strong supporter of Israel, and backs his support with cash, as well as, when the occasion demands it, letters to his congressman or to the President. The semantic complexities of the situation are illustrated by a 1959 poll of a large Southern congregation. When asked, "Should we raise money for Israel?", 89 percent who replied said yes, 8 percent no. When asked, "Should we belong to a Zionist group?", 45 percent said yes, 50 percent said no. The

term *Zionism* still carries with it implications of controversial political agitation and propaganda; but the aim of Zionism was to create
and sustain an independent Jewish nation in Palestine, and there
is scarcely an American Jew or an American Jewish organization
today that does not subscribe to that aim.

10.

The most obvious kind of support that American Jews give to
Israel is financial. It is doubtful that Israel could have survived at
all without the dollars that flowed from the United States.

At the time of her birth, the economy of Israel—as measured by
per capita income—was on a level with those of underdeveloped
countries like Colombia and Argentina, or of backward European
countries like Ireland and Italy. Despite limited natural resources,
the need to remain constantly on a wartime footing, and the influx
of great numbers of unskilled or unemployable immigrants, Israel
managed to show one of the highest economic growth rates in the
world over the two decades that followed; by 1962, she had increased her national product by 350 percent above 1948, and had
raised her per capita product by 90 percent even after a doubling
of the population in 14 years. This was achieved through a deliberate governmental effort. Israel has a quasi-socialist economy in
which the government is the major investor in most commercial
enterprises and is thus able to control and direct its industrial
development.

But a small country like Israel is not able to stimulate such an
extraordinary rate of growth through planning alone, nor is hard
work sufficient by itself; there has to be an inflow of capital. Since
most developing nations import more than they can export, securing capital is a difficult task. Israel, which was forced to import not
only goods but raw materials as well, could never have generated
the capital she needed for development if she had not been able
to draw on the checkbooks of the Diaspora.

Between 1949 and 1959 some $3,100,000,000 of foreign capital
was transferred to Israel—more than $1,500 per Israeli. This huge
inflow provided the fuel for Israel's remarkable industrial growth.
The bulk of this money came from three sources—the governments of West Germany and the United States, and the private
donations of the Diaspora, mainly the Jews of America.

The German contribution was in the form of war reparations.

In 1951, Chancellor Konrad Adenauer declared, "Unspeakable crimes against Jews were perpetrated in the Third Reich and they make it obligatory to extend moral and material reparation for injuries and damages suffered by individuals."

Negotiations in 1952 led to West Germany's agreement to pay $714,000,000 over a period of years to the government of Israel; in addition, Germany pledged to make restitution to individuals who had lost property or suffered injuries during the war, at rates to be determined in courts. From 1952 to 1964, when the governmental payment was complete, Israel received from $70,000,000 to $80,000,000 a year in reparations payments from West Germany. The flow of court-decided restitution money exceeded $100,000,000 in some years. Over the first decade of Israel's existence these German payments amounted to about 23 percent of Israel's total capital import.

Another $500,000,000—some 18 percent of the total—came in during that decade under various United States foreign aid programs. President Truman, after conferring with Chaim Weizmann, had requested such aid to Israel in the spring of 1948, but months passed while governmental agencies studied the financial and political risks involved. At last, in January, 1949, the Export-Import Bank agreed to lend Israel $100,000,000 for developmental purposes: $20,000,000 for expanding existing industries and establishing new ones, $35,000,000 for agricultural expansion, $20,000,000 for transportation and communications, and $25,000,000 for housing. In December, 1950, the Export-Import Bank advanced another $35,000,000 for further agricultural development, and there were additional loans of $27,500,000 in 1958 and $35,900,000 in 1961. Most of this money has now been repaid.

Aside from these loans, Israel received substantial grants from the United States for technical development, the resettlement of refugees, and other purposes. Under the Mutual Security Act of 1951, Israel was granted $64,400,000 in 1952, $72,500,000 in 1953, $53,900,000 in 1954, and diminishing sums thereafter. By 1961, Israel had received a total of $831,000,000 from the United States under all aid programs.* But in the 1960's American aid to Israel was phased out altogether, since Israel now was considered a developed country, and in fact had begun to provide its own foreign aid for other countries. (At present some seventy nations

*This represented the highest per capita rate of aid to any country.

are receiving help of some kind from Israel. Israeli technicians have planned a water-development project for Iran and an agricultural program in India. Israelis have trained the police force of Ethiopia, the parachutists of the Congo, and the armed services of Uganda. And Israeli advisers have helped with the building of hotels, highways, airports, and hospitals in a score of African and Asian countries.)

Though German war reparations were necessarily a vanishing account and American aid was subject to the whims of Congress, the bulk of Israel's inflow of capital came from an inexhaustible source: world Jewry. Between 1949 and 1959, 47 percent of Israel's import of capital—$1,469,000,000—represented the loans, investments, and donations of foreign Jews, chiefly those of the United States. Remittances from the United States have traced a rising curve, and now run at the rate of hundreds of millions of dollars a year.

Private investment is a relatively small part of this flow of cash, though it is not inconsiderable. The Israeli government welcomes foreign investment, within the framework of the mixed public-private Israeli economy, and the capital of American Jews has found its way into Israeli real estate, commerce, and industry, usually by way of partnership or other collaboration with private Israeli investors or the government. American Jews of lesser means have been able to underwrite the growth of the Israeli economy by purchasing stock in American corporations specifically chartered to invest in Israel. The best known of these is the PEC Israel Economic Corporation, founded in 1926. It has more than 10,000 stockholders in the United States, a board of directors that includes some 50 American Jewish philanthropists and industrialists, and has invested over $25,000,000 in Israeli enterprises. Its portfolio contains the shares or debentures of banks, canning companies, a computer manufacturer, a wine company, a firm that extracts potash from the Dead Sea, a tour agency, and real estate developers. Generally PEC takes a large equity position, often with the government as its senior partner, and provides financial advice as well as funds to the companies it controls.

More recently, American Jewish businessmen have been establishing branches of their companies in Israel, setting up commercial links with Israeli firms, or using their influence to persuade large American corporations to open plants in Israel. The Jerusalem Economic Conference of April, 1968, called by Israel in an attempt to stimulate this kind of investment, was attended by 500 foreign businessmen and trade experts, 216 of them from the United States and nearly all of them Jewish. The American delegation, led by Victor Carter, former chairman of Republic Pictures, arrived with 32 American-Israeli projects ready for implementation and 25 more in early stages. They ranged from the plans of Paprikas Weiss, an American importing firm, to market Israeli-made gefilte fish and other canned foods in the United States, to the proposal of the Motorola Company to triple its production facilities in Israel and that of Berkey Photos to establish a processing facility for Israel's movie industry. The new projects would bring in $17,000,000 in foreign capital, would employ 1,800 Israelis, and would export 90 percent of their output, thereby adding to Israel's hard-currency reserve.*

A different form of economic aid to Israel by American Jews has been the purchase of Israel bonds, which are sold throughout the world but are bought mainly in the United States. Israel floated her first bond issue, $500,000,000, in 1951. A $350,000,000 issue followed in 1954, a $300,000,000 issue in 1959, a $400,000,000 issue in 1964, and a $500,000,000 issue in 1967. None of these bond issues ever attained its authorized limit; but actual sales of Israel bonds from 1951 to 1968 came to more than $1,200,000,000. Proceeds of the bond issues go to agriculture, industry, transportation, pipelines, schools, and other developmental needs.

These bonds are loans, of course, which eventually must be repaid; several hundred million dollars' worth have already been redeemed. They are sold in various denominations from $100 to $100,000, and carry interest rates that are considerably below the rates available in other comparable securities. American Jews frequently purchase them to use as wedding or confirmation gifts; some bond-buyers are in the habit of putting their certificates away as souvenirs of Israel, and never present them for redemption,

*An organization engaged in similar projects is American Trade and Industrial Development With Israel, Inc., an American nonprofit corporation financed by the government of Israel; its full-time staff and network of volunteers seek to find American markets for Israeli products. Its guiding figures are Eugene Ferkauf, the founder and retired head of the E.J. Korvette retailing chain, and Allan J. Bloostein, the former president of New York's Stern Brothers department store. The American-Israeli Marketing Corporation, established in 1967 to provide assistance to Israeli exporters, is another such enterprise.

which in effect transforms their purchase into an outright contribution.

The central agency for the sale of the bonds in the United States is the Israel Bond Organization, which opens each year's campaign with a "conference" at which thousands of American Jewish leaders announce their pledges of purchases. The 1968 International Inaugural Conference, held in Miami Beach, Florida, produced initial pledges of $41,272,000—a 37 percent increase over the $30,150,000 pledged at the opening of the 1967 campaign. Such year-by-year increases are customary in these bond drives.

While American Jews may purchase bonds as individuals, the organizations to which they belong run bond-selling campaigns, through which members are encouraged by means of honor rolls and other public acknowledgments to subscribe for bonds. A typical bond campaign is that of B'nai B'rith, which in 1954 set for itself a three-year quota of $7,500,000 in bond purchases, representing 10 percent of the expected total sales of Israel bonds in the United States over those years. The quota was oversubscribed, and in each year since 1956 B'nai B'rith has adopted a larger quota; the aggregate sales of Israel bonds through this one organization now total over $100,000,000. Individual lodges and chapters of B'nai B'rith compete for leadership in the bond drives.

The most remarkable manifestation of American Jewish support for Israel is to be seen, however, in the vast sums raised not for bonds or investments but as outright contributions. In a hundred ways—giant fund drives, temple bazaars, lotteries, testimonial dinners—the Jews of America channel many millions of dollars a year to Zion. The total donations of American Jews to Israel since 1948 are rapidly approaching $2,000,000,000—this from a community of fewer than 6,000,000 people.

Charity, of course, is not a Jewish monopoly. Private charitable contributions by Americans in general now run to billions of dollars a year. More than 975,000 agencies are considered eligible for tax-deductible gifts; 30,000,000 Americans serve as volunteer workers for these organizations; 40,000,000 citizens a year give to them. What is unusual about the Jewish philanthropies is how much money they are able to extract from a relatively small group of people, and how broadly they are supported within that small group. For example, the Jewish community of Detroit numbers about 85,000. In 1964, Detroit's Allied Jewish Appeal received donations from 21,000 people—nearly every adult Jew in the city. Among professional people and businessmen, the response was 95 percent; out of 648 Jewish lawyers, 638 made contributions.

About half the money raised by the Jewish philanthropies goes to Jews overseas, mainly in Israel. The rest is used for domestic purposes—American Jewish hospitals, old-age homes, cultural institutions. The structure of the collection system varies from city to city. In New York City, the largest source of funds, two independent fund-raising groups operate. The United Jewish Appeal and its subsidiary, the Joint Distribution Committee, collect money for overseas; the Federation of Jewish Philanthropies collects for domestic beneficiaries. Elsewhere, a single united drive is the rule.

The division of funds by the united drive is a matter for local option. Atlanta's Jews send close to 70 percent overseas; those of St. Louis retain 60 percent for local needs. Detroit Jewry awards unusually large grants to Jewish educational and cultural institutions. Denver gives heavily to the Anti-Defamation League of B'nai B'rith, which combats anti-Semitism. Cleveland, where fund-raising is a powerful force (its Jewish community of about 85,000 gives as much each year as the Jewish community of Los Angeles, which is five times as large), allots about half of its annual intake to overseas agencies, and divides the rest among the Anti-Defamation League, the American Jewish Committee, the local Mount Sinai Hospital, the Cleveland Jewish Community Center, a local Family Service organization, and similar recipients.

There is no formal tithing among Jews, as there is, say, among Mormons. But many Jews customarily give away 10 percent or more of their incomes each year. Why?

They give, basically, for the uncomplicated reason that they think it is a decent, worthy, and necessary thing to do. They know that the comfortably affluent American Jewry of today is something quite exceptional in Jewish history, and in acknowledgment of their ancestors' centuries of poverty, hardship, and persecution, they share their wealth with the less fortunate. They give to Jewish causes because, as a B'nai B'rith pamphlet puts it, "An historic feeling of kinship, a sense of identity of fate and a mutually beneficial relationship of interdependence of Jews everywhere, are a natural part of the make-up of the American Jews and the American Jewish community."

But there are subtler elements to their charity. One of them is a fierce pride in Israel. Prior to 1948, the great events in Jewish history were all disasters: the Babylonian captivity, the Roman conquest of Palestine, the holocaust of the Nazi death camps. The birth of Israel showed the world—and the Diaspora Jew—a different kind of Jewish event, in which armed men created and defended a nation. By giving money to Israel, by strengthening that remarkable Jewish republic, the American Jew acquired a vicarious share of Israel's glory. Israel became "his" country. Each time Israel clashed with her Arab enemies and emerged the victor, that unearned increment of pride grew greater. How glorious it was, for America's vicarious Israelis, when after the Suez conflict of 1956 Israel offered to trade 5,800 Egyptian prisoners for 4 captured Israelis! How splendid it felt to see Israel in 1967 smash the Arabs on three fronts at once! The military victories of Israel, as well as Israel's accomplishments in making the desert fertile and building a modern industrial state amid the backwardness of the Near East, made Jews everywhere feel that they had gained in stature and self-respect. And so they were willing to pay out cash to keep Israel going, for Israel was a valuable source of pride and pleasure to them.

Beyond this lies another feeling, of which many American Jews perhaps have no conscious awareness: the hidden fear that someday Israel may be *necessary* to them as a place of refuge. Michael Selzer, an anti-Zionist spokesman, speaks rather derisively of the Jews who "continue to support Israeli fund-raising drives for no other reason than that they view the State as a kind of insurance against renewal of anti-Semitism and are just about as conscious of Israel as a healthy man who sends his premium to the insurance company each month and then forgets all about his policy." But the feeling is a real one, concealed though it may be. Those Jews old enough to remember the rise of Hitler live with a kind of mild paranoia, a numbing knowledge that ancient evils may come back to life at any time. Who knows what the future holds, even in the United States? Who can safely say that no danger of fanatic anti-Semitism remains? Many Jews believed they saw the birth of a new American Hitlerism in the presidential candidacy of George Wallace in 1968; others point with alarm to the increasingly violent anti-Semitic outcries of black militant leaders. Therefore they send cash to keep Israel strong. It is good to know that somewhere in the world there is one place where Jews will always be welcome.

Another component of the Jewish charitable impulse is a naïve, earthy, pardonably vulgar species of boastfulness. Most of America's well-to-do Jews are self-made men, men with first-generation money. They have done well in the world, and they want the world to know it. The *nouveaux riches* of other cultures and other eras built flamboyant palaces for themselves, draped their wives in furs and jewels, clad their servants in rich liveries. Jews do those things too; but a large number of them, shunning the customary types of conspicuous consumption, seek applause instead through feats of philanthropy. Their motives may be ignoble, but their deeds, at least, are not.

The techniques of Jewish fund-raising lean heavily on arousing this spirit of competitive giving. Potential donors are exposed to the scrutiny of their professional peers, their business associates, their neighbors, their friends. Fund appeals are made openly so that a man's gifts may be measured against his known resources and against his donation of the previous year. Woe betide the man who gives less than he is able to give, or who fails to exceed last year's offering! He must endure the silent—or not so silent—reproaches of his closest companions; he is labeled a miser, a hoarder, an enemy of Israel; he will probably be in trouble with his wife, whose status among her friends is measured in part by her husband's charitable donations.

One method that works particularly well in congregations where incomes are modest is the publication of a local philanthropic yearbook, called *The Book of Life* or something similar. This is a slick brochure that contains, usually, an essay on the joys of giving by an eminent rabbi, some photographs of hospitals or housing projects in Israel, reproductions of letters of thanks for last year's gifts from some high Israeli or American Zionist official, and advertisements—pages and pages of advertisements. If there are large Jewish business establishments in the area, they will take full page ads ("The management and employees of XYZ Markets, Incorporated, wish to extend greetings to all of their patrons for the New Year"). Smaller businesses, such as family-run shops, may take quarter-page or half-page ads. Wealthy individuals—doctors, lawyers, brokers—may also buy display ads, which of course never promote professional services, but simply say things

like "Dr. and Mrs. Sidney Jacobs" or "Compliments of the Bernsteins of Highland Road." Finally comes a list of names headed
"Friends" or "Boosters" or "Loyal Supporters of Israel." Here the
minimal contributors get their recognition: a line of agate type in
return for five or ten dollars. Even in this humble category, pres-
tige-gaining ploys are possible; one may buy entries for everyone
in one's family, so that a solid bloc of Schwartzes or Rosenblatts
or Liebermans leaps up from the page. The booklet establishes a
pecking order for local Jewry; the big men are the ones who buy
the display ads, the small men are the ones listed under "Friends,"
and the contemptible men are those whose names cannot be found
in the booklet at all.

Another technique, suitable only for large donors, is to offer "a
piece of the action" in Israel—the promise of one's name on some
building, work of art, or structure there. The range of opportunities in this sort of self-commemoration is immense. Thus the Israel
Museum in Jerusalem contains the splendid Billy Rose Art Garden and the imposing Samuel Bronfman Biblical and Archaeological Museum; Tel Aviv offers the Helena Rubinstein Pavilion of
Modern Art; the Hadassah Hospital complex on Mount Scopus
has a Daniel and Florence Guggenheim Rehabilitation Pavilion
and a Judith Riklis Building.

But one need not endow a museum or a hospital wing in order
to win this kind of immortality. Lesser plaques are available at
lesser prices, testifying that this piece of sculpture, this bench, this
garden, this scroll, this painting, this staircase, or these auditorium
seats were the gifts of Mr. and Mrs. So-and-So of Congregation
Such-and-Such in New York or Chicago or Cleveland. Such gifts
win attention twice: in the United States, where they are publicized in local newspapers and Jewish-organization periodicals, and
in Israel, where the commemorative plaques are seen by the thousands of American tourists that arrive annually. (They also draw
some sharp comments about American ostentation from the Israelis, who are not pleased to find such tags strewn all over their
public buildings.)

The most effective way of raising money for Israel, though, has
proven to be the fund-raising luncheon or dinner, at which pledges
are openly wrung from willing victims. "The universal objective,"
one veteran fund-raiser puts it, "is to make it impossible for a man
not to give. You appeal to whatever you think is best: fear, vanity,

sympathy. You want results. Vanity is usually the best of all." And another fund-raiser says, "Giving is a form of boasting, too."

The format of a fund-raising dinner varies very little within a general framework. A meal of no great distinction is served, the usual banquet food—rubber chicken, plastic roast beef, frozen vegetables. Speakers are arrayed on a dais. Among them, generally, can be found a rabbi, a business leader, and a judge or municipal official. If possible, a Jewish congressman is there, or a visiting Israeli diplomat. Some distinguished member of the community (that is, a big giver) may be designated as a guest of honor, and will be lavishly praised by each speaker. Someone who has recently come back from Israel will describe either the wonderful progress being made there, or the severe economic problems being encountered, or both. A film may be shown. Newsreels of Nazi death camps, accompanied by a can-this-happen-again? narration, used to be tremendously effective, but it is more common now to show battle scenes from the 1967 war. An amateur or professional comedian may reel off a string of jokes. Some of them will be standard double-entendre material, some the traditional self-deprecating Yiddish humor (favorite topics: overprotective mothers, spinster sisters, unscrupulous businessmen, terrifying Jewish waiters), and some of the jokes will be of a new species altogether, glorifying the Israeli David at the expense of the Arab Goliath.

Then comes the main item of business. "We all know how critical the situation is this year," the master of ceremonies invariably says. "The demand for funds has never been greater. The problems faced by Israel have never been more serious. The plight of our fellow Jews in Rumania [or Morocco, or the Soviet Union, or wherever] is extreme. How can we be satisfied with last year's level of giving? We have to boost this year's quota by 15 percent."

The fund-raisers have previously contacted the biggest givers and have elicited pledges from them for this year's drive. Now the master of ceremonies produces a sheaf of cards and begins to read from them the names of the important donors and the increase of this year's pledge over last year. The largest gift—perhaps ten thousand dollars, perhaps fifty thousand—comes first. Then comes the next level, and the next, and the next. At each level, members of the audience may rise and announce revised pledges of their own; a man who has promised to give five thousand may up his offer to ten, when he finds that some business competitor is giving ten. The master of ceremonies may single out people he knows, tease them, play on their pride, even order them to be more generous. "I don't mean to twist anybody's arm," he may say, but he is twisting arms, and everyone there knows it, and no one really minds, for it is all part of the ritual.

The atmosphere of these functions may seem superficially cordial, yet there are subterranean tensions. Rabbi Morris N. Kertzer of New York offers this description of a fund-raising luncheon in which members of the New York ladies' undergarment industry came together to make contributions to the United Jewish Appeal:

"The luncheon was held at a leading New York hotel and the mood was far from solemn despite the fact that we were brought together by the needs of the starving and the tempest tossed. These men who were locked in bitter competition in their offices on Seventh Avenue were transformed into a pleasant social group very much like a Lions Club luncheon meeting. . . . But they remained in competition—and no one dared *not* give, with the eyes of the whole industry upon them. Any suggestion of a decrease from last year's generous level would be regarded as a sign that their particular business was on the decline! Might as well tell Wall Street as inform the U.J.A. that things were not going too well at Adorable Undergarments!"

The folkways of Jewish fund-raising may seem as bizarre to outsiders as the potlatch ceremonies of the Kwakiutl Indians, but the results are undeniably impressive. Taking a masochistic pleasure in the process of extraction, often giving more than they can really afford for the sake of winning community status, America's Jews contribute huge sums to their charities. A big donation may be necessary in order to gain the approval of the admissions committee of some Jewish country club; charity-minded Jewish manufacturers may use large contracts as bait to draw contributions from other businessmen; irregular devices of all sorts may be used to blast checkbooks open. The end, to the fund-raisers, justifies the means. Every American dollar that goes toward Israeli education, social welfare services, or industrial development frees an equal amount of Israeli money that can be spent on national defense.

American money reaches Israel through a host of organizations. The bulk of it comes through the United Jewish Appeal; but Hadassah, the women's group, now transmits more than $10,-000,000 a year to Israel, and other important conduits include the

American Committee for the Weizmann Institute, the American Friends of the Hebrew University, the American Technion Society, the National Committee for Labor Israel, the American-Israel Cultural Foundation, and the Women's League for Israel, among many others. Those who give to these special funds also normally support their local united Jewish fund-raising federation.

The United Jewish Appeal overshadows all the others, however. Its collections have risen phenomenally since 1939, its first year of effective operation, when it took in $14,500,000. It thrives on crisis; the revelation of the Nazi extermination program sent the UJA's intake above $25,000,000 for the first time in 1944; the dramatic year of 1948 saw collections rise to $150,000,000; the relatively peaceful years that followed found the total sagging well below $100,000,000, with an upsurge recorded in 1956–57 at the time of the Sinai war. The 1967 war brought the UJA more than $200,-000,000 within a matter of weeks, and in December, 1968, the UJA announced that Israel would ask the Jews of the Diaspora to contribute $365,000,000 in 1969. ($100,000,000 of this was budgeted for social welfare services, including absorption of immigrants; $75,000,000 for housing of immigrants; $75,000,000 for education; $50,000,000 for health services; and lesser sums for youth care and training, higher education, and agricultural development.)

The process by which UJA money reaches Israel is somewhat complex. To begin with, the organization is actually an amalgamation of the Joint Distribution Committee, which aids needy Jews all over the world, and the United Israel Appeal, which is specifically Zionist. The United Israel Appeal is the successor to the United Palestine Appeal, which was founded in 1927 as a vehicle for transmitting funds to the Palestine Foundation Fund. The Joint and the United Palestine Appeal had experimented with combined fund drives in 1930, 1934, and 1935, but the United Jewish Appeal, though incorporated in 1935, did not begin permanent operations in its present form until 1939.

The funds taken in by the UJA are allotted by formula to the two subsidiary funds, with the United Israel Appeal getting by far the larger share of the income. The rest, allotted to the Joint Distribution Committee, is spent in part in Israel, but Israel is only one of some 30 countries in which the Joint currently renders assistance to Jews. Of the Joint's 1969 budget of $24,665,000, about 25 percent went to its health and welfare program for aged, ill, and handicapped recent immigrants in Israel, but much of its income went to the Jewish communities in Rumania, Yugoslavia, and the Arab states.

All of the money allotted to the United Israel Appeal finds its way to Israel, by one of several routes. It is not given directly to the government of Israel, which undertakes to meet its own regular expenditures (for defense, administration, industrial development, etc.) by taxation of Israeli citizens and by borrowing. Rather, it is channeled to various nongovernmental agencies within Israel, and used mainly for the costs of absorbing and housing Jewish immigrants. Thus the continued growth of Israel —the recruiting of new Israelis from among the world's Jewish population—is underwritten largely by contributions from the United States.

II.

The bulk of the money given to the United Israel Appeal by its parent, the United Jewish Appeal, is transferred by means of a network of interlocking corporations and instrumentalities to the offices of the Jewish Agency, in Jerusalem. This is a sore point among those Jews who still find Zionism a disturbing ideology. To them, the continued existence of the Jewish Agency after May 15, 1948, is objectionable, and the conveyance to it of so much of the money raised by the United Jewish Appeal seems at best sinister, at worst criminal.

When it was brought into being by Britain under the terms of the mandate in 1922, the Jewish Agency's function was quasi-governmental; the text of the mandate designated it "as a public body for the purpose of advising and cooperating with the Administration of Palestine . . . and, subject always to the control of the Administration, to assist and take part in the development of the country." Under the mandate, the Jewish Agency served in effect as the government of Palestine's Jews, representing them in their dealings with the British authorities; it also had the specific responsibility of overseeing the immigration of Jews to Palestine and their settlement in the Holy Land. Its members were drawn at first from the ranks of the World Zionist Organization. Weizmann's attempt in 1929 to enlarge the Jewish Agency by taking in representatives of other Jewish groups failed, and by the late 1930's the Jewish Agency and the World Zionist Organization were again synonymous.

Upon the termination of the mandate in 1948, the Jewish

Agency lost its major function. It could no longer represent the Jews of Palestine to their government, because now the Jews of Palestine *were* the government. Weizmann and Ben-Gurion, the two highest officers of the Jewish Agency, became the President and the Prime Minister of Israel, and the upper levels of the new state's government were staffed almost entirely from the ranks of the Jewish Agency.

The remaining functionaries of the Jewish Agency now had to adopt a different and somewhat curious function: they became the representatives in Israel of those Jews who lived *outside* Israel. The assumption was made, covertly and sometimes openly, that the Jews of all the world were in some fashion citizens of Israel, and in need of representation there. This attitude was voiced most clearly by Dr. Nahum Goldmann of the Jewish Agency in 1954 when he said of Israel, "There is no other state in the world where 90% of the people live outside of it." The effect of such remarks on non-Zionist and anti-Zionist Jews was considerable.

The change in the Jewish Agency's functions only gradually became apparent. For several years after Israel's independence it remained officially in limbo, serving as the chief recruiter of new immigrants without having any formal public existence. Israel at this time was taking great pains to protect the Jews of the United States against any accusations that they might have a dual national allegiance. This, of course, had always been a sensitive point among Diaspora Jews, but was of more than theoretical concern now that a Jewish nation actually existed. In the past, it had been possible to argue that a Jewish American's attitude toward a Jewish homeland was something different in kind from an Irish-American's special attachment to Ireland or an Italian-American's concern for the welfare of Italy. Those hyphenated Americans, the argument ran, were merely showing an understandable interest in the land of their birth or their ancestors' birth; but a Jew's yearning for Jerusalem was something much more tenuous and abstract than an Irishman's yearning for County Cork. If a Jewish homeland came into being, the Zionists said, an American Jew would no more consider himself a citizen of it than an American Roman Catholic would deem himself an honorary citizen of Vatican City.

But then a Jewish homeland did come into being, and since so many American Jews had worked so strenuously to create it, a good many Gentile Americans concluded that some special relationship had to exist between Jews everywhere and the new State of Israel. Nobody saw anything evil about this. It was self-evident that American Jews were strong supporters of Israel, and that seemed as natural as Irish-American support for the Ould Sod. But it upset non-Zionist American Jews to have Gentiles make such assumptions about them, and in 1949 the American Jewish Committee sent a delegation to Israel, headed by its president, Jacob Blaustein, to confer with Ben-Gurion about the semantics of Zionism. Ben-Gurion agreed to provide a clarifying statement, which was released on August 23, 1950:

"It is most unfortunate that since our State came into being some confusion and misunderstanding should have arisen as regards the relationship between Israel and the Jewish communities abroad, in particular that of the United States. . . . To my mind, the position is perfectly clear. The Jews of the United States, as a community and as individuals, have only one political attachment and that is to the United States of America. They owe no political allegiance to Israel. . . . We, the people of Israel, have no desire and no intention to interfere in any way with the internal affairs of Jewish communities abroad."

Under the circumstances, it would not have been appropriate for the Jewish Agency to emerge just then as an arm of the government of Israel whose purpose was to induce Diaspora Jews to emigrate to Israel. Nevertheless, despite Ben-Gurion's disavowal of any claim to the allegiance of American Jews, the leaders of Israel did indeed feel that such a claim existed—that Jews outside Israel were "exiles" whose duty it was to return to Zion now that the gates were open. This attitude had two sources. One was idealistic: the feeling that all Jews should come together again after millennia of dispersal. The other was severely practical: the more Jews who came to Israel, especially young and strong ones, the more secure Israel would be against her unfriendly neighbors.

Thus it was important not merely to have the dollars of the American Jews, but also the American Jews themselves; and if the Americans would not come, the money that they contributed in the name of Zionism should most fittingly be used to induce other Jews to Israel. "The basis of Zionism," said Ben-Gurion at another time in 1950, "is neither friendship nor sympathy, but the love of Israel, of the State of Israel. . . . It must be an unconditional love.

There must be a complete solidarity with the state and the people of Israel." And in August, 1951, he spoke of "the Ingathering of the Exiles" as one of Israel's most important tasks. "When we say 'one Jewish nation' we must ignore the fact, favorable or unfavorable as the case may be, that this Jewish nation is scattered over all the countries of the world and that Jews living abroad are citizens of the states in which they live—desirable or undesirable, no matter which—and that they possess rights or demand rights or we demand rights for them. They also have duties. And we, for whom this duplicity has ended and who are residents of the State of Israel living here and talking its language and fighting for the State of Israel, must not disregard the situation of those Jews who are not among us. . . . "

The wish to gather in the exiles prevailed over the desire to avoid offending non-Zionist Jews, and the relationship between the Israeli government and the Jewish Agency was embodied in Israeli law. The World Zionist Organization, at its 23rd Congress in August, 1951, called upon Israel to recognize it "as the representative of the Jewish people" outside Israel. This touched off some hot debate in Israel's parliament, the Knesset, including Ben-Gurion's assertion that while Israel "has itself become the chief and most potent instrument to fulfill the vision of Zionism and forge the Jewish people into one," it still must behave "as does every other State, and its power outside its frontiers is limited. It is just there that the Zionist Organization . . . has the occasion and ability to do what the State is neither able nor authorized to do." On November 24, 1952, the Knesset passed "The World Zionist Organization/Jewish Agency for Palestine Status Law," which formally set forth the policy that Zionists see as natural and proper, and that anti-Zionists regard as a conspiratorial transgression on their rights as Americans. These are the relevant clauses of the Status Law:

1. The State of Israel considers itself as the creation of the entire Jewish people and in accordance with its laws its gates are open to every Jew who wishes to immigrate thereto. . . .

3. The World Zionist Organization, which is also the Jewish Agency for Palestine, applies itself, as in the past, to the promotion of immigration into Israel, and directs absorption and settlement enterprises in the State.

4. The State of Israel recognizes the World Zionist Organization as the authorized agency which shall continue to work in the State of Israel for the settlement and development of the country, for the absorption of immigrants from the Diaspora and for the co-ordination of the activities in Israel of Jewish institutions and associations operating in these spheres.

5. The mission of the Ingathering of the Exiles, being the central task both of the State of Israel and of the Zionist movement in our days, necessitates continued efforts of the Jewish people in the Diaspora; and therefore the State of Israel looks forward to the participation of all Jews and Jewish bodies in the upbuilding of the State and in assisting mass immigration thereto, and recognizes the need for uniting all Jewish communities to this end. . . .

Whether the Status Law makes the Jewish Agency part of the government of Israel is hard to determine. Israel insists that it does not. In 1954, when the Jewish Agency's American branch registered with the United States Attorney General, as required of all foreign agents operating in the United States, it declared, "The Jewish Agency for Palestine is not an instrumentality or a subdivision of the State or the Government of Israel." Yet it certainly has official standing of a governmental sort in Israel, and American anti-Zionist Jews look upon it in that way. In an attack on the Jewish Agency published in 1956 by the American Council for Judaism, the California lawyer Moses Lasky declared, "The true conclusion is that the Status Law and Covenant in fact reflect a double relationship: juridically the World Zionist Organization is an organ of the State; ideologically the two are a duumvirate purporting to preside over a unique Nation spread throughout the globe."

What upsets the anti-Zionists, primarily, is that some of the money raised by the United Jewish Appeal filters down to the Jewish Agency and is used to spread the concept that the world's Jews belong to a single "people" whose proper place of residence is Israel. This, they say, is a fraud perpetrated upon those who think that their donations to the United Jewish Appeal are going only for charitable purposes, not for the dissemination of propaganda. Since the Jewish Agency's goals are political and ideological, they say, it should not be permitted to have access to the coffers of philanthropy. "While we favor liberal aid for Israel," said the American Jewish Committee in 1951, "we oppose the use for programs and activities in America not consistent with these views, of any funds collected for such aid."

A good deal of the money given to the United Jewish Appeal does return to the United States to underwrite Zionist propaganda here. The Jewish Agency's main subsidiary here is the American Zionist Council, which has helped to organize a number of other groups. The Herzl Foundation is one of them; it publishes a scholarly quarterly, *Midstream*, for the Zionists of the academic world. Another pro-Zionist academic group is the Council on Middle Eastern Affairs, which publishes *Middle Eastern Affairs*. The Inter-University Committee on Israel prepares textbook material on Israel for social science courses. The Hebrew Culture Foundation makes grants to American colleges and universities for the purpose of establishing chairs in the Hebrew language, Israeli studies, Jewish studies, or Near East studies. And there are others.

In 1963, the Senate Foreign Relations Committee examined the propagandizing activities of the Jewish Agency and the American Zionist Council as part of a general investigation of "non-diplomatic representatives of foreign principals in the United States." It concluded that the Jewish Agency uses the American Zionist Council as a " 'conduit' for propaganda funds to create a favorable climate in the United States for Israeli and Zionist policies." Zionists and anti-Zionists agree that the fundamental purpose of these propaganda activities is to fortify the concept of an indivisible world-wide Jewish people, and so to convince American Jews that it is their duty as Jews to emigrate to Israel, or, if they must remain in the Diaspora, to work for Israel's interests.

A dispute over whether this policy is justifiable has split the Jewish world ever since Israel was formed. Few Israelis have doubts on the issue; they want an *aliyah* from the Diaspora, and they want it instantly. They desire such immigration chiefly for reasons of security, although it is sometimes stated in more soaring terms, as when Ben-Gurion told a World Zionist Congress in 1960, "Since the day when the Jewish state was established and the gates of Israel were flung open to every Jew who wanted to come, every religious Jew has daily violated the precepts of Judaism and the Torah by remaining in the diaspora. Whoever dwells outside the land of Israel is considered to have no God."

But such furiously Zionist statements have had to be tempered frequently, for tactical reasons, by more moderate remarks. The American Jews who take strong exception to Zionist propaganda efforts are a small minority, consisting of the membership of the American Council for Judaism and to a lesser extent the American Jewish Committee. Even a pro-Israel Jew, though, is likely to be offended by the suggestion that he is transgressing against Judaism by continuing to live in the United States. So Ben-Gurion's contradictory statements of 1950, one denying that Diaspora Jews have any special tie to Israel, the other affirming it, have been followed by many similar statements attempting to retract or at least blur the most extreme positions. Thus, when the American Jewish Committee again protested ultranationalistic propaganda in 1957, Ben-Gurion replied soothingly, "The State of Israel represents and speaks only on behalf of its own citizens, and not on behalf of Jews of any other country. The attachment of Jews throughout the world to Israel is based on a joint spiritual and cultural heritage, and on a historical sentiment toward the land which was the birthplace of the Jewish people. . . . Jews throughout the world give expression to this attachment in various ways. But in whatever form they may be expressed, they carry no political connotation."

On the other hand, when Israel captured the Nazi death-camp official Adolf Eichmann in Argentina in 1960, he was spirited off to Jerusalem to stand trial for "crimes against the Jewish people." And, although the State of Israel had not even existed at the time he was committing those crimes, nor were the crimes committed in Palestine, Israel claimed jurisdiction over him because—as it was expressed in the court's verdict against him—"a crime intended to exterminate the Jewish people has a very striking connection with the State of Israel. . . . The connection between the Jewish people and the State of Israel constitutes an integral part of the law of nations."

The contradictions within post-1948 Zionism remain unresolved. American Zionist leaders continue to repudiate the idea that Israel holds any *political* claim over American Jews, while at the same time insisting that there is a *religious* claim, an obligation laid upon all Jews everywhere to immigrate to Israel or else to aid it from the Diaspora. (When one asks American Zionist leaders why they don't move to Israel themselves, they usually reply that they intend to, once their work among the brethren of the Diaspora is done.) They realize that the problem of defining an American Jew's relationship to Israel is a complex semantic tangle, and they devote a good deal of effort to arriving at an understanding of that relationship.

Thus Dr. Philip Baum, director of international affairs of the American Jewish Congress—a strongly pro-Israel group that prefers to maintain a formal distance from organized Zionism—told me late in 1968, "In the first place, we believe in the concept of Jewish peoplehood. We believe that central to this concept is the recognition of a certain affinity between Jewish life abroad and the State of Israel, the people of Israel." But, he added, "We have *no* political association with the State of Israel. We have no sense of political obligation to the State of Israel. The domestic policies of the State of Israel are theirs and not ours. We are frequently in intense disagreement with those policies. We are Americans concerned principally with policies of this government to which we belong, to which we owe exclusive political allegiance and fealty. ... We are part of the Jewish people but not part of the Jewish state." Dr. Baum went on, though, to say that Israel "is a place for not only the political working-out of the destiny of a sovereign state, but also a place where we think Jews have a place to live effectively, fully, freely, without inhibition of any kind, as Jews; it allows for a fuller renaissance of Jewish culture and Jewish life than any other place in the world. ... [Israel] is the most intensely Jewish of all the segments of the Jewish people. Naturally, we have a certain feeling of regard and concern for their well-being. Not political. Not philanthropic either. It is a sense of connection."

The Zionist Organization of America advocates large-scale emigration of American Jews to Israel. At its seventy-first annual convention in Washington, D.C., in September, 1968, it heard its former president, Emanuel Neumann—now the head of the American branch of the Jewish Agency—predict that "thousands of American Jews" would settle in Israel. "As Zionists we wish to believe," Dr. Neumann said, "that these are but the vanguard, moved by the sacred desire to become part and parcel of Israel reborn, men and women who want their children to grow up in the Jewish environment, free of the complexities and inner conflicts [of the Diaspora], rooted in the soil and each contributing his bit of strength to the total that is Israel." Dr. Neumann asserted that it "must be a point of honor with every Zionist family, with every Jewish family, to be represented in the land of Israel by one of its members." A few weeks earlier, Jacques Torczyner, the current head of the Z.O.A., had told me, "I honestly believe that you can lead a full Jewish life only in Israel. I believe that when Bernstein composes music here, when Irwin Shaw writes a novel, when Norman Mailer analyzes Chicago, these are American music, American literature; Jewish art, Jewish literature, you can only have in Israel. You can be a very good American and a very good Jew here but . . . you have to maintain your connection with the State of Israel." He observed also, "The Jew in America is worried. The Jew in America is disturbed. And because he is not religious and because he has no spiritual values, he has such a tremendous amount of love for Israel, because Israel gives him something meaningful in life."

The range of attitudes on the proper relationship of the Diaspora Jew to Israel is wide, then: from Ben-Gurion's fiery denunciation of Jews who remain outside Israel as Jews who have no god, to the American Jewish Congress' position that American Jews should feel "a sense of connection," but not necessarily anything more, with the people of Israel. The implication that American Jews are somehow failing in their Judaism by refusing to make the *aliyah* is unmistakably present in much Zionist thinking, and so is the assumption that all the Jews of the Diaspora are bound by powerful ties, either spiritual or political, to the state of Israel. (This assumption was codified in Israel's Law of Return, under which any Jew arriving in Israel was entitled to demand and receive instant Israeli citizenship.*)

The feeling among some Israelis on the subject of "the Ingathering of the Exiles" is extraordinarily strong. At a meeting of Zionist leaders of the world in Jerusalem in the early part of 1968, Itzhak Korn of Israel, secretary of the Labor World Zionists, proposed that membership in the World Zionist Organization be limited to those Jews who pledge themselves and their families to emigrate to Israel within five years. If enacted, this would force the resignations of nearly all members and officers of the American Zionist organizations, and so it met with sharp rejections from the leaders of those organizations. Mrs. Mortimer Jacobson, the president of Hadassah, denied "that a Zionist is only one who is committed to living in Israel," and insisted that Jews living outside Israel have

---

*In August, 1966, the Knesset modified the Law of Return to require a year's residence before citizenship could be granted. This was done to curb the abuse of the law by foreigners who under the old regulations came solely to acquire an Israeli passport, departing as soon as it was issued—usually within a week or two of their arrival.

a "significant role to play in the collective survival of the Jewish people." Rabbi Israel Miller, chairman of the American Zionist Council, also opposed the plan, though he was willing to see the establishment within Zionism of "special elite groups who intended to eventually settle in Israel." Korn's proposal was turned down.

The idea that Israel holds a claim—whether messianic or nationalistic—on Diaspora Jews is bitterly and steadily fought by the American Council for Judaism, which denies that any special Jewish nationality exists, or that it is possible for Jews to live a truly Jewish life only in Israel. The council regards itself as the spokesman for those Jews who see themselves as members only of a religion, not of an ethnic or national group. From its presses come rebuttals of all Zionist dogma. In 1964, the council went to the trouble of seeking a ruling from the State Department on the question of the legal status of the Jewish "people." Assistant Secretary of State Phillips Talbot replied, in a letter widely circulated by the council, "The Department of State recognizes the State of Israel as a sovereign State and citizenship of the State of Israel. It recognizes no other sovereignty or citizenship in connection therewith. It does not recognize a legal-political relationship based upon the religious identification of American citizens. . . . Accordingly, it should be clear that the Department of State does not regard the 'Jewish people' as a concept of international law." To which an editorialist in the Yiddish newspaper *The Day* replied, "The concept of a Jewish people and of Jewish peoplehood may be new . . . to Mr. Talbot . . . ; that does not alter the fact that the concept is recognized by international law." The Jerusalem *Post* commented that the recognition by the United States of Israel "as a sovereign state, and of Israel citizenship, which derives its legal basis in part from the Balfour Declaration, is ultimately also based on the recognition of the Jewish people as a national unit."

The storm over Israel's claim on the Diaspora has generally left the average American Jew untouched. Quite probably he contributes to the United Jewish Appeal; very likely his wife is a member of Hadassah. Chances are he has never heard of the American Council for Judaism. He knows a good deal about Israel, mainly about its military prowess, and he admires the Israelis' valor. But he does not contemplate emigrating to Israel; it has never occurred to him to do such a thing.

So far as most American Jews are concerned, the propaganda efforts that the Jewish Agency and other Zionist groups have conducted here have succeeded overwhelmingly in one respect, and have failed just as emphatically in another. They have instilled in American Jews (and in Americans in general) a feeling that the State of Israel is a necessary and permanent national entity, deserving of American support and, if needs be, of American military protection. But no momentum whatever has been created for an American *aliyah*, an American migration to Israel, an *aliyah* not of dollars but of Jews.

The desire for such an *aliyah* is intense in Israel and among American Zionists, and the disappointment over its failure to materialize is correspondingly keen. "Israel is the center of Jewish life and the source of the main values on which the communities in the diaspora will live spiritually," declared Nahum Goldmann, Weizmann's successor as head of the World Zionist Organization, in 1963. "Acceptance of the 'centrality' of Israel is certainly not yet fully shared by all the Jews of the world, and in particular is not shared by many in the United States who generously help with funds. The Zionist movement in the United States has failed to fulfill its task." The Jerusalem *Post*, later that year, also criticized American Zionism, saying that cash donations "have come to appear less the wholehearted participation of committed brothers than apologetic charity." In 1964 Dr. Sidney Marks, the national secretary of the Zionist Organization of America, said, "I know American Jewry. I know it well. I know its wealth, its comfort, its complacency, its demoralizing luxury. I know it all and I tell you that from this American Jewry it is possible to bring thousands of young people to *aliyah*." He admitted, though, that young Americans "must be induced, actually induced, to settle in Israel," and conceded that he did not intend to make the *aliyah* himself: "I am an American Jew; my family has had many generations in this country."

According to the Jewish Agency, the number of Americans who emigrated to Palestine between 1919 and 1945 was 8,057, or 2.3 percent of total Jewish Palestinian immigration. Nearly half of these arrived in 1933–35. Only sixteen came between 1940 and 1945. There has been no great increase in the rate of American *aliyah* since the end of World War II and the subsequent creation of Israel, nor is there even much wishful thinking about moving to Israel. The only formal survey of the situation, apparently, was made in 1952 by Marshall Sklare and Marc Vosk in a New Jersey industrial town with 130,000 inhabitants, 6,500 of them Jews, to which they refer by the pseudonym of "Riverton" in their report, *The Riverton Study*, published by the American Jewish Committee in 1957. Sklare and Vosk asked the Jews of "Riverton" if they would like to live in Israel; only 7 percent said they would, but few of them appeared to have any real intention of emigrating. Asked about an *aliyah* for their children, 8 percent were in favor, 59 percent opposed, and 33 percent felt it should be left to the children to decide.

Determining how many American Jews actually live in Israel today is not easy. Israel makes no data available on the subject. The American embassy in Israel has estimated, unofficially, that there are about 6,000. The Association of Americans and Canadians in Israel, an organization formed by those who had made the *aliyah*, said in 1966 that there were "over 20,000 Americans and Canadians in Israel," of whom 90 percent were Americans. Others feel that this figure is somewhat exaggerated, since it classes as "Americans" a number of Eastern European Jews who had lived in the United States for a while before settling in Israel. A more realistic total of Americans who have come to Israel not merely to retire but to take an active part in the building of the Jewish homeland is about 10,000.

The figure fluctuates because only some of the immigrants from America remain. The Association of Americans and Canadians reckons that American immigration to Israel between 1948 and 1960 resulted in a net gain to Israel of 7,595 settlers—out of perhaps 35,000 who had come. In recent years, some 1,500 to 2,000 prospective settlers from the United States have been coming to Israel per year, and about 1,000 have been going home. (The counter-*aliyah* from Israel to the United States is much greater, to the chagrin and distress of Zionists. In 1961, for example, 2,441 Israelis applied for emigration to the United States.)

Those American Jews who do settle in Israel lead, in general, a curiously uncomfortable life. Some have married Israelis, have become fluent in Hebrew, have adopted new Hebrew names; they have succeeded in being absorbed entirely into the culture of Israel, just as immigrants from Poland, Germany, Russia, or anywhere else have been absorbed. Many Americans, though, remain oddly isolated. Other Israelis look upon them as a bit strange because their *aliyah* was voluntary; they did not *have* to come to Israel. They were untouched by the Nazi holocaust; they had families and homes intact after the war, they lived in a country where persecution of Jews was unknown, they had good jobs and infinite opportunities. To give up the air-conditioned comforts of the United States and settle in tiny, unluxurious, enemy-encircled Israel seems to some Israelis like the deed of an unworldly idealist, and to others like the act of a fool. To some degree, American settlers in Israel are resented as slummers, as people who have—for whatever reason—condescended to live among the less fortunate.

Thus the Americans in Israel are derisively labeled "Anglo-Saxons," which seems wildly ironic to anyone who knows what meaning that term carries in the United States. A *shikun*, or housing development, in Jerusalem that was sponsored by the Association of Americans and Canadians in Israel as a cooperative project for its members is universally known as "the Anglo-Saxon *shikun*." Another, near Tel Aviv, is called "the American *shikun*," which is a little more satisfactory to its occupants, but not much. As one remarked unhappily, "In America we were 'Jews.' In Israel we become 'Americans.'"

Despite such sociological dilemmas, the Americans in Israel find their lives fulfilling to a considerable degree. About a fifth of them live in *kibbutzim* or other agricultural settlements, away from the intricate caste structure of the cities. Others—mostly in Jerusalem, Tel Aviv, or Haifa—are professional people, doctors, scientists, engineers, teachers, whose special skills afford them prestige in the community. A few, nearly all in Tel Aviv, have gone into private business; another small group is in the Israeli civil service. A good many of these Americans lead active, busy lives, and are well integrated into the society around them.

But the "Anglo-Saxon" community in Israel is small, and it is not growing rapidly. Many young American Jews go to Israel for summer work programs, through the American Zionist Youth Foundation or similar groups, and some may remain for a year or two; but few of them have any intention of becoming Israeli citizens. The 1967 war brought thousands of young volunteers to Israel to aid in civilian work while the Israelis themselves were mobilized; but when the emergency ended, all but a fraction of these volunteers returned to their homes.

The failure to develop an *aliyah* of Americans is part of a larger crisis of Israeli immigration, one that is causing great concern in that country. In 1948, when Israel was at last thrown open to Jews after a decade of White Paper restrictions, a tremendous pool of European displaced persons was ready to emigrate. Between 1948 and 1951, some 680,000 Jews entered the country, doubling Israel's Jewish population. This great influx created such economic difficulties that for a while it was actually necessary to impose some selectivity in new admissions; immigration in 1952 dropped to 23,375, in 1953 to 10,347, and in 1954 to 17,471. (In those years several Soviet-bloc nations imposed restrictions on Jewish emigration, which, along with the recession in Israel and the depletion of the European refugee pool, helped to cause the sharp drop in immigration.) An economic upturn in 1955 brought an increase in immigration to 36,303, with further increases in 1956 (56,234) and 1957 (71,224). The annual totals fluctuated between 30,000 and 80,000 for some years thereafter. In 1961 Israel received her millionth immigrant since the establishment of the state.

But the recent trend has been a dropping-off in the number of new immigrants, and a sharp upsurge in the outflow of Israelis to other countries. In 1967, when Israel was the focus of more attention than at any time since she gained her independence, the total immigration was 18,065, while about 11,000 Israelis left the country, for a net gain of only 7,000. At the 27th World Zionist Congress, held in Jerusalem in June, 1968, the failure of Israel to attract more Jewish immigrants was the major topic of discussion. How had it happened that in a year when the Jews of the world contributed $359,000,000 to Israel, 445 fewer Jews came to settle there than the year before? "This was the year when every Jew in the world discovered his personal identification with Israel," declared one delegate to the World Zionist Congress. "This was the year when world Jewry gave financial and moral support as never before. This was the year when immigration to this country should have jumped. And what happened? Nothing. The Jewish Agency completely failed to capitalize on the outpouring of emotion for Israel, and a tremendous opportunity was lost."

There was talk of revamping the Jewish Agency to make it more effective, although privately the delegates wondered whether the Jewish Agency was really to blame. The heart of the problem lies in the drying up of potential sources for immigrants. The Jews of the United States—now nearing 6,000,000 in number —are simply too secure, too comfortable, to want to live in Israel. Another million in Great Britain, Canada, and France are in a similarly cozy position. The Jews of Russia—numbering about 2,500,000—are not at all secure or comfortable, but they are forbidden by their government to emigrate, as a political move designed to soothe Arab fears of the sudden growth of Israel's population that an *aliyah* of Russian Jews would cause.

Aside from the simple desire for the strength that exists in numbers, Israel has a special reason, a somewhat embarrassing one, for wanting an *aliyah* of American, Western European, or even Russian Jews. This is the problem caused by the wholesale immigration of "Oriental" Jews into Israel. It is Israel's version of the race problem.

To Israelis, "Orientals" are Jews who come from the Arab lands —mainly Egypt, Iraq, Yemen, and North Africa. Most of them are poor. Few are well educated. They speak Arabic and French, rather than the Hebrew and Yiddish that are the primary languages of occidental Israelis. The Orientals are generally swarthy or dark-skinned. To a European Jew, they look very much like Arabs, and the treatment accorded them is not very sympathetic. As the American anthropologist Raphael Patai, a Jew who is one of the leading authorities on the culture of the Near East, expressed it in his book *Israel Between East and West*, "In addition to instability, emotionalism, impulsiveness, unreliability, and incompetence, the Oriental Jew is accused [by European-born Israelis] of habitual lying and cheating, laziness, uncontrolled temper, superstitiousness, childishness, lack of cleanliness and in general, 'primitivity' and 'lack of culture.' "

The Orientals, then, are Israel's Negroes. They are poorly integrated into Israeli society, are regarded as undesirable neighbors by white-skinned Israelis, and have little power in the government, which still is dominated by elderly European-born settlers who came to Palestine forty to sixty years ago. The harsh treatment the Orientals receive seems to indicate that discrimination and persecution are human constants; even the Jews, buffeted by irrational hatred for so long, have managed to find an "inferior" caste whom they can oppress, now that they have a country of their own.

The United States was able to ignore its black problem for so long because Negroes comprise a relatively insignificant percentage of the population. It is easy to pretend that a minority does not exist, if the suffering members of the minority do not cry out loudly enough. But Israel's Orientals are a majority, and their numbers grow greater every year; and in this lies one powerful source of Israel's passionate wish for an *aliyah* of Americans.

Of those Jews who came to Palestine before 1949, 88 percent were Europeans. The first rush of post-independence immigration brought with it a tide of Asian and African Jews, but Europeans still were in the preponderance: 198,000 out of the 340,000 immigrants of 1948–49, and 130,000 out of the 342,000 immigrants of 1950–51. Since then the percentage of Orientals in each year's inflow has risen steadily. The oppressed Jews of non-Communist Europe have all been collected by Israel by now; those of the Near East took longer to redeem. Since 1948, half of the total immigration has been Oriental; since 1955, two-thirds or more.

Worse yet, from the point of view of the now outnumbered European-born Israelis, the immigrants from Europe were generally old, while the Orientals are young and fertile. Their birth rate is one of the highest in the world. Their families average 4.9 members, as against 3.2 for the families of other Israelis.

At present, Israelis who were born in Europe or other centers of Western civilization make up one-third of the population. Their average age is about 45, so that many are past childbearing age. Israelis born in Asian or African countries constitute another third of the population; but their average age is only 25. The remaining third of the population consists of *sabras*, native-born Israelis. The average age of this group is only about 10, reflecting the urgent need of this country to be fruitful and multiply. But 7 out of 10 of these young *sabras* are Orientals. The demographic consequences are obvious; in another generation Israel will be a land whose people will be, in the main, ethnically indistinguishable from those of the Arab nations surrounding it.

Most enlightened Israelis—and most Israelis, knowing more than a little about persecution, *are* enlightened—are working toward solving the problem of the Orientals through educational programs that will lift these former Yemenites and Moroccans to their own level, without necessarily destroying the values of the Orientals' own cultures. They see the problem largely as one of assimilation. In some parts of the country, the results of this policy have been encouraging; in others they have not, and some Israelis are bleakly predicting a severe split within the country and the emergence of "two Israels"—or even the engulfing of the Western-minded, industry-oriented Israeli minority by the culturally stagnant Oriental majority, until Israel sinks to the level of her Arab neighbors and becomes vulnerable to destruction.

The solution, as these Israelis see it, lies in the immediate emigration of a million or so American Jewish college graduates to Israel: a bulwark against medievalism, a vanguard of progressiveness. What would happen to an Israel in which a million American boys and girls were turned loose does not seem to have entered their calculations, or else, perhaps, they prefer the transformations that this would bring to the transformation the Orientals appear to be working. But the point is moot; American Jews are second to none in their affection and support for Israel, but no *aliyah* from the United States is imminent.

12.

American Jews do go to Israel in great numbers, young ones as volunteer workers, older ones as tourists. Tourism is one of Israel's most important industries; in 1968, 432,000 tourists visited Israel, 145,000 of them from the United States. (Some 60 percent of the Americans, Israeli officials believe, were Jews, though no official statistics are kept on that.)

What American Jews see in Israel fascinates, excites, inspires, and sometimes surprises them, not necessarily in a favorable way. The historical aspect, Israel as the Holy Land, is of course irresistible, even more so since the 1967 war brought under Israeli control the shrines of Jerusalem, Bethelem, and Hebron, and such ancient archaeological sites as the mound of Biblical Jericho. Names out of the Old Testament take on new meaning for the Jewish tourist as his tour bus carries him through the country: here is Ashkelon of the Philistines, here is Samson's Gaza, here is Sodom, here is Megiddo, here is Beersheba. Then there are the holy places of the Christians, which cast a spell even for Jews—Nazareth, Bethlehem, Golgotha; there are the desert cities of the Nabataeans, and the ruined churches of the Byzantines, and the shattered but awesome fortresses of the Crusaders. And it is impossible not to respond to the achievements of the Zionists: lovely Haifa, glittering above the Mediterranean, and huge sophisticated Tel Aviv, and the sleek buildings of the Hebrew University and the Israel Museum rising near Jerusalem on the barren Judaean hills, and the orange groves next to the sand dunes along the coast, and the power plants, the factories, the highways, the bustle. To one who knows what Palestine was before the Jewish pioneers came, even a Tel Aviv traffic jam can be reason to rejoice.

The tourist in Israel is startled by the *Jewishness* of it all. On my first night in Tel Aviv I felt an odd and preposterous amazement, again and again, as I saw Hebrew signs on every storefront, Hebrew letters on traffic signals, Hebrew menus posted outside every restaurant. It seemed incredible to me that everyone hurrying across the street at one busy intersection should be Jewish, and that children tossing a ball should cry out to one another in Hebrew.

In the United States, even in a city like New York, Jews learn not to make themselves too conspicuous; it is a reflex, an exaggerated reaction to the fear of anti-Semitism, perhaps. A Jew remembers that he is Jewish, and therefore somehow different from most of the other people on the street. He knows that these strangers, wearing their crucifixes or thinking about last Sunday's church service, these Methodists and Baptists and Episcopalians and Roman Catholics at his elbow, share neither his childhood background nor, probably, his opinions on a thousand questions. In the United States, the Jew can remember meeting friendly, wholly sympathetic Gentiles who questioned him about his beliefs and his outlook on life as though he were a Martian.

In Israel, where Jewishness is universal, the American Jewish tourist has to make an effort at first to understand that he does not need to feel like an alien. In Tel Aviv it is the *goy* who is the alien. The Jew does not have to make, here, the little explanations that he was always making in the United States. ("A Jew doesn't take his hat *off* when he enters an important place. He puts his hat *on*." "The Jewish Sabbath is Saturday, not Sunday. Actually, it starts on Friday at sundown." "There isn't really a priesthood in Judaism any more. A rabbi is more of a community leader than a priest.") In Israel everybody knows all that—knows it a good deal better than he does himself.

That first night in Tel Aviv was strange indeed. I understood less than a dozen words of spoken Hebrew. I could scarcely make out the letters of the Hebrew alphabet. Only because nearly everyone in the city spoke English was I able to find my way. And yet, for some incomprehensible reason, I felt that I was among my own people, that I had come home. I was not prepared for that.

But the American Jewish tourist, as his stay in Israel lengthens, discovers some perplexing things about the supposed Jewishness of the unique nation. Yes, there is Hebrew everywhere. Yes, all the restaurants are kosher, and the whole country shuts down when the Sabbath begins on Friday. Yes, one hears familiar Yiddish inflections and sees familiar shrugs and winks. The Jewish cultural milieu is there, despite the presence of the Orientals, whom the American—with his German or Polish or Russian ancestry—finds hard to recognize as Jewish. Jewishness is there; but where is the Judaism?

The evidences of religious orthodoxy are all about. The immense skyscraper-headquarters of the Israeli rabbinate towers over New Jerusalem; lighthearted Israelis speak mockingly of the colossal edifice as "the Third Temple," although it is an administrative building and not a sacred shrine. There is no separation of church and state. The Israeli government has a Ministry of Religious Affairs at Cabinet level. The Knesset includes members who belong to religious parties standing for inflexible Orthodoxy in national life. The three religious parties draw about 15 percent of the total vote, and are strongly represented in the government.

Though Israel has a system of civil courts, there is a parallel system of eight regional rabbinical courts and a rabbinical court of appeal; these religious courts hold jurisdiction over many aspects of every Israeli's life. Marriage, divorce, and adoption are completely under the control of the religious courts. It is impossible, as a result, for a Jew to marry a non-Jew in Israel, since the rabbinate will not condone such unions and civil marriage does not exist. The children of mixed marriages are legally classified as bastards in Israel. A Jew who has come to Israel from another country faces an infinity of complications if he wishes to marry. If he has never been married before, he must produce a letter to that effect from a rabbi in his native country. If he was married before in a civil ceremony only, he is free in the eyes of the rabbinate to marry again in Israel, since that earlier marriage has no religious validity, but if he does marry again, he is subject to civil prosecution for bigamy. If he was married in a Jewish ceremony abroad but obtained a civil divorce, he will not be able to marry again in Israel, since the rabbinate does not recognize civil divorces. (If he obtained a Jewish divorce overseas, but not from an Orthodox rabbinical court, the Israeli rabbinate will not recognize that either.)

The laws of Judaism are the law of the land. All government offices close on the Sabbath and on holy days. All public transportation halts. Stores, businesses, and places of public entertainment must be shut. Israel enters a kind of suspended animation every Friday evening and does not emerge from it until sundown on Saturday. Ships and commercial airliners that arrive in Israel on the Sabbath may not unload their passengers until Saturday night. In some ultra-Orthodox sections of the cities, anyone who drives a car on the Sabbath runs the risk of being stoned. Even the army is required to halt most activity on the Sabbath except in times of national emergency. The army, too, must observe the Jewish dietary laws. So also must El Al, the Israeli airline, and all other public institutions. Hotels must keep kosher kitchens. The raising of pigs is prohibited except in certain areas of the state that are inhabited by Christians.

Beneath the surface of this seeming theocracy, though, the country seethes with revolt. Anti-Judaism is common, particularly among the tough, bouncy, materialistic, self-confident *sabras*, the native-born Israelis. (*Sabra* is a nickname derived from the Arab word for the desert cactus know as the prickly pear; *sabras* take pride in their thorniness.) There is little patience among the younger Israelis, and little fondness for the rituals and the constricting regulations of Orthodox Judaism. They are willing to tolerate the obligatory Bible lessons taught in all schools to children from the age of five onward, for in Israel the Bible is history and every citizen is an amateur archaeologist who gets keen pleasure from exploring the sites of Old Testament events. But they are unable to abide the interference of the rabbinate in their private lives—particularly in the matter of marriage and divorce— and they regard Israel's large ultra-Orthodox community as a useless drain on the nation's resources.

Some insight into Israeli attitudes toward religion is provided by a study published in 1963 by Aaron Antonovsky of the Israeli

Institute of Applied Social Research. A representative sampling of the population was asked, first, "Do you observe the religious tradition?" Fifteen percent replied that they observed all of its commandments; the same percentage indicated observance of most of the religious laws, but not all. The largest group—46 percent—said they observed the traditions "to some extent," but 24 percent declared themselves completely secular, not at all observant. (On the *kibbutzim*, the agricultural communes, the secularized Jews amounted to 76 percent.)

The second question was, "Should the government see to it that public life is conducted in accordance with Jewish religious tradition?" "Definitely not," replied 37 percent of those asked. "Definitely yes," said 23 percent. About 16 percent answered "probably not" and 20 percent "probably yes."

Where they can, young Israelis escape the Sabbath restrictions by finding enterainment in the Arab sections of Israel and now in the occupied territories. The Arab-owned night clubs and restaurants of Jaffa do booming business on Friday nights while Tel Aviv is dark; discotheques now thrive on Israeli trade in what formerly was the Jordanian half of Jerusalem. On the *kibbutzim*, many of which are openly atheistic, the Sabbath is simply a day off. However, many Israelis chafe under the Sabbath laws, and a much greater number live in continual anguish over the rabbinical intrusion into civil law. Yet there is little they can do about it except complain. Thanks to the Israeli system of proportional representation, the Orthodox religious parties are guaranteed a substantial bloc of seats in the Knesset, and thereby play powerful roles in the coalition governments that Israel must of necessity have. No prime minister could hope to remain in office if he attempted to strike a real blow at the control of national life by the religious groups. Then, too, the Oriental Jews are deeply religious. Though their mode of observance is quite different from the *shtetl* Orthodoxy practiced by Israel's dominant religious figures, the Orientals are unwilling to see any dilution of Israel's quasi-theocratic nature.

This engenders a frustration that has led to some angry language. Many young Israelis defiantly distinguish between "Israeli" and "Jew," and insist that simply because one is an Israeli, one does not also have to be a Jew. A "Jew," to those thorny *sabras*, is something miserable, pathetic, and timid; an "Israeli" is robust, modern, vigorous. In this scheme of things "Jews" are the prayer-muttering victims who walked meekly into Nazi gas chambers without the slightest show of resistance, while "Israelis" are the lean, tanned warriors who periodically send terrified Arab soldiers fleeing through the desert. An article published in an American Jewish Congress periodical in 1963 quotes an American resident of Israel who said, "When I first came to Israel, I had a discussion with an Israeli girl. She firmly denied being Jewish and identified herself as an 'Israeli.' She said: 'What have I in common with some Jew in Paris who has a long beard and stinks from garlic?' That kind of remark we often hear from . . . young Israeli Jews; and only yesterday one of them admitted to me that they are the worst anti-Semites around. . . ." Harold Isaacs, in his study of American Jewish settlers in Israel, mentions one who, in speaking of the unending Arab threat to the country, said, "If they come in, they'll have to come in fighting, and if we have to die, we'll die as Zionists and Israelis, *not as Jews*!"

The natural rebelliousness of youth is one explanation for talk of this sort. Young Israelis are not the only young Jews who, finding the Orthodox habits of their elders absurd or obsolete, loudly deny that they themselves are Jews. But there are special reasons for Jewish anti-Judaism in Israel.

One is the resentment kindled by the attitude of the ultra-Orthodox community—a resentment going beyond mere annoyance over the imposition on everyone of religious laws that only a few desire. Ordinary Israelis look upon the ultra-Orthodox as traitors to the nation, because they will neither recognize the existence of the State of Israel nor do anything to defend it.

The most extreme faction among the Orthodox is the Neturei Karta, "Guardians of the City," a group of several thousand people who live in the Mea Shearim district of New Jerusalem. In dress and in thought they seem like wanderers out of time, lifted bodily from some Eastern European ghetto of the eighteenth century. Like other ultra-Orthodox Israelis, the Neturei Karta are still awaiting the Messiah who will proclaim the redemption of the Jews and rebuild the Temple, and they regard the present State of Israel as an illegitimate usurpation of the Messiah's function. They are the only Jews in Israel who continue to recite the Passover lament, "This year we are slaves. Next year we shall be free men." They have torn down the Israeli flag, smashed radios playing the Israeli national anthem, and decreed Israel's Independence Day to be a time of mourning and fasting. They do not even recognize the chief rabbi of Israel, since he is chosen by the legislature of the state whose existence they reject. (In return, the chief rabbi will not grant official recognition to the rabbis of Mea Shearim, which is one of the stranger paradoxes of the religious situation in Israel.)

Most of the time, the Neturei Karta are no more than nuisances in Israel, blocking automobile traffic on the Sabbath, inveighing against miniskirts, demonstrating against such violations of Jewish law as the opening of a swimming pool for both sexes. (During that incident, in 1958, a group of ultra-Orthodox sympathizers in the United States picketed the White House to protest the "fascist" tactics of the mayor of Jerusalem, who had not only authorized the pool but sent police to break up the demonstration against it.) But in times of military crisis, few Israelis can forgive the religious fanatics for their refusal to serve in the armed forces. In Israel, military service is universal; men must serve for thirty months, women for two years. Since Israel's existence is in a state of more or less constant peril, the necessity for this is never questioned, and Israeli children look forward eagerly and enthusiastically to their opportunity to defend the homeland. But exemption from military service is available to the devout on grounds of conscientious objection, and the ultra-Orthodox avail themselves of this privilege. They will not fight for a secular republic. To them, suicide is preferable to conscription, and they would rather be massacred by Arab hordes than lift a hand in self-defense.

Most Israelis are bitter over this mass avoidance of a citizen's first responsibility, and they show it by a general loathing of Orthodoxy. It is bad enough, they say, that the fanatics constitute a nonproductive entity, giving Israel nothing but useless Talmudic scholars; but they leave the fighting to others. When I visited Israel shortly after the 1967 war, I saw a vivid example of this bitterness in the occupied Arab town of Hebron, which contains one of Judaism's holiest places, the burial place of Abraham, Isaac, and Jacob. For two decades Hebron had been in Jordanian hands, forbidden to Jews; now, as a result of the war, it was possible for the devout to travel down from Jerusalem to worship there. I saw a row of ultra-Orthodox Jews standing by the holy burial place, their eyes closed, their bodies swaying in the frenzied, convulsive movements with which they express their religious exaltation, their lips occasionally touching the wall of the holy building now restored to them. Most were old men, but some were no more than twenty years old. All were clad in the wide-brimmed hats and fur-trimmed cloaks of the ghetto, all wore the beards and ringlets of their sect. Nearby sat several Israeli soldiers, armed with submachine guns, assigned to the spot to protect these worshipers against possible harm by Hebron's Arabs. They looked on in boredom; sometimes they shook their heads in wonder and revulsion at some especially ecstatic outcry from the men at the wall; and they looked at the young worshipers—slender, unworldly, remote—with particular anger. These Israeli soldiers were proud of having made it possible for Jews to pray in Hebron again, but they were unable to conceal their disdain for the manner of those prayers or for the unwillingness of the ultra-Orthodox to aid in the liberation.

Another reason for the rise of anti-Judaism among Israelis is the almost total absence of alternatives to the Orthodox brand of worship. The grip of Orthodoxy on the country is so tight that the rabbinate has not permitted schismatic Jewish groups to thrive. There are nearly six thousand synagogues in the country. But only seven Reform and three or four Conservative congregations are among them. Their members are chiefly American and Canadian. Their rabbis have no official status and are forbidden to perform such rabbinical functions as marriage. The Reform rabbis are not allowed to serve as chaplains in the armed forces. Only one congregation owns its own building; the others meet in cramped rented quarters. The non-Orthodox sects, unlike Orthodox Judaism, get no financial support from the government.

There is not much impulse among the members of Israel's Reform and Conservative congregations to change this system. As one American rabbi living in Israel put it, "Unfortunately, the Conservative or Reformed person is by definition not a zealot. If they pushed hard there would be a great opportunity. But there are all kinds of obstacles."

Attempts by American Reform and Conservative groups to gain a better foothold for their brands of Judaism in Israel have come to very little. In December, 1967, delegates to the 49th Biennial General Assembly of the Union of American Hebrew Congregations, the Reform lay group, voted to form a National

Committee on Israel, and to ask each of the million Reform Jews in the United States to contribute a dollar to finance its program. The aim was to attack the void in Israeli religious life that many Israelis define by saying, "Here you're Orthodox or else you're nothing. There isn't anything in between."

In the autumn of 1968 the Reform rabbinical organization, the Central Conference of American Rabbis, met with the leaders of the Rabbinical Assembly, a Conservative group, to discuss a joint Reform-Conservative assault on Israel. Rabbi David Polish of Illinois told the gathering, "We are and must continue to be intimately identified with Israel and its fate and destiny. So far we have manifested this identity not only financially but by bringing influence to bear on Israel's economic policies. We have no less a right and a claim to influencing, for a time, its religious policies." Rabbi Polish called for Israel to evolve "a liberalized Judaism that goes beyond the legalistic to a more creative stance, such as a responsible concern for the moral and social issues of the day."

But so long as the Orthodox establishment holds political power in Israel, it does not seem likely that the other branches of Judaism will be permitted to develop there. Israelis almost certainly will be forced to continue to choose between Orthodoxy and secularism, and many will opt to be "Israelis" rather than "Jews."

American Jews who visit Israel naïvely expect it to be the most truly Jewish place on earth, and are shocked to find that it is not. They hear such Israeli leaders as Uri Avneri, head of the Semitic Action Movement, declare, "Religion is a stage in the development of human society in exactly the same way as feudalism or witchcraft: and frankly, it represents just about the same level of evolution as they do." They come upon anti-Judaic demonstrations in which marchers carry banners that depict caricatures of Orthodox Jews as cruel as anything ever found in Nazi propaganda sheets. They listen to earnest young *sabras* who say that religion has become irrelevant in Israel, that it was maintained in the lands of exile only as a way of keeping the national identity alive.

What is happening in Israel, American visitors come to realize, is a denial of one of the basic tenets of Zionist theory. Herzl and others had taught that Jews needed a homeland of their own because they were so alien in their customs that they could never hope to win acceptance in the Gentile world. Without a homeland,

Herzl argued, Jews would more and more camouflage themselves as Gentiles. But if a Jewish nation should arise again, everyone could practice the teachings of the religion openly and without fear of mockery.

Instead, Jewish nationalism has led to a withering away of Judaism in Israel. The only religion practiced is an Orthodox version so formalistic, so ritualized, so devoid of relevance to daily life, that a majority of Israelis have fallen away from it. The kind of Jewish life known in America, where the synagogue has become not so much a religious center as a social center, at which one meets the other members of the minority group to which one belongs, is unknown in Israel. Jews are not a minority there. They are free from the subtle uneasiness that Jews feel in the Diaspora. They do not need to cope with anti-Semitism, but only with the belligerent anti-Zionism of their Arab enemies, which is quite a different thing, being political and not religious or racial in origin. And so they have freed themselves from religion, too. They can establish their identity as Jews merely by being citizens of Israel, and need never set foot inside a synagogue. Of all the complexities arising from the existence of the State of Israel, perhaps the most extraordinary is this: that Jews from other lands, when they visit Israel and meet the vigorous, hardy Israelis, go away saying, "But they don't seem Jewish at all!"

13.

If American Jews are often baffled and disturbed by what they find in Israel, it must also be noted that Israelis are not delighted by all that they see in Americans. They look upon us with a kind of affection, but not with much respect; and often not with a great deal of affection, either. Though Israelis are charming and cordial to individual American visitors, extending hospitalities to them far beyond their means, the consensus of Israeli private opinion is that Americans as a class are spoiled, lazy, self-indulgent, cowardly, arrogant, and hypocritical—and brash and vulgar as well.

Part of this is standard anti-Americanism, not unique in any way to Israel. The United States is the strongest and wealthiest nation in the world, and this is bound to arouse some resentment, particularly since the United States does not always use its strength or its wealth in tactful ways. No one loves Goliath. Everyone envies Midas. When Midas and Goliath are one, a certain amount of jealous sniping from less fortunate peoples is inevitable.

Then, too, the Americans that Israelis see are tourists—not our most successful export. The tourists we send abroad include a good many loud, aggressive, boastful, and insensitive people, for we are a very young nation and we react poorly to ways of life we do not understand. The things tourists say and do are no more maddening to the natives of Tel Aviv than they are to those of Paris, Vienna, or Puerto Rico, but they win few friends for the United States.

Israelis have a special reason for feeling uncomfortable about the Americans: they owe us so much, and we never let them forget it. Israel is not economically self-sufficient, and could not have survived without foreign assistance, both from governments (mainly those of the United States and West Germany) and from individuals (mainly American Jews). There is deep gratitude in Israel for the billions of dollars this country has provided, and also for the political aid, from the days of the United Nations debate over partition onward. But Israelis cannot help feeling uncomfortable about their position as clients dependent on our benevolence. "We come to you and ask for money, because we need it," an Israeli told me. "And you give it, because you have so much. And then we feel like *schnorrers* [beggars]. So we resent your help. *Schnorrers* always resent the people who help them." The Israeli does not want to think of himself as a *schnorrer*. He prefers the image of an invincible warrior. But circumstances force the Israelis to be warriors and *schnorrers* simultaneously, and their anguish over this finds an outlet in a barely understood dislike of their benefactors.

We make things worse by taking a proprietary interest in Israel, which Israelis hate. American Jews, Israelis frequently charge, inspect the country as though they own it. "It's the old ones who get me, the one's who've given a few dollars, " I heard one young Israeli remark. "They'll go into a school or a kibbutz building and tap the walls, feel the draperies, open the drawers. They want to make sure they've had their money's worth." The myriad donor plaques all over Israel call forth much contemptuous humor from Israelis. The plaques seem to symbolize the American concern over money and the American love of claiming status. "See," a plaque cries, "I have been a success in business, and so I have sent my dollars to pave this courtyard, and now I affix my name in bronze to this wall so that future generations may know how successful I was, and how generous." This urge to derive prestige from worldly success strikes an Israeli as a specifically *Jewish* trait, and it is part of the Jewishness he is trying to reject. There is not much of a capitalistic impulse in Israel, and money is valued only for what it can buy, not for the prestige it can bring. In his effort to build a new kind of Jewish culture in Israel, the Israeli wants to get away from the stereotype of Jewish acquisitiveness as much as he does from the long beards and ringlets of Orthodoxy, and he places a vast psychological distance between himself and the sort of people who memorialize their own wealth with large plaques in his homeland.

Israelis regard American Jews as hypocrites because of their failure to make the *aliyah.* The continued existence in the United States of a Jewish community more than twice the size of that of Israel seems scandalous in Israel, and the huge sums raised by Zionist organizations in the United States on Israel's behalf make the anomaly all the more shocking. Israelis tend to look upon Zionism in the United States as a pleasant diversion for middle-class ladies with time on their hands, rather than as any sort of movement of commitment. If Americans are such great Zionists, they ask, why don't they move to Israel? Are they salving their consciences by sending all that cash? Obviously they don't want to leave their fine homes and their comfortable businesses, but in that case why do they call themselves Zionists?

It is a widespread belief among Israelis that many of the religious restrictions under which they must live are kept in force by the government solely to impress American Jews, who might withhold their donations if they saw Israel becoming too secular. This is an exaggeration of the actual situation, but there is no doubt that the government is extremely sensitive to the opinions of American Jews, and does its best to sustain Israel's image of Jewishness. This became obvious in the celebrated *Shalom* affair of 1962–64. The *Shalom*, a luxurious new ship of Israel's Zim Line, was under construction at a French shipyard when word got out that the blueprints called for two kitchens, one kosher, one non-kosher. The idea was to encourage non-Jewish Americans to visit Israel; the Zim Line felt that it might be able to induce some Gentile traffic on the *Shalom*'s voyages between Haifa and New York if non-kosher cooking were available.

Instantly a storm of controversy blew up. American Jews wrote
thousands of letters to the directors of the Zim Line. Some applauded them for a wise commercial move, others expressed horror that a ship flying the flag of Israel should violate the laws of
Moses. The Jerusalem *Post*, Israel's English-language newspaper,
published a long series of letters from its American readers, who
advised Israel to take a harder line generally on the matter of
religious observance. Many of the correspondents warned that if
Israel failed to measure up to their idea of what a Jewish state
ought to be, they would have to withhold their customary contributions.

In December, 1963, the chief rabbi of Israel informed Zim that
if the line persisted in contructing a non-kosher kitchen on the
Shalom, he would withdraw the rabbinical certificate of kosherness
not only from that ship but from all other vessels of the line,
making it impossible for Orthodox Jews to travel on them. The
minister of religious affairs indicated that the government was
backing this ultimatum. In a desperate moment Zim considered
getting a certificate from an association of Conservative rabbis in
the United States, but this would obviously have been intolerable
to Israel's Orthodox leaders, and the plan was canceled. Then a
Boston rabbi announced that he would lead a boycott of the Zim
Line and even of El Al, the Israeli airline, unless the *Shalom*'s
non-kosher kitchen were dropped. Zim capitulated under stern
government pressure.

"It is because of the American Jews," one Israeli commented.
"At home they eat pork and lobster, but here they are worse than
the rabbis."

Exactly so. The observance of Jewish dietary laws is in eclipse
in the United States. But the American Jew expects to find the
laws flourishing in Israel. Pork chops on the menu of the Tel Aviv
Hilton would be as unwelcome to a traveler as brassieres on the
girls of Bali or the replacement of calypso by rock-and-roll in
Trinidad. Israelis do not enjoy having to maintain customs that
they look upon as archaic, for the sake of pleasing their American
benefactors.

The tendency of an Israeli to view everything from his own
embattled nation's special situation is another cause of misunderstanding between Israelis and Americans. In the United States in
the late 1960's American college students—many of them Jewish

—devoted a great deal of effort to finding ways of resisting military conscription. The general belief that United States involvement in the war in Vietnam was immoral led to the corollary that it was an act of the highest moral value for a young American to elude the draft—that if only *every* American boy would defy the draft boards, the unjust and immoral war would come to a halt through lack of manpower. The draft-resistance movement was championed by the New Left, many of whose leaders are Jewish.

Israelis find the concept of resisting the draft incomprehensible, and are amazed that so many young Americans see anything virtuous about refusing to take up arms for their country. A good many Israelis point to the draft-resistance movement as yet another example of America's flabbiness, decadence, and cowardice.

In Israel, of course, military service is a sacred obligation, and no one avoids it except the ultra-Orthodox. Until the 1967 war, it was possible for the people of Jerusalem to look just across the street and see Arab soldiers on patrol in Jordan, armed and waiting; to the north, on the border with Syria, agricultural settlements accepted frequent shellings by the Syrians as a normal condition of life. Even in cosmopolitan Tel Aviv no one forgot that the enemy frontier was only a dozen miles to the east. Some of the pressures of that era have lifted, now, but Israel has no reason to relax even if her foes have been pushed back a bit from her borders. Israelis, boys and girls both, are ready to fight and if necessary to die for their country. Israelis look with distaste upon the pacifism of so many young Americans.

The Vietnamese war itself is translated into Israeli terms, with surprising results for an American visitor. Americans who traveled abroad during the worst years of that war wearily grew accustomed to being taken to task by foreigners for it, as though they were personally responsible for each escalation. But in Israel, I noticed, the only people who said much about the war were former Americans, who were, like a large number of American Jews, strongly opposed to it. Israelis themselves rarely ventured opinions on the subject.

I asked one Israeli friend why. "We know very little about your war here," he said—and he is a very well-informed man. "We feel it is not our business."

"But of course," I said, "you think it's a deplorable thing for the United States to be mixed up in."

He looked at me strangely. "How can I say that? How can you say that? In the judgment of your government, Vietnam is an outpost that must be defended. Here we believe in defending outposts. We have to rely on the government's military judgment."

His attitude, I learned later, was something of an extreme one, but far from unique. Israelis know the value of outposts. In the 1948 war, dozens of tiny border settlements played major roles in holding back the Arab invaders. If the government of the United States chooses to regard South Vietnam as a vital outpost, so be it; it is not the ordinary citizen's place to offer a contrary decision. Questions of morality did not enter into my friend's opinion of our war. He saw it purely in strategic terms, and in terms of the faith that one should place in one's leaders. The fact that it was a war against Communists helped shape his views; he is bitter over the aid that the Soviet Union had given the Arabs prior to the 1967 war. In Israel, the friend of your enemy is your enemy also.

The relationship between the Jews of Israel and the Jews of the United States, then, is a complex and unpredictable one. We have done a great deal to help them, both financially and politically; in some ways they are indebted to us for survival itself. But they have done a great deal to help themselves, too—more than many Americans will grant them credit for having done. Many of us like to think of the Israelis as bright children, living in a wonderful experimental playground that we have built for them. But in fact they are proud, independent, self-confident, strong people, who do not regard themselves as colonial dependents of American Jewry, and who find our attitude toward them often much too patronizing, insensitive, and crude. They fight their own battles, and fight them well, and want all the world to know it. They alone, they say, are responsible for what Israel does, and they show it in a variety of ways—such as the devastating 1969 raid on the Lebanese airport—that may shock and startle the cautious Jews of the Diaspora. We will go on helping them, for it suits our needs to be generous to them; and they will go on accepting our aid, because they must. But we have tried to smother Israel in our love, and Israel is not grateful for that. Her people look to us in mingled fondness and exasperation.

TEN

The Unending War

THE LONG political struggle to create a Jewish homeland in the Near East has given way to what promises to be an even longer military struggle to insure that homeland's survival. The tensions between Israel and the Arab world seem irremovable, because they are fundamentally irrational. This is not a quarrel that can be settled by an appeal to sweet reason.

There were many opportunities for settlement in the past, but all of them were lost. There was no enmity between Arab and Jew under Turkish rule. More enlightened planning in 1918 could have brought forth a binational Palestine capable of sustaining several million Zionists in the midst of the Arabs. But the conflicting imperialisms of Great Britain and France doomed that hope. It might yet have been possible to evolve some kind of shared Palestine, or else some peaceful and equitable partition, but for the alternating and sometimes simultaneous intransigeances of the Arabs and the Zionists. Eventually a point was reached where emotions prevailed over logic, and the Palestinian problem was settled by force of arms. Hundreds of thousands of Arabs fled their homes and could not return.

Even after 1948 a kind of peace was available. The Arab leaders could have swallowed their bitterness, accepted Israel's existence as a *fait accompli*, and come to terms of some sort with the Zionist state. (The 8,000 square miles occupied by the state of Israel are not at all vital to Arab interests, and the Arab refugees from Palestine—now numbering more than a million—could easily have been absorbed into the neighboring lands.) Despite its oil, the Arab world is not so wealthy that it can afford to squander resources on perpetual warfare; with Israel's aid, the whole Near East might now be enjoying an economic renaissance.

But the Arab nations, themselves emerging from colonial subjection, could not make peace with Israel. For political reasons of their own, they needed an external enemy. Loathing for Israel serves to distract the Arabs from their own poverty and from the incompetence, corruption, and pettiness of their leaders.

Israel is a convenient symbol by which the Arab rulers hold the support of the masses; anti-Zionism is an abstract crusade in the Arab world, kept alive for political purposes. Through a constant campaign of small provocations and terrorisms, Israel's enemies vent their rage and sustain what little unity they have. Sundered by personal rivalries among their leaders, split by strife that is itself irrational and incomprehensible to outsiders, the Arab states are held together only by their shared hatred for Israel.

Twice since Israel attained her independence, the war of nerves erupted into a shooting war. Each time it was Israel that by the ordinary rules of warfare could have been called the aggressor, but each time Israel was sorely provoked before going to war. Both wars were surrounded by controversy. Both ended in unexpectedly sweeping Israeli triumphs. When Israel goes to war, it is a time of testing for her friends in the United States. In 1956 and again in 1967, the behavior of American Jews cast revealing light on the bonds that link millions of Americans to the fortunes of this Near Eastern country.

2.

During Harry Truman's second term in the White House, the policy of the American government toward Israel was generally one of strong support. The infinite hesitations and reversals of the 1946–48 period gave way to almost unqualified approval for the new Jewish nation. All of the State Department's fine calculations turned out to be worthless. The Arabs were annoyed with us, but they had not evicted us from their oil fields, nor could they without wrecking their own economies.

The American public, so carefully indoctrinated by Zionist spokesmen, welcomed Israel enthusiastically. The United States has a natural sympathy for oppressed peoples struggling to attain independence; the battles in the Negev and the Galilee seemed not too different from those of Valley Forge and Saratoga. Then, too, the Israelis were a briskly progressive sort, very American in their drive and ambitions. The pace of industrial development in Israel pleased and impressed Americans, who saw only feudalism, poverty, and ignorance in the Arab countries. Our liking for Israel was not merely a matter of religion in 1949; it sprang from a genuine affinity of national outlook.

The year 1949 was part of the era when the world was polarizing into American and Soviet blocs, and American foreign policy was conceived with the intent of gathering as many nations as possible into the American bloc. The liberation movements in Asia and Africa had not yet begun. Scores of present-day United Nations members were not then independent, and Israel, as one of the first of the "new" nations, received a great deal of attention from the United States.

Israel, however, tried at first to remain neutral in the struggle between East and West. She had been aided by the Soviet Union as well as by the United States in her battle to win United Nations support for the partition of Palestine, and her leaders hoped that by staying on good terms with Russia they would be able to induce Stalin to permit the emigration of Russia's Jews to Israel. (Expediency had led the Russians to support the Zionists in 1947–48, thereby helping to throw the British out of Palestine. But there had been no change at all in Stalin's harsh repression of Russia's own Jews. A mass emigration of Jews from Russia to Israel would be too biting a repudiation of the Soviet system; Stalin would not allow it.) By early 1950, though, it was apparent to Israel that she did not have much to gain from friendship with Russia, and it was also becoming clear that no state of peace with the Arabs was going to materialize. She began thinking about entering into some formal relationship with the United States that would insure her national security.

Thus, early in 1950, Foreign Minister Moshe Shertok asked the United States to sell Israel a quantity of surplus war material. In spite of the new American policy of friendship toward Israel, the request was turned down; the State Department felt that to grant it might touch off an arms race in the Near East, with the Arabs rushing to buy new weapons from the British. A few months later Israel requested arms again. Again the request was refused, even though American Jewish leaders mobilized strong political support on Israel's behalf. Instead, the Truman administration sought to stabilize the Near Eastern situation by joining with Great Britain and France—the region's other chief arms suppliers—in a pact governing the sale of weapons to the entire area.

This was the Tripartite Declaration of May 25, 1950, under which the three great powers pledged to sell Israel and the Arab countries only such weapons as were needed to meet legitimate needs of self-defense. Any attempt to modify the boundaries of the 1949 armistice agreements by force, the three powers warned, would be opposed by them, either within the United Nations or outside it. Since Israel had declared herself content with her 1949 borders, while the Arab countries had continued to voice their determination to destroy the Zionist state, the Tripartite Declaration amounted to a formal guarantee to Israel that her territorial integrity would be defended.

A few weeks later the Korean War began. Israel, now firmly in the Western bloc, supported the United Nations American-led intervention in Korea, causing a further estrangement between herself and the Soviet Union. As the United States extended its involvement in the Near East in 1951 through an unsuccessful effort to draw Israel and the Arab countries together as members of the Western defense system, Russia began to regard Israel as a captive of American imperialism. The Arab nations, too, saw Israel as America's creature, and moved closer to alliance with Russia.

An attempt by Israel in February, 1952, to repair her relations with the Soviet Union proved a failure. Later that year a wild outburst of anti-Semitism and anti-Zionism erupted in Russia, which destroyed all hope of Russo-Israeli friendship and foreclosed the chance of an *aliyah* of Russian Jews. The climax of this campaign came in January, 1953, with the revelation in Moscow of the Doctors' Plot: four Jewish physicians were accused of conspiring with the Joint Distribution Committee, the "well-known agency of the American intelligence," to assassinate Soviet leaders and bring about the downfall of the Soviet Union. This led to the bombing by angry Israelis of the Soviet legation in Tel Aviv the next month, and to Russia's severing of diplomatic relations with Israel. Accusations of a Zionist conspiracy ended abruptly with the death of Stalin in March, 1953, and his successors indicated that the "plot" had been a figment of the old man's imagination, but the damage was done.

Though diplomatic relations between the two countries were

resumed in July, 1953, Russia now was committed to a policy of winning power in the Near East by backing the Arabs against Israel; and Israel was moving steadily closer to outright alliance with the United States. Such an alliance seemed a virtual necessity, for, swamped by hundreds of thousands of impoverished immigrants, Israel was close to economic collapse and badly in need of help. The currency was deteriorating, inflation was out of control, morale was low. In 1952 and 1953 Israel actually lost through emigration more citizens than she gained by *aliyah.*

But just as Israel was committing herself to a close relationship with the United States, the government of the United States changed. Out of office went the Democrats, with their traditional concern for the rights of minorities. Into office after twenty lean years came the Republicans, who were thought to be the party of the rich, the secure, the established. What changes would this bring in the American outlook on Israel?

Harry S Truman, at 68, had chosen not to run for office again in 1952. His miraculous victory in 1948 had not been followed by any miracles of administration, and he realized that the country was probably ready to let him go, after seven years in the White House. There was discontent in the land—over American involvement in the Korean War, over the supposed existence of a Communist conspiracy in the government, over the undeniable corruption of many of Truman's appointees, over inflation, over the fact that one party had held the presidency so long. The Democrats chose as their nominee a little-known but attractive figure, Governor Adlai Stevenson of Illinois. The Republicans selected General Dwight D. Eisenhower.

In their usual fashion, Jews discussed the candidates not only in a context of national affairs, but in terms of what their election might mean for the Jews—and for Israel. But there was no way of knowing. Stevenson was eloquent, intelligent, adequately liberal, and had a good sense of humor. These are characteristics that Jewish voters respect. On the other hand, Eisenhower was the hero of the war against Hitler. He was clearly a man of good will, and he had done a good deal to ease the conditions of the displaced persons under his jurisdiction in Europe after the war. Neither candidate had ever been involved in the making of foreign policy and neither had ever taken a public stand on American support for Israel.

In the end, most Jews remained true to their customary voting

habits, and cast their ballots for Stevenson, although not as universally as they had for Roosevelt and Truman. About 75 percent of
the Jewish vote went to the Democrats in 1952, compared with the
80 percent to 90 percent pluralities achieved among them by the
two previous Democratic candidates. Nevertheless, Eisenhower
won the election easily. He received 55 percent of the national
vote and led in 39 states, including all of those that had heavy
Jewish populations. Stevenson's nine states were all in the south,
where the majority of people normally voted Democratic no matter who ran. The country had been ready for a change in leadership.

President Eisenhower's Cabinet appointees reflected the traditional image of Republicanism: they were nearly all sedate, stol-
idly conservative men, most of them drawn from the business
community. American Jews were particularly uneasy about Eisenhower's Secretary of State, John Foster Dulles, a rigid, sternly
puritanical man who viewed the conflict between capitalism and
Communism as though it were a war between angels and demons.
Dulles' anti-Communism did not seem to pose any special threat
to America's friendship with Israel, but the inflexibility of his
harsh and pietistic view of the world distressed the Jews, who tend
to have more faith in men who understand the arts of compromise
and are willing to accommodate their ideas to reality. In addition,
when Dulles had sought a Senate seat in New York in 1949 he had
given New York's millions of Jews no reason to think that he was
their friend. Appointed by Governor Dewey to fill the four-month
vacancy left by the death in office of Senator Robert F. Wagner,
Dulles ran for a term of his own against Herbert Lehman. Largely
abandoning New York City's Jews to his Jewish opponent, Dulles
waged most of his campaign among the conservative people of
upstate New York. Frequently he hinted to them that Lehman's
followers were dangerous left-wingers, as when he said to a group
of farmers, "If you could see the kind of people in New York City
making up this bloc that is voting for my opponent, if you could
see them with your own eyes . . . you would be out, every last man
and woman of you, voting on Election Day." Jews, Negroes, and
members of other minority groups took exception to the tone of
Dulles' upstate campaigning, and Lehman won the election.

Soon after Dulles became Secretary of State in January, 1953,
he announced that he was going to re-examine United States

policy toward the Near East. This seemed ominous to Israel and her friends, since it necessarily implied a movement away from the present United States pro-Israel alignment and some sort of shift toward the Arabs. In May, 1953, Dulles undertook a 21-day tour of the Near East; he was an indefatigable traveler who believed in working from firsthand information whenever possible. He returned firmly convinced that the United States had to reshape its Near Eastern policy and work toward winning the good will of the Arab states through programs of military and economic aid.

Dulles had no wish to see Israel overwhelmed by her enemies. He supported the Tripartite Pact and defended the territorial *status quo* in the Near East. He was under no illusions about Arab intentions. He had heard Jordan's 18-year-old King Hussein declare on April 18, 1953, "We shall take back what was lost to us and we shall prove to the world that we are a strong nation," and he knew that such thoughts were shared by the other Arab leaders.

It was for the sake of preserving peace that Dulles decided to woo the Arabs. He believed that the United States would be in a position to exert a restraining influence over them only by first gaining their favor. This would mean some retreat from the recent close ties between the United States and Israel, but Dulles felt that in the long run his policies would work to Israel's benefit. One of the tragic ironies of his Near East policy-making is that nearly everything he did was done for the sake of avoiding war, but merely served to bring war closer.

Aside from helping to diminish Arab-Israeli tensions, the Secretary of State had other reasons to aid the Arabs. The Arab world was just beginning to emerge from colonialism; the French had been squeezed out of Syria and Lebanon, the British from Iraq, and Britain now was losing her hold on Egypt as well. Although a large British army still was camped on Egyptian soil to protect the Suez Canal, Egypt in 1952 had seen a nationalistic uprising led by idealistic young military officers, who had thrown out the corrupt King Farouk and proclaimed a republic. Colonel Gamal Abdel Nasser, who had emerged as the leader of the revolutionary junta, impressed Dulles as a progressive, dynamic statesman capable of lifting Egypt out of her backwardness. Dulles's puritan nature was stirred by the prospect of salvaging the Arabs from

sloth; he wished to do all in his power to help the emerging
ex-colonial nations achieve self-sufficiency as modern industrialized nations. The Arabs were a worthy reclamation project for
him, and Nasser seemed like the right agent of progress for the
task. Dulles resolved to back the Egyptian leader with enthusiasm
—even to the extent of helping Nasser evict the 80,000 British
soldiers camped by the canal. Guiding the Arab states into the
twentieth century would not only be a virtuous deed in its own
right, but it would give Dulles the opportunity to rescue them
from the perils of atheistic Communism.

In June, 1953, therefore, Dulles announced the new policy of
"friendly impartiality" in the Near East. The United States, he
said, would endeavor to help everybody. This country would work
toward the orderly establishment of self-government in the former
colonial territories; it would supply technical assistance to improve
the living standards of the inhabitants of the area; it would strive
to foster peace between Israel and the Arabs on the basis of the
1949 armistice boundaries; and it would endeavor to strengthen
the defenses of the entire Near East against possible Communist
aggression.

To Israel, "friendly impartiality" meant American abandonment of Israel. The subtleties of Dulles' aims were lost on the
Israelis, who could not see how a policy of cooperation with those
who loudly cried for their destruction was going to help them.
American Jews likewise took alarm at this retreat from the Truman policies. But they had little political leverage in Washington
now. A Republican President felt no strong obligation to look after
the interests of Jewish voters who, almost alone in the nation, had
resisted the Eisenhower magic in the 1952 election.

The first real test of our new impartiality came in the autumn
of 1953. Early in September, Israel began to dig a canal westward
from the Jordan River for a hydroelectric project. A mile and a half
of the canal was to pass through a demilitarized zone near the
Syrian border. This zone was under the jurisdiction of the United Nations, which had established a Truce Supervision Commission.

Several weeks after construction began, Syria protested to the
Truce Supervision Commission that the canal would give Israel a
military advantage, would take water from Arab-owned mills east
of the Jordan, and would deny irrigation water to certain Syrian

farms south of the canal. Israel denied these charges. General Vagn Bennike, the head of the Truce Supervision Commission, asked Israel to halt work on the canal "until agreement is reached." On September 28 and again on October 15, Israel offered to suspend construction while the Truce Commission or the Security Council investigated the matter; but she certainly was not going to make resumption of the work conditional on the consent of the Syrians, for that consent would never be forthcoming. Israel continued digging. Syria lodged a complaint with the Security Council.

While this dispute was going on, trouble broke out along Israel's frontier with Jordan, where there had been hundreds of minor episodes of Arab terrorism since 1948. On October 12, 1953, Arab raiders entered the village of Yahud, 10 miles from Tel Aviv, and murdered a Jewish woman and her two infants. Two nights later, an Israeli force crossed the border into the Jordanian village of Kibya, which was believed to be the place from which the raiders had come, and carried out a harsh reprisal, killing 53 Arabs and destroying 40 houses. Jordan charged that regular troops of the Israeli army had attacked Kibya. Prime Minister Ben-Gurion insisted that the reprisal had been a spontaneous act of the Jewish settlers along the frontier.

On October 17 Secretary of State Dulles, who was in London, expressed his shock over the Israeli raid at Kibya and called on the United Nations to condemn Israel for the killings. In an apparently unrelated move, Dulles announced three days later that $26,-000,000 in economic aid to Israel appropriated by Congress under the Mutual Security Act would be held back. The reason given was Israel's failure to comply with the United Nations Truce Supervision Commission's order to halt work on the hydroelectric canal. Since the United States not long before had declined to act on an Israeli request for a $75,000,000 loan, it appeared that "friendly impartiality" meant using American monetary leverage to keep Israel in line. Dulles denied that the suspension of economic aid had anything to do with the Kibya affair, but admitted that there was "a certain cumulative effect" to Israel's actions. At a press conference on October 21, President Eisenhower backed Dulles' decision to cut off the aid.

There were quick protests from Israel's friends in the United States. The next day, James G. McDonald, who had been our first ambassador to Israel, told the American Friends of the Hebrew University: "Secretary Dulles, in persuading President Eisenhower to approve economic sanctions against Israel, has intensified the crisis he sought to ease. He has deeply hurt the feelings of the Israelis and markedly encouraged the intransigeance of the Arab leaders. These Arab spokesmen, welcoming this official American rebuff to Israel, have hastened to express their delight. Adroitly they are interpreting this action as an indication of a fundamental change in the United States' policy toward Israel. . . . Of course, the Secretary did not intend thus to unleash forces seeking Israel's humiliation and dismemberment; but he has done so and, therefore, made a bad situation worse. In the name of 'impartiality'—the Secretary's avowed aim—he encourages Arab resistance to peace with Israel. Both expediency and justice require drastic and prompt modifications of Mr. Dulles' policy of 'impartiality.' "

As in the old days, Zionist leaders converged on Washington. Louis Lipsky and Mrs. Rose Halprin, on behalf of the Zionist Organization of American and Hadassah, led a delegation that included New York's Senator Irving Ives and Representative Jacob Javits. They called on Dulles on October 26 to urge reconsideration of recent American decisions. Stressing that it was to the advantage of the United States to sustain Israel "as a secure bastion of peace and freedom in the Near East," and emphasizing the economic damage that would be caused by withholding the aid funds, they argued that to weaken Israel would not serve the cause of peace. They also expressed sympathy for the victims of the deplorable attack on Kibya, but observed that the Israelis were not without provocation, since 421 of their own people had been slain or wounded in border incidents in that area over the previous four years.

The United Nations now took up the questions of the Kibya raid and the Israeli canal. General Bennike of the Truce Supervision Commission testified that the raid had been carried out by Israeli troops. Abba Eban, Israel's ambassador to the United Nations,* denied this charge and accused the Arabs of using guerrilla raids as a new form of warfare against his country. Then, on October 27, Eban declared that Israel was willing to halt work on the canal temporarily, pending consideration of the case by the

*And simultaneously Israel's ambassador to the United States.

Security Council. This was the same offer that Israel had made twice before. Eban still said nothing about making resumption of digging contingent upon Syrian approval, as General Bennike had urged.

But President Eisenhower decided to use Eban's offer as a face-saving device. He was embarrassed and disturbed by the furor the Zionists were raising over the aid cutoff, and, though he was hardly intimidated by their attempts at exerting pressure, he began to feel that his Secretary of State might have gone a little too far in his quest for "impartiality." So on October 28, the day after Eban's speech, Eisenhower announced that the order holding back Israel's Mutual Security Act money had been rescinded, in view of Israel's newly cooperative attitude.

With this discreet withdrawal under fire, the Eisenhower regime's first brush with American Zionist political power came to an end. It had been instructive for the President; and it was galling to Dulles, who had ordered the suspension of aid as a major act of policy, only to see it canceled on a flimsy pretext within eight days. At the Cabinet meeting of November 12, Dulles raised the Israel issue, saying that the best policy at home was to do the right thing abroad, even though this might temporarily alienate "extremists" in the United States. He warned against "playing politics" with foreign affairs. Eisenhower, too, commented that the Truman administration had used foreign policy for domestic political advantage during the Palestine crisis, and that he did not propose to do the same. And there the matter rested for a while.

But relations between the Eisenhower administration and the American Jewish community were badly strained by the affair. *The American Zionist*, published by the Zionist Organization of America, commented that the government "has blundered alarmingly in its dealings with Israel," and similar editorial attacks came from other Jewish publications.

In the spring of 1954 relations between America's Jews and the new administration were further strained when Assistant Secretary of State Henry A. Byroade, one of Dulles' experts on Near Eastern affairs, offered some pessimistic views on the future of Arab-Israeli relations. Byroade suggested that it might be useful for Israel to clamp a voluntary limit on immigration in order to ease Arab fears of Israeli expansionism. Israel was, at the time, not taking in many immigrants because of economic conditions, but

Byroade appeared not to realize that, and the tone of his comments seemed unnecessarily pro-Arab to Israel's supporters. On May 13 Ambassador Eban met with Dulles to get a clarification of Byroade's remarks. Dulles defended his Assistant Secretary but reaffirmed American friendship for Israel.

A casual statement by President Eisenhower at a 1954 gathering of Jewish leaders in Washington did not really inspire much confidence among his listeners, either: "I don't know what I would have done had I been President when the question of Israel's independence came up . . . but Israel is now a sovereign nation to which we do have obligations. We shall keep them."

American Jews continued to protest over "impartiality" and "Byroadeism." Many of them shared the views taken by a writer in the liberal weekly, *The Nation*, under the heading, "Stiletto Into Israel: The State Department Plot": "The purpose of Mr. Dulles's policy is to satisfy the Arabs by destroying Israel's viability and independence. In withholding economic aid to the Jewish state on the basis of the Syrian complaint, the State Department proposed to cripple Israel's power to become self-sustaining, to make it completely dependent on United States dollars—and thus to assure its greater amenability to United States pressures."

The State Department went forward with its policy of reaching toward the Arab world. In the spring of 1954 Dulles placed strong pressure on the British to withdraw their troops from Egypt, even letting it be known that if the Egyptians attacked the British base at the Suez Canal, the United States would give Britain no support. On July 27, 1954, an Anglo-Egyptian agreement was signed under which Britain promised to evacuate her forces from Egyptian territory within two years, ending generations of British occupation of Egypt.

By this move, Dulles believed he had won the support of Egypt for the Near Eastern defense alliance that he hoped to create. But he had done considerable harm to Israel by forcing the British out of Egypt. For while Britain was no friend of Israel, the presence of her troops along the Suez Canal acted as a buffer discouraging Egypt from invading the Jewish state. Furthermore, now that Egypt and not Britain held physical control of the canal, it would be easy for Nasser to deny the use of the waterway to Israel, in violation of international agreements on free passage.

In reality, Israel had not tried to send a ship of her own through the canal since 1949, although Israeli cargo in non-Israeli ships had been allowed passage. When the treaty of British withdrawal was announced, Israel tested the new status of the canal by sending the *Bat Gallim*, flying the Israeli flag, into the canal. The Egyptians seized the ship and imprisoned her crew. Soon afterward, Egypt served notice that no ship of any country that carried Israeli cargo would be permitted to use the canal. By the summer of 1954, the Suez crisis was in the making.

Dulles made other overtures to the Arab states in 1954, notably by awarding military and economic assistance to Iraq, and granting $40,000,000 in aid to Egypt. By the fall of 1954 it was clear that Dulles intended to sell arms to all of the Arab countries by way of strengthening them against Communism. That the Arabs planned to use their new weapons against Israel, not Russia, did not seem to occur to him. As the 1954 congressional elections drew near, though, the Republicans began to hear a good deal about their Near East policies from the Jewish organizations, and from Democratic candidates for office.

Senator Estes Kefauver of Tennessee, a Democrat who was running for re-election, visited the Near East in the summer of 1954, stopping in Israel. (A trip to Israel was becoming obligatory for American political figures.) On his return, Kefauver released a letter addressed to Mortimer May, the president of the Zionist Organization of America, in which he said, "The Israelis are gravely concerned and shocked by the one-sided policy of our State Department in supplying arms to the Arab states, which threatens to upset the status quo and the precarious balance of military power in the area. They are equally disturbed by the effects of the coming evacuation of the Suez Canal Zone by the British, which greatly increases the striking power of Egypt's armed forces, while Egypt persists in maintaining an illegal blockade of the Canal against Israeli shipping."

Kefauver said that he felt that Israel's alarm was well founded. He did not favor befriending the Arabs at the expense of our friendship with Israel or of endangering Israel's security, and promised to work toward a more balanced American policy in the Near East.

The American Jewish leadership elicited similar pledges from many other congressional candidates. Under the auspices of the American Zionist Committee for Public Affairs, a pro-Israel statement that included a declaration of opposition to the arming of the Arab states was presented to all of the nearly seven hundred candidates of both parties for the Senate and the House of Representatives. Three hundred and twenty-six of them signed it.

In October, 1954, the Zionist Organization of America sponsored some two dozen rallies across the United States to protest the Dulles policy. A delegation consisting of the presidents of most major Jewish organizations—the American Jewish Congress, B'nai B'rith, Hadassah, the Jewish War Veterans, the Zionist Organization of America, and eleven others—called on Dulles on October 25 to express its views. It was, said *The New York Times,* "the most powerful [Jewish] delegation to call upon the State Department since 1947."

It offered a statement that said, "We question whether the cause of Middle East peace or stability is served by military assistance to governments which maintain open hostility toward their neighbor. ... Military aid to the Arab states may well result in armed conflict, rendering the Middle East vulnerable to totalitarian subversion and infiltration."

Dulles assured his visitors that their memorandum would be given "careful consideration." However, he insisted that nothing would be done to upset the balance of power in the Near East. Nor was he willing to be drawn into any discussion of how he proposed to support Israel, saying that this was a matter for discussions between himself and Ambassador Eban and that he did not intend to see Eban until after the congressional elections. He expressed the hope that the Jewish leaders would not make Israel an election issue, and reminded them of his services to Zionism while a United Nations delegate. But for his friendship for Israel, he claimed, "the situation would have been even worse."

The Jewish delegation returned to New York City that evening to address a mass meeting of protest against American shipment of arms to the Arabs. Reporting on the meeting with Dulles, Louis Lipsky said, "Two years ago, when the present government in Washington was elected, it was not anticipated that today, close to the second anniversary of the event, we would assemble under the depression of grave anxieties, to face what seems to be a reversal of the traditional American approach to the problems of the Middle East. ... The radical change has not come about, we are convinced, by design to cause injury to Israel or to bring grief to its American friends. It has happened as a consequence of accepting, in haste, for reasons of state, rough and ready conceptions in which high-sounding slogans have been given the right of way. . . . The obsession which seems to have captured the imagination of our State Department was to win the so-called friendship of the Arab states by any and all means. For convenience and brevity (and to allay the suspicions of the parties concerned), the slogan adopted was called *impartiality.* . . . To show their impartiality, State Department officials thought it proper to issue public statements advocating Arab claims. The policy as it finally emerges is a travesty of American tradition and a breach of American pledges." At the same meeting, Emanuel Neumann declared, "Our complaint against the high level leadership in the Administration is that they have failed to correct the distorted vision of their subordinates and to check the irresponsible trend of their policies."

Suddenly Israel was very much a political issue again. Dulles, who was known to be bitter over his defeat at the hands of New York's Jewish voters in the 1949 senatorial contest, angrily rejected now the idea of making concessions to Israel for the sake of winning those voters. But other Republican leaders were more perturbed. President Eisenhower attended a dinner commemorating the three-hundredth anniversary of the landing of the first Jews in North America, made a grand show of eating gefilte fish, and pledged not to alter the balance of power in the Near East. Vice-President Nixon, a few days later, denounced the "whispering campaign" by which enemies of the Eisenhower administration were trying to make the President and the Secretary of State seem to be foes of Israel. Nixon said that he had spoken with Dulles and could assure everyone that the United States would do nothing to endanger Israel's security.

One figure caught in the political crossfire was Senator Irving Ives of New York, who was running for governor, a post being vacated by Thomas E. Dewey. Though Ives was a Republican, he had always enjoyed the backing of New York's Jewish voters, who approved of his liberalism and his support for Zionist goals. Since New York normally chose Republicans to be governor, it was considered certain that Ives would defeat his Democratic opponent, W. Averell Harriman, a veteran diplomat who had never run for public office before and had no familiarity with the complexities of New York politics. But as the debate over the Arab arms shipments warmed up, Ives began to see that he might be made the scapegoat for the Dulles policies toward the Near East.

The idea emerged that a group of Republican senators, including Ives, should go to Dulles and get from him some unequivocally pro-Israel statement that would reassure the New York voters. But when word came that Dulles did not welcome the plan, it was dropped. Next, Ives submitted his own draft of a statement to Dulles. The Secretary of State would not release it. Desperately, Ives joined with Jacob Javits, who was running for Attorney General of New York against Franklin D. Roosevelt, Jr., in an open appeal to Dulles not to send arms to the Arabs until friction between Israel and the Arabs ended. "We would defer taking the matter up with you until after the election campaign," they said, "but the urgency of the situation is such that we must address you now." Dulles made no response. He was determined not to appease the Jewish voters at the expense of his foreign policy.

On Election Day the Jewish voters made their displeasure felt. Harriman defeated Ives by less than ten thousand votes. Javits' Jewishness evidently was more of an asset than his Republicanism was a liability, for he triumphed over Roosevelt despite the magic of the latter's name. Another significant contest saw Richard Neuberger, a Jew, a Zionist, and a Democrat, elected to the Senate in Oregon by some two thousand votes; Neuberger's victory gave the Democrats control of the Senate by a 49–47 margin. The Democrats also regained control of the House of Representatives, though this was not an unqualified gain for Zionism, since the chairmanships of several important House committees thereby passed from Republicans who were warm friends of Israel to southern Democrats who were not.

The Republican leadership was shaken by the impact of the Near East question on the election; for a while there was talk of unloading Dulles by naming him to the Supreme Court. But in the end the President remained loyal to his Secretary of State. Dulles remained in his job; and the Near East moved in a circuitous way toward war.

3.

History is made by men, not by vast impersonal forces, though we sometimes tend to lose sight of that. The Suez crisis of 1956

was, in one sense, an inevitable collision between Jewish nationalism and Arab nationalism. But nearly every phase of that collision
emerged as a result of the individual strengths, weaknesses, stub-
bornnesses, piques, and tantrums of the handful of leaders involved.

The beginning of the chain of events that led to Suez, perhaps,
lies in the return to power in Israel of David Ben-Gurion in February, 1955. The peppery Ben-Gurion had retired as Prime Minister
at the end of 1953, and was succeeded by Moshe Shertok, who had
by then Hebraicized his name to Sharett. Prime Minister Sharett,
a more conciliatory man than Ben-Gurion, had hoped to work
toward some kind of peaceful accommodation with the Arabs.
Though Nasser at one point referred to him as "my brother Sharett," nothing substantial emerged. During 1954 and early 1955,
Arab *fedayeen*, or suicide raiders, repeatedly crossed the border
between Israel and Egypt; between September 1, 1954, and February 1, 1955, the Israel-Egyptian Armistice Commission censured
Egypt 27 times for armistice violations of this sort. Sharett urged
a policy of moderation in the face of these provocations.

Late in 1954, an internal political crisis in Israel forced a Cabinet
shuffle. Egypt arrested a group of Jews who, it was charged, had
plotted to blow up the United States Information Service library
in Cairo in order to damage relations between the United States
and Egypt. Nasser claimed that the affair was a scheme instigated
by Israel; and, to the embarrassment of the Sharett government,
it turned out that this was so. Certain subordinates of Defense
Minister Pinhas Lavon had given orders for the bombing, without
informing Lavon. In the scandal that followed, Lavon was forced
to resign, and Ben-Gurion replaced him as Defense Minister.

A tougher line was immediately evident in Israel's policies. In
February, 1955, Egyptian *fedayeen* raided Israel several times, and
on February 28—eleven days after Ben-Gurion's appointment to
the Defense Ministry—two platoons of Israeli paratroops crossed
the armistice line near Gaza and, in a rocket attack on a military
camp, killed 38 Egyptian soldiers. Alarmed by the ferocity of this
reprisal, Nasser turned to his friend John Foster Dulles, and asked
for $27,000,000 worth of arms.

Dulles hesitated. He still regarded Nasser as a benevolent and
progressive figure, but he was less willing now to sell weapons to
Arabs than he had been in 1954, when prospects of peace between

Israel and the Arabs had had at least a theoretical existence. To buy time, Dulles agreed to the arms sale, but hedged it with conditions he knew Nasser would not accept: that the weapons be paid for in dollars, a commodity in short supply in Egypt; that the arms not be used for aggression; and that Nasser permit an office of U.S. military aid to be opened in Cairo to supervise the use of the weapons. As expected, Nasser refused to meet the terms. What Dulles did not anticipate was that Nasser now would turn to the Soviet Union for arms, making pointless all of Dulles' seductive wooing of Egypt under the policy of "friendly impartiality."

In May, 1955, Nasser learned that the Russians were willing to make weapons available to Egypt, via her satellite of Czechoslovakia, on easy terms—barter of Egyptian cotton for tanks, jet planes, and guns. The next month Nasser again asked the United States for arms, threatening that if the U.S. did not comply he would get them from the Soviet world. Dulles regarded this move by Nasser as a poor attempt at blackmail; thinking Nasser was bluffing, he turned down the Egyptian request again. In July, Nasser closed his deal with Russia, and the first shipments of arms began secretly to leave Prague for Egypt on July 26. On September 27 Nasser publicly confirmed the rumors of the arms shipments, explaining that he had entered into agreement with Russia only after being refused arms by the United States, Great Britain, and France, who had made "demands" that would have cost Egypt her "freedom."

Dulles felt humiliated. Israel felt frightened by the entry of the Soviet Union into the Near Eastern situation, and asked the United States to restore the military balance by selling arms to her. "After considerable deliberation," President Eisenhower wrote, "we concluded that in the circumstances a United States shipment of arms would only speed a Middle East arms race; therefore we decided against it for the moment." Thereupon Israel began to look for help elsewhere. Foreign Minister Sharett* flew to Paris and obtained a pledge of help from Prime Minister Edgar Faure of France. France then was entangled in an Arab nationalist uprising in Algeria, and feared that a victory by Nasser over Israel might lead to an Arab unity movement that would endanger the French position in Algeria.

*After the Israeli election of July, 1955, Ben-Gurion had again become Prime Minister, with Sharett as his Foreign Minister.

In Israel, Prime Minister Ben-Gurion began to consider the possibility of launching a preventive war against Egypt. If the Russians arms shipments made it seem likely that Nasser would be able to carry out his boasts of destroying Israel, Ben-Gurion felt that Israel should strike first. On October 23, 1955, while Sharett was still in Paris, Ben-Gurion told the chief of staff of the Israeli army, Moshe Dayan, to begin drawing plans for such an attack. However, full-scale war did not break out even though border incidents and Israeli reprisals occurred repeatedly through the remaining months of 1955.

Alarmed by Russia's intrusion into the Near East, Dulles sought to salvage his friendship with Nasser by backing the Egyptian leader's pet engineering project, a giant new dam on the Nile at Aswan. This huge power and irrigation scheme had been in the planning stages for years, but Egypt had no way of meeting its costs—estimated at $1.3 billion—without foreign help. Nasser yearned for the dam as a symbol of Egypt's new modernism and dynamism, and Dulles saw it as a way of winning him back from his flirtation with Moscow.

In December, 1955, the United States and Great Britain announced that they were willing to help Egypt build the dam. Of the first $70,000,000 in costs, 80 percent would come from the United States and 20 percent from Britain as outright gifts; the next stage in the work would be financed by loans of $200,000,000 from the World Bank, $130,000,000 from the United States, and $80,000,000 from Britain, and so on until the dam was complete. "This, after all, is a cheap price to pay for peace and progress," Dulles said.

The offer carried considerable domestic political risk. "The Aswan Dam was not a popular project in this country, especially in the Congress," Eisenhower later wrote, "particularly in view of Nasser's apparent tendency to move closer to the Soviets; it would take all the pressure Foster and I could bring to bear to obtain congressional approval for our contribution, and we had little zest for an all-out legislative fight. . . ." Sherman Adams, Eisenhower's administrative assistant, noted in his own memoirs that "the members of Congress were acutely aware of the strong popular sentiment in this country for Israel" and that any pro-Nasser move such as this was bound to bring pro-Israel lobbies that were always effective and influential in the Capitol." When Dulles discussed the proposed Aswan financing with the leaders of Congress, Senate Democratic leader Lyndon B. Johnson was among those who questioned the wisdom of giving aid to Nasser. Dulles responded that Egypt might drift into the Soviet camp if the United States ignored her needs.

To the embarrassment and fury of Dulles and Eisenhower, though, Nasser reacted coolly to the Aswan offer when it was made public. He objected to certain conditions of the loans, such as the World Bank's standard requirement that it be given a voice in Egypt's economic policies in order to protect its investment. Nasser let it be known that the Soviet Union, too, was interested in financing the Aswan Dam, and that he was weighing the relative merits of the rival offers. By the spring of 1956, a dismayed Dulles realized that Nasser had deftly drawn him into a bidding contest with the Russians over Aswan.

Israel looked on apprehensively during the great powers' courtship of Nasser. She felt isolated and imperiled; her reprisals against Egyptian border raids grew more fierce as her insecurity deepened. In January, 1956, the Security Council censured Israel for the intensity of these reprisals, and warned that if she launched a preventive war against the Arabs, the UN would adopt economic sanctions against her. But Ben-Gurion continued to warn that Israel might be forced to wage such a preventive war if she did not get the arms she needed to match Nasser's new Russian weapons; Israel could not afford to wait until Egypt became invincible, but might have to strike within the next few months while she still stood a chance of victory with her present armaments. By March, Ben-Gurion was making such statements every few days.

Israel's fears had grown in February when news emerged that eighteen American tanks were waiting on a pier in Brooklyn for shipment to Saudi Arabia. Unable to obtain American arms herself, Israel protested this departure from the Tripartite Pact; in the uproar that followed, President Eisenhower investigated and reported that he found "nothing amiss" in the deal. Some restoration of the arms balance came in March, when France notified Eisenhower that she was selling twelve Mystère jet fighter planes to Israel. Objections from Eisenhower could have held up the transaction, but he let it go through.

The question of the Aswan Dam remained open, and Dulles was beginning to have second thoughts about his offer to finance the project. He was offended by the way Nasser seemed to be holding an option on the offer while prodding the Russians to better it; he had received a skeptical comment from Secretary of the Treasury George Humphrey about Egypt's ability to keep up the payments on the dam loans; and he was beginning to believe that not even a bribe the size of the Aswan Dam was sufficient to keep Nasser loyal to the West. Dulles was particularly wounded by Nasser's recognition of Communist China on May 15, 1956. To Dulles, that amounted to a recognition of the Antichrist. During the weeks that followed, the Secretary of State commenced the inner process of backing away from his Aswan commitment.

On June 13, 1956, the last British soldiers departed from Egypt, in accordance with the 1954 treaty. Five days later, Foreign Minister Shepilov of the Soviet Union joined Nasser at Port Said to help celebrate this triumph over the ancient evils of colonial imperialism, and a story was permitted to leak out to the effect that Shepilov had offered to provide Russian financing for the entire cost of the dam, at little or no interest and with 60 years to repay. On June 20, negotiations between Egypt and the World Bank over an Aswan loan came to a halt after Nasser put forth a series of conditions that were unacceptable to the bank and to the United States and Great Britain.

The new United States fiscal year began on July 1, and an appropriation for the Aswan work was included in the budget. But on July 10, Dulles told a press conference that it was "improbable" that Egypt would get the loan, and three days later he told Egypt, according to Eisenhower's account, that "we were not now in a position to deal with this matter because we could not predict what action our Congress might take and our views on the merits of the matter had somewhat altered. He told the Egyptians that we would consult with them the next week."

Nasser's next move in the daring game he was playing was to declare, unexpectedly, his willingness to accept the Western offer that he had been disdaining for the past six months. On July 16, he sent Ambassador Ahmed Hussein to Washington with instructions to settle the terms for the loan.

There are two interpretations of Nasser's motive. Perhaps the terms the Russians had given him were not as satisfactory as he had been telling the world, and, with the United States about to call his bluff, he suddenly wished to grab the better offer while it was still available. More probably, Nasser knew that his chances of getting the Aswan money from the West were now hopeless, and he was staging the charade in Washington so that he could use the inevitable rebuff from Dulles as the pretext for a dramatic new ploy—the seizure of the Suez Canal.

On July 19, Ambassador Hussein paid his call on Dulles. The day before the United States, chagrined over the rebirth of Nasser's interest in the Aswan loan, had conferred with Great Britain and France. The British Prime Minister, Sir Anthony Eden, had said he was willing to leave it to Dulles' judgment whether to grant or rescind the loan, but had warned, "We do not wish you to be precipitate; we wish you to play it long." Maurice Couve de Murville, the French ambassador in Washington, had said, "Beware how you handle the situation with the loan, because a most likely consequence of a refusal is the seizure of the Suez Canal." Dulles did not appear to believe that a seizure of the canal was likely.

Dulles' own intentions, as Ambassador Hussein entered his office, are difficult now to determine. Dulles himself claimed two months later that he had planned from the outset to tell Hussein that the deal was off, and he insisted that there was nothing abrupt about the cancellation, since Egypt should have sensed from American statements all during June and July that the offer was being withdrawn. A different version, though, is to be found in Herman Finer's massive study, *Dulles Over Suez*, which relies on the statements of "two very high State Department career officials" who were present at the meeting.

According to Finer, "Dulles began to explain the many difficulties he was encountering in clinching the loan. This took him a little time, as he always spoke very carefully, in rather pedantic language and syntax." Ambassador Hussein questioned him about certain aspects of the proposal. Dulles replied in a way that still left open the possibilities of further negotiations rather than total refusal. "Then, as Dulles appeared to be bringing the various reasons against the loan to a head, all in tones rather sad and firm, the Ambassador became excited. . . . He leaned forward over the table, gesticulating. 'Don't please say,' he blurted out, 'you are going to withdraw the offer, because . . .' (and he pointed to his pocket) 'we have the Russian offer to finance the dam right here in my pocket!'" Stung, Dulles retorted instantly, "Well, as you have the money already, you don't need any from us! My offer is withdrawn!"

Nasser's retaliation came a week later, on July 26. In a three-hour harangue against the treacheries of the West he announced that he was taking possession of the Suez Canal intending to apply its revenues to the costs of the dam. He imposed martial law in the canal zone and ordered all who worked at the canal, including foreigners, to remain at their jobs on pain of long-term imprisonment. Thus he boldly wiped out the last vestige of colonialism in Egypt and gained tremendous prestige throughout Africa and Asia.

The Suez Canal was then owned by a private corporation, most of whose stockholders were British and French. An international treaty of 1884 had guaranteed free access to the waterway—which links the Mediterranean Sea and the Indian Ocean by way of the Red Sea—to all nations, in peace and in war. Britain, regarding the canal as the lifeline of her empire, had guarded it since Queen Victoria's time, only to be pushed out by Nasser, with Dulles' help, in 1954–56. Nasser promised compensation to the Suez Canal Company's shareholders, but indicated that from now on he would be the arbiter who decided which nations could use the canal and which could not.

The affair of the Aswan loan had been transformed into an international crisis. The United States was not greatly affected by the fate of the canal, but Nasser's action caused consternation in Great Britain and France, where there was immediate talk of using military force to keep the canal out of Nasser's hands.

Here, again, Dulles' *a priori* beliefs played an important role. Though angry with Nasser, he, Dulles still held strong feelings about the importance of treating the emerging new nations with justice. An Anglo-French invasion of Egypt would be nothing more than an old-fashioned colonialist adventure. It would cause outrage through the entire noncommitted world, and allow the Russians to denounce the sins of the imperialist interventionists. If only as a matter of good public relations, Dulles would not tolerate the use of force against Nasser, and throughout the long, tense summer of 1956 the Secretary of State did everything in his power to prevent Britain and France from resorting to war as a remedy for the situation that Dulles' own maneuvers had helped to create.

Britain stood to lose the most from the seizure. A third of the ships that used the canal were British. Nearly a quarter of Britain's imports came through the canal, including most of her oil. At the time of the seizure she had about six weeks' reserves of oil on hand, at best. It seemed suicidal to Prime Minister Eden to let an Egyptian dictator have control over so vital an artery.

The French were aroused not so much by direct economic losses (although many Frenchmen were stockholders in the canal company) as by the desire to knock down Nasser, who was providing aid and comfort to the rebels in Algeria. Premier Guy Mollet, who viewed Nasser as an Arab Hitler, felt that the seizure of the canal by Egypt could serve as an excuse for ending Nasser's power before he consolidated his grip on the entire Arab world, to France's great injury.

Newspapers in Britain and France called for an invasion of Egypt. On July 27, the day following Nasser's harangue against the West, Eden cabled Eisenhower, "We are all agreed that we cannot afford to allow Nasser to seize control of the Canal this way. . . . If we take a firm stand over this now, we shall have the support of all the maritime powers. If we do not, our influence and yours throughout the Middle East will, we are convinced, be finally destroyed." Eden suggested the use of political pressure against Egypt first, but added, "we must be ready, in the last resort, to use force to bring Nasser to his senses. For our part we are prepared to do so." Eisenhower replied that he was convinced of "the unwisdom even of contemplating the use of . . . force at this moment," and was sending Dulles to London to work out a peaceful settlement.

Eisenhower later wrote, "We doubted the validity of the legal position that Britain and France were using as justification for talk of resorting to force. The weight of world opinion seemed to be that Nasser was within his rights in nationalizing the Canal Company. All considered the Canal to be a utility essential to global welfare rather than a piece of property to be operated at the whim of a single government; nevertheless, the waterway, although a property of the Canal Company, lay completely within Egyptian territory *and under Egyptian sovereignty.* The inherent right of any sovereign nation to exercise the power of eminent domain within its own territory could scarcely be doubted, provided that just compensation were paid to the owners of the property so expropriated. The main issue at stake, therefore, was whether Nasser would and could keep the waterway open for the traffic of all nations. . . ."

Aside from his basic distaste for a military solution in Suez, Eisenhower had a political reason for wanting to see the matter solved without shooting. This was a presidential election year. He intended to run again; his opponent, once more, would probably be Adlai Stevenson. The whole thrust of his first term in office had been toward world peace: first a disengagement from Korea, then the establishment of a close and relatively warm relationship with Russia's post-Stalin leadership. He did not want to see the end of his term marred by conflict.

In London, Dulles persuaded the British and French to take no action on Suez until after a conference of 24 nations that used the canal. The conference opened on August 16, 1956, with 22 nations present. Greece had declined to attend, and so, unhappily, had Egypt. Dulles put forth an involved and ultimately futile plan for a "Suez Canal Users' Association," which would be an international board to run the canal in cooperation with Egypt.

The labyrinthine negotiations over the users' association consumed many weeks, although everyone quickly saw that the association would have no power to compel Nasser to do anything he did not care to do—such as to allow Israeli shipping through the canal. While the talking continued, Britain and France quietly began to plan a joint military operation to overthrow Nasser and restore the canal to international control. The first meetings were held early in August.

Although Dulles himself had told the British in August that Nasser must be made "to disgorge" the canal—a phrase that the British interpreted as American sanction for force if diplomatic means failed—Eisenhower continued to urge moderation. A letter to Eden on September 2, signed by Eisenhower but written by the President with Dulles' aid, pointed out, "I believe . . . we can expect the Arabs to rally firmly to Nasser's support . . . [if] there should be a resort to force without thoroughly exploring and exhausting every possible peaceful means of settling the issue. . . ." The President noted that "Nasser thrives on drama," and suggested "deflating him through slower but sure processes," although he added, "I assure you we are not blind to the fact that eventually there may be no escape from the use of force. . . . But to resort to military action when the world believes there are other means available . . . would set in motion forces that could lead . . . to the most distressing results. . . ."

The Prime Minister of England, Anthony Eden, was a tense, restless man, who had spent most of his career in the shadow of Winston Churchill. He felt under severe pressure to demonstrate that he had mettle of his own, and chafed and writhed as weeks went by and Nasser continued to hold the canal. All of Britain cried out to Eden to do something about Nasser; but Eisenhower's warnings against war held him back. So Eden put his faith first in the users' association scheme, and when that collapsed, in a settlement imposed by the United Nations. On September 23, the Security Council decided to take up the Suez problem, with debate to begin within two weeks.

By then, however, Britain and France were seriously considering a way of making war against Nasser by proxy—using Israel as their standard-bearer.

Israel too was in an explosive mood. Cocky over his capture of the canal, Nasser had stepped up the pace of border raids against the Jewish state. The *fedayeen* raiders were striking at least once a week, and in the summer of 1956 had killed more than twenty Israelis while doing heavy damage to installations and crops. Worse, the Arabs seemed to be preparing for more orthodox warfare: Egypt and Syria, long bitter rivals, had established a joint military command late in 1955, and both countries now were receiving Russian arms as well as the services of Russian military experts. As the Arab military buildup continued, Ben-Gurion began to feel that the time for preventive war had come.

There were tentative discussions of military collaboration between Israel and France as early as August. Eden, still nervous about the American insistence on keeping the peace, would not hear of the idea. But gradually he began to see that the scheme had possibilities. Given enough arms, Israel might well bring Nasser down, and no one could say that it had been a war of shameless European imperialist powers against a struggling new nation. By the end of September, serious Franco-British discussions over a secret alliance with Israel were under way, and an assortment of generals and diplomats began to commute between Tel Aviv and Paris.

France seems to have been the dynamic force. Eden by nature

was inclined to hesitation and self-doubt, and Ben-Gurion, for all his ferocity, wondered if Israel were quite ready for this adventure. But France pushed the plan forward, and insisted that the war must begin just before November 6. That was the date of the American election. The French believed that Eisenhower, mindful of the Jewish vote, would be unable to condemn any Israeli military action at that time.

On September 29, Moshe Dayan and Shimon Peres of Israel flew to Paris to discuss strategy and to complete negotiations for tanks and trucks. When they returned to Israel, Dayan told his staff on October 2 that the war could begin as early as October 20, and would probably last about three weeks.

Still hoping to win Eisenhower's support, Eden telegraphed the President on October 1, "Nasser . . . is now effectively in Russian hands, just as Mussolini was in Hitler's. It would be as ineffective to show weakness to Nasser now in order to placate him as it was to show weakness to Mussolini." Dulles replied the next day with a strong attack on the Suez policies of Britain and France; he said the United States would have nothing to do with "colonial powers." On October 5, when the foreign ministers of Britain and France were in New York for the UN debate on Suez, they told Dulles that they did not believe any peaceful way to resolve the crisis existed. They regarded this as fair warning that war was coming.

During the next few days, UN Secretary-General Hammarskjöld developed a six-point peace formula. The Security Council approved the plan unanimously, and there actually appeared hope of a settlement for a moment. "A very great crisis is behind us," Eisenhower told the nation.

But Nasser showed no disposition to accept the Hammarskjöld formula. "It was no use to fool ourselves on that account," Eden's memoirs comment. "We had been strung along over many months of negotiation, from pretext to pretext, from device to device, and from contrivance to contrivance." It was time to act, before the rising fury in Great Britain over Nasser's impudence forced his hand. On October 16, Eden and his Foreign Secretary, Selwyn Lloyd, flew back to London from the United States to make final plans for war.

One day earlier, Eisenhower had received a disturbing intelligence report. High-flying reconnaissance planes had discovered

Israel to have, not the twelve Mystère jets the French had announced they were selling her, but *sixty* Mystères. Evidently France was surreptitiously shipping arms to Israel! Eisenhower and Dulles concluded that Israel was thinking of seizing some of Jordan's territory, perhaps the West Bank area that was, geographically if not ethnically, a natural part of Israel. The idea that Israel might be planning an attack on Egypt did not occur to them, nor did they imagine that collusion among Britain, France, and Israel was developing. "Both Foster and I," Eisenhower wrote, "suspected that Ben-Gurion might be contemplating military action during these pre-election days because of his possible overestimate of my desire to avoid offending the many voters who might have either sentimental or blood relations with Israel. I emphatically corrected any misapprehension of this kind he might have." Dulles did the actual correcting, by calling in Israeli ambassador Abba Eban, who was about to depart for home, and telling him that the sympathies of American Jews would not have "any iota of influence" on Eisenhower's judgment in foreign policy matters.

On October 22, Ben-Gurion and Dayan flew to Paris for secret meetings with the French leaders and Foreign Secretary Selwyn Lloyd of Great Britain. Over the next few days the actual structure of the action against Egypt evolved; only the highest-level members of the three governments took part in the planning. It was arranged that Israel would invade the Sinai Peninsula on the quite legitimate excuse that Egypt was preventing the free movement of Israeli shipping through the Gulf of Aqaba. (Egyptian gun emplacements at Sharm el-Sheikh at the tip of the Sinai effectively had sealed the Strait of Tiran, the outlet from the Gulf of Aqaba to the Red Sea.) The Israelis would claim that in order to keep the Strait of Tiran open they needed to sweep the Egyptians out of all of Sinai, and so, turning east, they would march to the Suez Canal. At that point, Britain and France proposed to intervene, calling upon Israel and Egypt to withdraw from the canal zone. Israel would at once do so, but Egypt, of course, would not, giving the two great powers their opportunity to attack Nasser in order to "protect" the canal.

By Thursday, October 25, these arrangements were complete. That night, having returned to Israel, Dayan issued a directive setting the time of attack for sundown on Monday, October 29. He noted that the purpose of the operation was "(1) To create a military threat to the Suez Canal by seizing objectives in its proximity. (2) To capture the Strait of Tiran. (3) To confound the organization of the Egyptian forces in Sinai and bring about their collapse."

Keeping these plans secret was virtually impossible. American reconnaissance planes must have observed Israeli troop movements; the CIA, it is thought, picked up some details of the plot by cracking diplomatic codes; even *Pravda,* on October 27, reported that military intervention in Egypt was about to begin. But President Eisenhower, already somewhat distracted from day-by-day surveillance of the situation by the demands of the election campaign, suddenly was compelled to turn his attention away from the Near East altogether toward an even more explosive situation. Suddenly, unexpectedly, Russia's empire in Eastern Europe seemed to be breaking up in a popular revolt!

The trouble had begun in Poland on October 19. Under the leadership of Wladyslaw Gomulka, the Polish Communist Party demanded greater independence for Poland from Russia, ousting pro-Russian officials and even defying Soviet leader Nikita Khrushchev, who flew to Warsaw to try to end the coup. Students paraded in Polish cities, crying, "Long live free Poland!" The unrest quickly spread to Hungary, which on October 23 went even further than Poland, launching an actual armed revolution to drive the Russians out.

The same day, Democratic candidate Adlai Stevenson, speaking in New York, called for a "new U.S. foreign policy" and demanded that Israel be given the arms needed to guarantee her territorial integrity; but Eisenhower had no time to think about Israel now. One day later news came that 10,000 Russian troops and 80 tanks had entered Budapest to crush the Hungarian uprising.

For years, Secretary of State Dulles had urged Eastern Europe to throw off the Soviet yoke, promising American aid if a liberation movement began. Now the liberation movement was under way, and Hungarian patriots were dying; what would the United States do? Dulles' bluff had been called. Any aid to the rebellious Hungarians would be an act of war against Russia. The thought of beginning World War III ten days before the election was unattractive to Eisenhower.

As Eisenhower followed the events in Hungary and Poland,

reports came to him of an Israeli arms buildup and of gossip in London that some action against Egypt was coming. On October 27 he cabled Ben-Gurion: "I renew the plea . . . that there be no forceable initiative on the part of your Government which would endanger the peace." Then he entered Walter Reed Hospital in Washington for a pre-election checkup. Dulles went to Texas to deliver a speech. The next day, Sunday, Eisenhower was still in Walter Reed and Dulles was flying back from Texas when word came from the American ambassador in Tel Aviv that war was imminent. Undersecretary of State Herbert Hoover, Jr. took the message to the hospital. Eisenhower responded with another message to Ben-Gurion urging that Israel take no hostile actions. On Monday, October 29, at 4 P.M. Israel time (9 A.M. in Washington), 16 planes dropped 395 Israeli paratroopers at the Mitla Pass in the Sinai Peninsula, 30 miles east of the Suez Canal. The war was on.

4.

It was a short war, shorter than anyone expected. On the first day, Israeli ground troops plunged through the Sinai Desert to reinforce the paratroopers at Mitla, while other striking units headed into the Gaza Strip and down the west coast of the Gulf of Aqaba toward Sharm el-Sheikh. The Israelis had 50,000 troops and 200,000 ready reserves. Egypt had an army of 75,000 equipped with Russian-made jet fighters and bombers, but the advantage of surprise aided the Jews, and before the war was 16 hours old the Egyptians were in disarray all over the Sinai.

Dulles, shocked and angered, called for United Nations condemnation of Israeli aggression. Adlai Stevenson assailed Dulles' "incredible blunders" in a campaign speech the evening of October 29, and Republican leaders went to Eisenhower to tell him that they believed that the Israeli affair could cost him the election. They reasoned, Eisenhower later wrote, that it might be necessary for the United States, "as a member of the United Nations, to employ our armed strength to drive them back within their borders. If this turned out to be the case, much of the responsibility would be laid at my door. With many of our citizens of the eastern seaboard emotionally involved in the Zionist cause, this, it was believed, could possibly bring political defeat." But no one urged the President to draw back from condemnation of Israel.

Eisenhower was puzzled over British and French intentions in the crisis. On the evening of October 29, Henry Cabot Lodge, the American ambassador to the UN, met with Sir Pierson Dixon, the British ambassador to the United States, to ask British backing for a UN resolution against Israel. Dixon was completely unsympathetic, saying bluntly that Britain would not consent to any anti-Israel action whatever. The next morning, Eisenhower cabled Eden for a clarification. What, he wondered, had become of the 1950 Tripartite Pact, pledging the United States, Great Britain, and France to maintain the territorial *status quo* in the Near East? His message crossed with a cable from Eden saying, "Egypt has to a large extent brought this attack on herself . . . we cannot afford to see the Canal closed. . . ."

Later in the day, Britain and France made the prearranged next move, by delivering ultimatums to Egypt and Israel. This was the text of the note to Egypt:

"The Governments of the United Kingdom and France have taken note of the outbreak of hostilities between Israel and Egypt. This event threatens to disrupt the freedom of navigation through the Suez Canal, on which the economic life of many nations depends. The Governments of the United Kingdom and France are resolved to do all in their power to bring about the early cessation of hostilities and to safeguard the free passage of the Canal. They accordingly request the Government of Egypt:

(a) to stop all warlike action on land, sea and air forthwith;

(b) to withdraw all Egyptian forces to a distance of ten miles from the Canal; and

(c) in order to guarantee freedom of transit through the Canal by the ships of all nations and in order to separate the belligerents, to accept the temporary occupation by Anglo-French forces of key positions at Port Said, Ismailia and Suez.

"The United Kingdom and French Governments request an answer to this communication within twelve hours. If at the expiration of that time one or both Governments have not undertaken to comply with the above requirements, United Kingdom and French forces will intervene in whatever strength may be necessary to secure compliance."

A similarly worded note was presented to Israel, requesting the withdrawal of Israeli troops to a point ten miles east of the canal.

The United States did not learn of the ultimatums until after they had been issued. A few months later, French Premier Mollet

admitted that the customary diplomatic courtesy of notifying the
United States had been dispensed with out of fear that the United
States, if forewarned, might have been able to cause a fatal delay
in the operation, during which Israel could be destroyed. If the
United States had been allowed to interfere, Mollet said, "we
should have been weeping for Israel annihilated, as we today
weep, impotent, for Hungary martyred."

Since Israel had not yet driven within ten miles of the canal, she
interpreted the October 30 ultimatum as a warrant to keep going
forward. Egypt, naturally, rejected the ultimatum. That afternoon
Ambassador Lodge presented a resolution to the Security Council
calling on all members of the UN to refrain from using force in
the Near East. Russia supported it, but it was vetoed by Britain and
France. They also vetoed a Soviet resolution asking Israel to pull
back to the 1949 armistice lines. The United States now turned to
the General Assembly, where vetoes were impossible, to obtain a
cease-fire resolution.

The Anglo-French ultimatum to Egypt expired at midday on
October 31. Within a few hours, French fighter planes had established a defense umbrella over Israel's cities. French destroyers
were already patrolling the coast. One of them attacked an Egyptian vessel an hour before the deadline. The French vice-admiral
then wired Paris, "Have crippled Egyptian destroyer. But not
entirely sure Egyptian. If this should prove a mistake it is not a
deliberate attack ... on the [U.S.] 6th Fleet." As night fell, 200
British and 40 French planes took off from aircraft carriers in the
Mediterranean and from bases on Malta and Cyprus and bombed
Egypt's airfields, catching most of the planes on the ground, and
eliminating the entire Egyptian air force in a few hours. That day,
the Egyptians had succeeded in holding Israel back at one vital
road junction in north-central Sinai and were bringing up reinforcements that might well be able to break the Israeli advance.
But now that Nasser realized he was at war with Britain and
France, he hurriedly ordered a general withdrawal of his troops
from the Sinai, pulling all forces back to defend Cairo, Port Said,
and Alexandria. As dawn came on November 1, the Israelis realized that the Sinai was theirs. They moved at will through the
whole region, cutting off and capturing thousands of the retreating
Egyptians.

Eisenhower and Dulles were aghast. Dulles guessed at once that there had been a coordinated Anglo-French-Israeli plan—he got confirmation of that from his ambassador to France on November 2—and he was angered by this treachery on the part of America's two most important allies. He became aware that all summer, while he and the President had urged peace, Britain and France must have been plotting war with the Israelis. The United States had been mocked.

The timing of the attack was appalling, too. The Russians were on the verge of sending in a major force to put down the revolt in Hungary, in the face of warnings issued by the West about the immorality of large nations crushing the nationalistic aspirations of small nations. Suddenly here were Britain and France destroying the West's position of moral superiority through an unabashedly imperialistic attack on helpless Egypt!

On the evening of November 1, Dulles drafted a statement announcing that the United States was suspending all military and some economic aid to Israel until an end came to the hostilities. That night, in a campaign speech in Philadelphia, Eisenhower spoke sadly of the present necessity of the United States to disagree with "those great friends," Britain and France, but said, "There are some firm principles that cannot bend—they can only break. And we shall not break ours." With five days to go before the election he canceled all further campaigning to concentrate on the foreign emergencies. The next morning the General Assembly called for a cease-fire by a vote of 64 to 5, with Britain, France, Israel, Australia, and New Zealand voting nay. Israel, that day, occupied the coastal town of El Arish, which the Egyptians had abandoned in such haste that wounded soldiers had been left on operating tables in mid-surgery.

Saturday, November 3, saw Prime Minister Eden reject the cease-fire resolution, saying that Britain and France intended to send troops into Egypt and keep them there until the United Nations sent a peacekeeping force into the Near East to maintain order. Estes Kefauver, the Democratic vice-presidential candidate, charged that the entire crisis had originated in the American "preoccupation with oil," while Eleanor Roosevelt asserted that Israel had gone to war in self-defense, and that the Eisenhower administration was pro-Arab. In the afternoon, Dulles, whose health had been weakening throughout the crisis, was taken to Walter Reed Hospital for emergency surgery; the doctors discovered that he was suffering from cancer. Eisenhower, a man of great good will but little experience with statesmanship, would have to carry on alone.

As though the Anglo-French attack on Egypt had given them license to do so, the Russians launched a particularly brutal suppression of the Hungarian revolt that Sunday: 200,000 troops and 4,000 tanks entered Budapest. Mopping-up operations continued in the Sinai. Israel had occupied the whole Gaza Strip and had taken control of the Strait of Tiran. In Washington, Undersecretary of State Herbert Hoover, Jr. summoned Reuben Shiloah of the Israeli embassy (Ambassador Eban was at the UN) and told him, according to an account by Ben-Gurion, "We are on the brink of war. Israel's refusal to comply with the Assembly's [cease-fire] decision is endangering the peace of the world. Israel's attitude will inevitably lead to grave consequences, such as the stoppage of all governmental *and private* aid to Israel, sanctions by the U.N., and perhaps even expulsion from the United Nations Organization." (Emphasis added.) Whether Eisenhower knew that a member of his government was threatening, two days before the election, to prohibit American Jews from giving aid to Israel, is uncertain.

At dawn on Monday, November 5, 600 British paratroopers were dropped west of Port Said, and 487 French paratroopers landed south of the city. By seven that evening the Egyptian commander had surrendered. Israel, that day, completed her conquest of the Sinai. Her victory over Egypt had been strikingly swift, though it would have been far more difficult to attain if the Anglo-French bombings on October 31 had not forced Nasser to call home his troops.

Russia, which had been preoccupied with Hungary all week, now stepped into the Near Eastern conflict. On Monday night, Russian Premier Nikolai Bulganin sent Ben-Gurion a harsh note expressing "unqualified condemnation" of "the armed aggressions of Israel," which Russia said was "acting as an instrument of external imperialistic forces." Bulganin went on, "The Government of Israel is criminally and irresponsibly playing with the fate of peace and with the fate of its own people. It is sowing hatred of the State of Israel among the Eastern peoples, which cannot but leave its impression on the future of Israel and which puts a question mark against the very existence of Israel as a State."

Simultaneously Bulganin informed France and Great Britain that if they did not get out of Egypt, Russia was ready to crush them with "every kind of modern destructive weapon." Another Russian note, to Eisenhower, suggested that the Soviet Union and the United States join forces to enter Egypt and put an end to the fighting. But of course it was inconceivable that Eisenhower would agree to form an alliance in a war against Israel with those who had just raped Hungary.

Nevertheless, the Russian threats gave Eisenhower some leverage in his attempt to halt the attack. He sent word to Ben-Gurion that if Israel did not retreat from the Sinai Peninsula, she could expect no help from the United States in the event of a Soviet attack. Then the United States put pressure on Britain. Eden was exhausted by now; there was genuine alarm in Britain over the possibility of war with Russia; in Parliament, the opposition Labour Party was enraged over British "aggression" in Egypt, and many members of Eden's own Conservative Party were dismayed by the doubtful morality of their leaders' secret maneuvers that had led to war. Also, suddenly, the pound sterling had come under selling pressure in the world's financial markets. Britain's gold reserves had fallen by £100,000,000 since the outbreak of the war, and Eden now learned that the United States Treasury Department had refused to take certain steps to protect Britain's currency, but that aid would be forthcoming if Eden agreed at once to a cease-fire.

The economic pressure from Washington was the final shove. On Tuesday, only a day after the Anglo-French forces had gone into Egypt, and before Nasser could be overthrown, Eden capitulated and ordered a cease-fire effective at midnight, so that a United Nations military force could take command in the Near East.

The war was over. Nasser still ruled in Cairo, though his prestige had been greatly tarnished. France and Britain had gained none of their policy objectives, having allowed the United States to frighten them out of Egypt when they were at the point of achieving triumph. The only apparent victor was Israel, which held the Sinai.

Tuesday, November 6, was also Election Day. Eisenhower's stern attitude toward Israel made no difference at all in the outcome of the presidential race. Most Jewish voters cast their ballots for Adlai Stevenson, which they probably would have done re-gardless of world events. But Eisenhower drew the biggest popu-lar-vote total in American history, carried 42 states, and collected 457 electoral votes to 73 for Stevenson. However, both houses of Congress had Democratic majorities: the Senate by 49 to 47, the House of Representatives by 234 to 201. Never before had the voters chosen a President of one party and a Congress of the other.

Eisenhower now turned to the task of undoing by diplomacy what Israel had won by force. The government of the United States had ceased to regard Israel as a valiant and heroic bastion of Western civilization in the midst of Arab backwardness. Israel had a new image now: an aggressor state, a modern Sparta popu-lated by Jewish militarists. The Eisenhower administration took upon itself the task of mobilizing world opinion against Israel to compel her to give up what she had won.

5.

American Jews, during the Suez affair, had found themselves singularly unable to influence the course of events. They had been, like nearly everyone else, largely unaware of the highly personal nature of the diplomacy of the summer, whereby great actions were governed by Dulles' puritanism, Nasser's braggadocio, Ben-Gurion's belligerence, Eden's uncertainty. They had applauded Dulles when he spurned Nasser on the question of the Aswan Dam money; they had cheered on France and Great Britain when those nations called for the overthrow of Nasser by force after the Suez Canal seizure; they had been thrilled by Israel's lightning victory. (Universally they ignored the fact that Israel had struck the first blows in the war. To them the Sinai campaign was a justifiable act of self-defense made necessary by innumerable and intolerable provocations, and not an act of aggression in any way.) America's Jews had looked on with some perplexity as the Eisen-hower administration labored to halt the war that seemed so just and so satisfying to them; and now their perplexity turned to outrage as they watched the President trying to compel Israel to surrender the fruits of victory.

Anthony Eden, weary and drained and full of self-doubt, ter-rified of American threats to knock down the value of the pound if he did not cooperate, had given in to Eisenhower on November 6, calling off the Anglo-French invasion of Egypt. Thus the Suez adventure, the final flourish of British imperialism, became a political catastrophe, abortive and pointless. It shattered Eden's own career and sent Britain reeling into a devastating re-examination of her role as a world power.

But David Ben-Gurion attempted to hold firm. He announced on November 7 a rejection of the United Nations order to withdraw Israeli forces from the Sinai Peninsula and the Gaza Strip. Israel had been intoxicated by her victory; in eight days she had routed some 75,000 Egyptians and captured a vast tract of territory, placing a huge buffer zone between herself and Egypt and opening the vital Strait of Tiran. Just 172 Israelis had been killed, 817 wounded, four captured. Egypt's losses had been some 3,000 dead, 7,000 captured. More than 100 tanks, nearly 200 pieces of artillery, and immense stocks of gasoline and ammunition had been abandoned to the Israelis during the flight from the Sinai.

But on the same day, November 7, that Ben-Gurion announced Israel's determination to stay in the captured territory, he received Eisenhower's note of November 5, dealing with Russia's threat to intervene against Israel. It spoke of Eisenhower's "deep concern" over Israel's refusal to withdraw, and expressed "the greatest regret" that Israeli policy might "impair the friendly cooperation between our two countries." But it also indicated bluntly that if Israel continued to maintain the posture of an aggressor, in defiance of the United Nations, she would get no American aid should Russia move in.

Ben-Gurion met with his Cabinet for nine hours on the following day. He was shaken by the tone of Eisenhower's note, and finally sent word to Washington via Ambassador Eban that Israel would withdraw her forces "upon conclusion of satisfactory arrangements with the United Nations in connection with this international force entering the Suez Canal area." Ben-Gurion also declared, "We have never planned to annex the Sinai Desert." Golda Meir, who had replaced Moshe Sharett as Foreign Minister of Israel, sent a similar message to the United Nations. She stressed that an Israeli pullback had to be accompanied by a show of good will by Egypt, which would have "to abandon its policy of boycott and blockade, to cease the sending into Israel of murder gangs, and in accordance with its obligations under the U.N. Charter to live at peace with Member States, to enter into direct peace negotiations with Israel."

Creation of the United Nations Emergency Force, as the peace-keeping army was to be called, did not immediately materialize; the UN would spend many months in debate before bringing it into existence. Nor did Nasser make any gesture of seeking peace with Israel. But Israel carried out a voluntary withdrawal from almost the whole of the Sinai in December, 1956, and January, 1957. However, she insisted on keeping possession of two places. One was the Gaza Strip, which directly adjoined Israel proper and had never been part of Egypt in the first place; it had been Palestinian territory until seized by Egyptian troops in 1948. The other was the region at the southern tip of the Sinai around Sharm el-Sheikh, which controlled the outlet of the Gulf of Aqaba. Israel maintained that she could not afford to give back to Egypt a place so vital to the free flow of her maritime commerce.

Several things motivated Israel's evacuation of the Sinai. One was fear of Russian intervention. Another was respect for international opinion. Also, Ben-Gurion, who knew Eisenhower well, regarded the President as a warm, responsive man who would not let Israel down if Israel made some show of cooperation. Possibly Ben-Gurion was influenced by a telephone call he received from a well-known American Jew who was a generous contributor to the United Jewish Appeal. Supposedly this man told Ben-Gurion that Israel would jeopardize the status of the American Jewish community by defying the wishes of President Eisenhower.

But United Nations Secretary-General Hammarskjöld was not satisfied with the Israeli withdrawal, nor was Eisenhower. They wanted a complete pullback to the 1949 armistice lines—which meant giving up Sharm el-Sheikh and the Gaza Strip. Here a deadlock developed, for Israel would not budge from those two places. On January 23, 1957, Ben-Gurion suggested that a withdrawal was possible, but only if Israel received guarantees that the United Nations would safeguard her against raids from Egyptian guerrillas based in the Gaza Strip and would insure her the right of free passage through the Strait of Tiran. These guarantees were not forthcoming, and Israel held on.

She grew even more determined after King Saud of Saudi Arabia—the son and successor of Ibn Saud—came to the United States on January 29 to confer with Eisenhower. The visit of this powerful monarch, and the pomp with which he was received by the American government, left Israel fearful that Eisenhower would sell out her interests to insure the continued flow of Arabian oil. (Saud got a bumpy greeting when he arrived in New York. There were Jewish demonstrations against his presence, and New York's Mayor Wagner, mindful of the sensitivities of his many Jewish constituents, announced that the customary formal reception given by the city to visiting heads of state would be omitted.)

The American Jewish community was growing restless over the Eisenhower administration's handling of the war's aftermath. On December 30, 1956, Emanuel Neumann, the president of the Zionist Organization of America, had made a nation-wide radio broadcast attacking the Eisenhower policies. "What we are witnessing," he said, "is the contemplated restoration of all occupied territory to Nasser's control. Having suffered a crushing military defeat, he is now to gain an undreamed-of political triumph. Not only is Israel to give up the fruits of victory—but the fleeting chance to establish a stable peace will have been thrown away. Nasser's prestige would not only be re-established, but enhanced, his power consolidated and his capacity for mischief immensely increased. If this be the policy of the United Nations and the United States, it is not statesmanship, but incredible folly."

Neumann saw "no reason in law or justice" why Israel should relinquish to Nasser the Gaza Strip, "a dagger pointed at her very heart—reaching as it does to within 35 miles of Tel Aviv." As for the Strait of Tiran outposts, "These points are nothing but rocky wilderness without human habitation. They are of no possible use to anyone except for one purpose and one purpose only: to be used as gun positions for maintaining unlawful blockade of an international waterway. ... Are we now going to insist that Egypt's illegal blockade be restored?"

Neumann noted that "in a democracy like ours, government policy is subject to the corrective influence of public opinion"— a signal that Jews well understood. Once more a letter-writing campaign began. Most of the correspondents defended the entire Anglo-French-Israeli intervention in the Near East, denying that any collusion had been involved or that aggression against Egypt had occurred. Many of them quoted editorials from Jewish publications, such as *Jewish Frontier*'s January, 1957, comment that "it might have been more politic if the United States government had been less rigidly moralistic in regard to its allies, and had shown a more sympathetic readiness to appreciate the causes which individually impelled Britain, France and Israel to oppose Egyptian designs."

Several powerful Senate figures spoke out against the pressure being placed on Israel to complete her troop withdrawal. They included such prominent Democrats as Lyndon B. Johnson, Hubert Humphrey, and J. W. Fulbright. Another strong supporter of Israel was the Senate Republican leader, William F. Knowland of California. To Knowland, a political conservative noted for his bitter anti-Communism, it seemed "immoral and in good conscience unsupportable" for the United Nations and the United States to be prodding Israel to pull out of Sharm el-Sheikh and the Gaza Strip while doing nothing at all to force Russia to withdraw from conquered Hungary. On January 29, 1957, members of both parties introduced a joint resolution in the Senate and the House, calling on the United States to seek guarantees in the United Nations against "a resumption of border raids and blockades of international waterways" in the Near East.

Secretary of State Dulles, who had returned to action following a period of convalescence, indicated that he too felt it was proper for the United Nations to offer Israel such guarantees. Dulles had learned a great deal about the Near East in the hardest possible way in 1956. Having seen his efforts to stave off war end in total disaster, he now recognized to a large extent the justice of Israel's case against Nasser and the equity of Israel's demand for protection in return for military withdrawal.

Secretary-General Hammarskjöld, though, took a narrower view of the situation. He felt that the prestige of the United Nations had been severely damaged by the Russian crushing of Hungary and the Anglo-French-Israeli war against Egypt. Since the UN was plainly powerless to chastise Russia, Hammarskjöld was determined to make a stand over the Near East. With Eisenhower's help he had forced Britain and France to pull out, and he wanted Israel out too, without any further discussion. Hammarskjöld began to talk about the necessity of imposing economic sanctions on Israel if she continued to defy the United Nations order to withdraw. Eisenhower and his ambassador to the UN, Henry Cabot Lodge, appeared to share this stern, simplistic view.

On February 2, Lodge offered two UN resolutions. One called on Israel to complete her withdrawal to the 1949 armistice lines. The other asked Israel and Egypt to abide by the terms of the 1949 armistice and directed the Secretary-General to place the United Nations Emergency Force on the 1949 boundaries to maintain peace. Both resolutions were passed. The next day Eisenhower wrote to Ben-Gurion to press for withdrawal, saying, "You know how greatly our nation values close and friendly relations with yours, and we wish to continue the friendly cooperation which has contributed to Israel's national development. . . . Such continued ignoring of the judgment of the nations, as expressed in the United Nations Resolutions, would almost surely lead to the invoking of further United Nations procedures which could seriously disturb the relations between Israel and other member nations." Eisenhower meant economic sanctions.

On February 5, Dulles told a news conference, "We would not take any action in the way of sanctions unilaterally. If there was action by the United Nations calling for sanctions, we would of course have to give them very serious consideration. . . ." In fact, the United States was already applying economic sanctions of a sort against Israel, as *The American Zionist* pointed out in its February, 1957, issue: "All U.S. economic aid for Israel, amounting to some $30 million in the current fiscal year, has been stopped. Technical aid has likewise been stopped. Military purchases, though very small, are not being honored. No passports are issued for travel to Israel, thus hurting its income from tourism. Negotiations for a $75 million loan by the Export-Import Bank were stopped. The sale of American surplus foods to Israel was also stopped. What is this, if not economic pressure in the form of sanctions? On several occasions recently the State Department had promised to call off these sanctions and resume economic and other assistance, but it was not done. Instead, there is talk of more and stricter sanctions to give Israel 'the economic squeeze.' "

The impetus for sanctions, actually, was coming not from the United States but from a General Assembly majority made up of the Soviet Union and her various satellites and subsidiary republics, and more than two dozen Asian and African nations demonstrating solidarity with Egypt against "colonialism." But Eisenhower was willing to follow the lead of these nations if no compromise avoiding sanctions could be worked out. And Ben-Gurion, on February 8, sent word that he would not submit to the UN resolutions of the previous week. Israel would withdraw her troops, but only if she retained civil administration and police power in the Gaza Strip, and if the United Nations guaranteed freedom of passage in the Gulf of Aqaba.

"Are we not, like other states, entitled to security from attack?" Ben-Gurion asked in a letter to Eisenhower. As for sanctions, "Is it conceivable that the United States, the land of freedom, equality, and human rights, should support such discrimination and that United Nations 'procedures' should be invoked to force us back into a position which would again expose us to murder and blockade? . . . Mr. President, in the Law which we received more than three thousand years ago on Mount Sinai and which has become part of mankind's heritage, the message went forth that there shall be no discrimination between man and man and between nation and nation. Throughout millennia of persecution our people have not lost faith in ultimate justice, peace and human equality. It is unthinkable now that we have recovered our independence in our ancient homeland we should submit to discrimination. . . . The question is not a legalistic one. It affects the very foundations of international morality: will the United Nations apply one measure to Egypt and another to Israel?"

On February 11, Dulles and Eban met to discuss the situation, and Dulles offered to back Israel's demands at least in part. He presented Eban with a memorandum acknowledging that the Gaza Strip had been a base for armed infiltration into Israel, and Dulles committed the United States to ask the United Nations to establish its peacekeeping force on the boundary between Israel and the strip, so that further such infiltration could be prevented. With regard to the Gulf of Aqaba, the memorandum said, "The United States believes the Gulf comprehends international waters and that no nation has the right to prevent free and innocent passage in the Gulf and through the Straits giving access thereto." The United States claimed free passage in the gulf for vessels of United States registry, and "is prepared . . . to join with others to secure general recognition of this right. It is of course clear that the enjoyment of a right of free and innocent passage by Israel would depend upon its prior withdrawal in accordance with the United Nations Resolutions."

Dulles warned Eban that this was as far as the United States was willing to go toward guaranteeing that the Strait of Tiran would be kept open to Israeli shipping. If Israel did not accept this February 11 pledge and forthwith withdraw from the two disputed areas, Dulles implied, the United States was likely to support the United Nations in any unfriendly action against Israel, such as sanctions or even the use of force. But on February 15 Eban received word from Ben-Gurion that Dulles' promises were unacceptable to Israel; the guarantee of free passage lacked real substance, and the Gaza statement committed only the United States, not the United Nations.

Unaware of their government's behind-the-scenes efforts to end the impasse, the American Jewish community kept up the pressure on Eisenhower for a softer line on Israel. Among the many communications the White House received was a lengthy telegram from the Midwest Conference on the Middle East, a meeting of delegates of seventeen major Jewish organizations (B'nai B'rith, American Jewish Congress, Hadassah, Jewish War Veterans, etc.) of eleven states. Referring to the "defensive action of Israel in the Sinai Desert initiated on October 29, 1956," the cable expressed the hope that the conditions making that action necessary would not be permitted to reappear. It asked the President to persuade the United Nations to guarantee the freedom of passage of all ships through all international waterways, including the Strait of Tiran and the Suez Canal, and to take the Gaza Strip under its own direct supervision. The Jewish leaders also requested the United States, "through its good offices directly and through the United Nations indirectly," to bring about direct peace negotiations between Israel and her Arab neighbors. Other communications from American Jews accused Eisenhower of applying a double standard, requiring Israel to live up to one code of behavior and Egypt another. Fair play for Israel, they asked—and many Gentile Americans echoed that demand.

The Eisenhower administration was baffled. Nasser apparently would not consent to having the United Nations Emergency Force enter the Gaza Strip and Sharm el-Sheikh if Israel withdrew; Ben-Gurion would not withdraw unless the United Nations pledged to occupy the two disputed zones. Sherman Adams, the key White House adviser, wrote some years later, "Now the United States had to make the hard choice whether or not to join the United Nations majority in imposing sanctions on Israel. Supporting Nasser on this issue would be unpopular both in Congress and throughout much of the nation, but all the legal arguments favored it."

On February 15, after Ben-Gurion's latest refusal came through, Dulles and Lodge flew to Georgia, where Eisenhower was vacationing. They agreed on the necessity to take a strong stand against Israel despite the trouble this would stir up in Congress. The United States had gone as far as it could, Dulles maintained, in meeting Israel's conditions for withdrawal. Since Israel still would not withdraw, the United States now must support the UN move toward economic sanctions.

Eisenhower went even further. Secretary of the Treasury George Humphrey, who was present at the meeting, provided the information that American private gifts to Israel amounted to about $40,000,000 a year, and the current annual sales of Israel bonds in the United States ran from $50,000,000 to $60,000,000. Eisenhower's memoirs relate that the President proposed "a resolution which would call on all United Nations members to suspend not just governmental but *private* assistance to Israel. Such a move would be no hollow gesture." Two days later, the White House released a statement from Georgia that revealed the text of Dulles' February 11 memorandum, cited Ben-Gurion's rejection of its terms, and asserted that the United Nations now must take firm steps to end the stalemate.

There were quick senatorial reverberations. Lyndon Johnson, as Senate Democratic leader, wrote to Dulles protesting, "The U.N. cannot apply one rule for the strong and another for the weak; it cannot organize its economic weight against the little state when it has not previously made even a pretense of doing so against the large states." His Republican counterpart, Senator Knowland, threatened to resign as an American delegate to the General Assembly if sanctions were voted against Israel. On February 19, the Senate Democratic Policy Committee backed the Johnson statement and urged President Eisenhower to resist any UN attempt to impose sanctions on Israel. Eisenhower decided to end his vacation and return to Washington for a conference with the rebellious congressional leaders on the following morning.

Dulles, at this point, hit on a curious device for making Ben-Gurion more cooperative. He asked a Jewish friend in New York to supply him with a list of prominent American Jews who would come to Washington and receive a direct briefing from him on the Israel problem. Then, Dulles hoped, these leaders would see that only Ben-Gurion's recalcitrance was blocking a solution, and they would put pressure on Israel to withdraw from the two disputed areas without demanding stronger guarantees than had already been offered.

Eight names were proposed, but the group was an odd one, since it included no representatives at all of the American Zionist movement, and quite a few Jewish philanthropists who had once been considered non-Zionist. Those on the list were: Irving Engel and Jacob Blaustein, president and a former president of the American Jewish Committee; Barney Balaban, the head of Paramount Pictures; Philip M. Klutznick, president of B'nai B'rith; Samuel D. Leidesdorf, treasurer of the United Jewish Appeal of Greater New York; Louis Novins of Paramount Pictures; Mendel Silverberg, a Los Angeles philanthropist; and William Rosenwald, the national chairman of the United Jewish Appeal. These eight agreed to see Dulles on February 21.

At 8:30 on the preceding morning Eisenhower met with 26 congressional leaders, including Democratic Senators Johnson, Fulbright, Mike Mansfield, and Carl Hayden, Republican Senators Knowland, Styles Bridges, Eugene Millikin, and Everett Dirksen, and such formidable House figures as Speaker of the House Sam Rayburn, Charles Halleck, and John McCormack. Lodge and Dulles were present at the meeting. So was Vice-President Nixon, who remained silent throughout the two and a half hours of discussion, for he was unwilling to get between two such powerful Republicans as Eisenhower and Knowland.

The President opened the meeting by explaining why he favored putting pressure on Israel for an unconditional withdrawal. Sherman Adams, who was there, tells us that Eisenhower felt that "such compliance was needed for Israel's own good," since "Ben-Gurion's government would soon be in a dangerous financial crisis unless it obtained help from the Export-Import Bank, which would be possible only if peace were restored." Also Eisenhower warned that failure to force Israel to comply with the withdrawal order would bolster Russia's influence among the Arabs, and might wreck the United Nations. It could even lead to a general war. "Nobody likes to impose sanctions," Eisenhower concluded, "but how else can we induce Israel to withdraw to the line agreed on in the 1949 armistice? The Arabs refuse to discuss a permanent settlement until that move is made."

The congressional leaders looked impatient, unconvinced, and stubborn. Lyndon Johnson in particular, Sherman Adams says, wore "a determined expression which seemed to say that he was not going to yield an inch."

Dulles took over, stressing the damage that would be done to the UN if Israel were allowed to remain defiant. Britain and France had withdrawn from Egypt at a considerable cost of prestige and political power, Dulles said, but Israel stayed on, questioning the good faith of the UN and insisting on impossibly ironbound pledges as a condition of departure. Sanctions now had to be imposed, or some other forceful alternative found. Dulles said, Adams relates, that "the rest of the world believed that on any crucial question such as this one Israel could control United States policy because of the strong favor it enjoyed in America. Therefore, Dulles asserted, the Arabs were watching us intently and, if we confirmed this belief, they would feel compelled to turn to Russia. 'But this does not mean that we have to follow an anti-Israel policy,' he added."

Knowland wanted to know why the United Nations had not applied sanctions against Russia over Hungary. Lodge replied that the facts of political life made such a move unlikely. Knowland then asked if the UN's debate on sanctions could be postponed a few weeks while new efforts were made toward a settlement with Ben-Gurion. Lodge said that if the United States asked a postponement, it would appear as if we were opposing sanctions.

Eisenhower now attempted to get the support of the group for, as he put it, "a statement setting forth our convictions and intentions." No one else in the room realized that any "convictions and intentions" had taken form that morning. Eisenhower, Lodge, and Dulles still seemed to favor sanctions, and most of the congressional leaders did not. The Democrats—Johnson, Rayburn, McCormack, notably—made it clear they were not going to sign any statement calling for a crackdown against Israel. Neither would Knowland and most of the other Republicans present. If the government wished to take an unpopular stand, the congressional leaders indicated, Eisenhower would have to bear all the responsibility for it. Senator Richard Russell of Georgia summed up the discussion by suggesting that since unanimity was impossible, the President "should simply shoulder the burden alone and make a statement to the people similar to the one he had made at the beginning of the meeting." Eisenhower answered that he intended to do just that, and read off the main points of a speech already scheduled for national broadcasting that night.

As he left the meeting room, Lyndon Johnson told the reporters outside, "Our views have not changed." Senator Johnson went on, "I regret that the Administration still feels that there is no choice but to bring pressure on one side in a two-sided dispute in the Middle East."

Eisenhower and Dulles spent the rest of the day polishing the President's speech, and at nine in the evening on February 20 Eisenhower went on the air. He called for Israel to withdraw unconditionally: "Should a nation which attacks and occupies foreign territory in the face of United Nations disapproval be allowed to impose conditions on its own withdrawal? ... If the United Nations once admits that international disputes can be settled by using force, then we will have destroyed the very foundation of the organization. ...."

Israel, Eisenhower said, should rely on the United Nations and the United States to see that guerrilla raids from the Gaza Strip ceased and that the Gulf of Aqaba remained open to Israeli shipping; but she did not have the right to *insist* on these conditions as a necessary prelude to withdrawal. He did agree that Israel had every reason to expect safeguards against attack from Gaza, although it would not be proper for Israel to maintain civil control over the strip.

As for the Gulf of Aqaba, Eisenhower reaffirmed Dulles' February 11 words: "The Gulf constitutes international waters and ... no nation has the right to prevent free and innocent passage in the Gulf." Then Eisenhower took a position that went somewhat beyond Dulles' statement: "We should not assume that, if Israel withdraws, Egypt will prevent Israeli shipping from using the Suez Canal or the Gulf of Aqaba. If, unhappily, Egypt does hereafter violate the Armistice Agreement or other international obligations, then this should be dealt with firmly by the society of nations."

Turning to the question of why the UN was being so tough toward Israel while seemingly condoning the far more flagrant Soviet attack on Hungary, Eisenhower said, "I do not believe that Israel's default should be ignored because the U.N. has not been able effectively to carry out its resolutions condemning the Soviet Union for its armed suppression of the people of Hungary. Perhaps this is a case where the proverb applies that two wrongs do not make a right." He passed over the point that Israel's aggression, if such it had been, had been undertaken to preserve her national existence, while that of Russia had been aimed at destroying the national existence of another country. But Eisenhower did concede that the UN's condemnations of Israel and Russia did not necessarily mean that the two "aggressors" had committed crimes of equal magnitude: "There can, of course, be no equating of a nation like Israel with that of the Soviet Union. The people of Israel, like those of the United States, are imbued with a religious faith and a sense of moral values. We are entitled to expect, and do expect, from such peoples of the free world a contribution to world order which unhappily we cannot expect from a nation controlled by atheistic despots."

The speech, for all its efforts at fair-mindedness, was indisputably a call for strong pressure against Israel. Though Eisenhower had not actually spoken of sanctions, the implication that he favored them was clear, and letters began flowing toward the White House as soon as he went off the air. Some of them were curious documents, such as the communication from a Christian lady in Texas who supplied a cluster of Biblical quotations to prove that God had promised Palestine to the Jews. Others were closely reasoned essays by well-known Republican Jewish industrialists, attempting to show Eisenhower how he had misunderstood Israel's position.

The day after the speech, the delegation of eight prominent American Jews that Dulles had summoned arrived in Washington in a state of high outrage. They spent an hour and a half with Dulles. The Secretary of State explained the complexities of the American position, and expressed resentment over the accusation that he himself was anti-Semitic. As a practicing Christian, he said, he could not hold such unworthy sentiments. His visitors were not mollified. One of them said, "I don't know anything about politics or diplomacy. But I do know that for our country to try to bludgeon Israel against its own vital interests is morally wrong." When Dulles offered to take them to talk with the President, they refused, because of their anger over his speech.

Though this meeting was not supposed to have been publicized, the newspapers quickly found out about it. The stories made it appear as though Dulles had been looking for an obliging array of non-Zionist Jews to give their blessing to America's hard line on Israel, and thousands of American Jews promptly wrote in to say that whatever Dulles' visitors might have told him, the majority of Jews in the United States were firmly behind Israel. There was hostile editorial comment, too, such as this Philadelphia *Inquirer* editorial:

Secretary of State Dulles' action in calling into conference certain U.S. leaders in Jewish humanitarian activities, presumably to exert pressure in the Israeli situation, is an arrogant intimidation of one group of American citizens.

It is also as stupid a device as could possible be imagined to advance State Department ends in trying to resolve current differences with the Israeli Government.

It has, additionally, overtones of illegality in seeking to exert the influence of private citizens upon a foreign power. Secretary Dulles may have forgotten about it, but U.S. law provides that no U.S. citizen may seek to influence a foreign government in any dispute involving the United States.

What the Secretary was doing in calling his extraordinary conference was establishing an alarming and thoroughly unjust precedent.

It would contain the implication of dual citizenship—as though certain influential Jews have as earnest a devotion to the State of Israel as they do to the United States.

The firmness of Eisenhower's February 20 speech led Ben-Gurion to seek a settlement more eagerly; he was probably also influenced by the action of Lebanon, Iraq, the Sudan, Pakistan, Afghanistan, and Indonesia in introducing a General Assembly resolution that would have cut off all foreign aid to Israel, including private contributions.

The issue of sanctions appeared to be moving toward a showdown. Eban, who had been in Israel for consultations, returned to the United States and held a series of meetings with Dulles, out of which came, on February 28, an agreement between the United States and Israel over Israel's withdrawal from the occupied territories. The next day, Foreign Minister Golda Meir announced this agreement at the United Nations in a speech that had been drafted by Eban and another Israeli in collaboration with two members of the State Department. It provided that any interference with Israeli passage in he Gulf of Aqaba and through the

Strait of Tiran would be regarded by Israel "as an attack entitling it to exercise its inherent right of self-defense" under the UN Charter, thus sparing Israel from condemnation as an aggressor if she found it necessary someday to evict hostile forces there. As for the Gaza Strip, it was agreed that the United Nations Emergency Force would have exclusive jurisdiction there until a peace settlement or some other definitive treaty emerged. Israel reserved the right to step in if there was any return to "the conditions of deterioration which existed previously."

Under this agreement Israel withdrew from the Gaza Strip and from Sharm el-Sheikh. By March 7, 1957, no Israeli troops remained in the strip, and the United Nations Emergency Force, made up of Danish and Norwegian troops, moved in. The UNEF also soon took over at Sharm el-Sheikh. On March 11, Egypt appointed a civil administrator for Gaza, claiming the right to do so under the 1949 armistice agreement. The UN commander, to Israel's consternation, allowed the Egyptians to take control of the Gaza Strip two days later. Golda Meir pointed out that Israel, in agreeing to leave Gaza, had certainly not contemplated the immediate arrival of the Egyptians, but no one now shared Israel's concern over the betrayal. For the next ten years, the United Nations Emergency Force would be present in the strip, but Egypt would administer it.

Short of going to war all over again, there was nothing the Israelis could do about it. They had been played for fools; they would never again trust the United Nations, nor would they be greatly impressed by the promises of the United States. They had been cleverly and cynically induced to give up virtually everything they had gained in the 1956 war. All that remained to them was the freedom to use the Gulf of Aqaba—for the UNEF did take over the administration of the Strait of Tiran—and the quiet confidence that they would be able to smash Nasser again if he gave them sufficient provocation. The Suez crisis thus came to its anticlimactic end. The Near East grew quiet; but nothing, nothing at all, had been settled.

6.

The seeds of the 1967 war were planted by the 1957 "settlement." Israel had submitted to international coercion and had allowed herself to forfeit her newly won advantages. She had even chosen to accept Nasser's coup in Gaza, after she belatedly realized that the United States had never pledged to do anything more about Gaza than recommend United Nations occupation of it. The UN had been overridden there by Egypt, and could do nothing about it, and there was no American obligation to set things to rights. So Israel gave in. But at the Strait of Tiran she drew the line. Late in March, 1957, Ben-Gurion told an American journalist, "I don't want any of our young people to die. Nor do I want one Egyptian boy to die because of Nasser's mad schemes. But if Nasser tries to block our historic and legal passage into the Gulf of Aqaba, we will meet him not at a peace table, but elsewhere with our armies."

The decade that followed before that confrontation took place was marked by the tortuous efforts of the great powers to arrive at a consistent Near Eastern policy. The goal of the United States was to maintain peace and international stability there. The goal of the Soviet Union was to achieve maximum Communist penetration through the fomenting of disorder. Neither policy was an outstanding success.

The initial United States reaction to the Suez crisis was the Eisenhower Doctrine, conceived late in 1956 and formally approved by Congress in March, 1957. This committed the United States to use its armed forces in defense of any Near Eastern country asking help against "overt armed aggression from any nation controlled by international Communism," and provided $200,000,000 for economic and military aid to all countries of the Near East.

Egypt and Syria, now dependent on Soviet arms shipments, could be deemed "controlled by international Communism" in terms of the Eisenhower Doctrine, and American protection thus became available to any state that felt menaced by the nationalistic ambitions of these two lands. This included not only Israel but also some of the moderate, pro-Western Arab countries, whose conservative rulers feared the radical socialist ideas emanating from Cairo and Damascus. By making fervent declarations of anti-Communism, these Arab countries could (and did) receive arms from the United States under the new doctrine.

Iraq, Lebanon, and Libya immediately endorsed the Eisenhower Doctrine. Saudi Arabia, Yemen, and Israel offered more cautious support. Egypt and Syria were silent. Jordan was a special case. The British, who had invented the country, finally had been evicted, and the Jordanian government was rapidly transforming the state into a pro-Soviet satellite of Egypt. In the spring of 1957, the youthful King Hussein dismissed his country's Nasserite leaders and took personal command. The United States, invoking the Eisenhower Doctrine, warned Egypt and Syria to keep their hands off Jordan, and declared that Jordan's independence and integrity were "vital" to world peace. The American Sixth Fleet moved into the eastern Mediterranean to underline those statements. Hussein prevailed, and Jordan was drawn into close association with the United States.

Continued upheavals in the Arab world kept the patterns shifting. In 1958, Syria and Egypt entered a short-lived merger under the name of the United Arab Republic. A revolution in Iraq later that year swept away the pro-Western government and the Hashemite monarchy and created a belligerent dictatorship that was at once pro-Soviet and anti-Nasser. To prevent disorders from spreading, the United States was forced to send troops to Lebanon, and Britain landed paratroopers simultaneously in Jordan. The net effect of all of these maneuvers was to draw the United States deep into the maelstrom of Near Eastern politics without gaining much real influence.

Israel, meanwhile, had settled back to a business-as-usual way of life, undergoing systematic shellings from Syrian gun emplacements in the hills above the Galilee and *fedayeen* raids from terrorists based in the Gaza Strip, and striking back with occasional reprisals. The Suez Canal, which Nasser had retained after the 1956 uproar, still was closed to Israeli shipping. The Strait of Tiran remained open.

Nasser, who had come within a day or two of destruction in the 1956 war, now was demonstrating not only his extraordinary capacity for survival but also his ability to manipulate the two superpowers at will. In 1958 he visited Moscow and obtained Russian financing for the Aswan Dam; but in 1959 he began to court the United States once more. Nasser had no more interest in turning Egypt into a Russian satellite than he had in making it an American one. He was one of the first neutralist leaders to realize how to exploit the Soviet-American rivalry for his own nation's benefit. Thus, while taking Russian money and skill for his dam, Nasser persecuted the domestic Communists of Egypt and Syria, who represented a threat to his own authority. And, while unfailingly denouncing the United States as a stooge of Israeli imperialism, Nasser coyly moved into a position where he might become eligible again for American foreign aid.

John Foster Dulles, of course, would have no dealings with Nasser after the contretemps of 1955–56. But Dulles resigned as Secretary of State in the spring of 1959, to die of cancer soon afterward, and his successor in the waning days of the Eisenhower administration, Christian Herter, explored in a far more flexible way the possibility of closer relations between the United States and Egypt. That exploration continued after John F. Kennedy became President in 1961. Although Kennedy recognized a strong United States commitment to Israel, he did not see that as a barrier to the development of American ties with Egypt. Kennedy viewed Nasser as a legitimate and important nationalist leader, and, like Dulles, thought there was a chance to wean him from anti-Israeli and pro-Russian attitudes through a policy of friendship.

The Israel issue was intimately involved in the exceptionally close 1960 election. Indeed, it may have been the deciding factor in Kennedy's narrow victory over Richard M. Nixon. Kennedy himself apparently believed it was.

Neither candidate had generated much enthusiasm when the campaigning season began. Nixon was regarded by Democrats and a good many Republicans as generally unscrupulous, untrustworthy, and unfit for high office; the Democrats nicknamed him "Tricky Dick," with damaging political effect. But Kennedy, a 43-year-old Massachusetts senator, did not inspire much greater confidence; he seemed too young, too ruthless, too ambitious. The sentimental favorite among Democrats still was Adlai Stevenson, one of the many men Kennedy had pushed aside in his rush to the nomination. Kennedy's rugged good looks and youthful vitality made older voters suspicious. The personal magic that he exerted had nothing to do with politics, but seemed more like the appeal of a movie star. Democrats, particularly Jews, also questioned Kennedy's credentials as a liberal. He had failed to speak out against Senator Joseph McCarthy's reign of terror in the early 1950's; he was a Roman Catholic, who presumably might let the Vatican dictate his policies; and his father, Joseph Kennedy, was widely thought to have been sympathetic to Hitler while serving as President Roosevelt's ambassador to Great Britain. Kennedy realized that he could not win the election, despite Nixon's general unpopularity, unless he convinced the country that he was mature enough to be President, and unless he convinced the liberal Democrats that he deserved their support.

He had, in fact, begun his quest for Jewish votes as far back as 1956, when he first started to work toward the 1960 Democratic nomination. Speaking at the annual banquet of Histadrut, the Israeli labor federation, in Baltimore on November 27, 1956, Kennedy declared, "It is time that all the nations of the world, in the Middle East and elsewhere, realized that Israel is here to stay." He reiterated that theme in frequent appearances before other Jewish groups. In February, 1959, addressing the Golden Jubilee Banquet of the fraternal order of B'nai Zion in New York, Kennedy praised the "magnificent achievement" of the Zionist pioneers, and denied the "myth . . . that it is Zionism which has been the unsettling and fevered infection in the Middle East."

Later that year, speaking in Oregon, he said, "Let us make it clear that we will never turn our back on our steadfast friends in Israel, whose adherence to the democratic way must be admired by all friends of freedom. But let us also make clear throughout the Middle East that we want friendship, not satellites—and we are interested in their prosperity as well as ours."

But in the summer of 1960 Kennedy still had not succeeded in establishing an identity liberal enough to satisfy the Jewish voters. In New York City, particularly, there was much talk of simply staying home on Election Day, since Nixon and Kennedy seemed indistinguishable and equally unacceptable. (There was so much talk, indeed, that Arthur M. Schlesinger, Jr. hurriedly turned out a pro-Kennedy book intended to show that there *was* a difference between the two men.)

An opportunity to make some dramatic move toward the Jewish sector of the electorate came when the Zionist Organization of America invited both candidates to address its national convention in New York in August, 1960. Nixon, always prudent, refused to speak, apparently on the advice of his campaign managers that the Zionists represented only one rather controversial faction of American Jewry; he had no wish to get involved in someone else's quarrels. Kennedy did not seek anyone's advice. He accepted the invitation and told his aides to draft the strongest pro-Israel speech possible.

When he received the draft, Kennedy tightened it himself to

make it even more outspoken. Then he showed it to Philip M. Klutznick, the head of the Business Men's Committee for Kennedy and Johnson, and Kennedy's unofficial adviser on Jewish affairs. Klutznick said, "You must remember you're committing yourself 'way out.'" Kennedy was undismayed.

He addressed the Zionists on August 25, 1960, telling them of his visit to Palestine in 1939, when he had seen how "the neglect and ruin left by centuries of the Ottoman Empire was slowly being transformed under conditions of the utmost difficulties by labor and sacrifice," and how he had returned in 1951 to see the promise of Zionism fulfilled: "I left with the conviction that, though the United Nations had given international status to Israel, nevertheless Israel had been made a nation by its own efforts. And it has claims to immortality." Repeating his observation that "Israel is here to stay," Kennedy criticized Arab leaders who called for Israel's destruction, and then attacked the Eisenhower administration—of which Nixon had been part—for its treatment of Israel:

"Our policy in Washington and in the United Nations has permitted defiance of our 1956 pledge with impunity—indeed, with economic reward. The Israelis surrendered their 1956 victory only because the United States and the United Nations committed ourselves to the fulfillment of a pledge of free transit in the Suez Canal. So this is a United Nations resolution in which we have a particular moral obligation."

Kennedy stressed the universality of our commitment to Israel:

"It is worth remembering ... that the cause of Israel stands beyond Jewish life ... it has not been merely a Jewish cause, any more than Irish independence was the cause merely of those of Irish descent, because wherever freedom exists, there we are all committed. And wherever it is endangered, there we are all endangered.

"The ideals of Zionism have, in the last half century, been endorsed by both parties, and Americans of all ranks in all sections. Friendship for Israel is not a partisan matter. It is a national commitment.

"Yet within this national obligation of friendship there is a special obligation on the party of which I am a member. It was President Woodrow Wilson who prophesied with great wisdom a Jewish homeland. It was President Franklin Roosevelt who kept alive the hope of Jewish redemption in the days of the Nazi terror. It was President Harry Truman who first . . . recognized the status of Israel in world affairs.

"And may I add that it would be my hope and pledge to continue this great Democratic tradition, to be worthy of it, to be associated with it, for what is needed now is leadership—impartial but firm, deliberate but bold; leadership instead of rhetoric."

He restated the Tripartite Pact of 1950, declaring, "We will act promptly and decisively against any nation in the Middle East which attacks its neighbor. I propose that we make clear to both the Israelis and the Arabs our guarantee that we will act with whatever force and speed is necessary to halt any aggression by any nation." He asked an end to the arms race in the Near East; and he promised economic and technical assistance to Israel and her neighbors: "The Middle East needs water, not war—they need tractors, not tanks—and they need bread, not bombs."

The speech caused a sensation in the Jewish community, and its ringing phrases of praise for Israel were to be quoted conspicuously in Democratic leaflets distributed in Jewish neighborhoods. The Jewish voters talked less and less about McCarthyism, the Pope, and Ambassador Joseph Kennedy. On Election Day they turned out heavily for Kennedy, giving him margins of 75 percent, 80 percent, even 90 percent in some areas. The Jews of Illinois voted more solidly for Kennedy than they had for Truman; Kennedy won Illinois' 27 electoral votes by a popular-vote margin of less than 9,000 out of 4,750,000 cast. In New York, with 45 electoral votes, a strong Nixon surge upstate was overwhelmed by the ballots of New York City, with its millions of Jews; Kennedy carried the state by 384,000 votes out of 7,380,000 cast. Had New York and Illinois gone Republican, Nixon would have become President in 1961.

A short while before his inauguration Kennedy met with Prime Minister Ben-Gurion, and—so Ben-Gurion later told C. L. Sulzberger of *The New York Times*—Kennedy declared, "I was elected by the Jews of New York and I would like to do something for the Jewish people." Ben-Gurion was shocked. "Why should he say such a thing to a foreigner?" he asked Sulzberger.

But during his tragically brief term in office, Kennedy disappointed his Jewish supporters by taking what seemed like an excessively sympathetic position toward Arab nationalism. He corresponded frequently and warmly with Nasser, expressing his pleasure over the Egyptian leader's program of industrialization and modernization; he tried to persuade a reluctant Congress to appropriate foreign aid for Egypt and other declared enemies of Israel; in April, 1962, the United States was one of the sponsors of a UN resolution strongly condemning Israel for a reprisal raid on Syria the previous month. American Jewish groups sharply criticized Kennedy for the American role in securing adoption of this resolution of censure, and spoke out harshly against the President's proposals for financial and military aid to the Arabs. They did not accept Kennedy's argument that showing good will to the Arabs would ultimately allow the United States to exert an influence in the Near East beneficial to Israel. Dulles had used the same argument, with catastrophic results. Nor did the American Jews know that in 1961 Kennedy had secretly sent his special assistant, Myer Feldman, to Israel to pledge American military protection in the event of an attack on the Jewish state. Feldman also was authorized to offer Israel Hawk antiaircraft missiles in return for an Israeli promise not to develop nuclear weapons. (The story of Feldman's visit did not become public until 1968.)

By the autumn of 1963, Kennedy was in serious political trouble with the American Jews over his gentle treatment of the Arabs and his apparent coolness toward Israel. With less than a year to go before the 1964 presidential election, there was speculation that Kennedy might begin to move toward stronger support of Israel, if only for purposes of domestic politics. And when he agreed to speak in New York on December 5, 1963, at the annual dinner of the Friends of the Weizmann Institute, it was generally assumed that he would use this opportunity to take some stand favorable to Israel.

An assassin's bullet prevented President Kennedy from keeping his date with the Friends of the Weizmann Institute. When the dinner—postponed because of the period of national mourning—finally was held in February, 1964, President Lyndon B. Johnson was the main speaker. During his Senate career, Johnson had been one of Israel's strongest friends. No one was surprised, then, when he said, "Tonight, as I speak to you with affection and share with you pride in Israel's achievements, I speak the warm sentiments uttered by every American President since Harry Truman." Then he astounded his listeners and threw the Arab world into confusion by declaring that the United States "has begun discussions with the representatives of Israel on cooperative research in using nuclear energy to turn salt water into fresh water."

Johnson, a Texan with a keen appreciation of the problems of desert life, was genuinely eager to collaborate with Israel in an attack on the problem of desalinizing water with nuclear energy. But he had no intention whatever of helping Israel make atomic bombs. (Actually, Israel already had the technological capacity—if not the economic resources—to produce nuclear weapons.) The Arabs, though, interpreted Johnson's speech as a sharp and frightening break with the Kennedy policies. Even if it did not imply —as some Arab leaders feared—that Johnson was going to instruct Israel in atomic warfare, it certainly meant a much greater commitment by the United States to Israel's development than had been evident under Kennedy. A day after Johnson spoke, Nasser told an Indian interviewer that war was inevitable in the Near East because Israel was bent "on expanding her empire from the Nile to the Euphrates." A week later, on February 22, Nasser said over Radio Cairo, "The prospects are for war with Israel. But this time it is we who will dictate the time; we who will dictate the place."

Belligerent announcements by Arab leaders had long been part of the normal climate of discourse in the Near East, but now they became more frequent and more violent. Late in 1964, President Abdul Salem Aref of Iraq said, "We must put an end to Israel's existence, and with the help of Allah, and the support of all nations that believe in justice, we shall." Syrian Chief of Staff Salah Jedid declared, "Our army will accept nothing short of the disappearance of Israel."

The Soviet Union, whose influence in the Near East had been gradually diminishing, reasserted itself. In February, 1964, Premier Khrushchev received a royal reception on a state visit to Egypt. He promised hundreds of millions of dollars' worth of new military aid to Nasser, and the promise was kept by Khrushchev's successors after his fall from power eight months later. Syria, too, was the recipient of Soviet benevolence.

A new and more violent cycle of raids and reprisals began as the Near East drifted toward another war. Between January, 1965, and May, 1967, guerrilla raiders trained in Syria carried out 113 acts of sabotage in Israel, killing 11 Israelis and injuring 62. There were 50 bombings in the first six months of 1966 alone. Egyptian raiders continued to cross into Israel from the Gaza Strip, though much less often than they had in 1955–56. Jordan, though less militantly anti-Zionist than her Arab neighbors, nevertheless permitted the use of Jordanian territory as jumping-off places for the guerrillas. So did Lebanon.

Israel had little appetite for a new war; she was politically divided and in serious economic trouble. Prime Minister Ben-Gurion had retired in 1963, choosing another veteran Zionist, Levi Eshkol, as his successor. Eshkol immediately angered Ben-Gurion by refusing to continue the investigation into the scandalous Lavon affair, growing out of the 1954 attempt by certain Israeli officials to stir up trouble between Egypt and the United States by blowing up an American library in Cairo. When Eshkol laid the venerable *cause célèbre* to rest, Ben-Gurion denounced him from his place of retirement on a *kibbutz* in the Negev, seriously damaging Eshkol's authority in the nation. The gentle and grandfatherly Eshkol, a man who eternally searched for ways of compromise, seemed too mild a leader to many Israelis, particularly with war increasingly likely. Eshkol refused to step down under fire, but the feud among the country's highest leaders left the Jewish state demoralized.

Nor did the economic problems help Eshkol's position. Israel's standard of living had long been rising more rapidly than her output of goods, and the result was a steady and widening gap between exports and imports. The problem was aggravated by Israel's continuing need to import fuel and arms, and by the end of the war reparations payments from West Germany, which for years had bolstered Israel's reserves of hard currency. Severe inflation was one result. And much of the blame fell on Eshkol, who had been Finance Minister during the decade when the economic crisis had been building up. By 1966 he found it necessary to deal with the situation by halting the growth of the economy. The deflationary measures brought on a steep recession, a wave of bankruptcies and unemployment, and a general disruption of Israel's economic progress. Immigration fell sharply and the emigration of Israelis to other lands increased. Watching Israel's internal difficulties worsen all through 1966, the Arabs began seriously to think that the moment had come to rid themselves of their unwanted Jewish neighbors.

7.

The Arab menace was the salvation of the Eshkol government. The threat from without served to unify the quarreling Israelis and distract their attention from their domestic troubles.

The process of rebuilding national morale began with a savage attack on Jordan, intended as a retaliation for recent terrorist activities. Jordan was a relatively benign Arab country, conscious of her military weakness and looking for no trouble with Israel. But the Israelis found Jordan's willingness to harbor Syrian guerrillas objectionable, and hoped to intimidate her into withdrawing that hospitality. Between July and November, 1966, Jordan-based terrorists had carried out 40 raids on Israel; now Israel administered a reprisal designed to discourage further such adventures.

Early on the morning of November 13, 1966, two Israeli armed columns escorted by 17 tanks and 80 armored half-tracks crossed into Jordan east of Beersheba, heading for the village of Es Samu, four miles over the border. Es Samu, with some 4,000 people, was suspected of being a base for terrorists. The Israeli invaders were under orders not to take lives. As dawn broke, the villagers found grim Israeli soldiers in their midst; they were ordered from their homes, and dynamite squads began blowing up buildings as a punitive measure. Some 125 houses, a school, and a clinic were destroyed. While this was going on, a Jordanian battalion blundered into Es Samu, believing that the Israelis were actually attacking a different town several miles away. With a long convoy of Jordanian trucks coming straight toward them, the Israelis had no choice but to open fire. The first Israeli volleys hit 15 of the trucks and killed 15 of their 70 occupants. The rest of the Jordanian force was allowed to retreat, and the Israelis returned to their own land.

The Es Samu raid was a tremendous success in Israel—the first sign that the unpopular Eshkol government had any muscle—but the rest of the world reacted badly. The United States, Britain, France, and the Soviet Union all called on the United Nations to censure Israel. Some of the strongest language came from the American ambassador to the UN, Arthur J. Goldberg, who, although Jewish, spoke out sharply against the Israeli action. Though the earlier terrorist raids were "deplorable," he said, "this deliberate governmental decision must be judged as the conscious act of responsible leaders of a member state and therefore on an entirely different level from the earlier incidents which we continue to deplore." Goldberg accused Israel of having authorized "a raid into Jordan the nature of which and whose consequences in human lives and in destruction far surpass the cumulative total of the various acts of terrorism conducted against the frontiers of Israel." The Security Council voted to censure Israel, a move denounced by American Zionist groups as "one-sided."

The Arab nations failed to comprehend the extent to which the Es Samu raid had buoyed Israeli spirits. Instead, convinced that Israel was on the brink of internal collapse, they intensified their acts of aggression in the early months of 1967. Provocation of an all-out war does not seem to have been their intention. Regarding Israel as too weak to launch a major attack, they hoped to drain her further by constant attrition and harassment until she was so feeble she could be occupied without a real struggle.

Border tensions were greatest along Israel's short frontier with Syria. In the first three months of 1967, Israel filed 790 formal complaints of Syrian violations of the 1949 armistice, which was still in effect. Then, losing patience, the Israelis sent planes out to defend their settlements along the Syrian border, and on April 7 an air battle took place in which the Syrians lost six Russian-made Mig fighters, a significant portion of their entire air force. This did not halt the Syrian raids, and Israeli leaders began to make threatening statements. On May 10, Israel's chief of staff, Yitzhak Rabin, suggested that Israel might have to march to Damascus and overthrow the Syrian government. Four days later, Prime Minister Eshkol said, "In view of the 14 incidents in the past month alone, we may have to adopt measures no less drastic than those of April 7."

In truth Israel had no plan to invade Syria. But Russia saw an opportunity to stir some trouble by claiming that such an invasion was imminent. Early in May, Russian officials in Cairo asserted that Israeli forces were massing along the Syrian border, and over the next two weeks Egypt received more detailed information indicating the presence of perhaps 11 Israeli brigades there. Actually Israel had only one company—120 men—on the Syrian border, to intercept terrorists. The United Nations truce-supervision teams were unable to find any trace of the alleged 11 brigades. President Nasser of Egypt, however, citing his country's mutual-defense pact with Syria, immediately went into action.

Nasser's prestige in the Arab world had been sagging for some time, and he had been accused in some quarters of being soft on Israel. In recent years he had withdrawn Egypt almost entirely from the war of terrorism against Israel, leaving the Syrian extremists to carry on alone. He ruled the only Arab country strong enough to take on Israel in a real war, but he had shown no inclination lately to become involved in such a war. Nasser also was the butt of Arab jeers because he had, for ten years, permitted the United Nations Emergency Force to occupy Egyptian territory. That force—some 3,700 troops from seven nations, commanded by General Indar Jit Rikhye of India—still patrolled the Gaza Strip and Egypt's long desert border with Israel all the way down to Sharm el-Sheikh.

Now Nasser decided to confound his detractors, using the supposed Israeli military buildup on the Syrian border as his pretext. On May 15, large numbers of Egyptian troops began crossing the Suez Canal into the Sinai Peninsula. In the publicity accompanying this move, Egypt said it was a defensive maneuver aimed at blocking Israel's planned aggressions. The next day, Egypt asked the United Nations troops to withdraw from Sinai—for their own safety, Cairo said, so that they would "not be harmed if hostilities break out." General Rikhye relayed the request to Secretary-General Thant in New York.

When the United Nations Emergency Force was created in 1956, it was with the understanding that it would be withdrawn immediately from Egyptian territory if Egypt ordered it out. Later that year, Nasser and Secretary-General Hammarskjöld had come to a private agreement under which no withdrawal of the UN troops would be executed without approval of the General Assembly. But this agreement had never been made public, and Hammarskjöld's successor, U Thant, evidently did not regard it as binding on him, since it had not been ratified by the General Assembly.

Thant, who had never demonstrated much firmness of purpose, asked Egypt to "clarify" the request. But this attempt to win time failed, because India and Yugoslavia, having been notified of Nasser's wishes, announced instantly that they would withdraw their soldiers from UNEF. These nations' contingents constituted about half the total force. By the evening of May 17, Egyptian troops were taking over Yugoslav observation posts along the border, and on the following day Thant gave recognition to the existing situation by ordering the complete withdrawal of UNEF. Syria's Foreign Minister said, "The withdrawal of the U.N. forces in this manner, which means 'make way, our forces are on their way to the battle,' proves that there is nothing that can stand in the way of the Arab revolution."

Israel had displayed little concern over Egypt's May 15 troop movements in the Sinai, assuming it was meant for show; Israeli strategists were contemptuous of the ability of the Egyptian army, and felt that Nasser, for all his Russian tanks and planes, would be afraid to start a war. Foreign military experts felt the same way. The Tel Aviv correspondent of the London *Times* reported on May 20, "The Egyptian Army in Sinai is seen in Tel Aviv mainly as a defensive force, not organized for invasion but more to stop a possible Israel invasion similar to the Sinai campaign. A big land campaign is thus ruled out." The eviction of the UN force disturbed the Israelis, and they filed a formal protest with Thant; but they interpreted the move as another show of bravado by Nasser, designed to bolster his prestige among his fellow Arabs. Israel did, however, order a partial mobilization of reserves.

Then, on May 22, Nasser declared that Egyptian troops had occupied Sharm el-Sheikh. The Strait of Tiran would thereafter be closed to Israeli shipping and also to non-Israeli vessels bearing strategic materials to Israel. "The Israeli flag will no longer pass the Gulf of Aqaba," he said. "Our sovereignty over the Gulf is indisputable. If Israel threatens us with war, we will reply thus: You are welcome, we are ready for war." Nasser offered as legal justification for this move the fact that the Strait of Tiran is only some nine miles wide, and thus within Egyptian territorial waters.

But the terms of Israel's 1957 withdrawal had guaranteed Israel's "free and innocent passage" through the Gulf of Aqaba; she would never have withdrawn from Sharm el-Sheikh without that pledge. Her port of Eilat, at the head of the gulf, had developed into a major maritime center with a cargo-handling capacity of three million tons. Eilat was essential to the Israeli economy. Closing the Strait of Tiran was indisputably an act of war. Obviously Nasser was testing Israel, discovering how far he could push the Eshkol government.

Israel waited expectantly for Prime Minister Eshkol to order the army into battle. This seemed the moment to strike, now, while Nasser's brazen defiance of international law was on the front page of every newspaper in the world. But the order did not come. To the amazement of all Israelis and the open disgust of many, Eshkol held back the waiting legions, and put his faith in aid from outside—specifically, aid from Washington. He looked to the United States now to make good its 1957 commitment to keep the Strait of Tiran open.

President Johnson was in an acutely uncomfortable position when word came of the Tiran closure. He was well aware of the extent of the American commitment with regard to Tiran, for he had helped create it as a senator in 1957. He knew that if Israel's existence were seriously threatened, the United States would be expected to intervene, unilaterally if necessary, to save it. But the United States was already engaged in one unilateral intervention on behalf of a small and friendly state; and the war in Vietnam not only had become a tremendous drain on American resources, but by the spring of 1967 was a colossal domestic political liability, virtually destroying Johnson's effectiveness as President. This would hardly be an apt moment for the United States to go to war in the Near East as well.

Johnson also was worried about the Soviet position. Russia's first official reaction to the crisis had come on May 23: a rehash of the rumored Israeli "aggression" against Syria and a comment that Israel's actions were being encouraged by "certain imperialist circles which seek to bring back colonial oppression to Arab lands." If the United States sent troops to reopen the Strait of Tiran, would the Soviet Union send troops to back Nasser? Johnson could not take the chance. He attempted to play for time.

On May 23, then, Johnson released a statement that declared: "The United States considers the Gulf [of Aqaba] to be an international waterway and feels that a blockade of Israeli shipping is illegal and potentially disastrous to the cause of peace. The right of free, innocent passage of the international waterway is a vital interest of the international community. . . . To the leaders of all the nations of the Near East, I wish to say what three Presidents have said before—that the United States is firmly committed to the support of the political independence and territorial integrity of all the nations of the area." In a separate message to the Israeli government, he asked a 48-hour delay in taking action while the

United States sought some peaceful means of reopening the strait. Prime Minister Eshkol, eager to avoid war, agreed to the delay.

It was important for Israel to know, though, how far the United States was prepared to go if peaceful means failed. Abba Eban, now Foreign Minister, set out for Washington on the day after the President's statement to meet with Johnson and, if possible, to extract some firm agreement from him. The same day also saw Nasser announce that Egypt had completed the task of closing the entrance to the Gulf of Aqaba through mines, armored sea and air patrols, and shore batteries.

In New York, the Conference of Presidents of Major American Jewish Organizations formed an emergency committee on the Near East crisis, headed by Mrs. Rose L. Halprin. She held a news conference on May 24 at the Jewish Agency's Park Avenue office to discuss a "solidarity with Israel" parade along Riverside Drive the following Sunday. At the United Nations, Canada and Denmark called for a Security Council meeting "to consider the extremely grave situation in the Middle East which is threatening international peace and security." American ambassador Arthur Goldberg told the Security Council, "I have been authorized to announce that the United States, both within and outside the United Nations, is prepared to join with all the other great powers —the Soviet Union, the United Kingdom, and France—in a common effort to restore and maintain peace in the Near East." But the Soviet Union refused to join that "common effort," and the Security Council adjourned without a date being set for the next meeting.

Eban arrived in Washington on May 25. He had stopped off en route in Paris and London to confer with President de Gaulle and Prime Minister Harold Wilson. France, which had been Israel's main supplier of arms in the past, now offered no help at all, for de Gaulle's attempt to resurrect French national grandeur had led him to turn against many old friends. "You must on no account start a war," he told Eban brusquely. "The country that fires the first shot will lose the friendship of France." When Eban reminded him of the 1956–57 alliance and of France's support for the right of free passage in the Gulf of Aqaba, de Gaulle said, "Times have changed since then. And, besides, I wasn't President then." Prime Minister Wilson was somewhat more encouraging, but pointed out to Eban that Britain could not act alone. The final decision on action would have to come from the United States.

When Eban landed in Washington he found a garbled message from Israel waiting for him, which seemed to imply that the Tiran blockade was no longer the prime issue; apparently the government now feared an Egyptian attack from the Sinai. But when Eban met with Secretary of State Dean Rusk on the afternoon of May 25, Rusk took a cool approach to this, shrugging off the Israeli fears by saying that the United States did not regard Egypt as ready to strike a quick blow. (Rusk did, however, send word to Cairo that night asking Nasser not to resort to force.) Rusk was vague and unclear on the subject of what help the United States was prepared to give Israel. His advice seemed to be to let the United Nations handle the crisis. When Eban met with Undersecretary of State Eugene V. Rostow and other American officials that evening, he heard the same thing.

The Israeli Foreign Minister had been in Washington for nearly 24 hours before he got to see President Johnson. Eban at once went on the offensive, producing a sheaf of documents detailing the 1957 United States pledges of "free and innocent passage" in the Gulf of Aqaba and speaking of Johnson's own role in forcing the Eisenhower administration to make concessions to Israel in that crisis. Johnson was sympathetic—"I want to see that little blue and white Israeli flag sailing down those Straits"—but would make no firm promises. Congress would have to approve any use of American troops, he said, and that would take time. (It might take forever, he could have added, considering the attitude of some powerful senators toward the unilateral American involvement in Vietnam.) Rather than acting alone on Israel's behalf, Johnson said, he preferred to organize a group of forty or fifty maritime powers who would sign a guarantee of free passage through the Strait of Tiran. This, he thought, would force Nasser to back down. He asked Eban if Israel could wait another two weeks while he made this further attempt at a peaceful settlement.

Eban returned to Israel in distress. He realized now that Johnson's hands were tied by the Vietnam situation, and that unless some good came out of the maritime-power scheme, Israel would have to deal with the Tiran blockade herself. And the maritime-power scheme seemed as futile an idea as Dulles' 1956 Suez Canal Users' Association project. But he put a brave front on things. Stopping in Paris on his way home, he told reporters on May 27

that in Washington he had noted "the particularly firm and vigorous feeling of those responsible for American policy, in favor of
free access to the Straits of Tiran by ships of all nationalities,
without distinction of flag or cargo."

Nasser, the day before, had made a boastful speech to the Pan-
Arab Federation of Trade Unions that was virtually a declaration
of war. Explaining his past hesitation to strike at Israel as a tactical
maneuver, Nasser said, "Recently we have felt strong enough that
if we were to enter a battle with Israel, with God's help we could
triumph. On this basis, we decided to take actual steps." Thus he
had evicted the UN Emergency Force; thus he had seized Sharm
el-Sheikh: "Taking such action also meant that we were ready to
enter war with Israel. It was not a separate operation." If war
comes, he went on, "The battle will be a general one and our main
objective will be the destruction of Israel. I probably could not
have said such things five or even three years ago. If I had said such
things and had been unable to carry them out my words would
have been empty and valueless. Today, some eleven years after
1956, I say such things because I am confident." He praised the
"magnificent" position of the Soviet Union, which he said "will
resist any intervention and aggression." And he asked, "What
is Israel? Israel is the United States. The United States is the
chief defender of Israel. As for Britain, I consider it America's
lackey."

His words created furor in Israel, especially after Eban returned
without the hoped-for pledge of immediate American military
backing. The country had polarized into hawks and doves, those
who wanted war at once and those who were willing to continue
searching for a peaceful settlement. The hawks felt that Eshkol's
delaying tactics were turning the blockade into a new *status quo*,
which Israel must resist now, while the world still viewed her as
victim and not as aggressor. They wanted to bring fierce old
former Prime Minister Ben-Gurion back into the government; he
would, they felt, instantly smite Nasser and reopen the Strait. The
doves argued that Johnson's request for a new two-week stay of
action should be heeded while the last avenues of settlement were
explored. Then, and only then, should war be considered.

The combination of Egyptian belligerence and Israeli impa-
tience led the United States into a frantic diplomatic effort on
Saturday and Sunday, May 27 and 28, to persuade Israel and

Egypt not to go to war. The Soviet Union, too, suddenly began to work toward maintaining peace, as though realizing that an outbreak of hostilities might lead directly toward a clash between Russia and the United States. The Soviet ambassador in Cairo saw Nasser at 3:30 A.M., Saturday, and strongly urged him not to be the first to open fire.

But Nasser had no intention of opening fire. He had thrown down the gauntlet; the next move was Israel's. If Israel capitulated, leaving him in command of the Strait of Tiran, victory was his without a shot. He would have obliterated his defeat of 1956 and taken a huge step toward the economic strangulation of the Jewish state. But he did not expect Israel to capitulate. He hoped Israel would choose to go to war—thus branding herself as an aggressor before the United Nations—and then, once attacked, Nasser could strike back with all the force at his command. This time, he was certain, he had the power to destroy Israel.

So he continued his goading tactics. At a press conference on Sunday he spoke of Israel's "false victory" in 1956: "In that year we did not fight Israel, we fought against Anglo-French aggression. We withdrew our forces from Sinai in order to face Britain and France. One day we stood in the face of Israel with a small force, and on that day Israel was unable to penetrate any Egyptian position. In spite of that, the American press published articles glorifying the Israeli Army, the Israeli might, and so forth. This was all nonsense. . . . Today we are alone face to face with Israel, and if Israel wants to try war I would again say to it, 'Welcome.' " And the following day he said, "The issue now at hand is not the Gulf of Aqaba, the Strait of Tiran, or the withdrawal of U.N.E.F., but the rights of the Palestinian people. It is the aggression which took place in Palestine in 1948 with the collaboration of Britain [!] and the United States. . . . We are not facing Israel, but those behind it. We are facing the West, which created Israel."

While pressure built up within Israel to go to war, American Jews mounted a pressure campaign of their own to lead the Johnson administration toward a stronger stand in Israel's defense. The tremendous and astonishing swell of support for Israel in the United States had begun almost immediately after the May 22 Tiran blockade; nothing was heard now of the old charge of dual allegiance as thousands of Americans swung into action on behalf of a foreign state. Congressmen were inundated with requests for

American military aid to Israel. Meetings were held in hundreds of synagogues; scores of local fund drives for Israel began, several days before the United Jewish Appeal launched its nation-wide emergency campaign on May 29. There was a swift and sudden mobilization of opinion, all but unanimous.

Non-Jewish Americans, too, displayed great concern over Israel's fate. It was common for Gentile Americans to tell Jewish Americans how worried they were over the safety of "your people over there"—and no one doubted that American Jews had some special stake in the welfare of Israel. "Your people !" The worst fears of the anti-Zionist Jews were realized; but the Gentiles were not denouncing American Jews for their identification with Israel. Rather, they seemed to envy them for having a connection with such a brave and beleaguered state. Even political conservatives of the far right, whom American Jews had always regarded with uneasiness, spoke out now in favor of Israel; they saw the Jewish state as the Near East's only bulwark against the international Communist conspiracy.

On Sunday, May 28, thousands of New Yorkers marched along Riverside Drive to express their support for Israel. The parade included members of Orthodox, Conservative, and Reform congregations, delegates from Jewish organizations, and a good many non-Jews; the Police Department Emerald Society's bagpipe band marched past the reviewing stand playing "Hava Nagila," the Israeli song of rejoicing, and a short while later the same tune came from the band of St. Benedict's High School in the Bronx. Dr. Joachim Prinz, chairman of the Conference of Presidents of Major American Jewish Organizations, estimated the number of Riverside Drive marchers as 125,000. A cheering crowd heard him read a statement that said, "We call on our President to enforce his vigorous denunciation of the illegal blockade of Israeli shipping in the Gulf of Aqaba." When a reporter asked him if he advocated unilateral American intervention, he said carefully, "We have not used the word 'unilateral.' " What is sought, he said, is "consideration of independent action."

About 50 Arabs staged a counterdemonstration, shouting, "Palestine is Arab!" and "Down with the Zionists!" They waved a white sheet that bore the inscription, "In the Name of Peace, We Appeal to American Jews to Invite Their Kin, Now in Israel, to Immigrate to America." Jeering supporters of Israel threw eggs, tomatoes, oranges, and shoes at them as they chanted, "We love Nasser," but police protected the Arab picketers from harm.

The anti-Zionist Jews of the American Council for Judaism found themselves more isolated than ever during this show of American support for Israel. The council, though it had fought vigorously against the creation of any Jewish state, had brought itself to accept the existence of Israel in the years since 1948. As Norton Mezvinsky, then the council's executive director, put it shortly after the 1967 war, "That Jews throughout the world constitute a common grouping is obvious. Those who affirm that they are Jews acknowledge this common grouping by that affirmation. . . . American Jews and Israeli Jews are part of the same grouping, a grouping that the great majority of both acknowledge and accept. . . . Both should stand ready to help the other appropriately and legitimately."

Thus the council—whose 250-man national advisory board included such prominent Jews as Stanley Marcus of the Neiman-Marcus Company, Henry A. Loeb of the brokerage house of Loeb, Rhoades and Company, and Donald S. Klopfer of Random House—no more wanted to see the Jews of Israel in peril than it did the Jews of any other part of the world. But the council had always been opposed to the idea that American Jews owed any allegiance to Israel, or that it was their duty to lobby on Israel's behalf with their own government.

As the May crisis intensified, many members of the American Council for Judaism found their emotional involvement with the plight of Israel overwhelming their abstract anti-Zionist beliefs, and they chose to maintain a discreet public silence. Not so Rabbi Berger, who was regarded as an extreme anti-Zionist even within the council, one who looked upon Israelis as "racists" for their advocacy of a Jewish state, and who had spoken out frequently against the injustices perpetrated on the Palestinian Arabs by Israel. On May 20, Berger had released a statement calling on the United Nations to resolve the disputes in the Near East. "We are deeply concerned," he said, "because more than 2,000,000 of our coreligionists live in Israel, many of them because they or their forebears were uprooted from their homes years ago and either had nowhere else to rebuild their lives or were under the impression that they had no other reasonable choice." But he also spoke sympathetically of the Arabs: "The peaceful progress of their lives again appears threatened by conflict over historic forces the origins of which reach back beyond their lives to a wholly different era of half a century ago."

On May 29, seeing what he viewed as "hysteria" building up among American Jews, the council's president, Richard Korn, issued a somewhat stronger statement in which he urged American Zionists, "most of whom are fellow Jews, to cease and desist from their perhaps well-meaning but ill-advised efforts to pressure the United States government into always taking absolute and militant pro-Israel positions." He called on Egypt and Israel to come to a peaceful resolution of the Tiran blockade, and to halt all raids across the armistice lines. But, despite Korn's reference to the "illusion" created by American Zionists "that their pressure tactics represent all American Jews," it was obvious that he was very much a minority voice that day. American Jews had already pledged millions of dollars for Israel, and thousands of young Americans were trying to volunteer for the defense of the Jewish state.

The Johnson administration continued to search for a diplomatic solution to the crisis, while resisting American Jewish pressure for some form of direct intervention. Much of this pressure fell upon Senator Jacob Javits, who met with Dean Rusk on Monday afternoon, May 29, and told a press conference afterward, "There is no question of unilateral United States action at this time."

From Jerusalem, on Tuesday, came a new statement of faith from Abba Eban in the great powers' ability to settle the conflict without war: "Now it is clear from the contacts we've had with the major powers that there are others in the world who are prepared to make common cause for the restoration of the legal situation in the Gulf of Aqaba." But, somewhat more realistically, he observed that the Israelis would pry the Strait of Tiran open "alone, if we must." He was scornful of the United Nations, which he said "does not emerge from the events of the past two weeks with brilliance or credit," and warned, "Let there be no mistake about the crucial character of this issue or about the unlimited effort that Israel is prepared to invest. This is the kind of interest for which a nation stakes all it has." Eban described Israel as a "coiled spring."

The coil grew unexpectedly tighter later on Tuesday when

word came that King Hussein of Jordan had flown to Cairo to sign
a mutual defense pact with Egypt. For years Nasser's agents had
worked to topple Hussein from his throne, but this subversion was
apparently forgiven now. The Jordanian king, aware of the tension in Israel and mindful of what had happened at Es Samu,
feared that when Israel finally did go into action she would strike
not at Egypt but at Jordan, an easier target. And so he offered his
troops to Nasser in the hope that Egypt would protect him against
the Jews.

With Hussein, the most liberal and enlightened of the Arab
rulers, suddenly joining forces with Egypt, Israel's situation became infinitely more precarious. Israel was ready for war with
Egypt along the Sinai frontier, and anticipated a possible Syrian
attack also. But Jordan's border with Israel ran virtually the whole
length of the country, and an attack from Jordan along Israel's
narrow waist could cut the Jewish state in half within hours. The
Israelis realized that they now faced the most dangerous contin-
gency of all, the one that in their planning they had labeled *Mikre
Hakol*, "the Eventuality of Everybody"—a simultaneous attack by
all the Arab countries. On June 1, President Aref of Iraq declared,
"Brethren and sons, this is the day to wash away the stigma. We
shall, God willing, meet in Tel Aviv and Haifa." The same day,
Ahmed Shukairy, the head of the clandestine Palestine Liberation
Organization, discussed in the Jordanian sector of Jerusalem what
would happen to Israel's Jews after the war. The foreign-born
ones, he said, would be allowed to return to their countries of
origin. "As for those born in Palestine, they can remain—those
that survive. I estimate that none of them will survive."

The news that Iraqi troops and armored units were entering
Jordan on June 1, and that Egyptian generals had arrived in Amman that day to take command of the Jordanian army, greatly
intensified the demand within Israel for immediate war. Israel had
been mobilized for most of May, now, which meant—with 80
percent of her army consisting of civilian reservists—that the
whole country had been at an economic standstill for weeks. It was
costly to keep up the mobilization, perhaps indefinitely, while
waiting for the Arabs to begin real fighting. And the cost in
nervous tension was even greater. End the suspense, the Israelis
told their leaders: strike now!

The Eshkol government had lost the people during the endless

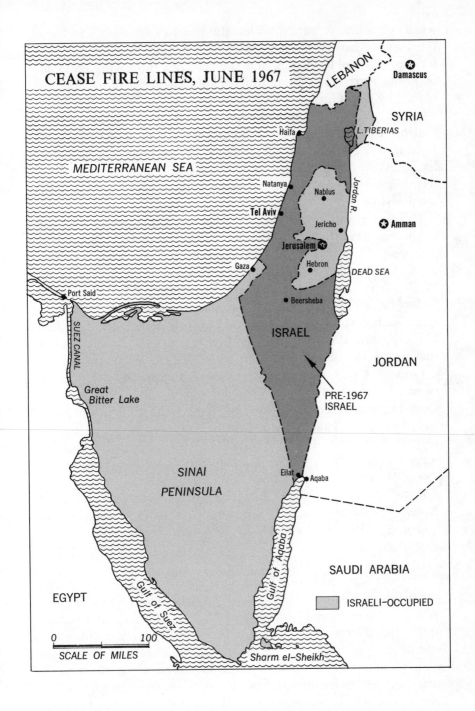

CEASE FIRE LINES, JUNE 1967

LEBANON

✪ Damascus

SYRIA

MEDITERRANEAN SEA

Haifa ● L. TIBERIAS

Natanya ● Nablus ●

Tel Aviv ● Jordan R.

Jericho ● ✪ Amman

Jerusalem ✪

Gaza ● Hebron ●

DEAD SEA

● Beersheba

ISRAEL

JORDAN

PRE-1967
ISRAEL

Port Said

SUEZ CANAL

Great
Bitter Lake

SINAI
PENINSULA

Eilat ● Aqaba
Gulf of Aqaba

SAUDI ARABIA

EGYPT

Gulf of Suez

ISRAELI-OCCUPIED

0   100
SCALE OF MILES

Sharm el–Sheikh

weeks of delay. A faction within the Knesset attempted to force the Prime Minister to step down. Menachem Beigin, the grim former leader of the Irgun, now the head of a right-wing nationalist political party, suggested to Eshkol that he let himself be replaced by Ben-Gurion. This Eshkol would not do, nor would he offer the post of Defense Minister, which he also held, to Ben-Gurion. But the overnight Arab unity move compelled Eshkol to yield in order to save his government, and on June 1 he agreed to let Ben-Gurion's protégé, Moshe Dayan, become Defense Minister. Beigin also was taken into the government as a Minister without Portfolio.

Dayan was one of the strongest advocates of a preventive war in the country. Born in Palestine in 1915, he joined Haganah at the age of 14, was jailed by the British for underground activities in 1939, and was released after a year to serve in the British army. While on a commando raid against Vichy French forces in Syria he lost his left eye and adopted the black eye patch that made him seem such a swaggering, piratical figure. He had distinguished himself in the 1948 War of Liberation and was the Israeli chief of staff in the 1956 Sinai campaign.

Now that this master tactician was a member of the government, the question was not whether war would come, but how soon. He took office on Friday, June 2. By Sunday night the plans were complete. Israel would strike at dawn on Monday, June 5. During the same weekend the United States continued to look for ways to open the Strait of Tiran by negotiations. Haunted by thoughts of a "second Vietnam," President Johnson wanted passionately to live up to his pledges to Israel without employing American military force. It was a hopeless struggle. But on the morning of June 5 Moshe Dayan took him off the hook.

8.

The war was short and extraordinary, a classic military maneuver that will be studied by strategists for centuries to come, just as the campaigns of Hannibal and Napoleon are studied today. While Israel's remaining civilians carried museum specimens to safe places and began to take down Chagall's celebrated stained-glass windows at the chapel of the Hadassah Hospital, ground units began to move into the Sinai Peninsula and the air force went into action in a precisely coordinated raid of ten Egyptian airfields.

All planes reached their targets. All bombs exploded. Most of the Egyptian air force was caught on the ground. Other Israeli bombers raided the airfields of Jordan and Syria, and struck also at those of Iraq, 500 miles away. By sundown, nearly 400 Arab planes had been destroyed, the entire air force of Israel's four enemies. The counterstrike that Nasser had been planning to deliver when the Israelis finally went on the offensive thus was prevented. Israel had complete freedom of the skies. There was no longer any danger of an attack on her own territory, for she could blast any invading columns at will from the air. The war could be carried to the enemy.

The ground war began with a replay of the 1956 Sinai campaign. Three Israeli divisions entered the Sinai. El Arish fell on Monday, the first day of battle. After a stubborn fight, the Egyptians yielded Gaza on Tuesday. As the Egyptian lines of defense broke, the war again became a rout, with Nasser's men in wild flight and the Israelis pressing westward without pausing for breath. On the third day of fighting, Israel closed in on the critical Mitla Pass, and when it fell, the only gateway for escape was shut for thousands of trapped Egyptians. A terrible tank battle was the last effort of the Egyptians; they took a harsh pounding and finally collapsed, opening the way to the Suez Canal.

Meanwhile another Israeli unit had landed at Sharm el-Sheikh on Wednesday, June 7, only to find the place empty. The Egyptians had fled, or, as Radio Cairo put it, "regrouped." The Strait of Tiran was taken without firing a shot. On Thursday the Israelis finished the job of destroying the Egyptian army in the Sinai, and at one in the morning on Friday, the first Israeli troops reached the banks of the Suez Canal. The Sinai war was over. It had been even shorter than in 1956.

In the north, the new Egyptian commanders of Jordan's army, prevailing over Hussein's men, had launched an attack with machine guns and mortars in the divided city of Jerusalem on the first day of the war. This was followed by a general attack all along the border between Israel and Jordan. Israel reacted with delight; at last she had the proper pretext for reunifying partitioned Palestine. She struck back enthusiastically against Jordan, and by Tuesday, June 6, the northern part of the Jordanian front had crumbled. A murderous air attack eliminated most of the Jordanian army on Wednesday, giving Israel the entire bulge of the West Bank—

Nablus, Jenin, Bethlehem, Jericho, Hebron. Within 48 hours Israel had taken back all that had been carved out of Palestine in 1948.

On Wednesday, too, the Old City of Jerusalem fell to Israel—the greatest single triumph of the war. It was a harsh struggle, for Israel spared the historic buildings of the Old City by refraining from heavy bombing, and this cost her the lives of many soldiers. But the Wailing Wall, a wailing wall no longer, was Jewish again. Though sniper fire still threatened them, the Israeli warriors rushed to the wall, kissing it, embracing it, dancing before it. Many of the soldiers scribbled prayers on scraps of paper and thrust them between the crevices of the wall, in accordance with an ancient custom. One, looking a trifle abashed, for he was not an observing Jew, told a reporter that he had written his son's name on the paper: "It was what my father wished to do for me, and my grandfather for him, and all the generations of my ancestors for two thousand years, and *I* am the one who has come." Dayan visited the wall, and Ben-Gurion, and Eshkol. General Shlomo Goren, the chief rabbi of the Israeli army, came up to it bedecked with battle ribbons, and jubilantly sounded the *shofar*, the ceremonial ram's horn. Asked if Israel would ever relinquish the Old City, General Goren said, "We took an oath today, while capturing the city. On our blood we took an oath that we will never give it up, we will never leave this place. The Wailing Wall belongs to us. The holy place was our place first, our place and our God's place. From here we do not move. Never. Never."

The final phase of the war opened on Friday afternoon, June 9. All was quiet then along the Jordanian front. Jordan, which now was once again nothing but Transjordan, was in a state of shock. The Sinai, too, was still, with dazed Egyptians shuffling through the sands, looking for someone to whom to surrender, someone to give them water.

Then it was the turn of the Syrians. They had been Israel's most ferocious assailants in the war of words, but when the war began they did very little—staying behind their own lines, and contenting themselves with showering shells on Israel from their bunkers in the hills above the Sea of Galilee. The shelling continued all week, and at noon on Friday, Israel chose to reply to it. In a brief but exceptionally bloody encounter Israeli soldiers overran the Syrian bunkers and plunged into enemy territory; the road to

Damascus lay open as the Syrians fled, and only a decision by the Israeli government to end the war prevented the capture of the enemy capital. When the soldiers were stopped, they were 25 miles from Damascus.

By sundown on Saturday, the Six-Day War was at its end. Israel held all of the Sinai, the richest territories of Jordan, and a corner of Syria. The entire political structure of the Near East had been turned upside down, not by Israel in collusion with two great powers, but by Israel alone, Israel erupting when her patience was exhausted.

9.

The outside world learned of these heroic events gradually and fitfully, and it was not easy at first to understand what was taking place. Nearly all the early reports came from the Arabs: declarations of war by more than a dozen Arab states, announcements of the heavy damage that had been inflicted on Israel. The annihilation of the Jewish state seemed to be in process. Only later did it become apparent that Israel had begun hostilities, that the war had been one-sided and was over almost as soon as it was under way, and that the damages inflicted on Israel had been slight. (A single Iraqi plane had bombed suburban Natanya, the Syrian air force had dropped bombs near the Haifa oil refineries and at an airfield at Megiddo, and Jordan had bombed the Israeli air base at Kefer Sirkin, all on the first two days of the war. The Jewish half of Jerusalem came under Jordanian fire on the second and third days. Thereafter Israel went unscathed.)

The news that the war had begun reached the White House at 2:50 A.M. on Monday, June 5. State Department officials quickly came together to discuss the situation. Soon an intelligence report arrived that said that five Egyptian airfields had been knocked out. Some of the younger State Department men showed evident pleasure at this blow to Nasser, and one senior official reminded them jokingly that "we are neutral in thought, word, and deed." Robert McCloskey, the State Department's press officer, overheard the phrase, with unfortunate consequences later.

By 4:30 A.M. President Johnson was awake and receiving a briefing on the situation. By then a message from Soviet Premier Kosygin had come in over the "hot line" communications system that links the Kremlin and the White House. Kosygin made it

clear that the Soviet Union did not want to intervene in the Near
Eastern war, and would stay out if the United States did. Johnson
immediately replied that there would be no American intervention. This was the first time the hot line had been used except for
routine exchanges of greetings since it was established in August,
1963.

At 5:55 A.M., Presidential Press Secretary George Christian
issued the first White House statement on the war: "The United
States will devote all its energies to bring about an end to the
fighting and a new beginning of progress to assure the peace and
development of the entire area. We call upon all parties to support
the Security Council in bringing about an immediate cease-fire."
At 8:15, Johnson, Rusk, and Secretary of Defense Robert
McNamara met to discuss the possibility of cooperating with
Russia to bring about a cease-fire. In the early afternoon, the State
Department held a press briefing at which press officer McCloskey, remembering the lighthearted phrase of the early morning
hours, declared that "our position is neutral in thought, word and
deed."

By this time the war—which seemed to be so grave a threat to
Israel's existence—had begun to exert its strange grip on the emotions of American Jews. Students at New York's Yeshiva College,
learning the news at 3:30 that morning, had rushed to their synagogue to pray; by daybreak they and some 2,000 students from
other colleges were parading in front of the UN, carrying signs
asking that Israel be preserved. Volunteers swarmed to the Israeli
consulate in New York and to the offices of the Jewish Agency.
Impromptu fund drives got under way. The reaction to the crisis
was far more intense, far more widespread, than anyone had expected. Somehow every Jew in America felt that he was himself
threatened by the menace that he believed was descending on
Israel. They could not remain passive in the face of such danger.
They had to do something—anything, if only to give money, to
parade, to cry out for justice for Israel.

The "neutral in thought, word, and deed" line seemed particularly inappropriate in view of this passionate partisanship, and
many Americans swiftly let the State Department know about it.
Congressmen expressed their outrage and the outrage of their
constituents. Calling on Dean Rusk to repudiate the McCloskey
statement, Representative William Fitts Ryan of Manhattan, a

Democrat, said, "I perceive a serious danger developing that, as various nations consider their own narrow interests, they will find it expedient to sacrifice their commitments to Israel." Senator Joseph S. Clark, Democrat of Pennsylvania, declared, "Morally as well as legally we are an ally of Israel. We are not neutral." Republican Senator Jacob Javits of New York described the McCloskey statement as something that "slipped out," and asked the President to restate American policy in his own words. Hurriedly Dean Rusk explained that the United States was merely "nonbelligerent." He said, "This word neutral—which is a great concept of international law—is not an expression of indifference, and indeed indifference is not permitted to us."

But the briefing that Rusk, McNamara, and Richard Helms of the CIA gave congressional leaders left them unsatisfied. "They never got around to policy at all," complained Everett McKinley Dirksen, the Illinois Republican. "It was a chronological recital." He offered a quotation from Revelation: "I know thy works, that thou art neither cold nor hot: I would thou wert cold or hot. So then because thou art lukewarm, and neither cold nor hot, I will spue thee out of my mouth." In fact there was no American policy, except one of waiting and hoping that the Israelis would be able to look after themselves.

By the time Dirksen made his comments—on the afternoon of Tuesday, June 6—it was apparent that the Israelis were doing quite well. The news of the destruction of the Arab countries' total air strength had filtered out of the Near East and had been verified by several reporters, though not by any government. It was known that Lebanon, after a token entry into the war, had withdrawn, that Iraq had sent troops to Jordan but that they were not doing any fighting, and that the contributions of Saudi Arabia, Kuwait, and most of the other Arab allies had been limited to messages of support and exhortations to fight bravely. The Arab newspapers and radio stations still claimed tremendous victories, but the claims were unconvincing. (On the fourth day of the war, when Israel had taken the West Bank, Jerusalem, and Sharm el-Sheikh, and was nearing the Suez Canal, the *Egyptian Gazette*'s lead story declared, "Arab forces on all fronts inflicted heavy losses on the Israeli enemy yesterday.")

But no one outside the Near East, on the second day of the war, realized how successful Israel had been, and the prospect that the

United States might have to send troops to save the Jewish state from destruction still was under serious discussion here. A group called Americans for Democracy in the Middle East sought the signatures of scholars, artists, poets, and writers for a full-page advertisement in *The New York Times* of June 7, which called the crisis "a moment of truth for our own country and for the whole world. Aqaba is a test from which all nations who are watching our performance will take their cue. If we fail to act to maintain the principle of freedom of navigation, every one of these countries will take note." The advertisement went on, "We therefore urgently call upon the President of the United States, supported as we have no doubt he will be by the people and the Congress, to act now with courage and conviction, with nerve and firmness of intent, to maintain free passage in those waters—and so to safeguard the integrity, security and survival of Israel and its people, and to uphold our own honor."

Many of those who were invited to sign were among the strongest opponents of American military action in Vietnam. Now, asked to support possible American intervention in the Near East, they found themselves confused and embarrassed. Arthur Schlesinger, Jr. refused to sign on the grounds that it would be inconsistent of him to oppose one intervention and favor another. Poet Robert Lowell, another who would not sign, said simply that he opposed all war. Those who did sign included many well-known Jewish and Gentile intellectuals: novelist Robert Penn Warren, poet Marianne Moore, critic Lionel Trilling, sociologist Daniel P. Moynihan, economist Robert Heilbroner. A White House aide, amused, suggested that the group should call itself "Doves for War." Conservative William Buckley, who approved Israel's anti-Communism, was amused at the way the Near East war had "most of the critics of our policy in Vietnam on the run." Theodore Draper, a Stanford University historian and one of the signers of the advertisement, later commented that he saw no inconsistency in his position: "There is no inherent reason why one cannot criticize the abuse of power in Vietnam and the abdication of power elsewhere."

The youthful members of the New Left movement, many of them Jewish, also had difficulty arriving at a position. Paul Booth, former national secretary of Students for a Democratic Society—and a Jew—said, "Our people do not believe the U.S. should be the policeman in the Mideast or the Far East." Deirdre Griswold of Youth Against War and Fascism declared, "Israel, in fact, is acting as a pawn of Western interests. Our people, with their sympathies, are for the Arab revolution. Israel is artificial." Her group had a sizable number of Jewish members. But Michael Myerson, director of the leftist Tri-Continental Information Center, suggested that "the strategy that if we want Johnson to support Israel, we'd better keep our mouths shut about Vietnam" might still the opposition of many Jews of the New Left to the Vietnamese war.

On the evening of Wednesday, June 7, thousands of Jews began to arrive in Washington. They had been summoned there by Dr. Joachim Prinz of the Conference of Presidents of Major American Jewish Organizations in order "to mobilize support for vigorous United States action to protect Israel's security and America's own vital interest in the Middle East." The next day, while a mass demonstration began to take shape in Lafayette Park, across the street from the White House, smaller Jewish groups called on the White House and on members of Congress to present their views. Ordinarily, the White House sends junior officials or staff aides to receive petitions from demonstrators, but this time, because of President Johnson's sensitivity to the delicate political situation, the petitioners were greeted by Undersecretary of State Nicholas deB. Katzenbach and Bromley Smith, executive secretary of the National Security Council. "Even in times of crisis, when so much of the President's time and that of his advisers is devoted to efforts to bring peace in the Middle East, we are always happy to hear the views of our citizens," Katzenbach said. (He said the same thing half an hour later when a delegation of Arab counterdemonstrators arrived.) Some three hundred New York City Jews called on Senators Robert F. Kennedy and Jacob Javits. Kennedy— whose constant avowal of an American commitment to Israel was a factor in his assassination by a Jordanian-American twelve months later—told the group, "There must be an unequivocal recognition, on the part of all countries in the Near East, that Israel is a nation, and that she exists. She has a permanent right to exist and grow and prosper. This is no longer open to doubt, and it can never again be open to question." Javits added that despite Israel's apparent military triumph, "there remains a glassy, glassy mountain still to climb. . . . It is our hope that our government will see that Israel is not disadvantaged."

At the rally, amid the singing of the Israeli national anthem and the waving of Israeli flags, a small group of pickets shouted pro-Arab slogans; they included some American Negroes wearing Arab robes. (The antipathy of black extremists for Israel was only just becoming evident. Several months after the war, though, the militant Student Nonviolent Coordinating Committee accused Israel of inflicting Nazi-style atrocities on the Arabs: "The Zionists conquered the Arab homes and land through terror, force, and massacres. . . . Zionists lined up Arab victims and shot them in the back in cold blood." Black anti-Zionism appears to be a reaction against all forms of white "imperialism," the Arabs being considered nonwhite in this instance; it also seems to be part of a general upsurge of anti-Semitism in the Negro community.) The high spirits of the demonstrators could not be dampened by the chants of "Nasser, Nasser" from the dissidents. Several senators spoke, as did two black leaders, Whitney M. Young, Jr. and Bayard Rustin.

Shortly after 3 P.M. the rally turned into an unofficial victory celebration when Joachim Prinz announced, "From the United Nations in New York we have the report: the United Arab Republic has just accepted the cease-fire. The war is over." The crowd began to dance the hora, the Israeli folk dance. One boy scrambled up the statue of Lafayette to plant an Israeli flag on top, then climbed it again to put an American flag beside it.

At a news conference elsewhere, Dr. Norton Mezvinsky of the American Council for Judaism told reporters that the sponsors of the rally "do not speak for all of American Jewry," and termed the rally "a Zionist show" aimed at "pressuring the government into an inflexible position of being 100 per cent behind Israel right or wrong." But the rallyers would not have agreed. They heard William A. Wexler, president of B'nai B'rith, tell them, "We are assembled here not as neutrals—but . . . as partisans in the great American tradition—to urge our government to act resolutely in support of a sincere, face-to-face, final and enduring peace settlement between Israel and her neighbors—a peace between equals. To urge our government that it do so with clarity and firmness—in word—in thought—in deed." And the gathering heard Rabbi Israel Miller of the American Zionist Council cry, "We meet as Jews to affirm a fact that becomes more and more visible each day. Israel does not stand alone. The Jewish people stands by her side. We are bound by ties of faith and fate, history and destiny, to Israel and its brave people, and the Jewish citizens of our country have responded today—and will respond in the future—to Israel and its needs. Israel does not stand alone. People of goodwill of all faiths stand by her side. Israel lives and will live—*am yisrael chai, v'yichheh.* To our brethren we say, *chazak, chazak, v'nitchazek:* Be strong, be strong, and we will strengthen one another."

Thousands of miles away in the eastern Mediterranean, a different aspect of the relationship between Israel and the United States had been explored that day. The U.S. Navy's electronic intelligence ship *Liberty*, flying an American flag and bearing other identifiable markings, was traveling west-north-west some 14 miles off the Sinai coast near El Arish. In mid-afternoon—early Thursday morning, Washington time—Israeli jet fighter planes appeared and opened fire.

"We didn't even have a chance to load the guns because the rockets hit us so fast," one of the *Liberty's* seamen said two days later. "It was incredible how fast they hit us." While the aerial attack was going on, three Israeli torpedo boats arrived. Two torpedoes were fired, one striking the *Liberty's* starboard side and ripping a 20-by-25-foot hole below the waterline. By the time the Israeli onslaught halted, nearly an hour after it began, 34 officers and men of the *Liberty* were dead and 75 had been wounded; the ship had been hit repeatedly and was ablaze in several places. One of the Israeli torpedo boats then asked if the *Liberty* needed assistance. The offer was refused and the wounded ship headed north to join the U.S. Sixth Fleet.

What had happened? Why had Israel attacked an American ship?

The official Israeli explanation was that it was all a mistake: that the *Liberty* bore no identification and was thought to have been an Egyptian vessel. When the truth was realized, one of the torpedo boats had signaled, "Terrible error. Can we help?" The Israeli ambassador to the United States expressed "deep regret for the tragic accident," and his government offered to pay compensation for the loss of American lives and the damage to the ship. (An initial payment of $3,325,000 was made by Israel in May, 1968, to the families of the 34 men killed.) The United States was quick to accept the apology and the explanation. Senator Robert F. Kennedy called the incident "a miscalculation that could take place any place in the world," and Senator Jacob Javits said, "With Israel, we know it was a mistake."

However, a survivor of the attack declared, "We were flying the

Stars and Stripes and it's absolutely impossible that they shouldn't know who we were. This was a deliberate and planned attack and the remarkable thing about it was the accuracy of their air fire." A naval court of inquiry subsequently ruled that the attack had been "unprovoked" and that Israel had had "ample opportunity to identify the *Liberty* correctly." The investigation also determined that the Pentagon had attempted to order all American vessels out of the war zone some hours before the attack, but through communications errors the message was not relayed to the *Liberty*.

The ostensible purpose of the *Liberty*'s presence off the Sinai coast was to serve as a communications center if the Sixth Fleet were needed to evacuate American civilians from the Near East. However, the elaborate electronic equipment on board would have been capable of monitoring Israeli or Egyptian transmissions. The possibility that the *Liberty* was eavesdropping on the war from the presumed safety of international waters is a strong one.

Since the American and Israeli official governmental responses to the incident were contradictory and inconsistent, we may not know the true story for a long time. But a story widely circulated in Israel is not out of keeping with the nature of Israeli military tactics. According to this account, Israel knew quite well that the intelligence ship was American—and ordered it to clear out. No espionage vessels, even friendly ones, were wanted just then. When the *Liberty* replied that she was outside the 12-mile-limit and free to do as she pleased, Israel gave orders to blast her out of the water. This was Israel's war, all the way, and she meant to win it without foreign intrusions of any sort.

10.

By Saturday, June 10, 1967, the war was over on all fronts. The United States had not had to intervene, nor had there been any confrontation with Russia. Israel, acting alone, moving in sudden swift fury, had routed Egypt, Syria, and Jordan; she had no need to share the credit for her victory this time. Premier Levi Eshkol, no longer shaky in his office, told members of his party how "President Johnson promised great things," first asking for a 48-hour delay, then for two weeks more, insisting to Abba Eban that up to 50 maritime powers would guarantee free passage through the Strait of Tiran. "We examined the situation," Eshkol said, "and found that it really came down to a dozen and finally to only two countries and then, perhaps, to only one—Israel." He added that he once had told President Johnson, "It is likely that when we are attacked you will be very busy with other matters."

Israel could be permitted a little boastfulness. In late May she had been threatened with obliteration; by early June, she was supreme in the Near East. She had lost only 679 men—a great many, in a country of two and a half million, but yet far less than the 35,000 or more Arab dead. The victory was almost numbing in its completeness. A British reporter quoted one Israeli leader as saying, "Israel is still in a state of shock. The only analogy I can think of is if Britain had found herself in occupation of Berlin just three days after Dunkirk."

Around the world there was shock, too—happy amazement, a feeling of vicarious pride in Israel, an admiration bordering on awe. The Arabs, of course, did not share these feelings; Nasser shortly was trying to prove that American and British aircraft had aided Israel in the war, a claim that he eventually withdrew, and the Soviet Union, greatly embarrassed by the failure of her Arab friends to make efficient use of the billion dollars' worth of military equipment she had supplied, spoke harshly of Israeli aggression. Soon would come a subtle shifting in world opinion as Israel annexed what had been Jordanian Jerusalem and settled down for a lengthy, perhaps permanent, occupation of the West Bank, the Sinai, and Syria's Golan Heights. Puny no longer, Israel now had become a substantial power, and the sight of her formidably armed soldiers patrolling Arab villages made it impossible to think of her any longer as a hare ringed by hounds.

The June War did not settle all of Israel's old problems, and it created some new ones for her—such as what to do with the huge Arab population she had acquired through conquest, and her difficulty in maintaining her image before the world in the aftermath of smashing victory. There is not likely to be real security for Israel for a long time to come.

But Israel exists.

Created in fulfillment of a Viennese dilettante's dream of a return to an ancient homeland, brought into being by years of crafty political maneuvering and by years of bloody fighting, nurtured by a global network of overseas "citizens" whose status, unofficial and intangible, is certainly unique, Israel has become a tough, uncompromising, extraordinary nation, able at last to fight its own battles and win. Israel is very much of the twentieth century, and yet, in many important respects, it is an archaic land, a throwback to Biblical times, to Joshua and David and the Maccabees. Israel has shown the world that Jews know how to farm; she has shown the world that Jews know how to fight.

She has shown American Jews something about themselves, too. Those six days in June awoke feelings long buried, feelings that some Jews scarcely knew existed in themselves. Even as they slip into assimilation, as they turn away from the Yiddishness of their fathers, America's Jews have discovered now that they retain some link to their Jewish past. They are, deny it though they may try, part of that dispersed nation that spilled forth upon the world thousands of years ago. They now have allegiances to another nation, an adopted nation in the New World; and they have no intention of undoing that ancient dispersion and returning to the ancestral land. But yet there is a tie, difficult to comprehend, difficult to explain even to one's self.

Once only a small group of American Jews understood and acknowledged such a tie: the Zionists of fifty and sixty years ago, turning mimeograph-machine handles in dusty lofts. At that time few of their fellow American Jews knew or cared greatly about the demand for reconstituting the ancestral Palestinian homeland. To other Jews, Zionists then seemed like fanatics, even cranks, clinging obsessively to a mystical and abstract desire to fulfill the unfulfillable.

In President Wilson's day, the idea that Zionism could ever become a potent force in American political life seemed absurd. A man like Louis Brandeis could succeed in prodding the government into issuing a few hesitant and qualified pro-Zionist statements, but Brandeis was an exception, virtually unique, a Jew who moved in the highest circles of power. As we have seen, most American Jews of that era were indifferent to the Zionist dream, since they had found their own Zion in the New World. And some —many—were passionately hostile to the prophets of the Return, fearing that talk of building a Jewish nation would damage their own standing in their adopted land.

But the tireless fanatics kept the mimeograph machines turning. They welded the American Jewish community, so fragmented, so faction-ridden, so hampered by timidities and insecurities and uncertainties, into the first of the vocal minority groups. They advocated the Zionist position—part mystical, part spiritual, part cultural, part political—until a majority of American Jews came to accept it as desirable and proper that a Jewish nation should exist. And then those Jews conveyed their wishes to their government.

The noble, if somewhat remote, figure of Louis Dembitz Brandeis was a key factor in bringing about this transformation. He showed the community at large that Zionism need not be the private movement of immigrants from Eastern Europe. The charismatic figures of Chaim Weizmann and David Ben-Gurion, inspiring American Jewry from abroad, certainly aided the growth of the movement. On the home front a pair of dedicated but dissimilar rabbis, the fiery Abba Hillel Silver and the diplomatic Stephen Wise, were the chief spokesmen for a movement that grew in impact and breadth from year to year. Behind them stood a legion of tacticians and strategists, drafting petitions, organizing mass meetings, publishing books, pamphlets, and periodicals. And gradually the ranks of this army were filled with recruits from synagogues and community centers and schools—part-time warriors for Zionism, giving time, money, and passion for the sake of restoring Jewishness to a land that had not known it for twenty centuries.

It took decades for American Zionism to become something other than the cloistered and futile pastime of a little band of zealots. The emergence of strong and eloquent leaders had much to do with that growth, but external forces also operated. Certainly the rise of Hitler gave Zionism powerful impetus. The nightmare that began in 1933 supplied an immediate and urgent reason why Jews should have a special place of refuge in the world. Zionism ceased to be solely an abstract and obsessive cause. The singular reluctance of the democratic governments in the 1930's and early 1940's to find room for Hitler's victims on their own soil enhanced Zionism's vitality. In the face of a bland bureaucratic refusal to give aid to the homeless, American Jewry discovered in its fury a need to create a home for the wanderers. The closing of Palestine by the 1939 White Paper, the hostility of the Arab world to Jewish settlement in the Holy Land, the political tensions surrounding the creation of Israel, the precariousness of the Jewish state's continued existence—all these have served to goad and urge American Jews into renewed activity on behalf of their coreligionists overseas.

We have seen how American Zionism gradually came to take form as a force capable of exerting political pressure in the United States, and we have seen the varying response of successive Presidents to the exertion of that pressure. The pattern of these responses shows that Zionism is a strong but by no means omnipotent center of power in the determination of American foreign policy.

Before World War II, when Jews themselves were deeply divided on the propriety of establishing a Jewish state, and hesitant to make demands of any sort on Gentile America, their power to influence foreign policy was slight. From President Wilson onward, the White House was open to Zionist delegations, and offered polite acknowledgment for their manifestos and petitions. But Zionists were considered merely one of many obscure pressure groups, whose requests were to be courteously received and promptly forgotten. So long as it was clear that Zionism spoke for only a fraction of the Jewish electorate, it was accorded no more respect in Washington than were the groups lobbying for the establishment of a state religion or for the liberation of Transylvania.

Even after Franklin Delano Roosevelt—who had been given the nearly unanimous support of American Jewry—entered the White House, Zionism had little political impact. Roosevelt tacitly conceded that the Jews had a claim to his attention, but he met all Jewish nationalist demands with pacifying words, not with actions. Only vaguely aware of the ideological background of Zionism, not at all convinced that even a majority of Jews wanted a Jewish state in Palestine, and highly sensitive to the explosive reactions of the Arab leadership, Roosevelt took care to balance each promise of support for Zionism with a private reassurance to the Arabs that he did not intend to meddle in Near Eastern matters.

The Roosevelt years were years of consolidation and growth in the Zionist world. As late as 1940 many American Jews were fearful of provoking trouble by advocating a Jewish state in Palestine. But the work of the militant core of leadership had its cumulative effect, as did the weight of world events. Great Britain converted more Jews to Zionism with the 1939 White Paper than

Theodor Herzl had ever reached. The revelation of the Nazi death-camp atrocities, coupled with the realization that few refugees were getting through the American bureaucracy into the United States, intensified the development of Zionism among American Jews. Roosevelt died just as this movement was nearing its climax, and the full force of it fell upon his beleaguered successor, Harry S Truman.

Truman was the first President to see that the Zionist goals had the support of millions of American Jews, and he was the first President to give meaningful backing to the attainment of those goals. Reluctantly at the outset, with many reversals and hesitations, Truman ultimately involved himself far more deeply in the creation of the Zionist state than anyone had ever expected. Now that Zionism was a mature and politically sophisticated force in American life, commanding the sympathy of a majority of Jewry, it seemed certain thenceforth to hold a dominant position determining American policies in the Near East.

Yet the Eisenhower administration showed that this was not the case. When the Republicans took over in 1952, they sent the obligatory warm messages to Zionist gatherings, but they felt no political obligation to serve the wishes of American Jews, and the foreign policy assumptions of Secretary of State Dulles were conceived without much regard for the domestic pro-Israel bloc. American Zionists, who had led Harry Truman to give them their highest desire, now watched in dismay as Dulles and Eisenhower demonstrated their independence from Zionist pressures. This process reached its culmination in the Suez crisis of 1956-57, when the Eisenhower government aborted the Anglo-French conquest of Egypt and sternly compelled Israel to withdraw from territory she had seized. The belief that American Zionists controlled the American government was exposed as a myth.

John F. Kennedy, elected by a hairsbreadth margin and plainly beholden to American Jewry for the presidency, restored at least in words the cordial relationship between the White House and Zionism that had existed under President Truman. But in his short term of office he satisfied few Zionist demands and attempted to reopen contact with the Arab world. Lyndon Johnson, when he succeeded Kennedy, appeared to show a greater willingness to satisfy the friends of Israel; but in the one moment of real peril in June, 1967, Johnson's hands were tied by domestic political considerations, and it is difficult to say if he would have backed words with deeds if Israel had been in need of American aid.

The 1968 election saw further erosion in the supposed political base of American Zionism. Richard Nixon, educated under the tutelage of Eisenhower and Dulles, received no more than 17 percent of the Jewish vote, yet succeeded in winning the presidency. No one can claim that Nixon's political future will be determined by his attitude toward Israel.

Nixon's path to the White House may well have been made easier by the way in which the injection of the Israel question into American presidential campaigns has become obligatory and ritualized. Nixon himself had made the standard gestures toward the American Jewish community in the 1968 campaign, advocating military superiority for Israel and distributing pamphlets showing himself meeting with David Ben-Gurion, Moshe Dayan, and Levi Eshkol, but it would be an exaggeration to say that he laid any real stress on this theme. The candidate most vigorously identified with American support for Israel in the 1968 contest was Robert F. Kennedy, who in his brief quest for the Democratic nomination issued a long series of strong statements backing Zionist aspirations. The most conspicuous of these were inserted, almost as *non sequiturs*, in Kennedy's television debate with his rival for the nomination, Senator Eugene McCarthy, on Saturday, June 1, 1968. To many sophisticated observers, Kennedy's declaration of support for Israel, virtually irrelevant to the flow of his discussion with McCarthy, seemed like the transparent attempt of a worried politician to harvest some Jewish votes during a program getting maximum national exposure. To Sirhan Bishara Sirhan, however, an embittered young Jordanian living in Los Angeles, Kennedy's words were a promise of continued oppression for the Arab world. When Sirhan's bullets took Kennedy's life a few days later, they removed the man who was perhaps Nixon's most formidable potential opponent; and at his trial Sirhan made it clear that it was for his Israel views and nothing else that Kennedy had been assassinated.

During his early months in office, Nixon showed no clear position on the Arab-Israeli conflict, but indications began to emerge that his administration would show no favoritism toward Israel. Though the Kennedy and Johnson administrations had been officially neutral in regard to Near Eastern questions, that neutrality had generally been handled in a way that favored Israel's interests. But even before the 1968 election, Republican leaders began speaking of a more "even-handed" policy toward the Near East, which could mean only a shift toward greater sympathy for the Arabs.

As a Republican President, Nixon is more likely to respond to the needs of the business community than to those of organized Zionism, and the business community began speaking out in favor of a new effort to improve relations with the Arabs almost as soon as Nixon took office. Early in 1969 Hugh M. Hyde, head of Johnston International Publishing Corporation, declared, "To express our friendship with the Arabs wouldn't jeopardize our interests in Israel, whereas the appearance of one-sided support of Israel does threaten our influence and investments in the Arab world." Hyde was a member of an eight-man delegation of businessmen that went to Algeria in search of ways to increase American trade with that country. Another member of the delegation, J. B. Sunderland of the American Independent Oil Company, commented, "Many people in this country know only one side of the Middle East question. In fact it is because of Israel that we have lost our good relations with the Arab world."

These statements are reminiscent of some of the thoughts expressed by James Forrestal and others in the Truman era who believed that it made good economic sense to keep from too strong a commitment toward Zionist ideals. The pressures of the American balance-of-payments problem may yet lead the Nixon government to explore ways of increasing American trade with the Arabs by decreasing Arab resentment of American foreign policy.

Toward the close of Nixon's first year in office, his administration began to say things that reminded Israelis and American Jews uncomfortably of the Eisenhower-Dulles era, and led them to think that Republicans were friends of Israel neither in word nor deed. Throughout much of 1969, as the Near East seemed once more to be drifting into war, Secretary of State William P. Rogers spoke frequently of "four-power talks" in which the United States, the Soviet Union, Great Britain, and France would devise some sort of scheme to insure the peace of the region. Those who remembered how the great powers had handled things after the 1956 war regarded any such suggestion as the first step in a new betrayal of Israel; and so the Israelis shrugged off Rogers' idea repeatedly, insisting that the Near Eastern tensions would have to be resolved by direct negotiation between Israel and the Arabs, not by any cabal of superpowers.

Nevertheless Rogers continued to pursue the scheme of a four-power solution. On October 28, 1969, he handed the Russians a secret note expressing a possible formula for peace in the Near East; after further refinement of his plan, he presented it openly in a speech on December 9, and expanded it even more in a note given to a four-power meeting at the United Nations on December 18. The heart of the proposal involved a pullback of Israeli forces to the 1967 boundaries. The whole West Bank region would be returned to Jordan, bringing Arab guns once more within a dozen miles of Tel Aviv; Jerusalem would somehow come under joint Israeli-Jordanian control; the Sinai Peninsula would revert to Egypt; Isreal would agree to admit unlimited numbers of refugee Arabs who previously had lived in Palestine. In return for these concessions, the Arab nations were to sign peace treaties with Israel, recognizing her sovereignty and guaranteeing the freedom of her ships in the Suez Canal and the Gulf of Aqaba. A system of demilitarized zones would be instituted to reduce tensions along the borders, and such complex issues as control of the Gaza Strip and the Golan Heights would be the subject of further negotiation.

The Israeli reaction was overwhelmingly negative. "Look," said Premier Golda Meir to a *New York Times* reporter, "Israel won't accept this. We didn't survive three wars in order to commit suicide so that the Russians can celebrate victory for Nasser." She spoke of "a deep feeling of injustice. After all that's happened, we're asked ... to start all over again, as though it were 1948. Why?" Deputy Premier Yigal Allon told *Time,* "To go back to the old demarcation lines of 1949, as the American plan envisages, leads Israel into a potential strategic trap. It is an invitation for another war, because it will create new illusions among the Arabs of prospects of victory. We need borders that will give us the possibility of real self-defense." Pointing out that the unacceptable American plan now was likely to become the minimum Arab expectation, Allon said, "The American initiative put an end to any hope of compromise in the foreseeable future. This is a great tragedy."

In the United States, predictably, the Jewish community denounced the Rogers plan. The Board of Governors of B'nai B'rith, at its annual meeting in January, 1970, said that the State Department scheme hoped to win peace "at the expense of Israel's security and bargaining position." The same month, the American Jewish Committee and the Zionist Organization of America attacked the proposal. Senator Charles E. Goodell, a Republican from New York, went before an American Jewish Congress rally in early January to accuse the Secretary of State of unfairly favoring the Arabs. And Mayor John Lindsay of New York City, addressing a Z.O.A. rally on on January 15, warned against "the danger of a misguided shift" in American policy toward Israel.

The Nixon administration seemed to be taken off guard by what should have been the expectable response of the American Jewish community. Secretary of State Rogers repeated that the United States was merely being "even-handed," and pointed to the words of his December 9 speech, in which he said, "Our policy is and will continue to be a balanced one. We have friendly ties with both Arabs and Israelis. To call for Israeli withdrawal . . . without achieving agreement on peace would be partisan toward the Arabs. To call on the Arabs to accept peace without Israeli withdrawal would be partisan toward Israel. Therefore, our policy is to encourage the Arabs to accept a permanent peace based on a binding agreement and to urge the Israelis to withdraw from occupied territory when their territorial integrity is assured. . . ." He added, "We have to conduct our foreign policy in a way that we think is best for our national interests."

American Jews remained unappeased. Zionist leaders commented privately that it was the old story: business-oriented Protestants in charge of the American government, with strong political ties to the oil industry and none at all to the Jewish voters, were again trying to placate the Arab world at the expense of Israel. Rogers' reference to "our national interests" translated directly, in the eyes of these Jewish leaders, into "the interests of the oil companies." The fact that a group of businessmen with substantial investments in the Near East had met with Nixon late in 1969 to discuss the situation—among them David Rockefeller, president of the Chase Manhattan Bank, who had just come from a meeting with Nasser—served to inflame their suspicions. So the next stage in the familiar scenario began, with a delegation from 14 Jewish organizations going to Washington to speak out on behalf of Israel.

At the beginning of January these leaders had a stormy two-hour conference with Rogers, at which he discovered how articulate and impassioned American Jews could be on the subject of Israel; but there were no concrete results. Weeks of rallies and demonstrations followed, the climax coming on January 25 with a meeting of 1000 Jewish community and organization leaders at the Statler-Hilton Hotel in New York. The meeting had been convened by the Conference of Presidents of Major American Jewish Organizations, a coalition of 24 religious and secular groups, for the purpose of expressing "deep concern and apprehension" over recent American statements of policy toward the Near East.

A message from President Nixon was the highlight of the meeting. He was, he said, aware of the "deep concern" of American Jews that Israel might become "increasingly isolated." But he asserted that this was "not true as far as the United States is concerned. The United States stands by its friends. Israel is one of its friends." The President went so far as to say that the United States was "prepared to supply military equipment necessary to support the efforts of friendly governments, like Israel's, to defend the safety of their people."

Although the promise of American military aid to Israel was unexpected, the rest of Nixon's message followed the traditional lines of presidential reassurance of uneasy American Jews. The chairman of the meeting, Dr. William A. Wexler, the president of B'nai B'rith, made an equally traditional conciliatory reply: Nixon's message, he said, "shows that the President understands and shares our concerns. It indicates that he wants no further erosion in American policy."

Yet the tensions between Nixon and the American Jewish community remained. Most members of that community had little faith in Republicans in general or in Nixon in particular, and, while they doubted that any expression of American policy could have much effect on the increasingly steadfast Israelis, they did not feel that the current administration was likely to do much to help the embattled Jewish state. The elaborate efforts Nixon had made to give a traditionally Jewish seat on the United States Supreme Court to a southern conservative Christian seemed a more accurate indication of his independence from Jewish political pressures than any number of friendly messages to pro-Israel rallies.

But the political power of American Zionism, though it has been greatly overestimated—particularly by the enemies of Israel—exists nevertheless. It is folly to think that Presidents will be made or cast down solely by their outlook toward Israel. It is certainly clear, though, that American Jews, through their energetic and persistent support of the creation and development of Israel, have established a permanent beachhead for Zionism within the American government. There will be times when the United States appears to turn against Israel—as in 1957—but under normal circumstances American Jews may take it for granted that their government shares their concern for Israel's welfare. Perhaps more to the point, Zionist activities over a span of many years insured that nearly all American Jews came to share that concern.

This is a remarkable achievement. It demonstrates the potency of an idea, the unique nature of the Jewish spirit. Two thousand years of exile could not destroy the yearning for a lost homeland, and in our times a series of powerful personalities as varied as Herzl and Hitler served, knowingly and unknowingly, to bring about the return to that homeland. Even in the United States, where the Zionist dream might not have been expected to flourish, a little band of zealots became, in the end, a powerful movement, until, at the climax of the long and harrowing struggle to give Israel birth, the Jews of America lent themselves almost universally to the effort. And in 1967's brief and terrifying and ultimately thrilling days of conflict even those who had earlier held back suddenly found in themselves an identity with Israel, a reservoir of pride and faith and admiration.

American Jews are not Israelis. Israel is not a part of the United States. The relations between American Jews and Israel have never been fully harmonious, nor can they ever be. Yet nearly six million Americans of the Jewish faith now find themselves intimately involved with the destinies of this curious and fascinating nation on the Mediterranean's eastern shore. There once was a definition of a Jew that went, "You're a Jew when a Jew in Minsk is hurt and you feel the pain." That definition needs to be brought up to date: "You're a Jew when a Jew in Israel is shot at and you want to shoot back."

For David's sake did the Lord his God give him a lamp in Jerusalem, to set up his son after him; and suddenly, unaccountably, astonishingly, the glow of that lamp reaches across the continents.

List of Jewish Organizations
in the United States

American Council for Judaism. Anti-Zionist group, founded in 1943.

American Jewish Committee. Founded in 1906 to prevent any "infraction of the civil and religious rights of Jews, in any part of the world." Leadership drawn primarily from the German-Jewish community in the United States; Reform Judaism a common bond. Originally a non-Zionist organization, with many members strongly opposed to Zionist program; gradual development of sympathy for the idea of a Jewish state began during World War II as outgrowth of refugee crisis.

American Jewish Conference. Quasi-legislative representative assembly of American Jews, first convened in 1943 to discuss problems of postwar status of Jews and Palestine; most American Jewish groups represented, but predominant outlook was Zionist. Further sessions held through 1947.

American Jewish Congress. Originally a representative assembly summoned in 1917 by Wise, Brandeis, Lipsky, and other Zionist leaders. Reorganized in 1922 as a continuing body "to deal with all matters relating to and affecting specific Jewish interests." Strongly Zionist in orientation.

American Jewish Relief Committee. Founded during World War I to coordinate American Jewish charitable efforts in war emer-

Note: This does not pretend to be a comprehensive listing of all the American Jewish organizations, or even of all the major ones. It is intended simply to provide a guide to the organizations which are most frequently mentioned in this book, indicating in one convenient location the general nature of their involvement with the question of the Jewish homeland in Palestine.

gency. Parent organization of Joint Distribution Committee; non-Zionist.

American League for a Free Palestine. Organized by Peter Bergson and other leaders of the Revisionist faction of Zionism during World War II to serve as the American fund-raising arm of the Palestinian underground military force, Irgun Zvai Leumi.

American Palestine Committee. Organization of pro-Zionist Christians, first organized in 1932, reactivated in 1941.

American Trade Union Council for Histadrut. American affiliate of Histadrut, the General Federation of Jewish Labor in Palestine and later Israel.

B'nai B'rith. Fraternal and philanthropic organization founded in 1843; initially oriented toward German-Jewish and Reform interests. Long active in economic development of Palestine, but not involved in political aspects of Zionism until World War II.

Central Conference of American Rabbis. Official association of Reform rabbis, founded 1889; originally anti-Zionist, but by 1935 sympathetic to the development of Palestine as a Jewish homeland.

Federation of American Zionists. Early American Zionist group, succeeded in 1918 by Zionist Organization of America.

Hadassah. The Women's Zionist Organization of America, founded in 1912, and for many years the largest of the Zionist groups in the United States.

Joint Distribution Committee. Founded in 1914 for the relief of Jewish war victims, later a general philanthropic organization. Active in the development of Palestine and Israel, but not involved in political Zionism.

Mizrachi. The Religious Zionist Organization of America, founded in the United States in 1913; strong Orthodox orientation.

National Committee for Labor Israel. American fund-raising arm of Histadrut, Israel's labor federation.

National Council of Jewish Women. Founded in 1893 to carry out a broad program of social services; officially non-Zionist, but committed to support for a Jewish homeland in Palestine since 1943.

United Jewish Appeal. Fund-raising group; since 1939 has served as coordinator for Zionist and non-Zionist charitable collections in the United States, allocating a portion of its receipts to Zionist bodies and the rest to general Jewish welfare programs. Composed of Joint Distribution Committee and the United Israel Appeal.

Zionist Organization of America. Organized in 1918 as the American wing of the World Zionist Organization, and for many years the most active group in the political campaign for a Jewish homeland in Palestine.

Acknowledgments

This book was written during a remarkably chaotic year of its author's life, when unusual circumstances forced him to rely in great measure on the assistance of others. This is not meant to excuse any flaws the book may have, only to emphasize the debt I have to the people listed here. Without their aid there most literally would not have been a book.

I am grateful, particularly, to my agent, Scott Meredith, for an infinity of services; to Lawrence Hughes and Hillel Black of William Morrow for their patience, forbearance, and encouragement; to my research associate, Stephen Crane, for his indispensable cooperation; and to Bill Adler for his suggestions and contributions. I must also thank my wife Barbara, not only for her help in the mechanical aspects of preparing the manuscript, but for putting up with the whole exhausting enterprise for so many months while her husband was submerged in the intricacies of Zionist history.

I am indebted to the hundreds of people both in the United States and in Israel who allowed me the opportunity to discuss with them their feelings about Israel, Zionism, Judaism, and related topics. In particular, I wish to thank the officers of several Jewish organizations who made themselves available for extended conversations. They include Jacques Torczyner, president, Zionist Organization of America; Dr. Simon Segal, director of the foreign affairs department, American Jewish Committee; Stuart Gottlieb, executive director, and Harold B. Attin, public relations director, of the American Council for Judaism; David Ariel, consul for political affairs, Israeli Consulate, New York City; Joseph Elron, Hebrew University, Jerusalem, Israel; and Dr. Philip Baum, director of international affairs, American Jewish Congress.

Other Jewish organizations also were generous with information, publications, and answers to innumerable questions. Among them were the America-Israel Cultural Foundation; the American Jewish Joint Distribution Committee; the American Trade Union Council for Histadrut; the American Zionist Council; B'nai B'rith; Histadrut National Committee for Labor Israel; PEC Israel Economic Corporation; and the Union of American Hebrew Congregations.

The facilities of the Zionist Archives and Library in New York were essential to the completion of this work, and I thank Mrs. Sylvia Landress, the director and librarian, and her capable staff —Rachael Schechtman, Esther Togman, Rebecca Zapinsky, and Akiva Horne. The staff of the Columbia University Library was also of considerable assistance. The Franklin Delano Roosevelt Library at Hyde Park, New York, the Harry S Truman Library in Independence, Missouri, and the Dwight D. Eisenhower Library in Abilene, Kansas, all made available to me unpublished documents and correspondence concerning the involvement of those Presidents with Zionist and Israeli problems; I owe special thanks to John E. Wickman, director of the Eisenhower Library, for performing tasks of selection above and beyond the call of duty.

Bibliography

Unpublished documents consulted for this book include correspondence received by Presidents Roosevelt, Truman, and Eisenhower; the Jacob de Haas files at the Zionist Archives; innumerable press releases, leaflets, brochures, circulars, and similar transient matter, also at the Zionist Archives; and assorted papers and memoranda shown me by the Jewish leaders who granted interviews.

Among published sources, aside from such periodicals as *The New York Times*, the New York *Herald-Tribune*, *Time*, and other repositories of news, I consulted the files of the following periodicals of specifically Jewish or Zionist interest:

American Israel Review
American Zionist
B'nai B'rith Magazine
Bulletin of the American Zionist Council
Commentary
Congress Bulletin
Congress Weekly (and *Congress Bi-Weekly*)
Hadassah Magazine
Hadassah Newsletter
Histadrut Foto News
Issues
Jerusalem Post
Jewish Affairs
Jewish Frontier
Jewish Herald
Jewish Observer and Middle East Review

Jewish Spectator
Menorah Journal
New Palestine
Student Zionist
Zionews

Among the books, pamphlets, and periodical articles consulted, the following were of special value:

ACHESON, DEAN. *Present at the Creation.* New York, Norton, 1969.

ADAMS, SHERMAN. *Firsthand Report: The Story of the Eisenhower Administration.* New York, Harper & Brothers, 1961.

AGAR, HERBERT. *The Saving Remnant: An Account of Jewish Survival.* New York, Viking, 1960.

AMERICAN COUNCIL FOR JUDAISM. *Statements by the American Council for Judaism on the Israeli-Arab Crisis and War of May-June, 1967.* New York, American Council for Judaism, 1967.

ANTONOVSKY, AARON, AND BERNSTEIN, S., editors. *Hechalutz Builders and Fighters, 1948.* New York, Hechalutz Organization of America, 1949.

BAUM, BERNARD H. "Zionist Influence on American Higher Education." *Issues,* Autumn, 1965.

BEN-GURION, DAVID, with MOSHE PEARLMAN. *Ben-Gurion Looks Back.* New York, Simon and Schuster, 1965.

BENTWICH, NORMAN. *Israel Resurgent.* London, Ernest Benn, 1960.

BERGER, ELMER. "Briefing for the Congress." *Issues,* Summer, 1965.

―――. *The Jewish Dilemma.* New York, Devin-Adair, 1951.

―――. *Realities of United States National Interests in the Middle East.* New York, American Council for Judaism, n.d.

BERKMAN, TED. *Cast a Giant Shadow: The Story of Mickey Marcus.* New York, Doubleday & Co., 1962.

BERKOWITZ, RABBI WILLIAM. *Ten Vital Jewish Issues.* New York, Thomas Yoseloff, 1964.

BIRMINGHAM, STEPHEN. *Our Crowd: The Great Jewish Families of New York.* New York, Harper & Row, 1967.

BISGYER, MAURICE. *Challenge and Encounter.* New York, Crown, 1967.

BLAU, JOSEPH L. *The Spiritual Life of American Jewry.* New York, Jewish Education Committee Press, 1965.

B'NAI B'RITH. *B'nai B'rith Israel Program.* Washington, B'nai B'rith, 1967.

BRANDEIS, LOUIS DEMBITZ. *Brandeis on Zionism.* Washington, Zionist Organization of America, 1942.

CELLER, EMANUEL. *You Never Leave Brooklyn.* New York, John Day, 1953.

CHURCHILL, RANDOLPH S. and WINSTON. *The Six Day War.* London, William Heinemann, 1967.

COLEMAN, CLARENCE L. "Aspirations of U.S. Jews." *Issues,* Winter, 1962–63.

CROSSMAN, RICHARD H. S. *A Nation Reborn.* New York, Atheneum, 1960.

CRUM, BARTLEY C. *Behind the Silken Curtain.* New York, Simon & Schuster, 1947.

DARMS, ANTON. *A Jew Returns to Israel.* Grand Rapids, Zondervan Publishing House, 1965.

DIMONT, MAX I. *Jews, God and History.* New York, Simon & Schuster, 1962.

DONOVAN, ROBERT J. *Eisenhower: The Inside Story.* New York, Harper & Brothers, 1956.

DRAPER, THEODORE. *Israel and World Politics.* New York, Viking, 1968.

EDITORS OF FORTUNE. *Jews in America.* New York, Random House, 1936.

EISENHOWER, DWIGHT D. *The White House Years.* Two volumes. New York, Doubleday & Co., 1963, 1965.

ELLIS, H. B. *Israel and the Middle East.* New York, Ronald Press, 1957.

FINER, HERMAN. *Dulles Over Suez.* Chicago, Quadrangle Books, 1964.

FINK, REUVEN. *America and Palestine.* New York, Herald Square Press, 1945.

FREEDMAN, MAX, editor. *Roosevelt and Frankfurter: Their Correspondence, 1928–1945.* Boston, Little, Brown, 1967.

FRIEDMANN, GEORGES. *The End of the Jewish People?* New York, Doubleday & Co., 1967.

FRIEDRICH, C. J. *American Policy Toward Palestine.* Washington, Public Affairs Press, 1944.

FUCHS, LAWRENCE H. *The Political Behavior of American Jews.* Glencoe, Illinois, Free Press, 1956.

GERVASI, FRANK. *The Case for Israel.* New York, Viking, 1967.

GOLDING, DAVID. "United States Foreign Policy in Palestine and Israel 1945–49." Unpublished doctoral dissertation, New York University, February, 1961.

GOLDSTEIN, ISRAEL. *American Jewry Comes of Age.* New York, Bloch, 1955.

HABER, JULIUS. *The Odyssey of an American Zionist.* New York, Twayne, 1956.

HALPERIN, SAMUEL. *The Political World of American Zionism.* Detroit, Wayne State University Press, 1961.

HALPERN, BEN. *The American Jew—A Zionist Analysis.* New York, Theodor Herzl Foundation, 1956.

HANDLIN, OSCAR. *A Continuing Task.* New York, Random House, 1964.

HECHT, BEN. *A Child of the Century.* New York, Simon & Schuster, 1954.

HERTZBERG, ARTHUR. "Israel and American Jewry." *Commentary,* August, 1967.

HERZL, THEODOR. *The Jewish State.* New York, Scopus Publishing Company, 1943.

ISAACS, HAROLD R. *American Jews in Israel.* New York, John Day, 1967.

JASTROW, MORRIS, JR. *Zionism and the Future of Palestine.* New York, Macmillan, 1919.

JOSEPH, DOV. *The Faithful City: The Siege of Jerusalem, 1948.* New York, Simon & Schuster, 1960.

KAGAN, BENJAMIN. *The Secret Battle for Israel.* Cleveland and New York, World Publishing Company, 1966.

KAHN, ROGER. *The Passionate People: What It Means To Be a Jew in America.* New York, Morrow, 1968.

KERTZER, MORRIS N. *Today's American Jew.* New York, McGraw-Hill, 1967.

KIMCHE, DAVID, and BAWLY, DAN. *The Sandstorm: The Arab-Israeli War of 1967.* New York, Stein & Day, 1968.

KIMCHE, JON and DAVID. *A Clash of Destinies: The Arab-Jewish War and the Founding of the State of Israel.* New York, Praeger, 1960.

KORN, RICHARD. "Analysis of Eshkol's Official Plan for 'Israel and the Diaspora.'" *Issues,* Winter, 1965–66.

————. *The Writing on the Wall.* New York, American Council for Judaism, October 19, 1968.

LASKY, MOSES. *Between Truth and Repose.* New York, American Council for Judaism, 1956.

LAZARON, MORRIS. "Are Judaism and Jewish Nationalism Inseparable?" *Issues,* Winter, 1962–63.

LEVINGER, LEE J. *A History of the Jews in the United States.* Cincinnati, Union of American Hebrew Congregations, 1944.

LIPSKY, LOUIS. *A Gallery of Zionist Profiles.* New York, Farrar, Straus & Cudahy, 1956.

————. *Thirty Years of American Zionism.* Two volumes. New York, Nesher Publishing Company, 1927.

LITVINOFF, BARNET. *Road to Jerusalem: Zionism's Imprint on History.* London, Weidenfeld and Nicolson, 1965.

MALLISON, W. T., JR. "The Zionist-Israel Juridical Claims to Constitute 'The Jewish People' Nationality Entity." *George Washington Law Review,* June, 1964.

MANUEL, FRANK E. *The Realities of American-Palestine Relations.* Washington, Public Affairs Press, 1949.

MATOVU, BENYAMIN. "How Zionism Threatened the Peace at Suez." *Issues,* Autumn, 1965.

———. "The Zionist Wish and the Nazi Deed." *Issues,* Winter, 1966–67.

McDONALD, JAMES G. *My Mission in Israel 1948–51.* New York, Simon & Schuster, 1951.

MEZVINSKY, NORTON. *What Should Be the Relationship of American Jews to the State of Israel?* New York, American Council for Judaism, November 3, 1967.

MILLIS, WALTER, editor. *The Forrestal Diaries.* New York, Viking, 1951.

MORSE, ARTHUR D. *While Six Million Died.* New York, Random House, 1968.

OXMAN, SHIMSHON. *The Government of Israel.* New York, Zionist Organization of America, 1948.

POLIER, JUSTINE W., and WISE, JAMES. *The Personal Letters of Stephen Wise.* Boston, Beacon Press, 1956.

PROSKAUER, JOSEPH. *A Segment of My Times.* New York, Farrar, Straus & Co., 1950.

RABINOWITZ, EZEKIEL. *Justice Louis D. Brandeis: The Zionist Chapter of His Life.* New York, Philosophical Library, 1968.

REICH, BERNARD. "Israel's Foreign Policy." Unpublished doctoral dissertation, University of Virginia, 1964.

ROBINSON, LLOYD. *The Hopefuls: Ten Presidential Campaigns.* New York, Doubleday & Co., 1966.

SACHAR, HOWARD MORLEY. *Aliyah: The Peoples of Israel.* Cleveland and New York, World Publishing Company, 1961.

SAFRAN, NADAV. *The United States and Israel.* Cambridge, Harvard University Press, 1963.

SAKRAN, FRANK C. *Palestine Dilemma.* Washington, Public Affairs Press, 1948.

SCHECHTMAN, JOSEPH B. *The United States and the Jewish State Movement.* New York, Thomas Yoseloff, 1966.

SCHWARTZ, LEO W. *The Redeemers: A Saga of the Years 1945–1952.* New York, Farrar, Straus & Young, 1953.

SELZER, MICHAEL. *The Aryanization of the Jewish State.* New York, Black Star, 1967.

SHERMAN, C. B. *Israel and the American Jewish Community.* New York,

Labor Zionist Organization of America Poale Zion, 1951.

SIDORSKY, D. "The United States and Israel." *Current History,* March 1958.

SILVER, ABBA HILLEL. *Vision and Victory: A Collection of Addresses, 1942–1948.* New York, Zionist Organization of America, 1949.

STEINER, GEORGE. "How U.S. Jews View the Jewish State." *Life,* August 12, 1957.

STEVENS, R. P. *American Zionism and U.S. Foreign Policy 1942–1947.* New York, Pageant Press, 1950.

STEVENSON, WILLIAM. *Strike Zion!* New York, Bantam Books, 1967.

SYKES, CHRISTOPHER. *Crossroads to Israel.* Cleveland and New York, World Publishing Co., 1965.

TAYLOR, ALAN R. *Prelude to Israel: An Analysis of Zionist Diplomacy 1897–1947.* New York, Philosophical Library, 1959.

THOMAS, HUGH. *Suez.* New York, Harper & Row, 1967.

TOYNBEE, ARNOLD. "Pioneer Destiny of Judaism." *Issues,* Summer, 1960.

TRUMAN, HARRY S. *Memoirs.* Two volumes. New York, Doubleday & Co., 1955, 1956.

UNION OF AMERICAN HEBREW CONGREGATIONS. *Israel and American Jewry—1967 and Beyond.* Union of American Hebrew Congregations, n.d.

WEIZMANN, CHAIM. *Trial and Error.* New York, Harper & Brothers, 1949.

WEYL, NATHANIEL. *The Jew in American Politics.* New Rochelle, N.Y., Arlington House, 1968.

WOLFE, BURTON H. "How Can a Liberal Support Zionism?" *Issues,* Winter, 1962–63.

ZAAR, ISAAC. *Rescue and Liberation: America's Part in the Birth of Israel.* New York, Bloch, 1954.

INDEX